Alfred Moquin-Tandon, Robert Thomas Hulme

Elements of medical Zoology

Alfred Moquin-Tandon, Robert Thomas Hulme

Elements of medical Zoology

ISBN/EAN: 9783743343610

Manufactured in Europe, USA, Canada, Australia, Japa

Cover: Foto ©ninafisch / pixelio.de

Manufactured and distributed by brebook publishing software (www.brebook.com)

Alfred Moquin-Tandon, Robert Thomas Hulme

Elements of medical Zoology

WORKS

PUBLISHED BY

H. BAILLIERE, 219, REGENT STREET, London.

[*Sent Free on Receipt of the Prices.*]

Anatomy (The) of the External Form of the Horse, with Explanations by JAMES I. LUPTON, V. S. The Plates by Bagg. Part I., containing 9 Plates and Explanations. Large folio. Price, plain, £1 11s. 6d.; on India paper, £2 5s.
This Work will be completed in Two Parts, consisting of 18 to 20 Plates, with their Explanations, and one volume 8vo. of Text, giving the Study of the External Form of the Horse and the Physiology of Locomotion.

A Practical Treatise on Coal, Petroleum, and other Distilled Oils. By A. GESNER, M.D. 8vo., with 20 Woodcuts. New York, 1861. 7s. 6d.

Compendium of Human Histology. By C. Morel. Illustrated with 28 Plates. Edited by W. H. VAN BUREN, M.D. 8vo. New York, 1861. 14s.

Illustrated Manual of Operative Surgery and Surgical Anatomy. By BERNARD AND HUETTE. Edited with Notes and Additions by W. H. VAN BUREN. 8vo. with 113 Plates, half bound morocco, gilt top. 1861. Plain, £2 4s.; Coloured, £3 4s.

American Medical Times. Published Weekly in New York, and received in London free. Subscription for the year, £1 5s.

Bell (A. N.)—Knowledge of Living Things, with the Law of their Existence. 12mo., with 2 coloured Plates, and 60 Wood Illustrations. New York, 1860. 7s. 6d.

Canton (A.)—The Teeth and their Preservation, in Infancy and Manhood to Old Age. 12mo. with Woodcuts, 4s.

Flourens (P.)—On Human Longevity, and the Amount of Life upon the Globe. By J. P. FLOURENS, Perpetual Secretary to the Academy of Sciences, Paris. Edited by W. C. MARTEL. 12mo. London, 1855. 3s.

Kæmtz.—A Complete Course of Meteorology. By L. F. Kæmtz, Professor of Physics at the University of Halle. With Notes by CH. MARTINS, and an Appendix by L. LALANNE. Translated, with Additions, by C. V. WALKER, 1 vol. post 8vo. pp. 624, with 15 Plates, cloth boards. 1845. 12s. 6d.

Knox (R.)—Man: his Structure and Physiology popularly explained and demonstrated, by the aid of 8 moveable dissected coloured Plates, and 5 Woodcuts. 2nd Edition, revised. Post 8vo. London, 1858. 10s. 6d.

Moquin-Tandon.—Manual of Medical Zoology: being a Detailed Description of Animals useful in Medicine, and the Species hurtful to Man; with General Considerations on the Organization and Classification of Animals, and with a Resumé of the Natural History of Man. Edited, with Notes and Additions, by T. HULME, Esq. With 124 Wood Engravings, post 8vo. 1861. 12s. 6d.

Owen.—Odontography; or, a Treatise on the Comparative Anatomy of the the Teeth, their Physiological Relations, Mode of Development, and Microscopical Structure in the Vertebrate Animals. By RICHARD OWEN, F.R.S., Corresponding Member of the Royal Academy of Sciences, Paris and Berlin; Hunterian Professor to the Royal College of Surgeons, London. This splendid work is now completed. 2 vols. royal 4to., containing 168 Plates, half-bound russia. London, 1840—45. £10 10s. Reduced to £6 10s.

Richardson (B. W.)—On the Medical History and Treatment of Diseases of the Teeth and the Adjacent Structures. 8vo. 1860. 8s.

Quekett (J.)—Lectures on Histology, delivered at the Royal College of Surgeons of England, containing Elementary Tissues of Plants and Animals, the Structure of the Skeletons of Plants and Vertebrate Animals. 2 vols. illustrated by 340 Woodcuts. London, 1852, 1854. £1 8s. 6d.

―――― **Practical Treatise on the Use of the Microscope.** Illustrated with 11 Steel Plates and 300 Wood Engravings. 8vo. 3rd Edition. London, 1855. £1 1s.

Trousseau and Reveil.—The Prescriber's Complete Handbook: the Principles of the Art of Prescribing, with a List of Diseases and their Remedies, a Materia Medica of the Medicines employed, classified according to their Natural Families, with their Properties, Preparations, and Uses, and a Concise Sketch of Toxicology. By M. TROUSSEAU, Professor of the Faculty of Medicine, Paris, and M. REVEIL. Edited, with Notes, by J. B. NEVINS, M.D. London, 1852. Roan limp, 6s. 6d.

Day (G. E.)—Chemistry: in its Relations to Physiology and Medicine. By GEORGE E. DAY, M.D., Professor of Medicine in the University of St. Andrews. 8vo. illustrated with Thirty Engravings. £1.

Gill (J. B.)—Epitome of Practical Surgery. 32mo. 1860. 1s.

Cooper and Suckley.—Natural History of Washington Territory: Minnesota, Nebraska, Oregon, and California. 4to. with 55 Plates and a Map. £2 10s.

Ganot.—Elementary Treatise on Physics. Edited on the Ninth Original Edition by Dr. ATKINSON. With 500 Illustrations. Post 8vo. 1861. *(In the Press.)*

Technology; or Chemistry applied to the Arts. By Knapp, Richardson, and H. WATTS. Vol. IV., 8vo. containing the Alkalies and Acids. Illustrated with Wood Engravings. *(In the Press.)*

Jones (J.)—The Natural and Supernatural: or, Man Physical, Apparitional, and Spiritual. 500 pages, 1860. 10s. 6d.

Fau.—The Anatomy of the External Forms of Man, for Artists, Painters, and Sculptors. Edited with Additions by R. KNOX, M.D. 8vo. text, and 28 4to. plates. London, 1849. Price Plain, £1 4s; Coloured, £2 2s.

Chemical Society (Quarterly Journal of the). 13 vols. 8vo. London, 1848—60. Vols. 1 to 7 have been reduced to 8s. each; Vols. 8 to 13, 13s. each; or in Quarterly Parts, price 3s. each.

Prichard.—The Natural History of Man; comprising Inquiries into the Modifying Influences of Physical and Moral Agencies on the different Tribes of the Human Family. By JAMES COWLES PRICHARD, M.D., F.R.S., M.R.I.A., Corresponding Member of the National Institute, of the Royal Academy of Medicine, and of the Statistical Society, &c. 4th Edition, revised and enlarged. By EDWIN NORRIS, of the Royal Asiatic Society, London. With 62 plates, coloured, engraved on steel, and 100 engravings on wood. 2 vols. royal 8vo. elegantly bound in cloth. London, 1855. £1 18s.

―――― **Six Ethnographical Maps.** Supplement to the Natural History of Man, and to the Researches into the Physical History of Mankind, folio, coloured, and 1 sheet of letter-press, in cloth boards. 2nd Edition. London, 1861. £1 4s.

Graham.—Elements of Chemistry; including the Application of the Science in the Arts. By T. GRAHAM, F.R.S., L. & E., Master of the Mint, late Professor of Chemistry at University College, London. 2nd Edition, revised and enlarged, copiously illustrated with woodcuts. 2 vols. 8vo. 1850, 1857. £2.

Berkeley (Rev. J. M.)—Introduction to Cryptogamic Botany. 8vo. Illustrated with 127 Woodcuts. 1857. £1.

ELEMENTS

OF

MEDICAL ZOOLOGY.

BY

A. MOQUIN-TANDON,

MEMBER OF THE ACADEMY OF SCIENCES, AND OF THE IMPERIAL ACADEMY OF MEDICINE;
PROFESSOR OF MEDICAL NATURAL HISTORY TO THE FACULTY OF MEDICINE AT PARIS.

With One Hundred and Twenty-four Illustrations.

TRANSLATED AND EDITED BY

ROBERT THOMAS HULME, M.R.C.S.E., F.L.S.,

LECTURER ON DENTAL SURGERY;
MEMBER OF THE BOARD OF EXAMINERS OF THE COLLEGE OF DENTISTS OF ENGLAND.

LONDON:

H. BAILLIÈRE, PUBLISHER, 219, REGENT STREET.

NEW YORK:	MELBOURNE:
BAILLIÈRE BROTHERS, 440, Broadway.	FERDINAND F. BAILLIÈRE.
PARIS:	MADRID:
J. B. BAILLIÈRE & FILS, Rue Hautefeuille.	BAILLY BAILLIÈRE, Calle del Principe.

1861.

PRINTED BY W. H. COX,
5, GREAT QUEEN STREET, LINCOLN'S INN FIELDS.

EDITOR'S PREFACE.

THE intimate relations which exist between the various departments of Zoology and practical medicine render a work embracing these subjects of considerable value to the medical man. This is especially the case in a country like England, possessing numerous colonies scattered over the surface of the globe, in one or other of which the young practitioner is frequently destined to commence his career of responsibility and usefulness.

At the present time there is no standard work in the English language upon Medical Zoology, the only book especially devoted to this subject being Dr. Stephenson's Medical Zoology and Mineralogy, which was published as far back as 1832. The numerous treatises on Materia Medica refer only to those animals which are employed as remedial agents, while the writers on practical medicine seldom give more than a mere outline of the Entozoa and of those Animals which are injurious to man.

The work of M. Tandon contains a more complete account of the Human Entozoa, and of those Animals which are either injurious or beneficial to man in a medical point of view, and is furnished with a larger number of illustrations, than any previous publication on the same subject.

In the translation the text and arrangement of the original work have been closely followed; only a few passages and two short chapters, the one on "False," and the other on

"Fabulous Helmintha," have been omitted. The place of these omissions has been more than occupied by other matter; all which additions are distinguished by being placed in brackets. The weights and measurements have been reduced from the French to the English scale, and are generally given in parts of the pound avoirdupois, or in fractions or decimals of the English inch. The principal responsibility which the Translator has taken upon himself in the way of alteration has been the addition of the passages already referred to. Some of the numerous synonymes of the names of the animals which M. Tandon has included in his work have been omitted, as being of little use to the student and apt to produce confusion. In one or two instances a different name has been made use of to the one proposed by the author; in all such cases the one adopted is that by which the animal has been generally known in England, and of which the use has been recently confirmed by its being retained in Küchenmeister's Manual of Entozoa. In no department of Zoology has greater confusion arisen from the want of a uniform nomenclature than in Helminthology.

The Translator desires to return his best thanks to Professor Quekett for the information he kindly afforded him, particularly with regard to the Bothriocephalus latus; an obligation which will be found specially mentioned in its proper place. His acknowledgments are no less due to Mr. Chatto, the librarian of the College of Surgeons, for his ready and valuable assistance in searching for names and references in the books of the library. The illustrations have been accurately copied by Mr. Joyce from the original wood cuts, and three additional engravings have been added from other sources.

21, JOHN STREET,
BEDFORD ROW.

AUTHOR'S PREFACE.

THESE *Elements of Medical Zoology* have been written principally for the use of those who are intended for the profession of medicine or the practice of pharmacy.

I have been desirous of including within the limits of a small volume, a clear and comprehensive description of those portions of Zoology which have any bearing upon medical science.

In such an undertaking there were two errors to be guarded against. One was to avoid entering too much into the details of either Comparative Anatomy or of Zoology. The majority of students are already bachelors of science, and, therefore, possess a general knowledge of the structure and classification of the Animal Kingdom. I did not consider that it fell within the limits of the present work, when speaking of the *Cantharides*, for example, to enter into a minute account of its nervous system, or when describing the *Viper*, to dilate upon the affinities of the genus or the family to which it belongs. The other error was not to describe at too great length the parts of animals or their products which are employed in medicine, and thus to infringe upon another department.

Most authors who have written upon Medical Zoology have adopted a purely Zoological arrangement. This plan undoubtedly possesses the advantage of imparting to their works a more scientific and less arbitrary arrangement, but, nevertheless, it has also certain disadvantages; it subordinates the Medical Zoology too much to Zoology proper, and deprives it of that professional spirit which should govern all the studies of either a medical or a pharmaceutical school. A writer on Medical Zoology, who arranges his chapters according to the "Animal Kingdom," of Cuvier, for example, will be compelled to speak of the *Quadrumana* and of the *Lepidoptera*, merely because these animals constitute two important divisions in the Zoological series. But the medical practitioner and the pharmaceutist make no use of either *Monkeys* or *Butterflies*... If on the other hand the writer adopts a Zoological plan, but omits those divisions or families in which the medical practitioner has no direct interest, his arrangement becomes disconnected and incomplete, and ceases in fact to be an arrangement. Again, there are animals distinguished from each other by their characters and structure, which the Zoologist places in different groups, often far apart, but which the medical practitioner, on the contrary, brings together for the purpose of studying them collectively, in consequence of the organs they inhabit, the diseases they give rise to, or the remedies which they require. Such is the case with the *Internal Parasites*, animals which are dispersed through the system of the Zoologist, but which are associated in the works of medical authors.[1]

These considerations have induced me to adopt an arrangement founded upon the characters of the animal or its Medico-Zoological relations. Such an arrangement is more practical than scientific; but it is simple, convenient, and well adapted for the purposes of medical or of pharmaceutical study, and avoids leading the reader into details which are foreign to his daily occupation.

I shall briefly point out the order and the family to which each animal belongs, and as the commencement of the work contains a special chapter on the subject of classification, it will

[1] Under the name of *Entozoa* or *Helmintha*.

be easy for the student, who desires further information upon this point, to ascertain either the class or the branch to which the animal belongs, and even to learn the affinities and the differences which arise from such an arrangement compared with other arrangements.

Many animals and many animal productions, which were formerly in use, are no longer employed in medicine. These might have been omitted, but as it' is useful to have a knowledge of this ancient Materia Medica, and to be acquainted with the history, the revolutions, and the progress of therapeutics, I have given a short description of these animals and of their productions in a separate chapter.

For a long time Medical Zoology was made to include only those animals or those parts of animals which are employed as remedies. Thus, in the *Materia Medica* of Linnæus about thirty pages are occupied with the animals which, in his time, were employed in medicine (*Cantharides, Leeches, Cochineal insect*). Bernard Peyrilhe, in his *Lectures on Medical Natural History* (first edition), has devoted forty-six pages to the description of these animals, but he has somewhat extended the list and includes the Internal Parasites, as the *Tæniæ*, the External Parasites, as the *Lice*, and also those animals which, without being parasites, injure man either by sucking the fluids of his body or by their poisonous properties, such as the *Flea* and the *Viper*.

Medical Zoology ought also to include the Natural History of man, and should investigate some of those more difficult questions which are merely touched upon by the sciences of anatomy and physiology. This important division of the subject has not been neglected.

In a still more extended sense Medical Zoology should embrace the relations which exist between the various branches of the science of animals, and the different departments of the healing art. Thus Zoological anatomy, physiology, teratology, and pathology are intimately connected with human anatomy, physiology, teratology, and pathology, and are capable, in many instances, of elucidating, or even of explaining, some of the important problems connected with them; but to have examined such matters in an efficient manner would have led me beyond the intentions of the present work.

I shall commence with the Natural History of Man or *Anthropology*. Under this head I shall examine the principal characters of our species, its perfection, its accidental degradations, its unity, its races, and the manner in which it has been classified by various writers.

This will be followed by a summary of the organization and classification of the animal kingdom.

I shall then describe, under the following heads:

I. Animals and the actual products employed in medicine.
II. Noxious animals, but which are not poisonous nor yet parasites.
III. Poisonous animals.
IV. External parasites or *Epizoa*.
V. Internal parasites or *Entozoa*.

PARIS, *September* 1, 1859.

CONTENTS.

PART THE FIRST.
NATURAL HISTORY OF MAN, OR ANTHROPOLOGY.

	Page
CHAPTER I.—CHARACTERS OF MAN	1
CHAPTER II.—ANATOMY OF MAN	3
CHAPTER III.—OF A SUPPOSED WILD MAN	19
CHAPTER IV.—THE UNITY OF THE HUMAN SPECIES	25
CHAPTER V.—OF THE RACES OF MAN	27
CHAPTER VI.—THE HUMAN KINGDOM	35

SECOND PART.
MEDICAL ZOOLOGY PROPER.

BOOK I.—Organization of Animals — 37
  I. Organs and functions of nutrition — 42
  II. Organs and functions of reproduction — 46
  III. Organs and functions of relation — 49

BOOK II.—Classification of Animals — 52
  I. Ancient — 52
  II. Linnæus — 53
  III. Lamarck — 55
  IV. Cuvier — 56
  V. Present state — 58

BOOK III.—Animals and the Animal products employed in medicine — 63

  SECTION I.—Animals or Animal Productions formerly employed in Medicine — 64

  SECTION II.—Animals and Animal Productions occasionally employed in Medicine — 68
    CHAPTER I.—ANIMALS EMPLOYED WHOLE — 68
    § I. Scink — 68
    § II. Wood Lice — 69
    § III. Cochineal Insect — 71

CONTENTS.

	Page
CHAPTER II.—ANIMALS EMPLOYED IN PART	80
§ I. Pachydermata	80
§ II. Sepiadæ	81
§ III. Snails	83
§ IV. Oysters	86
§ V. Coral	87
§ VI. Sponge	89
CHAPTER III.—ANIMAL PRODUCTS	91
§ I. Spermaceti	91
§ II. Bile	95
§ III. Crabs' eyes	96
§ IV. Spider's web	98
SECTION III.—Animals or Animal Productions which are constantly employed in Medicine	100
CHAPTER I.—LIVER OIL	100
§ I. Oil from the liver of the Cod	101
§ II. Oil from the liver of the Skate	105
§ III. Oil from the liver of the Shark	108
CHAPTER II.—MUSK	110
§ I. Musk	110
§ II. Civet	114
§ III. Beaver	118
§ IV. Hyraceum	122
§ V. Ambergris	125
CHAPTER III.—VESICATING INSECTS	127
§ I. Cantharides	128
§ II. Mylabris	134
§ III. Cerocoma	135
§ IV. Meloe	136
CHAPTER IV.—Leeches	137
CHAPTER V.—Galls	148
§ I. Galls	148
§ II. Cases	154
CHAPTER VI.—THE TREHALA	156
SECTION IV.—Animals or Animal Products employed as Accessories in Medicine	159
§ I. Bones	159
§ II. Blood	160
§ III. Flesh	162
§ IV. Albumen	179

	Page
§ V. Gelatine	179
§ VI. Fat	186
§ VII. Oils	188
§ VIII. Milk	189
§ IX. Eggs	193
§ X. Honey	196
§ XI. Wax	206
§ XII. Hair and other Corneous substances	210

BOOK IV.—Noxious Animals, but which are not poisonous nor yet Parasites — 212

  CHAPTER I.—ANIMALS NOXIOUS DURING THEIR LIVES — 212

    § I. Serra-salmes — 214
    § II. Hæmopis — 215
    § III. Cimicidæ — 219
    § IV. Nepa — 226
    § V. Hippoboscidæ — 227
    § VI. Tsetse — 228
    § VII. Gnats — 230
    § VIII. Stinging Animals — 234
    § IX. Larvæ of Flies — 237
    § X. Other Insects which may be accidentally introduced into the natural cavities of the body — 242

  CHAPTER II.—ANIMALS INJURIOUS AS FOOD — 244

BOOK V.—Poisonous Animals — 247

  SECTION I.—Animals which convey their poison by the mouth — 247

    CHAPTER I.—POISONOUS ANIMALS WITH FANGS — 248
      § I. Vipers — 248
      § II. Foreign Serpents — 255

    CHAPTER II.—POISONOUS ANIMALS ARMED WITH ANTENNÆ IN THE FORM OF CLAWS, OR WITH FOOT JAWS — 260
      § I. Spiders — 260
      § II. Scolopendra — 265

  SECTION II.—Animals which inoculate their poison by means of a special organ — 268

    CHAPTER I.—ORNITHORYNCHUS — 268
    CHAPTER II.—SCORPIONS — 270
    CHAPTER III.—HYMENOPTERA — 275
      § I. Bees — 275
      § II. Humble Bee — 279
      § III. Wasps — 279

	Page
SECTION III.—Animal poisons	281
Humours analogous to poisons	287

BOOK VI.—External Parasites or Epizoa — 291
- SECTION I.—Epizoa living on the skin — 291
  - CHAPTER I.—LICE — 291
  - CHAPTER II.—COMMON FLEA — 297
  - CHAPTER III.—CHIGOE — 300
  - CHAPTER IV.—TICKS — 302
  - CHAPTER V.—ARGADES — 304
  - CHAPTER VI.—HARVEST BUG — 305
- SECTION II.—Epizoa living beneath the skin — 307
  - CHAPTER I.—SARCOPTUS — 307
  - CHAPTER II.—ACAROPSE — 319
  - CHAPTER III.—DEMODEX — 320
  - CHAPTER IV.—SOME OTHER SPECIES OF ACARI — 323

BOOK VII.—Internal Parasites or Entozoa — 324
- SECTION I.—Insect Entozoa — 325
  - Œstridea — 325
- SECTION II.—Crustaceous Entozoa — 329
  - Linguatula — 329
- SECTION III.—Entozoic Worms or Helmintha — 330
  - CHAPTER I.—ASCARIDES — 335
  - CHAPTER II.—OXYURIS — 343
  - CHAPTER III.—TRICHOCEPHALUS — 348
  - CHAPTER IV.—ANCYLOSTOMUM — 353
  - CHAPTER V.—STRONGYLUS — 355
  - CHAPTER VI.—SPIROPTERA — 359
  - CHAPTER VII.—FILARIA — 359
  - CHAPTER VIII.—THECOSOMA — 368
  - CHAPTER IX.—FLUKES — 370
  - CHAPTER X.—FESTUCARIA — 375
  - CHAPTER XI.—TÆNIA — 376
  - CHAPTER XII.—BOTHRIOCEPHALUS — 386
  - CHAPTER XIII.—CYSTIC HELMINTHA — 391
    - § I.—Cysticerci — 391
    - § II.—Echinococci — 394
    - § III.—Acephalocysts — 394
    - § IV.—Transformations of the Cystic Helmintha — 395
  - CHAPTER XIV.—ZOOLOGICAL VIEWS — 403
- SECTION IV.—Infusorial Entozoa — 405

LIST OF ILLUSTRATIONS.

Fig.		Page
1. Head of European	- -	5
2. Head of Negro	- -	5
3. Abd-el-Kader	- - -	28
4. Yeh	- - - -	29
5. Soulouque	- - -	30
6. Head of Negro	- -	30
7. Scink	- - - -	68
8. Wood-louse	- - -	70
9. Armadillo	- - -	70
10. Cochineal insect	- -	72
11. Kermes	- - - -	77
12. African Elephant	- -	80
13. Helix pomatia	- -	84
14. Cachalot	- - -	92
15. Greenland Whale	- -	93
16. Whalebone plates	- -	93
17. Crabs' eyes	- - -	97
18. Cod	- - - -	101
19. Thornback Ray	- -	106
20. Squalus Acanthias	-	109
21. Musk Deer	- - -	111
22. Musk apparatus	- -	112
23. Musk sack	- - -	113
24. Civet	- - - -	115
25. Civet apparatus	- -	116
26. Zibeth	- - - -	117
27. Beaver	- - - -	118
28. Apparatus of the Castor		120
29. Glands of the Castoreum	-	120
30. Daman	- - - -	123
31. Cantharides	- -	129
32. Mylabris	- - -	134
33. Cerocoma	- - -	135
34. Meloe	- - - -	137
35. Grey Leech	- -	139
36. Green Leech	- - -	140
37. Dragon Leech	- -	140
38. Jaws of a Leech	- -	142
39. Leech bite	- - -	144
40. Cynips	- - - -	149
41. Terebra of Cynips	-	149
42. Common Gall	- -	151
43. Section of Gall	- -	151
44. Chinese Gall	- -	155
45. Turpentine Gall	- -	156
46. Larinus of the Trehala	-	157
47. Trehala	- - -	157
48. Helix pomatia	- -	175
49. Common Sturgeon	-	183
50. Sperm Whale	- -	189
51. Common Bee	- -	197
52. Mouth of Bee	- -	201
53. Leg of Bee	- - -	207
54. Whalebone	- - -	211
55. Hæmopis	- - -	215
56. Jaw of Hæmopis	- -	216
57. Common Bug	- -	220
58. Rostrum of Bug	- -	221
59. Reduvina	- - -	222
60. Rostrum of Reduvina	-	223
61. Notonecta	- - -	224
62. Rostrum of Notonecta	-	225
63. Nepa	- - - -	226
64. Rostrum of Nepa	- -	227
65. Horse Fly	- - -	227
66. Beak of Horse Fly	- -	228
67. Tsetse	- - - -	228
68. Trunk of Tsetse	- -	229
69. Gnat	- - - -	230
70. Proboscis of Gnat	-	231
71. Proboscis in action	-	232
72. Stinging hairs	- -	235

LIST OF ILLUSTRATIONS.

Fig.	Page	Fig.	Page
73. Portuguese Man of War	236	100. Grooves formed by the Sarcoptus	316
74. Larvæ of Fly	237		
75. Hominivorous Fly	238	101. Acaropsis	319
76. Common Viper	248	102. Demodex	321
77. Vipera Ammodytes	250	103. Linguatula	330
78. Vipera Pelius	250	104. Ascaris	336
79. Head of a Viper	250	105. Structure of Ascaris	338
80. Poison apparatus	251	106. Oxyuris	343
81. Cerastes Ægyptiacus	256	107. Trichocephalus	349
82. Crotalus Durissus	256	108. Ancylostomum Duodenale	354
83. Poison fang	258	109. Strongylus	356
84. Mouth of Spider	261	110. Head and tail of Strongylus	357
85. Gland and Claw of Spider	261	111. Filaria	363
86. Scolopendra	266	112. Fluke	370
87. Head and claw of Scolopendra	266	113. Common Tænia	376
		114. Head of Tænia	377
88. Common Scorpion	272	115. Segment of Tænia	379
89. Gland and spine of Scorpion	272	116. Sexual organs of Tænia	381
		117. Bothriocephalus latus	387
90. Poison apparatus of Bee	275	118. Head of Bothriocephalus	388
91. Head Louse	292	119. Segments of Bothriocephalus	389
92. Rostrum of Head Louse	294		
93. Body Louse	294	120. Sexual organs of Bothriocephalus	390
94. Pubic Louse	296		
95. Flea	298	121. Cysticerci	393
96. Mouth of Flea	299	122. Echinococci	395
97. Female Sarcoptus	310	123. Acephalocysts	396
98. Male Sarcoptus	312	124. Trichomonas vaginalis	408
99. Rostrum of Sarcoptus	313		

ELEMENTS

OF

MEDICAL ZOOLOGY.

PART THE FIRST.
NATURAL HISTORY OF MAN, OR ANTHROPOLOGY.

CHAPTER I.
CHARACTERS OF MAN.

MAN is the chief of living beings.

Buffon considered him as the only animal *with two hands and two feet.*

Blumenbach gave as his attributes: *the erect position and the possession of two hands.*[1]

Other writers have combined these characters and have said of man: *Situs erectus, manus duæ, pedes bini.*

To these principal characters, others have been subsequently added, which, although less determinate and occupying a subordinate rank, acquire a certain value by being associated together: such are the want of organs of defence (*inermis*), the absence of any natural covering against the inclemencies of the seasons (*nudus*), a projecting chin,[2] the contiguity of the teeth, or absence of any vacant space between them,[3] their evenness, that is, they are all of nearly the same height,[4] the vertical position of the lower incisors,[5]

[1] *Erectus et bimanus.* (Blum.)
[2] *Mentum prominulum.*
[3] *Dentes utrinque reliquis approximati.*
[4] *Dentes æquales.*
[5] *Incisores inferiores erecti.*

B

the hands being provided with a distinctly opposable thumb,[1] the feet having a strong projecting heel,[2] the breasts being two in number and placed on the chest,[3] and lastly, the possession of an extremely short coccyx.[4]

By combining the preceding characters, man may be said to possess a body erect, unarmed, and almost naked; a projecting chin, teeth touching each other, and of nearly the same height (the lower incisors vertical), two perfect hands (on the upper limbs), that is to say, having a distinctly opposable thumb; two feet (on the lower limbs) plantigrade, and with a well-developed projecting heel; two pectoral mammæ, and the coccyx not projecting.

All these are, however, physical characters: there are others of a far higher order, which establish an immeasurable interval between our species and all other animals. Man is especially distinguished from even the most highly organized beings by his understanding,[5] his perfectibility, his knowledge of God, his idea of the infinite, his love of the beautiful, and by his moral sentiment.[6] Thus, the great Linnæus, in his *Systema Naturæ*, after bestowing upon man the name of SAPIENS, did not draw up for our species a series of distinctive characters taken from the number, the proportion, or the form of the bodily organs, in the manner he has done for all other living beings. He justly despised the hands, the feet, the teeth, and the mammæ; he confined himself to writing after the generic name *Homo*, and repeated after his specific name these profound and significant words: NOSCE TE IPSUM![7]

---

[1] *Manuum pollex planè oppositus.*
[2] *Calcaneum prominens et validum.*
[3] *Mammæ pectorales, duæ.*
[4] *Coccyx abbreviatus.*—To these have also been added the lobule of the ear, and the presence, in the woman, of the hymen and the menses.
[5] "Man surpasses in dignity all created things by that emanation from the Divine nature, which animates and enlightens him." (Daubenton.)
[6] "In him we find religion, justice, prudence, piety, modesty, clemency, valour, endurance, faith, and numerous other virtues which are not met with in animals." (A. Paré.)
[7] "NOSCE TE IPSUM *gradus est primus sapientiæ, dictumque Solonis, quondam scriptum litteris aureis supra Dianæ templum.*" (Linn.)—Erxleben does not give the words *nosce te ipsum* as the specific character. After the generic name, he distinguishes man by the following attributes: "*Dentes primores incisores, supra et infera IV. Laniarii conici longitudine æquales. Manus in palmis, non in plantis: Mammæ pectorales II. Cauda nulla.*" This is a very complete and scientific description.

CHAPTER II.

ANATOMY OF MAN.

Man is provided with an internal osseous skeleton. This skeleton has an axis or column formed of 32 vertebræ, consisting of 7 cervical, 12 dorsal, 5 lumbar, 5 sacral, and 3 coccygeal.

The head is placed at the upper part of the vertebral column: it is composed of the cranium and face. In the cranium there are 8 bones: 1 occipital, 2 temporal, 2 parietal, 1 frontal, 1 ethmoid, and 1 sphenoid. In the face there are 14 bones: 2 superior maxillary, 2 malar, 2 nasal, 2 palatine, 1 vomer, 2 inferior spongy bones, 2 lachrymal, and 1 inferior maxillary. Each jaw possesses 16 teeth: viz., 4 incisors in the centre, 2 canines, 1 on either side, and 10 molars or tuberculated grinders, 5 at each extremity, divided into false molars and true molars; the canines are somewhat pointed and project slightly beyond the edges of the incisors and the tubercles of the molars.

Man has 12 pairs of ribs articulated with the vertebral column, 7 superior pairs or true ribs, which are united anteriorly to the sternum by cartilaginous processes, and 5 inferior pairs or false ribs which anteriorly are free.

A portion of the vertebral column with the ribs and the sternum bound the chest or thorax, a large conical cavity which occupies the anterior and superior part of the trunk.

The inferior extremity of the vertebral column or coccyx has above it a large pyramidal and triangular bone, termed the sacrum; this bone is united at the sides with the iliac or hip bones.

The coccyx, the sacrum, and the two ossa innominata form another large irregular cavity, which is open above and below, but closed in front, and is known as the pelvis.

Between the pelvis and the thorax is the abdomen.

In man, the upper or thoracic limbs are attached to the superior and lateral parts of the trunk; each consists of a shoulder, arm, fore-arm, and hand.

The shoulder is formed in front by the clavicle and behind by the scapula. The arm consists of the humerus; the fore-arm has the radius on its outer and the ulna on its inner side. The hand is divided into the carpus, metacarpus, and fingers. The carpus has 8 bones arranged in two rows: in the first row, passing from without inwards, is the scaphoid, the semilunar, the cuneiform, and the pisiform bone; in the second and in the same order is the trapezium, the trapezoid, the os magnum, and the unciform bone. The metacarpus is formed by 5 bones, named according to their numerical order from without to within. The fingers are 5 in number in each hand; they are named thumb, index, middle, ring, and little finger, or in their numerical order, passing from without inwards; each has three phalanges, except the thumb, which has only two.

The lower or abdominal limbs are articulated with the inferior or lateral parts of the trunk, and consist, like the superior, of four divisions—the hip, thigh, leg, and foot.

The hip bone, the analogue of the scapula, forms a part of the pelvis, which has been previously spoken of. The thigh has only a single bone, the femur. The leg has the fibula on its outer, the tibia on its inner side, and the patella in front and above. The foot is divided into the tarsus, metatarsus, and toes. The tarsus is composed of 7 bones: viz., the calcaneum, the astragalus, the scaphoid, the cuboid, and the 3 cuneiform bones. The metatarsus is composed of 5 bones, arranged parallel to each other, and named according to their numerical order, from within outwards. The toes are 5 in number, and are also named after their numerical order and in the same direction: each has three phalanges, except the great toe, which has only two.

In man, the length from the bend of the body to the sole of the foot is generally equal to half his height. The distance from the extremity of one middle finger to that of the other, when the arms are extended, is equal to the height of his body.

When the body is of average stoutness, the height is equal to five times its diameter.

The head and neck equal the sixth, and the head alone the seventh and a half part of the entire height of the body. The long diameter of the face represents the tenth part, and the latter is equal to the length of the palm of the hand.

Man is remarkable for the general weakness of his organs at the period of birth, and for the length of time required for his physical education. He is partly naked and partly covered; his hair is distinguished for its length.

The human species is especially frugivorous. Man drinks without being impelled to it by thirst, and he alone makes use of compound and fermented liquors. The latter he obtains from the grape, the sugar-cane, barley, rice, dates, the cocoa-nut, the berries of the juniper-tree, from the twigs of the pine and the birch, from the sap of certain trees, and from the milk of several of the mammalia.

His frugivorous nature accords with the character of his teeth, while his stomach is simple, and his alimentary canal of moderate length. The intestines are divided into the small and large intestines, the latter being provided with a rudimentary cæcal appendage. The great omentum hangs in front of the abdominal viscera, as far as the pelvis. The heart is placed obliquely upon the diaphragm, with its apex inclined towards the left side.

The human head has a facial angle which varies between 85° and 64°. The maximum of 85° occurs in the European (fig. 1);

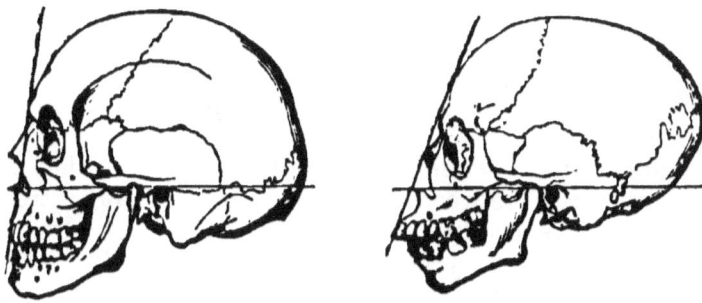

Fig. 1.   Fig. 2.

it is 75° in the Chinese; and 70° in the Negro (fig. 2). [In the adult Chimpanzee, the facial angle is only 35°, and in the Orang 30°. Professor Owen has shown that the measurements, which assigned a higher development of the facial angle to these anthropoid apes, were made on young animals, before the enormous canines of the second set of teeth had made their appearance and before the large elongated muzzle of the full-grown animal had become developed.]

The human brain is distinguished by several important characters; such as the great development of its anterior lobes, and of the corpus callosum, by the number of its convolutions and anfractuosities, by the depth of the latter, and, as a necessary consequence, by the great extent of the cerebral surface; it has been calculated that the volume of the encephalon is to that of the body as 1 to 28.[1] Its average weight

---

[1] In the Saimiri [a small species of monkey inhabiting Brazil, scarcely more than 10 inches in length, exclusive of the tail] the proportion is as

is about 44oz. 80grs. avoirdupois.[1] The posterior portions of the hemispheres overlap the cerebellum.

[The following tables of the average weight and relative size of the brain are taken from a paper by the late Dr. John Reid, in the London and Edinburgh Monthly Journal of Medical Science, for April, 1843.

TABLE I.

Average Weight of the Encephalon between 25 and 55 years of age, in the two Sexes. Males, 53 brains weighed. Females, 36 brains weighed.

	MALES.	FEMALES.	DIFFERENCE IN FAVOUR OF MALES.
	lb. oz. dr.	lb. oz. dr.	oz. dr.
Average weight of encephalon	50 3½ or 3 2 3¼	44 8¼ or 2 12 8½	5 11

Tiedman says, "The female brain is lighter than that of the male. It varies between 2lbs. 8oz. and 3lbs. 11oz. troy. I never found a female brain that weighed 4lbs. The brain of a girl, an idiot, sixteen years old, weighed only 1lb. 6oz. 1dr. The female brain weighs on an average from 4 to 8oz. less than that of the male; and this difference is already perceptible in a new-born child.

"The brain arrives, on an average, at its full size towards the seventh and eighth year. Soemmering says, erroneously, that the brain does not increase after the third year. Gall and Spurzheim, on the other hand, are of opinion that the brain continues to grow till the fourteenth year. The brothers Wenzel have shown that the brain arrives at its full growth about the seventh year. This is confirmed by Hamilton's researches.

"Desmoulins is of opinion that the brain decreases in old people. From this circumstance he explains the diminution

---

1 : 22; in some birds as 1 : 20 : 18 : 16 or : 12. The last proportion occurs in the tom-tit. (Is. Geoffroy Saint-Hilaire).

[1] That of Dupuytren weighed 50oz. 286 grains, avoirdupois, which is probably the maximum weight. The weight of 64oz. 191grs. avoirdupois, which has been assigned to Cuvier's brain, must be regarded as an exaggeration; while that of 78oz. 606grs. and of nearly 79oz. avoirdupois, which are supposed to have been the weight of the brains of Byron and of Cromwell, are impossible. [The brain of the late Dr. Ambercrombie weighed about 68oz. avoirdupois. See Cormack's Journal, Dec., 1844.]

of the functions of the nervous system and intellectual powers. The truth of this assertion has not as yet been determined. The brothers Wenzel and Hamilton deny it.

"It is remarkable that the brain of a man, eighty-two years old, was very small and weighed but 3lbs. 2oz. 3dr.; and the brain of a woman, about eighty years old, weighed but 2lbs. 9oz. 1dr. I have generally found the cavity of the skull smaller in old men than in middle-aged persons. It appears to me, therefore, probable that the brain really decreases in old age, only more remarkable in some persons than in others."[1]

The following are the results obtained by Dr. Reid, with reference to the weight of the brain at different periods of life.

TABLE II.

Males: number of brains weighed, 154.				Females: number of brains weighed, 97.			
Age. Years.	Number weighed.	Encephalon. oz.	dr.	Age. Years.	Number weighed.	Encephalon. oz.	dr.
1 to 4	5	39	$4\frac{2}{5}$	2 to 4	6	37	9
5 " 7	3	43	10	5 " 7	3	39	$9\frac{1}{3}$
7 " 10	6	46	$2\frac{1}{6}$	7 " 8	3	42	$7\frac{1}{3}$
10 " 13	3	48	$7\frac{1}{3}$	—	—	—	—
13 " 16	5	47	$8\frac{2}{5}$	—	—	—	—
16 " 20	6	52	10	16 " 20	8	44	$11\frac{1}{2}$
20 " 30	25	50	$9\frac{1}{2}$	20 " 30	18	45	$2\frac{2}{9}$
30 " 40	23	51	15	30 " 40	23	44	$1\frac{1}{2}$
40 " 50	34	48	$13\frac{1}{2}$	40 " 50	18	44	$10\frac{1}{9}$
50 " 60	29	50	2	50 " 60	5	45	$4\frac{1}{5}$
60 " 70	8	50	$6\frac{6}{8}$	60 " 70	11	42	$14\frac{6}{7}$
70 & upw.	7	48	$4\frac{2}{7}$	70 & upw.	2	38	$8\frac{1}{2}$

This table shows that the brain attains its greatest absolute weight at an early age. The maximum is found in the table of the male brains at between 16 and 20. Dr. Reid, however, states that this apparent excess of weight at that period over the next forty years must have arisen from sources of fallacy incidental to insufficient data. And in the group between 40 and 50, Dr. Reid states that some brains much below the

[1] Tiedman on the Brain of the Negro compared with that of the European and the Orang Otang, Phil. Trans. 1836.

average were found, so as to leave no doubt that the average weight in that group was to be attributed to that circumstance.

A decided diminution in the weight of the brain was noticed in females above 60 years of age, but among the males this was not apparent until a later period.

"Anatomists," says Tiedman, "differ very much as to the weight of the brain compared with the bulk and weight of the body; for the weight of the body varies so much, that it is impossible to determine accurately the proportion between it and the brain. The weight of an adult varies from 100 to 800lbs., and changes both in health and when under the influence of disease, depending in a great measure on nutrition. The weight of the brain, although different in adults, remains generally the same, unaltered by the increase or diminution of the body. Thin persons have, therefore, relative to the size of the body, a larger brain than stout people.

"From my researches I have drawn the following conclusions:

"1. The brain of the new-born child is, relatively to the size of the body, the largest; the proportion is 1 : 6.

"2. The human brain is smaller, in comparison to the body, the nearer man approaches to his full growth. In the second year the proportion of the brain to the body is as 1 : 14; in the third, 1 : 18; in the fifteenth, 1 : 24. In a full-grown man, between the age of 20 and 70 years, as 1 : 35 to 45. In lean persons the proportion is often as 1 : 22 to 27; in stout persons as 1 : 50 to 100 and more.

"3. Although Aristotle has remarked that the female brain is absolutely smaller than the male, it is nevertheless not relatively smaller compared with the body; for the female body is, in general, lighter than that of the male. The female brain is for the most part even larger than the male, compared with the size of the body."

The brain of a man, eighty-two years old, was very small and weighed but 3lbs. 2oz. 3dr.; and the brain of a woman, about eighty years old, weighed 2lbs. 9oz. 1dr.[1]

The following table gives the results obtained by Dr. Reid from the examination of 92 bodies.

[1] *Opus cit.*

Table III.

Relative Weight of the Encephalon to the entire Body.

Males: number of brains weighed, 57.			Females: number of brains weighed, 35.		
Age. Years.	Number weighed.	Encephalon. oz. dr.	Age. Years.	Number weighed.	Encephalon. oz. dr.
1 to 5	4	1 to 8½	2 to 4	4	1 to 8⅖
at 5	2	1 ,, 9$\frac{15}{19}$	5 ,, 7	—	—
at 7	2	1 ,, 10$\frac{2}{11}$	7 ,, 10	3	1 ,, 13$\frac{1}{23}$
13 to 15	3	1 ,, 15$\frac{10}{11}$	13 ,, 15	—	1 ,, 22
—	—	—	16 ,, 20	3	1 ,, 30½
20 ,, 30	11	1 ,, 35$\frac{22}{44}$	20 ,, 30	4	1 ,, 33$\frac{4}{23}$
30 ,, 40	6	1 ,, 37$\frac{6}{11}$	30 ,, 40	8	1 ,, 34⅝
40 ,, 50	14	1 ,, 38	40 ,, 50	5	1 ,, 35
50 ,, 60	11	1 ,, 36¼	50 ,, 60	2	1 ,, 38$\frac{1}{33}$
60 ,, 70	4	1 ,, 30⅓	60 & upw.	6	1 ,, 38⅓

Man's face is more or less flat (*os sublime*), while that of animals is provided with a *snout*, which is more or less projecting (*os bestiale*). The human face is small relatively to the size of the cranium; it is short, and has a vertical or slightly oblique direction. The forehead projects, and the features portray every thought and every change of feeling.

The organs of the senses are well developed. That of touch is extremely fine, owing to the form of the hand, the softness and flexibility of the skin, and the various positions which the thumb is capable of assuming.[1] Taste is very delicate; and that of smell easily distinguishes between different odours. The ear has a marvellous power of appreciating the different intonations of sound; and sight, although restricted to a short distance, is nevertheless clear and distinct. The latter acts in front, and not at the sides of the body, thereby producing greater concentration and unity in its action.

Man alone is cosmopolitan; for he only is acquainted with the use of fire and clothing. He appreciates and seeks for causes. He observes the actual, he conceives the possible, and doubts the supernatural. (Bourdon.) He delights in amuse-

---

[1] In the monkeys it is the posterior pair of extremities which are best adapted for prehension, and not the anterior or superior pair, as in man.

ment and luxury; he hopes and repents; he laughs and weeps; he has the wonderful faculty of expressing abstract notions by the aid of sound, and it is upon this faculty that his memory and his power of reasoning depend. (Cuvier.) The distinction which reason establishes between man and animals is so great [1] that the most degraded Hottentot is capable of governing the most perfect of the mammalia, whether in the form of a mischievous monkey or of the sagacious elephant; he commands them, he compels them to obey him, and renders them subservient to his use. (Adanson.)

Man has been justly pronounced the chief of animals and the king of nature.[2] He has no other masters than his own passions and his fellow-men; his superiority does not depend upon the strength of his body or the perfection of his senses, but upon the faculties of his soul and the powers of his mind.[3]

He has measured the course of the stars, and calculated the period of their return. He has invented signs in which to embody his ideas, and by which he can preserve and transmit them to posterity.[4] Lastly, the multiplicity of his industrial occupations bears a direct relation to the variety of his amusements and the extent of his dominions.

Man's body is adapted to the erect position. His uprightness results partly from the central situation of the occipital foramen (Daubenton), and to an arrangement of the vertebral column, which is peculiar to himself (Serres). [In a well-formed European skull, the plane of the occipital foramen is horizontal, and its anterior extremity is about half way between the tuberosity of the occipital bone and the incisors of the upper jaw. This central position of the occipital foramen and the condyles is one of the great peculiarities of man, who is destined to stand erect. His head, therefore, is almost equally balanced on the top of the spine. In monkeys, who hold a middle rank between man and quadrupeds, the foramen magnum is placed farther back; in the orang-utan, it is about twice as far from the foramina incisiva as from the back of the head. Consequently, although monkeys can stand erect for a

---

[1] "He comes naked upon the earth . . . to his great profit and advantage he is armed with understanding and clothed with reason." (A. Paré.) "Man is a *philosophical animal*." (Virey.)

[2] "Man is more excellent and perfect than all the animals." (A. Paré.)

[3] "*Robur et vires in sapientia.*" (Eustachi.)

[4] "He has reduced to writing the doctrines and speculations of philosophers, so that by this means we are still able to converse and to dispute with Plato, Aristotle, and the other writers of antiquity." (A. Paré.)

time, they cannot do so long.[1]] Man's back is less covered, or, more correctly speaking, it is more naked than his chest or his abdomen; a character which does not belong to any other mammalian animal. (Blumenbach.) His foot is large and provided with a projecting heel, upon which the leg is placed in a vertical position; the toes are short and possess but little flexibility, and the great toe, although larger and longer than the others, cannot be opposed to them. The muscles which maintain the foot and the thigh in a state of extension are exceedingly powerful, and form the calf and the buttock. The pelvis is large, the legs are placed apart and give firmness to the bipedal and erect position. Man could not, even if he wished it, move conveniently upon all four limbs. The inferior extremities, now become posterior, would be too long relatively to the superior, which would be similarly converted into anterior extremities. The length of the thighs would always bring the knees against the ground. The shoulders, placed too widely apart, and the arms carried too far from the medium line, would ill support the anterior part of the body. The heel would not rest upon the ground. The weight of the head would not be properly sustained. The eyes, instead of looking forward, would be directed towards the ground. The arteries which supply the brain not subdividing as in most quarupeds, the blood which is requisite for the supply of so large an organ would be poured into it with too much force, and frequent apoplexies would be the result of the horizontal position. (Cuvier.)

The straight and erect attitude of man is that of command. His head, directed towards the heavens, offers an august and dignified countenance. (Adanson.) It has been truly observed, that the erect attitude of man constitutes one of his great physical distinctions, even as his intelligence forms a moral distinction.

The nearly equal number of individuals belonging to the two sexes proves that monogamy is the natural condition of man.

The male organ contains no central bone; it hangs in front of the pubis, and the prepuce does not attach it to the abdomen. This fold of the skin covers the gland more or less completely, and is provided with its proper frenum. The scrotum is placed externally, and is lax and wrinkled.

[1] *Human Osteology*, by Luther Holden, p. 117, 2nd edition. London, 1857.

The womb is a simple oval cavity; at the entrance of the vagina there is generally a hymen or carunculæ myrtiformes. The mammæ are placed on the chest, and thus accord with the facility with which the female carries her infant in her arms. (Cuvier.)

The human female has usually one young at a birth. Out of 150 to 200 deliveries there does not occur above one example of twins. It is extremely rare to meet with more. The duration of pregnancy is nine months. Children born before the seventh month seldom live.

A fœtus of a month old is from .02 to .03 of an inch in length; at two months it measures from an inch to an inch and a half; at three months from two to two and a half inches; at five months from eight and a half to ten and a half inches; at seven months from thirteen to fourteen inches; at eight months from nearly fourteen to fifteen inches; and at nine months eighteen inches and a half.

[According to Müller an embryo of the *fourth week* measures $3\frac{1}{2}$ lines. At the commencement of the *second month* the length of the embryo extends to a few lines or half an inch. The extremities are visible in the form of leaf-like appendages, and the cavity of the mouth exists, and is wide open. In the course of the *third month* the fœtus acquires the length of two and a half or three inches; in the *fourth*, during which the sex becomes distinguishable, it reaches to four inches; and in the *fifth* to twelve inches. At this period occur the formation of the fat, and the further development of the rudimentary horny structures, the nails and the down, lanugo, which appears over the whole surface, and the eyelids coalesce. In the fifth month, also, the movements of the embryo are felt by the mother. A fœtus born during the *sixth month* breathes, but does not continue to live. In the *seventh lunar month* the embryo acquires the length of 16 inches or more, and if expelled from the uterus is sometimes capable of living. In the *eighth lunar month* its length is $16\frac{1}{2}$ inches; the testes at this period descend from the abdominal cavity through the inguinal ring into the scrotum, which had hitherto the form of empty folds of the skin, and the eyelids become free. In the *ninth month* the hair appears on the head, and the embryo measures 17 inches in length. In the *tenth lunar month* its length reaches 18 or 20 inches.[1]]

The milk teeth begin to appear some months after birth

[1] See Müller's *Elements of Physiology*, transl. by Baly, vol. ii. pp. 1588 —1594. London, 1842.

[between the fifth and eighth.[1]] The incisors are the first teeth which are cut [those of the lower jaw generally preceding the upper by a week or two]. At two years of age [or from that to two and a half] the healthy child is provided with twenty teeth. These teeth begin to be shed about the seventh year, and are replaced by others. Of the twelve molar teeth, which are never shed, four make their appearance at the age of four years and a half, four at nine years of age, and four much later. The latter, termed the wisdom teeth, sometimes show themselves towards the twentieth year, but occasionally not until after the fortieth.

[The periods mentioned in the preceding paragraph for the appearance of the permanent molars differ materially from those at which they occur in this country. The first permanent molars do not appear before the seventh year, and sometimes the four are not through the gum until the ninth year. The second are in place between the twelfth and thirteenth years. These numbers were obtained by Mr. Saunders from the examination of a large number of children, for the purpose of ascertaining how far the teeth might be trusted for the purpose of determining the age of children employed in factories, and to prevent any infringement of the Factories Regulation Act. From all the cases which came under his notice, Mr. Saunders has drawn the following conclusions.

"Thus then it appears, that of 708 children of nine years of age, 389 would have been pronounced, on an application of this test, to be near the completion of their ninth year; that is, they presented the full developments of that age. But on the principle already stated, that of reckoning the fourth tooth as present when the three are fully developed, a still larger majority will be obtained, and, instead of 389, the proportion will be as follows: of 708 children, no less a number than 530 will be fully nine years of age. What then are the deviations exhibited by the remaining 178? They are the following: 126 would be pronounced eight years and six months, and the remaining 52 eight years of age, so that the extreme deviations are only twelve months, and these only in the inconsiderable proportion (when compared with the results obtained by other criteria) of 32 in 708.

"Again, of 338 children, of thirteen years of age, no less than 294 might have been pronounced with confidence to be

---

[1] T. Bell: *The Anatomy, Physiology, and Diseases of the Teeth*, p. 60, 2nd edit. London, 1835.

of that age. The remaining 44 would have been considered as follows: 36 in their thirteenth, and eight near the completion of their twelfth year."[1]

The fœtus increases the more rapidly as it approaches the period of birth. The child increases less and less as it passes from that period.

At birth the infant weighs from 3 kilogrammes (6·6lbs. avoirdupois) to 3 kilogrammes and a half (7·7lbs avoirdupois). It has attained more than one quarter of its full height; at two years and a half it has acquired the half, and at nine or ten years of age the three quarters. At thirty years of age it ceases to grow.

[The length of the new-born infant varies from about 16 inches to 22; the average, probably, being between 18 and 19, though Roederer states it to be 20½ inches. The mean weight is about 7lbs. avoirdupois, or one twentieth of that of the adult. Dr. William Hunter states, that of many thousand new-born perfect infants weighed at the British Hospital, in London, by Dr. Macaulay, the smallest was about 4lbs., the largest 11lbs. 2oz., while the greater number varied from 5 to 8lbs. The average weight of 26 children at the natural period, weighed by Roederer, was about 6¼lbs.; the lightest 5¼lbs.; and the heaviest 8lbs. The length of male slightly exceeds that of female children, while the difference in weight is estimated by Dr. Clarke at about 9oz. avoirdupois. In the case of twins, the average weight of each twin is in general less than that of children born at single births, though the combined weight of both is greater. Dr. Clarke found that the average weight of twelve twins was 11lbs. avoirdupois each pair; the heaviest being 13lbs., and the lightest 8½lbs.[2]]

The average height of a man is 5·378 feet.[3] A man is considered to be of the ordinary height when he measures from 5·249 to 5·754 feet. The woman is somewhat shorter. A man is said to be short when he is much under 5·249 feet, and is called tall when he is above 5·754 feet in height. Men who do not measure 3·280 feet are *dwarfs*, while those who exceed 6·560 feet are *giants*.[4]

---

[1] *Medical Gazette*, vol. ii., 1837-38, p. 492. See also Mr. Saunders's work, entitled, *The Teeth a Test of Age*.
[2] T. H. Tanner, M.D., F.L.S.: *A Practical Treatise on the Diseases of Infancy and Childhood*, p. 16. London, 1858.
[3] According to Tenon it is 5·495; according to Lélut, 5·436; and according to Silbermann, 5·429 feet.
[4] By raising his arms in the air a man measures from the sole of his

[The skeleton of O'Byrne, the Irish giant, which is preserved in the College of Surgeons, measures eight feet from the vertex to the sole of the foot. In the annual Register Chronicle, for June, 1783 (vol. xxvi. p. 209), it is stated that in August, 1780, O'Byrne measured eight feet, that in 1782 he had gained two inches, and after he was dead he measured eight feet four inches. He died in 1783, aged only 22; his death was hastened by excessive drinking, to which he was always addicted. None of his family were of more than ordinary stature.]

The varieties of the human race which differ most as regards height are the Boschesmans and the Patagonians. Putting aside the exaggerated statements of some travellers, we find that the proportion of their heights is as 8 to 27.[1]

[Darwin, in his interesting narrative of the voyage of the Beagle, when speaking of the Patagonians, says: "Their height appears greater than it really is, from their large guanaco mantles, their long flowing hair, and general figure: on an average their height is about six feet, with some men taller and only a few shorter; and the women are also tall; altogether, they are certainly the tallest race we anywhere saw.[2] The skeleton of a male Boschesman in the College of Surgeons (No. 5,357) measures four feet five inches from the vertex to the sole of the foot. If we assume that there is the same relative difference between the length of the skeleton and the body of the Boschesman as there was in the case of O'Byrne (viz., the one twenty-fifth of the whole height), then the owner of the foregoing skeleton must have been four feet seven inches high.]

The average weight of mankind, without reference to age or sex, is 115lbs. avoirdupois. That of a man is 121lbs., and that of a woman, 110lbs. Man attains his greatest weight at about forty years of age, and begins to diminish very perceptibly at sixty. The average weight of the old person, in both sexes, is about the same as that of the individual at nineteen years of age.

foot to the tips of his fingers 6·560 feet, and from the sole of his foot to the umbilicus 3·280 feet. (Silbermann.)

[1] It has been calculated that the difference in size between the Shetland pony and the large English brewer's horse is as 1 to 27. Thus the variation in the size of the human race is eight times less than what occurs in the horse.

[2] Charles Darwin, M.A., F.R.S. : *Journal of Researches into the Natural History and Geology of the Countries visited during the Voyage of H.M.S. Beagle round the World*, p. 232. 2nd edit. London, 1845.

[M. Quetelet[1] has given the following table of the variation in the weights of full-grown and well-formed persons in kilogrammes; the value of the number in avoirdupois has been placed beside them, omitting fractional parts when under half a pound.

	Maximum.	Minimum.	Medium.
	kil. lbs. av.	kil. lbs. av.	kil. lbs. av.
Male weight	98·5 218	49·1 108	63·7 140
Female ,,	93·5 206	63·7 140	55·2 121½

A healthy child begins to talk when he is from twelve to fifteen months old, the first sound which he utters amongst nearly all nations and in almost every language are the syllables *ba, pa, ma*, because they are the sounds which are most easily pronounced. Some children will articulate very distinctly at two years of age, and will repeat nearly all that is said to them; but the majority do not talk until they are two years and a half old, and frequently not until much later. (Adanson.)

When the body has attained its full height and size, it begins to spread and to become fat. The minute vessels are gradually filled up, the solids are rendered more dense, and after a life of longer or shorter duration, passed amidst more or less excitement and anxiety, there comes old age, feebleness, decrepitude, and death. (Cuvier.)

According to Duvillard (1806) the average duration is 28¼ years. According, however, to the more recent statistics, it is 33·63 years.

Men who have passed the average period of life usually attain to 70 years of age. Persons who live to a hundred are exceedingly rare, and still more so those who exceed that age.

[The returns of the Registrar General's *Fifth Annual Report* show, that in England the average duration of life at birth is 41·18 years; and in children who have attained the age of one year it is 47·71 years for the male, or 48·55 years for the female; and for all children without reference to the sex it is 48·13 years.

The following remarks are taken from Dr. Tanner's work on the diseases of children:[2]

"Let us suppose," says this writer, "that 100,000 children were born alive on the 1st January, 1841; and that

[1] "*Annales d'Hygiene Publique*," &c., tom. x. p. 27.
[2] *Op. cit.* p. 6.

they were the offspring of all ranks and classes of Englishmen. From the usual proportion of the two sexes registered, it will appear, that 51,274 were boys, and 48,726 girls. Of the 100,000 children, 14,631 have perished during the first year, leaving 85,369 alive on the 1st January, 1842; they were exactly a year old, and are placed against the age '1' in the table. On the 1st January, 1843, the survivors were two years old, and in number 80,102; so that 5,267 have died in the second year. On 1st January, 1846, the fifth birthday was attained, and there were 74,201 living. Consequently, in the first five years, 25,799 children out of 100,000 have died. During the next five years, when the children leave home more, and when—as it appears from the parliamentary returns—great numbers pass part of the day at school, the mortality becomes considerably less, so that we find 70,612 alive at the age of ten; while from ten to fifteen the loss is small, 68,627 living to the latter age. The loss of life among girls now becomes rather greater than among boys, and it continues so for the ensuing five years, when both sexes are more detached from the care of their parents, and the majority pursue the professions or trades by which they afterwards gain a livelihood. The mortality appears to increase rather rapidly from twelve to fifteen; and then at a slow regular rate from the age of fifteen to fifty-five: 66,059 attained the age of twenty. It was stated that 51,274 boys were born alive to 48,726 girls; but the mortality in infancy is greater among boys than girls; so that 31,958 males attain the age of twenty-five, and 31,623 females attain the age of twenty-four. This is about the average age of marriage in England, and the number of the two sexes is then nearly equal. The chance of living from twenty-five to forty-five is rather in favour of English women; the violent deaths of men counter-balancing the dangers of child-bearing. At the age of sixty 37,996 will be still alive, while 24,531 attain the age of seventy; *i. e.*, 11,823 men, and 12,708 women, the mortality of the latter being less than that of the former after fifty-five. At the age of eighty, there is but little doubt that about 9,000 of the 100,000 will still be found alive; but after this period the observations grow uncertain, although we may calculate that 1,140 will attain the age of ninety, 16 will be centenarians, and 1 man and 1 woman, out of the 100,000, may remain to complete their one hundred and fourth year.

" For convenience of reference, these calculations are arranged in the following table, which also contains a register showing the *expectation of life*; i. e., the mean number of years which, at any given age, the members of a community, taken one with another, may expect to live. The *mean duration of life* is found by adding the age to the expectation of life: thus, the mean duration of a boy's life at five years is 5 + 49·64 = 54·64. The *probable duration of life* is the age at which a given number of children born into the world will be reduced one half; so that there is an equal chance of their dying before or after that age. Thus, out of 51,274 males and 48,726 females, a total of 100,000 new-born infants, about one-half of each sex will have died before completing the age of forty-five; so that the probable lifetime of an infant at birth is 45 years.

LIFE TABLE FOR ENGLAND.

Age.	Living.	Males.	Females.	Expectation of Life.		
				Persons.	Males.	Females.
0	100,000	51,274	48,726	41·18	40·19	42·18
1	85,369	43,104	42,265	47·13	46·71	47·55
2	80,102	40,388	39,714	49·19	48·82	49·57
3	77,392	39,018	38,374	49·89	49·52	50·29
4	75,539	38,064	37,475	50·11	49·74	50·48
5	74,201	37,385	36,816	50·01	49·64	50·38
10	70,612	35,564	35,048	47·44	47·08	47·81
15	68,627	34,573	34,054	43·74	43·35	44·13
20	66,059	33,324	32,735	40·34	39·88	40·81
25	63,295	31,958	31,337	36·99	36·47	37·52
30	60,332	30,473	29,859	33·68	33·13	34·25
35	57,172	28,867	28,305	30·40	29·83	30·99
40	53,825	27,145	26,680	27·14	26·56	27·72
45	50,301	25,311	24,990	23·86	23·30	24·43
50	46,621	23,376	23,245	20·55	20·02	21·07
55	42,796	21,355	21,441	17·16	16·68	17·63
60	37,996	18,808	19,188	14·00	13·59	14·40
65	31,852	15,589	16,263	11·20	10·86	11·52
70	24,531	11,823	12,708	8·78	8·51	9·03
75	16,664	7,867	8,797	6·74	6·53	6·92
80	9,398	4,316	5,082	5·07	4·92	5·20
85	4,021	1,780	2,241	3·75	3·64	3·83
90	1,140	481	659	2·74	2·68	2·77
95	174	69	105	2·13	2·22	2·06
100	16	7	9	—	—	—
104	2	1	1	—	—	—

"This table reads thus: Of 100,000 births, 51,274 will be male children, and 48,726 females; of which number 85,369 will be alive at the end of one year, or 43,104 males, and 42,265 females. So again, of the 100,000, one male and one female will live to the age of 104.

"To learn the expectation of life the table should be read as follows: At birth, a child's expectation of life is 41·18 years; if a boy, 40·19 years; if a girl, 42·18 years. Again, at the age of 40, a person's expectation of life is 27·14 years; hence the mean age to which persons who attain the age of 40 live, is $40+27·14=67·14$ years."]

The period when man is capable of reproducing his species is that of puberty; this occurs at from twelve to sixteen years in the male, and from eleven to fourteen in the female. The circumstances being otherwise the same, this period occurs earlier in hot climates than in those which are temperate, and in the latter sooner than those in which are cold.

Puberty is the spring-time of human life. Up to this period nature has only supplied the child with what was necessary for its nourishment and for its growth. His life has been confined to himself, he has been incapable of transmitting it; but the moment when puberty arrives he has acquired, not only all that is necessary for his individual existence, but he can also impart existence to others. (Adanson.) This superfluity of life, which seeks to extend itself without, is marked by several signs, such as a change in the voice, the growth of the beard, the enlargement of the throat, and the development of the sexual organs.

CHAPTER III.

OF A SUPPOSED WILD MAN.

DOES man exist, or has he ever existed, in a wild state? The answer is, and should be, in the negative. Man (*Homo sapiens*) is essentially a social being.[1] If when he first appeared upon the earth, he remained for a time in the so called state of nature he must rapidly have emerged from that condition. But this early stage of society was never similar or analogous to the kind of life which is led by even the most perfect of the

[1] Ζῶον πολιτικὸν. (Aristotle.)

mammalian animals. The least enlightened populations, and the lowest islanders, have always presented themselves in the condition of a society more or less perfectly organized; sometimes even remarkably so, and manifesting, not only a craving for civilization, but also the capacity of attaining it. In fact, even in the smallest tribes, it is easy to recognise the presence and influence of those important moral instincts which relate to family, to property, and to religion.

Human society is essentially distinguished from every association of animals, such as those of beavers, bees, or ants, both by the motives which produce it, the advantages which are derived from it, and by its progress towards perfection. (Rullier.)

It is with regret that we find a great naturalist admitting for the noblest of living beings the existence of a savage type (*ferus*),[1] to which he gives as characters the quadrupedal station, the absence of speech, and a covering of hair (*tetrapus, mutus, hirsutus*).[2]

Several writers have published apocryphal histories of miserable individuals belonging to our species, who, having been abandoned either through poverty or crime, have lived in woods, and caverns, amidst the beasts of the fields. These persons, having lost the power of speech, could only utter discordant and inarticulate sounds, and approached to a state of imbecility.

It would be folly to seek with Lamettrie,[3] in these rare and happily exceptional cases, the primitive type of the human race. These degenerated beings are physical and moral aberrations from the normal or civilized man, and not individuals who have returned to the primitive condition from which civilization originated.

Linnæus mentions nine of these cases; but he does not inquire into their origin, their authenticity, or their scientific value; he gives them without order or date, and without detail or comment. All these unhappy beings are children, not a single adult is amongst them;[4] a very remarkable circum-

---

[1] *Homo ferus* (Linn.) *non est varietas.* (Exerleben.)
[2] Aristotle and Pliny also believed in the existence of a wild type of the human race.
[3] De Lamettrie has related several examples, and from them he has drawn the six characters which he assigns to man *in a state of nature.*
[4] Larrey has spoken in a vague manner of a wild man whose skeleton he saw at Wilna. His description, which was probably taken from some hasty notes made at the time, seems to have been written under the pre-

stance, and one which shows that a state of isolation is not that which is adapted to our species. Some of these children have been found with herds of sheep and oxen, and others even amongst wolves and bears! It is on this account that Linnæus has characterized them by epithets indicative of their singular association (*juvinis ovinus, bovinus, lupinus, ursinus*).

When we inquire into the origin of these cases, we are astonished at the contradictions, the falsehoods, and the absurdities which we meet with.

The following are two of the best authenticated examples: *The Young Girl of Champagne, and the Young Savage of Tarn.*

1. The *young girl of Champagne* (*puella Campanica*, Linn.) had lived in the woods, in the midst of the wild animals, but it was not known what were the circumstances which led to this. She was captured and taken to a chateau in the neighbourhood where she was brought up. She resided for a long time in Paris, and was known by the name of *Mademoiselle Leblanc*. We are indebted for her history to M. Racine.

In the month of September, 1731, the servants of the Chateau de Sogny, near Chalons-sur-Marne, one night perceived a sort of phantom on an apple-tree in the garden; they approached without noise and succeeded in surrounding the tree. But, suddenly, the phantom leaped over their heads, then over the wall of the garden and fled to the woods, where it mounted a large tree. The master of the chateau directed his servants, with the assistance of the country people, to cut down the tree; it was necessary to serve several in the same way, in consequence of the phantom throwing itself from tree to tree. It was suspected that it was a young savage of the female sex, and the people endeavoured to pursuade her to descend. The mistress of the chateau, thinking that hunger and thirst would soon induce her to do so, ordered a bowl of water and some food to be placed at the trunk of the tree. The young girl, for such it proved to be, tempted by the sight, partly descended and then remounted. At length she came down and proceeded to drink; she performed this act by dipping her chin in up to the mouth, and swallowed the liquid in the same manner as a horse.

When she was secured, the nails both of her hands and feet were very long and exceedingly strong, giving her great facility in grasping the branches of the trees, and probably assisting her to destroy the wild animals. The colour of her body was

conceived notion that the skeleton bore a strong resemblance to that of the *Orang-utan!*

of a blackish cast, but this disappeared with the change in her mode of living.

Taken to the chateau, she immediately seized upon some raw fowls, which the cook had in his hands. She was not acquainted with any language, or articulate sound, but merely uttered harsh gutteral cries. She was, however, able to imitate the voices of certain quadrupeds and birds.

In winter time she was compelled to cover herself with the skins of animals; but at all seasons of the year she must have worn a girdle, to which she attached a short round club, which she made use of to protect herself from the wild beasts. She once, as she afterwards related, felled a wolf with a single blow on the head. When she killed a hare with her stick, she skinned it and eat it; when, however, she had hunted one down, she opened a vein with one of her nails, drank the blood and threw the rest away. Her mode of running was very surprising; there appeared to be scarcely any motion in her feet and body, so that she seemed to glide along rather than run. She exhibited the same agility in swimming and secured fish by diving. She ate the latter with great relish. She was able to remain a long time beneath the water, so that one would have supposed that the water was her natural element.

When she acquired the power of speech, she related that she had lost a companion of her own age, with whom she used to live. They were both swimming in a river (no doubt, the Marne) when they heard a noise which induced them to dive: it was a sportsman, who having mistaken them at a distance for water-fowls, had fired at them; they came out some way off and went into a wood, where they found a chaplet, which both of them wanted for the purpose of making themselves bracelets, her sister having struck her on the arm, she returned it by a blow on the head, so violent, that as she expressed it her sister *became red*. Prompted by that natural impulse which leads us to succour those of our own kind, she immediately went in search of a tree which yielded a gum that, according to her, would cure the injury she had inflicted; when she returned her wounded companion was gone, and she never saw her again.

The exact age of the girl could not be ascertained, nor the locality from whence she had come. When questioned by signs as to where she was born, she pointed to a tree. She gave the persons, however, to understand that she had traversed a great expanse of water. Condamine conceived the idea of ascertaining the place of her birth, by presenting to her the roots and the fruits of various American plants, in the hope that she might recognise amongst them some of the objects which she had seen in her childhood, but the experiment was unsuccessful.

For a long time she refused to be clothed.

At Paris she was placed in a convent, a solitude which was very different from that of the woods, and rendered her extremely melancholy.

This girl was not an idiot like most of the *wild* children which have been described by writers. She knew how to cover herself with skins to protect her from the cold, and could arrange them with skill. She had made a belt in which to place her stick; she entertained the idea of ornamenting herself with a chaplet; she desired to cure the wound she had inflicted on her sister, and she was acquainted with the virtues of a certain gum. Has the most perfect and the most exalted of the mammalia ever exhibited such signs of intelligence, or such a combination of ideas, as was presented by this unhappy girl, who, from having been deserted, had fallen into her degraded condition?

2. *The young boy of Tarn*, commonly called the *wild boy of Aveyron*, was the subject of public curiosity at the beginning of the present century. All Paris went to see this unfortunate being. He had received the name of *Victor*. The Abbé Bonnaterre and Dr. Itard, have each of them published a full and most interesting account of him.

The child was eleven or twelve years old, and had been seen several times in the wood of Lacaune (Tarn) tearing up the ground in search of potatoes, which he eat raw; he also collected acorns and chesnuts; he slept upon dry leaves, and upon any one approaching would climb into the trees.

Towards the end of the year 1799 he was met by two sportsmen, who managed to secure him.

The child was quite naked, and his habits most disgusting; he was ferocious and irritable, he was subject to spasmodic movements, which were often of a convulsive character, and he balanced himself to and fro like the animals in a menagerie. He would endeavour to scratch those who thwarted him, but he evinced no kind of affection, or recognition of those who had charge of him. He appeared to be indifferent to almost everything, but continually endeavoured to escape from the habitations of men, in order that he might return to the woods.

He was incapable of uttering any sound, and the nervous system was probably diseased.

This unhappy being was taken to a village in the neighbourhood. He contrived to escape at the end of a week, and regained the mountains, where he wandered about for fifteen months, covered only with a ragged shirt, enduring the most bitter cold and the most intense heat.

He was again captured upon his entering a lone house in the Canton of Saint Sernin, most probably being driven to it by want of food. He was taken to the hospital of Sainte Affrique, thence to Rodez, and lastly, by the order of the minister, to Paris.

He arrived in the capital towards the end of the year 1800.

His height was about four feet three inches; his skin was white and delicate; his hair was of a dark chesnut colour; his face was rounded, his physiognomy agreeable, but with little expression; his eyes were deep set and black, and the eyelashes largely developed; the nose long and somewhat pointed; his smile was pleasing; the tongue was without any malformation.

His body was covered with scars and lacerations from the spines and branches of the trees. At the upper part of the trachea was a transverse mark, about an inch and a half long, which seemed to have been caused by some cutting instrument. . . . . !

Pinel regarded the little savage of Tarn as a miserable idiot, attacked by an incurable disease, and pronounced him to be incapable of instruction, or of becoming fitted for society.

Dr. Itard did not agree with this opinion, he ventured to entertain some hopes of him, and endeavoured to bring him up in an establishment for the deaf and dumb. He has published a long account of the results which were obtained at the end of nine months. It must be admitted, that, in spite of the apparent satisfaction of the doctor, these results were far from brilliant. All that can be said is, that the little savage was not entirely wanting in intelligence. But the purely animal functions predominated in him over all others, and his look had always a certain amount of vacancy, which is well expressed in the engraving of his portrait. His voice was never capable of producing more than certain discordant and almost inarticulate sounds.

He manifested great dislike to sitting in a chair, or sleeping in a bed. He often crawled on his knees, almost in the manner of a monkey. It was with difficulty that he was taught to walk slowly. For a long time he refused all food, either raw or cooked.

He smelt all his food before eating it. He had not the slightest idea of modesty.

One morning after a fall of snow he uttered a cry of distress, and quitting his bed ran first to the window, then to the door, then impatiently from one to the other, and at last escaped, half dressed, into the garden. There he manifested his joy by the most piercing cries, rolled himself in the snow, and gathering it up in handfuls swallowed it with an incredible avidity. (Itard.)

The origin of this child is uncertain; it was suspected that he had been deserted when he was between four and five years of age, and that he had, therefore, passed seven years in the forests. Some persons, who were worthy of credit, declared that he was the legitimate child of a notary, who had been inhumanly abandoned, because nature had deprived him of the power of speech.

Whatever he might have been, Pinel has justly observed that the child was an idiot; but in the history of this idiot there are two circumstances related by Dr. Itard, well deserving of attention:

1. The child sometimes went by himself into the garden belonging to the establishment of the deaf and dumb, and seating himself on the edge of a reservoir, his balancing motion gradually diminished, and his body became perfectly quiet; his countenance then assumed all the appearance of a profound and melancholy revery; he would remain in that state for hours, closely watching the surface of the water, upon which, from time to time, he would cast the fragments of the dried leaves.

2. If during the night the bright rays of the moon entered his chamber he seldom failed to rise and place himself before the window; there he would remain standing during a considerable part of the night, motionless, his neck extended, and his eyes fixed upon the distant view illuminated by the moon, in a state of ecstatic contemplation! . . .

Has anything ever been observed in the most intelligent monkey which could be compared to the state of revery exhibited by this diseased and idiot child?

CHAPTER IV.

THE UNITY OF THE HUMAN SPECIES.

MAN inhabits all the climates of the earth, with the exception of those of the polar regions. The populations of the various countries present certain differences in the form of the head, the expression of the countenance, the height of the body, the proportions of the limbs, the characters of the hair, the quantity of the beard, and in the colour of the skin. Nevertheless there exists but *one species of man*, and the populations of every country and of every period have descended from a common stock.

Some naturalists have endeavoured to establish several distinct species of men.

Linnæus in his *Systema Naturæ* (1766) admits two species of men, the *Homo Sapiens* and the *Homo Troglodytes*. Under the latter title he includes the *Albino;* these, however, are persons in a state of disease, and in the present day they are not regarded as even constituting a variety. Linnæus imagined that this supposed second species lived in caverns, and for this reason he bestowed upon it the name of troglodytes, characterizing it by the epithet of nocturnal (*nocturnus*). At the end of his *Mantissa plantarum altera*, which appeared five years after the twelfth edition of the *Systema Naturæ*, the illustrious naturalist of Sweden committed the serious error of including in the genus *Homo* an ape, the *Gibbon* of Buffon, which he names *Homo Lar;*[1] "a surprising error committed by a great genius, which should never find imitators." (Pouchet.)

Virey (1821) also admitted two species of men, distinguished by the difference of aperture in the facial angle; in the one it varies between 85° and 90°; in the other between 75° and 82°. In the apes it never exceeds 40°. These two species of men include six races characterized by their colour, and these again comprise eleven sub-races, which are arranged according to the regions they inhabit.

Desmoulins (1824) divided the genus man into eleven species more or less distinct; the characters he gives them are often established with considerable ability, but they are always insufficient to induce us to reject the unity of the human race. He names these species: 1st, the *Celto-Scyth-Arabs;* 2nd, the *Mongols;* 3rd, the *Ethiopians;* 4th, the *Euro-Africans;* 5th, the *Austro-Africans;* 6th, the *Malays* or *Oceanians;* 7th, the

[1] *Pithecus Lar*, Geoff. Saint-Hilaire; *Simia Lar*, Gmelin; *Simia longimana*, Schreb.; *Hylobates Lar*, Bory de Saint-Vincent.

Papous; 8th, the *Negro-Oceanians;* 9th, the *Australasians;* 10th, the *Columbians;* 11th, the *Americans.*

Bory de Saint-Vincent (1825) goes even farther than Desmoulins; he admits fifteen species of men. These are: 1st, the *Japetic;* 2nd, the *Arabian;* 3rd, the *Hindoo;* 4th, the *Scythian;* 5th, the *Sinic* (Chinese); 6th, the *Hyperborean;* 7th, the *Neptunian;* 8th, the *Australasian;* 9th, the *Columbian;* 10th, the *American;* 11th, the *Patagonian;* 12th, the *Ethiopian;* 13th, the *Caffre;* 14th, the *Malanian;* 15th, the *Hottentot.* He arranges these fifteen species into two tribes: 1st, the LEIOTRIX, or those with smooth hair; this division includes the *Japetic, Arabian, Hindoo, Scythic,* and *Sinic* species belonging to the Old World; the *Hyperborean, Neptunian,* and *Australasian* species, common to the Old and the New, and the *Columbian,* the *American* and the *Patagonian* species, peculiar to the New World; 2nd, the OULOTRIX, or those with crisp hair, containing the *Ethiopian, Caffre, Malanian,* and *Hottentot* species.

In the present day man is generally regarded as constituting a simple species, in which all the individuals are capable of mingling indiscriminately, and are able to produce an offspring which is as fruitful as its parents.

CHAPTER V.

OF THE RACES OF MAN.

WHILE fully admitting the unity of the human species it is impossible not to perceive the existence of numerous distinctions between the various nations which people the globe, and of hereditary peculiarities which are more or less permanent. It is a matter of convenience to designate these particular modifications by the title of *race,* and thus, while maintaining the unity of the species, to recognise the existence of varieties. These races are sometimes propagated and preserved by the act of generation, while at other times they become united together, and are transformed by intermixture.

The idea of these modifications is extremely ancient. Moses, and at a later period Ephorus of Cumæ, divided mankind, the one into three races, after the three sons of Noah; the other into four, after the *four cardinal points.*

Linnæus recognised four varieties of his *Homo sapiens,* corresponding to the four quarters into which, in his time, the earth was divided.[1]

---

[1] His variety, *monstrosus,* cannot constitute a race.

Blumenbach proposed to establish five races: 1st, the *Caucasian;* 2nd, the *Mongolian;* 3rd, the *Ethiopian;* 4th, the *American;* 5th, the *Malay.*

M. Dumeril makes six: 1st, the *Caucasian* or *Arab-European;* 2nd, the *Hyperborean;* 3rd, the *Mongolian;* 4th, the *American;* 5th, the *Malay;* 6th, the *Ethiopian* or *Negro.*

Bory de Saint-Vincent, whom we have previously seen distinguishes fifteen species of men, admits also the existence of races and sub-races. Thus the *Japetic,* to which we belong, is divided as follows:—

Japetic species.
{ A. *Gens togata.* { a. *Caucasian Race* (western).
                    { b. *Pelasgic Race* (southern).
{ B. *Gens braccata.* { c. *Celtic Race* (western).
                      { d. *Germanic Race* (northern).

1st variety. 2nd variety.
Teutonic. *Sclavonic.*

Many naturalists, of whom we are one, admit with Cuvier three principal races: 1st, the *White* or *Caucasian;* 2nd, the *Yellow* or *Mongolian;* 3rd, the *Black* or *Ethiopian.*

The *Caucasian Race* (fig. 3) occupies the whole of Europe,

Fig. 3.—*Abd-el-Kader.*

the North of Africa, and Western Asia as far as the Ganges. It appears to have descended from the mountains of the Caucasus, from whence it derives its name.

The head is oval, and the forehead well developed, the eyes are placed horizontally, the cheeks scarcely project, the jaws are but little advanced, the hair is long and smooth, and the skin is of a pinkish white. This race is the most intelligent.

The *Mongolian Race* (fig. 4) is found in Eastern Siberia,

Fig. 4.—*Yeh.*

Kamtschatka, Russian America, China, Japan, and the Ladrone and Phillipine islands. It seems to have originated in the Altai mountains.

The face is flattened, the forehead low, oblique, and square set; the eyes straight and oblique, the cheeks projecting, the hair straight and black, the beard thin, and the skin of an olive colour.

The *Ethiopian Race* (fig. 5) inhabits Africa to the south of the Atlas mountains. It principal centre is Ethiopia, to which it has given its name.

The skull is compressed (fig. 6), the nose flat, the jaws projecting, the lips thick, the hair woolly and crisp, and the skin more or less black. This race is the least intelligent.

There are several intermediate varieties between these three races distinguished by characters more or less strongly marked;

ANTHROPOLOGY.

Fig. 5.—*Soulouque.*

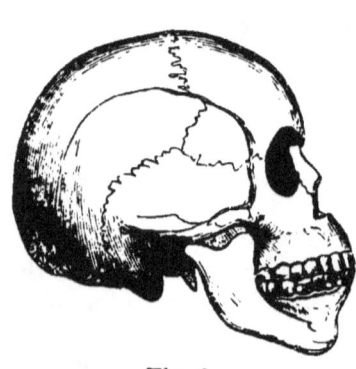

Fig. 6.

these may be regarded as sub-races. This has induced some ethnologists to enumerate as many as eleven varieties or sub-varieties of the human race. To the *Caucasian, Mongolian,* and *Ethiopian* they have added the *Alleghanian, American, Hyperborean, Malay, Australasian, Malanian, Hottentot,* and *Caffre* races. These divisions are contained in the most recent and important works which have been published in this science. Their distinctive characters accord very closely to their geographical distribution.

The following is a summary of the characters of the several sub-races of mankind as presented by my friend M. Is. Geoffroy Saint-Hilaire, in his last course of lectures before the Faculty of Sciences at Paris. I have arranged them in very nearly the same manner as this learned naturalist.

Table V.

Synoptical Table of the Human Races.

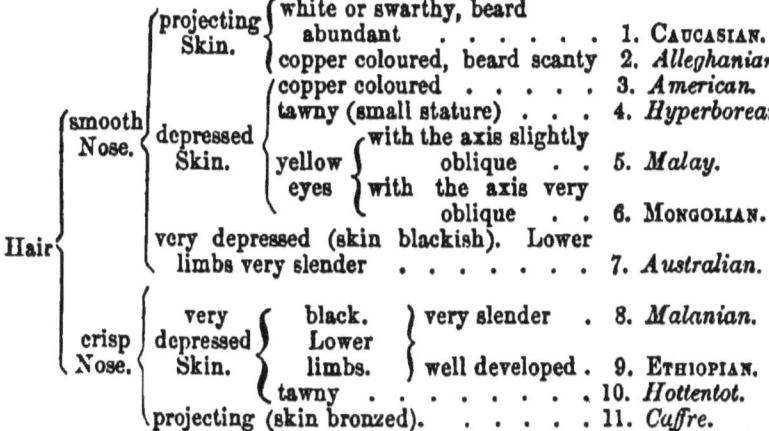

```
                     ┌ projecting  ┌ white or swarthy, beard
                     │   Skin.     │   abundant . . . . . . 1. Caucasian.
                     │             └ copper coloured, beard scanty  2. Alleghanian.
        ┌ smooth   ──┤             ┌ copper coloured . . . . . 3. American.
        │  Nose.     │             │ tawny (small stature) . . . 4. Hyperborean.
        │            │ depressed   │          ┌ with the axis slightly
        │            │   Skin.     │ yellow  ┤      oblique . . 5. Malay.
        │            │             │ eyes    │ with the axis very
Hair ───┤            │             │          └      oblique . . 6. Mongolian.
        │            └ very depressed (skin blackish). Lower
        │              limbs very slender . . . . . . . 7. Australian.
        │            ┌  very     ┌ black.     ┐ very slender . 8. Malanian.
        │  crisp   ──┤ depressed ┤ Lower      │
        └  Nose.     │   Skin.   │ limbs.     ┤ well developed . 9. Ethiopian.
                     │           └ tawny      . . . . . . . . 10. Hottentot.
                     └ projecting (skin bronzed). . . . . . 11. Caffre.
```

[Dr. R. G. Latham, the latest English authority on the races of men, in his work on the "Varieties of Man" has divided the human species into three primary varieties, the Mongolidæ, the Atlantidæ, and the Japetidæ. In his "Varieties of the Human Species," published in Orr's "Circle of the Sciences,"[1] he has arranged them into nine principal groups. Before enumerating these, it is necessary to observe that—

Ethnological facts are either physical or moral: physical, as when a class is determined from the colour of the skin; moral, as when one is determined from the purity or impurity of the habits.

Moral characteristics are either philological (that is, connected with the language), or non-philological (that is, not so connected).

The variations which occur in the different languages allow of their being arranged under the four following heads:

1. *Aptotic* (from *a* not, and *ptosis* a case).—Languages without inflections and monosyllabic, as the Chinese:

2. *Agglutinate*.—Languages which are inflectional, but which have become so from the juxtaposition or composition of different words.

3. *Amalgamate*.—Languages with inflections, which cannot be shown to have originated in separate and independent words.

[1] Vol. i. p. 308.

Anaptotic (from *ana* back, and *ptosis* a case).—Languages which, like the English, once possessed inflections, but have fallen back or lost them.

GROUP 1.—*Physiognomy*: Mongol. *Language*: Monosyllabic. *Area*: Ladakh, Bulistan (or Little Tibet), Tibet, Nepal, Sikkim, Butan, Northern India, Arakhan, the Burmese Empire, Siam Cambojia, Cochin China, Tonkin, China, the Islands of Adaman, Nicobar, Carnicobar, Hainan, and the Mergui Archipelago. *Divisions*: Tibetan (or Bhot), Siamese (or Thay), Burmese, Peguan (or Mord), Kambogian Anemitic (or Cochin Chinese), Chinese; various tribes imperfectly distributed and described as Sub-Himalayans, Nagas, and Sifan; Mincopie (or Adaman Islanders), and Nicobarians.

GROUP 2.—TAURAINANS.—*Physiognomy*: Mongol. *Language*: Agglutinate. *Area*: Mongolia, Mantshuria (the parts north of Pekin—the valley of the river Amur, Selinga, or Saghalin), Siberia, Independent Tartary, Chinese Tartary, Turkistan, Anatolia, Roumelia (or Turkey in Europe), parts of Bokhara, Persia, Armenia, Syria, the Crimea, Lapland, Finland, Esthonia, Livonia, the Russian governments of Archangel, Olonetz, Novrogood, St. Petersburgh, Tver, Yaroslav, Vologda, Permia, Viatka, Kazan, Simbirsk, Saratov, Astrakhan, Caucasus, Nizhninovogorod, Penza, Tambov, Hungary, the Kurile Isles, Japan, Kamskatka. *Divisions*: 1. The Mongolian Stock; 2. The Tungusian Stock; 3. The Turk Stock; 4. The Ugrian Stock; 5. The Peninsular Stock.

GROUP 3.—THE CAUSACIAN STOCK IN THE LIMITED MEANING OF THE TERM (DIOSCURIAN—*Latham*).—*Physiognomy*: European rather than Mongol. *Language*: Monosyllabic rather than European. *Area*: Caucasus. *Divisions*: 1. The Circassian; 2. Mizhjeji, The Irou; 4. The Georgians; 5. The Lesgians; 6. The Armenians.

GROUP 4.—THE PERSIAN STOCK.—*Physiognomy*: Caucasian rather than Mongol. *Language*: in its present state with but few inflexions. *Area*: Kurdistan, Persia, Beluchistan, parts of Bokara, the Kohistan of Cabul, Kafrestan. *Divisions*: Kurds, Persians, Biluchi, Afghans (Pushtu), Paropamisans (populations of Kaffristan and the Kohistan of Cabul).

GROUP 5.—THE INDIAN STOCK.—*Organization referable to two types*: in one the skin is dark, the face broad, the features coarse; in the other, the features are regular, the head dolikhokephalic, the skin brunette rather than black. *Language*: Modified by foreign admixture; most so in the northern parts of India. *Area*: India, Ceylon, the Maldive islands, parts of the Monosyllabic frontier, the mountains of the southern parts of Beluchistan, *i. e.*, the country of the Brahui.

GROUP 6.—THE OCEAN GROUP.—*Area:* The Peninsula of Malacca, Sumatra, Java, and the chain ending in Timor and Rotti; Borneo, and the chain leading to the Philippines; the Philippines; the Bashi and Babyani Isles; Formosa, Celebes, and the Moluccas; the islands between Timor and New Guinea; Madagascar.

GROUP 7.—THE AMERICANS.—*Area:* The Aleutian Isles, North and South America; remarkable for the comparative absence of domestic animals. *Physiognomy:* Modified Mongol; the departure from the type being the most marked on the water system of the Mississippi and the coast of the Atlantic, *Languages:* Agglutinate.

Dr. Latham remarks upon this series that he finds "no such misgivings as to the origin and affinities of the great American group as find place in most works on the subject." He neither finds difficulty in connecting them with the Old World, nor doubt as to the part thereof from which they came. Thus he finds in North Eastern Asia just what the *à priori* probabilities of the geographical relations of the two continents indicate.

His reasons for thus making short work of a hitherto long question, lie in the recent additions to our geographical and ethnograpical knowledge for the parts to the west of the Rocky Mountains, for the northern parts more especially; for Russian America, for New Caledonia, and for the Oregon. It is only lately that we have known much of these districts, especially in respect of their ethnology. More than this, it is only recently that the *Far West* of the parts between the Rocky Mountains and Atlantic has been at all carefully explored. What followed from this want of information? It followed, as a matter of course, that our notions of the so-called Red Man of America were formed upon the Indians of the Alleghany Mountains, the Mississippi, and the St. Lawrence. But these were extreme samples; samples of the American in his state of greatest contrast to the Asiatic. No wonder, then, that the connection between them was mysterious and uncertain. If investigators doubted, the want of *data* justified them. The populations which were the likeliest to supply the phenomena of transition were unknown or neglected.

Again, there was only one population common to the Old and New World. This was the Eskimo, a population which at one and the same time occupies the Aleutian Islands, the Peninsula of Aliaska, the Island of Kadiak, the greater part of

Russian America, the coast of the Arctic Sea, Greenland, and Labrador. Here it comes in contact with the so-called Red Indian of the Algonkin class.

Now, between this so-called Red Indian of the Algonkin class, and the Eskimo in geographical contact with him, there is a broad line of demarcation—a line of demarcation so broad as to suggest the idea of contrast rather than connection. Hence, as long as we studied America on its eastern or Atlantic side, we got nothing from the Eskimo; nothing from the fact (apparently so important) of his being common to the two hemispheres, and (as such) being likely to supply the connecting link between them. He was anything but such a link. He was rather a knife to separate than a band to bind. Yet, on the *Western* or *Pacific* side of the continent, this same Eskimo so graduates into the American Proper, and the Indian Proper so graduates into the Eskimo, as to make the distinction between the two groups as difficult as, on the east, it had been easy."[1]

GROUP 8.—THE AFRICAN STOCK.—*Organization*: Head rarely other than dolikho-kephalic; hair rarely straight, always, with individuals resident on their native area, black; skin dark, in certain localities attaining the *maximum* amount of blackness. In such cases the hair is crisp, and the lips thick; *i.e.*, the physiognomy is Negro. *Languages*: Agglutinate. *Area*: Africa, *minus* the Island of Madagascar (wholly or in part), *plus* Arabia and parts of Persia and Syria.

GROUP 9.—THE EUROPEAN GROUP.—*Physiognomy*: Caucasian in the wider and more inconvenient sense of the term. *Languages*: Either unplaced, or Indo-European (so called). *Area*: Western, Central, and Southern Europe. *Divisions*: A 1, The Basks; B 2, The Skipitar; C 3, The Kelts; D 4, The Greeks and Latins; 5, The Sarmatians; 6, The Germans. The three divisions marked D are easily, conveniently, and accurately looked on as sections of some higher denomination —species (so to say) of a genus. To this most writers add the Kelts; some the Albanians. All exclude the Basks. The name of this higher class, when it is limited to the divisions under D, is Indo-Germanic; when extended to D and C as well, Indo-European. The present writer objects to it in either form; holding it to be a word as erroneous and inconvenient as *Caucasian in the wide sense of the term*. Each, however, keeps its place and must be used, however unfit for use.]

[1] *Opus cit*, p. 349.

CHAPTER VI.

THE HUMAN KINGDOM.

MANY naturalists have regarded man merely as an *animal;* although it is true, they have pronounced him to be the *most perfect* and the *first of animals.*

Linnæus and his school [1] place man in a distinct *genus* under the name of *Homo*. This genus is the first of the order *Anthropomorpha* or *Primates* of the class *Mammalia*, which is itself the first of the animal kingdom.

According to Cuvier (1800), M. Dumeril (1806), Ch. Bonaparte (1839), and Lesson (1840), man should be placed apart in a separate family. The two first and the last designate this family by the name of *Bimana*, and the third by that of *Hominides*.

Blumenbach (1779), Illiger (1811), and Blainville (1816), arrange man in a distinct *order;* this order is termed *inermis* by the first, *erecti* by the second, and *man* by the third. According to Zenker (1828), and Carus (1834), he constitutes the *Class Homo*.

A small number of philosophical naturalists have regarded man, not as the head of the animal kingdom, but as constituting one of the *great divisions* of nature; they did not, however, give to this division the title of *kingdom*. Amongst these are Aristotle, Albert le Grand, Neander (1585), Ozanam (1691), Ch. Bonnet (1764), Adanson (1772), Daubenton (1782), Herder (1784), Vicq d'Azyr (1792), Geoffroy Saint-Hilaire (1794), Lacépède (1799), and others. Voltaire seems to have been the first who looked upon man as constituting a *separate kingdom*.[2] (Is. Geoffroy Saint-Hilaire.)

De Brabançois (1816), Treviranus (1820), and Fabre d'Olivet (1822), admitted this kingdom; but they named it, the first, *moral kingdom*, the second, *human kingdom* (Menschenreich), and the third, *regne hominal*. The Abbé Maupied (1851) substituted for these titles that of *social kingdom*. Most naturalists and ethnologists of the present day have adopted this *moral, human,* or *hominal kingdom*. Amongst

---

[1] See amongst others Erxleben (1777), Gmelin (1788), Fischer (1829).
[2] HE (the Eternal artificer) has bestowed upon man organization, feeling, and reason; upon animals feeling, and that which we term instinct; and upon vegetables organization only. His power, therefore, acts continually over these THREE KINGDOMS. (Voltaire, edit. Pallisot, Paris, 1792, tom. xxxvi. p. 628.—*Dialogues et entretiens philosophiques*, Sophronime et Adelos.)

them, it is sufficient to mention the names of MM. Is. Geoffroy Saint-Hilaire, Grimaud, Hollard, Horaninow, Longet, Lordat, Neas d'Esenbech, Jean Raynaud, Runge, and Serres.

Considered in regard to his *organization*, man approximates closely to the mammalia; but, considered with respect to his intelligence, he is far removed from them. If we wish to obtain a correct knowledge of his zoological relations, and of his proper classification, we must contemplate him in both points of view—that is to say, in his entirety. Pascal has said: " Man is neither angel nor beast, but belongs to both."

In establishing a distinct kingdom for the reception of man, and in placing it immediately above the animal kingdom, the lord of creation is not confounded with the beasts, and yet he is always in close affinity with the mammalia; that is to say, with the most perfect of the vertebrated animals.

Amongst living beings, or in the *organic world*, there are therefore *three kingdoms*: the *vegetable*, the *animal*, and the *hominal*.

In the first, says M. Is. Geoffroy Saint-Hilaire, LIFE is altogether vegetative; in the second, to the *vegetative* life is added *animal* life; in the third, to the *vegetative* and *animal* life is superadded the *moral* life.

It may be said, the plant *lives*, the animal *lives* and *feels*, but man *lives, feels*, and *thinks*. In the first kingdom life is *simple*, in the second *twofold*, and in the third *threefold*. *Vegetability, anamality*, and *humanity*, are three terms which succeed each other in a progressive order, as simple as it is logical. It is a series, in which, not only can none of the terms be transposed, but in which neither can any of them be added to. We have no conception of anything in the organic word below the plant, and what organized being are we able to imagine higher than man? There may be degrees in the development of the vital, the sensitive, and the intellectual faculties; but there is no intermediate condition between *living* and *not living*, between *feeling* and *not feeling*, and between *thinking* and *not thinking*. (Is. Geoffroy Saint-Hilaire.)

Man is the highest and ultimate term of creation. He occupies the summit of the living pyramid. In the kingdom which he constitutes (HOMINAL), there is but one genus (HOMO), and in this genus but one species (SAPIENS). This species presents three varieties or principal races (CAUCASIAN, MONGOLIAN, and ETHIOPIAN), and eight sub-varieties or secondary races (*Alleghanian, American, Hyperborean, Malay, Australian, Melanian, Hottentot,* and *Caffre*).

SECOND PART.

MEDICAL ZOOLOGY PROPER.

BOOK I.

ORGANIZATION OF ANIMALS.

ANIMALS are living beings, containing a large amount of nitrogen, having the power of digestion, and possessed of sensation and locomotion.

Like all living beings, the body of an animal is the seat of a double and continuous internal movement of molecular composition and decomposition (Blainville), by means of which it incorporates into its substance materials derived from without, and which take the place of other particles that are discharged from within; in this way every part of the body is insensibly renewed. This double movement, by which the individual perpetually takes from and gives to the external world, is one of the distinctive characters of life.

The duration of life in each species is definitely fixed, but circumstances may prolong it, or accidents or disease may shorten or arrest it.

Life presents a series of phenomena, which are capable of transmission. Every animal receives it from an animal, or from two animals denominated its *parents;* for life comes from life. (Cuvier.)

That portion of the animal which is capable of becoming a new individual is called a *germ,* and the separation of this constitutes its *birth.* So long as life continues, the body undergoes a series of changes, which mark what is termed its *ages.* The time which elapses between the birth of an individual and the period when he attains his normal size is his *youth;* his increase during this interval determines his amount of *growth.* When he has attained his full dimensions, the time during which his body and his energies appear to remain in a stationary condition, constitutes his *adult* age. Lastly, the time during which he becomes enfeebled, and his body seems to diminish, forms the period of his *old age.*

At a certain stage of their existence all animals are capable of producing their like; and they thus transfer to other animals that life of which they are permitted to have the temporary enjoyment.

When life ceases, the animal is said to be *dead*.

To be born, to live, to reproduce, and to die, are four characters which are common to all living beings.

After death, the physical and chemical laws, which have previously been rendered subservient to the life of the individual, now become predominant, and the constituent elements of the body are speedily decomposed.

All animals are ultimately composed of *Oxygen*, *Hydrogen*, *Carbon*, and *Nitrogen*, which constitute their essential chemical ingredients.

[There are, however, several other elementary bodies which enter in larger or small quantities into the composition of different animal structures. Müller enumerates seventeen as having been met with in the animal kingdom:

1. Oxygen.
2. Hydrogen.
3. Carbon.
4. Nitrogen.
5. Sulphur, met with principally in the hair, albumen, and brain.
6. Phosphorus . . in the bones, teeth, and brain.
7. Chlorine
8. Fluorine
9. Potassium
10. Sodium   } . in the teeth and bones.
11. Calcium
12. Magnesium
13. Manganese } found in the hair.
14. Silicum
15. Iron   . . in the blood, pigmentum nigrum.
16. Iodine   } . in some marine animals.]
17. Bromine.

The four elementary substances above mentioned combine in various ways and in different proportions; they give rise to a liquid element and to certain solid elements, which form the foundation of the general structure of animals, or of their *organization*. The liquid element is the *blood;* the solid elements are the tissues.

The *blood*, or nutrient fluid, is a liquid of a more or less intense red, sometimes of rose, lilac, yellow, blueish, or even

---

[1] *Elements of Physiology*, by J. Müller, M.D. Trans. by W. Baly, M.D. 2nd edit. vol. i. p. 2. London, 1840.

green colour, at other times it is almost colourless [as in most of the invertebrated animals]. Examined beneath the microscope it is seen to consist of two portions, a yellowish transparent liquid, the *serum*, and of solid corpuscles, of a more or less regular form, the *globules*. These globules are extremely small. They are of a circular form in nearly all the *Mammalia*, oval in the *Reptilia*, and always flattened. Their surface is smooth, rarely granulated (*framboisée*). They contain a central spot, surrounded by a kind of dark border. In the higher animals the globules are composed of a nucleus (*noyeau*), and an envelope. The latter is much the largest, and generally forms a more or less attenuated border around the nucleus. In the lower animals, particularly those with colourless blood, these two parts cannot be distinguished.

[The exceptions to the circular form of the blood corpuscles of the mammalia occur in the Camel and the Llama; in these animals the globules are elliptical like those of birds and the cold-blooded Vertebrata. This peculiarity of the Camelidæ was first pointed out by Mandle. There is a considerable difference in the size of the blood globules in the different Mammalia, a fact which should be borne in mind in reference to the operation of transfusion. According to Mr. Gulliver[1] the average diameter of those of man is the $\frac{1}{3356}$ of an inch, that of the Elephant as much as $\frac{1}{2745}$ of an inch, while in those of the Napu musk deer it is not more than $\frac{1}{13325}$, and sometimes as small as $\frac{1}{15000}$ of an inch. Müller says the diameter of the red globules in Man varies between the $\frac{1}{4013}$ to $\frac{1}{2537}$ of an inch. In others of the Mammalia the diameter of the blood globules ranges between the extreme dimensions which are given above. There is, however, no absolute relation between the size of the animal and that of his blood globules; thus they are nearly the same in the Horse as in the Bat; while in the Sloth they are larger than those of the Ox. Mr. Gulliver has pointed out that in investigations of this kind it is necessary to compare together those animals which most resemble each other in their organization, and which consequently belong to the same natural family. By proceeding in this manner, he believes he has been enabled to detect a certain relation between the size of the individual and that of the blood corpuscles. Thus, in the class Mammalia, the Elephant and the Whale possess the largest globules; whilst the Chevrotain, the most diminutive of the Ruminants, has the smallest.

---

[1] See Gerber's Anatomy by Gulliver. Appendix, p. 5 et sequent.

The following is the description which Kolliker has given of the human blood globule in his Manual of Microscopic Anatomy.[1]

The red globules, when examined individually, present the following structure: Their form is mostly that of a biconcave or flat circular disc, with rounded margins, and they accordingly appear to the observer to vary in shape, according as their surfaces or their sides are directed towards him. In the former case they are pale yellow, circular corpuscles, which almost always have a slight central depression, and this sometimes has the aspect of a clear central spot, sometimes of a dark central body, according as the corpuscle is in or out of the focus of the microscope; the appearance in the latter case is apt to be confounded with that of a nucleus. When seen from the side, however, the blood corpuscles show themselves as dark red-shaped structures, of the form of an elongated narrow ellipse, or like a biscuit seen edgewise. With regard to their intimate structure, every blood globule consists of a very delicate yet tolerably firm and elastic colourless cell membrane, composed chemically of a protein substance nearly allied to fibrine; contained in this envelope is a viscid coloured substance, which in the separate blood globules appears yellow, and is composed principally of globuline and hœmatine. In the adult, the contents of the blood globule present no trace of morphological particles of granules, or of a cell nucleus; they are accordingly true vesicles, and on that account, as well as from their shape not being globular, the name of "blood cells" is to be preferred. The elasticity, softness, and pliability of their envelope are so considerable, that they ere enabled to accommodate themselves to vessels which are narrower than their own diameter, and for the same reason, when they are elongated, flattened, or otherwise altered in form by pressure under the microscope, they are able to resume their previous shape. The blood globules are rendered the more capable of adapting themselves to the vessels, by the fact that their surface is quite smooth and slippery, so that they easily glide along the similarly constructed walls of even the narrowest capillaries.

In examining the blood corpuscles the nature of the fluid in which they are immersed must be borne in mind. If placed in water, the specific gravity of which is less than that of the

[1] *Manual of Microscopic Anatomy*, by A. Kolliker. London, 1860, p. 518-19.

serum of the blood, they become biconvex in consequence of the water passing into the envelope by endosmose. If, on the other hand, the fluid should be denser than the serum, as in the case of a strong saline or saccharine solution, the corpuscles part with a portion of their contained fluid by exosmosis, they put on a shrivelled aspect, and become granulated on their surface; this shrivelled appearance may again be got rid of by diluting the menstruum and reducing its specific gravity to the lowest point.[1]]

The organic *tissues* are three in number: 1st, *cellular* tissue; 2nd, *muscular* tissue; and 3rd, *nervous* tissue.

Cellular or *areolar tissue* is composed of numerous Camellæ, which by their interlacement intercept a number of open spaces termed *cells*. The whole of this tissue has been compared to a sponge having the form of the entire body, and in which the other parts of the animal are placed. When this cellular tissue becomes condensed it forms layers of greater or less extent *(membranes)*, or tubes more or less ramified *(vessels)*, or filaments of greater or less thickness *(fibres)*.

Muscular tissue is composed of bundles of fibres, striated or smooth, sometimes dotted, which have the property of contracting with more or less force.

Nervous tissue, sometimes called *medullary matter*, may be compared to a soft pultaceous mass, in which may be distinguished a number of microscopic fibres and vesicles of various forms[2] containing a fatty substance *(medullary nervous matter)*, which readily changes into globules.

Some writers admit other organic tissues as distinct from cellular; such, for example, as the *fatty, glandular*, and the *elastic* tissues.

The *fatty* or *adipose tissue* consists of vesicles having extremely delicate, colourless walls, filled with an oily fluid, which is generally of a yellow colour. This fluid solidifies after death in consequence of the diminished temperature.

Glandular tissue presents an infinity of minute delicate ramified tubes, which by their interlacing constitute a parenchyma of a peculiar nature. All these tubes unite into a common duct.

Elastic tissue is composed of homogeneous fibres, not striated nor dotted, but ramifying and anastomozing together. These fibres form ligamentous fasciæ remarkable for their physical elasticity, but which have no power of spontaneous contraction.

[1] See Todd and Bowman's *Physiological Anatomy*, vol. ii. p. 298.
[2] Stellated, fusiform, and ovoid. (Jacubowitsch.)

These tissues blend together, interlace, and combine for the purpose of forming the various *organs*. The organs are of three kinds: some serve to nourish the individual; others bestow upon him the power of perpetuating his species; while a third bring him in relation with the external world. These are respectively named, the *organs of nutrition*, the *organs of reproduction*, and the *organs of relation*. The functions which are accomplished by the first two are common to animals and vegetables, and are termed the *vegetative* or *organic function*; those which are fulfilled by the third are named the *animal functions*.

I.—Organs and Functions of Nutrition.

Nearly every animal possesses an internal cavity for the reception and digestion of its food. In the simplest species, this receptacle is the essential and almost only organ with which they are provided, while in the most perfect it is merely an accessory apparatus. Nevertheless, it becomes more and complicated in proportion to the perfection of the entire organism of which, properly speaking, it forms the foundation.

Food consists of liquids and solids.

The first are taken into the mouth and comminuted by means of the *jaws;* these are sometimes two in number, placed one over the other, and act vertically; at other times there are as many as four [insects]; these have a lateral position, and act horizontally. The jaws, which have a vertical position, are generally osseous; they are covered by a pair of *lips*, and furnished at their margins with hard ossicles or *teeth;* these are divided into *incisors, canines*, and *molars*. At other times, a layer of corneous matter takes the place of the lips, the jaws project, and become converted into *mandibles*, and the whole forms a *beak*. The lateral jaws are calcareous or corneous. The two superior are also termed *mandibles;* and the two inferior *jaws* properly so called, or *maxillæ*. In the *crustacea*, the latter are accompanied by auxiliary jaws, termed *foot jaws*. The inner margin of these organs is frequently serrated or provided with teeth, or at other times with a small moveable hook, or pointed *claw*.

Liquids are drawn up by means of a beak or *rostrum*, a *sucker*, or a *proboscis*.

. After the food has been taken into the mouth, it passes to the fauces or *pharynx*, and from thence it is conveyed into the digestive cavity. This cavity varies greatly in its form and in its capacity. In the simplest animals, it is a sac with a single opening, which serves both for the reception of the food, and for the discharge of the indigestible materials. Subsequently, the sac becomes elongated into a muscular membranous canal, provided with two openings, a *mouth*, and and an *anus*, each of which fulfils a separate function. This canal dilates at a certain part and forms a *stomach*. This dilitation divides the digestive canal into three parts; viz., that which precedes the stomach, the stomach itself, and the part which comes after it. The anterior portion forms the *œsophagus*, and the posterior the *intestine*. The opening of the œsophagus into the stomach is termed the *cardia*, that of the stomach into the intestine the *pylorus*. These openings may be brought close to each other, or placed some distance apart.

In general, the œsophagus is not very long. This is especially the case in those animals which have little or no neck. In the *ostrich*, the œsophagus is remarkable for its length, while in the *oyster* it does not exist. In some birds, this portion of the canal dilates towards its lower part into a *crop*, and into a second gastric cavity or glandular stomach, the *ventriculus succenturiatus*.

The stomach is a regular or irregular cavity, with very thin or with very thick walls. It has, usually, the form of a globular or oval sac, or resembles that of the common bag-pipe. There may be observed one or two *culs-de-sac;* when there are two, one is often large and the other small. The stomach may be simple or compound. If we regard the dilitations of the œsophagus in the granivorous birds as gastric cavities, these animals will then have three stomachs—the *crop*, the *glandular stomach*, and the *gizzard*. In the *Ox*, and in all the ruminating animals, there are four stomachs—the *ingluvies* or paunch, the *reticulum* or honey-comb stomach, the *omasum* or many-plies, and the *abomasum* or reed. The common *Dolphin* (Delphinus Delphi) has also four stomachs placed in succession. The *medicinal leech* has eleven pairs of stomachs, of which the last are very large, and were for a long time mistaken for a pair of enormously developed cæcums.

The intestine is the longest portion of the alimentary canal; it forms numerous folds or reduplications, named its *convolutions*. This arrangement allows the canal to acquire considerable dimensions. It is generally longer in the herbivorous animals than in the carnivorous. In the first it is occasionally as much as thirty times the length of the animal's body, while in the latter it is often reduced to the same length. In some of the lower animals it is even shorter than the body. In those species in which the nature of the food is changed, in passing from the larval to the perfect state (Frog), the length of the intestinal canal changes with the period of life; the tube is long while the creature is herbivorous, and is shortened when it becomes carnivorous. The intestine is divided into the *small intestine* or *anticæcal*, and into the *large intestine* or *postcæcal*. These two divisions are separated by the *ileo-cæcal valve* or *valve* of Bauhin. The first is divided into the *duodenum, jejunum,* and *ileum;* and the second into the *cæcum, colon,* and *rectum*.

The food is permeated by certain fluids which serve to dissolve and adapt it for digestion; these fluids are furnished by four kinds of secreting organs which are true appendages of the digestive canal; these are the *salivary glands*, the *liver*, the *pancreas*, and the *gastric glands*, which secrete the gastric juice.

The *salivary glands* are placed in the neighbourhood of the mouth or of the œsophagus. They are usually two in number and are more developed in the terrestrial than in the aquatic animals.

The *liver* is a large gland situated at the commencement of the intestine or near the stomach; it sometimes surrounds the latter. In the *leeches* it is reduced to a network or thin layer of a brownish or blackish matter. The fluid secreted by the liver has received the name of *bile;* it is discharged into the intestine or into the stomach. It is sometimes retained in a special reservoir, the *gall bladder*.

The *pancreas* is another gland, smaller than the liver, and very variable in its form; its secretion enters the duodenum, and its duct occasionally unites with that of the bile.

The *gastric glands* consist of minute tubuli situated in the thickness of the digestive mucous membrane; one end terminates in a blind extremity, while the other opens on the inner surface of the stomach, into which the tubuli discharge an acid secretion, which acts principally on the animal portions of the food.

Besides the glands now spoken of, there are others which eliminate certain excrementitious fluids from the blood; amongst the latter are the *kidneys*, which secrete the *urine*.

The alimentary matter, thus altered and transformed, become separated into two portions—the *chyle* and the *excrement;* the former is absorbed by the walls of the digestive cavity, while the latter is discharged by the anus. The *chyle* is a white opaque fluid, which becomes absorbed or conveyed by the venæ lactea to the different organs, where it is mixed with the blood with which the latter are supplied. Similar canals, termed *lymphatics*, convey to the blood the residue of the nutritive particles and the products of cutaneous absorption.

The blood is everywhere present in the substance of the organs. In a great number of animals it is, moreover, contained in a system of ramifying tubes or vessels: these tubes being of two kinds—*the one conveys* the nutrient fluid to the different parts of the body, and is named *arteries; the other converges* to the centre, or towards the centre of the animal, and is called *veins*.

The movement of the nutritive fluid is sometimes irregular, and at other times regular and circular. In the latter case it is spoken of as the *circulation*. The current of the circulation may be simple or double, or even triple. In the *sanguisuga* it is in a manner multiple; for independently of the general circulation, these animals present partial circulations between every five rings.

The circulation of the nutrient fluid is frequently assisted by one or several special motor organs termed *hearts*. These organs are more or less muscular, sometimes placed in the middle of the body, at other times at each of the centres of impulsion. Generally speaking there is only a single heart provided with one, two, three, or four cavities. The cavities which receive the blood are termed *auricles*, and those which propel it *ventricles*. The latter are always thicker, stronger, and more robust than the former.

In order that the blood may be capable of nourishing the body, it requires to undergo a particular modification from contact with the atmosphere. Hence a function arises which may be regarded as an act of nutrition by means of gaseous food (the complement of the nutrition, by solid and liquid aliments), and which has received the name of respiration. When the animal lives surrounded by the air, the respiratory organ is hollow, and is termed a *lung*; when the animal resides in the water, it projects from the rest of the body and constitutes a *branchia*. In the most perfect species, the lung appears to be parenchymatous, but in reality it consists of an immense number of microscopic cells. In the *snails* this organ assumes the form of a large sac, which is covered on its inner and upper surface by a network of vessels. This sac may be considered as one of the constituent cells of the parenchymatous lung enormously developed. In *insects* there are neither lungs nor branchiæ, but a series of elastic tubes called *tracheæ*, which convey the air to every part of the body. The openings of the tracheæ are placed along the sides of the body, and have received the name of *stigmata*. In the animals which are provided with lungs, or with branchiæ, the blood is conveyed to the air, while in those which have tracheæ the air is carried to the blood. The most perfect species, although they are provided with a special organ of respiration, at the same time absorb the air by the cutaneous surface of their bodies. The animals which are most simply organized breath exclusively by means of the skin.

When the blood is perfectly formed it diffuses itself through the cells, or by the ramification and sub-division of the vessels, into the tissues of the organs, and then becomes converted into the various structures which enter into their formation. Several of the most important organs in the animal economy appear to be provided for the production of special secretions, all of which concur in the act of *assimilation*.

II.—Organs and Functions of Reproduction.

Reproduction is one of the most important functions of nature, for life is only given for the purpose of bestowing life.[1] It is by reproduction that species are preserved, that races are propagated, and that the general balance of life is maintained. There are animals which seem formed solely for the fulfilment of this function; they are born, they reproduce, and die.

Reproduction may be accomplished in several different ways.

In the species which are most simply organized, the animal sometimes divides into several portions, each of which forms a new individual; this is termed *fissiparous reproduction*; at other times the creature gives off from certain parts of its body buds or *gemmæ*, which at a fixed period become detached and give rise to young animals; this is *gemmiparous reproduction*. The latter is said to be *external* or *internal*, according as it takes place on the exterior of the body, or in a particular cavity within which the buds are formed. The animals which arise from the *fissiparous* and *gemmiparous* modes of reproduction are termed by some writers *agamic generations*.

In the higher animals the act of reproduction is accomplished by means of special organs; this is *generative reproduction* or *generation*. These organs are termed *sexual*, and consist of

[1] *Omne vivum ex vivo.*

the *female* organ, which furnishes the rudiments of the new individual (the *germ*), and of the male organ, which produces the fecundating liquor (*seminal fluid*) which vivifies the former and determines its development.

The *female apparatus* is essentially composed of the organ which produces the germ, the *ovary*, and of a canal which conveys them to without, and which has received the name of *oviduct*.

The *male apparatus* is always provided with a gland which secretes the seminal fluid, the *testicle*, and of the excretory canal of the gland, called *ejaculatory duct*.

In some of these animals the sexes are united in the same individual: these are named *unisexual* or *androgynous*. In this case either one individual may be sufficient of itself (*Oyster*) for reproduction, or it may require the union of two individuals. When two androgynous individuals unite for the purpose of reproduction, sometimes the two organs fulfil their functions at the same time, and each individual fecundates the other and is itself impregnated; such is the case with the *Snail* (*Limax*). At other times, the association of several, or at least three, individuals is required, the central animal performing the office of the male to the one in front of him, and that of the female to one behind him, as in the case of the *Water snail* (*Lymneus*). More rarely the two portions of the double sexual organs do not act at the same time; each individual, notwithstanding its bisexual nature, only fulfilling one office; but having performed for example the office of male, at a later period it acts as a female either with the same individual, or with another (*Ancylus*).

In a great number of animals the sexes are separated and placed on distinct individuals: these are said to be *unisexual*.

The *males* externally resemble the *females*, or differ from them more or less distinctly. In a small number of cases the two sexes would be taken to belong to different groups of animals. The unisexual character necessitates the conjunction of two individuals in the generative act; nevertheless these animals present two modes of union, which are very distinct from each other: in the one the fecundating fluid of the male is not applied to the germ until it has passed out of the body of the female (*Carp*), or at the moment of its discharge (*Toad*); in the other its application takes place in the body of the mother (*Beaver*). Sexual generation may therefore occur without connection of the sexes, or this connection may be very slight and accompanied by *simple contact*, or it may be accompanied with love, and followed by true *intromission* (*copulation*).

Animals, which have a complicated sexual apparatus, besides the parts already mentioned, present others which are charged with important functions. The females are provided with a uterus or *womb*, in which the germ resides for a longer or shorter time before its birth; *tubes*, or excretory canals, which receive the germs from the ovaries, and conduct them to the uterus; and a *vagina* or sheath, for the reception of the excitory organ of the male. The orifice of the vagina is termed the *vulva*. The males have *vesiculæ seminales* or reservoirs, in which the seminal fluid is accumulated; canals, or *vasa differentia*, which convey this fluid from the testicles to the reservoirs; and a verge or *penis*, for its introduction into the apparatus of the female. The extremity of the male organs is named the *glans penis*.

In some few of the lower animals, the female can produce young without contact with the male. This form of reproduction constitutes *parthenogenesis*, and occurs in the *Aphides* or plant lice. Under certain circumstances the eggs, which thus become fruitful without the co-operation of the opposite sex, produce only males; this is termed *arrenotokia*, and takes place in the honeybee (*Apis mellifica*).

In the reproduction of some of the higher animals, the fecundated ovum is deposited by the female; but it is not until some time afterwards that it gives rise to a new individual; these animals are *oviparous* (*Birds*). At other times the egg is hatched at the moment of its expulsion, and the young animal issues from the body of its parent with the fragments of its former covering; such animals are said to be *ovoviviparous* (*Viper*). Lastly, the fecundated egg is not expelled from the body of the parent, but is retained within the uterus, and there grows, develops itself, and is hatched. This constitutes the *viviparous* reproduction of the *Mammalia*. In reality, all these animals are *ovigerous*. Their mode of reproduction only differs as regards the locality in which the development of the germ takes place, and as to the time which it occupies.

The *egg* is essentially composed of the germ-vesicle or *cicatricula*, and of a protecting envelope; the latter may be single and consist only of *membrane*, or it may be double and consist of *membrane* and *shell*. In the oviparous and ovoviviparous species it moreover contains a certain amount of nutritive matter (the *vitellus* or *albumen*). In the viviparous species the germ receives its nourishment direct from the mother.

When the egg is hatched it gives rise sometimes to an individual which resembles its parent (*Birds*), at other times to one which differs essentially from it (*Butterflies*). This intermediate form between the germ and the perfect animal is called a *larva*. The larvæ are always agamic, yet in some animals they have the power of reproduction, but it is then always gemmiparous or fissiparous. These forms of larvæ have received the name of *scolex*, and the existence of two modes of reproduction in the same species constitutes *alternate generation*. Some animals pass through two or three intermediate forms before arriving at the perfect state.

III.—Organs and Functions of Relation.

Most animals possess five *senses*.

The sense of *touch* is that which is most frequently present, and is seated in the general integument; but it also resides in certain special organs where it acquires a higher state of perfection. These organs are the *lips*, the *barbs*, and the *tentacles* of certain animals, and the *tail* and *feet* of others; but, above all, it is in the *hands* that the sense of touch becomes most acute.

Taste is a species of touch of a still more delicate character; it is placed at the entrance of the alimentary canal, principally in the floor of the mouth, in an organ termed the *tongue*. The tongue is an elongated muscular body endowed with greater or less motive power; it is covered with papillæ (*conical, fongiform, circumvallatæ*), *spines, hooks*, and even with true teeth. In some animals, in which the sense of taste is but slightly developed, the tongue is scarious, cartilaginous, or provided with a corneous investment.

Smell is the sense for the perception of odours. The olfactory organ is a single or double cavity provided with a great number of irregularities or anfractuosities, which are invested by a delicate membrane, the *pituitary*. This membrane communicates externally through the openings termed *anterior nares, nasal openings* or *nostrils;* in certain animals these openings are protected by cartilaginous plates, which form the *nose*. The nasal fossæ have also posterior openings, which lead to the cavity of the pharynx; these are named *posterior nares*.

In the *snails* the organ of smell is divided into two parts, which are placed at the extremities of the larger horns or *tentacles*. It is composed of an oval or pyriform ganglion, from which the short but extremely ramified nerves spread themselves over a peripheral pituitary membrane. There is no nasal cavity, and consequently no external opening.

Sight is the faculty which enables animals to perceive external objects by means of the rays of light, and to appreciate the colours with which they are clothed. Vision takes place

E

through the *eyes*. The eye is a small but complicated apparatus of a more or less globular form. It is essentially composed of a *retina* or nervous element, of a *choroid* or vascular element, and of a *sclerotic* or fibrous element. The latter becomes transparent in front of the globe of the eye, and forms the *cornea*. There exists in the eye a perfect dioptric apparatus; this consists of the *aqueous humour*, the *crystalline humour* or *lens*, and the *vitreous humour*. There are also some accessory parts, as for example the moveable membranes or *eyelids*, which protect the apparatus; they may be naked or provided with certain hairs termed *cilia* or *eyelashes*. These membranes are generally two in number, but occasionally (as in birds) there is a third, the *membrana nictitans*.

The higher animals generally possess two eyes, while some of the lower forms have four, six, eight, or even more. The *medicinal leech* has ten, but they are altogether rudimentary. In *insects* the eyes are of two kinds; the one small, simple, and adapted for seeing objects which are near—these are termed *ocelli stemmata* or *simple eyes*; the other kind consists of large compound eyes, generally adapted for seeing objects at a distance; they are composed of a variable number of simple eyes aggregated and united together—these are called *compound eyes*.[1]

Hearing is the sense which takes cognizance of those vibrations of external bodies which are transmitted through the surrounding medium, and give rise to *sound;* the organ through which this is accomplished is the *ear*. In the lowest animals the ear is reduced to a sack filled with a special fluid, through which the nerve is distributed, and which contains a number of small stone-like masses termed *otolithes*. This sack may or may not communicate externally. In the higher animals the auditory apparatus becomes more and more complicated. There is observed: 1st, the essential part or *vestibule;* 2nd, certain accessory parts which render it more sensitive; these are the *semi-circular canals*, the *cochlea*, and a chain of small bones, consisting of the *stapes*, the *os orbiculare*, the *incus*, and the *malleus;* 3rd, the part which collects the vibrations, or the *external ear*, consisting of the *external auditory foramen*, and the *concha*. The concha is sometimes replaced by a circle of feathers or hairs.

Several of the lower animals have neither nose, eyes, nor ears.

---

[1] In one of these compound eyes there are sometimes as many as 12,000 simple eyes (common dragon fly).

Those species which have no distinct head, or the *acephala*, are always ill provided with organs of the senses; many of them seem only to have that of touch.

In the very lowest animals the nervous matter would appear to be confounded with the general substance of the body. There is no centre of sensation. In animals whose structure is somewhat more complicated, the nervous matter accumulates at certain points, and produces *ganglions* or nervous centres. These accumulations are at first small and irregularly dispersed. When the organization is still further advanced the nervous centres become enlarged, and are brought near to each other; they then assume an annular arrangement around the neck, or form an enlarged mass in the interior of the head. The ganglions either isolated or united in small groups give rise to a rudimentary nervous system. The annular arrangement around the neck forms an *œsophageal ring*; while the accumulation of nervous matter in the head constitutes the *encephalon*. The superior ganglia of the œsophageal ring are named the *cerebral* ganglia, and the inferior the *sub-œsophageal* ganglia. This kind of nervous system is termed *ganglionic*. The encephalon is generally composed of the *cerebrum* or brain, the *cerebellum*, the *pons Varolei* or *mesencephalon*, and of the *medulla oblongata*, which is itself a continuation of the *spinal cord*. The whole of this nervous system is termed *cerebrospinal*.

The impressions which are received through the senses are transmitted by the nerves to the central masses of the nervous system. When the animal perceives a *sensation* it frequently gives rise to an act of *volition*, which is also communicated by the nerves, either to the organs of the senses, or to those of *motion*.

The *organs of motion* are the *limbs*. These are made up of two portions; the one active, the *muscles*; the other passive, the *bones*, or certain hard parts which supply their place.

The *muscles* are soft, of various shades of red, or of a greyish colour, and in some cases quite transparent; they are formed of irritable contractile fibres, having various degrees of consistency, and arranged parallel to each other. Some are destined to bend or shorten the parts (*flexors*); others to open or elongate them (*extensors*). There are also muscles which are not under the control of the will; these are frequently termed *internal* in contradistinction to the others, which are always situated, more or less, towards the surface of the body.

[The muscles are usually divided into the *voluntary* and the *involuntary*. The first, called also the muscles of animal life, include those of locomotion, respiration, and those of the face; these are under the control of the will. The second, which comprise the muscles of the heart, the intestinal canal, and some others, are not subject to the influence of the will. The ultimate fibres of these two sets of muscles differ in their anatomical structure.

The fibres of the voluntary muscles are marked by parallel transverse lines or striæ, and are known as striated muscular fibre. The fibres of the involuntary muscles, with some exceptions, are smooth and marked at intervals with oblong corpuscles or nuclei; the latter are best seen after the application of acetic acid. The principle exception to this character occurs in the muscles of the heart. The fibres of this organ resemble those of the voluntary muscles in having striæ, but they are less strongly marked, and are less regular, and the fibres themselves are smaller in diameter than in the voluntary muscles.]

The *bones* are hard, dry, and white. They are divided into the *long, short,* and *flat bones*; it is more particularly the first which are met with in the limbs. The whole forms the skeleton or solid framework of the animal. There are many species which have no internal skeleton; but the skin becomes impregnated with calcareous matter (*Crawfish*), or is converted into a kind of corneous material (*Beetles*), which takes the place of the osseous framework, and forms a kind of dermal skeleton. In other animals, the skin is provided with special folds (*mantle*), which are more or less developed, and secrete calcareous plates of various forms to which the muscles are attached, and which either partially or completely protect the usually extremely soft structures of the body; these plates are termed *shells*. The shell consists of a single piece in the *univalves,* as in the *Snails,* and of two pieces in the *bivalves,* as in the *Oyster*.

BOOK II.

CLASSIFICATION OF ANIMALS.

I. ANCIENT.—The ancients divided animals into those with blood, and into those without. They considered only those species were provided with this fluid, whose blood was of a red colour, such as that of *Birds* and *Fishes*, believing that it did not exist in those in which it was very pale or altogether colourless, as in *Insects* and many *Molluscs*. These latter animals were named by them *exsanguineous*.

[This was the classification of Aristotle, who divided animals into the *enaima* and into the *anaima*, literally into those with blood and into those without blood. It is not, however, correct to say that the Father of natural history disbelieved in the existence of a blood, or at least of a nutrient fluid analogous to it, in the lower animals, since he distinctly says: "Every animal possesses a vital fluid, the loss of which occasions its death;" but, as the colour of this fluid in the higher classes is always red, for the purpose of distinctive description, he assumed the colour as an essential quality, and named the two series as above.]

The first classifications were extremely arbitrary systems; the characters upon which they were established were sometimes taken from the nature of the food, sometimes from the limbs, and at other times from the integuments. If the classifications which were subsequently proposed were occasionally more happy in their arrangements, these improvements were rather the result of a kind of instinct, or of repeated attempts, than of careful observation and reflection.

II. LINNÆUS.—Linnæus was the first to establish a rational classification of the animal kingdom.[1] This great naturalist arranged the various animals into six classes: Mammalia, Birds, Amphibia, Fishes, Insects, and Worms.

Mammals (*Mammalia*) are animals whose bodies are provided with a covering of hair; they have two jaws, an upper and an under, generally furnished with *teeth*, and covered by a pair of lips; the respiration is pulmonary; the heart is quadrilocular; they have almost always four limbs, provided with *hands* or *feet;* they are viviparous.

To this division belong the *Apes, Bats, Bears*, the *Beaver, Musk Deer, Wild Boar, Whale, &c.*

[1] This expression is unjust towards the memory of our illustrious countryman Ray. Although his actual classification has been superseded by others, yet Cuvier, in his "Histoire des Sciences Naturelles," vol. ii. p. 454, after describing Ray's arrangement of the mammalia, says, "In this classification we meet with the germs of all those which have been made since. Linnæus, especially, has taken nearly all his characters from those which Ray had pointed out . . . . We are indebted to Ray as the pioneer and model of all the classificators who have succeeded him, so greatly was he endowed with the spirit of method." (*Trans.*)

Birds (*Aves*) are animals whose body is covered with feathers; they have two jaws, one superior, one inferior, without teeth or lips; they are converted into *mandibles*, and form the *beak*; the respiration is pulmonary; the heart quadrilocular; they have always four limbs, two *wings* and two *feet*; they are oviparous.

To this division belong the *Vultures, Woodpeckers, Ducks, Herons, Pheasants, Thrushes,* &c.

Amphibia (*Amphibia*) are animals whose body is generally covered with scales; they have two jaws, one superior, one inferior, sometimes furnished with imperfectly developed teeth, with or without lips; their respiration is pulmonary, rarely branchial; their heart trilocular or bilocular; they have sometimes four limbs, very rarely only two, and occasionally none; they are almost always oviparous.

To this division belong the *Tortoises, Lizards, Frogs, Vipers, Snakes, Sturgeons,* &c.

Fishes (*Pisces*) are animals whose bodies are covered with scales; they have two jaws, one superior, one inferior, sometimes provided with teeth and covered by lips; their respiration is branchial; their heart is bilocular; they have generally four true limbs (*fins placed in pairs*), and in addition to these accessory limbs (*single fins*); they are almost always oviparous.

To this division belong the *Eel, Cod, Sole, Tunny, Salmon, Carp,* &c.

Insects (*Insecta*) are animals whose body is covered with a coriaceous or calcified skin; they have four jaws placed laterally; their respiration is tracheal; their heart unilocular; they have generally six limbs (always *feet* and sometimes two or four *wings*), rarely more; they are provided with *antennæ*; they are oviparous.

To this division belong the *Cantharides* beetle, *Flies, Fleas, Tarantula, Scorpion,* and *Crayfish.*

Worms (*Vermes*) are animals whose body is covered with a soft skin, sometimes provided with a shell; the jaws vary in their number and arrangement, and are sometimes wanting; the respiration is accomplished with or without a special organ: the heart is unilocular or wanting; the limbs are rudimentary or absent; they are provided with *tentacles*; they are oviparous or reproduce without a true generative act.

To this division belong *Leeches, Snails, Slugs,* the *Oyster, Madrepores,* and *Corals.*

The following table contains a synopsis of the principal characters of these six classes:

$$\text{Blood} \begin{cases} \text{red} \begin{cases} \text{warm} \begin{cases} \text{Jaws} \dots \dots \dots \text{ 1. MAMMALS.} \\ \text{Mandibles} \dots \dots \text{ 2. BIRDS.} \end{cases} \\ \text{cold} \begin{cases} \text{Lungs} \dots \dots \dots \text{ 3. AMPHIBIA.} \\ \text{Branchiæ} \dots \dots \text{ 4. FISHES.} \end{cases} \end{cases} \\ \text{white} \begin{cases} \text{Antennæ} \dots \dots \text{ 5. INSECTS.} \\ \text{Tentacles} \dots \dots \text{ 6. WORMS.} \end{cases} \end{cases}$$

The classification of Linnæus is extremely important, in consequence of its scientific character, its simplicity, and its convenience. It affords an excellent summary of all that was known at the time of its appearance, and has served as the starting-point for the various classifications which have been proposed since the period of this illustrious naturalist.

It is, however, very evident that the first four classes of this classification are much more closely allied to each other than the fourth is to the fifth, or the fifth to the sixth. The last is moreover composed of very heterogeneous elements. It contains, for example, the *Leeches* and the *Earth Worms*, which are far more intimately allied to *Insects;* and the organization of the *Cuttle fishes* and the *Slugs* is much more complicated than that of the *Worms*, properly so called, and is more allied to that of *Fishes* than of *Corals*.

III. LAMARCK.—Lamarck, taking as his basis the presence or absence of the skeleton and the structure of the nervous system, divided animals into those without vertebræ or the *Invertebrata*, and into those with vertebræ or the *Vertebrata*.[1] The first he subdivided into the *apathetic*, which included part of the *Vermes* of Linnæus, and into the *sensitive*, which included the remainder of the *Vermes* and the *Insecta* of the same author. The *vertebrata* he termed *intelligent* animals, which corresponds to the first four classes of Linnæus.

Lamarck commenced with the simplest animals, and gradually proceeded to those which were more elevated in the scale of organization; thus following an inverse order to that of his predecessor.

[The taking these supposed endowments of the animals as the ground of classification was quite inadmissible, and hence the groups of Apathetic, Sensitive, and Intelligent animals have never been adopted. The grouping together of the first four

[1] Aristotle had termed these animals—*animals provided with blood*. [Lamarck's division of the animal kingdom into the Vertebrata and into the Invertebrata, corresponds to Aristotle's *Enaima* and *Anaima*.]

classes of Linnæus, under the title of the Vertebrata, has remained a permanent acquisition to science.]

IV. CUVIER.—Profiting by the observations of his predecessors and his own researches into the organization of the animal kingdom, G. Cuvier revised, corrected, and perfected the classification of Linnæus. Like Lamarck, he recognised the resemblance which existed between the first four groups, and united them under the name of *Vertebrata*, giving to this assemblage the title of *branch*. From the *Vermes* he separated such animals as the cuttle-fish, the snail, and the oyster, to form a second branch, which he termed *Mollusca*. Amongst the worms he discovered a small group with red blood (leeches and earthworms; these he associated with the *insects*, and formed of them a third branch, the *Articulata*. The majority of the remaining *Vermes* having the parts of their bodies arranged like rays around a common centre, he named them *Radiata*.

In Cuvier's classification there are, therefore, four principal branches—the *Vertebrata*, the *Mollusca*, the *Articulata*, and the *Radiata*. The first group includes the *Monkeys*, the *Dog*, the *Beaver*, the *Whale*, the *Birds*, the *Tortoises*, the *Frogs*, and the *Fish*. The second contains the *Poulps*, *Cuttlefish*, *Calamary*, *Snails*, *Slugs*, *Oysters*, and *Mussels*. In the third are the *Leeches*, *Earth-worm*, *Crayfish*, *Crabs*, *Spiders*, *Cantharides*, and *Bee*. Lastly, in the fourth are the *Star-fish*, *Tape-worm*, *Thread-worm*, *Corals*, and *Sponges*.

The following are the characters of each of these branches:

1. *Vertebrata*.—Animals symmetrical, consisting of two similar halves. Body supported by an internal skeleton, composed of a number of separate pieces placed one over the other (*vertebræ*), forming a spinal column and canal, terminating anteriorly in the head and posteriorly in a coccyx or tail.

Digestive canal complete; jaws two in number, one either before or above the other. A special organ of respiration frequently double; lungs or branchiæ. Heart thick, muscular, frequently with four cavities, never less than two; blood red, warm or cold. Nervous system cerebro-spinal; five senses. Limbs usually four, never more. Sexes separate.

2. *Mollusca*.—Animals seldom symmetrical; that is, they are composed of unequal portions. Body soft and without any internal skeleton, but covered with a cutaneous envelope provided with a particular fold (*mantle*), and often containing calcareous masses called *shells*.

Digestive canal complete; jaws one, two, or three in number, horny, sometimes rudimentary, and at other times wanting. A special respiratory organ sometimes pulmonic, sometimes branchial. Heart with two or three cavities; blood colourless or of a bluish cast, always cold. Nervous system ganglionic, rarely symmetrical, and with no abdominal chain; organs of the senses only slightly developed. Limbs imperfect or absent, often consisting of a large fleshy disc, at other times of a byssus, but never of wings. Sexes separate, or united in the same individual; in the latter case two animals mutually impregnate each other, or one animal may suffice of itself.

3. *Articulata.*—Animals symmetrical; that is, composed of two similar halves; marked by a series of transverse constrictions, which divide them into a number of segments, giving them the appearance of being formed of a series of rings. Body with no internal skeleton, but covered with a hard integument (*dermal skeleton*), which is either calcareous or corneous.

Digestive canal complete; jaws often four in number, always lateral. Heart replaced by a dorsal vessel, blood generally colourless, sometimes pinkish, cold. Respiratory organ mostly consisting of tracheæ. Nervous system ganglionic, always symmetrical, with an abdominal chain; organs of the senses only partially developed. Limbs perfect, with ginglymoid articulations, generally six in number, sometimes two or four wings. Sexes almost always separate.

4. *Radiata.*—Animals symmetrical, but not formed of two similar halves, generally consisting of parts having a radiated arrangement. Body soft, without either an internal or external skeleton. The animals sometimes live in societies, and secrete a horny or calcareous axis.

Digestive system extremely simple; sometimes consisting of a sac with two openings, at other times with only one. No heart. Circulatory system reduced to a few rudimentary vessels, blood colourless and cold. No special organ of respiration. No encephalon or œsophageal ring, rarely ganglions, sometimes nerves; no organs of the senses. Limbs represented by filamentary processes. Sexual organs very imperfect, often reduced to a simple ovary; many reproduce by gemmation and fission.

This classification may be tabulated as follows:—

Form	Body			
	binary	no segments	a skeleton	1. VERTEBRATA.
			no skeleton.	2. MOLLUSCA.
		segments		3. ARTICULATA.
	radiated			4. RADIATA.

This classification, like that of Linnæus, proceeds from the complex to the simple; but it is more even, regular, and natural. If the *Mollusca* were all formed of two dissimilar halves like the *Snails*, and if all the *Radiata* had a strictly radiated disposition, the classification of Cuvier might be symbolized by the four following figures, each of which corresponds to one of his branches:

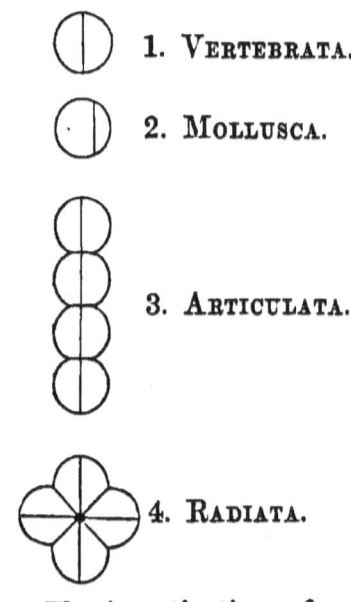

1. VERTEBRATA.

2. MOLLUSCA.

3. ARTICULATA.

4. RADIATA.

PRESENT STATE.—The investigations of modern anatomists and systematists have introduced some slight modifications into the Cuverian distribution; but these changes refer rather to the orders than to the branches, to the details rather than to the general arrangements. Although the names have been often changed, the principal groups have remained almost or entirely the same. Every one recognises the *Vertebrata* of Cuvier, or of Lamarck, in the *Osteozoaria* of De Blainville;[1] his *Mollusca* in *Malacozoaria* of the same writer;[2] his *Articulata* in the *Entomozoaria*;[3] and his *Radiata* in the *Actinozoaria*; so that it is still the classification of Cuvier which prevails.[4]

Nevertheless, this classification is far from perfect. If the

[1] These are the *Myeloneura* of Ehrenberg, and the *Hypocotyledones* of Van Beneden.
[2] M. Van Beneden has united them to the *Radiata* under the name of *Allocotyledones*.
[3] There are the *Epicotyledones* of M. Van Beneden.
[4] Mr. Milne Edwards has introduced some important changes.

CLASSIFICATION OF ANIMALS.

Mollusca seem more allied to the Vertebrata in respect to some parts of their organization than the *Articulata*, the latter certainly resemble them much more with respect to their faculties and their embryology, a fact which both Lamarck and De Blainville were fully conscious of. The division, *Radiata* especially, has been the subject of a great number of criticisms. It includes animals which are fixed to the earth after the manner of vegetables and also locomotive animals, animals which have organs of the senses and those that are without them. There is no appearance of radiation in the *Thread-worms* or in the *Flukes;* nevertheless, these animals have been placed in the same division as the *Sea Hedge-hogs* and the *Corals*. The *Tape-worms* and the *Bothriocephala* have segments placed end to end; why are they not arranged amongst the *Articulata?*.

A circumstance of the utmost importance, but one which has not been sufficiently considered in the classification of animals, is, on the one hand, their state of isolation or association, and, on the other, the unity of the organisms or their repetition.

Zoologists have long since shown that certain animals, as the *Polyps* for example, possess a kind of life very different from that of ordinary animals, inasmuch as, instead of being isolated, numbers of them are grouped together and live in societies. Linnæus terms them *animalia composita*. Cuvier, speaking of these associations, says, "The individuals are associated in large numbers to form compound beings." There are, therefore, *isolated* or *solitary* animals, and *compound* or *associated* animals. Again, between these two kinds of animals there are others which are intermediate, and which present neither the perfect isolation of the first, nor the multiplicity of the second. *Natura non facit saltus!* Such, for example, is the worm. Philosophical anatomy has taught us that this annelid is composed of segments or articulations placed in a linear arrangement, in each of which the same organs are regularly repeated. It is a series of particular organisms, each of which has a nervous centre, digestive, vascular, secreting, and reproductive organs. It may be termed a distinct series of animals, symmetrically and longitudinally arranged, but intimately united and governed by a common life. These special organisms have received the name of *Zoonites*. (1826.) Various physiological experiments have shown that it is possible, artificially, to render each organism more independent of the whole, and to a certain extent to isolate the particular life of the zoonites from that of the common life of the general association.

Nature even goes further, and in the tape-worm [1] exhibits these zoonites disengaging themselves, and becoming isolated at a certain stage of their existence. The same animal thus furnishes science with a kind of synthesis and analysis.

Lamarck perfectly understood the difference which separated a vertebrated animal from an insect when he arranged these animals in two series: the *Inarticulata* (that is to say, the *solitary* animals, and the *Articulata* (that is, the *zoonites*). But this illustrious naturalist appears to have lost sight of this fundamental idea, when he associated the *polype* or *compound animals* with *Inarticulated animals*.

I have therefore divided the animal kingdom into three sub-kingdoms: I. The *Isolated* animals; II. *Zoonite* animals; III. The *Associated* animals. I divide the sub-kingdoms into six branches, according to the characters of their nervous systems, which may be cerebro-spinal, ganglionic, rudimentary, or wanting. I have retained, as far as possible, the names generally admitted, especially those of Cuvier and De Blainville.

ANIMALS.

1st Sub-Kingdom.	2nd Sub-Kingdom.	3rd Sub-Kingdom.
ISOLATED.	ZOONITES.	ASSOCIATED.
1st. Branch. VERTEBRATA or OSTEOZOARIA. (Musk deer. Cod.)	—	—
2nd Branch. MOLLUSCA or MALACOZOARIA. (Cuttlefish. Oyster.)	**4th Branch.** ANNELIDA or ENTOMOZOARIA. (Blistering beetle. Leech.)	—
3rd Branch. HETEROMORPHA or PROTOZOARIA. (Ascidia. Volvox.)	**5th Branch.** RADIATA or ACTINOZOARIA. (Star-fish. Sea hedgehog.)	**6th Branch.** ZOOPHYTA or PHYTOZOARIA. (Coral. Sponge.)

[1] Linnæus has said of the *Tænias*: "*Animalia hæc sunt composita simplici catena . . . . latente intra singulum articulum animalculo cum sua fructificatione.*" He adds elsewhere: "*Omnis articulus propria vita gaudet.*" Vallisneri, Lamarck, and Duvernoy believed in the polyzoic nature of the *Tænias* and similar animals. MM. Leuckart, Eschricht, Steenstrup, Van Beneden, and Siebold, have illustrated the multiplicity of their organisms.

Amongst these branches, those of the *Vertebrata* and *Mollusca* of Cuvier remain almost without alteration. The Annelida represent the articulata of the great naturalist with the addition of the intestinal worms; but his fourth group has been altered and subdivided. Blainville had previously formed it into two sub-kingdoms: the *Actinomorpha* or the *Radiata*, properly so called, and the *Heteromorpha* or *Heterozoaria*. I have adopted this division; but I have considered it better to separate the truly *associated* animals from those which, like the *Tænias* and the *Star-fishes*, already begin to show a state of fusion; in other words, into the *radiated* zoonites and into the *compound animals* composed of distinct individuals.

A mere inspection of the table shows that a linear arrangement of the branches and classes cannot be natural. If we follow the order of the figures placed before each branch, the *Annelida* are separated too far from the *Mollusca*, and especially from the *Vertebrata*. If, on the other hand, a linear arrangement is adopted, and the *Articulata* are placed after the *Mollusca*, and the *Radiata* after the *Heteromorpha*, the latter are arranged at too great a distance from the *Mollusca*, and the *Radiata* too far from the *Annelida*. The three groups of ISOLATED or SINGLE animals (I., II., and III.) form a natural series. We pass in a natural manner from the first to the last through the *Mollusca*. The animals having a ganglionic nervous system (II. and IV.) are brought together on a horizontal line, and the question of the preeminence of the *Mollusca* or of the *Annelida*, decided sometimes in favour of the first (Cuvier), sometimes in favour of the second (Carus), obtains a solution. Blainville arranged these animals below the *Vertebrata*, giving to each the same rank; that is, he placed them at an equal distance. My method differs slightly from his, inasmuch as I place the *Annelida* at a somewhat greater distance. If in some respects the *Mollusca* are endowed with a less perfect organization and with a lower grade of instinct than the latter, yet on the other hand they are single animals and not zoonites. The animals with a rudimentary nervous system, or in which it is wanting, offer so many points of resemblance that they are arranged in a horizontal series (III., V., and VI.), which is quite as natural as that of the vertical series of the *isolated* animals. We pass from the *Heteromorpha* to the *Zoophytes* by means of the *Radiata* or *Actinozoaria*.

The following is the number and arrangement of the classes contained in each of the branches:—

ANIMALS.

1st Sub-Kingdom.—ISOLATED.

Classes.

I.—VERTEBRATA or OSTEOZOARIA.
- Allantoidians.
  1. MAMMALIA (Musk deer).
  2. AVES (Common fowl).
  3. REPTILIA (Viper).
- Anallantoidians.
  4. BATRACHIA (Frog).
  5. PISCES (Cod).
  6. MYELAIRIA [1] (Lancelet).

II.—MOLLUSCA or MALACOZOARIA.
- Mollusca properly so called.
  7. CEPHALOPODA (Cuttlefish).
  8. PTEROPODA (Clio borealis).
  9. GASTEROPODA (Slug).
- Conchifera.
  10. ACEPHALA (Oyster).

III.—HETEROMORPHA or PROTOZOARIA.
- Malacozoaria.
  11. TUNICATA [2] (Ascidia).
- Sarcodaria.
  12. INFUSIORIA [3] (Volvox).

2nd Sub-Kingdom.—ZOONITES.

IV.—ANNELIDA or ENTOMOZOARIA.
- Articulata properly so called. Vermes.
  1. INSECTA (Cantharides).
  2. ARACHNIDA (Scorpion).
  3. CRUSTACEA (Crayfish).
  4. ROTIFERA (Wheel ænimulis).
  5. ANNELIDA (Leech).
- Helminthes.
  6. NAMATOIDEA (Threadworm).
  7. TREMATODA (Fluke).
  8. CESTOIDEA (Tapeworm).

V.—RADIATA or ACTINIZOARIA.
  9. ECHINODERMATA (Star-fish).

3rd Sub-Kingdom.—ASSOCIATED.

VI.—ZOOPHYTES or PROTOZOARIA.
- free.
  1. ASSOCIATED properly so called [5] (Botryllus).
- fixed.
  2. BRYOZOA.
  3. POLYPIFERA (Corals).
  4. SPONGIARIA (Sponge).

---

[1] Is. Geoffroy Saint-Hilaire, C. Bonaparte.
[2] First section of the *Shelless Acephala* of Cuvier.
[3] *Homogeneous Infusoria* of Cuvier.
[4] *Turbellaria* of some writers.
[5] *Compound Acephala* of Cuvier.

BOOK III.

ANIMALS AND THE ANIMAL PRODUCTS EMPLOYED IN MEDICINE.

In the earlier ages of medicine, the remedies derived from the animal kingdom were exceedingly numerous. It is only necessary to examine the catalogues which have been left us by the ancients to be convinced of this fact. These catalogues, which were mere compilations of receipts, contain the most extravagant remedies, brought together without any order; and, generally speaking, unaccompanied by any critical remarks.

Physicians having made the organization of man the subject of their special study at a very early period, it is hardly to be wondered at if they sought to obtain from his body various remedies against disease. Man was long regarded as an animal *par excellence*, and it was, therefore, thought that this animal ought naturally to furnish a number of valuable medicines.

Amongst other ancient remedies which were seriously recommended, was the use of *tanned human skin* as a belt, the *nails* and *hairs* either burnt or distilled,[1] the *teeth, brain, saliva*,[2] *wax*,[3] *urine*,[4] the *excrements*, the *fat* (especially of a person who had been hanged), the *blood* of a man who had been beheaded drank while it was still warm,[5] and filings of the *human skull* (*hominis cranium raspatum*)! Lémery observes, "The skull of a person who has died a violent death forms a quicker and better remedy than that of a person who has died from a lingering disease, or who has been taken from a cemetery, because the first contains all his spirits, while in the others they have been exhausted either by the disease or by the earth." Boyle believed that powdered human skull, applied to the skin, had permanently cured him of bleeding from the nose.

---

[1] The hair of children eased the gout; that of adults was employed against the bite of a dog!

[2] The saliva of a man who had fasted was a specific against the poison of serpents! . . .

[3] Wax cured the sting of the scorpion!

[4] The urine of eunuchs rendered women fruitful!

[5] At Rome, the warm blood of the gladiators was ordered in various diseases! In Egypt, kings attacked with elephantiasis were ordered baths of human blood!

The progress of medical science and of common sense has long since freed us of these therapeutical extravagancies.[1]

SECTION I.

ANIMALS OR ANIMAL PRODUCTIONS FORMERLY EMPLOYED IN MEDICINE.

A LARGE volume might be formed of the statements which are to be found in different authors, relating to the animals or their productions which were formerly used in medicine, but which are now abandoned.

Linnæus very properly discarded many of the false and absurd statements of his predecessors. But one is surprised to find still included amongst his *Materia Medica* the *fat of the wild cat (cati sylvestris axungia)*, the *testicles of the horse (equi testiculi)* and the *penis of the whale (ceti priapus)* ! . . . The most celebrated men have always, to a certain extent, been enslaved by the prejudices of their time.

The ancient therapeutists often sought for what they termed correspondence between the disease and the remedy, but it is impossible to conjecture what were the relations upon which they founded the virtues of many animal substances. Thus, in spitting of blood, they recommended the patient to drink kid's blood mixed with vinegar; in diseases of the kidneys they prescribed the back of a hare to be eaten raw or cooked, *but without touching it with the teeth;* in diseases of the spleen, they applied the spleen of a dog over the region of the affected organ; in disorder of the liver, they ordered the dried liver of a wolf in wine sweetened with honey, or that of an ass bruised in honey with two parts of celery and three nuts! . . .

The following are some of these therapeutic agents which belonged to the ancient medical zoology, arranged in three series :

I. THE ENTIRE ANIMAL.

    1st. *Simply opened or bruised.*—Bat, mole, pigeon, toad, tree-frog, spider, scorpion.

    2nd. *Dried or reduced to powder.*—Hedge-hog, tit-mouse, water-wag-tail, wren, goat sucker, plover, snake,

[1] See the work of J. W. Pauli, entitled, *De medicamentis e corpore humano desumptis, merito negligendis.* Lipsiæ, 1721, in-4.

toad,[1] earthworm, bug, cricket, grasshopper, ant. . . . . .

3rd. *Calcined and reduced to ashes.*—Badger, mouse (*mus combustus*), crow, cuckoo, kingfisher, lizard, salamander, slug, scarabœus.

4th. *Infused in water.* Magpie (*aqua picarum compositum*), swallow (*aqua hirundinum*).

5th. *Boiled in milk.*—Toad.

6th. *Infused in oil.*—Dog (*oil of young dogs*),[2] fox, hawk, cameleon, scorpion (*oil of Matthiole*), cockroach, earthworm.

7th. *Distilled.*—Ants (*water of magnanimity*).

II. BONES of the dog, wolf, hare (*astragalus*), horse, stag, eagle (*skull, vertebræ*), toad (*left humerus*), carp, shad, and whiting.

III. BLOOD of the bat, lion, dog, mole, weasel, hare, rat, horse, ass, elephant, rhinoceros, bull, camel, stag, goat, goldfinch, lark, pigeon, cock, pheasant, quail, ostrich, swan, duck, tortoise, lizard, frog, tree-frog, and snake.

IV. FAT of monkey, dog, wolf, fox, wild cat, hedge-hog, badger, rabbit, hare, marmot, beaver, porcupine, dormouse, ass, elephant, stag, fallow-deer, camel, eagle, falcon, kite, common fowl, pheasant, cassowary, heron, frigate bird, pelican, lizard, snake, frog, tree-frog,[3] carp, pike, eel-pout, and lamprey.

V. COVERING.

1st. *Skin* of mole, horse, ass, rhinoceros, eagle, tench, and eel.

---

[1] Zwelfer states that cakes (*a*) composed of the toad preserved him from the plague, and that the same remedy had relieved, and even cured, some of his domestics and friends of malignant diseases. Van Helmont also applied this singular remedy to the skin.

[2] *Catellos recens natos numero tres*, in three or four pounds of olive oil. Some used them while they are alive (*vivos*), others after they were dead (*necator*).

[3] Oligans Jacobœus pretends that the fat of the tree-frog causes teeth which have been rubbed with it to fall out without pain.

(*a*) The term cake has been used instead of the obsolete word troche, by which the older pharmaceutists designated certain compounds composed of various powders, made up with any convenient medium, not containing sugar, into little cakes of various forms, and afterwards dried. The word trochiscus or troche is derived from trochos, a wheel, the cakes being very often made up into that shape. See the section on the so-called crabs' eyes, p. 96.

2nd. *Hair* of cat, fox, hare, horse, ass, elephant, goat, camel. .
3rd. *Feathers* of eagle, lark, partridge. .

VI. SHELLS.
1st. *Univalves*—snail, rudimentary shell of slug, whelk, dentalium.
2nd. *Bivalves*—common mussel.
3rd. *Epiphragma* of the large Roman snail.
4th. *Pearls* of the pearl oyster and the mussel.

VII. NUTRITIVE ORGANS.
1st. *Jaws* of the pike, trout. .
2nd. *Teeth* of wolf, badger, wild boar, cod, &c.
3rd. *Tongue* of grouse, flamingo. .
4th. *Stomach* of hedge-hog, pigeon, common fowl, crane, ostrich, eel-pout. .
5th. *Intestines* of wolf. .
6th. *Spleen* of dog, ass. .
7th. *Liver* of wolf, mole, bear, badger, weasel, otter, hare, porcupine, elephant, goat, roebuck, eagle, swan, duck, lizard, frog, eel. .
8th. *Kidneys* of ass. .
9th. *Lungs* of fox (*pulmones preparati*), weasel, hare, pig. .
10th. *Heart* of monkey, lion, mole, stag, crow, peewit, kingfisher, toad. .

VIII. BILE, URINE, EXCREMENTS.
1st. *Bile* of monkey, cat, dog, hedge-hog, martin, weasel, bear (*fel inspissatum*), hare, ass, pig, elephant, goat, roebuck, fallow-deer, camel, eagle, peewit, nightingale, bee-eater, pheasant, partridge, crane, wood-cock, snipe, tortoise, lizard, frog, salmon, pike, carp, eel-pout, eel. .
2nd. *Urine* of ass, mule, rhinoceros, cow, goat, stag, camel, lizard. .
3rd. *Excrements* of cat, dog (*fed upon bones*),[1] wolf, fox, martin, weasel, hare, mouse,[2] ass, mule, pig, elephant, ox, sheep, goat, roe-buck, fallow-deer, camel, eagle, hawk, crow, kite, pee-wit, swallow,

---

[1] *Album græcum, spodium græcum, album canis, nihil album, cynocoprus.*—Libavius gives the method of preparing and preserving the *album græcum*.
[2] *Album nigrum stercus nigrum, muscerda.*

ANIMAL PRODUCTIONS, ETC. 67

cuckoo, pigeon, common fowl, peacock, quail, bustard, swan, goose, tortoise, lizard.[1] .

IX. ORGANS OF REPRODUCTION.
1st. *Testicles* of badger, weasel, otter, horse, ass, hare, common fowl. .
2nd. *Penis* of ass, bull, stag (*priapus cervi*), whale, sea tortoise. .

X. EGGS.
1st. *Covering of the eggs* of the frog.[2] .
2nd. *Entire eggs* of lizard, barbel, pike, cuttle-fish. .
3rd. *Shell* of crow, common fowl, quail, ostrich. .

XI. ORGANS OF RELATION.
1st. *Brain* of badger, hare, stag, camel, eagle, hawk, crow, pee-wit,. common fowl, partridge. .
2nd. *Eye* of hare, quail, crane. .
3rd. *Ear-bone* of carp, whiting, cod, pike. .
4th. *Foot* of hare (*leporis tali*). .
5th. *Hoof* of horse, mule, ass, elephant, rhinoceros, tapir, elan (*ungula preparata*).[3] .
6th. *Claws* of hawk. .
7th. *Claws* of crab. .

XII. ACCESSORY ORGANS.
1st. *Horn* of rhinoceros, ox, sheep, goat. .
2nd. *Appendages* of flying stag (*horns*). .

XIII. VARIOUS PRODUCTION.
1st. *Suet* of sheep. .
2nd. *Dried tears* of stag. .
3rd. *Ink* of cuttle-fish. .
4th. *Cocoons* of silk-worm (*English drops*), spider (*Montpellier drops*). .
5th. *Bezoars.* A. *Stony* (*intestinal concretions*)[4] of the monkey, wild boar,[5] Indian hog,[6] ox,[7]

---

[1] See the Stercoral Pharmacopeia of C. F. Paullini (*Heilsame Drek-Apotheke*, Frankfort, 1696, in-8).
[2] *Ranarum sperma exsiccatum, sperma ranæ.*
[3] It was especially the *hoof of the left foot* which was employed.
[4] The name bezoar is given to calcareous masses, more or less solid, generally formed of concentric layers, and found in the stomach, intestines, and urinary passages of quadrupeds.
[5] *Pig stone, lapis porcinus.*
[6] *Malacca stone, lapis porci Malacensis, yellow bezoar.* The bezoar of *Ceylon* (*lapis porci Ceylanici*) was larger and not so scarce.
[7] *Masang de vaca, Indian yellow, glate stone.*

goat of Peru,[1] ibex,[2] camel, serpent,[3] viper.[4] B. *Hairy (agagrophiles)*[5] of horse, ox, and sheep.

SECTION II.

ANIMALS AND ANIMAL PRODUCTIONS OCCASIONALLY EMPLOYED IN MEDICINE.

CERTAIN animals and animal productions formerly in use are still occasionally, though very rarely, prescribed by medical men.

They may be divided into three groups: 1st, *Animals employed whole;* 2nd, *Parts of animals;* 3rd, *Animal productions.*

CHAPTER I.

ANIMALS EMPLOYED WHOLE.

THESE animals are: 1st, the *Scink;* 2nd, *Wood Louse;* 3rd, *Cochineal Insect.*

I. Scink.

The *Scink* of the pharmaceutist[6] is a small Saurian reptile

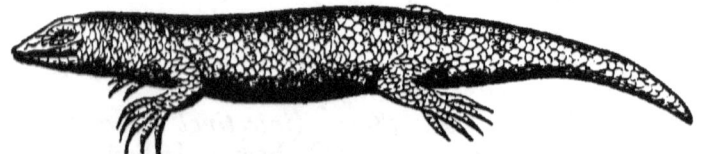

Fig. 7.—*Scink.*

belonging to the family Scincoides; it is very common in

---

[1] *Western bezoar.*
[2] *Oriental bezoar,* green resinous bezoar.
[3] *Serpent stone, cobra de capello.*
[4] Bezoar of France.
[5] Concretions which form in the stomach and intestines of various quadrupeds, from the accumulation of hairs swallowed by the animals in licking themselves. The hairs become felted together in balls.
[6] *Scincus officinales,* Schreb. (*Lacerta Scincus,* Linn.). The Arabs term it *el Adda.*

Nubia, Abyssinia, Egypt, Arabia, and in the south of Algeria and Morocco.

The body is from nine to twelve inches in length; it passes gradually into the tail, which is thick and conical, and forms nearly one third of the entire length. The colour of the animal is of a silvery yellow, with dark transverse bands. The muzzle is wedge-shaped. The teeth are small, close set, and pointed. The feet are short, the toes free, flat, and unguiculated.

Before it is brought to Europe it is dried, the intestines having been previously removed, and the end of the tail cut off. The space that was occupied by the intestines is filled with aromatic plants, and it is then wrapped up in leaves of wormwood.

The *Scink* was long regarded as a most useful and valuable remedy. In the Materia Medica it was said to be stimulant, restorative, and antisyphilitic, but especially serviceable in restoring the powers of the body when they had been exhausted by voluptuous indulgences.[1] (Dioscarides.) It entered into the composition of several complicated formulæ.

The *common Lizard*[2] has been proposed as a substitute for the *Scink*. A species of *Anolis*,[3] and an *Iguana*,[4] have also been mentioned for the same purpose.

Very recently Dr. Gosse, of Geneva, has advocated the therapeutic properties of the Scinks. He maintains that the ancients were justified in employing them, and that these animals possess powerful stimulant and sudorific properties, which might be usefully employed in various diseases.

§ II. Wood-lice.

Under this name of *Woodlice*[6] are included two small

---

[1] *Corpus officinale pro aphrodisiaco*, Linn.

[2] *Lacerta agilis*, Linn. [The common lizard of this country is not the Lacerta agilis of Linnæus, but the Zootica vivipara of Bell, or scaly lizard of Pennant. See Bell's Brit. Reptiles.]

[3] *Anolius bullaris*, Cuv. [This species was first described by Catesby in his Natural History of Carolina, under the name of the Green lizard; it is a very beautiful species, of a greenish gold colour.]

[4] *Iguana delicatissima*, Laur. (*I. nudicollis*, Cuv.).

[5] The *Saurians* are not the only reptiles whose medicinal virtues have been extolled. The old therapeutists made use of a volatile salt containing a powder composed of *vipers*, also cakes (see note, p. 65), as well as a wine, a syrup, a jelly, and an oil. The fat of these animals was recommended in nervous affections, and was considered to be a good cosmetic.

[6] *Onisci, Aselli*.

species of isopod crustacea, belonging to the family of the Oniscidæ: the *common Wood-louse* (fig. 8), and the *officinal Armadillo* (fig. 9).

1st, The *common Wood-louse*[1] is constantly found in cellars, in the crevices of walls, under stones, and in old wood.

The body is oval, oblong, of a grey colour, and composed of a number of imbricated rings. It has four antennæ, the lateral ones being provided with eight joints. It is provided with two pointed appendages at its posterior extremity.

Fig. 8. *Wood-louse*.

Wood-lice avoid the light and frequent damp situations, where they feed upon decomposing animal and vegetable matters; their walk is naturally slow, but they can move quickly when irritated. When alarmed they have the singular power of rolling themselves up into a ball; they are ovoviviparous. At birth the young have only twelve feet [the adult animal has fourteen, one pair being attached to each of the seven rings, which form the thorax].

2nd, The *officinal Armadillo*[2] is met with in France, but it belongs especially to Italy.

The *Armadillo* is closely allied to the preceding species. The rings are smooth and polished, and of a grey colour. The lateral antennæ have only seven joints. The posterior appendages of the body are not projecting.

The medicinal properties of the *Wood-louse* and the *Armadillo* were long spoken of in high terms. Those individuals were preferred, which lived on walls and on stones covered by saline particles. Galen speaks of their beneficial effects in obstructions of the abdominal viscera; Baglivi considered them as lithontriptics, Vallisneri as antiscorbutic, and Geoffroy as anti-rheumatic. . . . Most writers have mentioned them as being aperient, laxative, and diuretic. It has been ascertained that they contain the hydrochlorates and nitrates of potash and lime, which may possibly explain their former reputation in medicine. These minute crustacea entered into the composition of numerous prescriptions. Patients swal-

Fig. 9. *Armadillo*.

---

[1] *Oniscus asellus*, Linn. In the old pharmacopeias it was called *Cutio* and *Porcellio*.
[2] *Armadillo officinalis*, Cuv. It was known as prepared wood-louse or armadillo of the shops.

lowed them raw, and that even while they were alive, consuming as many as two hundred in the course of the day. De Haen seriously relates that in certain cases of weak sight, patients had eaten these animals with bread, and that this extraordinary remedy had been exceedingly efficacious.

§ III. Cochineal Insect.—Coccus Cacti, Linn.

The *Cochineal* is an insect belonging to the order Hemiptera, the tribe Homoptera, and to the family Gallinsecta. They constitute the genus *Coccus* of Linnæus; they are characterized by a pectoral beak, an abdomen terminated by setæ, and by the presence of two wings in the male—none in the female.

1st. COMMON COCHINEAL (fig. 10).—The *Common Cochineal*, or *Cochineal of the Nopal*,[1] is an insect which is held in considerable estimation, on account of the beautiful and brilliant colour which it furnishes.

This animal was employed in medicine and in the arts long before its true nature was ascertained. It was supposed to be a small berry or grain, known as *shining grain*.[2] Lopez de Gomara, in 1525, gave the first description of this insect, and of the plant upon which it fed. Thierry de Menonville, in 1787, published an excellent treatise on the *Cochineal*. Reaumur has given some details respecting the generation and metamorphoses of those species which are met with in France.

Habitat.—The *Cochineal* of commerce is found in different parts of Mexico. It lives on several species of *Nopal*, particularly on the *common*,[3] the *cochineal* bearing,[4] and the *Tuna*[5] species.

Description.—The *Cochineal of the Nopal* is a small insect. The male and the female are not alike, and might be supposed to belong to different genera. It has even been stated that the individuals which had been taken for the male were parasites.

The body of the male is elongated, short anteriorly nar-

---

[1] Adanson has seen students when herborizing eat some dozens of these insects and find them very good.
[2] Pomet said (1694) that the Spaniards exposed them to the action of heat, so that the young should not become developed in France.
[3] *Opuntia vulgaris*, Mill (*Cactus Opuntia*, Linn.).
[4] *Opuntia cochenillifera*, Mill (*Cactus cochenillifera*, Linn.).
[5] *Opuntia Tuna*, Mill (*Cactus Bonplandia*, Kunth).

rowed behind, and of a deep red; the head is small, with a rudimentary beak; the antennæ are of moderate length, filiform, and composed of eleven joints. The abdomen is terminated by two setæ, longer than the body, diverging, and very slender. The wings reach beyond the abdomen and cross each other horizontally on the back; they are oblong and perfectly transparent. The limbs are long, with a single joint to the tarsus, terminating in a hook. The animal is quick and active.

The female is at least twice the size of the male, the body is oval, obtuse anteriorly, slightly attenuated behind, convex above, and flat below. It has ten distinct rings, of a brown colour, covered with a white powder. It is provided with an extremely narrow, slightly conical, and very pointed rostrum from 3 to 4 lines in length. The abdominal setæ are shorter than the body. The limbs are small, and the animal very slow.

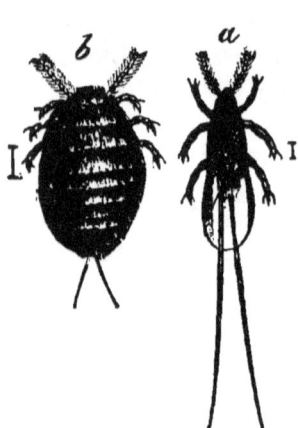

Fig. 10.—*Cochineal.*[1]

The larval stage in both sexes does not last more than ten days; that of the pupa fifteen. The male does not live more than a month. As soon as he is born he seeks the female and when impregnation is accomplished he dies. The female lives a month longer, and during this time her abdomen becomes considerably enlarged. When the period for laying the eggs has arrived she fixes herself to the plant. The eggs remain adherent to the under surface of her body, so that the laying is hardly evident externally. As the abdomen empties itself its inferior parietes approaches the upper and thus forms a considerable cavity below. Very soon the parent insect dies, her abdomen dries up, the skin becomes hard and shrivelled and serves as a kind of shell for the protection of her offspring.

The eggs are from 250 to 300 in number, and are united into a narrow band; they are oval, of an intense red colour, and are covered with a farinaceous secretion. They are hatched in a few days. The larvæ issue from beneath the dried-up remains of the parent by an opening at the posterior part, and spread themselves over the nopals. During the first days of

[1] *a*, male; *b*, female.

their existence they traverse the tenderest parts of the plants, and seek out a suitable spot to attach themselves to. Having decided upon this, about one third of the individuals cover themselves with a white powder, which assumes the form of a cacoon open at one end; beneath this covering the larva becomes transformed into a chrysalis, and then into the perfect insect. The abdominal setæ soon make their appearance through the opening previously mentioned, and the animal comes out backwards: these are the males. The other two-thirds are the females, whose bodies daily increase in size, while the males flutter around them, or walk over their backs.

Cultivation.—The Cochineal is found wild in the woods, but it is usually propagated and reared artificially. A certain number of nopals are planted around the houses to form a nopalry. It is usually placed in an open situation, where there is no shade, but where it is sheltered from the west winds. It is surrounded by a hedge of reeds, as much to break the currents of air as to guard the plantation from the attacks of wild beasts. A nopalry ought not to be more than two acres in extent. The ground having been properly prepared, the plantation is formed by cuttings of the nopals planted about half way in the ground. The cuttings are placed a foot apart and arranged in rows, with intervals of rather more than a yard between them.

Females obtained from the woods, just before they are about to lay their eggs, or insects filled with eggs, which have been preserved through the winter on the sheltered nopals, are placed, to the number of ten or twelve, in small nests, composed of the fibres of the cocoa nut, or in small cylinders open at the ends formed of the leaves of the dwarf palm, and suspended to the spines of the nopals; at other times they are placed in the crevices of the plant. This is called *sowing* the cochineal. The larvæ soon come out of the nests and spread themselves over the nopals. They are afterwards arranged in groups on the most succulent and vigorous parts of the plant.

The principal care which is required in raising the *Cochineals* is, to shelter them from the effects of the wind and the rain; this is done by simply placing matting over the nopals.

Thierry de Menonville introduced this valuable insect into Saint Domingo, but the revolution of Haiti prevented the success of the experiment, and the insects were allowed to perish.

The Dutch succeeded in naturalizing them in Java. In 1845, that is, in about ten years after their introduction, the quantity sold on account of the government amounted to 5,513lbs.

Living individuals have, on several occasions, been introduced into Europe. Linnæus tells us that Rolander presented some to the Botanic Garden at Upsal in 1756.

The *Cochineal* has become acclimated in Spain, more particularly in the neighbourhood of Malagar and in the kingdom of Valencia.

In 1806, M. Souceylier, a naval surgeon, brought home some living Cochineals, which he transmitted to M. Robert, professor of botany at Toulon.

In 1827, the naturilization of the Cochineal was attempted in Corsica, but without success. The same year it was introduced into the Canary Isles, where it met with the most perfect success, for the eight and a half pounds of Cochineal which these islands exported in 1831, amounted to no less than 882,200lbs. in 1850. The diseased vines, upon which the insects lived in the Canaries, have been lately rooted up and replaced by nopals.

The Spanish Government, fully appreciating the value of this branch of industry, forbade the exportation of the precious insect under the penalty of death. In spite, however, of this, in 1831, M. Simonnet, a pharmaceutist of Algiers, had the courage to run the risk of the undertaking and introduced the first Cochineals into the French settlements. He procured the insects from Valencia; but in consequence of bad weather he had the mortification to find his endeavours unsuccessful. Two years afterwards, Dr. Loze, a naval surgeon, brought several pots of the cactus, each having from thirty to forty of the Cochineal insects living upon them. At the end of 1834, he presented to the Academy of Sciences samples of his first crops, which were pronounced to be of an excellent quality. Recalled in 1836, M. Loze was obliged to leave his cacti and the Cochineals in the garden of Hussein Bey, where they were exposed to every kind of risk. Some time after, M. Hardy, director of the central Nursery Garden, endeavoured to save what might be left of them. It was with difficulty he could find two or three of the nopals, with a few impregnated females upon them; it was with these fragments that he was enabled to establish the valuable cultivation of which we are speaking. In 1846, 37lbs. were sold at Marseilles by order of the Minister of War. M. Chevreuil stated, that the produce from Algeria was equal in value and in quality to that of Mexico. From that time the cultivation of the Cochineal was rapidly developed.

In 1853, in the province of Algiers alone, there were fourteen nopalries, containing 61,500 nopals, and their produce sold at 15 francs the kilogramme (2·2055lb. avoir.).

Collecting.—The collecting of the Cochineals takes place in the fine weather, shortly before the time for laying their eggs, when the abdomen has attained its greatest size. Their size at this period is nearly that of a pea.

The Cochineals which are sown in April are collected in the June following. From these are chosen females which are intended for the rearing of the summer crop; this begins towards the end of May and is completed in September; from the second gathering females are again put aside for the winter crop. In a favourable season, three gatherings may be obtained during the year.

When the time for collecting has arrived, cloths are spread beneath the nopals, their joints are cut off and the insects detached by passing a fine brush or the blunt edge of a knife over the plant. This operation is repeated several times. Some growers do not mutilate the nopals, and scrape the joints without separating them from the trunk.

The Cochineals from the first gathering are considered the most valuable.

The insects are killed in several ways; one is to place them in baskets and steep them in boiling water, they are afterwards spread out on hurdles covered with cloths, and dried, first in the sun, and afterwards in the shade, where there is a free current of air. By this method the insects lose in the water the white powder with which they are covered. The Spaniards term these *cochinella renagrida*. At other times the insects are merely baked in an oven; when prepared in this way, they have an ashengrey colour, and are named *jaspeada*. Lastly, the cochineals are killed by being heated on iron plates, when they turn of a dark colour; this variety is known as the cochinella *nigra*.

Reaumur says that it takes 65,000 insects to weigh a pound Fr. (1lb. 1oz. 10¼dr. avoir.) while, according to M. Fée, it does not require more than from 42 to 45,000.

Three varieties of cochineal are distinguished in commerce: 1st, The *Mesteque*[1] *fine* or cochinella *Jaspeada* of the Spaniards; it is of a purplish grey colour and covered with a whitish powder. 2nd, The *Black* cochineal; this is the largest; it is

---

[1] Mesteque is the name of a Mexican province. (Ed.)

of a reddish or purplish black colour, and is almost or quite devoid of the white powder. 3rd, The *Sylvestre* cochineal or *grana Sylvestria;* this consists of the smallest insects; it is of a dullish red colour, and is of the least value. This variety is obtained from the nopal plants which grow wild in the woods.

In order to give the cochineals the farinaceous appearance which distinguishes the finest qualities, powdered talc or white lead is mixed with them. In this way the black variety is made to resemble the mesteque or fine variety.

Uses.—Cochineal has been recommended in hoopingcough and dysury. It has also been used in the form of a drink as a remedy for the troublesome form of cough which follows measles.

Carmine and lake carmine are formed from cochineal.

The colouring principle of cochineal (*cochinella* or carmine) is a crystallizable substance of a brilliant purplish red colour. It fuses at 112° F. It is insoluble in ether, but very soluble in alcohol and water. Alkalies change it to a violet colour, and acids to an intense red. Cochineal will preserve its colouring properties unchanged for a century. (Hellot.)

In 1736, there were imported into Europe 771,161 lbs. of cochineal of the value of fifteen millions of francs. At the present day, in the General Table of the commerce of France, that country alone receives about 761,776 lbs., valued at three millions of francs.

[A syrup of Cochineal has been introduced into the last edition of the Pharmacopœia.

SYRUPUS COCCI (*Syrup of Cochineal*).—Take of bruised cochineal ℨiv, boiling distilled water Oj. The cochineal is to be boiled for fifteen minutes in the water in a closed vessel, frequently stirring it; then strain. Add of sugar twice the weight of the strained liquid, and dissolve with a gentle heat. Lastly, when the syrup has cooled, mix with each fluid ounce half a fluid drachm of spirit.

Various properties have been assigned to cochineal, but without the least foundation; its only real use is as a colouring matter. It is for this purpose that it is ordered to be added to the *tinctura cardamomi composita,* and to the *tinctura cinchonœ composita.*]

2nd. *Other species of Cocci.*—Three other species of Cocci which are now almost entirely neglected were formerly used in medicine. These are: 1st, the Kermes; 2nd, the Coccus Polonicus; 3rd, the Coccus Lacca.

ANIMALS OCCASIONALLY EMPLOYED IN MEDICINE. 77

1st. The *Kermes* or *Coccus* of the oak[1] lives upon a particular species, peculiar to the South of Europe, known as the Quercus coccifera (fig 11). This is generally obtained from Montpellier, Provence, and Spain.

This species of Coccus is larger than that of the nopal, the female attaining the size of a large pea. It has no trace of rings, is of a globular form, and at first is of a bright red, but afterwards of a dark violet colour, and is covered with a white powder. It surrounds itself with fine threads, out of which it forms a kind of cocoon. Each female lays from 1,800 to 2,000 eggs.

By analysis *kermes* yield a red colouring matter similar to carmine, a peculiar animal principle termed coccine, a yellow fatty matter, and some phosphates and salts. (Lassaigne.)

2nd. The *Coccus Polonicus*[2] is found in Poland and Russia, and occasionally in France, attached to the roots of a small plant, the *Scleranthus perennis*; it is also found on the *Potentilla reptans* and *P. alba* of Linnæus.

The male has 13 to 14 joints to the antennæ and is provided with a bushy tail. The female is of an oval form and reddish colour; the first pair of feet are inserted near the antennæ and are very short and strong. The insect is collected in the Ukrane towards the end of the month of June,

Fig. 11.—*Kermes.*

---

[1] *Coccus Ilicis*, Linn.; commonly known in commerce and in pharmacy as *animal kermes, vegetable kermes*, kermes of the oak, *shining grain*.

[2] *Coccus Polonicus*, Linn. (*Porphyrophora Polonica*, Brandt), commonly termed *Saint John's blood*. [In Germany, during the ninth, twelfth, thirteenth, and fourteenth centuries, the rural serfs were bound to deliver annually to the convents, a certain quantity of kermes, the *coccus polonicus*, among the other products of industry. It was collected from the trees, upon Saint John's day, between eleven o'clock and noon, with religious ceremonies, and was therefore called *Johannisblut* (Saint John's blood), as also the German cochineal. At the above period a great deal of the German kermes was consumed in Venice for dyeing the scarlet to which that city gives its name. (Ure's Dic. of Arts and Sciences, art. Kermes.)] Another species is found in Armenia, *P. Hamelii*, Brandt (P. Armenica, Burmeister), which also yields a colouring matter used in the arts.

when the females are ripe. The abdomen is at this time swollen and filled with a purple fluid. The plants are rooted up with an iron instrument having the shape of a trowel. The cocci are freed from dirt by shaking them in sieves. The insects are sprinkled with vinegar, or with hot water, and are then dried in a warm place, or by the heat of the sun, but very slowly and with great care. If they are dried too quickly the colour is changed. (Bernitz.)

3rd. The *Coccus Lacca* (Kerr) lives on several trees in India; amongst others, upon the *Ficus religiosa*, the *F. Indica*, the *Rhamnus jujuba*, the *Croton lacciferum*, and the *Butea frondosa*.

The lac insect has the body oblong, flattened below and convex above, narrowed towards the posterior extremity, and furnished with a thickened ridge around the thorax and abdomen; the antennæ are filiform and bifurcated; the eyes are placed towards the inferior part of the head; its rostrum is placed beneath the thorax; the abdominal rings are obscure; according to Kerr there are fourteen rings; but according to Roxburgh there are only twelve; the body is terminated by two diverging setæ. (Kerr, Swagermann.) The male is furnished with two large membranous wings.

The insects attach themselves to the twigs and the young branches, which are about the thickness of the finger.

It has been supposed that the insect pierces the bark of the trees upon which it lives, for the purpose of depositing its eggs, and that a resinous matter oozes out of the wound, which dries upon the surface. The females of this species have the same habits as those of the *Cochineal* insect, and like them they become fixed at the period of laying, and cover the eggs with their dead bodies. As, however, they exist in great numbers they become closely packed together and arranged in lines. It has been stated that the resinous matter sucked up by the insect is transuded through the pores of its body. (Latreille.) It seems, however, more probable that the single puncture of the bark made at the time when the insect becomes fixed is sufficient to allow of the exudation of the resin, in which the creature becomes enveloped, and to which it imparts its red colour.

When a branch covered with lac is examined a rough irregular crust is seen on the bark, pierced by a number of small holes, which communicate with cells placed beneath. These cells are oval and terminate in a fine point towards the wood and in a blunted extremity externally; they are about $\frac{3}{25}$ of an inch in their greatest diameter; they seem to be moulded upon a very delicate shell (*utricule*, Virey). In the interior there is seen in the centre a red fluid, a cottony material of a white or rose colour, dark red globules, and small oblong bodies of the same colour. The shell is the abdomen of the parent insect, the globules are the eggs, and the oblong bodies the young larvæ.

It is the dead bodies of the females filled with eggs, and united together by the resinous matter previously spoken of, which form the substance known as *lac, lac resin*, or *gum lac*.

There are four kinds of lac known in commerce: 1st, *Stick Lac*, in which the lac is still attached to the branches, where it forms an irregular crust of variable thickness, and of a dark opaque red colour. 2nd, *Seed Lac* is that which has been removed from the branches and pounded; it generally occurs in small fragments, and the colour is not so dark as that of the first. [Seed lac is prepared by removing the resinous concretion from the twigs; it is then coarsely pounded and triturated with water in a mortar; the greater part of the colouring matter is thus dissolved, and the granular portion which remains after being dried in the sun constitutes Seed lac. See art. Lac in Ure's Dic. of Arts and Sciences.] 3rd, *Shell Lac* is that which has been melted in boiling water, and then poured on to smooth polished stones. These plates resemble glass of antimony, but they vary much in their colour, according as they have been more or less deprived of the colouring matter; they are consequently distinguished as the *brown*, the *red*, and the *white*. [In India the *Seed Lac* is put into oblong bags of cotton cloth, which are held over a charcoal fire by a man at each end, and as soon as it begins to melt the bag is twisted so as to strain the liquified resin through its substance, and to make it drop upon smooth stems of the banyan tree (*musa paradisa*). In this way the resin spreads into thin plates, and constitutes the substance known in commerce by the name of *shell lac*. (Ure.)] 4th, *Thread Lac* is a preparation made in England, which has the appearance of a number of reddish semi-transparent threads closely pressed and packed together.

[Although no longer employed in medicine, lac is extensively used in the arts and manufactures; it enters into the formation of sealing wax, of certain varnishes, of French polish, and is used in the manufacture of waterproof hats. In addition to this resinous matter, a dyeing material, known as *lac-dye*, is obtained from Stick lac. This is procured from a watery infusion of the ground stick lac evaporated to dryness. The residue is then made up into cakes about two inches square, and half-an-inch thick, which are stamped with the trade mark of the manufacturer. In England this colouring matter is employed for dyeing scarlet cloth, and is found to yield an equally brilliant colour, and one less easily affected by the perspiration than that produced by cochineal.]

CHAPTER II.

ANIMALS EMPLOYED IN PART.

THESE are animals which furnish certain calcareous or horny structures which are employed in medicine. They consist principally of—1st, *Pachydermata;* 2nd, *Cuttle fishes;* 3rd, *Oysters;* 4th, *Corals;* 5th, *Sponges.*

§ I. Pachydermata.

Amongst these animals is the *Elephant* (*Elephas*), one of the proboscidian mammalia, whose tusks are formed of an osseous substance known as *ivory.*

There are two species of Elephant: that of *India* (*Elephas Indicus*),[1] in which the summit of the head forms a sort of pyramid; the forehead is concave, and the ears small; that of Africa (*Elephas Africanus*, Cuv.), in which the head is round, the forehead convex, and the ears large, so as to cover the shoulders. These animals are provided with tusks implanted in the inter-maxillary bone. They are two very long pointed teeth, curved and hollow to the extent of half their length. Those of the *African Elephant* (fig. 12), are much larger than those of the *Indian Elephant*. The *ivory* of both is characterized in a transverse section by curved lines passing from the centre to the circumference, crossing

Fig. 12.—*African Elephant.*

---

[1] Some writers consider that there are two species of Indian Elephant and have named them *Elephas Asiaticus* and *Elephas Sumatranus.*

each other, and by that means intercepting lozenge-like or rhomboidal interspaces.

Ivory calcined until it becomes white has been regarded as absorbent, astringent, and anthelmintic; some therapeutists have termed it *spode* or *spodium*; others designate it as *caput mortuum*. The various preparations into which it formerly entered have now fallen entirely out of use.

The beautiful velvety black, known to painters as *Ivory black*, is obtained by calcining this material in closed vessels. [The calcined matter is afterwards ground and then levigated on a porphyry slab; it is much used in copper-plate printing.]

The tusks of the Elephant are used in the making of artificial teeth. It is also used in the manufacture of artificial teats, pessaries, and other surgical instruments.

The tusks of the Hippopotamus (*Hippopotamus amphibius*, Lin.) and Wild Boar (*Sus Scropha*, Lin.) are also used in the manufacture of artificial teeth.

[The tusks of the Elephant are never used in the present day in the construction of artificial teeth, whatever they might have been formerly: the objections to this material are that it is more easily destroyed by the fluids of the mouth, and at the same time is more costly than the teeth of some other animals, which are better adapted for the purpose. The tusks of the Wild Boar, on account of their size alone, could seldom be made available for the manufacture of artificial teeth. The only teeth which have ever been extensively used are the tusks of the Hippopotamus and the Walrus.]

§ II. Sepiadæ.

The *Sepiadæ* or *Cuttle-fishes* are molluscous animals belonging to the decapod division of the cephalopoda; they constitute the genus *Sepia* of Linnæus. The body of the animal is fleshy, depressed, and contained in a mantle, having the form of a sac, terminated posteriorly in a blunted extremity, and bounded on either side by a narrow lateral fin. The mouth is terminal and surrounded by ten arms provided with suckers; two of these arms are pedunculated, and are much longer than the others.

The most familiar species is the *common Cuttle-fish* (*Sepia officinalis*, Lin.), which is extremely abundant in all parts of the ocean and in the Mediterranean sea.

The *Common Cuttle-fish* varies in length from three to twenty-eight inches. Its body is oval and spread out at the sides; the upper surface is marked by purplish or reddish spots, and with white undulating lines upon a greyish or leaden coloured ground. The aperture of the mantle is imperfectly divided into three lobes; the two fins are united posteriorly. The orifice of the mouth is circular, membranous, and more or less fringed. There are two hard corneous jaws which shut into each other and resemble the beak of a parrot. (Rondelet.) The eyes are very large. The elongated arms or tentacles are nearly the length of the body, and their dilated extremities are furnished with a number of small pedunculated suckers. The other arms are furnished on their inner surface with several [four] rows of concave suckers.

The *Cuttle-fish* feeds upon crabs, squills, and various mollusca; it breaks down the carapace or shells of these animals with its beak-like jaws, and their further comminution is accomplished by means of its strong muscular stomach, which acts like a gizzard.

At the bottom of the abdominal sac is a bladder containing a black liquid, known as the ink of the *Cuttle-fish*. This bladder communicates by a small canal with the rectum. When the animal is pursued or threatened with danger it discharges some of this black fluid, which diffuses itself through the water, and in the midst of the obscurity which it produces the creature endeavours to escape.[1] The pigment used in water colour painting and known as *Roman Sepia*,[2] is obtained from this black liquid; it has been stated that the Chinese colour, commonly known as Indian ink, is prepared from a species of cephalopod allied to the *Cuttle-fish*. It is, however, almost certain that this ink is prepared from a kind of soot.

Cuttle-fishes are bisexual and oviparous. Their eggs are soft, of a blackish colour, and collected together like a bunch of grapes, and hence the name of *sea grapes*, which is commonly given to them.

The *Cuttle-fish* encloses in its dorsal region a solid body, known as the *Cuttle bone Sepium*, or *shell of the Cuttle-fish;* the French give it the name of *biscuit de mer*.[3] Blainville has proposed to call it *Sepiostaire*. This body is of an elongated oval form, somewhat broader behind than before, depressed,

---

[1] *Atramentum quo se occultat* (Linn.).
[2] *Eo litteræ pinguntur* (Linn.).
[3] *Os officinale* (Linn.).

extremely porous, and very light. Its superior surface is convex and granulated; its inferior is partly convex and partly concave; it terminates posteriorly in a thin dilated aliform margin, composed of calcareous and horny matter, which, becoming everted, forms a wide and shallow concavity. Quite at the extremity is a more solid portion, which has the form of a conical hook or apophysis; it is sometimes straight, sometimes curved. The thickened part of the *sepium* is composed of thin parallel calcareous plates, which are deposited in such a manner that the last formed covers the greater part of all the others, but leaves their posterior margins uncovered. The principal ingredient is carbonate of lime.

The bone of the *cuttle-fish* was formerly employed as an antiacid and absorbent. It enters into the preparation of certain tooth-powders.

[The following is the formula of the tooth powder in the French codex:

Bol armeniac		
Red coral		
Bone of cuttle-fish	*aa*	℥j, gr. xiv.
Dragon's blood		ʒiv, gr. vii.
Cochineal		ʒj, gr. ij.
Cream of tartar		℥j, ʒiv, gr. xxi.
Powdered cinnamon . . .		ʒij, gr. iv.
Cloves		ʒij, gr. viij.

The cellular structure of the bone of the *cuttle-fish* renders it so light that it floats on water. It was analysed by John, who gives the following as its composition:—

	Hard, Upper or Outer Portion.	Porous Part.
Carbonate (with a trace of phosphate) of lime	80	85
Non-gelatinous animal matter soluble in water with common salt	7	7
Gelatinous membrane not soluble in water	9	4
Water, with a trace of magnesia	4	4
	100	100

It is used in the arts as a polishing material, for forming moulds for fine silver castings, and as a pounce to prevent ink from spreading after erasures.]

§ III. Snails.

Snails are gasteropodous mollusca, belonging to the genus *Helix*, the family *Helecidæ*, and to the order Pulmonifera. The characters of the animal are—1st, an elongated body, with a thick collar bilobed inferiorly; four cylindrical tentacles; a crescent-shaped dentated upper mandible or jaw; an oval elongated foot; the respiratory orifice on the right side; reproductive orifice near the base of the right large or ocular tentacle. 2nd, Shell dextral, globose or depressed, the spire usually short, with the last turn generally large; umbilicus perforated or unperforated; the columella straight or spiral; aperture transverse, oblique, and semilunar; a thick peristome, terminating in an abrupt or reflected margin.

Snails live in hedges, on dry plants, on the trunks of trees, in the crevices of walls, and on stones. They feed principally upon vegetable substances. Their generative organs are androgynous; they contain a copulative pouch, the dart enclosed in a sac, numerous vesicles, and a flagellum. At the period of copulation a large spermatophora issues from the male organ, and penetrates the female apparatus of another individual. These animals are oviparous and deposit their eggs in moist earth. The use of snails as a medicine has been advocated at various times. At the commencement of the present century Dr. Chrestien, of Montpellier, recommended them to be used boiled or in the raw state after removal from the shell. Other writers have recommended them to be sprinkled with sugar; this causes them to give out a large quantity of their viscous slime, which is to be taken by the patient.

The species which is best known is the *Helix pomatia* (Linn.) or Roman snail. The shell of this species (fig. 13) is 1½ inch in

Fig. 13.—*Helix Pomatia*.[1]

height, globose, obliquely bowed below, with fine and unequal

[1] The animal in a state of extension, and a separate view of the jaw.

longitudinal striæ, tolerably thick, very strong, smooth, shining, opaque, of a reddish or dirty yellow, and with three or four indistinct yellow bands. The spire is composed of five or six convex turns, which rapidly increase up to the last, which is large; the suture is deep, the summit elevated, and the umbilicus oblique; the aperture is interrupted by the penultimate curves, and is provided with an erected margin, which is thickened and of a reddish white internally. During winter this aperture is closed by a membrane called the epiphragm, which is convex, thick, cretaceous, and of a greyish colour.

These molluscs live in gardens, vineyards, and forests.

The *Helix pomatia* formerly entered into the composition of several pharmaceutical preparations. They were made into broth, into a mucilage, a syrup, a jelly, and a pomade. These preparations have long since fallen into disuse. Snails were recommended in herpes; they were allowed to crawl over the surface of the skin and deposit their mucus upon it, or they were pounded and applied to the part. (Adanson.) Dr. Gœlis, of Vienna, has extolled the efficacy of the pounded shell in epilepsy and in intermittent fevers (1815).

M. Oscar Figuier, of Montpellier, prepared a snail paste, which enjoyed a certain amount of repute. The species employed in the formation of this paste were the large garden snail, *H. aspersa* and *H. vermiculata*. The *H. pomatia* and the wood snail, *H. nemoralis*, might also be employed for this purpose; but these species, which are so common in the northern and temperate parts of France, are not met with in the south.

According to M. Soubeiran, a hundred individuals of the *Helix pomatia*, which weigh two pounds, when they have been freed from their shells, yield about one pound three ounces of flesh, while one hundred of the *H. nemoralis* of the average size do not give much more than ten ounces.

Snails contain a peculiar mucilaginous principle, whose characters are imperfectly known, but which seems to have some resemblance to gelatine and mucus. M. Oscar Figuier thinks that the properties of these molluscs are partly owing to an oil with a sulphurous odour, which may be extracted by means of ether, and to which he has given the name of *helicine*. He recommends that this principle should be retained as much as possible unaltered in all the pharmaceutical preparations. According to a recent analysis of M. Gobley, *helicine* cannot be considered as a proximate principle; it does not contain sulphur; it consists, like human venous blood, of oleine, margarine, cholesterine, lecithine, and cerebrine.[1]

In a work presented some months back to the Academy of Medicine, M. Eugene Fournier has examined the proportions of mucilage, of iodine, of sulphur, and of phosphorus, which are contained in snails. He shows that these proportions vary according to the localities in which animals live and according to the nature of their food. He is of opinion that these principles might be artificially increased, and that the animals might even be made to assimilate other principles, such as doses of opium, belladonna, digitalis, and of arsenic. It is known that these molluscs can feed without inconvenience upon various substances, which exercise a more or less decided action upon man.

M. Chatin considers that the *Limneus stagnalis* of our ponds and marshes may be substituted for snails in the formation of syrups and lozenges. It is true that this mollusc has less mucilage, but an equal weight of them contains four times as much iodine.

The English obtain from Prince's Island a large species of Achatina (*A. carinata*), which they have introduced into Europe as a remedy in phthisis.

§ IV.—Oysters.

Oysters are acephalous conchiferous molluscs, with only one adductor muscle (Monomyaria); they belong to the genus Ostrea, which may be regarded as the type of the family Ostreidæ.

The body of the animal is of an oblong oval form, flat, often irregular, and covered by a thick mantle, which is fringed at its margins. The mouth is furnished with elongated triangular palpi. No foot. The branchiæ are large curved, nearly equal, the external shorter than the internal. The shell is attached, bivalved, irregular, foliaceous, rough, and generally thick; upper valve short, flat, and moveable; lower valve larger and convex. Hinge toothless. Ligament partly internal, and inserted on both sides into an oblong cavity.

Oysters live near the shore, at moderate depths, where the water is tranquil. They are sometimes developed in vast numbers, forming what are termed *oyster banks*. Some of these banks are miles in extent, and seem to be inexhaustible.

---

[1] Dr. Lamare has recently recommended *helicine* in phthisis.

In 1819, a bank was discovered near one of the islands of Zealand, which for the space of a year supplied the inhabitants of the Low Countries with such abundance of oysters, that the price of these shell-fish fell to tenpence a hundred; as, however, this bank happened to be situated almost on a level with low water, the winter being very severe, it was entirely destroyed. (Deshayes.)

Of all shell-fish, oysters are probably those whose faculties are the most limited. Fixed to the rock or to some submarine body, the only food which they obtain is that which is brought to them by the currents of the ocean, and they give no other signs of life than that of opening and closing their valves. Nevertheless, it appears that under certain circumstances they may have the power of removing themselves from the spot to which they have been attached.

These animals are androgynous, but the male and female organs do not perform their functions at the same time. The seminal fluid makes its appearance before the ova.

The young oysters are lodged in the mantle of the mother, from whence they sally forth and swim around her, by means of their vibratile cilia, but take refuge between the maternal valves on the approach of the slightest danger.

The shell of the oyster, like all others, consists of carbonate, with a small quantity of phosphate, of lime; it was formerly extolled as a powerful absorbent and antiacid, and even as a lithontriptic. The shells were calcined and reduced to a very fine powder. In the present day the carbonate of lime or of magnesia is used instead. They are still, however, used in the preparation of certain dentifrices.

If, however, the valves of these molluscs are but little thought of as a remedy, the animal on the contrary is highly prized as an article of food. The oyster fishery has for many years been an important branch of industry and commerce. These molluscs will be noticed again when speaking of the flesh of animals.

§ V.—Coral.

Red coral[1] is a marine production, distinguished by its hardness, its capability of receiving a high polish, and by its fine red colour.

Coral is found attached to rocks at the bottom of the sea.

---

[1] *Corallium nobile* (*Gorgonia nobilis*, Ellis; *Isis nobilis*, Linn.; *Corallium rubrun*, Lamk.).

It is met with in different parts of the Mediterranean and in the Red Sea; it exists at various depths, but never less than three yards, nor more than three hundred.

Coral was for a long time regarded a marine plant; it is now known to be the production of polyps which live in societies. When seen in the ocean this kind of coral resembles the trunk of a small leafless shrub.

The central part of the coral is as hard as marble, and its surface is marked by parallel but irregular striæ. This axial portion is covered by a soft fleshy layer, formed of delicate membrane and fibres reticulated together, and inclosing a number of glandular bodies, filled with a milky fluid, which seem to unite it to the calcareous portion. In the fleshy mass are depressions in which the bodies of the polyps are lodged; these consist of a globular portion which is fixed, and of a free exsectile cylindrical portion terminated by a mouth surrounded by eight tentacula or arms, which are notched at their margins.

The *Coral* from the coasts of France is considered to have the brightest and deepest colour, probably because it is more carefully selected than that of other countries. That of Italy rivals it in beauty; that of Barbary is larger, but not so brilliant. Five varieties of *coral* are known in commerce, and are distinguished by the following fanciful titles:—1, *The Froth of Blood;* 2nd, *The Flower of Blood;* 3rd, 4th, and 5th, *Blood of the First, Second,* and *Third* quality.

According to Vogel *Coral* contains nearly four-fifths of its weight of carbonate of lime; it also contains magnesia and oxide of iron.

[Witting states that 100 grains of red coral yield the following constituents:—

Carbonate of lime	83·25
Carbonate of magnesia	3·50
Oxide of iron	4·25
Animal gelatine and sand	7·75
Loss	1·25
	100·00]

Coral was formerly employed medicinally, and was looked upon as a tonic and an absorbent. M. Desbois, of Rochefort, pretends that it is tonic, because its colour is owing to a *martial principle,* that is to say, to a salt of iron; but there are so many better ways of administering this metal that the sooner the pretended tonic properties of coral or its colouring matters are forgotten, the better. It has, moreover, been shown that this colour does not depend upon iron, but upon a red matter containing nitrogen, similar to that which decorates various shells, and which is deprived of all colour by the action of the feeblest acids. (Fremy.) With regard to its absorbent properties, there are several bodies which are better adapted for this purpose, so that even in this respect coral could not long continue to be used.

The old practitioners administered coral in the form of a powder, bolus, electuary, as a drink, and as a tincture; they also made use of a magestry or precipitate of coral, which was held in considerable repute. Lémery considered it adapted to *renovate* the *heart*.

At the present time, coral is only used as a mechanical agent for the purpose of cleaning the teeth. It can only act very slightly as an absorbent, and still less as a tonic.

Other species.—The old Materia Medica also included Black coral, the *Gorgonia Antipathes* of Linnæus, and White coral, which was a mixture of *Oculina* and the *Caryophyllia;* the *Oculina virginea* (Lamk.) being the species which was principally made use of.

The same virtues were attributed to these corals as to the Red.

The Black coral is distinguished from the Red by the horny nature of the stem, and by its flexibility and smoothness.

White coral differs still more; the axis is stony or calcareous, but the polyps are contained in lamellated star-like cavities, and not in the fleshy cortical substance.

§ VI. Sponge.

Sponge consists of aggregations of animals belonging to the class of Polyps.

The species which is best known is the common domestic sponge or *Spongia officinalis*. Like the corals it is an inhabitant of the sea; it is very abundant in the Mediterranean, especially around the islands of the Grecian Archipelago. It is found attached to the rocks where they are least exposed to the action of the waves and currents.

The *Common sponge* presents itself in masses of various forms and sizes; it is of a brown colour, and composed of a light elastic and resisting tissue, which is traversed in every direction by numerous interspaces. This tissue consists of delicate flexible interlaced fibres provided with pores (*oscula,*

Lamk.) and irregular canals, which communicate freely with each other. In this tissue there is found a number of silicious or calcareous particles (*spiculæ*), having a slender, simple, or tricuspid form.

In its living state the *Common Sponge* is covered with mucous layers consisting of a kind of animated jelly. The most opposite opinions have been entertained with regard to the nature of sponges. Amongst the ancients, some regarded them as plants; others as being of a twofold nature, that is to say, as vegetables which served as a residence for certain polyps. Dioscorides, Pliny, and their commentators, have divided *Sponges* into males and females. Rondelet, the two Bauhins, Ray, Tournefort, Vaillant, Marsigli, and others, have placed them in the vegetable kingdom; while Nieremberg, Peyssonel, Tremblay, Ellis, Lamouroux, and others, have maintained their animal nature. In the present day, the latter opinion is generally admitted to be the correct one. Five different hypotheses have been held as regards this animal nature: 1st. That the fibrous portion and the muco-gelatinous layer constitute a single animal. 2nd. That the muco-gelatinous layer alone forms the animal. 3rd. That the sponge is a compound being, consisting of an aggregation of polyps, living in the substance of the enveloping muco-gelatinous substance. 4th. That these polyps exist only in the interspaces of the fibrous mass. 5th. That the polyps are found both in the muco-gelatinous layer and in the fibrous mass. The fourth hypothesis is the true one.

The animalcules of the *Sponges* are a species of membranous tubes, capable of extending and retracting themselves. They have been compared to polyps deprived of tentacles and reduced to their most simple conditions.

Sponges have yellow or whitish seed-like eggs, from which non-ciliated embryos are produced, in the interior of which contractile cells become developed, and subsequently spicules, which are ultimately covered with vibratile cilia. (Lieberkuhn, Bowerbank.) Several of these embryos unite together to form a colony, in which their individuality becomes exceedingly indistinct.

Sponge is composed of an animal matter which has been compared to albumen and to mucus (*fibroine*, Mulder). It is soluble in sulphuric, hydrochloric, and nitric acids, and in liquor potassa. These solutions give a precipitate with nut-galls. Besides carbon, hydrogen, oxygen, and nitrogen, sponge contains iodine, sulphur, and phosphorus. It also contains bromine, carbonate, and phosphate of lime, sea salt, and traces of silica, magnesia, and alumina.

Formerly *Sponges* were strongly calcined, or they were made hot and then reduced to a powder, which was used as a remedy in goitre and scrofula. Its curative properties were owing to the presence of iodine.[1]

Sponges were also used in surgery, to dilate certain wounds or natural cavities. For this purpose the sponge when perfectly dry was dipped into melted wax and then compressed between two iron plates until cold, the pieces of sponge prepared in this manner were called *tents*.

Every one is acquainted with the numerous domestic purposes for which sponge is used.

Other species.—Besides the last species, which is known in common as the *Fine Syrian Sponge*, there are seven others: 1st. *Fine Archipelago Sponge*, which is probably only a variety of the former; it is used for domestic purposes; it is also employed in the manufacture of porcelain and in lithography. 3rd. *Fine hard Sponge*, commonly called *Grecian Sponge;* this is employed for domestic purposes, and also in certain manufactures. 4th. *White Sponge of Syria*, called also *Venetian Sponge;* this is made use of for the same purposes as the former. 5th. *Gelatine (géline) Sponge*, which comes from the coast of Barbary. 6th. *The Brown Sponge of Barbary*, also called *Marseilles Sponge*, the *Spongia communis* of naturalists; this is used for cleaning rooms and similar purposes; it is fished on the coast of Tunis. 7th. *The Sponge of Salonica* (Gervais, Van Beneden).

CHAPTER III.

ANIMAL PRODUCTS.

The animal productions which require to be noticed are: 1st, *Spermaceti;* 2nd, *Bile;* 3rd, *Crabs' eyes;* 4th, *The Web of the Spider*.

§ I. Spermaceti.

Spermaceti is a substance which is obtained from several

---

[1] In ancient pharmacy the burnt bodies of the Alcyonia were also employed, the same virtues being attributed to them as to the sponges. The species which was principally used was the *Alcyonium Lyncurium* of Lamouroux, commonly called the Sea quince or Sea orange.

species of cetacean mammals, particularly from the cachalot or spermaceti whale. It is also obtained from the common or Greenland whale.

1. The *Great Cachalot* (*Physeter macrocephalus*, Linn.) is an enormous animal,[1] which is met with in all parts of the ocean. Anderson measured one which was 70 feet in length. This mammal (fig. 14) is of a blackish blue colour, darkest on the back [the under surface is whitish, and also around the eyes]; the head is very large, especially at its anterior part. The upper jaw has no teeth, or if they are present they are quite rudimentary and hidden in the gum. The lower jaw is narrow and about three feet shorter than the upper; it is provided on each side with from twenty to thirty cylindrical slightly curved teeth on either side. The vent is single, and not double, as in most of the Cetacea. The eyes are projecting and placed on eminences. The dorsal fin is reduced to a callous prominence. The tail is bilobed and is very flexible.

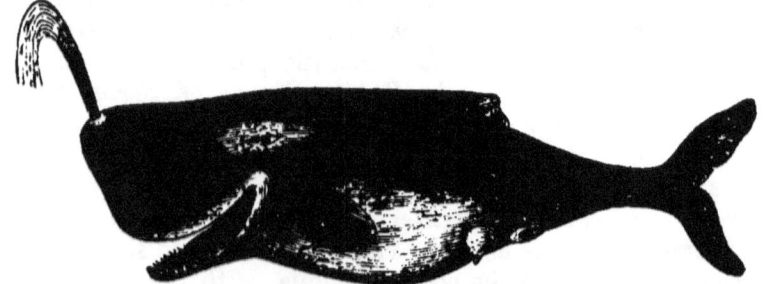

Fig. 14.—*Cachalot.*

The *Cachalot* in swimming usually produces a foaming of the water, showing its back and the fleshy eminence which surrounds the vent; its movements are not rapid.

[Beale states, that when undisturbed the animal passes tranquilly along, just below the surface of the water, at the rate of about three or four miles an hour, its progress being effected by a gentle oblique motion of the tail from side to side; when proceeding at its usual rate, the body lies horizontally; the water by its progress being somewhat disturbed, is known by the whalers under the name of "White water;" in this mode of swimming it is able to obtain a velocity of about seven miles an hour. When it swims at a more rapid rate, the action of the tail is altered, the water is struck directly upwards and downwards, and each time the blow is made with the inferior

---

[1] *Longitudo sæpe sexaginta pedum* (Linn.).

surface, the head sinks down eight or ten feet, and when the blow is reversed it rises out of the water presenting to it only the sharp cut-water portion.]

2. The *Greenland Whale* (*Balæna Mysticetus*, Linn.). This animal is usually regarded as the most voluminous of the Cetacea, and therefore, of all known animals.[1] Its dimensions

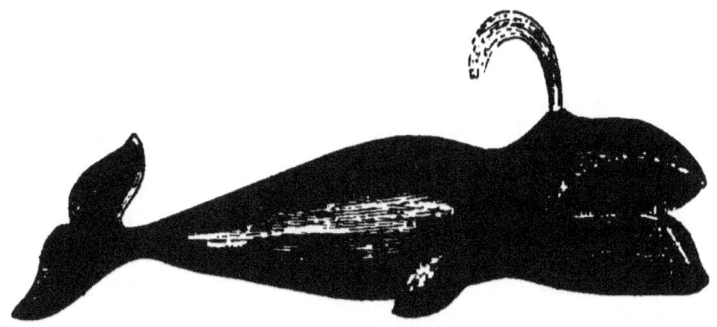

Fig. 15.—*Greenland Whale.*

have, however, been greatly exaggerated. Scoresby, who was present at the capture of three hundred and twenty-two individuals, has never seen one which measured more than from sixty-five to seventy feet in length.[2] Its greatest circumference is from thirty to forty feet.

The *Whalebone Whale* has no teeth, but there are rudiments of these organs in the lower jaw of the young animal. (Geoffroy Saint-Hilaire.) The upper jaw is keel-shaped, and is provided on each side with a series of thin transverse plates, upwards of three hundred in number, composed of the baleen or whalebone (fig. 16). These plates terminate at their inferior margin in a fringe of coarse hair. The tongue is fleshy and very thick. The animal has no dorsal fin.

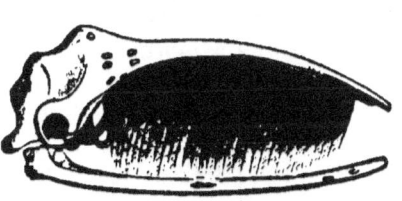

Fig. 16.—*Whalebone Plates.*

The *Whale* is an inhabitant of the Arctic regions. The species which is met with in the South Atlantic ocean, the *Balæna Australis* of Kleir, or Whale of the Southern Ocean, differs essentially from that of the North, the *Balæna mysticetus*; it is the smallest of the two

---

[1] *Maximus omnium animalium* (Linn.).
[2] Linnæus asserts that they occasionally attain the length of 100 feet (*sæpe* 100 *pedum*).

species, usually measuring from thirty-five to forty-five feet, but frequently extending to fifty.

3. *Spermaceti.*—This substance is found in the cellular tissue which separates the membranes of the brain in the *Cachalot*. The whole of the upper portion of the skull consists of large cavities covered in, and separated from each other, by cartilaginous walls. It is in these cavities that the *spermaceti* is contained.[1] The cavity which is occupied by the encephalon appears relatively small to the entire volume of the head. Camper found in a head, measuring eighteen feet long, that this cavity was only twelve inches in width, nine in length, and seven in depth.

In the living animal the *spermaceti* is dissolved in an oily liquid, but in the dead animal it becomes solidified. This is purified by being squeezed through coarse bags; it is then boiled in an alkaline ley, which frees it from any remaining oil; it is then washed and melted.

In a *Cachalot* from the Moluccas, which was sixty-four feet long, M. Quoy calculated there were twenty-four barrels of spermaceti, each containing two hundred and seventy-five pounds, so that the entire quantity amounted to more than six thousand six hundred pounds.

The *spermaceti* of commerce and of the pharmaceutists is a white, friable substance, soft to the touch, and breaking into shining greasy-looking scales. It melts at 113° Fah. Boiling alcohol will dissolve the one seven hundredth of it.

Chemists have long regarded spermaceti as a compound body, saponifiable by the action of alcohol, and to a certain extent analogous to the neutral fats.[2] M. Heintz, in works which he has recently published, assigns a more complicated composition to the substance. M. Chevreul obtained from spermaceti a peculiar body, to which he gave the name of *cetine*. This is a white, laminated, friable substance, which melts at 120° Fah., and has no action on litmus. Boiling alcohol will dissolve two and a half parts of it.

Spermaceti was formerly administered in diseases of the lungs and kidneys. In the present day it is no longer used internally, but it enters into the formation of certain cerates or pomades, which are applied to cracked breasts and to the pustules of small pox; it is also employed in the manufacture of lip salve.

[There are two preparations of *spermaceti* in the London

---

[1] *Spermaceti e ventriculis cerebri*, Linn.
[2] Chevreul, Dumas, Peligot, Lawrence, Smith.

Pharmacopeia, the *Ceratum Cetacei* and the *Unguentum Cetacei;* they are both composed of spermaceti, white wax, and olive oil, the latter being the softest in consequence of the smaller quantity of wax and larger quantity of spermaceti, which is used in its preparation. They are employed as dressings for blisters and excoriated surfaces.]

§ II. Bile.

Bile is a fluid which is secreted by the liver, and is received into a special receptacle termed the *gall bladder,* from whence it passes into the duodenum. Some of the mammalia are unprovided with this bladder, and the bile does not then remain for a time in the liver, but is immediately discharged into the intestine.

Bile is a limpid viscous fluid, heavier than water, usually of yellow or green colour, having a faint nauseous odour, which, by a certain change, approaches to that of musc, and a sweetish but at the same time a bitter taste. It may be evaporated without undergoing decomposition.

The *bile of the Ox* is sometimes employed in the form of an extract. Its specific gravity is 1·026 at a temperature of 42° Fah. When warmed in closed vessels *bile* becomes thickened, froths up, solidifies, and forms the substance known as extract of bile; it readily mixes both with water and alcohol.

[Ox Bile (*Fel Bovinum, seu Tauri*).—An extract of Ox bile was formerly used in medicine, and it has been lately reintroduced. Dr. Copland[1] says he has made use of the inspissated Ox gall for many years with advantage. He recommends it in mesenteric affections, and has found it exceedingly useful where the secretion of the bile has been deficient and the mucous membrane of the alimentary canal irritable and relaxed. Dr. Clay,[2] of Manchester, says, "its effect upon the system is not purgative; but it acts as a mere solvent of the material contained within the intestinal canal; producing no excitement to propel; but by liquifying the mass facilitates its excretion." It acts as an aperient, and may be given in doses of ʒj to ʒj daily.]

Bile contains 7 per cent. of solid matter, which is held in solution by mucus; it consists of two nitrogenous soaps, having a sweet but, at the same time, bitter taste; the choleic of soda and the tauro-choleic of soda. The first, the *biline* of Berzelius, is the most abundant; it contains an organic crystallizable

---

[1] Dic. Pract. Med. vol. ii. p. 725. [2] Med. Times, 1842.

acid, which has no sulphur amongst its constituent elements. The second is present in smaller quantities; its acid is uncrystallizable, and contains sulphur. Besides these substances, *bile* contains oleic and margaric acids, cholesterine, some colouring matter, and certain salts.

The *bile* of the sheep, the dog, and the cat differ slightly from that of the ox.

§ III. Crabs'-eyes.

The great reputation which *crabs' eyes* formerly enjoyed as a medicine, has greatly diminished since the commencement of the present century.

The *River Crab* or *Cray-fish* (*Astacus fluviatilis*) is a decapod crustacean, which inhabits the rivers and brooks of Europe. It hides itself beneath the stones at the bottom, or in the hollows of the banks. It seldom comes out of its hiding-place, except for the purpose of procuring its food, which consists of the dead bodies of submerged quarupeds, fishes, molluscs, the larvæ of insects, worms, and all kinds of decomposing animal matter.

The *Cray-fish* is an animal with an elongated body, varying in colour, according to the locality from which it comes, from a greenish or clear brown to a blueish green. The head is confounded with and united to the thorax. The carapace is semi-cylindrical, and terminates anteriorly in a curved pointed rostrum, which is marked in the centre with a transverse groove. The rostrum is dentated laterally, and has a double tooth on the upper part of its base. The four antennæ are thin and setaceous; the external large, and supported upon a pedicle with three joints; the internal short and bifid. The eyes are hemispherical, and their diameter is not greater than that of their pedicles. The mouth is furnished with six pairs of modified limbs; the first pair has received the name of *mandibles*, and the last that of *foot jaws*. The abdomen (improperly termed the *tail*) is large, composed of six segments, and curved inferiorly. The first pair of thoracic limbs are much larger than the others; they are of unequal size, and are armed on their inner edge with fine teeth; they support a pair of strong pincers, of which the external joint is fixed, while the internal, which is much the smallest, is moveable. The four last pairs of limbs are slender, and of nearly equal size; the second and third are also each of them provided with a pair of pincers; but in these it is the external joint, and not the internal, which is moveable. The five pairs of abdominal or *false feet* are adapted for swimming. The tail is formed of five large plates, rounded at their margins and ciliated; the external plates are divided into two distinct pieces by a transverse suture.

The *Crabs* moult at the end of the spring. These Crustacea copulate with their abdomens opposite to each other. Two months afterwards the female lays her eggs. The eggs, varying in number from twenty to forty, are collected together in bundles, and fixed to the false feet, by means of a slender flexible pedicle, which is slightly enlarged at its base. The eggs are spherical and of a reddish brown colour. The females carry these grape-like bodies about with them until the young are hatched.

When the *Crabs* are about to cast their shell, two calcareous masses are found in the lateral compartments of the stomach. These bodies have received the name of *crabs' eyes*.[1] They disappear after the moult has taken place. Reaumur ascertained that they served for the formation and hardening of the new skin. It appears, in fact, that the pouches of the stomach, which have just been mentioned, shortly before the casting of the shell occurs, secrete the calcareous salts, which exist in excess in the blood, and form these stony masses. At a later period the stones are gradually dissolved and serve to calcify and harden the new skin.

These concretions (fig. 17) are round bodies, convex on one side, and flattened on the other, compressed, narrow at their edge, and marked on one side with a circular groove. These masses are hard, smooth, and white, consisting of super-imposed layers of carbonate of lime and of a certain quantity of mucus. It is their form and the circular groove which have obtained for them the name of *crabs' eyes*. Their diameter varies from seven to fifteen lines in diameter, and their weight from seven and a half to twenty-two and a half grains. M. Guibourt has noticed that when these concretions are placed in boiling water they become of a rose colour, which is a modification of the colour that the shell acquires when similarly treated.

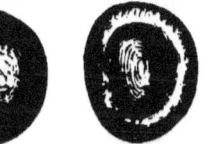

Fig. 17.—*Crabs' eyes*.

The *crabs' stones* which are most esteemed come from Astrakan. They have been prescribed as absorbents in acidity of the stomach. They were reduced to a powder, washed,

---

[1] *Crabs' stones, concrementa seu calculi cancrorum.*

ground with a small quantity of water, mixed into a paste, and made up in the form of lozenges, which were then dried and known as *prepared crabs' eyes*. Formerly these lozenges (called *trochisci*) entered into the composition of a number of pharmaceutical preparations, which are no longer in use.

Other substances producing the same effects, and more certain in their action, have been substituted for the *crabs' eyes;* as, for example, chalk and magnesia.

Some dentists still make use of these concretions in the manufacture of dentifrices.

§ IV. Spider's Web.

Spiders, or more correctly speaking the *Araneidæ*, constitute a numerous tribe belonging to the class Arachnida. Linnæus placed them all in the genus *Aranea*, and classed them with the insects. There are more than two hundred species in the neighbourhood of Paris.

These animals have the head united to the thorax, the abdomen distinct, and supported upon a short pedicle. The abdomen is very large, especially in the females; the skin is soft and flexible. *Spiders* have six or eight simple eyes in the form of hemispherical tubercles, which shine in the dark like those of cats. They have eight long slender legs, terminating in the male in two notched claws, and in the females in a single one. The organs of generation are placed in the former sex on either side of the head at the extremity of the palpi.

[Only a portion of the generative organs are situated at the extremity of the palpi, consisting of a kind of vesiculæ seminalis or sperm reservoirs, and of the intromittent organ. The true testicles are placed in the abdomen, between the lobes of the liver. They consist of two long simple interlaced cæca, from which two deferent canals pass to the anterior part of the under surface of the abdomen, and terminate by two approximate orifices, or else by a common opening between two apertures, which lead to the pulmonary organs. During the breeding season these testicles are found laden with spermatozoa in various stages of development. These must be first transferred to the extremity of the palpi, and afterwards applied to the vulva of the female.[1] The female organs are found at the middle and inferior part of the abdomen near to its commencement.]

---

[1] See Owen—*Lectures on the Invertebrata*, p. 460, 2nd edition, London, 1855; also Siebold—*Anatomy of the Invertebrata*, edited by W. T. Burnett, M. D., p. 394, London, 1854.

These animals are exceedingly ferocious and cruel, so that even the season of love does not alter the savageness of their nature. The males, which are much smaller and feebler than the females, are compelled to approach them with great caution. "One day," says De Geer, "I witnessed a male gently approaching his female, who was tranquilly reposing in the centre of her web; he made use of all the usual precautions, and several times retreated as if from fear... At length he placed himself beneath her, but at the cost of his life, for in a moment the female seized him with her claws, which she had only to close upon him; she then enveloped him in her threads, and began to suck his blood. "I declare," he adds, "the spectacle filled me with a kind of horror and indignation."

Some females carry their eggs under their abdomen. Others, when the young are hatched, place them on their back.

Most of the spiders can form a web, either for the purpose of ensnaring their prey, or for protecting their eggs.

Every one is acquainted with the *web* of the *spider*. The silk of which it is composed is secreted by irregular grape-like glands. (Treviranus.) From these glands nine pairs of tortuous canals are given off, which ultimately terminate in small reservoirs, in which the silky material is perfected. The three central pairs of reservoirs are the largest; the middle ones are placed very obliquely; the others are arranged nearly transversely. The excretory canals of the three central pairs are nearly straight and parallel; those of the remaining six are narrower and more or less tortuous. All of them converge to the posterior part of the abdomen.

Beneath the anus there may be observed six fleshy projections arranged in pairs; they are cylindrical or conical, and pierced at their extremities with an infinite number of minute apertures. These are the *spinnarets*. The two upper projections are the largest, the two inferior the smallest, and those in the middle the least prominent.

While in the body of the animal the material for the formation of the thread is a viscous liquid. This substance is transformed into a glutinous thread, which becomes firm as it dries.

Each thread, although extremely delicate, is, nevertheless, composed of as many filaments as there are pores in the different spinnarets.

Some *Spiders* form a large triangular horizontal web, with a small tubular chamber in one of the angles. Others construct a loose net-work, which is placed vertically, and in the centre of which they remain motionless. There are some which cover up a hole in the wall or the rock with a silken covering. Others construct an extremely delicate net-work, from which they hang suspended. Others throw off long threads, which trail along from the hinder parts of their bodies. Certain tropical spiders weave a net sufficiently strong to entangle some of the smaller birds, and even to offer a certain amount of resistance to man.

It is needless to repeat all the marvellous statements which have been made upon the medicinal properties of the *Spider's web*. Formerly it was used as a cataplasm in hysteria. They were administered internally in the form of pills in fever. The celebrated *Montpellier drops* were obtained from them by distillation, and were recommended as a preventative to apoplexy.

If the *web of the Spider* is ever employed in the present day, it is for the purpose of arresting hœmorrhage from the capillary vessels.[1]

SECTION III.

ANIMALS, OR ANIMAL PRODUCTIONS, WHICH ARE CONSTANTLY EMPLOYED IN MEDICINE.

THE animals, or animal productions, which are endowed with medicinal properties, and which are capable of exercising a decided influence over our bodies, and are therefore constantly employed in medicine, are but few in number.

These therapeutic agents will be arranged in seven divisions: 1. *Liver oil.* 2. *Musk.* 3. *Vesicating insects.* 4. *Leeches.* 5. *Galls.* 6. *Trehala.*

CHAPTER I.

LIVER OIL.

FOR some years the *oil from the livers of fish* have been frequently administered, so that its manufacture and commerce

[1] The *two-spined ant, Formica bispinosa* (Oliv.), of Cayenne, constructs with the down which accompanies the seeds of a cotton tree (probably the *Bombax globosum*, Aubl.,) a nest composed of a very fine kind of felt which is used with astonishing success in stopping hœmorrhage. (Lescalier.)

ANIMALS CONSTANTLY EMPLOYED IN MEDICINE. 101

have lately become of considerable importance. It is stated that on the coast of Malabar alone, in the year 1854, 721,095 gallons were exported, estimated in the official documents at the value of 517,167 francs.

§ I. Oil from the Liver of the Cod.

1. COD.—*Oil from the liver of the Cod*[1] is principally furnished by the *common Cod, Gadus Morrhua* (Linn.), *Morrhua vulgaris* (H. Cloq.).

This well-known fish belongs to the order Malacopterygii subbrachiata, and to the family Gadidæ.

It inhabits every part of the Northern ocean, between the 40° and 70° of latitude. An incalculable number are found every year on a submarine mountain, known as the *Bank of Newfoundland*, which extends for one hundred and fifty leagues in front of the island of the same name. England employs 10,000 men in this fishery. Thirty-six millions of *Cod* are salted on an average every year. One man will sometimes take from three to four hundred in a day, occupied from morning to night, in throwing his line, and in withdrawing the captured *Cod*. This fish is distinguished for its astonishing fecundity. Leeuwenhoek calculated that each female contained 9,344,000 germs. The germs or roe furnish a kind of caviare. [True caviare is the salted roe of the Sturgeon; it is much esteemed by the Russians, and is imported as a luxury into this country, but is an oily unwholesome kind of food.]

The *Cod* (fig. 18) varies in length from three to four and a half feet, and measures about one foot in circumference; it weighs from fifteen to more than twenty pounds. [The weight of the common cod varies between twelve and eighty, or a

Fig. 18.—*Cod.*

hundred pounds; see Griffiths's Cuvier.] The body of the fish is elongated, smooth, of a greyish yellow colour, brown on the

---

[1] *Oleum jecoris Morrhuæ*, or *oleum Aselli majoris*, of the older writers.

back, white on the ventral surface, and marked with a white line on either side. Its head is strong and compressed, the mouth large, and the lower jaw provided with a single barb. It has three dorsal and two anal fins. The thoracic fins are slender and pointed; the caudal fin is not forked.

The Cod is a most voracious animal; it feeds on fish, more especially on the herrings, and on various crustacea and molluscs.

2. *Oil.*—The liver of the *Cod* is very voluminous, and furnishes a large quantity of oil.

This oil was formerly employed for the purposes of illumination, and in the manufacture of chamois leather; but it was used in a very impure state, not being obtained exclusively from the Cod, but mixed with oil from the *Shark, Tunny, Conger eel,* and many other fishes. Since this oil has been employed in medicine the great object has been to procure it free from all such admixtures. Besides the *common Cod,* this kind of oil may be obtained from several other fishes, which were formerly arranged in the same group with it, and which have similar characters and properties.

The genus *Gadus* of Linnæus having been broken up by modern ichthyologists, unfortunately for science the name has disappeared, whereas it should have been retained for the group to which the typical species belongs.

The following are, however, the other *Gadoids,* which principally furnish the *Cod liver oil,* or *oleum jecoris Morrhuæ;* the *Dorse,*[1] the *Haddock,*[2] the *Capalan,*[3] the *Hake,*[4] the *Whiting,*[5] the *Coal-fish,*[6] the *Ling,*[7] the *Torsk,*[8] and the *Burbot.*[9] The flesh of these species is usually esteemed as food, both fresh and salted.

Cod liver oil is brought from Dunkirk, Ostend, England, and Holland. Large quantities are manufactured at Bergen, in Norway (Jongh), also on the islands of Lofodes and St. John, in Newfoundland (Hogg). From the latter locality alone there were exported in 1823, 415,000 kilogrammes of oil,

---

[1] *Gadus Callarias,* Linn. (*Morrhua Callarias,* Cuv.)
[2] *Gadus Æglefinus,* Linn. (*Morrhua Æglefinus,* Cuv.)
[3] *Gadus minutus,* Müll. (*Morrhua minuta,* Cuv.)
[4] *Merlucius vulgaris,* Cuv. (*Gadus Merlucius,* Linn.)
[5] *Merlangus vulgaris,* Cuv. (*Gadus Merlangus,* Linn.)
[6] *Merlangus Carbonarius,* Cuv. (*Gadus Carbonarius,* Linn.)
[7] *Molva vulgaris,* Cuv. (*Gadus Molva,* Linn.)
[8] *Brosmius vulgaris,* Cuv. (*Gadus Brosme,* Müll.)
[9] *Lota vulgaris,* Cuv. (*Gadus Lota,* Linn.)

and in 1828, 1,395,000 kilogrammes. Each kilogramme weighs 2·2053lbs. avoirdupois.

There are three varieties of Cod liver oil:—1. The *White*, 2. The *Brown*, and 3. The *Black*. The first is the colour of Madeira wine, or of a golden yellow, and has little or no odour. The second has the colour of Malaga wine, or is of a pale brown; the odour is more strongly marked, and its consistency is thicker than that of the first. The third is of a clear chocolate or dark brown colour; it has a very strong odour, and is still thicker than the second.

The *White oil* is that which is obtained first, by simply allowing the livers to drain in tubs pierced at the bottom with a number of holes, or provided with stopcocks, or they are placed in a kind of cage whose sides are formed of coarse linen cloth; the quantity which is procured of this kind of oil is equal to about half the weight of the livers employed. The blood and other impurities sink down, and the oil floats at the top.

The *Brown oil* is that which is separated afterwards, when the substance of the liver is beginning to decompose. The separation of the oil is sometimes hastened by pressure.

The *Black oil* is that which is obtained by boiling the livers in water, and by pressing out all the oil that remains in the putrid mass from which the two previous kinds have been extracted.

All these oils have undergone more or less fermentation, and, in the latter case, the oil has also been subject to the influence of heat.

In commerce, there is a fourth quality of the oil, called in England the *pale*, and in France the *white*. This variety has a yellow tinge, of the colour of champagne; it has very little odour or taste. It is the spontaneous production of the first stage of decomposition which the livers undergo at the ordinary temperature of the atmosphere, between the time of the fishing and the operation of extracting the oil. There is sometimes an interval of several days, which is a sufficient time for the commencement of decomposition.

It is only within these few years that these four kinds of oils, especially the three first, have been met with in a pure state in the shop of the druggist. They are now clarified and decolorized by chemical processes, rendered more limpid and less nauseous, part of their characteristic odour being removed, and probably at the same time some of their properties; they are also mixed with other oils. The consequence of this is, that many of the white or blanched oils of commerce are of very slight medicinal value.

Dr. Fleury has justly observed that all the processes of extraction, which have been just mentioned, depend upon the putrefaction and fermentation of the livers, and that this is the source of the dark colour, the nauseous odour, and repulsive flavour of the oil. He has therefore proposed a new method of preparation, which yields an oil that is clearer, has less smell, and is better flavoured, and, above all, produces it in greater abundance. This method consists in taking the fresh livers, washing, and then draining them, and putting them in a pan, in which they are submitted to the action of a hot water bath. In about twenty minutes the oil begins to swim at the top. The operation lasts about three quarters of an hour. There remains in the pan a quantity of refuse, which is strained through a flannel or coarse cloth; this part of the process may be aided by gently pressing the strainer.

Mr. Hogg also prepares an oil from the fresh livers, but he employs a vessel with a double bottom, and instead of hot water he heats his apparatus by means of steam. His oil is paler, more limpid, more transparent, and of a lighter yellow than that which is called *white* oil. It has the smell of the fresh fish, and has scarcely any taste. It is known as *Hogg's golden green oil*. (Jongh.)

Lastly, Dr. Delattre, of Dieppe, conceived the idea of guarding the livers from the action of the atmosphere during the extraction of the oil. For this purpose he has constructed an apparatus consisting of three large earthen vessels of a globular form, which are half buried in a large sand bath, heated by means of a thermo-syphon. These vessels communicate with a reservoir, from which a current of carbonic acid gas is given off, which expels the air from them. The sand-bath is not heated until all the air has been expelled. The use of this apparatus prevents the formation of oleic, sulphuric, and phosphoric acids.

M. Delattre distinguishes five varieties of *Cod liver oil*. 1st. The *Virgin;* 2nd. The *Pale yellow;* 3rd. The *White;* 4th. The *Brown;* and 5th. The *Black oil*. He has deposited selected samples of these five varieties in the museum of the Faculty of Medicine. The *virgin oil* is obtained by exposing the fresh livers, immediately after their extraction from the fish to a dry heat of the temperature of 104° Fah. The *yellow* and *white oils* are procured, the first by a temperature of 122° Fah., and the second by a temperature of from 140°

Fah. to 158° Fah. The *brown oil* is obtained from livers which have been kept three or four days; and the *black* from those which are from ten to fifteen days old.

According to M. Delattre the *brown oil* is the only one which should be used for medicinal purposes. The *virgin oil* is an unnecessary refinement. The *yellow* and the *white* have no better qualities than the brown; while the *black*, containing choleic and acetic acids, has a disagreeable acridity, which should cause it to be rejected.

Cod liver oil, however it is obtained, should have the characteristic odour of the sardine and a fresh flavour, without any acrid taste; at a temperature of 59° Fah. it should stand at 392° of Lefebvre's oleometer. When a few drops are poured on to a piece of glass placed upon white paper, on adding a very small quantity of concentrated sulphuric acid, it should produce a carmine tint, inclining to the colour of catechu. (Gobley.)

Cod liver oil is a compound of oleine, of margarine, chlorine, iodine, bromine, sulphur, phosphorus, and of various acids; there is also found a small quantity of lime, magnesia, and soda, and a particular principle called *Gaduine*.

Gaduine is a colouring matter, which is at first yellow, but becomes gradually darker upon exposure to the air. It is soluble in alkalies.

Some writers have endeavoured to refer the medicinal properties of *Cod Liver Oil* to the presence of iodine, and for this reason the proportion in which this substance is present has been very carefully inquired into. According to M. Berthi, there is 4·7 grs. in every 2·2 lbs. avoirdupois. According to more recent analyses, it is not more than 4 grs., but the quantity varies in different samples of the oil, and according to the time of year. The latter is the proportion which is found in the yellow oil. In the white oil there was found 3·9 gr., in the brown oil 3·7 gr., and in the black oil only 3·6 gr. (Delattre.)

Some practitioners consider that the bromine and the phosphorus may account for the action of this substance. Soubeiran says that a great part of its medicinal virtues depends upon the oil itself, and upon the aromatic and sapid bodies which are mixed with it.

§ II. Oil from the Liver of the Skate.

Several physicians have proposed to substitute the oil procured from the liver of the *Skate* for that which is obtained from the liver of the cod. They have even insisted upon the superiority of the latter for medicinal purposes; this supposed superiority depended partly upon the fact that the oil from the liver of the *Skate* was prepared with greater care, and was less repugnant to the patient, than the commercial oil derived from the liver of the cod, which was thick and black. (Guibourt.) It was also supposed that *skate oil* contained more iodine than that of the cod. Experience has shown that this is not the case.

1. *Rays.*—The *Rays* are fishes belonging to the order Selachia and to the family Raiidæ; they may be recognized by the flattened form of their bodies, which resembles a disc, arising from the enormous size of their pectoral fins, which join each other anteriorly, and extend backwards along the sides of the abdomen as far as the ventral fins. The eyes are placed on the dorsal surface of the disc; while the mouth, the branchial apertures, and the nostrils are on the abdominal.

This kind of oil is obtained principally from the *Thornback*, the *Skate*, the *Sting Ray*, and the *Eagle Ray*. The following is a brief summary of their characters:

```
        ⎧ no spine.  ⎧ armed with prickles   1. Thornback.
Tail ⎨   Back . . ⎨ unarmed . . . .        2. Skate.
        ⎩ spined . . ⎧ moderate . . . .     3. Sting Ray.
                    ⎩ very long . . . .     4. Eagle Ray.
```

The *Thornback*, *Raia clavata* (Linn.), from the shores of the Mediterranean, is of a brown colour, spotted with white and black. The body attains a length of twelve feet.

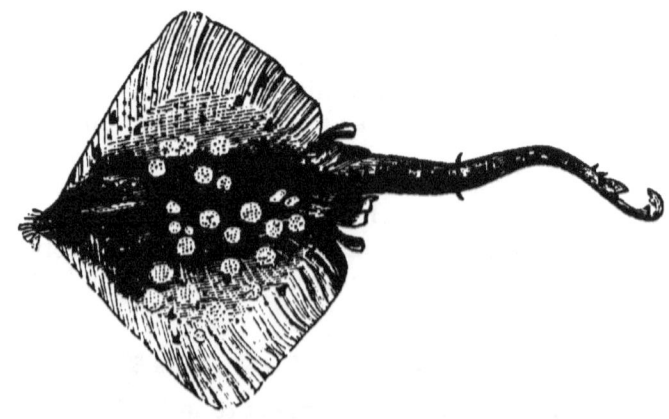

Fig. 19.—*Thornback Ray.*

The *Skate* (*Raia Batis*, Linn.) is a lozenge shape. The back is rough. It is larger than the preceding. Some have been caught weighing as much as eighty-five pounds. [Cuvier says, more than two hundred pounds.] Its liver yields a large quantity of oil.

The *Sting Ray* (*Raia Pastinaca*, Linn.) is not uncommon in the Mediterranean. The head is heart shaped; its body is of a brown or livid green colour above, and white below. It does not weigh more than from four to six pounds.

The *Eagle Ray* (*Raia Aquila*, Linn.) In this species the pectoral fins do not extend around the head, which is left free; and the tail is extremely narrow and long, and has been compared to a whip. This species is found in the Ocean and in the Mediterranean sea.

2. *The Oil.*—*Skate Oil* is of a clear yellow, or of a light golden colour: sometimes it has an orange or reddish tint. It has the same density as that from the cod, but not so strong a flavour.

This oil is manufactured on the coast of Normandy. When pure it is known in commerce as *Rouen oil*. It is sometimes mixed with cod oil.

Skate oil may be manufactured by the pharmaceutist. Two methods have been recommended. In the one the livers are boiled in water and the oil is collected, which swims at the top; in the other, which is that of M. Gobley, the livers are cut in thin slices, and then warmed in a vessel until the oil has separated. The liquid, which is obtained by this means, is then strained through a woollen cloth, making use of slight pressure. It seems to the writer that it would be better to prepare this oil in the same manner as that of the cod, either by means of a water bath, as in the plan pursued by M. Fleury, or by means of a vapour bath, as in that of Mr. Hogg's, taking care, according to the method of M. Delattre, to make use of glass globes instead of pans.

MM. Girardin and Preissier have compared together the oils obtained from the *liver of the Skate* and from that of the *Cod*. The first preserves its normal yellow colour in a stream of chlorine even at the end of half an hour, while the second rapidly assumes a dark brown tint. *Skate oil* becomes of a clear red by the action of cold sulphuric acid, and the mixture when shaken acquires at the end of a quarter of an hour a dark violet colour; while the oil from the cod rapidly turns black. These characters are far from being constant.

According to M. Personne *skate oil* contains less iodine

than the cod oil. One litre or 1·67 of a pint, prepared by direct heat, yielded M. Gobley 3·85 of a grain of iodide of potassium. This chemist was unable to find any trace of phosphorus. M. Delattre in some recent analyses obtained the following results:—1st. That the proportion of iodine in *skate oil* is one half the quantity of that in the cod oil. 2nd. That the sulphur is one quarter less. 3rd. That the phosphorus, on the contrary, is one third more.

The *oil of the skate* is very mild, and infants of a month old are perfectly able to bear it. (Delattre.)

§ III. Oil from the Liver of the Shark.

Dr. Collas has published an interesting account in the *Revue Coloniale* upon the medical and surgical employment of this oil in the French establishments in India.

1. *Shark.*—The *Sharks*, like the Rays, belong to the order Selachia.

The genus *Squalus* contains a large number of species, all of which are distinguished by the length of their bodies, and by the possession of a large muscular tail. The snout is supported by the cartilaginous processes which are appended to the anterior part of the skull; the branchial apertures are placed at the sides of the neck; the eyes are also situated on the lateral parts of the head; the pectoral fins are of moderate size.

These animals sometimes acquire a very large size; they are extremely voracious, and their gluttonous appetite leads them to seek with avidity after every kind of living prey.

The majority are ovoviviparous; some of them discharge their eggs surrounded by a horny case.

The genus *Squalus*, like the Raiidæ, belongs to the tribe of cartilaginous fishes; it seems, therefore, logical to admit *à priori* that the oil obtained from their liver should possess the same qualities as that from the latter group. But even supposing that *Shark oil* is inferior, it is not less important to know that, in case of necessity, it may be substituted for that of the Ray or the Cod family. (Collas.)

The *Sharks* are a very common fish, and are easily captured; they frequent the shores, and are seldom found in the open sea. In the tropics, however, they are met with at a great distance from land. In the bays they are said to live in shoals.

There are several species which are capable of yielding the oil. Dr. Delattre has obtained it from the *Squalus Acanthias* (fig. 20), from the *lesser spotted Dogfish* (*Squalus catulus*, Linn.), from the *Humantis* of Laciepede (or *Squalus centrina*, Linn.), from the *Monkfish* (*Squalus Squatina*, Linn.), *the Squalus Mustelus*, Linn., and from the *Fox Shark* (*Squalus vulpes*, Gmel.).

Fig. 20.—*Squalus Acanthias*.

2. *Oil.*—Dr. Collas gives the following directions for the extraction of the oil from the *liver of the shark*. After carefully washing the liver and removing the gall bladder, it is cut in pieces and boiled in water in a large earthen vessel for nearly an hour. The fire must not be too fierce. The liquid is to be constantly stirred with a wooden spoon. When the oil floats at the surface it is removed. The residue is allowed to remain for a couple of days in an open vessel. The liver is then boiled over again and the oil removed as it swims at the surface. These oils are next filtered in order to free them from impurities.

Shark's liver oil has a fine amber colour, like pale brandy. At a temperature of 86° Fah. it is perfectly limpid. Its smell and taste resemble that of cod oil. When it is left undisturbed for some time it throws down a considerable quantity of stearine, which appears as a white granular substance. Dr. Collas has given it the name of *squalin*, in order to distinguish it from the ordinary stearine of commerce. He believes that this substance might be useful as the medium for applying certain topical remedies, which are used in the treatment of wounds and ulcers. He recommends it as a substitute for certain local applications, which are made use of in diseases of the skin. Squalin does not seem to become rank like lard. It has also a much greater consistence than the latter kind of grease, which becomes fluid at the ordinary temperature of Pondicherry, and which requires to be mixed with suet in order to give it the consistency of pomade.

According to Dr. Delattre the active principles are present in larger proportions in the oil of the *shark* than in that of the cod; it is richer in iodine and in phosphorus, but it contains less bromine and sulphur. The increase in the quantity of iodine is double what is lost in the bromine.

Compared with the oil from the ray it contains one and a half times more iodine, and only one-fifth less phosphorus.

CHAPTER II.
MUSK.

In Medical Zoology the name of *musk bearing* is given to those animals which furnish medicine with the peculiar substance known as *musk*, and some other analogous productions.

True musk, and the substances which have the closest resemblance to it, such as *civet* and *castoreum*, are secreted by special organs. *Hyraceum*, which differs from the former in several respects, is furnished by the digestive organs. It is the same as regards *ambergris*.

All the animals which produce *musk*, or a substance resembling musk, belong to the class Mammalia.[1]

We shall examine in a separate chapter each of the following substances: 1. *Musk*; 2. *Civet*; 3. *Castoreum*; 4. *Hyraceum*; 5. *Ambergris*.

§ I. Musk.

1. *The Animal.*—The *musk deer* (*Moschus moschiferus*, Linn.)[2] is a mammalian animal belonging to the order Ruminantia, and to the family Moschida.

It inhabits the mountains and wooded districts of Thibet and China. Buffon has described one of these animals, which

---

[1] Secretions resembling musk are found in some other mammalia, as for example in the *Genette*, the *Desman*, the *Badger*, the *Musaraigne*, the *Musk Rat*, the *Ondatra*, and the *Musk Ox*. The Crocodile also gives off an odour of musk. The same is the case with the fluids of several of the *Cephalopoda*, and with that of some *insects*, especially the *Aromia moschata*; but neither these animals nor their secretions have been made use of as antispasmodics. The tail of the *Desman* of Muscovy, or *Musk Rat* of Russia (*Myygale Muscovita*, Geoffr.), is sought for as a perfume. It owes its odour to a substance which is secreted by two small follicular glands placed at its base. The odour is so strong that it penetrates the flesh of the pike and other fish which have fed upon this animal. Pallas states that a thermometer which he had made use of for ascertaining the temperature of an individual remained impregnated with it for fourteen years.

[2] In China its common name is *Che-hiang*, that is to say, the *Deer which discharges an odour*; it is also called *Xe*. It is the *Toorgo* or the *Gifar* of the Tartars, the *Kudari* of the Calmucs and Mongols, the *Dsaanja* of the Tungusians of the Yenisey, the *Houde* of those of the Baikal, the *Dsehija* of those of the Ceuta, the *Gloa* or *Glao*, or *Altah*, of the Tanguts of Thibet, the *Bjos* of the Ostiaks, the *Kaborga* of the Russians of the Yenisey, and their *Saiga* on the borders of the Baikal.

ANIMALS CONSTANTLY EMPLOYED IN MEDICINE. 111

the Duke of Vrillière preserved for three years at his chateau of the Hermitage near Versailles, where the creature seemed to have become acclimated.

This animal (fig. 21) is about the size of a young roebuck six months old. The colour of the skin is blackish with a mixture of yellow and reddish brown. It, however, varies considerably; in the young animal it is of a reddish grey, with patches of white arranged in lines, while in the old it is of a blackish brown colour. The most constant character of the fur throughout the life of the animal is the presence of two white bands bordered with black, and enclosing between them a black band, which extends along the under part of the neck from the throat to the chest. The tail and a heart-shaped space around it are naked in the male, and always moistened with a strong smelling humour. On the other hand, the females, during the whole of life, and the males, up to two years of age, have the tail covered with hair on its upper part, and with wool on its under part. The animal has no horns. The mouth opens as far back as the molar teeth. The male has two canines in the upper jaw developed into the form of tusks; these teeth project externally on each side of the mouth; they pass downwards, curving backwards, and have the posterior edge adapted for cutting. The eyes are proportionally of a large size, and have a long narrow pupil. The ears are moderately long, covered externally with reddish black hair, and internally with long grey hairs. The hinder limbs are longer and stronger than the anterior. An important osteological character is the presence of a slender fibula, extending from the head of the tibia to the extremity of the astragulus. The feet are small. The anterior have two spurs which touch the ground, the external being the largest. The posterior have two unequal hoofs, the internal being much longer than the external.

Fig. 21.— *The Musk Deer.*

The *Musk Deer* is a timid, nocturnal mammal, very rapid in its course; it has a leaping motion something like that of the hare; it leads a solitary life, except in autumn; it feeds upon the leaves, bark, and roots of trees; its flesh is good to eat.

Musk apparatus (fig. 22).—This consists of a sac, which is only present in the male; it is placed on the median line of the abdomen, between the navel and the orifice of the prepuce, but nearest to the latter. This sac is of a rounded oval form, flat on its superior or adherent surface, but convex and covered with hair on its inferior or free surface. In the adults this sac is from two to three inches long, an inch and a quarter to two inches in width, and from seven to ten lines in depth. When the skin is removed two bundles of muscular fasciculi are seen, which pass from the groin and surround the sac. (Pallas.) Immediately beneath is the proper envelope of the sac composed of three separate membranes. The first (*fibrous coat of* Pereira) has, on its external surface, some longitudinal folds, and in its interior numerous depressions; it receives branches from the iliac artery. (Pallas.) The second (*pearly coat of* Pereira) is thin, whitish, and with external projections, which correspond to the excavations of the first membrane; it has also numerous grooves, which are traversed by blood vessels. Lastly, the third (*Epidermoid coat of* Pereira) is still more delicate than the second; some have supposed they could distinguish an external silvery layer, and an internal layer of a reddish brown or yellowish colour. On the inner surface of

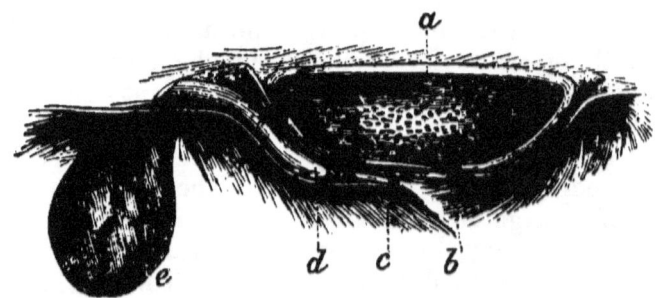

Fig. 22.—*Musk Apparatus.*[1]

the sac are strongly marked folds and excavations. Each excavation contains two or more oval corpuscles of a yellowish or reddish brown colour. These small bodies are glands for the secretion of the musk. They appear to be composed of a very

---

[1] *a*, musk sac cut vertically; *b*, its orifice; *c*, orifice of the prepuce with its brush of airs; *d*, the glans traversed by the filiform prolongation of the urethra; *e*, testicle.

thin membrane, containing a brownish coloured substance. Towards the middle of the external or convex surface of the sac is a short canal, which passes obliquely, is about a line in width, and has its internal opening surrounded by a number of converging hairs. A little behind this orifice is that of the prepuce, a kind of slit bounded by a brush of red-coloured hairs.

Musk.—In the living animal the *musk* has the consistence of honey, is of a brownish red colour, and has a very strong odour.

The Chinese missionaries pretend that this secretion drives the carnivorous animals from the musk deer and thus serves it as a means of defence. Pallas supposes that this matter is intended to excite voluptuous feelings in the female during connection. It appears that during this act, the musk sac is compressed, and that a portion of the semifluid matter escapes and lubricates the organ of the male. Oken compares musk to the sebacious matter secreted by the prepuce.

When the musk is dry it becomes almost solid, granular, and of a very dark brown. It feels unctuous and fatty to the touch. It has a bitter and aromatic taste. Its smell is still exceedingly powerful; a very small quantity will scent a large mass of any substance, and it will be retained for a long time. The scent is agreeable when much diluted.

Each sac (fig. 23) does not contain more than 370 grains in the adult, and 123 grains in the old animal.

Two kinds of musk are known in commerce: 1st. The *Tonquin* or Chinese Musk; and 2nd. The *Kabardin* or Russian musk. The Tonquin is more highly estimated than the Kabardin. This substance is not always surrounded by the natural sac, and druggists therefore distinguish between *musk in the sac* and *musk out of the sac.*

Fig. 23.—*Musk Sac.*

Musk contains ammonia, a volatile oil, stearine, oleine, cholesterine, an oil united with ammonia, gelatine albumen, fibrine, a substance soluble in water and insoluble in alcohol, hydrochlorate of ammonia, and several other salts. (Blondeau and Guibourt.) According to Dr. Hanle, bitter almonds, when mixed with a solution containing musk, entirely neutralize the odour of the latter. It appears, however, that the odour is not destroyed since it returns to its original strength when the hydrocyanic acid is dissipated. The golden sulphuret of antimony, when mixed with *musk*, also removes its odour. Kermes mineral gives it a smell of onions. (Bley.) The Arabs were the first who introduced musk into medicine.

Musk is adulterated by introducing earth, sand, and even iron and lead into the sac. Sometimes the scent is replaced by dried blood, muscle, gelatine, wax, asphalte, styrax, benzoin, &c.

[Musk is a remedy but little used in the present day. It acts as a stimulant on the nervous and vascular systems, but is liable to produce eructation and derangement of the stomach. It may be given in substance, either in the form of boluses, or suspended in water by means of saccharine or mucilaginous substances. Its dose is from eight to fifteen grains. (Pereira.)]

2. *Other species.*—Three other species of deer are mentioned as capable of yielding musk:—1. The *Napu*. 2. The *Kranchil*. 3. The *Chevrotain of the Altai*.

The *Napu* (*Moschus Javanichus*, Raffles) is found in the woods of Java and Sumatra, where it feeds on the berries of a species of *Ardisia*. It is twenty-one inches long and fourteen high; the colour is brown mottled with black on the back, grey mixed with white on the flanks, and white on the abdomen and the inner parts of the thighs. At the posterior angle of the lower jaw is a white line which extends to each side of the chin. A black line unites the eye with the nostrils. Its horns are short and straight. The tail is tufted, and white at its termination as well as below.

2. The *Kranchil* (*Moschus Kranchil*, Raffles) inhabits the forests of Sumatra, where it feeds upon the fruit of the *Gmelina villosa*; it is sixteen inches long and ten inches in circumference. The fur is of a reddish brown, passing into black on the back, and white on the inner parts of the thighs. The line on each side of the jaw reaches as far as the shoulder. It has no black line between the eyes and the nostrils. The tail is tufted, and white at its termination.

3. The *Chevrotain of the Altai* (*Moschus Altaicus*, Esch.) inhabits, as its name implies, the Altai mountains. (Jobst.) It has two white lines on its neck.

§ II. Civet.

The *Civet* belongs to the genus *Viverra* of Cuvier, forming part of the digitigrade division of the Carnivora. It is characterized by the possession of three false molars [premolars of Owen] above, and four below, of which the anterior are some-

ANIMALS CONSTANTLY EMPLOYED IN MEDICINE. 115

times lost, two large tubercular teeth [molars of Owen] above, and one below—in all forty teeth. This genus comprises two species which require to be noticed. 1st. The *Common Civet;* 2nd. The *Zibeth Civet.*

Common Civet (fig. 24).—The *Common or true Civet* (*Viverra Civetta,*[1] Schreb.) inhabits Guinea, Congo, and Ethiopia.

This small mammalia is about twenty-eight inches long, independent of the tail, and from ten to fourteen inches high at the shoulders. It has been compared to a fox, but it is longer and does not stand so high. The hair is coarse and long, forming a kind of crest on the back, which becomes blended with the tail; this crest rises up when the civet is irritated. The fur of the animal is of a dark brown, varied with patches and bands of a blackish brown. The spine of the back is of a black brown colour, and the flanks are irregularly spotted with the same. These patches become converted into black bands on the chest, the shoulders, and the buttocks. Two oblique bands of this colour are seen on the sides of the neck;

Fig 24.—*Civet.*

they are separated from each other by an interval of a greyish white colour. The head is elongated and of a whitish colour but the circumference of the eyes, the cheeks and the chin, are brown, as well as the feet and the posterior half of the tail; the latter has three or four light coloured rings towards its base. The muzzle of the Civet is pointed, but rather less so than that of the Fox; the animal has long whiskers, and a tail shorter than its body.

These animals are very ferocious, but are, nevertheless,

---

[1] In Darfour it is called *Gatt* (cat) by the Arabs, and *Mzouron* by the Negroes. It is also called *Kaukau* in Ethiopia, *Nzime* or *Nzfusi* in Congo, and *Kastor* in Guinea.

brought up in a domesticated state. They possess great activity and run like a dog. Their eyes shine in the dark. During the night they hunt after small quadrupeds and birds.

Civet apparatus (fig. 25.)—This consists of two sacs, situated in the neighbourhood of the genital organs. They are present in both sexes.

These sacs are each about the size of an almond. The inner surface is pierced with a number of apertures communicating with the glandular follicles, which secrete the scent. The follicles are surrounded by a very vascular membrane. A muscle covers the whole and has the power of compressing the secreting follicles as well as the sac, and thus expels the *civet*.

The sacs open into a kind of cloaca or shallow pouch, placed between the anus and the genital organs.

Besides the scent glands, there is, also, on each side the anal orifice, a small opening from which a blackish and very offensive humour is discharged. This opening communicates with a round gland smaller than that which produces the *civet*.

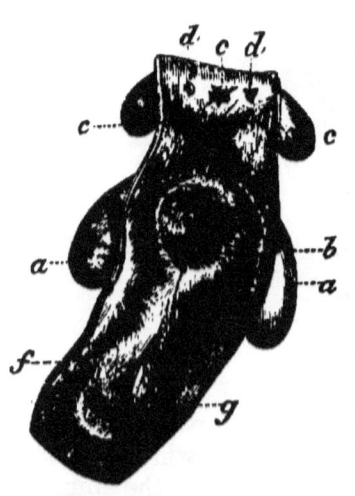

Fig. 25.—*Civet apparatus.*[2]

Civet scent.—Civet[1] is an unctuous substance of a fatty resinous nature, which is at first semifluid and of a yellow colour, but afterwards becomes very thick and of a brown colour. It has a disagreeable ammoniacal odour, often very strong, resembling a mixture of musk and fecal matter. Its taste is acrid and burning.

Civet is composed of ammonia, elaine, stearine, mucus, resin, a volatile oil, a yellow colouring matter of subcarbonate and phosphate of lime and of oxide of iron. (Boutron-Charlard.)

The *Civet* is reared in a domestic state in various parts of Africa, for the sake of its perfume. Some dealers have as many as three hundred. They are fed exclusively upon flesh, which gives a strong penetrating odour to the perfume. (Aucapitaine.) Every eight days the contents of the sac are scraped out by means of a

---

[1] *Zebed* of the Arabs (*Viverreum*, Gerv.).
[2] *a a*, glands which secrete the civet; their orifices opening into the pouch; *c c*, anal glands; *d d*, their orifices; *e*, anus; *f*, vulva; *g*, clitoris.

ANIMALS CONSTANTLY EMPLOYED IN MEDICINE. 117

small spoon, or a hollow piece of bamboo, the animal having been previously secured.

2nd. ZIBETH CIVET (fig. 26).—The *Zibeth Civet* or *Zibeth* (*Viverra Zibetha*, Linn.)[1] inhabits the Molucca and Philippine islands.

The animal is from twelve to sixteen inches long, and thirteen inches high; the fur is of a yellowish grey, marked with a number of black spots, sometimes so close together as to form lines, especially towards its posterior part. The tail is black along the whole of its upper part, but marked with black and white along the sides, giving it the appearance of half rings; the abdomen is grey; a black band commences behind the upper part of the ear, describes the segment of a circle as far as the fore limb, and forms the boundary of the spotted portion, separating it from the pure white of the sides and under part of the neck. Another band, somewhat larger, com-

Fig. 26.—*Zibeth.*

mences at the base of the ear, taking the same curve as the first, from which it is separated by a white band of equal width, and then unites with that from the opposite side underneath the neck. A third descends vertically, a little below the ear. Lastly, a fourth, which divides the grey of the cheeks from the white of the neck, corresponds to the ascending portion of the lower jaw.

The animal is nocturnal; it appears to be omnivorous, but gives the preference to fruits.

The *Zibeth* differs from the Civet, principally by the absence of the dorsal crest, by the shortness of its fur, by the lateral bands of the neck, and by the half rings on its tail. The animal is bred like the Civet, and its perfume is collected in the same manner; it is afterwards spread out on the leaves of the pepper plant, in order to separate the hairs from it; it is also said to be washed with salt and water or with lemon juice, before it is packed up in leaden boxes.

The *scent of the Zibeth* resembles that of the Civet. Both

[1] It is the *Goot* or *Baar* of the Arabs, and the *Sawadu Punee* of the Malabars.

these substances are adulterated with laudanum and storax; at other times with dried blood, grease, oil of nutmegs, and a small quantity of musk.

§ III. The Beaver.

ANIMAL.—The *Beaver* (*Castor Fiber*, Linn.) belongs to the order Rodentia and to the family Sciurida.

This animal inhabits the uncultivated districts of Canada and Siberia. A few are found in Prussia, in Poland, and in France, where it is named *Bievres*. It is supposed that the small river called Bievres, which empties itself into the Seine, at Paris, owes its name to its having been formerly frequented by these animals. The last Beavers which were met with in France were found upon the banks of the Rhone and the Gardon. Some writers consider that the Beaver of France is a different species from that found in Canada.

The Beaver (fig. 27) is from three to four feet in length from the muzzle to the end of the tail, and from twelve to sixteen inches in width across the chest; the fur consists of two kinds of hair, the one close set, very fine, and of a grey colour; the other longer, coarser, and of a brown colour. The head resembles that of the Marmot; it is nearly as long as

Fig. 27.—*Beaver.*

it is wide; the ears are short; each jaw has ten teeth, consisting of two incisors and four molars on each side. In a skull of the Canadian Beaver (No. 2160), in the College of Surgeons, the lower incisor measured $4\frac{1}{4}$ inches in the curve of the tooth, while the upper incisor from the same head was only $3\frac{5}{8}$ inches. All these teeth are bevelled off from within outwards so as to form a cutting edge; they are of a dark yellow colour on their anterior surface, and white internally. The crowns of the molars are flat and impinge vertically upon each other; they may be described as a lamina of bone folded upon itself so as to form three indentions on the outer edge and one on the inner; in the lower teeth this arrangement is reversed. (Cuvier.) The mammæ are four in number, two of which are situated between the anterior limbs near the neck, and two on the chest. The feet have five short toes, quite distinct, and provided on the fore limbs with very strong claws, those on the hind limbs are longer and are united by an intermediate membrane. The tail is oval, flat, thick, and covered with scales. This tail answers at the same time the purposes of a trowel and an oar; the animal constantly making use of it in swimming, and also to mould the earth with which constructs its habitation.

Beavers resemble land animals as regards the anterior parts of their bodies, and aquatic animals with respect to the posterior parts. During the summer time they live solitary or in couples in holes near the water. At the approach of winter, they assemble in large numbers on the borders of the river or lake. If the water is smooth and undisturbed they build their huts on the banks; if, however, the water is swift and shallow, they first construct a strong dam across it, formed of fallen trees, branches, stones, and mud; the whole being covered with a solid outer layer. The side of the dam next the stream is always perpendicular, while the opposite one is shelving. When it is built up the *Beavers* form their huts against it; they are made of the same materials, only of a smaller size; there are several stages of them; each is sufficiently large to contain eight or ten Beavers. The works are carried on only during the night, and executed with surprising rapidity. Yet the only implements which the Beavers possess are their claws, their teeth, and their tail.[1] When they have completed their dam and their dwelling-places, they lay up a store of bark for the winter and shut themselves in their houses.

Castor apparatus (fig. 28).—The *castor* is secreted by two large glands placed in the neighbourhood of the sexual organs. The ancients mistook these glands for the animal's testicles.

Beneath the tail of the *Beaver* is a shallow pouch, which may be compared to the cloaca of the bird (Adanson), and into which the arms and genital organs open. The anal orifice appears behind quite at the commencement of the tail. In the middle on either side are the openings of several small glands, termed the *anal glands*, which secrete an oily, yellow, disagreeable fluid, distinct from the *castoreum*. These glands are

[1] " *Architectura in construendo domos ad ripas superat omnium animalium excepta hominis.*" (Linn.)

oblong, lobed, and are each accompanied by one or two accessory glands. In front of the pouch is the genital orifice, which communicates with the preputial canal. The latter is cylindrical, and covered with small papillæ, which are pointed, of a blackish colour, and are directed backwards. It is to the right and left of this groove that the glands are placed which secrete the castoreum. These glands consist of two oval, pyriform sacs of unequal size, which open into the preputial groove by two large orifices. Those of the adult animal are at least three inches in length, and sometimes as much as five; they are larger than the testicles, and cannot be confounded with them. Moreover, they are present in the female as well as in the male, but they are somewhat less developed. The outer surface is irregular, and in the interior are a number of delicate cæcal processes which secrete the *castoreum*.

Castoreum.—In the living animal the *castoreum* is an almost fluid unctuous substance of a strong penetrating and even fœtid odour.

Fig. 28.—*Apparatus of the castor.*[1]   Fig. 29.—*Glands of the castoreum.*[2]

[1] *a a*, castor glands; *b b*, their orifices in the preputial canal; *c*, the penis with its peculiarly formed prepuce; *d*, opening of the preputial canal; *e e*, anal glands; *f f*, their orifices; *g*, anus; *h*, part of the tail; *i*, prostate; *k k*, Cowper's glands; *l l*, the vesiculæ seminales; *m m*, different canals; *n n*, the testicles; *o*, the bladder.

[2] *a a*, dried glands of the castoreum; *b*, a portion of the preputial canal.

The castoreum of commerce is dried in the two sacs still united together (fig. 29). These sacs are pyriform, elongated, somewhat compressed and wrinkled, of a blackish brown colour externally, and of a yellow or reddish brown internally. When cut into their contents resemble a compact resinous mass, intermixed with membrane or with whitish fibres. Its odour is very penetrating, and almost fœtid; its taste is acid and bitter.

Castoreum varies in value, according to its age, and to that of the animal which furnished it, and possibly according to how near the creature was to the period of heat. It loses its qualities very rapidly when kept in a moist situation.

Linnæus believed that this substance was better when obtained from Beavers which had fed principally on the bark of the poplar. M. Paul Gervais, having had the opportunity of dissecting Beavers from the Rhone, was struck with the resemblance between the odour of their *castoreum* and that of the young shoots of the willow-tree, or of its bark when macerated. These trees form a large portion of the food of the Beaver.

There are two qualities of *castoreum*: 1. *American*; 2. *Russian*. The first is divided into *Canadian castoreum* and *Hudson's bay castoreum*.

Castoreum contains castorine, a volatile oil, salicine, carbolic acid, benzoic acid, albumen, a fatty matter, mucus, carbonate of ammonia, and the salts of soda and potash.

Castorine was discovered by Brandt and Bizio; it crystallizes in long diaphanous crystals and fasciculi; its odour is the same as that of the *castoreum*; it has a coppery taste. It is insoluble in cold alcohol and in water, but dissolves in boiling alcohol and volatile oils.

Castoreum is adulterated in various ways: 1. The sacs are opened and the scent removed, its place being supplied with dried blood, galbanum, or gum ammoniacum. 2. Artificial sacs are manufactured with the scrotum of the goat, or from the gall-bladder of various animals; in this case the sac is falsified as well as its contents.

Castoreum is administered in several ways—in injections, in drinks, and in pills. From this substance is prepared a distilled water, a common tincture, an ætherized tincture, and a syrup.

[Castoreum was formerly employed in certain derangements of the nervous system, such as hysteria, apoplexy, &c. It was also supposed to exert a special influence over the uterus, and was used to promote the lochial discharge, and for the expulsion of retained placenta. In the present day it is but little employed, being generally regarded as an almost inert remedy. It is best given in substance, either reduced to powder, or in the form of a pill. The dose should be at least ʒij. (Pereira.)

The London Pharmacopœia contains a tincture of Castor (*Tinctura Castorei*), which is made by macerating two ounces and a half of castor in two pints of rectified spirits for fourteen days and then straining. This preparation, says Pereira, contains only half a drachm of castor in one fluid ounce of the tincture, and it would, therefore, be necessary to administer two ounces of the tincture to give a medium dose of castor (ʒj). The dose directed in the Pharmacopœia is xx ♏ to fʒij.]

§ IV. The Hyraceum.

ANIMAL.—The *Daman of the Cape*[1] (*Hyrax Capensis*, Ehr., *Cavia Capensis*, Pall.).—This animal was regarded by Pallas and Erxleben as a Rodent, and by Cuvier and Illiger as a Pachyderm. M. Is. Geoffroy Saint-Hilaire, founding his opinion upon its organization and habits, considered it as forming the connecting link between these orders. The toes have irregular corneous formations, partly resembling hoofs and partly claws.

The *Daman* inhabits the Cape of Good Hope, Abyssinia, and even as far as Lebanon. It never descends into the plains.

This small mammal (fig. 30) is the size of a Marmot. (Pallas.) With the exception of not having a horn it is almost a Rhinoceros in miniature. (Cuvier.) Its form is heavy, short, and low on its feet. The fur consists of long, close-set, soft, silky hair, and of very fine scanty woolly fibres. Its general colour is of a greyish brown. The head is thick and terminated by a short thick muzzle. The ears are short, round, and bordered by fine hairs; the neck is short and wider than it is long. The upper jaw has two strong incisors, which curve downwards; in the young animal there are two very small canines; the lower jaw,

---

[1] Commonly called *Badger of the rocks* (*Klipp-daas*, *Klip-dasje*, or *Klip-dasse*) or *Marmot of the Cape*. The Abyssinians call it *Gihe* according to Shaw, and *Ashkoko* according to Bruce; the Libanians, the *sheep of Israel* (*Gannim Israel*.)

ANIMALS CONSTANTLY EMPLOYED IN MEDICINE. 123

Fig. 30.—*Daman*.

somewhat shorter than the upper, has four incisors, but no canines. (Cuvier.) On the upper lip are a number of long stiff black hairs. There are also a quantity of large hairs beneath the eyebrows and beneath the throat. The abdomen is very wide. The palms of the feet are naked and covered with a soft skin. The fore feet have four toes, and the hind feet only three; these toes terminate in small round hoofs, excepting the innermost toe of the hind foot, which is armed with an oblique hooked claw. There is no visible tail; the coccyx is reduced to a small tubercle. There are three mammæ on each side, of which the anterior is axillary, and the two others inguinal.

The *Daman* is a very active animal and cleanly in its habits; although naturally savage and timid, it is easily tamed, and is even capable of forming attachments. Its food consists of the fruits and roots of aromatic plants; it is particularly fond of the *Cyclopia genistoides*, an elegant shrub belonging to the family of papilionaceæ.

Origin of hyraceum.—This substance is found in small masses on the sides of rocky mountains, in the clefts of the rocks, in caverns, and in those places generally which are frequented by the *Damans*. The inhabitants collect these fragments while they are fresh, soft, and somewhat glutinous.

Sparmann, Thunberg, Burchell, and Lichtenstein, all agree in regarding the *Daman of the Cape* as the animal which produces the *hyraceum*.

But how is this substance formed? Is it by special glands as in the *Musk-deer*, the *Civet*, and the *Castor?* The anatomy of the genital organs, which has been published by Pallas, is opposed to this conclusion.

Is the *hyraceum* merely the dried urine of the Daman? According to Sparmann and Thunberg the Dutch call this substance *Badger's urine* (*Dassen-pissat* or *dasjespis*); they believe that the Damans have the habit of always discharging their urine in the same place, and that the urine in drying deposits a certain substance, which gradually condenses and ultimately forms the *hyraceum*. It will be presently seen that this explanation is to a certain extent correct.

Krauss suspected that it might be the menstrual discharge of the animal, but there is nothing to confirm this notion.

Dr. Edward Martiny considers the *hyraceum* as the secretion of the preputial glands, and probably also of largely developed vaginal glands. But these glands would not have been overlooked by Pallas in his dissections.

Several modern writers admit, and it appears to the author correctly, that this substance is nothing more than the excrements of the animal mixed with its urine which have been deposited and dried in the crevices of the rock, and in caverns frequented by the animal. (Pereira, Verreaux.) The examination of the *hyraceum* made by L. Soubeiran, and its analysis by Schrader and by Reichel, fully confirm this view of the matter.

Hyraceum.—This is a solid, hard, heavy substance, of a blackish brown colour, with certain portions clearer or more brilliant, and having a resinous appearance. It can be cut with a knife and softened between the fingers. It has some resemblance to the bdellium of India and to black myrrh. (Guibourt.) When exposed to a moist atmosphere it softens and becomes more or less glutinous. Its odour is strong and disagreeable, somewhat analogous to that of castoreum, but not so strong, and somewhat urinous. Its taste is bitter, astringent, and acrid.

Hyraceum is very soluble in water, to which it imparts a yellow colour, especially when the water is hot; it leaves a clear brownish yellow coloured residue. It is but partially soluble in alcohol, and in ether, to which it imparts a very light yellow tint. (L. Soubeiran.)

When examined by the microscope it is found to contain particles of plants; as for example, the husks of grasses, fragments of cellular and fibrous tissue, and portions of tracheal vessels. There are also present hairs, particles of silicious sand, and granules of uric acid. (L. Soubeiran.)

Chemical analysis shows that *hyraceum* contains a yellow colouring matter soluble in common alcohol and in water, a brown matter soluble in water, a green resin soluble in alcohol, a small quantity of fatty matter, and a large amount of insoluble residue, containing the remains of vegetable fibres and quartz. (Schrader.)

The *hyraceum* of commerce is packed in cylindrical tin boxes, each containing about a pound.

This substance has been proposed as a substitute for castoreum; some years ago it was brought into use in consequence of the high price of castoreum. At the present time it is very rarely employed, and in all probability it will shortly be numbered with those substances which, after having been boasted of as panaceas, have been rejected from the list of the Materia Medica. (L. Soubeiran.)

§ V. Ambergris.

1. *Origin of Ambergris.*—Various hypotheses have been put forward with respect to the origin of *Ambergris*.

Avicenna and Serapion assert that it is a balm which grows upon the rocks, in the same manner as mushrooms do upon trees, and which afterwards falls into the sea.

Cardan pretends that it is the dried saliva of the sea-cow.

Fernandez Lopez considers it to be the excrements of certain birds which had fed upon odoriferous plants.

Others have regarded *ambergris* as the condensed froth of the sea, or as a kind of greasy earth which has become hardened, as bitumen, as a species of resin, as a kind of gum, as the sperm of the whale, or as the excrement of crocodiles, &c.

Virey pronounces *ambergris* to be a species of adipocire arising from the decomposition of various odoriferous Poulps, which reside in the open sea. A circumstance which appeared to give some support to this suggestion, was the discovery on several occasions of horny mandibles in the interior of the pieces of amber precisely similar to those of the Cephalopoda.

Pelletier and Caventou, who have given a good analysis of *ambergris*, describe it as a biliary calculus.

Serval Marel has the credit of first recognizing the true source of this odoriferous substance. According to this writer it is produced by several large animals of the whale species. It is a residue of digestion, a kind of intestinal calculus or *coprolite*.

This statement has been confirmed by Swediaur and by Romé Delile. It is known that the Japanese call *ambergris, kuusura no fuu;* that is to say, *excrement of the whale.* (Kæmpfer.)

Ambergris forms in masses in the alimentary canal of the Cachalots,[1] and is discharged with their excrements. Some

---

[1] See p. 92, and Fig. 14.

persons consider that this substance is a normal production of all the Cachalots; others suppose that it is a morbid and, consequently, an accidental formation.

The *Cachalots* are capable of furnishing it in large quantities. A whaleman obtained forty-four pounds from the intestines of one individual, and one hundred and fourteen from those of another.

Ambergris is sometimes found floating on the sea, at other times on the shore, mixed with the excrements of the Cachalots, occasionally, as has just been mentioned, in the intestines themselves. This substance is regularly collected on the coasts of Japan, of the Molucca islands, of India, of Madagascar, and of Brazil. When the Cachalots are opened the *ambergris* is found in the cæcum, and never in any other part of the intestinal canal.

The food taken by these Cetacea seems to influence the formation of the *ambergris*. It appears that there are some species of Poulps (*Eledons*) which have the odour of musk; that the Cuttle-fish and other molluscs, and even small fish, which have not been properly digested, give rise to this substance. It is known that amongst these animals there are some which exhale a musk-like odour. When the American fishermen discover *ambergris* in any part, they immediately conclude that it is frequented by some of the Cetacea.

Some have supposed that only the Cachalot has the property of producing *ambergris*; others, with more reason, admit that it is produced both by the Cachalot and the Balæna. The principal species which produce it are the *Physeter macrocephalus*[1] and the *Balæna mysticetus*.[2]

2. AMBERGRIS (*ambra cinerea*).—This is a tolerably hard, solid substance, of a greasy waxy nature; it is lighter than water, and melts at a low temperature. Its colour is a greyish black, sometimes yellow or brown; it is often covered with a white efflorescence, which forms on its surface and penetrates some little distance into the interior. *Ambergris* has a mild sweet odour, which extends to a considerable distance, and scarcely any taste. It is more or less soluble in water and in alcohol, according to its state of purity.

Ambergris forms irregular masses, sometimes composed of concentric superimposed layers, and at other times of small irregular roundish grains. In the interior there are occasion-

---

[1] See p. 92, and Fig. 14.
[2] See p. 93, and Fig. 15.

ally found the remains of molluscs and of fishes, such as the mandibles, scales, and bones. The masses are generally from two ounces to a pound in weight. They are, however, found weighing as much as from ten to twenty pounds. A spermaceti whale which was stranded in 1741 near Bayonne, had a mass of amber in its interior which weighed more than ten pounds. Masses have been mentioned of from one to more than two hundred pounds weight. The East India Company, in 1695, had a mass weighing one hundred and sixty pounds. In 1721, Valmont de Bomara saw a mass of more than two hundred pounds in weight. Another has been mentioned weighing eight hundred and sixty-six pounds, which, however, seems scarcely credible.

Ambergris contains ambreine, a sweet balsamic alcoholic extract, with benzoic acid, aqueous extract, benzoic acid, and chloride of sodium. (John.)

Ambreine was discovered by MM. Pelletier and Caventou; its properties are analogous to those of cholesterine. This substance is white, insipid, has a sweet smell, and is insoluble in water, but dissolves in alcohol and ether.

It has been stated that Foxes are very fond of *ambergris*, and that they come down to the coasts in search of it, eat it and return it in the same state as they swallowed it with regard to its perfume, but altered in colour. This propensity is supposed to account for the existence of pieces of whitish *ambergris* which are found at some distance from the sea on the Landes of Aquitain and which the inhabitants term *Fox amber* (Bory) ?

[In England ambergris is only used as a perfume.]

CHAPTER III.

VESICATING INSECTS.

VESICATING or *blistering insects* are those which have the power of producing a vesicular inflammation of the skin. These insects are valuable external agents. They are rarely administered internally.

The *blistering insects* consist of Cantharides, belonging to the order Coleoptera and to the tribe Heteromera.

These insects originally formed a portion of the genus *Meloe* of Linnæus, characterized by a rounded thorax and an inflected head. This group has been divided into thirteen genera. The *blistering insects* form nine of these genera, of which four are more important than the others, and require to be particularly noticed. These genera are: 1. *Cantharides;* 2. *Mylabra;* 3. *Cerocoma;* 4. *Meloe*. The characters which distinguish them are principally furnished by the wings and the antennæ. The following is a summary of these characters.

Wings { normally developed . { filiform .... 1. Cantharides.
  Antennæ . . { claviform
  Articulations { eleven 2. Mylabra.
  { nine 3 Cerocoma.
  absent .... 4. Meloe.

The five remaining genera which possess more or less vesicating properties are *Hycleus, Decatoma, Lydus, Œnas,* and *Tetraonix*.

Dorthes asserts that the ancients employed the caterpillar of the *Phalæna Pityocampa* as a substitute for the Cantharides.[1]

§ I. Cantharides.

1. COMMON CANTHARIDES (*Cantharis vesicatoria*, Lat.).[2] This insect is the principle blistering agent in use.

Aldrovandus, Johnston, Gesner, and others have described under the name of *Cantharides* several different species of coleoptera, sometimes even insects belonging to other orders.

1. *Habitation.*—Cantharides are common in the southern countries of Europe. They are found on the ash, lilac, privet, and jasmine. They are also met with on the elder, rose, apple, willow, and poplar trees. Richard found them on the honeysuckle and on the chamæcerasus. Others have observed them, but more rarely, on the walnut, the cynoglossus (dog's tongue), and even on wheat. They often assemble in large numbers, and devour the leaves of the plant very rapidly. Paul Hermann saw a large ash entirely destroyed by being deprived of its leaves by these insects.

2. *Description.*—The *Common Cantharides* (fig. 31) is a coleopterous insect, measuring from six to eleven lines in length, and from one to two lines in breadth. Its body is elongated and cylindrical; the head is large and cordiform; it

---

[1] According to Hentz, there is in the United States a species of Spider (*Tegenaria medicinalis*, Walck) which the inhabitants use as a blistering agent. This species is common in the neighbourhood of Philadelphia. Similar properties are attributed to the *Clubio medicinalis*, Walck.

[2] *Lytta visicatoria*, Fabr., *Meloe vesicatorius*, Linn., commonly called Cantharides of the shops .Spanish fly, Cantharides fly.

is furnished with long filiform antennæ, composed of eleven joints. The thorax is narrower than the base of the head; it is small, and has the prothorax almost square. A deep furrow is seen on the middle of the head and of the thorax. The elytra are as long as the abdomen, flexible, covered with fine markings, and provided with two longitudinal nervures along the inner margin; they cover up the membranous and transparent wings. The feet are slender, and the filiform tarsi terminate in a pair of very curved hooks which are covered with thick-set hairs on their under surface. There are five joints in the tarsi of the two first pairs of feet, and only four in the last. The body and the elytra are of a golden green colour with a metallic lustre, but the antennæ are black.

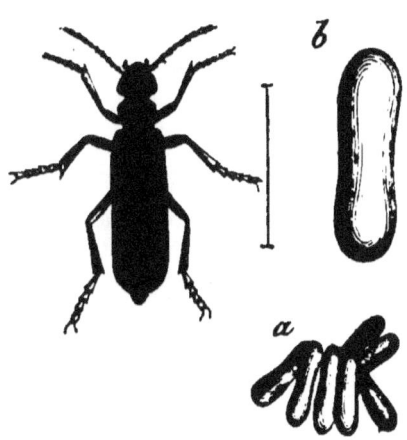

Fig. 31.—*Cantharides.*[1]

The animal gives off a very strong, disagreeable, poisonous odour, which spreads to a great distance.

The males are smaller than the females. Audouin has given an accurate description of the copulation of these insects, which he witnessed on the branch of a lilac tree. The male harasses the female, who at first sluggishly opposes him, but afterwards offers an active resistance. He then mounts on her back and seizes her antennæ with his fore feet. On the first joint of the tarsus of these feet there is a deep groove, and on the tibia a strong spine or hook, which, when the joint is flexed, enters the groove and forms a complete ring. It is with this kind of pincers that the male grasps the antennæ of the female, which he pulls and handles like a pair of horns. Having thus obtained the mastery, the act of copulation soon takes place. It lasts for about four hours. At the end of this time the female, who has hitherto remained immoveable, and apparently indifferent, struggles violently. The male, who is weakened, falls off, and the intromittent organ is torn away and remains in the vagina of the female.

---

[1] *a,* Several eggs adhering together, magnified; *b,* a single egg more highly magnified.

After copulation the females bury themselves in the earth, where they lay a considerable number of small eggs; these are cylindrical, somewhat flattened at their sides, slightly curved, of a yellowish colour, and agglutinated together (fig. 31 a, b).

The larvæ which issue forth have a soft elongated body, of a yellowish white colour, composed of thirteen segments and provided with six short scaly feet; the head is rounded, furnished with two small filiform antennæ, and a mouth armed with two strong jaws and four palpi. Some writers assert that the larvæ feed upon roots; others believe that they are parasites. Adanson says that they devour the ants.

3. *Collecting.*—The collecting of the *Cantharides* takes place early in the morning before sunrise, while the animals are still in an enfeebled state. For the purpose of collecting them, large cloths are spread at the foot of the trees and shrubs, which are then well shaken.

Some writers recommend the persons who are engaged in collecting the insects to provide themselves with a mask and gloves. These precautions are, however, altogether useless. (Berthoud.)

For the purpose of destroying the *Cantharides* they are steeped in boiling water or in hot vinegar, or they are exposed to the vapour of the latter after being placed in linen bags, or on horse-hair sieves. M. Lutrand recommends their being exposed to the vapour of chloroform. They are afterwards placed in a drying room.

In the process of drying the insects lose considerably in weight, so that each insect weighs very little more than a grain.

They are preserved in stoppered bottles.

In choosing *Cantharides* those that are fresh, dry, and whole should be selected. When they are three or four years old they are liable to be attacked by several small insects, which entirely destroy them, devouring even the elytra and the other hard parts. Even the best closed vessels will not always preserve them. They are eaten by a small coleopterous insect, the *Anthrenus musæorum*, by the *Ptinea*, and by the *Dermestes*. Various means have been proposed for preserving them, but unfortunately they are often insufficient. Camphor, which is effectual for the moths, is of no use in the case of the Anthrenus. Murcury placed at the bottom of the bottle is said to be an excellent means of preservation. (Soubeiran.)

[Dr. Pereira says he has found the addition of a few drops of acetic acid an effectual remedy against the attacks of the mites (*Acarus domesticus*).]

The *Cetonia aurata*, Linn., and the *Callichroma muscata* are often found mixed with *Cantharides*, as well as a species of *Chrysomela*. (Emmel.)

[These insects are mixed by the dealers with the Cantharides for the purpose of fraud; they have no blistering properties, and are easily distinguished by the form and proportions of their bodies.]

4. *Active part.*—The ancients believed that the vesicating properties of Cantharides resided in the hairs which cover their bodies. The active principle of these animals, *Cantharidin*, was discovered by Robiquet in 1840. This principle is a white crystallisable substance, with an extremely acrid taste. When applied to the skin it rapidly raises a blister; taken internally it is a virulent poison. Cantharidin is fusible, very volatile, and is entirely dissipated when exposed to the air at the ordinary temperature. It is insoluble in water, but dissolves in alcohol, more so in hot than in cold. Ether also dissolves it.

Is the cantharidin distributed indiscriminately throughout all parts of the animal? Hippocrates considered that the antennæ, the head, the elytra, tne wings, and the feet are inert, and recommended that they should be rejected. Schwilgue has revived this opinion. Linnæus, on the contrary, maintains that the vesicating property resides nearly equally in every part of the insect. H. Cloquet and Audouin are also of this opinion. M. Farines, however, has stated that a blister made from the powdered antennæ, elytra, wings, and feet, after being applied for thirty hours, produced no effect. M. Berthoud in some recent experiments found that 3858 grains troy (250 grammes) of the thorax and the abdomen, which he terms soft parts, yielded 6·5 grains of cantharadin; and that 1929 grains (125 grammes) of the antennæ, heads, elytra, wings, and feet, which he terms *corneous parts*, yielded ·817 grains, which is in the proportion of 4 to 1.

Do *Cantharides* lose their vesicating properties by age? Foster assures us that when these insects have fallen into the condition of dust their remains have no action.

Dumeril, on the other hand, has successfully employed *Cantharides* which had been preserved for twenty years. We must not suppose, as some pharmaceutists have done, that the active principle of these insects is not eaten by their parasites; if this were really the case, the *Cantharides* which had been attacked by them, instead of losing their qualities, would, on the contrary, become more active. Observation shows that the excrement and remains of these parasites have no vesicating properties, and as they become mixed with the fragments of the *Cantharides*, the refuse which remains in the bottles can have but a very slight action. According to M. Farines, the properties of the dust of the worm-eaten *Cantharides*, compared with the ordinary powder, diminish in the ratio of 7 to 10½. On the other hand, Robiquet, M. Guibourt, and Virey, in analysing this dust, have found but a very small quantity of cantharidin. M. Berthoud obtained 1·45 grs. of cantharidin from 1929 grs. of dust; that is, about three fifths the quantity which would be furnished by the same weight of sound Cantharides. It is, therefore, evident that the remains of the worm-eaten insects would not be altogether inert.[1]

2. OTHER SPECIES.—The genus *Cantharis* contains a large number of species. Dejean enumerates thirty; and Audouin raises the number to sixty-four. It is, however, very rarely that any other species is employed than the one which has just been spoken of.

In the South of France, a species termed *Cantharis dubia*, Fabr., *Lytta dubia* of Oliver, is found on the lucern. The body of this insect is black, and the head of a reddish colour, divided into two portions by a longitudinal black line.

According to M. Courbon the *punctated Cantharis*, *Lytta adspersa*, Klug, *Epicauta adspersa*, Dej., from Montevideo, is an excellent vesicant, and acts more quickly than the *common Cantharis*.

The latter species lives on the beetroot; it is from $\frac{5}{10}$ to $\frac{6}{10}$ of an inch in length. The head, thorax, and abdomen are of an ashen grey colour, covered with small black spots. The antennæ are black, and the feet of a reddish colour.

Other *Cantharides* have been mentioned possessing vesicating properties, as for example that of Syria, *Lytta Syriaca*, Fabr., and a species from Arabia, which lives on wheat, *Lytta segetum*, Fabr. . . . M. Leclerc describes in his thesis (1835) seven species, whose properties he had experimented upon. . . M. Courbon has also enumerated two species of *Cantharis*, the *Epicauta cavernosa*, Reiche, and the *Lytta vidua*, Klug, (*Causima vidua*, Dej.,) both from the neighbourhood of Montevideo.

[There are five preparations of Cantharides in the London Pharmacopieia.

[1] M. Limousin-Lamotte announced to the Pharmaceutical Society of Paris, that blisters made from the worm-eaten remains had acted well. This statement was strongly contested, but was subsequently confirmed by M. Dubuc.

1. Acetum Cantharidis (*Epispasticum*), *Vinegar of Cantharides* (*Epispastic*).—Take of Cantharides rubbed to powder ℥ij; acetic acid Oj. Macerate the Cantharides with the acid for eight days, frequently shaking; lastly press and strain.

This is used as an extemporaneous blister.

2. Tinctura Cantharidis, *Tincture of Cantharides*.—Take of bruised Cantharides ℥iv; proof spirit Oij. Macerate for seven days, then press and strain.

The action of this preparation is diuretic and stimulant; the dose is m10 to ʒj. It should be given in some demulcent liquid, as barley water or linseed tea. Its effects on the bladder must be carefully watched. (Pereira.) It is occasionally used externally as a rubefacient.

3. Ceratum Cantharidis, *Cerate of Cantharides*.—Cantharides rubbed to a very fine powder ℥j; spermaceti cerate ℥vi. Add the Cantharides to the cerate, softened by heat, and mix.

This is used to promote a discharge from a blistered surface and to stimulate issues and indolent ulcers. It is a more powerful preparation than the next, which is used for the same purpose, and consequently it is more liable to affect the bladder, and to produce inflammation of the lymphatics and general irritation.

4. Unguentum Cantharidis, *Ointment of Cantharides*.—Cantharides rubbed to a very fine powder ℥iij; distilled water ℥xij: cerate of resin lbj. Boil the water with the cantharides down to one half and strain. Mix the cerate with the strained liquor, afterwards let it evaporate to a proper consistence. This is milder but less efficacious than the former.

5. Emplastrum Cantharidis, *Plaster of Cantharides*.—Take of Cantharides rubbed to a very fine powder lbj: wax and suet each ℥viiiss; resin ℥iij; lard ℥vj. To the wax, suet, and lard, liquified together, add the resin previously melted, then remove them from the fire, and a little before they concrete, sprinkle in the cantharides and mix.

"In making blistering plasters, care must be taken not to add the cantharides while the melted lard is quite hot, as the heat greatly injures the vesicating powers of the insect. For a similar reason the plaster should be spread by the thumb, a heated spatula being objectionable. To prevent the blister moving after its application to the skin, its margin should be covered with adhesive plaster. In order to guard against any affection of the urinary organs, place a piece of thin book muslin or silver (tissue) paper between the plaster and the skin. The efficacy of the blister depends on the fatty matter dissolving the Cantharidin and transuding through the muslin or paper. Some recommended the paper to be soaked in oil, which is supposed to dissolve the cantharidin. Now oil, not being miscible with the blood, is not readily absorbed; and hence it is supposed arises its protective influence. The usual time requisite for a blistering plaster to remain in contact with the skin is twelve hours; the vesicle is then to be cut at its most depending part and dressed with spermaceti ointment. When we wish to make a perpetual blister, the cerate of cantharides is employed as a dressing, or, if we wish to excite less irritation and prevent the possibility of the urinary organs being affected, the cerate of savin." (Pereira.)]

§ II. Mylabris.

The number of insects belonging to the genus Mylabris is very considerable. Oliver has described something like sixty. At the present time there are nearly two hundred. There are few groups in which the species have been more confounded together, or in which the synonyms are in greater confusion. (Guerin.)

The body of these insects is generally black. Some have the elytra of a dark yellow with black bands or spots.

These insects are very timid, and when it is attempted to capture them they fold up their feet and antennæ, and, falling down, assume the appearance of death.

1. THE MYLABRIS OF THE CHICORY (fig. 32), *Malybris cichorii*, Fabr., *Meloe cichorii*, Linn.—This species is the one which is best known, and which has been most carefully examined. It is supposed to be the insect which Dioscorides and Pliny have mentioned under the name of Cantharis.

Habitat.—This *Mylabris* is found in several of the warm parts of Europe. It resides on the flowers of the wild chicory, and on several other plants belonging to the family compositæ.

Description.—The elytra are of an obscure yellow, with three large, somewhat zigzag, black bands. The first band is interrupted and sometimes reduced to three or four spots.

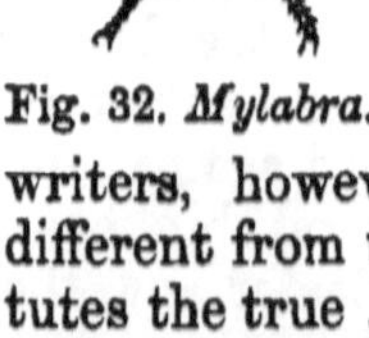

Fig. 32. *Mylabra.*

This species of Mylabris is employed in Italy, Greece, Egypt, and as far as China. Some writers, however, think that the one found in France is different from that of China, and that the latter alone constitutes the true *Mylabris of the chicory*. The others form one or two distinct species. It is at least certain that Linnæus has confounded several species under the name of *Meloe cichorii*.

2. OTHER SPECIES.—The species most nearly allied to the *Mylabris of the Chicory* are:

1. The *variable Mylabris, Mylabris variabilis*, Pall., to which Dr. Bretonneau has drawn attention.

2. The *Mylabris of Sida, Mylabris Sidæ*, Fabr., *M. pustulata*, Oliv., is a large species which lives in China, and forms an extensive article of commerce. According to Soubeiran it is largely employed in Germany, where it is imported by the English merchants.

3. The Blue Mylabris, *Mylabris cygnescens*, Illig., has been recommended by M. Farines, a pharmaceutist of Perpignan.

The following are the distinctive characters of these three species compared with those of the common species.

Having { Elytra . { bands . { ochre yellow
First band { interrupted 1. *Mylabris cichorii*.
              { entire . . 2. *Mylabris variabilis*.
reddish brown . . . . . 3. *Mylabris Sida*.
points . . . . 4. *Mylabris cygnescens*.

According to Dr. Collas, the *Indian Mylabris, Mylabris Indica*, Fussl., *M. punctum*, Fabr., is successfully employed at Pondicherry.

M. Guerin-Méneville has mentioned as a vesicating insect the *Mylabris of the olive tree, Mylabris oleæ*, Chevrol, which is found in Algeria.[1]

§ III. Cerocoma.

The Cerocoma of Schœffer (fig. 33) *Cerocoma Schœfferi*, Fabr. *Meloe Schœfferi*, Linn., is a small insect which lives on the gramineæ, umbelliferæ, and the compositæ. It buries its head in the flowers. It is found in the neighbourhood of Paris.

The insect is from five to seven lines in length; it is covered with down, and is of a golden green colour; the head is small and black; the thorax is of the same colour, while the antennæ and the feet are yellow; the elytra are the same length as the abdomen, and are very flexible. The animal is an active flyer.

There are several other species belonging to the genus *Cerocoma* in France, in Spain, and in the East, but their vesicating properties have not been investigated.

Fig. 33.
Cerocoma.

---

[1] The remedy for hydrophobia, which was administered at the monastery of Phaneromana, not far from Eleusis, according to M. Ch. Laurent, was

§ IV. Meloe.

The name of *Meloe* is given to insects allied to Mylabra and Cantharis; they are remarkable for the shortness of the elytra and the absence of wings.

These insects are generally of a black colour, but this is often mixed with shades of green and blue. The elytra are frequently punctated or rough.

The *Meloe* are very fertile. Godard saw a female deposit in two layings 2212 eggs. The eggs are very small.

When the larvæ are born they attach themselves to hymenoptera, which are searching for food; by this means they are transported to the nests of the bees, where they continue to live and complete their development. According to M. Fabre the larvæ of the *Meloe* pass through four distinct forms before arriving at the pupa stage; these consist of the primitive larval form, of a second larval form, of a pseudo chrysalis, and of a third larval form. The primitive larva is coriaceous, and attaches itself to the hymenoptera; the object of this is that the larva may be transported to a cell containing honey. When it reaches a cell it devours the egg of the hymenoptera. The second larva is soft, and differs altogether externally from the first; it feeds upon the honey. The pseudo chrysalis has the body covered with a corneous integument, and is deprived of motion; it is half invaginated in the cast-off skin of the second larval form. The third larval form resembles the second; it is half enclosed in the cast-off integument of the pseudo chrysalis, as the latter was in those of the second larval form. After the latter stage the metamorphoses follow the usual course; the larva becoming a true pupa, and the pupa a perfect insect.

When a Meloe is irritated or attempted to be captured, it discharges from the joints of its legs a viscid, acrid liquid, of a yellow colour, and having the odour of amber or of violets. An entomologist, at Montpellier, who had incautiously handled some of these insects, had his hands the next day covered with pustules. MM. Amoreux and H. Cloquet, however, assert that they have often handled them without experiencing any ill effects.

the *Mylabris bimaculata*, Oliv, pounded up with the *Cynanchum excelsum*, a plant belonging to the family Asclepiadaceæ, and upon which the insect lived. This pretended specific must be classed with the innumerable remedies which have been proposed without the least success against this fearful disease (Dumeril), amongst which are also found the *Cetoinia aurata*, the *Proscarabæus*, and the *Telophora*.

SPECIES.—Four species of *Meloe* are more particularly made use of; the following is a short summary of their characters:—

Antennæ { thick { the middle (dark violet) . 1. *Meloe proscarabæus*.
{ the apex (deep black) . . 2. *Meloe rugosus*.
{ the whole (greenish black) . 3. *Meloe variegatus*.
filiform { notched (deep black with red
{ bands) . . . . . . 4. *Meloe maialis*.

1. The *Meloe Proscarabæus*, Linn., (fig. 34) has the elytra slightly rugose. It is very common in France. The *Meloe Gallicus*, Dej., appears to be a variety.

2. The *Meloe rugosus*, Marsh, has the elytra extremely rugose. It is not uncommon in the south of France, as for example in the environs of Montpellier.

3. The *Meloe variegatus*, Donav., has the elytra slightly rugose. It is found in the neighbourhood of Paris.

4. The *Meloe maialis*, Linn., is distinguished from the three previous species by the presence of transverse bands of a red colour on the abdomen. This insect is found in Spain.

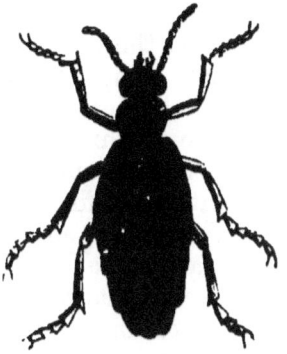

Fig. 34.—*Meloe*.

The use of the following species has also been recommended: the *Meloe autumnalis*, Oliv., which is found in the neighbourhood of Paris; the *Meloe punctatus*, Oliv., under which title two species have been confounded, viz., the *Tuccius* of Rossi, and the *coriarius* of Hofmansegg; and the *Meloe Algeria*, Linn., which inhabits Sardinia.

CHAPTER IV.

LEECHES.

LEECHES are abranchial Annelida belonging to the family Hirundinidæ and to the genus *Hirudo*.

They are found in ponds, ditches, marshes, streams, and rivulets.

The body of these animals is elongated, flattened, gradually narrowed anteriorly, and obtuse posteriorly; it is soft, viscous, and slippery to the feel, and is composed of ninety-five equal and very distinct rings, which project at the sides. Leeches, when they contract their bodies, assume the form of an olive. Their colour is more or less of a greenish cast. The back has six parallel longitudinal bands of a reddish or brownish hue, spotted with black, continuous or intercepted, and sometimes reduced to mere points. The ventral surface is either of a uniform colour or spotted with black, and bordered on each side by a straight or undulating band of the same colour.

The anterior extremity is provided with an oral sucker, not very concave, and with the upper lip almost lancet-shaped. Within the mouth are three jaws furnished with minute teeth. The eyes are ten in number, but are hardly visible; they are placed on the upper lip, where they form a curved line, the six anterior being the largest. The posterior extremity of the body is also terminated by a round obliquely placed sucker, at the base of which and at its upper part is the anal orifice.

Leeches are androgynous. The sexual orifices are placed on the anterior third of the belly; the male orifice between the twenty-seventh and twenty-eighth ring, and the female five rings farther back. The first is a minute pore, surrounded by a thickened margin, and the second a small transverse slit.

The copulation of these animals is double. In the act two individuals approach each other; their bellies are placed opposite to each other, but in the contrary direction, so that the oral sucker of each is turned towards the anal sucker of the other. In this position the leeches unite with each other and copulation takes place.

The period of gestation lasts from twenty-five to forty days. When a leech is impregnated an enlargement takes place around the sexual apertures, which has received the name of the girdle or *clitellum*.

At the time of laying their eggs the *Leeches* come from the water and seek for some moist earth, where they can make a hole or gallery; they then discharge from their muciparous sacs a clear white and transparent liquid. (Ebrard.) This froth has all the appearance of white of egg after it has been beaten up. (Wedecke.) The animal, by a series of contractions of the anterior part of its body, facilitates the discharge of this fluid (Ebrard), and becomes entirely surrounded by it. The clitellum swells, and a pellicle is formed upon its surface. The worm appears to suffer, it twists about in every direction, the posterior part of its body remaining almost stationary and serving as the point of resistance. At the end of a certain time, the *leech* quickly withdraws its head from the pellicle before mentioned, and at the same time this is detached from the clitellum. The *Leech* then extricates itself backwards from this kind of membranous case. It thus forms an oval sac, open at each end. The two orifices are then closed up by a thick brown mass. Before the animal comes out of the case, it has deposited a number of small eggs, accompanied by a large quantity of albuminous matter. The sac becomes more solid, assumes a darker colour, and forms a closed capsule (*embryophore*, Fermond). This kind of shell is not analogous to the covering of the eggs of the other oviparous animals; it is a simple secretion from the skin; a kind of structure which reminds one of the caducous membrane of the mammalia. The frothy matter surrounding the shell dries, becomes of a reddish colour, then brown, and ultimately forms a spongy network, which transforms the capsule into a species of cocoon.

The mere drying of the frothy mucus would not suffice to form the tissue of which we have been speaking. It is probable that the capsule exercises some influence on its formation, for the spongy tissues always begin to be organized from within outwards, so that the deepest portion is often found converted into the spongy tissue, while the superficial portion still remains in the frothy state. If the transformation into the spongy tissue arose solely from drying, it is evident that this change should commence on the exterior. (Weber.) Possibly the deposition of the frothy matter takes place at intervals, and the part which is not dried, is that which is last secreted?

Each *Leech* produces two cocoons, rarely three.

Every cocoon encloses from ten to eighteen eggs. Chatelain has counted as many as twenty-one, and Charpentier twenty-six.

The eggs are hatched between the twenty-fifth and twenty-eighth day. (Achard, Chatelain.) The temperature seems to exercise some influence on their development. At this time the young *Leeches* force off the flaps or opercula at the extremities of the capsule, pass through the spongy tissue, sometimes winding their way through the different laminæ, and emerge at various parts of the surface.

Fig. 35.
Grey Leech.

140   MEDICAL ZOOLOGY.

Fig. 36.—*Green Leech.*

Fig. 37.—*Dragon Leech.*

At birth the leeches are about $\frac{67}{10}$ of an inch in length. They are filiform, transparent, of an ashen colour approaching to white; some have a reddish cast. Their eyes are easily distinguished at the end of a few days; the dorsal bands or spots make their appearance; and by degrees the young animal assumes the livery of its parents. During the first days, when the young *Leeches* are alarmed or are pursued by their enemies, they return to their cocoon and hide themselves in the spongy tissue.

1. SPECIES.—Writers have described not less than fifty different species of *Leeches*; many of these are, however, mere varieties not distinctly characterized. In a recent work the number is reduced to seventeen, and even of these more than half are still very imperfectly known.

There are three principal varieties of *Leeches* employed in France. These are: 1st, The *Grey Leech*; 2nd, The *Green Leech*; 3rd, The *Dragon Leech*. The following is a summary of their characters:

	Lateral Bands	
straight.		zigzag.
Belly		
spotted.	not spotted.	
1. *Grey Leech.*	2. *Green Leech.*	3. *Dragon Leech.* [*True English or Speckled Leech.*]

1. The *Grey* or *Medicinal Leech*, *Hirudo medicinalis*, Linn., *Sanguisuga medicinalis*, Sav., (fig. 35) is an inhabitant of Europe and certain parts of northern Africa. The body is olive green, mixed with grey. On the back are six rusty red longitudinal stripes; the sides are olive green. The belly is spotted with black.

2. The *Green* or *officinal Leech*, *Hirudo officinalis*, Moq., *Sanguisuga officinalis*, Sav., (fig. 36) is found in the same

localities as the former. The body is of a clear olive or green colour. The back has six rusty red longitudinal bands, generally continuous. The margins are of an olive colour both on the back and on the belly. This species differs but very little from the *Grey Leech*.

3. The *Dragon* or *Trout Leech*, *Hirudo troctina*, Johns., *Sanguisuga interrupta*, Moq., (fig. 37,) is found in Algeria and the whole of Barbary. The body is of a clear brilliant green colour. The back has six rows of spots, which are generally very distinct; the margins are of an orange or reddish colour. The belly is sometimes spotted with black, sometimes not.

The last species has been long regarded as being of an inferior quality; but recent experiments have shown that it is quite as good as the *Grey Leech*. (Milton, Tripier.)

These three leeches offer numerous varieties, which have been described in special monographs on the subject. The colours of the bands, the way in which they are intercepted, and the form of the spots, have been made the ground for giving a number of names which are quite undeserving of serious attention. The climate, the water, and the soil seem to influence these points of difference. *Leeches* are sometimes named after the country from which they come; thus we have the Spanish, the Portuguese, the Hungarian, the African, the Algerian, and the Morocco *Leech*. The merchants divide the *Leeches* into *small, middle sized*, and *large*. The very small are called threads (*filets*); those which are just born sprouts (*germemont*); and the very large ones cows (*vaches*).

The dealers often gorge the *Leeches*, before selling them, with blood from the slaughter-houses, and thus convert the *filets* into small ones, and the small ones into the middle-sized.

Some years back, under the name of *Hæmenteria*, M. Fillippi introduced a new genus of American Hirundinidæ, which differs from the ordinary *Leeches* in the structure of the mouth; this organ is provided with a stiff, pointed, small, protrusile sucker instead of the three jaws. This learned zoologist has described three species: the *Hæmenteria Ghiliani*, *H. Mexicana*, and *H. officinalis*. The first is found in the river Amazon, the other two in Mexico. The advantages offered by these species will be referred to subsequently.

2. *Action on Man.*—It has been long known that *Leeches* can pierce the skin of man, and of other vertebrata, for the purpose of sucking their blood. The attention of observers was directed at a very early period to the organs with which these creatures are enabled to inflict their wounds. But the

first naturalists were unprovided either with the microscope or the magnifying glass, and these organs of the *Leech* are very small and deep-seated.

Arnaud de Velleneuve believed that the *Grey Leech* had a small *proboscis* in its mouth, similar to that of the Gnats; Gesner supposed that it was armed with a cleft and tubular tongue. Poupart imagined that the animal had no cutting instruments, and that it caused deep lacerations by a violent sucking action. Rondelet is one of the first who pointed out the presence of three small teeth or jaws; his knowledge of them was, however, very imperfect. Muralto examined them more carefully. Dom Allou, Morand, Braun, Kunzemann, and Brandt have described the jaws of the *Leech* more or less correctly.

1. *Jaws* (38).—The jaws of the *Leech* are three in number placed longitudinally: one superior and median, two others inferior and lateral. If the oral sucker is laid open, these organs are found closely approximated at their posterior extremity and diverging at their anterior.

The jaws of the *Leech* are semicircular, thin, cartilaginous, moderately strong, smooth and whitish bodies, having one straight margin, which is fixed, and provided with a process firmly imbedded in the muscles, while a second margin is free, rounded, and cutting.

The process enlarges after its commencement, but is not branched. The convex border is provided with a row of teeth arranged close together. Dom Allou and Carena believed there were two rows of teeth; this, however, was an optical illusion, caused by the curious form of these small bodies. M. Brandt has only represented thirty-five teeth; the writer has counted from forty-six to eighty-three; the average number is from sixty-six to sixty-seven. These teeth are chevron-shaped like the letter V reversed; they are arranged parallel to each other and are placed across the cutting edge of the jaw (fig. 38), having their angle turned towards

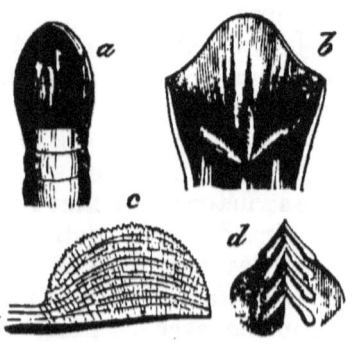

Fig. 38.—*Jaws of a Leech.*[1]

[1] *a*, oral sucker; *d*, oral sucker opened to show the three jaws; *c*, jaw magnified, seen in profile; *d*, portion of a jaw highly magnified, so as to show the chevron-shaped denticles.

the axis of the mouth. Viewed sideways, the teeth appear like a number of elongated processes, blunted and swollen at their bases, pointed at their summits, and arranged symmetrically like the teeth of a comb, but with a slightly radiated disposition. Viewed from above, and under a low magnifying power, their basal enlargements appear like two rows of parallel projections.

The denticles are unequal in size, the smallest being placed anteriorly. They increase in volume from before backwards, that is to say, towards the deepest part of the mouth. The two extremities of the jaws have no teeth. These denticles have been compared physiologically to the incisors of the mammalia.

The jaws are lodged in a kind of depression of which the margins barely rise above them.

Each jaw is provided at its base with a small fasciculus of muscular fibres, which diverge backwards and are intermingled with the muscles of the pharynx (fig. 38, *b*).

There is also observed in the tissue of these organs fibres, some of which are transverse and pass from one extremity to the other, while others are longitudinal and oblique, and pass from each denticle to the base of the jaw.

A little in front of the jaws, in the interior of the sucker, is a strong tendinous ring, which forms the circumference of the mouth.

2. *The manner of biting.*—When the *Leech* is about to bite it elongates the oral sucker; it then contracts the extremity of the two lips, which become everted. The upper is a little more shortened than the lower, so that the organ ceases to be elongated, and becomes more or less circular.

The *Leech* then draws a small papiliform piece of the skin into its mouth. (Poupart.)

The three jaws are brought forwards; they emerge from their cases, and are closely applied against the little papiliform portion of the skin. The muscular fibres of the sucker and the tendinous ring on its inner surface then contract and act alternately. At the same time, the special muscles of the jaws draw them forcibly from before backwards, and the process of skin is wounded in three places.

The denticles at the posterior extremity commence the incision, these being the strongest and the sharpest.

The points of resistance are the rings of the sucker which at that time are drawn very closely together, and are firmly applied to the surface of the skin.

In biting, the jaws act like small dentated wheels cut in halves, or like very fine curved saws.

The teeth of the *Leech* being so much softer than those of other animals, one is surprised to find bodies which have so little firmness producing such deep incisions. Blainville thinks that the fibrous cartilaginous tissue of the denticles owes its rigidity to the contraction of their muscular fibres, and this opinion is probably correct. If the transverse fibres and the longitudinal fibres, which cross them, are made to contract at the same time, the jaw must necessarily become rigid. Moreover, the longitudinal fibres passing obliquely, the effect of their contraction must be to elevate and render the points of the chevron-shaped denticles more projecting.

The person who is bitten has at first a sensation of pressure on the part where the *Leech* has fixed itself. This increases, and is soon followed by a sharp acute pain, resembling a combination of pricking and tearing.

3. *The wound.*—The wound of the *Leech* has a triradiate form produced by the three linear incisions, uniting in a common centre, and forming three nearly equal angles with each other (fig. 39). Aldrovandus has given a perfectly correct description of the wound.[1]

Fig. 39.
Leech-bite.

In consequence of the lines enlarging towards the centre, and their margins being somewhat undulating (the wound being rather jagged than cleanly cut), and as the little crust which covers them passes slightly beyond their edges, it often happens that the three angles are partially filled up, and the wound becomes somewhat of a triangular form.

Sometimes the wound inflames and loses its proper form; it may also give rise to a slight suppuration, or even to a partial erysipelas.

The *Hæmenteria* which have been mentioned previously do not produce a true bite. According to the experiments of M. Craveri, their wound is small and *leaves no traces behind.* (!)

4. *Suction.*—After a *Leech* has punctured the skin, the mouth, aided by the muscular fibres which constitute the sucker, and especially the ring by which it is surrounded, performs the act of suction.

Morand pretends that the anterior sucker acts like a pump, and that it is aided by the *tongue*, which performs the part of

---

[1] "*Sugendo trifidum vulnusculum imprimunt, ita ut radii ab uno centro terni æque distantes procedant.*"

a piston. Unfortunately for this explanation *Leeches* have no tongue; Morand having mistaken for the latter organ the suboesophageal ganglia placed on the exterior of the œsophagus.

Durondeau believed that the whole of the digestive system *from the tail to the head* served to draw the blood. But one simple fact suffices to destroy this theory; it is this—that when a *Leech* is cut in two, it will still continue to perform the act of suction. Moreover, the structure of the alimentary canal is physically opposed to this general act of imbibition.

The experiments of Swayne and Johnson have shown that in the operation of which we are speaking the animal does not withdraw its jaws from the wound, as many writers have asserted. We admit this fact, which we have also verified, but we believe that the muscular fibres which draw the jaws backwards and press them together towards a common centre, relax a little, the jaws then return to the beginning of the incisions, and as they diverge leave the centre of the wound exposed. This part of the wound is the largest and the deepest, and is that which principally furnishes the current of blood.

3. *The quantity of blood drawn.*—Writers have never been agreed as to the quantity of blood which a *Leech* is capable of drawing.

Tyson remarks that this animal eats more than its own weight at a meal. He compares it to a silk-worm, which, in the course of a day, will consume a quantity of leaves of a greater weight than its own body.

Ray says, that a *Leech* weighing 60 grs. will suck up three times that quantity of blood; while Adanson states that one weighing 30 grs. will absorb 240 grs., that is to say, eight times its own weight. Simon Bonnet believed the average quantity to be from 92 grs. to 138 grs.; but as a considerable quantity of blood oozes from the wound, if left to itself the patient probably loses from 118 grs. to 277 grs. of blood. According to M. Alphonse Sanson one *Leech* will consume 247 grs.; according to my own calculations it would be 231 grs.

Braun has remarked that the quantity of blood sucked up does not increase in proportion to the size of the animal. According to this writer a young *Leech* will consume three times its weight, and a full-grown one only twice its weight. According to M. Alphonse Sanson the small will consume three times and four-fifths; the middle sized small four times and two-thirds; the middle sized large seven times; and the large five times and one-third of their own weight. I have repeated these experiments with the following results. M. Sanson experimented on six individuals; my calculations are based upon the results obtained from twenty individuals. Small *Leeches*, two and a half times; the small middle-sized, four times; the large middle-sized, five and a half times; and the large, five times and one eleventh part of their own weight. We find, therefore, that the middle sized large *Leeches* are those which relatively consume the largest quantity of blood.

[Pereira says, "the quantity of blood a leech is capable of drawing varies considerably. I believe four drachms to be the maximum. On an average I do not think we ought to estimate it at more than one drachm and a half. Of course this has no reference to that lost after the animal has fallen off, which varies according to the vascularity of the part; in children being oftentimes very considerable. When the leech has had sufficient it drops off; but it is said if the tail be snipped, the animal will continue to bite, the blood passing out posteriorly as fast as it is taken in by the mouth. I have tried several, but they usually let go their hold the instant the tail is cut. H. Cloquet has made the same remark."] [1]

These results, however, will vary with the species and race of Leech employed; according also as to whether the individuals are strong or unhealthy; as to whether they are partially gorged or not, and also as to whether they have come direct from the waters of their native marshes, or from the artificial reservoir of a chemist's shop.

The digestive system of the *Leech* consists of eleven pairs of gastric pouches. These pouches increase in size as they proceed backwards, the last pair being very much larger than those which precede them. This arrangement accounts for the large quantity of blood which these animals are capable of retaining.

For a long time it was the custom to throw away all Leeches which had been used, but they are now disgorged and preserved for a future occasion. This disgorgement can be accomplished in various ways, as with salt, alum, sugar, ashes, tobacco, ipecacuanha, chalk, lime, charcoal, sawdust; or with salt and water, sea water, dilute vinegar, wine, beer, infusion of absinth, &c. Some have recommended friction, pressure, or even puncturing the animal. One of the best methods of disgorgement is to place the *Leeches* in a solution composed of

---

[1] Pereira, *Materia Medica*, vol. 2, pt. 2, p. 2197, 3rd ed. London, 1853.

sixteen parts of sea salt to one hundred of water at a temperature of between 104° Fah. and 113° Fah. The *Leeches* are then pressed gently, and afterwards placed in fresh water.

In some places the *Leeches* are simply thrown into the reservoirs, where they are left for some months.

The gorged *Leeches* are excellent for the purpose of reproduction.

3. HIRUDINICULTURE.—The enormous consumption of *Leeches* and their increasing scarceness have induced persons to rear them artificially. Hirudiniculture has for some years been an important branch of commerce, particularly in the Gironde and some other districts of the southern departments.

The *Leeches* are placed in large artificial marshes, in which the water is always kept at a uniform level. Care is taken to place a supply of clay or of peat at the bottom and on the margins. Aquatic plants are also provided for the purification of the water and on which the Leeches can rub themselves or take refuge.

M. Vayson, of Bordeaux, has recently suggested a small domestic marsh (a *vaysonier*), which will be exceedingly useful to the pharmaceutist and to persons who are desirous of raising *Leeches* on a small scale. This apparatus consists of a common earthen vessel, having the form of a truncated cone reversed. The lower part is perforated by a number of holes, but not so large as to allow of the *Leeches* passing through them; the vessel is then filled with peat earth, and a number of *Leeches* are placed upon it, which embed themselves in the earth. The upper opening of the vessel is then covered up with a piece of coarse canvas. When it is desired to send the leeches to a distance the earth is made as damp as possible, and the vessel is packed in a box or wicker basket. When it is only wanted to preserve the animals, the lower part of the vessel is placed in water to the depth of about four inches, and the creatures are left to themselves. In consequence of the infiltration, the lower layers of the peat are soon saturated with water, while the upper portion is almost dry. The *Leeches* know perfectly well how to choose between these two extremes the layer which is best adapted for them, and form in it galleries, in which they live, grow, and produce their cocoons. The *vaysonier* will answer both for the preservation, the conveyance, and reproduction of the *Leeches*.

CHAPTER V.

GALLS.

Galls[1] are excrescences or growths of the tissues of plants arising from the puncture of certain insects, and which are destined to lodge and nourish their larva. These excrescences are hollow and consist of an astringent tissue.

They may be divided into two kinds: 1. *Galls;* 2. *Cases.*

The first are more or less of a round form, have very thick walls, and are produced by different species of *Cynips*.

The second are more or less elongated, have very thin walls, and are produced by different species of *Aphides*.

§ I. Galls.

1. CYNIPS.—The *Cynips* are minute Hymenoptera, belonging to the subdivision Terebrantia and to the family Pupivora.

These insects have the head very small and the thorax dilated superiorly; they look as if they were deformed; the abdomen is compressed into a keel and cutting on its under surface, obliquely truncated, and obtuse at its termination.

The Cynips puncture the plants by means of a special instrument; and introduce one or several eggs into the small cavity they have formed. The eggs soon increase in size; the larvæ have no feet, but are often provided with fleshy tubercles in place of them. The larvæ are enclosed in the *gall*, which grows around them, and where they remain for five or six months; some of them undergo their metamorphoses in this kind of prison, while others issue forth and bury themselves in the earth.

Cynips of the common gall—Cynips gallætinctoria, Linn. (fig. 40).—This is one of the most interesting of these small insects. It is of a pale yellow colour, and is covered with a whitish silky down; the under surface of the abdomen is black and shining; the nervures of the anterior wings are brown.

Terebra (fig. 41).—The instrument by means of which the insect punctures the plant and produces the *gall* is only present in the female. It is a kind of auger or borer placed at the extremity of the body, having a curved form, and lodged

---

[1] These formations belong to botany as well as to zoology.

in the interior of the abdomen; its posterior extremity is placed beneath the anus, in a central canal, between two long ciliated valves, each of which forms a half sheath. The borer

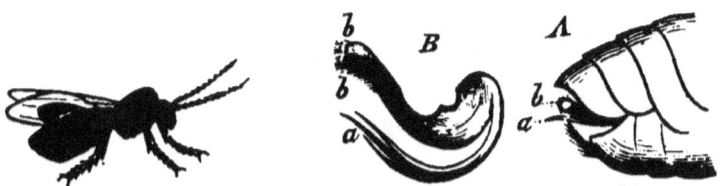

Fig. 40.—*Cynips.*   Fig. 41.—*Terebra of Cynips.*[1]

looks as if it consisted of a single and very delicate seta (Latreille), but when magnified it is seen to be composed of three capillary pointed threads, of which the central is somewhat longer than the two lateral.

The *Cynips* thrust this instrument into the tissues of the plant.

When a twig or a leaf has been punctured, the nutrient juices flow towards the wound, and an excrescence is formed, which gradually increases in size and hardness.

2. GALLS.—There are few plants which do not have *galls*, but they are found more especially on the oak, poplar, elm, birch, pine, rose-tree, ivy, &c.

These excrescences have sometimes only a single cavity, inhabited by one larva; at other times there are several cavities, either communicating with each other or separate, and forming the dwelling-places of a similar number of larva. The larva gradually consume the interior of their house, without however destroying it, as the latter continues to increase in proportion to the growth of the insect.

Réaumur noticed that the kind of insect exercised great influence over the form and consistency of the *gall*, so that where there are several of these excrescences growing on the same leaf, some may be woody, others herbaceous; some smooth or tuberculated, while others are granulated or haired.

In a medical point of view galls may be divided into the *common* or *true galls* and into the *hairy galls* or *bedeguars*.

1. *True galls.*—These well-known productions are of a more

---

[1] *A*, extremity of the abdomen, magnified; *a*, terebra; *b*, the valves; *B*, the terebra separate and still more magnified; *a*, the three threads of the terebra; *b b*, the valves.

or less rounded form, regular or irregular in shape, and more or less solid. The best known is the *Aleppo gall*[1] (fig. 42), which is found on the dyers' oak, *Quercus infectoria*. It is produced by the species of Cynips which has been previously spoken of. This *gall* is about the size of a nut; it is heavy, and of a globular form; the surface is smooth, but presents here and there some irregular tubercles. Its colour is a blackish or yellowish green; it has strong astringent properties. Care is taken to gather the gall before the insect has escaped.

The *galls*, which are left on the trees, and which are collected after the escape of the Cynips, may be recognized by the presence of a round hole, which is made by the insect, and by their lightness. These *galls* are only slightly astringent, and are of a lighter colour (white galls). The best galls come from Syria; those of Smyrna or the Morea are larger, but lighter, and not so good in quality.

When a gall is cut through there is seen—1, a small cavity in the centre, in which is the larva; 2, a not very thick, light, spongy layer, of a yellow or brown colour in its substance, but white at the surface around the central cavity; this layer contains a small quantity of starch (Guibourt), and appears intended for the nourishment of the insect; 3, three or four large cavities, which appear to be formed by the separation or folding together of certain fleshy curved scales; these provide for the respiration of the larva; 4, another substance which is present in large quantities, and has a compact radiating structure, which when magnified is seen to be made up of shining particles; 5, an external green layer containing chlorophus and a volatile oil.

The different species of oak produce a great number of galls more or less resembling the *common gall*.[2] Some of these have been carefully examined.

The *smooth gall*, which Reaumur termed gall of the petiole of the oak, grows on the young branches of the English oak (*Quercus sessiflora*, Smith), in the neighbourhood of Paris, and on those of the *Quercus Pyrenaica*, Willd., near Bordeaux. It is from $\frac{6}{10}$ to $\frac{8}{10}$ of an inch in diameter; it is light, spherical, without tubercles, of a reddish colour, and of a spongy texture.

---

[1] Commonly called *nutgall*, *painter's gall*, *Levant gall*, and *black* or *green gall*.

[2] The other galls owe their origin to different species of Cynips; amongst them is that of the common oak (*C. quercus folii*, Linn.), and that of the *C. quercus togæ* of Fabricius.

Sometimes it contains only a single cavity, while at other times there are three or four, and the same number of *Cynips*.

With this species may be associated the round galls on the leaves of the oak, those which Reaumur terms *currant galls*, and the *gooseberry seed galls*, which only differ in respect to their size.

Fig. 42.—*Common Gall.*   Fig. 43.—*Section of Gall.*[1]

The *crowned gall* is probably produced by the buds being puncturing at an early stage of their development. Its form is spherical, and it has a short pedicle; above there is a crown of blunt spines or tubercles. Such is the *small crowned gall of Aleppo*.

The *horned gall* of M. Guibourt appears as if it were attached by its centre to a very young branch. It is irregular, and seems to be formed by the union of several bodies, which are dilated at their bases, and horned at their summits. It is light, woody, of a yellowish colour, and hollowed internally into a number of chambers, each of which is surrounded by a

---

[1] *a*, the cavity; *b*, nutritive layer; *c*, air chambers; *d*, radiated substance; *e*, envelope.

radiating substance. Each chamber opens externally by a separate aperture.

The *gall of Hungary*, called also *gall of Piedmont*, is an irregular excrescence, which grows on the acorn of the English oak, after the ovary has been fecundated. The gall sometimes occupies half the cup, while the remainder of the acorn grows beside it; at other times, it occupies the whole cup. In the centre of the gall is a small cavity, surrounded by a layer of half-woody matter; air enters the cavity from its summit.

The *squamous gall*, which Reaumur called *artichoke* gall, is also found on the English oak. It resembles the cone of the hop; it arises from the abnormal development of the involucrum of the female flower previous to fecundation. Internally, there is a kind of woody receptacle, which Reaumur compared to the lower part of the artichoke; this also arises from the excessive development of the base of the involucrum. The receptacle projects slightly at the margin, which gives it a cup-like appearance.[1]

The characters of the several galls which have been mentioned might be arranged as follows:—

Galls	of one piece	regular	spherical	tubercular	1. *Aleppo.*
				non-tubercular	2. *Smooth.*
			non-spherical		3. *Crowned.*
		irregular	with horns		4. *Horned.*
			without horns		5. *Hungarian.*
	of several				6. *Squamous.*

Nutgalls contain tannin, gallic, ellagic, and luteogallic acids; chlorophyl, a volatile oil, extractive matter, woody fibre, gum, starch, liquid sugar, albumen, and various salts, amongst others the gallates of potash and lime. Berzelius also admits the presence of a small quantity of pectic acid, and combined with the tannin.

M. Pelouze has carefully studied the tannin obtained from nutgalls. It is a solid, colourless, inodorous, non-crystallizable substance; it has an astringent but not bitter taste; it reddens litmus; it is very soluble in water, but scarcely at all so in ether; and it gives a black or green precipitate with the

---

[1] Tournefort states that at Scio the galls of *Salvia pomifera*, Linn., are collected for the purpose of making a kind of sweetmeat of them. According to Lesson the same might be done with those of the ground ivy (*Glechoma hederacea*, Linn.).

salts of the peroxide of iron. It is one of the most powerful astringents known.

Nutgalls or tannin are made into pills, into an ointment, an electuary, and into various drinks and gargles; from them is prepared the antihœmorrhoidal ointment of Cullen, and a powder for the purposes of embalming.

[There are three preparations of galls ordered in the Pharmacopœia.

1. DECOCTUM GALLÆ, *Decoction of Galls.*—Bruised galls ℥ijss; distilled water Oij. Boil down to a pint and strain. Employed as a chemical antidote and test.

2. TINCTURA GALLÆ, *Tincture of Galls.*—Bruised galls ℥v; proof spirit Oij. Macerate for seven days, then press and strain. A powerful astringent. Dose from f℥ss. to f℥ij. Diluted with water, it forms a useful and convenient astringent, gargle, and wash. (Pereira.)

3. UNGUENTUM GALLÆ COMPOSITUM, *Compound ointment of Galls.*—Finely powdered nut-galls ʒvj; lard ℥vj. powdered opium ʒiss. Rub together. Astringent. Used in hœmorrhoidal affections. Mixed, says Pereira, with zinc ointment it is applied to piles after the inflammatory stage is passed.]

2. *Bedeguars.*[1]—This name is given to galls which are covered with numerous close-set fibres or hairs.

The *bedeguars* which are best known are those of the rose tree; they are caused by the *Cynips rosæ* of Linnæus (*Diplolepis rosæ*, Oliv.), a small hymenopterous insect of a shining black colour, with the feet and abdomen, excepting at its termination, of a feruginous brown colour; the wings are transparent, and of a smoky hue.[2] MM. Brandt and Ratzebourg have given a good description of them.

The *bedeguars* are round or oval, more or less irregular, excrescences, sometimes resembling medlars (Blanchard); they are covered with filiform or scale-like processes; they are often branched, and are of a green, reddish, or purple colour. In the interior are a number of larvæ living in separate cells, which are each provided with hard thick walls; in these the insects pass the winter as pupæ.

---

[1] Commonly called soft apples, or vegetable sponges. [In some parts of England they are called Robin's cushion.]
[2] In these excrescences there is often found the *Diplolepis bedegaris* of Oliver, a small insect of a bright golden green colour; this is a parasite on the first.

Formerly bedeguars were employed in medicine on account of their stringent properties.

§ II. Cases.

The *cases* or *vesicles* (*folliculi*, Linn.) not only differ from the galls by their less rounded form, their thinness, and the kind of insect which gives rise to them, but also with regard to their cavity, which is always much larger, and is capable of containing an entire colony of the insects.

1. APHIDES.—The *aphides or plant-lice* which reside in the cases are small hemiptera, belonging to the subdivision Homoptera, and to the family of the Hymenelytra.

The body is soft and ovate; the head small, with the antennæ longer than the body; the second segment of the thorax is large and elevated; the elytra and the wings membranous. At the extremity of the abdomen are two hollow tubercles, from which a saccharine fluid is discharged.

These insects feed upon the juices of the plants, upon which they live in large numbers. In spring and summer each colony contains demi-pupa, which are apterous, but afterwards acquire wings, and other individuals who are always apterous. All these individuals are females, who are ovoviviparous *without previous copulation*. The young emerge from the posterior part of the abdomen of the mother. The males only appear towards the close of summer; these are also apterous; they impregnate the last generation, which is produced by the preceding individuals; these impregnated females are oviparous. The influence of a single impregnation extends over several generations to the number of eight or nine. (Bonnet, Duvau.)

The *Aphides* multiply enormously. Reaumur calculated that five generations proceeding from a single mother, if no obstacle intervened, might give rise to the astounding number of 5,904,900,000 individuals.

Rostrum.—This organ, which is nearly perpendicular, arises from the under surface of the head, between the anterior pair of limbs; it is composed of three joints. The animal uses it to puncture the leaves and young twigs of the plant.[1]

2. *Cases.*—One of the most curious of these formations is that which is known as the *Chinese gall* (fig. 44).[2]

---

[1] The disease of certain trees, known as *honey dew*, is produced by different species of *Aphides*.

[2] In China it is commonly called *Yen-fou-tsze*.

This *case* grows on the leaves of *Distylium recemosum*, Zucc.,[1] a large tree of Japan, belonging to the family hamamelida. (Decaisne.)[2] According to M. Guibourt it is also developed on the buds of the tree.

The insect which produces these cases belongs to the genus *Aphis*, or to one which is closely allied to it (Doubleday); it has been named *Aphis Chinensis*, Bell.

It is a minute ovate insect, truncated posteriorly with moderately long antennæ, composed of five unequal joints.

The *Chinese Galls* are large: some equal a chesnut in size, others the closed hand. (Duhalde.) Their form is an irregular oblong, with angular protuberances, which sometimes have the appearance of horns; some are single, others are bifurcated, and occasionally they are divided into three or more lobes. The colour of these cases is at first a dull green, it then becomes yellow, and ultimately of a reddish grey. The surface has a soft feel like that of velvet; when examined by a lens it is seen to be covered with a very short compact down. The cavity of the excrescence is very large, arising from the thinness of its walls ($\frac{1}{25}$ to $\frac{2}{25}$ of an inch). The tissue of which it is composed is firm, hard, and brittle. When one of these galls is broken it has a whitish, translucent, and resinous appearance. Its taste is astringent without any flavour or smell of resin. (Guibourt.) The inner surface is covered with a substance, having a chalky appearance. (Pereira.) In the interior is found the remains of a large number of Aphides. The *Chinese galls* are gathered in before the occurrence of frost; the insects which they contain are destroyed by exposing them to the vapour of boiling water.

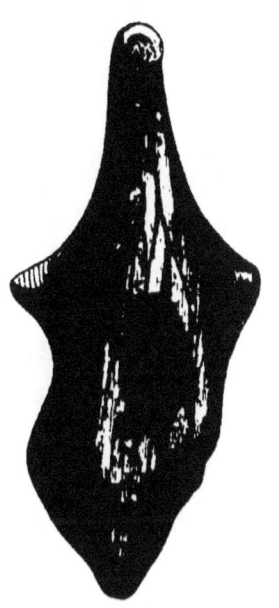

Fig. 44.—*Chinese Gall.*

These *cases* are of great use, and are held in high estimation in China as a powerful astringent, not only for medical purposes, but also for dyeing.

Allied to the *Chinese galls* are certain excrescences which are found in the East, and also in the South of France, and which are produced by another species of *Aphis*: these are the

---

[1] Commonly called in Japan *Ou-pey-tse, Ou-pei-tse, Woo-pei-tse.*
[2] According to M. Schenk it is a terebinthaceæ, the *Rhus semialata*, Murr. var. β *Osbekii* DC.

vesicles or *galls of the pistacias*. These false galls are found on the *Pistacia vera, P. Terebinthus*, and the *P. Lentiscus*. The insect which produces them is the *Aphis Pistaciæ*, Linn., a small black insect, with a roughened thorax, very long legs, and white wings.[1]

The cases from the pistacias are at first of a green and afterwards of a red colour, mammelated, light, with a turpentine flavour, and very astringent.

They are distinguished into three kinds, according to their form: the *siliquose*, which grow at the extremity of the branches; the *globular*, which occur on the peduncles; and those which are formed like a *cushion* on the surface of the leaves. The first are sometimes three inches in length and resemble the pod of a leguminous plant. They are known in Judea under the name of *caroub*. The second and third often resemble the fruit of the turpentine tree. These are known under the name of *baisonges*.[2]

These excrescences are eaten by the inhabitants of the East. They are often employed as a substitute for the common galls, and they are also used as a red dye.

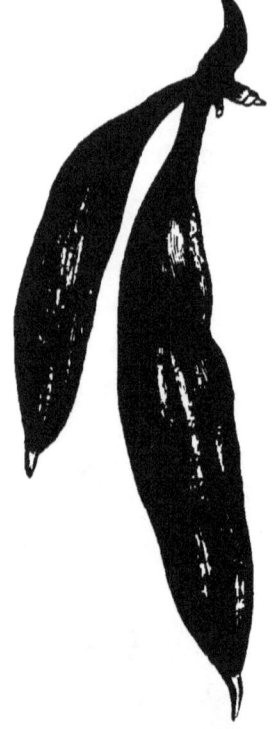
Fig. 45.—*Turpentine Gall.*

CHAPTER VI.

THE TREHALA.

THE *trehala* or *tricula*[3] is a singular case which is well known at Constantinople and in some some parts of the East.

At the last great exhibition some of these cases were sent from Turkey by M. Della Sudda as a particular species of *manna*, without any other explanation appended to them than the word *trehala*.

This production is described in the Persian Pharmacopœia

---

[1] It is probable that Linnæus has included several species under the same name, and that this character is peculiar to the *lentiscus*.

[2] In the Levant the Arabs call them *egi, engi*, or *basengi*, and the Turks *badzenge*.

of brother Ange, of Toulouse, under the name of *schakar tigal*, which means *sugar of nests*.

It was at first supposed that the *trehala* was obtained from an onopordon. It was afterwards ascertained that it grows on the branches of a Syrian echinops. (Decaisne.) It is produced by an insect, and is found principally in the desert between Aleppo and Bagdad. (Bourlier.)

1. LARINUS.—This insect is neither a Cynips nor an Aphis, but a tetramerous Coleoptera belonging to the family Rhyncophora. It belongs to the genus Larinus, and has been named by M. Chevrolat *Larinus subrugosus*. It is closely allied to the *Larinus onopordonis*, Germ.

The *Larinus subrugosus* (fig. 46) is of an oblong form and of a black colour. It has a projecting snout, to the middle of which the antennæ are attached. The elytra cover the whole of the posterior part of the abdomen; they are oblong, and terminate each in a soft and slightly recurved point. Their surface is marked by ten punctated lines, which commence at the anterior margin and unite before reaching the opposite extremity.

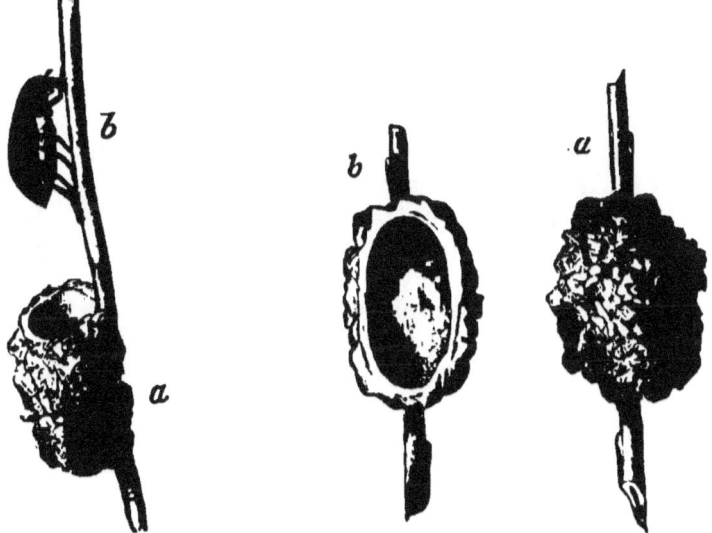

Fig. 46.—*Larinus of the Trehala.*[1]   Fig. 47.—*Trehala.*[2]

2. THE CASE (fig. 47).—This is of an oval form, and

[1] *a*, the case; *b*, *Larinus subrugosus* at the time of its escape.
[2] *a*, *trehala* before the escape of the insect; *b*, a vertical section of one of the cases.

attached in the direction of its length to a branch of the tree. Its greatest diameter measures from $\frac{6}{10}$ to $\frac{8}{10}$ of an inch in length; its external surface is very irregular, and of a light grey colour. The under surface is flattened and marked by a deep groove where it was attached to the branch. When separated a large circular hole is found at one extremity, by which the insect escaped.

The cavity of the *trehala* is large, and the perfect insect is often found in it just ready to escape.

The internal surface is smooth and of a whitish or reddish colour.

Its tissue is not very thick; it is irregular, hard, and has an amylaceous appearance. It cracks when bitten, has a sweet taste, and yields mucilage.

In water at the ordinary temperature the *trehala* swells, but only partially dissolves, and changes into a mucilaginous mass. Iodine changes it to a blue colour, and in some cases to that of red wine.

Analysis shows that it contains gum, a particular kind of starch which is much less soluble in water than that from the potato, and a new kind of crystallizable sugar, analogous to that from the sugar-cane, but much more solid; M. Berthelot has given this the name of *trehalose*.

It is during the larval stage of its existence that the *Larinus subrugosus* constructs this curious kind of case.

Does the *trehala* result solely from a wound inflicted by the insect? Is it an excrescence similar to the galls produced by the Cynipidæ, and to the cases of the Aphides? or is it a nest which is made by the *Larinus?* M. Guibourt admits the second mode as the way in which it is formed. A circumstance which supports this opinion is the fact that the *trehala* is not attached by a point or a pedicle like the galls, but is fixed along its whole length by the groove which embraces the point of support. It appears that the larva of the *Larinus* collects a considerable quantity of saccharine and amylaceous matter, which it procures from the echinops, and that it constructs its dwelling by disgorging this matter and moulding it with its rostrum.

M. Bourlier thinks that the formation of the sugar, which is found in the case, might be explained by the presence of albuminous matters in the saliva with which the insect binds together the starchy materials.

Brother Ange and M. Guibourt think that the nest serves the Larinus for a habitation during the whole of its life; I am, however, inclined to believe with M. Bourlier, that the insect emerges after it has assumed its perfect form. If it were otherwise, how could copulation take place, since each *case* contains only one individual? Moreover, most of the nests which I have examined were pierced at one end and were empty.

The *trehalas* are generally collected before the animal has escaped.

In Turkey and Syria a decoction is made of the nests of the *Larinus* by breaking up about an ounce of them, placing the pieces in a pint and a half of boiling water, and stirring them for a quarter of an hour. This preparation is given to persons in affections of the respiratory organs, particularly those who are attacked with bronchitis.

The *trehala* is also employed as food. The use of it is as universal in the East as that of salep and tapioca is in France.[1]

SECTION IV.

ANIMALS OR ANIMAL PRODUCTS EMPLOYED AS ACCESSORIES IN MEDICINE.

THERE are certain animal productions which are made use of rather as food than as remedies, and are interesting as a matter of hygiene rather than of therapeutics. It is true they sometimes enter into the formation of various medicines, but it is only as the medium through which the more active principles are administered; some of them are used merely to extract, clarify, or colour other medicines.

These substances may be arranged under twelve heads: 1st, *bones;* 2nd, *blood;* 3rd, *flesh;* 4th, *albumen;* 5th, *gelatine;* 6th, *fat;* 7th, *oil;* 8th, *milk;* 9th, *eggs;* 10th, *honey;* 11th, *wax;* 12th, the *hair*, and *other corneous parts.*

§ I. Bones.

Bones are employed in the manufacture of gelatine. There are two methods of extracting it. The first, which is the process of Papin, consists in breaking the bones in pieces and

---

[1] A closely allied insect, the *Larinus odontalgicus* of Dejean, out of which the genus *Rhinocellus* has been formed, has obtained a reputation as an odontalgic. (Gerbi, Latreille.) Some species of *Carabidæ*, *Chrysomelidæ*, and *Cochinellidæ* have been mentioned as possessing similar properties. (Caradori, Hirsch.)

boiling them at a temperature over 212° Fah.; this is done by placing them in an air-tight vessel termed a digester. [If such a vessel is half-filled with water and exposed to the heat of the fire, the steam which is formed has no means of escape, and therefore presses upon the water and prevents the further formation of steam till the temperature of the water rises above the boiling point]. In the second, the chondrin is first deprived of the phosphate and carbonate of lime by the action dilute hydrochloric acid, and is afterwards converted into gelatine by prolonged boiling under the ordinary pressure of the atmosphere. This method is not so good as the former.

When *bones* are calcined in closed vessels they leave a residuum of charcoal, and about seven tenths of their weight of calcareous salts. This charcoal is known as *animal charcoal* or *bone black*. It is impregnated with sulphuret of calcium, and empyreumatic matters, which enable it to decolorize liquids, but it imparts to them a disagreeable flavour. To deprive it of these matters, it must be acted on by hydrochloric acid, which not only frees it from all smell, but at the same time increases its decolorizing properties.

It is well known that animal charcoal is used for the purpose of decolouring various liquids, and especially syrups. M. Lebourdais has recently employed it in the extraction of the alkaloids.

The bones of the sheep are said to be more easily acted on by acids, and is therefore recommended for the preparation of phosphorus.

§ II. Blood.

The ancients recommended the use of the blood of animals, and even of man, in certain diseases. We have previously stated that the use of this fluid is entirely abandoned in the present day.[1]

The *blood* of the mammalia and of birds is eaten after it has been prepared in various ways, more particularly after it has been coagulated and mixed with spices.

Blood is employed in the preparing and clarifying syrups, by calcining it with the phosphate of lime, the chalk, and especially the potash of certain varieties of animal charcoal which possess decolorizing properties in an eminent degree.

Decomposed at a red heat with iron and carbonate of potash, *blood*, like all nitrogenous animal substances, produces ferrocyanuret of potassium.

[1] See page 63.

The serum of the *blood* has been largely employed in painting. (Carbonel.) Mixed with quick lime or with slacked lime reduced to powder, and to a suitable consistence, it forms a kind of glazing which resists the action of the sun and the rain.

[The *Animal Charcoal, Carbo animalis* of the Pharmacopœia, is directed to be prepared from bullock's blood by fire.

Transfusion.

The idea of injecting the blood of a living animal into the body of another appears to have been first suggested by a celebrated German chemist, Libavius, at the commencement of the 17th century. The operation was first actually performed in London by Lower on a dog in 1665, and for the first time on the human subject by a medical man in Paris of the name of Denis in 1667, the blood which he made use of being that of the sheep. Several fatal accidents having followed the operation, it was forbidden to be used in France by a decree of parliament, except by the previous permission of the faculty of medicine at Paris, and from that time it fell into disrepute. It was again brought into notice by Dr. Blundell in 1818, and a paper has recently been published by Dr. Waller[1] in the Transactions of the Obstetrical Society, advocating the use of Transfusion in certain cases of hæmorrhage.

It appears that in 1785 Dr. Harewood, afterwards professor of anatomy at Cambridge, drew attention in his "Thesis on Transfusion of Blood" to the value of this remedy in cases of hæmorrhage. He, however, asserted that the blood of an herbivorous animal might be substituted for that of a carnivorous animal, and *vice versâ*, without injury. Dr. Blundell,[2] on the contrary, maintained that the blood which is made use of must be from the same species of animal as that into which it is to be injected. Various experiments have now shown that this is the case, and that, although the injections of the blood of a different species may revive the animal for a time, it ultimately dies. This result may be accounted for by the difference which has been shown to exist in the size of the blood globules of different animals. Prevost and Dumas found that when the blood of the cow or the sheep was injected into cats or rabbits, the exsanguinated animals at first revived, but did not ultimately recover; the temperature of the body speedily diminished, the pulse became rapid, other fatal symptoms came on, and the animals died almost always before

[1] *Transactions of the Obstetrical Society of London*, 1859, vol. 1, p. 61.
[2] *Researches Physiological and Pathological*, 1824; see also *Medico-Chirurg. Trans.*, 1818, vol. 9, p. 56.

the sixth day. Blundell met with the same results from injecting human blood into the veins of a dog, while, on the other hand, he kept a dog alive for three weeks without food by the daily injection of a few ounces of the blood of one of its own species into the jugular veins. "Of all cases of hæmorrhage," says Dr. Waller, "none seem more favourable for a trial of this operation, than those which occur during the puerperal state, which from their severity are termed floodings." In performing the operation three things are necessary to be observed:—

First, that great care be taken to get rid of any air that may be contained in the syringe; secondly, to introduce the blood very slowly, experiments having proved that a sudden and large supply overwhelms the action of the heart, and causes immediate death; thirdly, to wait a few minutes between each injection. The syringe used by the author is lined with tin, and is capable of containing two ounces of fluid; it is furnished with a long tubule for the convenient injection into the vein; a funnel communicates with the barrel of the syringe, through which the blood passes without being received into an intermediate vessel.

It is seldom, if ever, necessary to inject a large quantity of blood: it is better to discontinue the operation as soon as the rally is decisive, and there is no returning collapse. In one case attended by the author, four ounces only were sufficient to produce this effect. As a general rule, from eight to twelve ounces may be safely injected].

§ III. Flesh.

The flesh of animals is of the utmost importance in hygieine and in medicine. It varies both as regards its nutritive properties and as to the easiness with which it is capable of being digested.

Meat contains a variable amount of:—1st, substances containing a proteine base (Albumen, fibrine, and caseine); 2nd, gelatine; 3rd, fatty matters; 4th, osmazome. Albumen, fibrine, and caseine are more or less easy of digestion, but have no great nutritive properties. Gelatine is a food which is easy of digestion, but neither has this much power of nutrition. Fatty substances are difficult of digestion and contain very little nutriment. Osmazome or extract of meat is a food easy of digestion and of excellent properties.

The meat which man makes use of may be arranged into seven principal groups:—1, *Meats properly so called;* 2, the *flesh of poultry;* 3, of *game;* 4, of *fish;* 5, of *Mollusca;* 6, of *Articulata;* 7, of *Radiata.* Those animals whose flesh is only eaten occasionally, and as it were exceptionally, have been omitted, as, for example, the *Turtles,* several large *Reptiles, Frogs,* and some *Insects.* Amongst these animals the principal are the *fresh* or *green Turtle, Chelonia Midas,* Latr., which is so common in certain portions of the Atlantic ocean, the *Iguanas* of the Antilles and Brazil, *Iguana delicatissima,* Laur., *tuberculata,* Laur., *cornuta,* Lacep., *cærulea,* Daud., and *fasciata,* Brongn., the *Basilisk* of the Moluccas, *Basilicus cristatus,* Bory, the migratory locust, *Gryllus migratorius, Ægyptius,* and *Tataricus,* Linn., &c.

1. *Meats properly so called,* or *butcher's meats,* are five in number, and stand in the following order as regards their capability of digestion:—1. *Mutton;* 2. *Beef;* 3. *Lamb;* 4. *Veal;* 5. *Pork.* The muscle or flesh of these animals contains in every 100 parts:

	Water.	Albumen.	Gelatine.
Mutton	71 parts.	22 parts.	7 parts.
Beef	74 —	26 —	6 —
Lamb	75 —	27 —	6 —
Veal	75 —	19 —	6 —
Pork	76 —	19 —	5 —

Very young animals yield a food which is easy of digestion, but which has little nutriment; this arises from their flesh containing a greater proportion of gelatine and fat, but less albumen, fibrine, and osmazome. Old animals yield the nutritive elements, but are difficult of digestion; their fibrine having become hard and dense, and their osmazome more abundant. The sucking pig is, however, less digestible than the mature animal, which is owing principally to the preponderance of the gelatine.

The part of the animal tissues, which is most easy of digestion and the most nutritious, is the muscular fibre or fibrine; after that the liver, kidney, pancreas, and brain; and lastly, the tendons, aponeuroses, and lungs.

[*Raw Meat.*—This was first recommended by Professor Weisse,[1] of St. Petersburgh, in the diarrhœa of children, which occurs during weaning. "Two teaspoonfuls," says Dr. Tanner,[2] " of finely chopped beef or mutton may be given daily to a child one year old: and if it crave for more, and evidence is afforded

---

[1] *Journal für Kinderkrankhecten,* herausgegeben von F. J. Behrend und A. Hildebrand, vol. 4, p. 99, Berlin, 1845.
[2] *Opus jam cit,* p. 345.

of its digestion, the quantity may be increased. It is very remarkable that debilitated children, who refuse all other kinds of food, will eagerly take this; but as the strength is regained the desire for it passes away."]

The quantity of meat consumed in France in 1830 has been estimated at 907,152,619 lbs. troy, of which 764,875,059 were furnished by the pig, ox, sheep, and goat (J. Reynaud); the names are arranged in the order of their importance.

[In London it is difficult to ascertain the quantity of meat, fish, and poultry which is brought for the supply of its two million and a half of inhabitants. The following calculations, which are taken from Dr. Wynter's interesting work, "Curiosities of Civilisation," can only be regarded as approximations to the truth; but in every case there is little doubt they are below the actual amount which is consumed.

According to the official account the number of live stock exhibited at Smithfield in 1853 was :—

Oxen, 294,571; sheep, 1,150,060; calves, 36,791; pigs, 29,593. Total, 1,893,888.

But this is far from giving a true idea of the whole amount brought into London. Much stock arrives in the capital which never enters the great mart. A more correct estimate of the flocks and herds which are annually consumed in London may be gathered from a report of the numbers transmitted by the different lines of railway, compiled from official sources by Mr. Ormanby, the cattle-traffic manager of the North Western Railway.

	Oxen.	Sheep.	Calves.	Pigs.	Total for 1853.
By Eastern Counties	81,744	277,735	3,492	23,427	386,398
,, L. & N. Western	70,435	248,445	5,113	24,287	348,280
,, Great Northern	15,439	120,333	563	8,973	145,308
,, Great Western	6,813	104,607	2,320	2,909	116,649
,, L. & S. Western	4,885	100,960	1,781	516	108,162
,, South Eastern	875	58,320	114	142	59,451
,, London & Brighton & S. Coast	863	13,690	117	54	14,724
,, Sea from North of England & Scotland	14,662	11,141	421	3,672	29,896
,, Sea from Ireland	2,311	3,472	21	5,476	11,280
Imported from the Continent	55,065	229,918	25,720	10,131	320,834
Driven in by road, and from the neighbourhood of the metropolis (obtained from the toll-gate lessees)	69,096	462,172	62,114	48,295	641,647
Total	322,188	1,630,793	101,776	127,852	2,182,609

The following table, obtained from the daily bills of entries at the Custom House, shows the continental sources from whence London derives a portion of its food.

From	Oxen.	Sheep.	Calves.	Pigs.	Total.
Holland	40,538	172,730	24,280	9,370	246,918
Denmark	9,687	7,515	60	..	17,062
Hanseatic Towns	4,366	37,443	1	632	42,442
Belgium	449	12,006	1,244	..	13,699
France	105	224	135	129	593
Portugal	100	..	..	..	100
Spain	17	..	..	..	17
Russia	3	..	..	..	3
Total	55,065	229,918	25,720	10,131	320,834

In addition to the live cattle which are thus brought to the London markets, there is a large quantity of country killed meat conveyed by the railways to the dead meat markets, the principal of which are Leadenhall and Newgate markets. According to the returns obtained from the different railway companies, the following was the weight of country killed meat conveyed by the undermentioned lines:—

Eastern Counties	10,398 tons.
North Western	4,602
Great Western	5,200
Great Northern	13,152
South-Eastern	1,035
South-Western	2,000
Brighton and South-Coast	100
	36,487

Thus no less than 36,487 tons of meat are annually "pitched" at Newgate and Leadenhall markets. As the Scotch boats convey about 700 tons more, there are at least 37,187 tons of country killed meat brought to London by steam.

Taking into account the quantity of meat derived from all sources, Dr. Wynter gives a summary of the grand total in the following table:—

	Beasts.	Sheep.	Calves.	Pigs.
Newgate meat	156,000	468,000	31,200	31,200
Leadenhall ditto	5,200	41,600	...	...
	161,200	509,600	31,200	31,200
Live stock brought to London	322,188	1,630,793	101,776	127,852
Total supply of live stock and meat to London	483,388	2,140,393	132,976	159,052

This, he says, he is convinced is still below the truth, for it does not include the country killed meat sold at Farringdon and Whitechapel markets. The total value of this enormous supply of flesh cannot be much less than fourteen millions annually.]

2. The *flesh of poultry* is obtained principally from four species, which stand in the following order as regards their easiness of digestion:—1, the *Fowl*; 2, the *Turkey*; 3, the *Duck*; and 4, the *Goose*.

These birds afford a fibre which has but little density, a very slight quantity of gelatine, and not much osmazome. Their flesh is easy of digestion. According to Brande 100 parts of the fowl yield 73 parts of water, 20 of albumen, and 7 of gelatine.

Like butcher's meat, the younger the animal the greater is the digestibility of these birds. Domestication generally renders the flesh tenderer, and more easily acted on by the gastric juice. When these birds are shut up and gorged they grow to a large size, and become charged with fat. Occasionally some of their organs, especially the liver, become hypertrophied (*Geese, Ducks*). The tissues are then more and more indigestible.

3. *Game.*—The principal species amongst the mammalia are the—1, *Goat, Cervus capreolus*, Linn.; 2, the *Hare, Lepus timidus*, Linn.; 3, the *Rabbit, Lepus cuniculus*, Linn.; and amongst the birds — 1, the *Partridge*;[1] 2, the *Pheasant, Phasianus Colchicus*, Linn.; 3, the *Grouse*;[2] 4, the *Pigeon*;[3] 5, the *Woodcock, Scolopax rusticola*, Linn.

The flesh of game is generally easy of digestion; but that of the birds with long beaks must be excepted; it contains very little gelatine or fat. To secure its being easily digested it must, however, be taken in moderate quantities.

In 1857 Paris alone consumed poultry and game to the value of 17,052,013 francs.

[The great emporiums for game and poultry in London are Leadenhall and Newgate markets. It is impossible to obtain anything like an acurate account of the quantity consumed in

---

[1] In France there are four species of Partridge: the *Common Partridge, Perdix cinerea*, Lath., the *Guernsey Partridge, P. sexatilis*, Mey., the *Red Partridge, P. rubra*, Briss., and the *Rock Partridge, P. petrosa*, Lath. The latter is of rare occurrence.

[2] In France there are three species of *Grouse*: the *Wood Grouse, Tetrao Urogallus*, Linn., the *Black Cock, T. tetrix*, Linn., and the *Common Grouse, T. lagopus*, Linn.

[3] In France there are four species of Pigeons: *Columba palumbus, C. Œnas, C. Livia*, and *C. Turtur.*

the metropolis. The following estimate was given to Dr. Wynter[1] by a dealer who turns over 100,000*l.* a year in this trade. As the list takes no account of the quantity which goes direct to the retailer, nor of the thousands sent as presents, it must fall short of the actual consumption.

Grouse	100,000
Partridges	125,000
Pheasants	70,000
Snipes	80,000
Wild Birds (mostly small)	150,000
Plovers	150,000
Quails	30,000
Larks	400,000
Widgeon	70,000
Teal	30,000
Wild Ducks	200,000
Pigeons	400,000
Domestic Fowls	2,000,000
Geese	100,000
Ducks	350,000
Turkeys	104,000
Hares	100,000
Rabbits	1,300,000
Total	5,759,000]

4. *Fish.*—Man uses a great number of fish as articles of food. Amongst these animals twelve principal species require to be mentioned; these are—1, Common *Whiting, Merlangus vulgaris,* Cuv.;[2] 2, the *Hake, Merlucius vulgaris,* Cuv.; 3, the *Cod, Morrhua vulgaris,* H. Cloq.; 4, the *Sole, Solea vulgaris,* Cuv.; 5, the *Plaice, Platessa vulgaris,* Cuv.; 6, the *Trout, Salar Ausonii,* Valenc., *Salmo fario,* Linn.; 7, the *Pike, Esox Lucius,* Linn.; 8, the *Carp, Cyprinus carpio,* Linn.; 9, the *Turbot, Rhombus maximus,* Cuv.;[3] 10, the *Salmon, Salmo Salmo,* Valenc.; 11, the *Mackerel, Scomber Scomberus,* Linn.; 12, the *Herring, Clupea harengus,* Linn.

According to Brande, 100 parts of haddock yield 82 parts of

---

[1] *Curiosities of Civilization,* by Andrew Wynter, M.D., p. 224, London, 1860.

[2] The *Coal Fish, M. Carbonarius,* Cuv., and the *Pollock, M. Pollachius,* are also used as food.

[3] The *Sole, Plaice,* and *Turbot* are commonly known as flat fish. Others of these fish which are eaten, are the *Brill, Rhombus vulgaris,* Cuv., and the *Flounder, Platessa Flesus,* Cuv.

water, 13 of albumen and fibrine, and 5 of gelatine; and the sole 79 parts of water, 5 of albumen and fibrine, and 6 of gelatine.

Placed according to their facility of digestion, fish might be arranged in the following manner: 1, Sea fish with white flesh; 2, Flat fish also with white flesh; 3, Fresh water fish; 4, Fish with red flesh.

The flesh of these animals usually contains less nourishment than that of the other vertebrata.[1]

5. *Flesh of Mollusca.*—Amongst these animals are—1, *Oysters;* 2, *Veneridæ;* 3, *Mussels;* 4, *Snails;* 5, *Various other fluviatile and marine species*. These animals are arranged in the order of their capacity for digestion.

The species of Oysters[2] which are eaten in France, on the Atlantic coasts, are the *Common Oyster, Ostrea edulis,* Linn.; and the *Horse Oyster, O. Hippopus,* Linn.; on the Mediterranean coasts, the *Mediterranean Oyster, O. rosacea,* Fav. non Desh., *O. Mediterranea* of *M. de Serres,* and the *O. lacteola* of Moquin Tandon. In Corsica is eaten the *O. lamellosa,* Brocchi. There is also found in the Mediterranean the *crested oyster, O. cristata,* Born, and the plicated oyster, *O. plicata,* Chemn.

Under the name of the *Common Oyster* are included several varieties; for those of *Cancale* of *Marennes,* and of *Ostend,* are altogether different from each other.

At Rome the *Oysters* from the Lucrin lake were held in high estimation (*nobilissimus cibus*). Nero preferred those from Corsica. Naples obtains *Oysters* from the lake Fusaro, which enjoy a certain reputation. (Coste.) Excellent *Oysters* are found in Algeria, near Bone. Those from the coast of Languedoc are of an inferior quality. At Paris and in the north of France there is an enormous consumption of *Oysters* from *Marennes, Cancale,* and *Ostend.*

Fresh *Oysters* are easy of digestion provided they are not eaten in too large quantities. Their capability of digestion is owing to the salt water they contain and to the bile which is present in their largely developed liver.

Oysters are generally eaten entire and while they are still alive.[3] Some persons reject the beard and fringes of the mantle in the larger varieties, and eat only the central portion.

Raw *Oysters* are a delicate, savoury, and strengthening kind

---

[1] In 1857 Paris alone consumed fish to the value of 9,169,547 francs.
[2] See page 86.
[3] *Vivæ epulæ,* Linn.

of food. Adolphe Pasquier and Sainte Marie have recommended them as remedies. They are suitable in dyspepsia and in chronic affections of the digestive organs, and even in diseases of the chest. They are often recommended to the convalescent.

Cooked *Oysters* are indigestible.

Ostreaculture.—The artificial production of *Oysters* has become an important branch of industry.[1] As far back as the time of Rondelet, the art of *sowing* these molluscs was known. In the present day this art has become greatly developed, and the multiplication of these animals is carried on on a large scale. The natural banks are divided into several portions, which are successively fished, and then allowed to repose for some time, in order that the animals may be replenished. Means are also taken to favour and hasten this process. Besides this, artificial banks are formed, which, like the natural banks, are divided into separate portions.

The *Oysters* are placed in large reservoirs, where they grow and become of a green colour; this is called *bedding the Oysters*. At Marennes these reservoirs are termed *claires*. They are like a number of fields, which have been inundated, placed along the banks of the Seudre; they differ, however, from the ordinary beds or reservoirs, inasmuch as they are not covered by the tides. (Coste.) An oyster, six to eight months old, when placed in the *claires*, requires two years before it arrives at its proper size and condition. By far the greater portion of those which are eaten never arrive at this state. The full-grown oyster when placed in the reservoirs becomes of a green colour in a few days. (Coste.)

The green colour of the Oyster does not affect the whole of the animal. It shows itself more particularly on the four branchial folds; there are also traces of it on the inner surface of the first pair of labial palpi, on the external surface of the second, and in a part of the alimentary canal.

For a long time it was supposed that the green colour of the Oysters was owing to the soil of the reservoirs, to the decomposition of the ulva and other water plants, or to a diseased condition of the liver, a kind of jaundice, which imparted a green colour to the parenchyma of the breathing organs. Gaillon asserted that it arose from one of the naviculæ, *Vibrio ostrearius*, which penetrated the substance of the animal. Bory de Saint-Vincent proved that this vibrio was not naturally of a green colour, but, that under certain circumstances,

[1] In 1857 Paris consumed 2,033,379 francs worth of oysters.

it became coloured like the Oyster, and by the same means. According to this naturalist, the green colour depends upon a molecular substance (the *green matter* of Priestley), which becomes developed in all waters under the influence of light. According to M. Valenciennes, this colour is caused by a peculiar animal production differing from every organic substance which has hitherto been examined. M. Berthelot has analyzed this substance, and finds that it does possess peculiar characters. It does not resemble either the colouring agent of the bile, of the blood, or of any of the ordinary organic colouring substances.

These green molecules enter the branchiæ during the act of respiration, where they become arrested, and ultimately gorge, obstruct, and colour the organ. At the same time, one of the principal functions of the body being interfered with, the animal becomes distended and subject to a kind of anasarca, which renders its tissues more tender and more delicate.[1]

[The London market[2] is principally supplied with *Oysters* from beds at Whitstable, Rochester, Milton, Colchester, Burnham, Faversham, and Queenborough, all artificial beds, furnishing *natives*. Those of the river Crouch, or Burnham oysters, are pre-eminent for their marine flavour; probably on account of the facilities for rapid importation of them in fine condition. Besides these, considerable quantities of sea oysters, or those which grow upon natural beds, and which are sometimes called rock oysters, are brought from various parts of the coast. The sea oyster is often, before being brought to market, kept for a time in artificial beds to improve its flavour. Much of the quality depends on the ground and condition of the beds, and oysters of different years from the same place often vary materially in this respect. They are considered full grown for the market when from five to seven years old; sea oysters at four years. The age is shown by the annual layers of growth or shoots on the convex valve. Up to three or four years, each annual growth is easily observed, but after their maturity it is not so easy to count the layers. Aged oysters become very thick in the shell. In the neighbourhood of fresh water the oyster grows fast, and improves in body and flavour.

In London the chief consumption of the common or rock oyster is from the 4th of August to January, and of natives

---

[1] See p. 86.
[2] *A History of British Mollusca and their Shells*, by Edward Forbes and Silvanus Hanley, vol. 2, pp. 313—319, London, 1853.

from October to March. The consumption is said to be greatest in the hottest months after the commencement of the oyster season; the warmer the weather, the more oysters are consumed. They are brought to market in craft of various sizes; they are packed in bulk closely in the hold; in some cases a cask of salt water is kept, from which to sprinkle them superficially. Those that come by rail are packed with their convex shells downwards, in bags and barrels. From the boats they are transferred to the salesmen, who keep them in a little salt and spring water, and shift them every twelve hours. Some pretend to improve them by "feeding" them with oatmeal. Oysters, like other bivalves, live chiefly on infusoria. The quantity consumed annually in London varies in different seasons. One informant states twenty thousand bushels of natives, one hundred thousand bushels of common oysters, to be about the mark; another estimates the quantity sold in the season, from the 4th of August to the 12th of May, to be nearly one hundred thousand London bushels, each bushel being three Manchester or imperial bushels; and that about thirty thousand bushels of natives are sold during the same period by various companies. During the season commencing on August the 4th, 1848, and ending May 12th, 1849, M. Wickenden estimates about one hundred and thirty thousand bushels of oysters to have been sold in London, though of that quantity about one fourth was sent away to various parts of the United Kingdom and the Continent.

Oysters of good repute are fished in the neighbourhood of the Channel Islands. There are two oyster-banks, the one off Guernsey, and the other off Jersey. The former is of little importance; the latter of considerable value. They belong to the region of oyster-banks, which extends along the coasts of Normandy and Brittany. Dr. Knapp states that the number annually procured here for the use of the Channel Islands and English markets cannot be less than eight hundred thousand tubs, each tub containing two English bushels; and in some years thrice that quantity is believed to be procured from those banks during the season. As many as three hundred cutters have been employed upon them dredging. The oysters, on the Jersey bank, are of large size, and are sold at from five to seven shillings the tub, or from three to four pence per dozen.

The oyster-fishery of most consequence in Scotland is that of the Frith of Forth. The oyster beds there extend about twenty miles, from the Island of Mucra to Lockenzie, and are dredged in from four to six or seven fathoms water. The price varies, wholesale (1853), from two shillings to two shillings and sixpence the hundred; the retail price from two and sixpence to four shillings and sixpence, or even five shillings. Mr. George Moffat, fish dealer in Edinburgh, estimates the number of oysters dredged in the Forth in the season at 2,027,520; only three fourth parts of which, however, it is believed, are sent to Edinburgh, being 1,520,640. The same gentleman has calculated that 7,346 oysters are daily consumed in Edinburgh during the season, from the beginning of September till the end of April.

On both sides of Ireland oysters abound in many places. There are oyster beds in the Shannon, said, in 1836, to yield a revenue of 1,400*l.* annually, and to employ seventy men and sixteen boats.]

The *Veneridæ* and the *Mytilidæ* are far from being held in such repute as *Oysters*. These mollusca are eaten both raw and cooked.

The *Veneridæ* are collected in considerable quantities, and are eaten by the poorer classes.

It is principally two species which are fished: the *Venus virginea*, Linn., and the *Venus decussata*, Linn., which is somewhat smaller than the former.

The *Common Mussel*, *Mytilus edulis*, are sought after in many countries. An apothecary of Orleans has published a work on the employment of these mollusca in affections of the air passages.

Other salt and fresh water bivalves are eaten, as the *Clams, Razor-fishes, Scollops, Cockles, &c.*

[In England the *common Mussel*[1] is much used in many places for food, and still more for bait. Dr. Knapp, of Edinburgh, has given a very interesting account of the quantities of this animal destroyed annually in the neighbourhood of that city. "As an article of food," he states these cannot be used fewer than ten bushels per week in Edinburgh and Leith, say for forty weeks in the year, in all 400 bushels annually. Each bushel of mussels, when shelled and freed from all refuse, will probably contain from three to four pints of the animals, or about 900 or 1000, according to their size. Taking the latter number, there will be consumed in Edinburgh and Leith about 400,000 mussels. This is a mere trifle compared to the enormous number used as bait for all sorts of

---

[1] Forbes and Hanley, *Opus cit*, vol. 2, p. 174.

fish, especially haddocks, cod, ling, halibut, plaice, skate, whiting, &c. In Newhaven alone there are four large deep-sea fishing boats, which generally go out three times a week, and fish for about thirty weeks in the year, excluding Sundays and bad weather. Each of these boats carries eight men, with eight lines of 800 yards in length, which, at a low calculation, take 1200 mussels to bait each time they are used; so that each boat will use 28,800 mussels per week, equal to 864,000 per annum. There are sixteen smaller boats, whose consumption of mussels comes to 3,456,000. The total consumption of mussels for bait annually in Newhaven alone may be reckoned at 4,320,000. At all the other fishing stations in this district a similar use is made of these abundant and prolific shell-fish, so that Dr. Knapp calculates that thirty or forty millions are used for bait alone by the fishermen of this district each year. The best mussels at Newhaven are fished in three fathoms of water, and are sold at 8*d*. per basket, each containing nearly a bushel. Supposing each bushel contained 1000 mussels, this quantity would be worth more than 1300*l*.

The *common Cockle* is a species of shell-fish held in little or no estimation by the rich, but to the poor it is in some parts almost a necessary of life, and in others it affords them a cheap and palatable luxury.

The following remarks are taken from the authors already quoted:

The *edible Cockle, Cardium edule,* inhabits most parts of the British coast, especially where there are large tracts of sand. The variety most common in our markets rarely exceeds an inch and four-fifths in length by an inch and a half in breadth, and comes in most instances from estuary sands. Everywhere this excellent mollusk is sought after for food, and it is one of the most savoury of its tribe; indeed, preferred by many persons to the oyster. It is equally good raw and cooked, dressed either by roasting or boiling, and gives a delicious flavour to fish sauce. In times of scarcity *Cockles* have afforded valuable supplies of food for the poor, and in the Zetland isles bushels of their shells may be seen near cottages. Lieut. Thomas informs us that in Sanda, among the Orkney isles, during the late failure of the potato crop many of the poorer people subsisted almost entirely on *Cockles*.

The following estimate of the quantity of fish of all kinds which are brought to the London market, is quoted from Mr. Mayhew's "London Labour and London Poor" by Dr. Wynter,[1]

---

[1] *Opus cit*, p. 212.

who remarks upon it, that the figures seemed to him to be so enormous, that he hesitatingly submitted the table to one of the largest salesmen, who assured him that it was no overstatement.

Description of Fish.	No. of Fish.	Weight of Fish.
WET FISH.		
Salmon and Salmon Trout (29,000 boxes, 14 fish per box)	406,000	3,480,000
Live Cod (averaging 10lbs. each)	400,000	4,000,000
Soles (averaging ¼lb. each)	97,520,000	26,880,000
Whiting (averaging 6oz. each)	17,920,000	6,720,000
Haddock (averaging 2lbs. each)	2,470,000	5,040,000
Plaice (averaging 1lb. each)	33,600,000	33,600,000
Mackerel (averaging 1lb. each)	23,520,000	23,520,000
Fresh Herrings (250,000 barrels, 700 fish per barrel)	175,000,000	42,000,000
Ditto in bulk	1,050,000,000	252,000,000
Sprats	...	4,000,000
Eels from Holland (principally), England, and Ireland (6 fish per lb.)	9,797,760	1,505,280 / 127,680
Flounders (7200 qrtns. 36 fish per qrtn.)	259,200	43,200
Dabs (7500 qrtns. 36 fish per qrtn.)	270,000	48,750
DRY FISH.		
Barrelled Cod (15,000 barrels, 40 fish per barrel)	750,000	4,200,000
Dried Salt Cod (5lbs. each)	1,600,000	8,000,000
Smoked Haddock (65,000 barrels, 300 fish per barrel)	19,500,000	10,920,000
Bloaters (265,000 barrels, 150 fish per barrel)	147,000,000	10,600,000
Red Herrings (100,000 barrels, 500 fish per barrel)	50,000,000	14,000,000
Dried Sprats (9,600 large bundles, 30 fish per bundle)	288,000	96,000
SHELL FISH.		
Oysters	495,896,000	...
Lobsters (averaging 1lb. each fish)	1,200,000	1,200,000
Crabs (averaging 1lb. each fish)	600,000	...
Shrimps (326 to a pint)	498,428,648	...
Wilks (227 to half bushel)	4,943,200	...
Mussels (1000 to half bushel)	50,400,000	...
Cockles (2000 to half bushel)	67,392,000	...
Periwinkles (4000 to half bushel)	304,000,000	...

The species of *Snails* which are sought for in France are, in the North, the *Edible snail, Helix Pomatia* (fig. 48); the *Wood snail, H. Sylvatica*, Drap.; and the *Grove Snail, H. nemoralis*, Linn. At Montpellier, the *common snail, H. aspersa*, Mull.;

the *H. vermiculata*, Mull.; the *H. Pisana*, Mull.; and even the *H. variabilis*, Drap. In the department of the Vaucluse, the

Fig. 48.— *Helix pomatia*.[1]

H. aspersa, H. vermiculata, H. Pisana, H. variabilis, the Heath snail, *H. ericetorum*, and sometimes the *H. Algira*, Linn. In Provence, the species just enumerated, and in addition *H. aperta*, Born, and *H. melanostoma*, Drap. In certain localities the *Helix cespitum* and *H. lineata* are also eaten; and in others the *H. hortensis*, Mull., and *H. arbustorum*, Linn., or *Shrub snail*.

All these snails do not produce exactly the same kind of flesh. Epicures set great store by the *Helix vermiculata*, which is known at Montpellier by the name of the *Morgueta* (modest), because it draws itself far into its shell. The *H. natica* is considered still more tender and delicate; it is called in Provence *Tapáda* (closed), on account of the calcareous lid which closes up the shell. The species which is hardest is the *Helix pomatia*.

Snails are principally collected towards the close of winter, before they have taken fresh food. It is said that those individuals which inhabit elevated situations are the best; it is also asserted that the animals retain the flavour and perfume of the plants they have eaten. This is, no doubt, the reason why the Snails of certain countries, or of certain districts, are held in high repute.

The flesh of *Snails* is generally tough and insipid. It is necessary to prepare them with strong seasonings, as with plenty of ham, anchovies, parsley, aromatic herbs, pepper, or garlic. It is moreover a kind of food which digests but slowly.

[1] The animal extended, with a separate view of the jaw.

At various periods considerable pains have been taken to obtain these mollusks in large quantities.

The Romans kept them in pens called *cochlearia*. (Varron.)[1] They were fattened with various plants. A small quantity of wine and some laurel leaves were added to give them a better flavour. The pens were situated in moist shady places, and were surrounded by a ditch or wall. Pliny has not forgotten to transmit to us the name of the person who invented the *cochlearia*.[2] Addison has given a full description of that of the capuchin monks at Fribourg.

Besides these, many of the marine Gasteropods are eaten, as, for instance, some of the *Murecidæ, Turbos, Littorinidæ, Buccinidæ, Strombidæ,* and *Patellidæ.*

6. *Flesh of Articulata.*—Amongst these animals is the *Cray-fish, Astacus fluviatiles;*[3] 2, the *Prawn, Palæmon serratus;* 3, the *Common spiny Lobster, Palinurus vulgaris;* 4, the *Lobster, Homarus vulgaris;* 5, the *Common shore Crab, Carcinus Mœnas.*

The flesh of all these animals is hard and fibrous, and is apt to resist the action of the gastric juice. Nevertheless, that of the *Cray-fish* is not very difficult of digestion; but the other species, especially the Lobsters and the Crabs, are frequent sources of indigestion.

[Enormous quantities of Lobsters are consumed in London; they are taken on various parts of the English coast, particularly on rocky shores. From the southern and western coasts a considerable number are constantly sent off to the London markets, by the South-Western Railway from Southampton, and by the Great Western from Bristol; also by steamers from Guernsey and Jersey; and again from the coast of Ireland to Liverpool. From the coast of Scotland, the Orkney and Lewes islands, it is computed that not less than 150,000 reach the market at Billingsgate; but the principal supply is from Norway, from whence there is sent not less than 600,000. There is often in the season a supply at Billingsgate of not less than from 20,000 to 25,000 lobsters in one day].[4]

7. *The flesh of Radiata.*—Amongst this group are several species of the Sea Hedge-hog. The inhabitants of Provence and of Languedoc are fond of the *Echinus esculentus,* Linn.; *E. lividus,* Deslong.; and *E. granularis,* Lamk. The latter

---

[1] *Cochlearium vivaria* (Pliny).
[2] He calls him *Fulvius Hispinus.*
[3] See p. 96, M. Lereboullet has recently described two new species, *A. longicornis* and *A. pallipes.*
[4] *A History of British Crustacea,* by Thos. Bell, p. 243, London, 1848.

species is also procured on the coasts of Naples and La Manche. In Corsica and Algeria the *Echinus melo*, Lamk., is made use of. Some species of Holothuria are also eaten at Naples, the *Holothuria tubulosa*, Blainv.; at the Ladrone islands, the *H. Guamensis*, Quoy and Gaim; and in China, the *Trepang, H. edulis*, Less.

BROTH.—The flesh of animals serves for the preparation of *broths*, a liquid and very nourishing kind of food, which is extremely useful both to the invalid and to the convalescent.

Broth is an aqueous solution, the base of which consists of some kind of flesh; it is made by boiling the meat for a long time over a slow fire. *Broth* always contains gelatine, fat, and osmazome. Some vegetables, such as carrots, turnips, or lettuces, are generally added, which somewhat alter its composition. The broth which is principally used is made from Beef. The more this kind of food is concentrated the greater is the amount of nourishment which it contains; 220 lbs. of meat will yield two hundred basins of broth of more than half a pint each, or altogether 176 pints of broth, and 110 lbs. of the boiled meat.

Broth is also made from bones, to which a small quantity of meat is added and a large quantity of vegetables. The quantity procured from the bones is to that which is obtained from meat as 3 to 2. One hundred pounds of meat, of which a quarter is employed to make broth, with two pounds and a quarter of gelatine obtained from bones, will give two hundred basins of broth and eleven pounds of boiled meat; while the remainder would furnish forty-four pounds of roast meat.

[In cases of irritable stomach, where the ordinary kinds of food cannot be retained, as, for instance, in the obstinate nausea and vomiting which sometimes accompany pregnancy, a preparation known under the name of *Liebig's New Soup for Invalids* is recommended as being often tolerated when every other kind of food is rejected. It is made as follows:—

Take $\frac{1}{2}$ lb. of newly killed beef or fowl, chop it very fine, add $1\frac{1}{2}$ lb. of distilled water, four drops of pure muriatic acid, 34 to 67 grains of common salt, and stir well together. After an hour the whole is to be thrown on a conical hair sieve, and the fluid allowed to pass through without any pressure. The first thick portions which run through are to be returned to the sieve, until the fluid filters through quite clear. On the flesh residue in the sieve pour slowly $\frac{1}{2}$ lb. of distilled water, and let it percolate through. There will be thus obtained rather more than a pound of cold fluid (cold extract of flesh) of a red colour, and possessing a pleasant taste of soup; of which from one tablespoonful to a cup may be taken at pleasure. It must not be warmed, since it is rendered muddy by heat, and deposits a thick coagulum of albumen and the colouring matter of blood. When the flavour is thought disagreeable it may be concealed by the addition of a little claret].[1]

There are several other kinds of *broth* which are occasionally made use of; these are:—

1. *Veal broth.*—This contains only a small quantity of gelatine, of fat, and of osmazome, and is not very nourishing. It is employed as a drink rather than as food. When much diluted it constitutes *Veal water*. A broth is also prepared from the lungs of the calf.

2. *Chicken broth.*—This contains gelatine, a small quantity of fat and of osmazome. It is still lighter and less nourishing food than the preceding.

3. *Tortoise broth* is prepared rom the flesh of the *Testudo Græca*, Linn., of the *T. Mauritanica*, Dumer, and of the *T. marginata*, Schœpf. These species are terrestrial, and common in Algeria; the third is also found in the Morea. Some of the fresh water tortoises may be substituted for them, such as *yellow Tortoise*, *Testudo Europœa*, Gray, from the south of Europe, or the *Emys Caspica*, Schw., and the *E. Sigris*, Dumer; the one inhabits the eastern parts of Europe, and the other Spain and Algeria.

4. *Viper broth*, *Vipera Aspis*, Merrem, is made from the animal after the head, skin, and intestines have been removed. This broth was formerly regarded as a powerful remedy in obstinate gonorrhœa, and as capable of restoring the powers of the body when they have been exhausted by excess. It is nearly banished from the list of materia medica.

5. *Frog broth.*—This contains gelatine and a small quantity of osmazome. It is insipid, and has very little nutriment. It is considered to be a cooling diet: it is made from the green or common Frog, *Rana esculenta*, Linn., and also from the *Rana temporaria*, Linn.: 125 grammes or 1928 grains of frog's thighs are put into 500 grammes or four times the same quantity of water.

[The common Frog of this country is the Rana temporaria: the R. esculenta, or edible Frog, does not exist in England.]

[1] *On the Signs and Diseases of Pregnancy*, p. 392, by T. H. Tanner, M.D., London, 1860.

6. *Snail broth.*—This is even less nourishing than the last. In the north of France it is made from the large *Helix pomatia;* in the south from *H. aspersa* and *vermiculata ;*[1] in the Isle of France the *Navicella elliptica,* Lamk., is made use of for this purpose.

7. *Oyster broth.*—This is regarded as a restorative and an aphrodisiac.[2]

8. *Cray-fish broth.*—This also ranks as a restorative, and was formerly recommended in phthisis, in leprosy, and other cutaneous affections.[3]

§ IV. Albumen.

Albumen is a colourless, inodorous, and tasteless substance, which is coagulated by heat. This coagulation commences at a temperature of 104° Fah., but it is not complete except at a temperature of from 140° to 158°. When its solution is extremely diluted, heat does not thicken it; but by boiling and evaporating it in *vacuo* a residue is obtained of insoluble *albumen.* Alcohol precipitates *albumen* from its solutions. If water is poured upon the precipitate, a portion of it is redissolved; another portion is converted into coagulated *albumen.* The latter contains all the properties of fluid *albumen,* except its solubility. *Albumen* contains a small quantity of sulphur and of phosphorus.

It is very useful in the treatment of the first stage of poisoning from the salts of copper and of mercury. Mixed with a large quantity of water it is successfully employed as an emollient. Some practitioners have recommended it in the treatment of certain cases of yellow fever. Mixed with oil it is stated to relieve the pain in parts which have been burnt; it has also been administered in diseases of the eyes. In some cases of fracture the limb is surrounded by lint bandages soaked in *albumen;* it has been used as a dressing for slight excoriations of the skin. It is, however, principally employed for clarifying wine, beer, and vegetable juices. Its nutrient properties, either alone or in combination with other animal principles, have been previously noticed.[4]

§ V. Gelatine.

This substance is obtained by boiling the skin, ligaments, tendons, membranes, cellular tissue, or bones of animals in

---

[1] See pages 83, 174.
[2] See pages 86, 168.
[3] See page 96.
[4] See page 162.

water.[1] It is first obtained in solution by evaporation; it is then concentrated, and as it cools it forms a tremulous jelly, and becomes *gelatine*.

A question arises as to whether *gelatine* exists ready formed in the animal structures which yield it, or whether the composition of these structures is changed by the action of the boiling water? The latter opinion appears to be the most probable; but the alteration is a simple molecular movement, for the composition of *gelatine* is the same as that of the tissue from which it is derived.

Pure *gelatine* is solid, but its hardness and consistence vary greatly; it is heavier than water, semi-transparent, colourless, inodorous, and tasteless. It possesses great adhesive properties, and it is from this substance that common glue, Flanders glue,[2] mouth glue, and food lozenges are made.

Gelatine is only slightly soluble in cold water, but readily dissolves in boiling water. In order that a hot solution should form a jelly in cooling, it must contain at least $2\frac{1}{2}$ parts of gelatine to every 100 of water. If it is boiled too long a certain quantity of water becomes united with the gelatine, which in consequence is changed, and will no longer form a jelly.

Gelatine is partially soluble in dilute, but not in strong alcohol; it is precipitated by tannin.

Ligaments and tendons by boiling yield a kind of *gelatine*, to which Mudler has given the name of *chondrin*. It differs principally from ordinary *gelatine* in not being precipitated by tannin.

It is chiefly the mammalia which furnish the *gelatine* of commerce and of pharmacy.

The purest *gelatine* is known under the name of *grenetine* [from *Grenet*, the name of the maker]; it is more especially employed in pharmaceutical preparations.

STAG'S HORN (*cornu Cervi*).—During the summer the fur of the *common Stag* is of a yellowish brown colour, with a black line along the back, while the sides of the animal are marked with numerous pale spots. In winter time it is of a uniform greyish brown colour. The rump, the buttocks, and the tail are always of a pale reddish colour. The head of the *Stag* is provided with horns, which were formerly used in the manufacture of medicated jellies and of emollient drinks. The horns are shed every year during the spring and are

[1] See page 159.
[[2] This is a very pure kind of glue, made from young animals.]

re-produced in the summer. At first the new horns are simple protuberances, and are known by the name of *dags*, but as they grow they branch into a number of projections termed *antlers*. The extremities of the antlers are known in pharmacy as horn tips. In the fourth year the horn terminates in an expansion termed the *palm*, which is provided with a number of points. The *burr* is a rough channelled projection at the base of the horn. The female of the *Stag* or *Hind* has no horns.

The horn tips are divided into small fragments by means of a knife or a file. They are then boiled for some time in water, to which they give up their gelatinous principle. Isinglass is now generally substituted for Stag's horn.

Besides gelatine, Stag's horn furnished several other preparations, which are now rarely made use of. These were:— 1. *Volatile essence of Stag's horn*, which is only an oleaginous subcarbonate of ammonia. 2. *Volatile oil of Stag's horn;* this is very similar to Dippel's animal oil, and consists essentially of subcarbonate of ammonia.

Stags' horns were also calcined (*cornu ustum*), ground up, and made into lozenges.

[A preparation of this kind is still retained in the Pharmacopœia.

CORNU USTUM, *Burnt horn*.—Burn pieces of horns in an open vessel until they become perfectly white; then powder and prepare them in the same manner as directed with respect to chalk.

In the older editions of the Pharmacopœia this preparation was termed *Cornu Cervi ustum* and *Cornu Cervi calcinatum*, and was accordingly directed to be made from Stags' horns.

This substance is sometimes used in the manufacture of tooth powder; it contains a large quantity of phosphate and a small quantity of carbonate of lime; it can only act mechanically as a fine powder, and is in no respect superior to the common prepared chalk.]

The same uses were formerly made of the horns of the Elk, *C. Alces*, Linn.; the Fallow Deer, *C. Dama*, Linn.; and of the Rein Deer, *C. Tarandus*, Linn.

ISINGLASS.—*Isinglass* or *Fish glue* is the prepared air bladder or swimming bladder of the *Sturgeon*. The *Sturgeons* (*Acipenser*) belong to the cartilaginous fishes and to the family *Sturionidæ*.

The flesh of these animals is held in high estimation. Their fecundity is extraordinary; a single female has been known to contain 1,467,857 eggs. When these masses of eggs or ovaries are salted, they form the article of food known as *caviare*.

The species from which *isinglass* is principally procured is the *Huso* or *Great Sturgeon*. It is also obtained from the *Sewruga*, the *Sterlet*, and the *Sturio* or *common Sturgeon*. The following is a summary of the characters of these four species:

The lips {entire Snout {short . . . . *The Huso.*
long {straight and narrow . *The Sewruga.*
curved and broad . . *The Sterlet.*
cleft . . . . *The Sturio.*

The *Huso*, *Acipenser Huso*, Linn., inhabits the tributary streams of the Caspian and Black seas. It is sometimes procured in the Po.

The back is of a dark blue, almost black colour, and the belly of a clear yellow; the body is long, the head large, and the snout very obtuse. It is from 10 ft. to 16 ft. long, and weighs upwards of 200 lbs.; it has been known to measure as much as 30 ft., and to exceed 2000 lbs. in weight.

The *Sewruga*, *A. stellatus*, Pallas, inhabits the rivers which empty themselves into the Black and Caspian seas, particularly the Volga and the Danube.

The back is of a brown colour, and the belly white. It is seldom more than 3½ ft. in length.

The *Sterlet*, *A. Ruthenus*, Linn., is found in the Caspian sea, in the Volga and the Ural.

It is distinguished by the black colour of its back, by its yellow plates, and by its white belly shaded with pink; its upper and caudal fins are grey, and the lower red. The plates which cover the body are arranged in three rows.

It is of the same size as the previous species; it is very rare to meet with individuals 4½ ft. in length. Its weight is from 30 lbs. to 37 lbs.

The *Common Sturgeon*, *A. Sturio*, Linn. (fig. 49).—This species is found in various parts of the ocean, in the Mediterranean, the Red, the Euxine, and the Caspian seas.

In the summer time it ascends the great rivers, particularly the Volga, the Danube, the Po, the Garonne, the Loire, the Rhine, &c. (Lacèpede.)

[This species has been caught in the river Thames.]

The plates on the body are arranged in five longitudinal rows. Individuals are commonly met with varying from 13 ft. to 16 ft. in length. One which was captured in the Loire, and presented to Francis I., measured nearly 20 ft.; some are said to have measured 25 ft.

GELATINE. 183

In the preparation of *isinglass*, the air bladder of the *Sturgeon* is first well cleaned, stripped of its external membrane, which is of a dark brown colour, and freed from all the blood which it contains. It is then split open longitudinally,

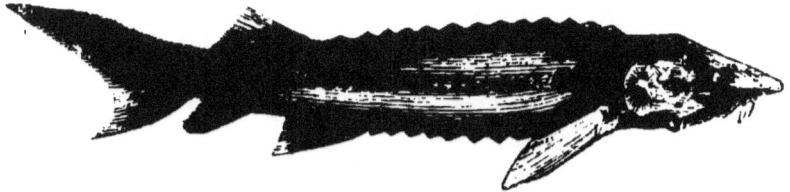

Fig. 49.—*Common Sturgeon.*

cut up into pieces, washed, kneaded by the hands, made up into different forms, and afterwards left to dry gradually in the shade.

Four kinds of raw *isinglass* are known in commerce: 1. *Lyre Isinglass* [*long* and *short staple* of English market]. This consists of small cylinders folded upon themselves so as to bear a rude resemblance to an ancient lyre. 2. *Heart-shaped isinglass* [also known as *long* and short *staple*]. This only differs from the former as to the manner in which the cylinders are folded. 3. *Book isinglass.* This consists of layers folded into squares and joined together by means of a steel which passes through them. 4. *Leaf* isinglass, which only differs from the former in the folds being separate. The first is the purest and the most valuable.

Isinglass is also sold in the form of *tablets*. This is of less value than the other kinds, and is made by boiling the fins, heads, and other parts of the Sturgeon, and then spreading them out on boards.

Isinglass is bleached by means of sulphurous acid. When cut up into long strips, a very excellent kind of fish-glue is made from it, which is known as *English* glue.

From purified isinglass is also formed another kind of fish-glue, known as glass glue or vitreous glue (*vitreuse*).

It is calculated that 1000 large Sturgeons yield 264 lbs. of isinglass, which is about 4 oz. 3½ dr. for each individual. The Sterlets would not produce more than 80 lbs., which is about one-third of the former quantity.

Isinglass is principally obtained from the parts of Russia on the borders of the Caspian Sea. The Dutch were formerly largely engaged in this kind of manufacture, but the article was of an inferior quality.

Isinglass is almost entirely composed of an animal substance which is readily converted into gelatine.

Isinglass is light, coriaceous, of a whitish colour, semi-transparent, and bears some resemblance to parchment; it is tasteless, inodorous, and insoluble in cold water, but dissolves in boiling water, and forms a transparent jelly in cooling. Fifteen grains of *isinglass* are sufficient to impart a firm consistence to an ounce of water.

Besides the various species of *Sturgeon*, *isinglass* may be obtained from the air bladder of several other fish, as this organ always contains a large quantity of gelatine; but this kind of isinglass is of an inferior quality to that from the *Sturgeon*. Thus it is obtained from some of the *Siluridæ*; and at Lyons a very transparent vitreous-like *isinglass* is made from the scales of the *Carp*.

An inferior kind of *isinglass* is known in commerce, which is made from the air bladder of the *Cod*, and also a false isinglass manufactured from the stomach of the calf. Pereira has described a kind of *false isinglass from Para*, which is nothing more than the ovary of some large fish, probably, he says, of the *Sudis Gigas*.

Isinglass is used for the purpose of clarifying numerous liquids. [*Court* or *Black sticking Plaster* is made with a solution of isinglass and tincture of benzoin laid upon black sarsenet.]

It is employed in the making of jellies, syrups, and blanc-mange. [Considered medicinally, it is emollient and demulcent. It is employed, dissolved in water or milk, and rendered palatable by acid and sugar, as a nutritious substance for invalids and convalescents. (Pereira.)]

Hippocolle is a kind of glue made from the skin of the *Ass*,[1] which comes from India and China, it is obtained from the cartilages of the *Ass* and the *Zebra*; it answers for the same purposes as isinglass. It is considered to be a mild astringent.

SKIN.—The skin of some of the mammalia is made use of for several purposes.

That of the *Chamois*, *Antilope rupicapra*, Pall., is valuable on account of its great pliability; it is used for the purpose of

[1] It is also known under the name of *hockiak* or *hokiak*. The Chinese call it *nyo-kiæo* or *hoki-hao*. It is a strongly aromatised gelatine.

separating mercury from other metals; by straining, the mercury passes through the pores of the skin while the impurities are retained.

That of the *Gazelle, Antilope Dorcas*, Pall., is used for packing the hepatic and socotrine aloes of commerce.

The skin of the *Sheep, Ovis Aries*, Linn., according to the mode in which it is prepared, furnishes parchment and chamois and morocco leather. In pharmacy it is used for the making of plasters.

NESTS OF ESCULENT SWALLOW.—The nests of these birds may be associated with isinglass, which they closely resemble in their appearance. The birds belong to the family of the Hirundinidæ.

There are five species of the *Esculent Swallow;* four of which belong to the Indian Archipelago. Only one species is found in the Isle of France. The principal species are the *Common Esculent Swallow*,[1] distinguished by a white patch at the base of the tail feathers, and the fucus-eating swallow,[2] which is of a uniform brown colour.

The nests have an oval cup-like form, they are from $2\frac{1}{4}$ to $2\frac{3}{4}$ inches in length and about an inch and a half in width. They are firmly attached to the rock. They have a yellow colour, are semi-transparent, and of a firm and tenacious consistence. The free edge of the nests is somewhat thickened, their surface is rough, and when broken they present a vitreous-like fracture. They are formed in successive layers.

Many naturalists have supposed that these nests were composed of the remains of certain fish, or of the mucilage of various Zoophytes; others have believed that the birds formed them from the juice of a tree, with the fronds of lichens, or from gelatinous sea weeds. It is now ascertained that at the period of nidification the birds disgorge a viscid humour, which is secreted by the salivary glands or by the follicles of the crop;[3] it is analogous to the fluid with which the European swallows cement the clay of which their nests are constructed.[4]

There are three gatherings of the nests in a year. Those which are intended for the first laying of eggs are the purest and the most valuable; those which belong to the last are

---

[1] *Callocalia esculenta*, Gray, *Hirundo esculenta*, Linn.
[2] *Callocalia fuciphaga*, C. Bonap., *Hirundo fucifaga*, Thunb., *Callocalia nidifica*, Gray.
[3] E. Home, Blyt, Laidley, Itier.
[4] According to a Chinese physician these nests are formed of the *consolidated gastric juice without any admixture*. (Itier.)

mixed with feathers and fragments of vegetation. In some there are found portions of algæ and lichens. (Guibourt.)

It is probable that the nests of the different species do not resemble each other.

The material of which the nests are composed is insoluble in cold water, but softens by moisture; it dissolves in boiling water in the same manner as gelatine. Every 100 parts contain 90·25 of animal matter and some salts. (Müller.) The nests are supposed to possess restorative properties. (Cuvier). They are used for the purpose of making soups and various kinds of ragouts. They are also prepared like mushrooms. Their substance softens and resembles vermicelli.

§ VI. Fat.

Fat is a secretion of the adipose tissue of animals. It exists in considerable quantities beneath the skin, on the surface of the muscles, in the omentum, at the base of the heart, and around the kidneys. It becomes fluid at a temperature of from 59° to 104° Fah.

The *fat of the Pig* has received the name of *hog's lard*, this term being more especially applied to it after it has been purified. The fat of the *Sheep* is termed *suet*.

Fat is freed from the foreign matters with which it is mixed by cutting it into small pieces, melting it at a moderate temperature in water, then pouring it off and filtering it through a fine cloth. Some persons recommend that the water in which the melting takes place should have a certain quantity of sulphuric acid mixed with it. [Many plans of purifying fats have been proposed; one of the best is to mix two per cent. of strong sulphuric acid with a quantity of water, in which the tallow is heated for some time with much stirring; to allow the materials to cool, to take off the supernatant fat, and re-melt it with abundance of hot water.[1]]

Fat is usually of a softish consistence, but varies in this respect according to the animal, and according to the part from which it is obtained. It is lighter than water, colourless, or of a yellow tint, sometimes odorous, sometimes inodorous, and has a bland insipid taste. It is essentially composed of elaine, a body which is liquid at a temperature of 46° Fah., and is only slightly soluble in alcohol even when boiling, and of stearine, which melts at a temperature of 100° Fah., [Brande says about 110° Fah.,] and is still less soluble in alcohol. Acted upon by a solution of caustic potassa these substances

---

[1] See Ure's Dic. of Arts and Sciences, art. Fat.

are converted into two acids: oleic acid, which is principally derived from the elaine, and margaric acid, which appears to be formed in a great measure by the stearine.

Lard is a white, soft, semi-transparent fat, with little or no smell; it melts at about 80° Fah. [In order to separate this fat from the membrane in which it is contained, it is melted over a slow fire, then strained through flannel or linen, and poured while liquid into a bladder, where it solidifies on cooling (*adeps præparatus*). Occasionally salt is added to preserve it; but unsalted lard should be employed for medicinal purposes. By melting in boiling water, lard may be deprived of any salt which may have been mixed with it. While solidifying, lard should be kept stirred, to prevent the separation of the stearine and elaine. (Pereira.)]

Suet is a white hard fat; it melts at from 98° to 125° Fah.

Beef fat is of a pale yellow colour; it has scarcely any smell, and melts at 100° Fah.

Bear's fat is of a yellowish white colour, semi-fluid, of a peculiar odour, and has a nauseous taste.

Goose fat is of a yellow colour and has a disagreeable smell; it melts below 80° Fah.

Ostrich fat, Struthio Canulus, Linn.—This is a fine, white, firm fat, with only a slight odour resembling that of the preceding; it melts at about 79° Fah.[1] (Duroziez.)

Writers mention several other kinds of fat, which were formerly used in medicine; a list of these has been given in the first book of this work.[2]

Lard is used in the manufacture of the various kinds of ointments and pomades.

After a certain time fat undergoes a change; it turns yellow and becomes *rancid*.[3] In order to prevent *lard* from turning rancid, it should be carefully covered up and kept in a cool place. M. Deschamp (d'Avallon) recommends that it should be impregnated with the odoriferous and resinous principles of the buds of the poplar or with benzoin. The first process consists in adding from twelve to one hundred of the buds. This fat is of a green colour, and cannot, therefore, be used for making white pomades. It becomes of an orange colour when mixed with an alkali. *Benzoinated fat* is prepared by heating in a water-bath for two or three hours four parts of pounded benzoin in 100

---

[1] An Ostrich will supply nearly one-third of its weight of fat. (Gosse.)
[2] See p. 65.
[3] MM. Fl. Prevost and Em. Rousseau state that the *fat of the Ostrich* has very little tendency to become rancid.

parts of fresh fat, and stirring while cooling. This fat becomes rancid sooner than that which has been mixed with the buds of the poplar. M. Soubeiran proposes to substitute, for the benzoin, the balsam of tolu, which is left in the preparation of the syrup. One hundredth part by weight of the tolu dissolved in alcohol is to be mixed with the lard; it is then to be warmed and stirred for the purpose of evaporating the spirit.

Lard is adulterated with inferior kinds of fat and with salt. Plaster of Paris is also sometimes mixed with *lard*. The two last adulterations are easily detected by melting the lard in water; the salt is dissolved, and the plaster is precipitated. (Chevallier.)

§ VII. Oils.

Animal oils[1] are fatty substances characterised by the great fusibility remaining liquid at a temperature below 60° or even 50° Fah.

Animal oil is produced in great abundance by the *Whale* and the *Porpoise*.

Whale oil, known under the name of *Fish oil*, is obtained from the *Common Greenland Whale*[2] and by the Rorqual, species of Whales in which the skin of the throat and the belly is arranged in folds or plicæ. The fat or blubber of these animals is first cut away with enormous knives; it is then divided into smaller pieces, packed in casks, and afterwards melted.

This kind of oil is thick, of a dark brown colour, and has a rancid fishy smell; it becomes congealed at a temperature of 32° Fah. The Whale produces an enormous quantity of oil; a single individual is capable of yielding a ship's cargo.[3] [A ship's cargo will, of course, vary with the size of the vessel and the quantity of oil, with the species of whale and the age and size of the individual; but, after making all allowance for the difference which may arise from these causes, the above statement seems exaggerated. The largest cargo ever known by Dr. Scoresby to have been brought to this country, was that by Captain Souter, of the Resolution, of Peterhead, in 1814. It consisted of forty-four whales, yielding two hundred and ninety-nine tons of oil, which sold at £9,368: and adding the whalebone and the bounty, which was at that time allowed to whaling vessels by the government, the entire returns amounted to £11,000. The total value of the British whale-

---

[1] See p. 101.
[2] See p. 92.
[3] *Pinguedo copiosissima, ut ex unico sæpe oneretur navis*, Linn.

fishery for the same year, which was a very favourable one, was £700,000.]

The oil of the Porpoise, Delphinus globiceps, Cuv., is of a citron colour, and its sp. gr. 0·91 at a temperature of 68° Fah. It is very soluble in alcohol. It contains less cetine [1] than whale oil, and much more phocine.

According to M. Berthelot the latter principle forms a tenth part; in another species, probably the *Delphinus marginatus*, Duvern., the same chemist found only the one hundredth part of this substance. In other Cetacea there are only traces of phocine.

Oil is obtained from the *Dugong* and the *Spermaceti whale*.[2]

Oil is also found in the organs or in the productions of some other animals; as, for instance, in the yelk of birds' eggs; this is easily extracted by compression.

In the distillation of nitrogenised organic matters, such as blood, bones, muscle, &c., a very thick, brown, extremely fetid oil is obtained. When this has been distilled several times, it

Fig. 50.—*Sperm Whale.*

forms a colourless liquid, which has long been known as *Dippel's animal oil*; it was formerly in great repute in the treatment of diseases of the nervous system.

§ VIII. Milk.

Milk is an emulsive fluid, which is secreted by the mammary glands of the female mammalia. It is a white, opaque, somewhat viscid fluid, with an agreeable odour, which is dissipated by heat, and has a mild sweet taste.

Milk consists of a mucilaginous solution, which holds in suspension a fatty matter composed of small spherical globules.

---

[1] See p. 94.
[2] See p. 92.

It is composed of caseum or caseine, albumen, butter, sugar of milk, and several salts.

When milk is evaporated, as in boiling, or even in warming it, a pellicle forms on the surface, and if this is removed it is replaced by a second. This pellicle is almost entirely composed of caseous matter and of cream.

The principal milks are those of the *Cow*, the *Sheep*, the *Goat*, the *Woman*, the *Ass*, and the *Mare*.

1. *Cow's milk* has a density of 1·0324. It is of a yellowish white colour, very opaque, and with a sweet taste. It contains in every 1000 parts, 885 parts of water, 35 of soluble and insoluble caseous matter and albumen, 30 of butter, 40 of sugar of milk, of the phosphates of lime, magnesia, potash, soda, and iron, of the chlorides of potassium and sodium, and of soda.

When milk is left undisturbed its surface becomes gradually covered with a thick, unctuous, yellow layer; this is *cream;* it consists of large globules, which, when united by the process of churning, forms butter. The cream separates but slowly, in consequence of its density differing but little from that of the milk; it is composed of butter (*butyrum*) and of milk. When agitated the butter separates and leaves a fluid termed *buttermilk*. This liquid contains all the elements of the milk, but only a very little caseum, and a large proportion of butyric acid. When nearly all the cream has been removed, it is *skimmed milk;* when this is left to itself acetic and lactic acids are formed and coagulate the casein. A clear yellow liquid with a sweet taste then separates, which is termed *whey*. The coagulation of the caseous matter (*curds*) is usually accomplished by artificial means.

When milk is filtered it leaves behind it the insoluble caseous matter and the fat globules; a clear fluid passes through, which becomes thickened and coagulated by heat in proportion to the quantity of albumen which it contains.

The caseous matter or casein exists in considerable quantity in milk under the form of very minute globules; it is insipid and inodorous. Its composition is the same as that of albumen.

Butter,[1] or the fatty matter of milk, is met with in the form of globules, varying in size from $\frac{1}{30000}$ to $\frac{1}{180000}$ of an inch. It is composed of three fatty bodies: oleine or elaine, stearine, and butyrine.

[1] In Paris there was consumed, in 1857, 10,551,366 francs worth of butter.

Sugar of milk or salt of milk (*lactine*) is solid, of a sweet flavour, and with no smell. It crackles between the teeth. It crystallizes in white, semitransparent, regular prisms. At the ordinary temperature of the atmosphere water will dissolve one ninth part of its weight. Occasionally a small quantity of blood is found in milk. (Lepage.) More rarely there is also found infusorial animalculæ which change its colour.

2. *Sheep's milk* has a density of 1·0409. It gives more cream and butter than that of the Cow; but its butter is softer, and melts more easily, while its casein is more greasy and more viscid.

3. *Goat's milk* has a density of 1·0340. It gives off the odour of the goat. Its fatty matter is thick, and its butter firm and white, but is less in quantity than in the two previous milks.

4. *Human milk* has a density of 1·023. It contains a considerable quantity of sugar of milk and very little caseine. The latter is very soft, viscous, and tremulous. This milk contains a good deal of cream.

5. *Ass's milk* has a density of 1·0355. It has the same consistence, smell, and taste as human milk. It contains less cream, and what there is is not so thick; its butter is soft, white, and insipid; its casein is less in quantity, and soft.

6. *Mare's milk* has a density of 1·0346. It contains very little butter; its casein is soft, and its serum tolerably abundant. The Kalmucks, by acidulating and fermenting this milk, obtain from it *araka*. (Pallas.)

LACTODENSIMETER.—Quevenne has invented an instrument for the purpose of determining the density of milk, which he terms a *lactodensimeter*. It is an areometer. The density of water being 1000, the average density of pure milk from the Cow is 1031, and when the cream has been separated 1033 (the temperature being 59° Fah.). As a matter of convenience the two left hand figures are omitted. Thus, when the instrument marks 25 or 30 degrees, it shows that the density of the milk which has been examined is 1025 or 1030, or in other words that a litre (1·760 pint) of the milk weighs either 1025 grammes (2 lbs. 8 oz. 478 grs. Troy), or 1030 grammes (2 lbs. 9 oz. 65 grs. Troy). The density of milk which has not been deprived of its cream should vary between 29 and 33 degrees, that of skimmed milk between 32·5 and 37·5. The addition of one tenth part of water to milk will lower the indicator three degrees, and in skimmed milk 3·25.

CREAMOMETER.—This is another instrument proposed by

Quevenne. As skimmed milk becomes more dense, its properties may be changed by removing a portion of the cream, and then adding a certain quantity of water. Unfortunately this is what happens every day. The lactodensimeter will not detect this double fraud, but the creamometer will.

The latter instrument consists of a kind of gage, of a tolerable size, and divided into 100 parts. This is allowed to remain in the fresh milk for twelve hours. The cream gradually rises to the surface. The average quantity of cream is 11 to 12 for every hundred parts of milk. All milk which yields a less quantity than this has been more or less deprived of its cream. One of the inconveniences of this instrument is that it only affords the required information after the lapse of twelve hours. It has been recommended to substitute for it simple agitation. A given quantity of milk is to be boiled for ten minutes, taking care that it is continually shaken during this time. It is then placed in a flask. When it is cooled down to —4° Fah., the mouth of the vessel is closed, and it is well shaken until all the butter is separated. It is then strained through a fine cloth. The butter is then to be washed, pressed, and weighed. Every litre (1·760 pint) of milk ought to yield at least 30 grammes of butter (462·6750 grs. Troy).

LACTOSCOPE.—This instrument is intended in certain cases to indicate the richness of the milk in butter. It was invented by M. Donné. Its action depends upon the opacity which the liquid receives from the presence of the fat globules. The instrument consists of two plain glasses, between which the liquid is placed; the instrument is then examined in a dark place by the flame of a candle through this layer. The glasses are separated from each other until the opacity is such that the flame ceases to be visible. The thickness of the layer which is required to produce this result should be thinner in proportion to the quantity of fatty matter present. One of the glasses is fixed; the other on a moveable foot, one turn of which corresponds to a thickness of $\frac{1}{500}$ of an inch. The circumference is divided into fifty equal portions, which constitute degrees; a good milk should mark 34 degrees. Unfortunately for the accuracy of the lactoscope, the opacity of the milk does not depend only upon the fat globules, but also upon the caseine held in solution: it also depends upon the various substances which are introduced by the dealers.

Adulteration.—Of late years the adulterations which are practised on milk have been carefully inquired into. One plan is to remove the cream, and then mix the milk with water; in order to restore to it its opacity and consistence, as well as to remove the blue tint which is induced by the adulteration, sugar, glucose, farina, and dextrine are added; various other substances are also made use of, such as infusions of rice, barley, &c.; gummy and albuminous matters, fish glue, liquorice juice, the colouring matter of the marigold, and baked carrots. (Chevallier.)

Preservation.—The lower the temperature the better milk keeps; but in order to preserve it for any length of time various plans have been proposed.

1. Concentrate the milk to one third or one half; put it into well-stoppered vessels and expose them to the heat of a water bath for a period of two hours. (*Appert's process.*)

2. Evaporate at a low temperature, and drive in air, which facilitates its thickening. (*Gallais's process.*)

3. The foregoing processes are now abandoned. The following are much better:—To every litre (1·760773 pint) of milk add from 75 to 80 grammes (1157 to 1234 grs.) of sugar. It is then concentrated in a flat-bottomed vessel in which the liquid is kept constantly moving in order to prevent the formation of a pellicle. When it has become reduced to one-fifth of its original volume, it is put into tin boxes, which are then treated according to Appert's method. (*Lignac's process.*)

4. The milk is charged with carbonic acid by the same kind of machine as is used in the manufacture of Seltzer water; it is then placed in bottles in the usual manner. (*Bethel's process.*)

5. Lastly, milk is preserved without the addition of any foreign substance, and without the abstraction of its cream, or the evaporation of its aqueous particles. It is simply placed in a tin vessel which is provided with a pewter tube. This is warmed for three-quarters of an hour in a water bath for the purpose of expelling all the air, and the tube is then hermetically closed by means of pincers. (*Mabru's process.*)

§ IX. Eggs.

The eggs which are employed in medicine are those of the common fowl, *Phasianus Gallus*, Linn.

Every egg consists of a calcareous covering or *shell;* of a semi-opaque membranous envelope which covers the internal surface of the shell; of the glairy ligaments or *chalazæ* which connect the envelopes with their contents; of the white or *albumen*, a transparent liquid with a very slight tint of a greenish yellow, and which is contained in a loose cellular tissue, varying in density in the different layers; of the yellow or *vitellus*, a globular opaque mass of a golden yellow colour surrounded by a very delicate membrane, the *vitelline membrane*, and suspended in the midst of the albumen; lastly, of the germ of the bird or *cicatricula*, a small white body which adheres to the yelk.

A hen's egg contains on an average 367 grs. Troy of the white, and 324 grs. Troy of the yelk.

The shell is composed of animal matter, carbonate of lime, a small quantity of carbonate of magnesia and of phosphate of lime, with slight traces of an oxide of iron. Sulphur is present in the animal matter and becomes liberated in the form of sulphuretted hydrogen, when shells which have been previously calcined are acted upon by the stronger acids.

The internal membrane appears to be of an albuminous nature. (Vauquelin.) This also contains a small quantity of sulphur. It readily dissolves in liquor potassæ without producing ammonia.

White of egg consists of a solution of albumen, with the presence of certain salts, a small quantity of sugar and probably also of carbonate of soda. It almost entirely dissolves in either cold or tepid water, leaving only a few particles of membrane. In boiling water the albumen becomes coagulated, and forms a white compact mass.

The yelk consists of a large quantity of water, of vitelline, of margarine, and of oleine, of a viscous matter, of cholesterine, of osmazone, of a colouring matter, of the salts usually present in animals, and contains traces of lactic acid. (Gobley.)

The oil of the yelk is composed of oleine, margarine, of a small quantity of cholesterine, and of colouring matter.

There are two kinds of colouring matter in the yelk; the one is red, contains iron, and resembles the colouring matter of the blood; the other is yellow, and appears to be analogous to the colouring matter of the bile.

Eggs are said to be *fresh* when they have not been laid more than two days in summer or six in winter.

Eggs change in proportion to the length of time they have been laid. The evaporation of the water in their interior takes place through the pores of the shell, and forms a space at one extremity (*air chamber*).

If the white of an egg is coagulated which is not fresh, when the shell is broken a depression is seen at one end. When eggs have been laid some time the chalazæ become relaxed, and lose the power of supporting the yelk; the latter, in consequence of its greater specific gravity, falls to the lowest part. Farmers and egg-merchants ascertain this fact by examining the egg before a lighted candle, or by the light of the sun.

Fresh eggs, when gently shaken in the direction of their length, give no evidence of any internal displacement. Stale eggs, on the contrary, give rise to a slight shock, arising from the displacement of their contents. M. Delarue, of Dijon, has given the following directions for ascertaining whether an egg is fresh or not:—Dissolve eight ounces of common salt in 1·760 pint of water, and when the water is dissolved place the egg in the solution. If it has been laid the same day it goes direct to the bottom of the vessel; if not, it does not sink so far; and if it is three days old it floats in the liquid; if it is more than five days old it comes to the surface, and the shell projects in proportion to the age of the egg.

Eggs may be preserved fresh for a whole year by covering the pores of the shell with varnish, with a layer of wax, or with some fatty substances. Cadet Gassicourt recommends the *eggs* to be placed in a vessel in layers, and then to pour in lime water, containing a small excess of the powdered lime, so that the eggs shall be covered to the depth of from six to seven inches of the liquid.

It is supposed that, in this case, a deposit of carbonate of lime takes place, which fills up the pores of the shell, rendering it thereby impermeable to air, and so preserving the animal matter in its interior.

The following process has been proposed by M. Delarue :— Take 1543 grs. of slack lime for every 200 eggs. Mix with the lime, as intimately as possible, 154 grs. of powdered sugar; the whole is then to be placed in sufficient water to cover the eggs. In fifteen days the operation is completed. The small quantity of saccharate of lime which is formed penetrates the shell, and prevents the entrance of air.

The Chinese place their eggs in water holding in solution a tenth part of sea salt until their density becomes greater than that of the liquid.

Eggs may also be preserved by placing them in ashes, dry sand, bran, millet seed, saw dust, powdered charcoal, &c.

The parts of the *egg* which are employed in medicine are the white and the yelk.

The white is used for clarifying syrups and many other liquids; this effect is produced by its coagulation by the heat from the liquid, or by the acids or the spirit contained in it. The coagulated albumen forms a kind of mesh, which, as it sinks to the bottom of the liquid, carries the impurities with it.[1]

The yelk enters into the formation of certain emulsions. It serves for making emulsions with resins, gum resins, and volatile oils. The yelk can be perfectly mixed with water.

Eggs form a valuable and plentiful source of human food. The annual consumption of hens' eggs in Paris is about 115 for each individual.[2] In the rest of France, especially in the country places, this number is doubled. It is calculated that 7,231,160,000 *eggs* are consumed in France independent of those which are exported to other countries, or which are used for the purpose of hatching.

[The white of egg is a valuable remedy in cases of poisoning by bichloride of mercury, sulphate of copper, and bichloride of tin. Its efficacy in these cases depends on the combination of the albumen with the oxide or chloride of the metal. (Pereira.) There is no necessity of separating the white from the yelk, as the latter is efficacious as well as the former.

Eggs beaten up with warm water, and to which a small quantity of brandy or port wine has been added, and then flavoured with sugar or nutmeg, are valuble adjuncts to the dietary of the sick room.

The MISTURA SPIRITUS VINI GALLICI consists of Brandy and Cinnamon Water each f℥iv, the Yelks of two Eggs, Purified Sugar ℥ss, Oil of Cinnamon ♏ij. Mix.—This preparation is stimulant and restorative, and is used in the last stage of low fevers and in cases of exhaustion. The dose is from f℥ss to f℥iss.]

§ X.—Honey.

The honey-producing animals are *Bees*, *Wasps*, and some allied insects.

The *Aphides* also secrete a sweet fluid by means of a pair of abdominal glands which communicate with two tubes on the upper surface of the abdomen.

It is stated that honey has been found in the galleries of certain exotic species of *Ants*, but it is doubtful whether they have not stolen it from some other animals. However this may be, the most perfect melliferous animals are the *Bees*.

1. *Bees.*—The *Common* or *Honey Bee, Apis Mellifica*, Linn., is an insect belonging to the order Hymenoptera, and to the family Anthophila.

---

[1] See p. 179.
[2] In 1857 Paris consumed eggs to the value of 9,524,111 francs.

The *Bee* appears to have come originally from Greece, from whence it has been transported to the different parts of Europe.

Every one is familiar with these insects; the body is covered with hairs, is of a brownish black colour and is marked with a transverse greyish band on the abdomen. The antennæ are filiform and shorter than the combined length of the head and the thorax. The simple eyes are arranged in the form of a triangle, placed in the females on the forehead, and in the males on the vertex.

Bees live in societies called swarms. When one of these swarms is artificially lodged it constitutes a hive. Each swarm constructs a very peculiar and complicated nest. It consists of partitions composed of hexagonal cells. These partitions are arranged perpendicularly; each consists of two rows of cells placed opposite each other and connected together by their bases, so that the cells themselves are placed horizontally. Each partition with its double series of cells forms a *comb*.

It is in the interior of these cells that the eggs are deposited and the food is stored up.

Each swarm consists of three kinds of individuals: 1, a *female*; 2, *males*; 3, *neuters* or *workers* (fig. 51).

Fig. 51.—*Common Bee.*[1]

The *female* which the ancients called a *king*, but which is now known as the *queen*, is found solitary in every swarm; she is large, strong, and has an elongated body; she possesses a sting, and upon her devolves the laying of the eggs.

[1] *Common bee—a*, male or *drone*; *b*, female or *queen*; *c*, worker or *neuter*.

The *males* or *drones* vary in number from 500 to 1000 in each swarm. They are smaller, less robust, and have a shorter abdomen than the female. They have no sting. Their office is to impregnate the female.

The *workers* or *neuters* number from twelve to twenty or even thirty thousand in each hive, and are the smallest members of the community. The working bees have a sting. The duties of these are to take charge of the eggs and of the young, and to construct the combs. They generally divide these labours amongst them: some attend exclusively to the young—these are the *nursing bees;* others collect the nectar and pollen of the flowers and form from them the honey and the wax, construct the combs, and lay up a supply of food—these are the *wax workers.*

Many writers regard the associations of *Bees* as a republic. Linnæus terms the government a gynocratic *republic*. This celebrated naturalist believed that the queen is guarded from sight by the workers, and that she is not able to emerge from her dominions; this, however, is an error. The association of *Bees* appears rather to be a true monarchy, at the head of which is placed a sovereign, who is the only one of her sex, and who is solely engaged in laying eggs. But who governs the society? It governs itself; each sex, each individual instinctively, necessarily, and blindly executes the functions which are assigned to it; and each displays the same zeal, skill, and perfection in the fulfilment of its duties.

Copulation takes place at the beginning of summer, out of the hive. The female rises into the air until she is lost to sight, surrounded by a crowd of males. (Huber.) One only of the latter is summoned to partake of her favours. This male usually belongs to another hive. (Hamet.) The female soon returns, bearing at the extremity of her abdomen the genital organs of the male.

As soon as the female is impregnated, and the males are no longer of any use to the community, the workers wound them with their stings, and put them to death. This slaughter usually takes place in the month of August, when the vicinity of the hive is covered with the dead bodies.

Two days after the queen has been impregnated she begins to lay her eggs, and becomes the object of the attention and solicitude of the entire colony. The workers clean her by rubbing her with their proboscs, and from time to time present her with the honey with they have disgorged.

There are several layings. Reaumur has calculated the

number of eggs which the female can lay in the course of three weeks at 12,000. She generally deposits from 200 to 400 a day.[1] The eggs are oblong, slightly curved, attenuated at the extremity, by which they are attached to the cell, and are somewhat transparent. These eggs produce workers and a single female.

It has been recently stated, that the queen has the power of laying eggs before copulation as well as after it has taken place, when the seminal fluid has lost its fecundating powers, but that these eggs only give rise to males. It is also supposed that, after she has been fecundated, she can prevent the seminal fluid from coming in contact with the eggs, and that she can thus deposit male germs at her pleasure.

The neuters are imperfect females; that is to say, individuals who have been arrested in their development, and do not possess the copulative vesicle. Nevertheless, under certain circumstances they do lay eggs, but they are always male eggs.

Suitable cells are prepared for the reception of the new generation. Each egg has its particular cell. The cells which are intended for workers are regular and perfectly equal polyhedra. Those for the males are somewhat larger, are less regular, nearly cylindrical, and as if they were engine-turned. The male cells are dispersed amongst those of the workers. The cells for the females hang down.

The eggs are hatched at the end of four or five days, when there comes forth a small whitish larva, composed of fourteen segments with a corneous head and no feet. The larva remains motionless within its cell. The workers feed it with a mixture of honey and pollen, of which the quantity varies according to the age of the individual.

Five or six days after they are born, the period for their metamorphosis has arrived, and the workers then close up the mouth of the cells with a convex lid or cup of wax.

The larvæ spin around their bodies a covering of silk, and at the end of three days they are transformed into nymphs.

When they have remained in this state seven days and a half, they undergo their last metamorphosis, and are changed into *Bees*. They then eat their way through the lid, and emerge from their cells.

The males are twenty-one days from the time they are hatched until they assume their perfect state. The females are thirteen days. The nature of the food exercises great influence over the duration of this period. By varying the

[1] Linnæus says that each queen lays 40,000 a year.

food of the larvæ, the workers can at their option produce workers or queens; that is to say, females whose development has been arrested, or females who are normally developed. When a swarm has lost its queen, the workers demolish several of the ordinary cells for the purpose of forming a royal cell. A larva is placed in this, and after being fed on the necessary kind of food, instead of producing a working bee, it is transformed into a queen.

When the young bees have come forth, the workers immediately clean out the cells, and prepare them for the reception of another set of eggs. This, however, is not the case with the royal cells; these are destroyed, and fresh ones formed for every laying.

When a queen is born in a hive, a great agitation is perceived, and the whole colony appears to be in motion; on the one hand, the old queen endeavours to reach her new-born rival for the purpose of plunging her sting into her body, while on the other hand crowds of workers interpose to defend her. Some are charged with wax, and seem desirous of enclosing the new queen in her cell, and to provide for her safety by making her a prisoner. In a short time the old queen issues forth from the hive, with all the appearance of anger, and is accompanied by a large number of the community. She and her partisans assemble together at some distance from the old hive, and become the founders of a new colony. The young queen remains behind, and is soon at the head of a numerous society by the successive development of the larvæ belonging to her generation. In this manner a young swarm is produced, which take possession of the first hive.

If two or three queens are born at the same time, they wage war against each other until only one of them is left alive, who, having conquered her rivals, becomes the sovereign of the new society.

When a second queen is introduced into a hive, she is either destroyed by the legitimate sovereign, or by a number of the workers, who precipitate themselves upon her, and plunge their stings into her body. (Huber, De Beauvoys.)

Sometimes one colony will attack another in order to rob it of its provisions. If it should be victorious, the honey belonging to the enemy is carried off, and transferred to their own hive. *Bees* pass the winter in a torpid state. It has recently been proposed to preserve them during their lethargy in a kind of pits.

2. ORGANS WHICH FORM THE HONEY (fig. 52).—*Bees* are furnished with a proboscis, which is the homologue of the lower lip of other insects.

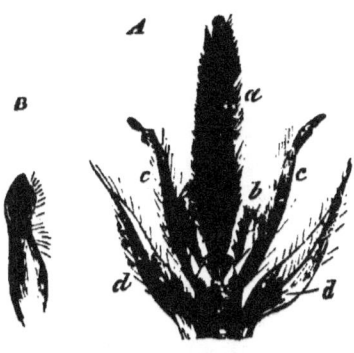

Fig. 52.—*Mouth.*[1]

Swammerdam thought the proboscis was tubular, and perforated at its extremity, and that thus it was organised to draw up the juices of the flower after the manner of a pump. According to this celebrated anatomist the most external pieces, which form the case, served only to separate the petals, while the inner portions were intended to compress the tube, and cause the ascent of the sugared fluid. This suction was favoured by the pressure of the atmosphere, and by the dilitation of the abdomen, which formed the vacuum of the pump.

Reaumur has given a more correct account of this apparatus and of the functions which are performed by the different pieces. He has shown that the proboscis is a kind of velvetty tongue, which by its movements becomes charged with the honeyed liquor; that this fluid then passes between the external pieces or jaws, and thus gains an opening at its base, which had escaped the notice of Swammerdam.

It appears, therefore, that the instrument with which the *Bees* collect the honey is not entitled to be termed a *proboscis*. Entomologists have named it the *ligula*.

The *ligula* is a long, lancet-shaped, slender, obtuse body, marked with transverse lines, and covered with hairs, which are directed from the base towards the apex. It is contracted at its commencement, and appears to be articulated by a pedicle, which is short and truncated anteriorly, while posteriorly it is attenuated, and then suddenly dilated. On either side of the contracted portion are two appendages, *paraglossa*, having the form of short obtuse processes furnished with hairs. Further back, where it becomes dilated are the *labial palpi*. These are longer than the paraglossa, but shorter than the tongue; they pass from behind forwards, and from within to without; they diminish in size towards their termination, and

---

[1] *A*, mouth of a working bee; *a*, ligula; *b b*, paraglossa; *c c*, labial palpi; *d d*, the jaws; *B*, mandible of a worker.

are composed of a number of unequal joints. Still further back are the narrow lancet-shaped *jaws*, looking as if they were provided with a median nervure.

The opening of the mouth is situated at the upper part of the base of the tongue; it is of a moderate size, and is closed by a small fleshy triangular lobe, which Reaumur[1] named the *tongue*. This aperture, which is the opening of the pharynx, communicates with a dilated esophagus. When a Bee is compressed between the fingers a drop of honey often issues from this spot.

The nectar of flowers and the various sweet vegetable juices after they have been imbibed and swallowed by the Bee become modified in the stomach (Reaumur), and transformed into honey. This is disgorged and deposited by the animals in particular cells prepared for the purpose in the layers of the comb.

3. HONEY.—*Honey* (*mel*) is a sugared, perfumed, semifluid substance of the consistence of syrup, and of a more or less golden yellow colour.

The collecting of the honey takes place during the months of September and October. There are various ways of obtaining it. The old method was not without danger to the operators as well as to the *Bees*. The head was covered with a mask, the hands with gloves, and the legs with cloths. The hive was then smoked. When the *Bees*, having been driven out by the smoke, had assembled at the top of their abode, the hive was turned topsy-turvy. The combs had then to be cut away, and, in order that the insects should not be injured in the operation, they were compelled to retire further off by again smoking them by means of a piece of smouldering tow or linen fixed to the end of a stick, so that it could be directed towards the comb to which the *Bees* had attached themselves. This method was exceedingly detrimental to the multiplication of the *Bees*. In the present day a different plan is adopted. In the evening the hive is gently raised from its support, laid upon its side, and left in this position during the night. Early the next morning an empty hive is rubbed with honey, and fixed with its opening upwards; the other hive is then placed upon it, so that the two openings correspond. By this means the full hive is placed below the other in a reversed position; it is then struck repeatedly with a small stick, and the animals, in consequence, pass into the upper hive. When all or the

---

[1] *Epipharynx* or *epiglossa* (Savigny).

greater number of the *Bees* are supposed to have entered the empty hive is detached, and placed where the full hive had been removed from. The latter is then reversed upon a cloth, on which the combs fall. The Bees which remain behind are driven off, either by moving them with a feather, or by smoking them. Some recommend the fumes of tobacco, and others that of chloroform.

In order to extract the honey from the combs they are placed upon sieves, or in coarse sacks, and exposed to a slight heat, or simply to the warmth of the sun; a viscous fluid drains from them, which is known as *virgin honey;* it is the most pure and the most valuable.

When no more honey comes away the combs are broken up, and then allowed to drain again, and this time the heat is somewhat increased.

After this the combs are pressed, care having first been taken to remove the eggs. By this means a larger supply of honey is obtained, but of an inferior quality, holding in suspension a certain amount of extraneous matter, which either swims at the top or sinks to the bottom. The honey must be left some time to settle, and then skimmed and carefully poured off.

The less heat and the less amount of pressure which are used the better the honey.

Good honey is soft, of a pale yellow colour, with granular particles dispersed through the semifluid portions. It is entirely soluble in water, and capable of undergoing alcoholic fermentation. It has a bland, sweet, pleasant, and more or less aromatic flavour.

Writers distinguish six kinds of honey: 1. that from Mount Hymetta, from Mount Ida, from Mahon, and from Cuba; 2. that of Narbonne; 3. that of Gâtinais; 4. that of Saintonge; 5. that of Burgundy; 6. that of Brittany.

The honey from Mount Hymetta was celebrated in the earliest ages of the world. Martial, Horace, and Silius Italicus have extolled its flavour and its perfume. It is a white, liquid, and transparent honey.

Narbonne honey enjoys a well-merited reputation in pharmacy. It is somewhat solid, of a whitish colour, very granular, with a strong smell and an aromatic taste, which is occasionally slightly pungent. It contains a small quantity of wax and acid. This honey comes almost exclusively from the little town of Corbières.

The honey of Gâtinais is next in esteem after that of

Narbonne. It is not so granular as the latter, and is of a darker colour, and less aromatic. It has a pale yellow tint, and a very sweet taste. It comes from that portion of the department of Seine et Marne which is to the south of the Seine, and from a part of Orleans. It is often sold in Paris under the name of Narbonne honey. It is the best for the preparation of syrups.

Saintonge honey is very thick, less granular than that from Narbonne, but nearly as white. It has a strong aromatic odour and an agreable flavour. It is very similar to that from Gâtinais, but it is not of so deep a colour. This honey is principally employed in the country where it is produced.

Burgundy honey is held in less repute than the former kinds.

The honey of Brittany is the most inferior of all. It is of a brown red colour. It has a sharp taste, and a smell resembling gingerbread, which sometimes is not at all agreeable. It contains a fusible granular matter, soluble in water and in alcohol. It is seldom employed in medicine. It is especially reserved for veterinary purposes. The nature of the flowers influences the colour, taste, perfume, and other qualities of the honey.

Some honeys are almost white; others are of a golden yellow, red, fawn, brown, and even black colour. A Bee belonging to Madagascar and the Isle of Bourbon (*Apis unicolor*, Latr.) produces a green honey.[1]

The honey prepared from the nectar of the labiata is generally very much perfumed; that from the South of France appears to owe its good qualities to the great number of these plants, which are found in that part of the country. The aromatic odour which characterises the honey from the neighbourhood of Montpellier, particularly that from the *sources of the Lez*, appears to be owing to this circumstance. Sauvage states, that having planted a hedge of rosemary before a hive, of which the honey had no particular smell, from that time it became perfumed. M. Biot noticed in the Balearic isles, and De Candolle in the Corbieres, near Narbonne, that the honey of these countries owed its superiority to the same family of plants. Olivier has stated, that the honey of Upper Provence, which is of an excellent quality, is collected from lavender. The good qualities of Cuban honey arise from the orange

[1] It is obtained from the *Mimosa heterophylla* and from the *Weirmanna glabra*.

flower. Bosc states that the deliciousness of the honey from the neighbourhood of the orangery at Versailles is owing to the same cause. It is said that it is the black or buck wheat which gives the inferior qualities to the honey of Brittany. The makers of gingerbread at Rheims are said to pay a higher price for the honey which is obtained in the spring from the willows, than that which is obtained in autumn from the buck wheat. (Allaire.) The aromatic flavour and odour of the honey from Gatinais appear to depend upon the flowers of the saffron, which are produced in large quantities in that country. The yew, according to Virgil, and the box tree, according to Pliny, imparted a better flavour to the honey of Corsica.

Aristotle pretends, that at a certain period of the year the honey from the neighbourhood of the Caucasus rendered those who ate it insensible. Xenophon and Diodorus of Sicily relate that the soldiers became furiously intoxicated after eating the honey in the neighbourhood of Trebizond. These statements have been confirmed by several modern writers. Tournefort believes that these deleterious properties are owing to the flowers of the *Azalea Pontica;* others that they depend in a great measure on the *Rhododendrum Ponticum.* Guldenstaedt tasted some honey which was collected from these shrubs. It was of a dark brown colour, with a bitter taste, and caused deafness and giddiness. Smith Barton has described the symptoms produced by a poisonous honey found in South Pensylvania, near the Ohio. During his voyage to the Brazils, Auguste de Saint-Hilaire remained in a state of delirium for several hours from only taking two teaspoonfuls of a mild pleasant honey gathered by a bee, *Polistes Lecheguana,* A. St.-Hil.; from a species of fir tree, the *Pallulinia australis.*

Various writers have published cases which show that honey collected from narcotic or poisonous plants may produce nausea, colic, and even actual poisoning. Lambert says that the honey collected from a certain tree in Colchis produced vomiting. Labillardière suspects that the poisonous effects in Asia Minor are caused by the *Cocculus suberosus.* In Brazil a drink called *grappe* is concocted from wild honey and certain fruits, which causes vomiting. (Roulox Baror.) The honey from Pensylvania, South Carolina, Georgia, and the two Floridas, when it has been collected from the *Kalmia augustifolia, latifolia,* or *hirsuta,* or from the *Andromeda mariana,* produces disorder of the stomach, vomiting, convulsions, and sometimes death. Haller mentions the case of two Alpine villagers who were poisoned by honey from the aconite. Seringe mentions another instance where two Swiss herdsmen having eaten some honey, collected from the *Aconitum Napellus* and *lycotonum*,[1] were seized with convulsions and delirium; one of them, who was unable to vomit, died discharging blood and froth from his mouth.

The qualities and effects of honey are very variable. A kind which is excellent at one period of the year may become noxious at another. Every bee-keeper knows that the same hive produces a somewhat different honey every month owing to the difference in the flowers upon which the *Bees* feed.

Honey is a mixture, in variable proportions, of two different sugars: glucose, which is solid, crystallisable, and perfectly resembles the solid sugar of the raisin; the other is liquid, non-crystallisable, and has a rotatory movement to the left. Soubeiran has mentioned a third sugar, distinguished from that in grains by being convertible by acids, and from the fluid sugar in having a rotatory motion towards the right. Small quantities have also been found of a vegetable acid, and of the colouring and odorous principles which exercise so much influence over the qualities of the honey. According to M. Guibourt, some honeys appear to contain manna.

Honey is adulterated by the addition of water, starch, the pulp of chesnuts, bean or maize flour; gum tragacanth and sand are also mixed with it. These adulterations are detected by dissolving the honey in water, when the starch and other matters sink to the bottom. The addition of iodine produces a blue colour. Honey is also adulterated with starch sugar. When this is the case, it has a peculiar appearance and a disagreeable taste. Dissolved in water it gives a copious precipitate with oxalate of ammonia and the salts of baryta, in consequence of the sulphate which it contains.

Under the name of Narbonne honey, various inferior kinds are sold, which have been whitened, and to which the perfume of the best honeys has been imparted by straining it over flowers of rosemary.

§ XI. Wax.

Bees[2] are the principal *wax*-producing animals.

It has long been known that certain vegetables, as, for example, the *Ceroxylon andicola*, and the *Benincasa cerifera*,

---

[1] This was the honey of the *Common Humble* Bee, *Bombus terrestris*, Fabr.
[2] See p. 196.

produce a substance consisting of *wax* and some other principles.[1] The twigs, leaves, and fruits of many plants are covered with a powder, which is a waxy matter differing very little from that which is produced by Bees. From these circumstances it was supposed that the insect received the *wax* already prepared from the plant; it has, however, been shown to be an animal formation. No doubt the Bee obtains the elements of the wax from the plants; but she modifies and transforms them.

Bonnet and Hunter maintained that *wax* was a secretion. It is, however, to the experiments of Huber of Geneva that we are indebted for a practical demonstration of the fact. He enclosed a swarm of Bees in a new hive, and gave them nothing but honey and water. At the end of some days the insects had constructed several layers of cells of a very pure *wax*. MM. Dumas and Milne Edwards repeated the experiment with both honey and sugar, and obtained the same result.

1. WAX ORGANS.—Hunter and Huber asserted that the elaboration of the wax took place by means of eight small pouches placed between the lower segments of the abdomen. M. Leon Dufour denies the existence of these presumed *wax* pouches. Some writers, guided by the fact that secretions of the nature of wax are met with in several other insects, conclude that the *wax* of the Bee accumulates by exudation on the inner surface of the delicate membranes, which bind the joints of their feet together. According to M. Leon Dufour, the Bee swallows the pollen and other vegetable substances which contain the elements of the *wax*. It then yields this matter fully elaborated from the mouth in a soft pulpy condition. This pulp is deposited and formed, as it were, in a kind of mould, in the wax receptacles placed along the lateral parts of the abdomen, where it assumes the form and consistency of plates. The legs of the Bee, and especially the posterior pair (fig. 53), are admirably adapted for

Fig. 53.
Leg of Bee.[2]

---

[1] The *wax* of Japan is found in the fruit of the *Rhus succedaneum*. Myrtle wax is obtained from the wood of *Myrica cerifera*. Other kinds of wax are extracted from the *Croton sebiferum*, *Celastrus ceriferus*, *Myristica sebifera*, and *Myristica Bicuhyba*.

[2] Hinder limb of a worker: *a*, *basket* seen on its outer or convex surface; the inner or concave is placed opposite to it; *b*, the *brush*.

the purposes for which they are required, and have the first joint of the tarsus dilated. This dilatation is most marked in the workers; it has a square form, and its inner surface is provided with several rows of stiff hairs placed transversely, which gives to this part the name of the *brush*. The leg is dilated, and forms a triangular cavity on its inner surface, which is known as the *basket;* the outer surface is somewhat convex, and bordered by long curved hairs.

It is by means of this simple apparatus that the workers gather the pollen and waxy secretions of the plant. The pollen is supplied by the stamens, and the waxy secretions, which cover the leaves and the fruit, readily adhere to the hairs of the Bee. These materials are gathered together in small pellets by means of the brushes, and are then deposited in the basket by the second pair of feet. The workers may be often seen returning to the hive with their *baskets* completely full. Reaumur calculated that eight baskets full of pollen would weigh ·771 of a grain. Each Bee will make four or five journeys in a day, carrying two baskets full each time; consequently, in the space of a month, 18,000 workers would accumulate 88 lbs. avoir. of this material.

Such are the instruments with which the Bees collect and transport the elements of the wax, and such is the manner in which they gather, accumulate, and carry away these precious materials.

It has been previously seen how the animal prepares, disgorges, and elaborates the wax, and how it deposits it in the cavities of its abdomen.

The plates of wax are small, and appear as if they were formed of perpendicular fibres. (Dujardin.)

The basket, or dilated portion of the Bee's leg, has a small hook with which it draws the plates of wax from the sides of its body. The insect deposits them one upon the other, like layers of bricks, and moulds them into the walls of its cells.

For this purpose the Bee makes use of its mandibles.[1] These organs are very small in the males and the females, but they are well developed in the workers. They are hollowed out, and divided into two portions by a longitudinal ridge. When the mandibles are approximated, they form a pair of cutting pincers, and at the same time a kind of groove. It is with these instruments that the animals construct the beautiful cells of their comb.

---

[1] See p. 201, fig. 52, *B*.

It has just been stated that 18,000 workers in the space of a month will bring to their hive more than 88 lbs. of pollen. But at the end of a year the same number of insects will only have yielded a little more than 2 lbs. of genuine wax. What then has become of the remainder of the pollen? It has evidently been either consumed as food, or rejected as useless.

2. WAX.—Wax is a combustible material of which the Bees compose the cells or comb, which is provided for the reception of their young and their food.

When the honey has been removed from the comb, it is melted at a moderate heat of from 143° to 145° Fah. It is then poured into moulds, and forms the *yellow* or *crude wax*. It owes its colour and its odour to foreign matters.[1]

For the purpose of purifying the wax, it is made up into thin ribbons or films, or it is melted and poured in the liquid state on to cylinders of wood, which revolve horizontally in the water, and divide it into lumps. The films or lumps of wax are then placed on webs of canvas, and exposed in a meadow to the action of air and sun light, care being taken that it is sprinkled every night with water. By degrees the wax loses its yellow colour and becomes bleached, the process commencing at the surface, and gradually proceeding inwards. This process has the inconvenience of occupying a long time, and in some establishments the process of bleaching by chlorine has been substituted for it. Immersion of the lumps or ribbons of wax in a solution of chlorine, or exposing them to the action of chlorine gas, produces in a short time the same effects as the former process does in a long time. The same thing may be accomplished by means of other chemical substances.

A small quantity of suet is often mixed with the wax in order to restore to it the suppleness it has lost.

Wax which has been completely deprived of its colour, is called *virgin* or *white wax*.

Virgin wax should be solid, opaque, white, brittle, and without any decided taste or smell. It softens and becomes malleable at a moderate temperature. It melts at about 149° Fah., and when thrown on red hot coals it inflames and burns away.

Thin slices of white wax seen beneath the microscope have the appearance of an amorphous substance. If, however, they are melted on the glass plate, and then allowed to cool, they

---

[1] It is sometimes adulterated with potato starch. (Delpech.)

assume a crystalline structure. This structure becomes more evident when it is examined by polarized light, and when one of the thin plates of gypsum, which M. Biot terms *sensitive plates*, is placed over it. (Dujardin.)

Wax contains three distinct principles—viz., cerine, myricine, and ceroleine. The cerine, or cerotic acid, forms the greatest part of the compound; it melts at 172° Fah.; it dissolves in boiling alcohol, which throws it down as a deposit in cooling. Myricine is white, inodorous, and tasteless; it melts at 161° Fah.; it requires 200 parts of boiling alcohol to dissolve it. Ceroleine forms only a very small proportion of the wax, about 4 or 5 per cent.; it melts at 84° Fah.; it is soft and very soluble both in alcohol and ether, even when cold.

Wax forms the basis of cerates. It also enters into the composition of a great number of unguents and plasters. It has even been recommended medicinally in the form of electuary, emulsion, and pills.

[Wax forms the hardening material of all the cerates of the pharmacopœia. The two simple cerates are the common cerate and the cerate of spermaceti; the latter has already been noticed under the head of spermaceti.[1]

CERATUM, *Cerate.*—Wax ℨxx, Olive oil Oj. Add the oil to the melted wax, and mix.

Wax also enters into the composition of several of the plasters and ointments of the pharmacopœia.]

OTHER KINDS OF WAX.—Certain species of *Cocci* exude a waxy material, which bears some resemblance to spermaceti, and from which bougies are made. The *Coccus Sinensis* (Westwood) furnishes the *Chinese Wax*. The *Coccus ceriferus* (Fabr.), which lives in Bengal, produces a similar substance. In the *Common Cochineal*,[2] principally in the variety known as *Silver Cochineal*, a white powder is seen on the females, which consists of wax.

§ XII. Hair and other Corneous Substances.

Hairs, hoofs, and feathers have long since been banished from the materia medica;[3] but the corneous parts of animals still render us important services in other respects.

Horsehair is employed in the manufacture of mattresses, chairs, and various kinds of elastic tissues.

[1] See page 94.
[2] See page 71.
[3] See page 65.

The hair of the ox, after being calcined, has been profitably employed for some years, by M. Liance, in the preparation of kermes mineral.

It is sufficient to recall the various uses to which whalebone[1] is applied. This material consists of corneous plates from 6 to 9 feet in length, arranged parallel to each other, and attached vertically to the palatine surface of the maxillary bones (fig. 54). These plates have their inner edges narrow, and terminating in a number of coarse fibres, which are the free ends of the fibres of which the plates are composed. When the mouth of the whale is closed on a swarm of mollusca, or on a shoal of small fishes, the water escapes through the intervals of the plates and the fringes of coarse hair. Thus the whole forms a kind of filter, which strains off the water, but retains what was in it.

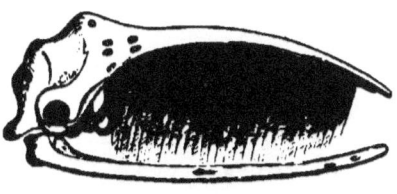

Fig. 54.—*Whalebone.*

The *feathers* of Birds are used for making mattresses, bolsters, quilts, and various kinds of ornaments. The body feathers (*Hen, Grebe, Penguin*), the down (*Goose, Eider duck*), the great wing and tail feathers (*Ostrich, Goose, Crow*), and the covertures which protect the base of the latter (*Peacock, Egret, Marabout*) are all employed for some purpose or another.

Feathers form an important branch of commerce: in 1833, there was imported into France 230,222 lbs. of feathers of the value of £29,318.

---

[1] See page 93.

BOOK IV.

NOXIOUS ANIMALS, BUT WHICH ARE NOT POISONOUS NOR YET PARASITES.

CHAPTER I.

ANIMALS NOXIOUS DURING THEIR LIVES.

General Observations.

THE noxious animals which are not poisonous nor yet parasites are those in which there is no special gland for the secretion of a poison, and which are not permanent inhabitants either of the interior or of the exterior of our bodies.

There are some, however, which not only cause pain, but also produce other symptoms, which seem to show that there is something more than a mere mechanical action in their puncture. The saliva which is deposited in the wound probably possesses some specific action.

The number of these animals is very considerable. There are many species, both large and small, which every one is acquainted with, which wound us with their horns, their teeth, their beak, their claws, or with particular instruments. It is unnecessary to enumerate their names. Generally speaking, they are animals which avoid man. They only wound him when they are attacked, tormented, or mutilated, or when they are endeavouring to escape from the hand which has seized them.

It has been asserted that several large tailless bats belonging to South America, and particularly the *Vampire*[1] and the *Javelin Bat, Phyllostoma haustatum,* Cuv., could destroy a man by sucking his blood. It is now ascertained that these animals only inflict small circular or elliptical wounds, which are painful, and are sometimes accompanied by a considerable amount of local inflammation (Azara Tschudi); in some rare cases this may assume a poisonous character from the state of the climate. (Cuvier.)

---

[1] *Vampyrus spectrum,* Spix, *Vespectilio Vampyrus,* Linn., commonly known in Brazil as the *Andiraguaça* or *Roussette*.

The *Musaraigne*, the *Rat*, and even the *Squirrel*, can bite so as to draw blood. It is the same with certain Birds, and some large kinds of Lizards.

Other Birds defend themselves with the spur attached to their foot, or with the points of their wings.

Several species of *Rays* inflict wounds with the toothed spine of their tail, and the *Weaver* with the spines of their fins.

The *Torpedo* and *Gymnotus* give electric shocks.

The *Crustacea* will seize the fingers or the skin with their strong dentated claws.

Many *Insects* bite, prick, or scratch, &c.

The injuries which can be inflicted by *Ants* have been greatly exaggerated. The bites of these minute animals are altogether insignificant, at least in our country. Some foreign *Ants* are more disagreeable, especially when they occur in large numbers; such as the *Ants* of Southern Africa, mentioned by Father Labat; the *Flaming Ants* (*Flammants*) of the woods of Cayenne, which, according to Barrere, give rise to febrile disturbances; and the *Fire Ant* of Surinam, of which Stedman has given an account. Adanson relates that certain *Red Ants* of Senegal live in the branches of a species of oak, where they compose their nest of the leaves, and that they throw themselves on persons who are so imprudent as to come near, and bite them severely. This celebrated naturalist was once attacked by these insects; his hands and face were covered with blisters as if they had been burnt.

It is known that a kind of acid vapour (*formic acid*) is exhaled from the bodies of the *Ants*. The vapour is not a poison, but it may produce some slight action on our bodies,[1] and may even produce small blisters, accompanied with a peculiar kind of itching. It is asserted that a large number of these insects assembled together on one spot, or the vapour arising from a formicary, is capable of producing a species of erysipelas.

The *Flies* in our country sometimes bite very disagreably, especially towards the autumn; but these insects are rather inconvenient than hurtful.

One of the *flies* most to be dreaded is a species of Stomoxys, which appears about the middle of the summer, and assembles in swarms around the heads of horses and of cattle; it also attacks man.

---

[1] When the *Red Ant* (*Formica rufa*, Linn.) crawls over a piece of litmus paper it produces a red track.

There are many insects which exhale a very disagreeable, stinking odour. This smell arises from a fluid which they disgorge, or transude from some part of their body, principally when they are touched. Some of the beetles belonging to the families of *Silphidæ* and *Carabidæ* discharge a very fœtid fluid from the mouth. The *Brachinidæ* or Bombardier beetles discharge a still more offensive fluid from the anus. The large *Cicadæ* pour out a fluid which is probably an urinary secretion. The *Blattidæ* have two vesicles at the side of the anus, which impart a most nauseous odour to our food. The *Cocci* exude a bitter and acrid liquid from between the articulations of the thorax and the tarsi of the anterior feet.

Lastly, the *Flies* and other insects which frequent putrid meat, and other kinds of filth, may convey to our bodies the germs of dangerous disorders.

The present division of the work will be devoted to the consideration of: 1. The *Serrasalmes*; 2. *Horse Leech*; 3. *Bugs*; 4. The *Nepa*; 5. The *Hippoboscidæ*; 6. The *Tsetse*; 7. The *Gnats*; 8. *Stinging animals*; 9. The *Larvæ of Flies*; 10. *Insects introduced accidentally into the natural cavities of the body.*

§ I. The Serra-salmes.

The *Serra-salmes* (*Pygocentrus*) are fishes belonging to the Salmonidæ. They live together in shoals, and are carnivorous. They attack with the greatest ferocity all animals which may chance to come into the same waters as themselves, not excepting even man himself. They fix themselves on to the skin and tear their victims with their triangular cutting teeth. Their bite is so sharp and so quick that it is not felt more than the cut of a razor. (A. de St. Hilaire.)

One of the best known species is the *Piranha* or *Devil Fish*[1] discovered by M. de Castelnau in Uruguay, in the rivers Tocantin and Amazon.

When any object is thrown into the water inhabited by the *Piranhas*, these fish immediately attack it. One of the companions of M. de Castelnau, being oppressed by the heat, wished to bathe, but no sooner had he entered the water than he was attacked by a shoal of the *Piranhas*, and he saw his blood pouring forth and discolouring the water. He made for the bank, which was fortunately close at hand, and he thus escaped what was otherwise certain death. (De Castelnau.)

---

[1] *Pygocentrus Piraya*, Mull. (*Serrasalme Piraya*, Cuv., *Serrasalmus Piranha*, Spix).

§ II. Hæmopis.

HÆMOPIS SANGUISUGA, Moq., or *Horse Leech* (fig. 55).—
This creature is met with in nearly every part of Europe. It
is found in Sweden, in the South of Spain, in Portugal, and in
Turkey. It is very common in the North of Africa along all
parts of the coast, and has been found in
all the waters which have been visited by
the French troops in their furthest advances into the desert. Larrey noticed it
in Egypt, and Barker Webb in the Canary
Islands.

The *Hæmopis* inhabits the marshes,
ditches, and smaller rivulets. The full-
grown animals usually bury themselves
in the mud. The young appear to prefer
the running waters, where they remain at
the surface ready to plunge below upon
the slightest disturbance. (Guyon.)

Description.—The body of the *Hæmopis*
is soft, depressed, elongated, and gradually
narrowed towards the anterior extremity;
when it is squeezed between the fingers it
feels like a dead or diseased medicinal
Leech. The body has from 95 to 97 short
and rather indistinct rings, and an upper
lip composed of three segments. The back
is of a brown or greenish brown colour,
sometimes approaching to a reddish or
Sienna earth colour, or to an olive or green
colour. It has generally longitudinal rows
of minute close-set black spots. There are
usually six of these rows, but sometimes

Fig. 55.—*Hæmopis.*

only four, and still more rarely only two. In many individuals these spots are replaced by one or two large bands
of a red colour, shaded off at the margins. Individuals are
occasionally met with, in which the back is of a uniform colour.
The margins are not very prominent, and are marked by a
very distinct[1] line of an orange, yellow, or reddish brown colour.
The belly is of a uniform blackish slate colour, generally darker
than the back, sometimes of a red or of an olive colour, and at
other times of a dull black; sometimes it is marked with obscure,
isolated, irregular spots, and at other times it is free from

[1] *Margine laterali flavo*, Linn.

them. The suckers are smooth, slender, and of the same colour as the belly; the anal is half the size of the ventral. The eyes are ten in number, very distinct, and arranged in a curved line; six are placed on the first segment.

At the period of reproduction the *clitellum*[1] is paler than the rest of the body; it commences at the 22nd ring, and terminates at the 28th. Of the male and female orifices the first is placed between the 24th and 25th rings, and the second between the 29th and 30th.

The cocoons are oval, smaller and shorter than those of the medicinal Leech, and covered with a looser and more irregular tissue. In one M. Tandon found eight embryos.

The *Horse Leech* has often been confounded with the true Leeches. It differs: 1, as regards its size, which is somewhat larger; 2, by its jaws, which are smaller, not so strong, and furnished with a smaller number of teeth (thirty instead of sixty), which are not so pointed (fig. 56); 3, by a softer and less contracted body; 4, by the rings being less marked, less coriaceous, and forming during their contraction ridges, which are less apparent; 5, by smaller and not such prominent cutaneous tubercles; 6, by the absence of the red or brown dorsal bands; 7, by the belly being darker than the back, and having no black marginal bands.

Fig. 56.—*Jaw of Hæmopis.*[2]

2. ITS ACTION ON THE VERTEBRATA.—Aldrovandus believed that nine of these Leeches were able to kill a horse. This statement, which has been repeated by Gisler, Weser, Müller, and many other writers, has latterly been disputed. It bears the impress of exaggeration, and is, therefore, rejected. It has even been asserted that these annelides do not pierce the skin of the vertebrata or suck their blood.

The *Horse Leech* has been clearly proved to be as eager after blood as the *Medicinal Leech*, but the latter is provided with the means of penetrating the skin at any part, even such skins as those of the pachydermata, while the *Hæmopis*, with its less developed and more feebly armed jaws, can only penetrate the mucous membranes. Hence the necessity which this species is under of introducing itself into the natural cavities of horses, oxen, and other animals.

[1] See p. 138.
[2] *a*, Jaw seen from the side; *b*, form and arrangement of the teeth.

Dr. Guyon has frequently found in the neighbourhood of Algiers *Horse Leeches* lodged in the nose, pharynx, and air passages of the animals which have been slaughtered for the use of the troops and the people. Amongst other instances an ox had twelve of these leeches in the mouth and fauces, five around the anterior part of the glottis, four in the ventricles of the larynx, and six about the fourth or fifth ring of the trachea; altogether twenty-seven. These Leeches were still attached twelve hours after the death of the animal.

The *camels* and the *mules* are frequently tormented by the *Hæmopis*, which penetrates into the nasal fossæ and into the air passages. These annelides easily gain entrance into the mouths of animals which come to the water they inhabit for the purpose of drinking. Whatever part of the body the *Hæmopis* may be lodged in, it is always attached by means of the anal sucker, which fixes itself firmly to the mucous membrane. The oral sucker applies itself to the surrounding parts according to the caprice of the leech. Thus, upon examining the mucous membrane in the neighbourhood of an *Hæmopis*, it is seen to be covered with a number of small wounds and cicatrices. (Guyon.) When the *Leeches* are sufficiently gorged, they detach themselves from their victims at the time of their visiting the watering places, and thus regain their natural habitation.

Dr. Guyon has made some experiments upon these animals. He introduced them into the æsophagus and oviduct of fowls, and into the nasal fossæ and the rectum of rabbits. At the end of thirteen days the animals appeared very much wasted; they eat but little, and had a melancholy appearance. The fowls perished in about thirty days, and the rabbits in about forty.

M. Tandon also made several experiments; he placed two large *Horse Leeches* at the back of the mouth of two small rabbits. The animals penetrated into the trachea; one stopped at the commencement of the canal, the other passed completely in. The first rabbit died in about an hour and a half, while the second was suffocated in three quarters of an hour.

The *Horse Leech* is one of the main causes of disease in the animals of Algeria. It is not, however, probable that nine of them would destroy a horse, as stated by Aldrovandus, since it has been seen that an ox was capable of supporting twenty-seven without receiving any material injury. At the same time they might cause the animal to be very unwell, and if nine full-grown leeches were to fix themselves on the same part of the air passages, the animal might be suffocated, as in the case of the rabbits mentioned above.

3. ACTION ON MAN.—The *Hæmopis* also introduces itself into the mouth, pharynx, nasal fossæ, larynx, and trachea of man. Most if not all the cases, which have been recorded by writers, of *Leeches* being lodged in the alimentary canal or air passages of our species, are to be referred to the *Hæmopis* in a country where these animals are abundant; great caution should be used in drinking water from the rivulets, and especially from the marshes.

The young worms, which are not more than $\frac{1}{10}$ inch in length and not thicker than a fine thread, are carried along by the water, and swallowed without being noticed. They become arrested and fix themselves to various parts of the mouth, especially to the back part of it.

At first a slight pricking is felt at the back of the mouth, and afterwards the presence of a foreign body.

It has been stated that the bite of the *Hæmopis* is more painful than that of the *Medicinal Leech*. (Savigny, Audouin.) M. Tandon at first supposed that the difference depended upon the jaws being less compressed, and the teeth being not so sharp, or in consequence of the mucous membranes which are wounded being very sensitive. But M. Guyon has satisfied himself that their wounds are not very serious; only the presence of the animals in the nasal fossæ, and still more so in the air passages, produces great inconvenience, and in some cases threatens the individual with suffocation.

The wounds inflicted by the *Hæmopis* heal very quickly when the animals which inflicted them are removed.

The *Horse Leech* was noticed in 1756 at the siege of Mahon. Since that time a great number of soldiers and travellers have suffered from imprudently drinking the water from ditches and marshes. Larrey in Egypt, Bory St. Vincent in Spain, and Barny in Algeria, have often been consulted by soldiers who had these animals attached to the back of the mouth or to the air passages.

Dr. Guyon once found one of these leeches on the conjunctiva of a soldier, where it had got while he was washing himself. On another occasion he extracted one from the vagina of a young girl who had been for some time in the water.

This gentleman could not succeed in inducing the *Hæmopis* to bite the external parts of the human body. M. Tandon also attempted the same thing on several occasions, but with no better success. He placed some of these leeches of different ages on the parts of his own body where the skin is most delicate, he also tried them on the arm and thigh of a child, but the animals never attempted to bite. On one occasion he bathed the inner surface of his arm with blood; the leech moved about and felt the blood, it even dilated its sucker, but it never cut the skin or made any attempt to do so.

The *Horse Leech* is never employed in medicine,[1] the reason for which is sufficiently evident. In the countries where they are abundant, they might be used instead of the common *Leech* in the few instances in which it is required to apply them to the mucous membranes at the entrance of one of the internal cavities of the body. It would, however, be very necessary to watch the animal, in order to prevent its entering too far.

§ III. Cimicidæ.

The *Cimicidæ*, or *Bugs*, belong to the order Hemiptera and to the family Geocores.

Linnæus, who was the founder of group *Cimex*, assigned as its characters—rostrum inflected; antennæ longer than the thorax; wings four, placed transversely, the upper pair coriaceous; the body flattened, and the feet adapted for running.

This genus, which is far from a natural one, contains 121 species. Linnæus was compelled to divide it into twelve sections, according to the presence or absence of wings, the nature of the elytra, the thickness of the body, and the form and characters of the antennæ. At the present time the Linnæan genus corresponds to more than forty genera, containing more than 1000 species.

1. COMMON BUG (fig. 57).—Every one is familiar with the *Common Bug* or *Bed Bug*, *Cimex lectularius*, Linn. There are few persons who have not at some time or another been bitten by this disagreeable and stinking insect.

The bug lives in the crevices and corners of old wood; behind curtains, looking-glasses, and picture-frames; in all kinds of old furniture, and especially in bedsteads. The flattened form of its body enables it to penetrate into the narrowest aperture.

The animal avoids the light,[2] hiding itself during the daytime. It seldom remains on our bodies or on our dress.

The *Bug* is said to have been introduced into Europe.

---

[1] Gisler pretends that the Norwegians employ this leech instead of the *Medicinal Leech*. This statement cannot be correct.
[2] *Nocturnum fœtidum animal.* (Linn.)

However, Aristotle, Pliny, and Dioscarides distinctly refer to it. The ancients gave it the name of *Coris*. The insect was not known in England before the 17th century. It is stated to have been imported from America in 1666, with a cargo of wood.[1] Others believe that it came from India.

Description.—The *Bed Bug* has an oval body, about $\frac{2}{10}$ inch in length, somewhat narrowed anteriorly, thin at the sides, very depressed, soft, and of a reddish or ferruginous brown colour. It is covered with very short hairs. The head is of a square form and provided at the commencement of the rostrum with a hood which serves as a sheath to the base of the latter. The eyes are round and black; the antennæ setiform and composed of four cylindrical joints; the first very short; the second thick, long, cylindrical, and partially covered with hairs; the third very long, much slenderer than the others, and slightly dilated at its extremity. The thorax has the first segment hollowed out anteriorly, and truncated posteriorly; the sides are dilated, rounded, and membranous. The animal has small rudimentary elytra. It has no wings. The legs are of moderate size and black at their extremities; the tarsi are short, and consist of three joints; the first is very slightly developed, the second is conico-cylindrical, the last is somewhat shorter than the second, cylindrical, and armed with two strong hooks. The abdomen is large, oval, composed of eight segments, fimbriated at its margins, very depressed, and easily crushed between the fingers. It is marked with a black spot posteriorly.

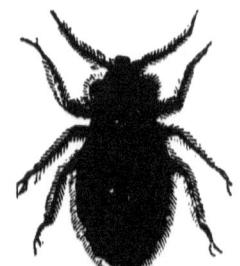

Fig. 57.—*Bug.*

The scent of these insects arises from a fluid, which is secreted by a pyriform reddish gland, placed in the centre of the metathorax, and opening between the posterior legs.

Bugs lay their eggs about the month of May. The eggs have an oblong form and are of a white colour. They are slightly narrowed at one extremity, where there is a small, round, slightly convex operculum, which closes up the orifice from whence the larva issues forth. When seen under the

---

[1] Linnæus, upon the authority of Southal, states that this insect was introduced into England shortly before 1670. Mouffet relates that in 1503, two ladies having been bitten during the night by two *Bugs*, inquired of a medical man to know *what these little animals were*. This circumstance proves that the introduction of these animals was prior to 1666.

microscope, the shell of these eggs is found to be covered with minute projections.

The larva differs from the perfect insect by the absence of the elytra, and by its paler colour, which is more or less of a yellow tint.

Mouth (fig. 58).—This consists of a short rostrum, which does not reach farther than the base of the first pair of limbs. In a state of repose it is lodged in a small groove directly under the thorax. The rostrum contains three joints; the first and second are cylindrical, somewhat depressed, and of nearly equal length; the second is stouter; and the third, which is conical, is somewhat longer than the others. This apparatus contains three stiff-pointed setæ.

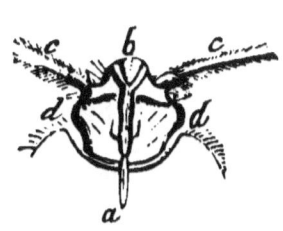

Fig. 58.—*Rostrum*.[1]

Action on Man.—All are aware of the avidity with which these animals attack man, and with what eagerness they suck his blood. They also torment young pigeons and some other animals.

The odour of man's body attracts these insects. When one has the misfortune to sleep in a room infested with *bugs*, they issue forth from their hiding-places as soon as the light is extinguished, and hasten in multitudes towards the bed. Some mount the walls and reaching the ceiling, let themselves fall down.

Having got to the sleeper, they seek out the parts of his body most favourable for their purpose, plunge their rostrum into his skin and gorge themselves with his blood.

These animals do not draw up the blood by suction, after the manner of the Leech. The buccal apparatus, which is nearly the same in all sucking insects, does not allow of this kind of action. The setæ of the mouth when placed together move alternately up and down, causing the blood to mount into the æsophagus, much in the same manner as water in a chain-pump. (Dumeril.) This ascent is favoured by the viscous nature of the fluid, and especially by its globules.

Bugs do not attack the parts about the genital organs or about the anus. They may, however, introduce themselves into the ears or nose, and gain entrance to the frontal sinuses, at

---

[1] *a*, end of the rostrum; *b*, its base; *c c*, portions of the antennæ; *d d*, the eyes.

least, when they are young (Raspail); they do not, however, remain there long.

M. Dumeril found the eggs of the *Bug* under the nail of the great toe in a dead body. This is, however, an exceptional case, as these insects are not permanent inhabitants of man's body. So soon as they have gorged themselves with his blood they leave him.

The bite of the Bug gives a kind of smarting painful sensation; it produces a red mark with a depressed spot in the centre; it frequently produces a small blister.

2. OTHER SPECIES.—M. Signoret has discovered a second species which lives in the Island of Reunion; he has described it under the name of the *Round Bug, Acanthia rotundata*, Sign.

M. E. Eversmann has described and figured a third species under the name of the *Ciliated Bug, Acanthia ciliata*, Eversm., which lives in the houses at Kasan.

It is smaller than the common species, and differs also in being of a more oval form and of a reddish grey colour. It is covered with grey or yellow hairs, and has a strong rostrum.

This species does not live in company in the crevices of old wood, but leads a solitary life on the walls and furniture. It is sluggish, and moves but slowly; it appears stupid, and like an insect benumbed with the cold.

Its bite produces a considerable amount of swelling, which lasts for some time; it is much more painful than that of the *Common Bug*. (Eversmann.)

3. ALLIED INSECTS.—With the Bugs may be associated the *Reduviidæ* and the *Notonectidæ*.

1. The *Reduvius personatus* (fig. 59) is a common insect in France. It is occasionally found in the neighbourhood of Paris; it lives in houses, taking up its abode in ovens and chimneys.

The animal is from half to three-quarters of an inch in length, oblong, flattened above, of a brownish colour, with obscure markings on the thorax. It resembles a long fly; the head is narrow, supported on a distinct neck, and is provided with compound eyes and with two simple eyes. The thorax is nearly triangular, very distinct, and almost bilobed; the anterior lobe, which is usually the smallest, is separated from the posterior by a groove. The elytra are as long as the abdomen, placed horizontally, very thin, and partially overlap each other. The

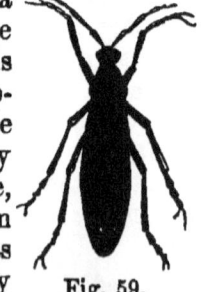

Fig. 59.
Reduvina.

wings are well developed and are used in flight. In flying the insect makes a slight noise, similar to that which is produced by the Crioceridæ and the Longicornes Beetles, but the separate sounds succeed each other more rapidly; this noise is produced by the friction of the head against the thorax. The legs are long and slender, the tarsi short and provided with three joints. The abdomen is flattened above and convex below.

The *Reduvina* gives off a disagreeable odour, which has been compared to that of a mouse. These animals nourish themselves by sucking the bodies of other insects, hunting them and piercing them with their pointed rostrum.

The larvæ, which are very hideous,[1] also lead a life of rapine; they even pursue the *Common Bug*. (Linnæus, Fabricius.) These larvæ resemble small spiders; they discharge from the whole of their body a viscid humour, to which all the dust, earth, and offensive matter adheres with which the animal comes in contact. They hide themselves in corners and in holes in walls, and in heaps of dirt;[2] they watch until some insect approaches and then throw themselves upon him; at other times, when pressed by hunger, they advance slowly or by sudden jerks, but cautiously, so as not to alarm their victim, upon whom they suddenly precipitate themselves and seize him with their fore feet. (De Geer.)

Mouth (fig. 60).—The beak of the *Reduvius personatus* is short (about $\frac{1}{10}$ inch) and curved; the surface is armed with stiff hairs; it consists of four joints, of which the first is the thickest, the third the longest, and the fourth the shortest; the base of it is covered by a rudimentary upper lip; its termination is received into a groove on the under surface of the thorax; the beak encloses four stiff lancet-like setæ. It appeared to M. Tandon as if two of these setæ were serrated at their edges.

Fig. 60.—*Rostrum.*[3]

Action on Man.—The *Reduvina* attacks man, and the wounds which it inflicts are very painful. Latreille was once bitten on the shoulder by one of these insects; his whole arm became swollen and continued so for some hours.

Entomologists are agreed that these insects are not provided

---

[1] *Larva horrida, personata,* Linn.
[2] *Cimex stercorarius,* Frisch.
[3] *a,* first joint; *b,* second joint; *c,* third joint; *d,* terminal joint; *e,* compound eye; *f,* single eye.

with a poison; and, in fact, at present no gland or reservoir for the reception of such a fluid has hitherto been discovered. If, however, the bite of the *Reduvina* was purely mechanical, how is it possible to explain the rapidity with which it kills or stupifies small insects (De Geer), and also the phenomena which it produces on our own species? These effects are probably caused by the saliva.

OTHER SPECIES.—There is a red and a black species, and also the *Reduvius cruentus*, whose bites are equally painful.

According to Major Davis, another species, *Reduvius serratus* (Fabr.), is met with in India, which produces slight electric shocks.

2. The *Notonecta glauca* is a species of water Bug, commonly known as the *Boat Fly* (fig. 61); it is very different from the species of *Bugs* which have been previously mentioned.

This animal is found in the neighbourhood of Paris and throughout nearly the whole of Europe; it is aquatic, and lives in ditches, ponds, and other masses of stagnant water; it usually maintains itself at the surface of the water, but immediately plunges beneath when any one approaches.

Description.—The body is about half an inch in length, oblong, narrow, nearly cylindrical, somewhat contracted posteriorly, convex above, flattened below, and has its sides fringed with long hairs, which spread out and sustain the animal in the water; the head is large and of a grey or greenish colour; the eyes are large, oblong, and occupy all the sides of the head; the antennæ are shorter than the head, and composed of four slender joints; the first is very short and cylindrical, the second is longer and slightly bent, the third is cylindrical and not quite so long or so thin as the second, the last is shorter and slenderer than the third. The thorax is wider than it is long, of a yellowish grey anteriorly, and of a dark grey posteriorly. The elytra are about the same length as the abdomen, and of a greenish grey colour, with black spots on their anterior margins; the wings are membranous, of the same length as the elytra, and of a white colour; the four anterior feet are short, and constructed in the usual manner; the posterior are double their length, they are strongly ciliated, and their tarsi are unprovided with hooks; the hinder limbs act as oars. The abdomen is black above, and greenish grey at the extremity.

Fig. 61. *Notonecta.*

The *Water Bugs* in the various stages of larva, nymph, and perfect insect, feed upon small aquatic insects, which they seize with the hooks of the anterior feet and pierce with their beak. These animals are exceedingly voracious, and when other insects are not present they will devour their own species. They have a very singular mode of swimming, placing themselves on their backs, and generally in an inclined position. From this circumstance they have received the name of *Notonecta*, which literally means *back swimming*. The head is somewhat higher than the rest of the body when the animal ascends through the water, and a little lower when it remains at the surface or when it descends; while in the act of swimming, the anterior limbs are placed against the thorax and only the posterior pair or oars are in motion; when, however, the animals are on the mud at the bottom of the water, or on a leaf, or when they are walking, it is the anterior feet which are brought into use, the posterior remaining motionless, and trailing after the insect.

De Geer has described the male organs of the *Water Bug;* they are contained in the last segment of the abdomen. If the belly is compressed, a large scaly piece issues forth of a black colour and cleft at its extremity; at this part a portion is seen projecting from between two plates, which is the penis.

In the act of copulation the male and the female place themselves side by side, the male being somewhat the lowest; they swim about joined together in this manner with great swiftness.

The eggs are deposited on the stems and leaves of aquatic plants, and even on the epidermis of the insects; they are oblong, cylindrical, and of a yellow colour; they are hatched at the commencement of spring.

The young larvæ immediately begin to swim about; they resemble the perfect insect, only they have no wings. The nymphæ have rudiments of the wings.

Mouth (fig. 62).—The beak is very strong and about $\frac{1}{10}$ of an inch in length; it has an elongated conical form and is composed of four joints, of

Fig. 62.—*Rostrum.*[1]

[1] *A*, head seen in profile; *a*, rostrum; *b*, first joint; *c*, second joint; *d*, third joint; *e*, terminal joint; *f*, rudiment of the upper lip; *B*, rostrum separate; *C*, seta with fringed margin; *D*, one of the two straight setæ.

which the first is thick, the third the longest, and the last very slender and not very pointed. The sucker is formed of a short, pointed, superior piece, and of three slender sharp-pointed setæ as long as the case. One of them is ciliated on one side and plumose towards its extremity.

Action on man.—The *Notonecta* bite strongly, but these insects do not emerge from the water, and consequently, unlike the *Ruduvina*, they do not enter into houses; they are only to be feared when the hand is incautiously placed into the element in which they reside; the pain they occasion is tolerably acute.

As the insects which are attacked by the *Notonecta* soon die, some writers have supposed that they discharge a poisonous fluid into the wound; but where is this poison organ to be found? Is it not the saliva which, in this case, also exercises a poisonous influence?

§ IV. Nepa.

The *Grey Nepa*, *Nepa cinerea*, Linn., (fig. 63,) commonly called *Water Scorpion* or *Water Spider*, is a Hemipterous insect belonging to the section Heteroptera and to the family Hydrocores. It is common throughout the whole of France [and England], where it lives in ditches, marshes, and other pools of fresh water.

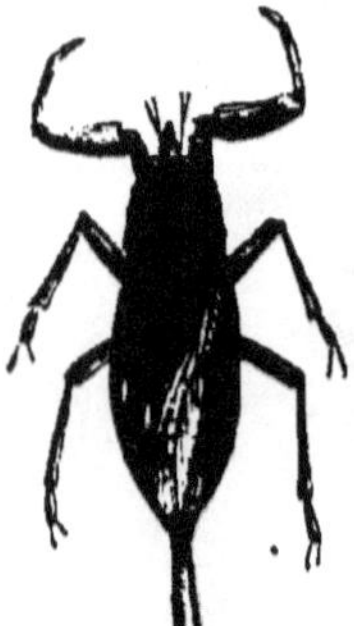

The body is three-quarters of an inch long, of an oblong oval form, very depressed, and of an ashen colour, with red on the upper part of the abdomen; it terminates in a tail consisting of two slender filaments, which are tubes, through which the animal breathes. The antennæ are short, three-jointed, and cleft; the thorax is nearly square; the elytra are horizontal, coriaceous, and of a dingy grey; the anterior limbs have the coxæ short, and the thighs large and terminated by strong pincers, which give the insect some resemblance to the scorpion.

Fig. 63.—*Nepa.*

The *Nepa* swims slowly and with difficulty (Lamk.), it often walks at the bottom of the water; it comes forth at night time, and flies with great agility.

The eggs resemble small grains surrounded by seven bands; the insect deposits them on the stems of the water plants.

The larvæ are hatched in the middle of summer; they differ from the perfect insect in the absence of wings and of the abdominal filaments; the nymphæ are provided with elytra.

Mouth (fig. 64).—This consists of a curved rostrum, placed almost perpendicularly (Lamk.); it is short, conical, pointed, and tolerably stout; the rostrum is composed of three joints, of which the second is the longest. It encloses four slender pointed threads; two are provided on one side with a kind of straight narrow blade, and are very finely notched towards the base; the others are finer, and have also a narrow edge, but less developed than in the former; one of them is provided at its termination with a number of fine hairs directed from behind forwards.

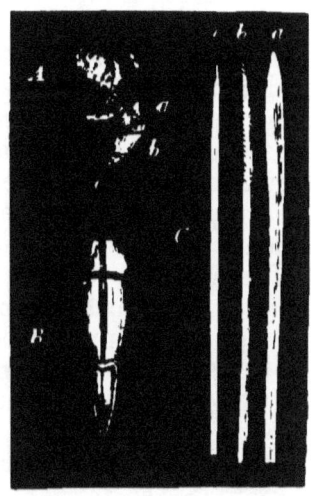

Fig. 64.—*Rostrum.*[1]

Action on man.—The *Nepa* bite very sharply, and cause a good deal of pain; the wound is not dangerous.

§ V. Hippoboscidæ.

The *Horse Fly*, *Hippobosca equina*, Linn., (fig. 65,) is an insect belonging to the order Diptera, and to the family Pupipara.

This insect settles on horses and cattle, generally beneath the tail near the anus; they select the parts which are devoid of hair.

Description.—The *Horse Fly* is of a brown colour mottled with yellow and white; it has a small head, a short thorax, and a flat abdomen; the antennæ have the form of tubercles, and are immersed within the head; the eyes are compound and occupy the entire side of the head; it has no simple eyes; the wings are horizontal, obtuse, partially cross each other, and extend beyond the abdomen; the balancers are placed beneath two flattened scale-like eminences; its limbs are well developed, and give the animal something of the appearance of a spider.

Fig. 65.—*Horse Fly.*

These insects walk quickly and often sideways; their flight is abrupt and rapid.

The female lays neither an egg nor a larva, but a true nymph;

---

[1] *A*, Rostrum seen from the side; *a*, first joint; *b*, second joint; *c*, terminal joint; *B*, rostrum separate; *C*, setæ contained in the rostrum; *a*, one of the two setæ with a lateral blade; *b*, ciliated seta; *c*, non-ciliated seta.

this is of a large size, and fills up the whole of the abdomen; its skin hardens after it is born. The *Horse Fly* emerges from the nympha by detaching a portion of the envelope. (Reaumur.)

Mouth (fig. 66).—This consists of a short, straight, cylindrical beak (*haustellum*), formed by the union of two modified palpi; these resemble a pair of small blades, or coriaceous valves; they are flat, oblong, straight, and terminate in a rounded extremity; they arise from the clypeus, which is hollowed out at its lower border, pass parallel to each other, and then form by their re-union a semitube, which covers the sucker.

The sucker is a large filiform, cylindrical, curved process, which commences from a kind of bulb in the mouth; this apparently simple process consists of two setæ, one superior, one inferior; the first has a canal on its under surface which covers over the second.

It is with this instrument that the *Hippobosca* so torments horses and cattle as to drive them frantic; it punctures the skin and eagerly sucks their blood.

Fig. 66.-*Beak.*

Action on man.—According to the experience of Reaumur, the *Hippobosca* is as eager after the blood of man as of the other mammalia. The same naturalist assures us that its bite is not more acute than that of a flea; Reaumur is, however, mistaken in this respect, as the bite of this insect is very painful.

§ VI. Tsetse.

The *Tsetse* or *Tzetse* (fig. 67) is a very formidable Fly which inhabits Africa. Bruce, who met with it in Abyssinia, has given a bad drawing of it, but has correctly described its habits.[1]

MM. Arnaud, Livingstone, Oswald, L. de Castelnau, and Anderson, have collected many curious details concerning this insect. Mr. Westwood has given a very good description of it.

The *Tsetse* belongs to the genus *Glossina*. It is named the *Biting Glossina, Glossina morsitans*, Westw.[2]

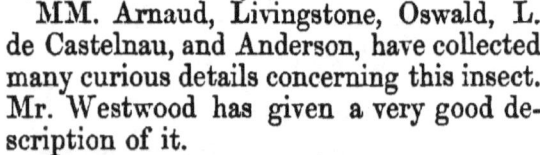

Fig. 67,—*Tsetse.*

[1] Mr. Anderson has given a very correct drawing of the insect in the *Cosmos*.

[2] This insect is called *Zebud* in the Chaldean version of the Bible, *Zimb* in the Arabian version, and *Tsaltsalya* in the Ethiopian; the Greeks give it the name of *Cynomya*, and the Negroes of *Tse-Tse*.

Nearly all the central countries of South Africa are more or less infested by the *Tsetse;* it is very common in all the countries situated to the north of Lake Ngami; and is again met with in Soudan and in the tropical districts.

This insect usually frequents the bushes and reeds on the borders of marshes. It is larger than the common fly, and of a whitish yellow colour; the thorax is of a pale chesnut on its upper surface, is covered with grey hairs, and has four longitudinal interrupted black bands in the centre; its proboscis (fig. 68) is twice as long as the head, and is extremely slender; it resembles a fine corneous thread; the palpi are straight, of the same length as the proboscis, and form a sheath for it; the abdomen is of a light yellow with darker spots or bands; the wings are smoke-coloured.

The buzzing of the *Tsetse* is a mixture of a dull and a sharp sound, producing a very discordant noise; this buzzing spreads a terror and disorder amongst men and animals which even the wild beasts of the country when they are twice their number will not produce. (Bruce.)

Its vision is extremely acute, and it darts like an arrow upon the animal that it intends to attack; it always makes its puncture between the belly and the thighs, when a swelling soon rises up around the wound.

Fig. 68.—*Trunk.*

The horse, the ox, and the dog, after they have been attacked by this insect, waste away and die in the course of a few days; those which are fat and in good condition soon die, while the others drag on a miserable existence for some weeks; three or four flies are sufficient to produce these disastrous results. The blood of the animals which die is altered and diminished in quantity; the fat in the neighbourhood of the wound is soft, viscous, and of a yellow colour; in general, some portion of the intestines is enormously swollen; the flesh putrifies very quickly (Castlenau); and the heart, the lungs, and the liver are more or less affected. The goat is the only domesticated animal which can live with impunity in the midst of these flies; dogs escape the danger when they are fed exclusively by means of the chase, but if these animals are fed with milk they invariably die; on the contrary, the calf has nothing to fear so long as it sucks.

The bite of the *Tsetse* is not dangerous to the wild animals;

the elephant, zebra, buffalo, and the various kinds of antelopes and gazelles which abound in the countries inhabited by this fly, do not experience any ill effects from it.

These insects do not bite when it is bright moonlight, or when the nights are very cold.

Action on man.—The *Tsetse* also attacks our species, but its action on man is attended with but little danger; its bite is very analogous to that of the gnat's,[1] but the pain does not last so long. (De Castelnau.) M. Arnaud, however, suffered for some months after being bitten by one of these insects.

M. Chapman, one of those who have penetrated the furthest into the interior of South Africa, states, that whilst he was hunting, having a small hole in his dress made by a pin, he has often seen one of the *Tsetse*, which appeared to know that it could not penetrate his dress, dart down, and, without ever missing its mark, wound him through the undefended opening.

Is the *Tsetse* a poisonous animal? Its effect on the domesticated animals would appear to answer the question in the affirmative, but its action on man declares the contrary. How then are we to explain its fatal effects on cattle? At the same time these results vary in different species, and in some they are of no consequence.

§ VII. Gnats.

The *Gnats, Culex*, are insects belonging to the order Diptera, to the tribe Nemocera, and to the family of the Culicidæ. Linnæus assigned as their character the possession of setaceous darts enclosed in a flexible sheath.

1. THE COMMON GNAT. (fig. 69), *Culex pipiens*, Linn., is the best known species.

This insect has a long body and limbs, covered with hairs, and of a grey colour; the antennæ are plumose in the males; the eyes are large, and converge posteriorly;

Fig. 69.—*Gnat.*[2]

---

[1] See page 232.
[2] *A, Common Gnat; B*, its larva.

the palpi are projecting, filiform, and covered with hairs; the abdomen has eight browncoloured rings.

These insects are very abundant, especially where there is much water. They assemble in swarms, which, as they ascend and descend, perform a variety of movements, and create a singing noise as they follow in the track of man and other animals. They are fond of blood, but they also suck the juices of flowers.

Copulation takes place towards the close of the day. The female deposits her eggs on the surface of the water, and, crossing the hinder legs, arranges them beside each other in a perpendicular direction; the eggs have the shape of a sugar-loaf, and the mass forms a small boat, which floats on the surface of the water; each female lays about 300 eggs a year.

The eggs are hatched in about two days; the larvæ abound in ponds, marshes, and stagnant waters, especially during the spring; the head of the *larvæ* is provided with ciliated appendages, which enable them to procure their food; the abdomen is long and cylindrical, and terminates in a respiratory tube. The animal suspends itself in the water with its head downwards for the purpose of breathing. These larvæ swim about by sudden darts; when the water is disturbed they precipitate themselves with great rapidity to the bottom, with a zig-zag motion. (Lamark.) They change into nymphæ, which can row themselves about by means of their tail and two fin-like appendages; they have two corneous tubes beneath the thorax. Lamark correctly observes that this second state of the *Gnat* is, properly speaking, neither a larva, a chrysalis, nor a nympha; all the metamorphoses take place in about three or four weeks.

Mouth (fig. 70).—Reaumur has given an admirable description of the mouth of the *Gnat*, and of the manner in which it acts. There is

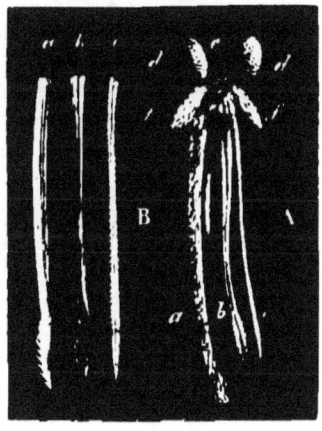

Fig. 70.—*Proboscis.*[1]

---

[1] *A*, proboscis; *a*, lower lip, forming a sheath; *b*, jaws and mandibles, having the form of filaments united together; *c*, upper lip, forming a fifth filiament; *dd*, eyes; *e*, head; *ff*, maxillary palpi; *B*, separate filaments; *a*, one of the two serrated filaments; *b*, one of the two with lancet-shaped points; *c*, upper lip,

a long, slender, projecting proboscis, composed—1, of a membranous cylindrical tube, terminating in two small lips, forming a slight enlargement or disc; 2, of a sucker or dart formed by the union of five scaly and setaceous threads. The tube is cleft superiorly, forming a half canal, but the terminal lips are united above so as to form a ring around the dart; of the five threads, two are terminated by a small lancet-shaped dilatation, two others have on their outer edge near the point very fine teeth directed from before backwards, while the fifth is setaceous and armed with fine spines throughout its entire length.

Action on man.—The bite of the *Gnat*, which is scarcely felt in temperate climates, becomes unbearable in hot countries.

These animals follow man everywhere; they enter his houses, particularly at night, announcing their presence by a loud singing noise, and pierce his skin, which even his clothes are not sufficient to protect.

When a *Gnat* has selected the part which he intends to suck, he applies the terminal expansion of the proboscis to the spot; he then thrusts out the dart from the centre of the expansion and penetrates the skin; in proportion as the dart is buried, the external protecting tube, whose expansion is fastened around the wound, becomes longer than the portion which is not inserted (fig. 71, A); as the tube is cleft on its upper surface it opens from above downwards, leaving the dart exposed; it becomes bent and forms at first an arch, of which the dart is the cord; it afterwards forms an angle, which is at first very obtuse, and afterwards very acute. At a certain time the head of the animal makes its nearest possible approach to the terminal expansion, and the groove forms between the latter and the bite a vertical fold (fig. 71, B).

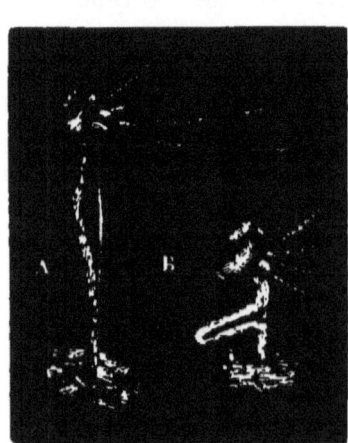

Fig. 71.—*Proboscis in action.*[1]

Amoreux regarded the Gnat as a poisonous insect; this is somewhat doubtful, since there is no gland for the secretion of a poison. It appears, however, that when the animal has punctured the skin it disgorges into it a drop of fluid, which

---

[1] A, proboscis when the setæ are first introduced; B, proboscis when the setæ are completely immersed.

is probably saliva; the setæ which form the dart leave a narrow space between them, but sufficient to give passage to this fluid. It is through the same channel that the blood is pumped up by the insect. Reaumur believed that the saliva poured out by the *Gnat* is also intended to render the blood more fluid. M. Dumeril thinks that it first exercises a narcotic action, which momentarily deadens the local sensibility; this enables the insect to suck without being perceived; afterwards it gives rise to an acute inflammation accompanied with considerable pain, and a small edematous spot, which every one is familiar with. Persons are sometimes completely disfigured by the bites inflicted by *Gnats* and the inflammation which accompanies them. These bites, when they are severe and numerous, produce restlessness and even fever; the insupportable itching caused by them compels the person to be perpetually scratching himself, but even this affords only a momentary relief; the more the person scratches himself the more the local inflamation and the pain seem to increase; the pain varies not only according to the size and vigour of the *Gnat*, but also according to the susceptibility of the part which is bitten.

2. OTHER SPECIES.—The principal *Gnats* in France besides the *Common Gnat* are the *Ringed Gnat*, *Culex annulatus*, Fabr., which is of a brown colour with transverse bands of white, and the *Culex pulicaris*, Linn., which has no bands, but three indistinct spots. The latter is the largest; it inhabits the southern parts, particularly in the neighbourhood of Cette.

The *Creeping Gnat*, *Simulium reptans*, Latr., which is black with a white ring, and about the size of a flea, is common in Sweden, and forms the type of the genus *Simulium*.

The Musquitoes of America are true *Gnats*; those of the French Colonies appear to belong to the genus *Simulium*. The bite of these insects is extremely painful; cloth clothes do not always preserve the person against their attacks. When these animals bite a person who is asleep he wakes up with his body covered with small pimples with a black spot, or a collection of dark serum in the centre surrounded by a ring of a deep fawn colour (Bouffiers); a severe itching is felt, the person scratches himself, the skin becomes abraided, and the inflammation continues to spread.

In the moist forests of the Isle of France and of Madagascar, there is an insect which appears to be closely allied to the *Gnats*, whose bite also causes intolerable pain; it is named *Bigaye* or *Bizigaye*.

In conclusion, it must be observed, that amongst the Diptera there are animals less known and less common than the Gnats which do not spare man when they have an opportunity of attacking him. Such is the case with the *Autumn Fly*, *Conops calcitrans*, Linn., which bites the legs, especially on the approach of rain; and also with the *Breese Fly*, *Tabanus bovinus*, Linn.

§ VIII. Stinging Animals.

The caterpillars of several of the *Bombycidæ*, or nocturnal moths, called *Processionary Moths*,[1] which live in societies on the oak and the pine, protected by a silken covering,[2] are clothed with fine hairs, which become blended with the covering of their nest and the tissue of their cocoons; these fine hairs penetrate the skin, and cause great irritation and even swelling of the part. Other species which are mentioned as producing similar effects are the *Bombyx of the oak*, *Phalæna quercus*, Linn.; a *Liparis*, *Liparis auriflua*, Ochsen, whose caterpillar resides in wood; and a *Lithosia*, *Lithosia caniola*, Fabr., whose caterpillar lives on walls.

The ancients were acquainted with urticating Caterpillars; Dioscorides mentions them under the name of *Eutoma;* the Romans called them *Erucæ*.

When Reaumur was engaged in studying the habits of the Processionary Moth, he experienced great irritation of the skin on his hands, fingers, and body, especially about the nostrils and around the eyes; he was constantly sneezing, and could only partially open his eyes; his skin became inflamed and covered with red patches and pustules; this state lasted for four or five days. When these hairs, says Reaumur, become buried in the skin, they are like so many small spines, which it is very difficult to remove.

On one occasion the celebrated naturalist inadvertently caused an exanthematous eruption on the neck and shoulders of four ladies who had assisted him in some of his experiments, yet the ladies had never touched either the caterpillars or their nests.

Charles Bonnet, after taking some of these Caterpillars out of the water in which they had been drowned, found that his fingers became numbed; they afterwards began to itch, followed by a burning sensation and swelling.

Charles Morren made some experiments which proved the

---

[1] The principal are the *Processionary Moths*, properly so called, *Phalæna processionea*, Linn., and the *Pityocampa*, *Bombyx Pityocampa*, God.

[2] There are 600, 700, and even 800 in a nest. (Morren.)

action of these hairs at a distance; like Reaumur, he saw the particles of scales and hairs fly off into the air from the vessels in which the Caterpillars were kept; these became dispersed about and produced the affection of which he speaks. These filaments are not the ordinary hair which covers the caterpillar, but are extremely small and invisible to the naked eye, and become detached when the animal changes into a chrysalis. (Reaumur, Morren.) These hairs (fig. 72) are of various lengths, and are more or less pointed, but they often get broken and are truncated; some are transparent, others are somewhat opaque and marked with longitudinal striæ, or are finely punctated; there are some which appear to be hollow, divided into compartments by transverse partitions, and filled with some peculiar substance. Reaumur says he has seen a hair in the centre of each swelling.

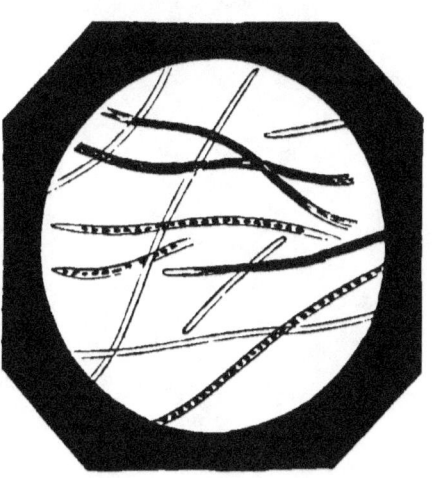

Fig. 72.—*Stinging Hairs.*

Do these hairs act merely in a mechanical manner, or has the matter which occasionally fills the interior of them anything to do with the irritation, as Charles Morren supposes? Is it true that the presence of formic acid has been detected in many of them? Whatever it may be, it is necessary to be on one's guard against the species of Caterpillars which have just been mentioned, and, generally speaking, of all those which are covered with hairs.

M. Borkhausen does not hesitate to say, that when the irritating action of the *Processionary Moths* takes place in the interior of the lungs, or of the alimentary canal, that death may ensue?

The ancients employed urticating Caterpillars in the formation of sinapisms. (Dioscorides.) Reaumur and Dorthes thought that when pounded they might, under certain circumstances, be made useful as a substitute for Cantharides.[1]

Certain marine animals, at the head of which are the *Actiniæ* and the *Medusæ*, have more or less urticating properties.

[1] See page 127.

These animals are commonly known by the name of *Sea Nettle*.[1]

A *Cyanea*[2] of Pondicherry is particularly mentioned as one which secretes an extremely acrid and irritating fluid.

The *Physalia*, or *Portuguese Man of War*, also causes a considerable amount of irritation; it is provided with an oblique wrinkled crest, which stands up like a sail; when they are taken hold of they produce a tolerably acute burning sensation, which continues for some time; sometimes it causes a feeling of faintness (Dutertre, Leblond); but generally speaking the effects do not extend beyond the hand. The commonest species is the *Physalia pelagica*, Bosc.

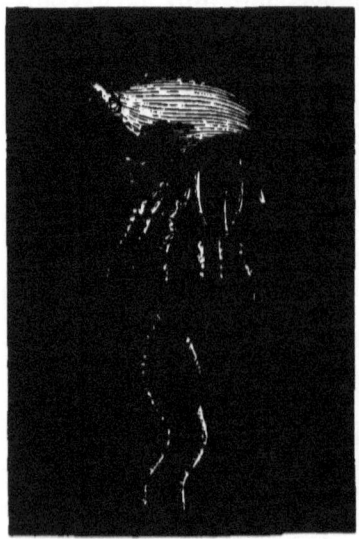

Fig. 73.
Portuguese Man of War.

The stinging apparatus of the Medusæ consists of microscopic capsules situated in the skin, on which they form minute projections; they are principally noticed on the extremities of the long tentacles. These capsules are hard and transparent; they contain a second thin and flexible membrane, at the bottom of which is a long slender thread coiled up when in repose; this thread can emerge from the capsule, and its base is then seen to be provided with a number of sharp points like the barbs of a hook (*hastæ*, Corda).

Certain capsules have a small dart, which is provided with gland and lateral muscles.

This apparatus serves the *Medusæ* as a means of attack and defence. The burning sensation which these animals produce when they are touched, and which is most perceptible on the mucous membranes, has been aptly compared to the effect of stinging nettles; it may even give rise to vesications.

The *Rhizostoma Aldrovandi*, which lives in the Mediterranean, and that of Cuvier, *Rhizostoma Cuvierii*, found in La Manche, secrete a slime which is extremely irritating; a single drop is sufficient to produce inflammation of the conjunctiva

[1] The offspring of these animals are Polyps.
[2] *Medusa (Cyanea) Caliparea*, Reyn.

and the eyelids; this slime produces a number of small papillæ on the hand, which are accompanied with an intolerable itching.

§ IX. Larvæ of Flies.

The *larvæ* of certain *Flies* often torment the human species. Mr. W. Hope has published an interesting work on the subject; he has given the name of *myasis* to the disorders produced by these animals and other Diptera.

1. SPECIES.—The *larvæ* which are most frequently met with in various parts of the body belong principally to four species: 1. The *Flesh Fly;* 2. The *Bluebottle Fly;* 3. The *Golden Fly;* 4. The *Hominivorous Fly.* The following is a summary of their characters:—

Eyes	widely separated behind		. . . .	1. *Flesh Fly.*
	very close behind	Thorax . . .	black, abdomen blue with black bands .	2. *Bluebottle Fly.*
			golden green, abdomen without bands	3. *Golden Fly.*
			dark blue, abdomen with purple bands.	4. *Hominivorous Fly.*

The *Flesh Fly*[1] is very common, and is the largest of the four. Its body is of a golden yellow anteriorly, and covered with long, stout, black hairs; the thorax is grey, with four longitudinal black bands; the abdomen is of a shining black colour, with four square white spots on each ring.

This insect flies rapidly, and produces a constant buzzing noise; it is ovoviviparous.

It hunts about for decomposing flesh for the purpose of depositing its larvæ upon it. These are soft, whitish coloured grubs, without feet, terminating in a pointed extremity anteriorly, but thick and truncated posteriorly. The mouth is a sucker, furnished with two hooks, adapted to tear and divide their food (fig. 74).

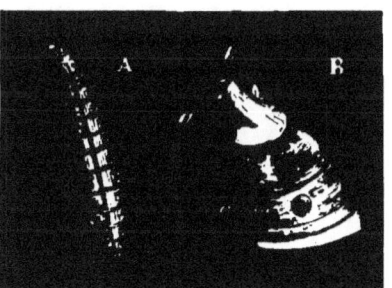

Fig. 74.—*Larvæ of Fly.*[1]

The *Blue* or *Meat Fly*[2] is one of the largest species found in France; its size is, however, less than that of the *Flesh Fly.* The head is of a brown colour,

---

[1] *Sarcophaga carnaria*, Meig., *Musca carnaria*, Linn.
[2] *Calliphora vomitoria*, Rob.-Desv., *Musca vomitoria*, Linn., *M. chrysocephala*, De Geer.

with yellowish reflexions; its presence is indicated by its loud buzzing noise; its sense of smell is very acute, and it recognises the presence of meat, especially when it is fresh, at a long distance off. It is oviparous as well as the two following species; its larva is called a *maggot*.

Fig. 75.
Hominivorous Fly.

The *Golden Fly*[1] is about the same size as the common house fly. It lays its eggs principally upon carrion. Its larvæ devour dead bodies, even those which have been injected. (Raspail.)

The *Hominivorous* Fly, *Lucilia hominivora*, Coq. (fig. 75), inhabits Cayenne. It is about the third of an inch in length; the palpi are of a yellow colour, and the head very large; the face is of a golden yellow, and the feet black; the wings are transparent and smoke-coloured, especially towards their base. (Coquerel.)

2. ACTION ON MAN.—It is well known that the *larvæ* of the three first species of *Flies* which have been mentioned may be deposited and developed in wounds, and in the natural cavities of the human body.

It is especially in hospitals that these untoward events take place. Several surgeons met with the same thing in Algeria and in the Crimea.

Instances of the *larvæ of Flies* being vomited or found in the stomach are not rare. Mr. Hope mentions seven or eight cases.[2] The presence of these animals in the intestines is less frequent. Brera mentions one example, and Mr. Hope a second.

Latham found the *larvæ of a Fly* in the maxillary sinus of a woman. Vohlfant and Mangles met with them in the frontal sinuses. A curious instance of the last kind has been published by Dr. Astros, of Aix. A woman, while sleeping in the open air, was attacked by *Flies*, which deposited their eggs, or their larvæ, in her nostrils. For three days she felt a slight dull pain, which appeared to commence in the frontal sinus and extended to the right temple. The pain was followed by a tingling sensation, and a peculiar kind of noise, resembling that produced by an insect gnawing a piece of wood. The noise was heard by other persons besides the patient. For two days after bleeding at the nose, the patient discharged a considerable

---

[1] *Lucilia Cæsar*, Rob.-Desv., *Musca Cæsar*, Linn.

[2] See Airel, Osiander, Phelsum, Joerdens.—The larvæ of the *Musca meteorica*, Fabr., is sometimes developed in the stomach of man.

number of the *larvæ* of a *Fly*. As many as one hundred and thirteen were counted.[1]

Dr. Chevreul, of Angers, saw ten of the *larvæ* of a *Flesh Fly* come out of the ear-passage in a child of dirty habits.

Ruysch found them in the urinary passages.

Professor Lallemand extracted upwards of twenty of the same kind of larvæ from the vagina of a female, who had had ulceration of the neck of the uterus for eighteen months.

In 1826, at the Hotel-Dieu, at Montpellier, a student removed in the presence of M. Tandon thirty *larvæ* of a *Fly* from a cancer at the bottom of the abdomen of an unfortunate patient who was dying.

Andry, Panarolus, Lieutaud, Bertrand, Alibert, and others, have recorded similar instances.

These examples are fortunately rare. The injuries which are inflicted by the *hominivorous Fly* are, however, more frequent. The larvæ of this species are often met with in the nasal and frontal sinuses in Guiana. M. Coquerel met with a considerable number in a condemned criminal, who was killed by them. Dr. Saint-Pair saw six similar cases in 1855 and 1856. Three of the patients died after great suffering; two of them had the nose entirely destroyed, and the last escaped with only the mutilation of this organ.[2]

At first the patients experience only a slight uneasiness in the nasal fossæ. This is followed by headache and ædema of the parts about the nose, which extends more or less on to the face; afterwards there is free hæmorrhage from the nose and acute pain in the suborbital region, which the patients compare to being beaten with a hammer. Ulcerations subsequently occur on the nose, through which some of the larvæ escape. The general symptoms are the same as those which accompany acute inflammation; this is followed by erysipelas of the head and face, sometimes by meningitis, and lastly by death.

In one of the cases recorded by M. Saint-Pair, 800 larvæ were expelled by means of injections; but it was impossible to get rid of them all. They soon gained the globe of the eye and crawled between the eyelids. The lower eyelid became gangrenous, and the inferior margin of the orbit was exposed.

---

[1] M. Legrand du Saulle has recently communicated a similar instance to the Institut. It occurred in a young girl nine years of age, whose frontal sinuses contained a number of *larvæ* which produced perpetual frontal headache, accompanied with convulsions.

[2] Dr. Daniel has recorded another instance which was fatal, and in which the left ear was filled with larvæ.

The larvæ entered the mouth and eat away the gums, laying bare the superior maxilla. The patient died seventeen days after he had entered the hospital.

Another patient, under the care of Dr. Chapuis, only lived between three and four days. More than *one hundred* larvæ were found in the nasal fossæ and in the pharynx. After death the mucous membrane of these cavities was found to be nothing but a black putrid mass.

Can, however, the *larvæ of the Flies* of our country, or of any other, penetrate the skin so long as it is healthy and the surface unbroken? Unfortunately it is too clearly proved that these animals are capable of abraiding the skin.

Leeuwenhoeck relates a case in which a number of tumours about the size of the end of the finger made their appearance on the leg of a lady; the limb ultimately became of a monstrous size. In one of the tumours there was found some of the larvæ of a *Flesh Fly*.

M. Hope states an instance of a young man in Jamaica, who had larvæ in the substance of the cheek and of the gums. It has just been seen that the larvæ of the *hominivorous Fly*, after having destroyed the nasal fossæ, produced similar ravages.

Saltzmann saw a young man in the hospital at Strasburg whose whole skin was penetrated by thousands of *larvæ*. In the groin and on the legs masses of flesh were completely destroyed. The left eye was eaten away. The patient died.

In June, 1829, John Page, a pauper, died from the injuries inflicted upon him by the larvæ of a *Fly* at Asbornby, in Lincolnshire. The man was in the habit of strolling about the country, and subsisted on the pittance he obtained from door to door; the support he usually received from the benevolent was bread and meat; and after satisfying the cravings of nature, it was his custom to deposit the surplus provisions, particularly the meat, betwixt his shirt and skin. Having a considerable portion of this provision in store so deposited, he was taken rather unwell, and laid himself down in a field; when from the heat of the season at that time, the meat speedily became putrid, and was of course struck by the flies; these not only proceeded to devour the inanimate pieces of flesh, but also literally to prey upon the living substance; and when the wretched man was accidentally found by some of the inhabitants, he was so eaten by the maggots that his death seemed inevitable. The surgeon who saw him declared that his body was in such a state, that dressing it must be little short of instantaneous death, and in fact the man only survived the operation a few hours. White maggots of enormous size were crawling in and upon his body, which they had most shockingly mangled, and the removing of the external ones served only to render the sight more horrid.[1]

M. J. Cloquet has published a still more remarkable case. A rag gatherer, about fifty years of age, was found sleeping in a ditch in the Boulevard of Paris, near Montfauçon, and taken to the hospital of St. Louis. The skin of his head was raised up in rounded tumours, which had irregular openings through which the flesh could be seen in a putrid state. An enormous number of the *larvæ of a fly* were moving about inside the tumours. Fifteen to twenty of the larvæ escaped from between his eyelids, which were swollen and closed up. The cornea were opaque and as well as the sclerotic had been perforated. The eyeballs appeared to be empty. Other larvæ issued from the nose and the ears. They were also lodged at the orifice of the prepuce and around the anus. The unhappy man personified all the horrors of the affliction of Job. Never, says M. Cloquet, had I seen a spectacle more horrible or disgusting than this miserable being, devoured alive by these *larvæ* of the carrion fly.

The previous cases must remove any doubt as to the statement of Plutarch with respect to the great criminals, who, he says, were condemned by the kings of Persia, to be eaten alive by the larvæ of Flies. The guilty person was placed between two boats of the same size, turned one over the other, the head, the hands, and the feet being left uncovered. His face was exposed to the sun, smeared with honey. The larvæ which were born penetrated into the flesh of the unhappy being. . . .Mithridates, who was exposed by Artaxerxes Longimanus to this horrible punishment, lived for seventy days in the most cruel agonies. When the upper boat was removed all his flesh and his entrails were seen to be eaten away by myriads of worms.

With the exception of the *Œstridæ*, which will be noticed in another chapter, neither the *Flies* nor their *larvæ* can be regarded as parasites. They are never observed on man except by accident. Even the *hominivorous Fly* does not form an exception to this statement. Generally these *larvæ* are introduced into our bodies, so to speak, in spite of themselves. In true parasitism, where one individual lives at the cost of

[1] M. Tandon relates this case on the authority of M. Roulin, but it is originally recorded in Brown's edition of *White's History of Selbourne*, p. 114, London, 1840. (Ed.)

another, the latter is not destroyed by it, except under peculiar circumstances. If it had been otherwise, the species of parasite, or of the animal which nourishes it, must necessarily have disappeared; a fact which is contrary to the general laws of nature. Kunzmann correctly observes that the wounds made by insects for the purpose of feeding at our expense, are never followed by such serious consequences as those which they inflict upon us in self-defence.

§ X. Other Insects which may be accidentally introduced into the natural cavities of the body.

All that has been said in the previous chapter with reference to the introduction of the *larvæ of Flies* into the natural cavities of man's body will also apply to other insects. As regards the latter, however, they are sometimes larvæ and sometimes the perfect insect. It must also be observed, that these false parasites are not always carnivorous animals; they are, therefore, not always able to nourish themselves at the expense of man's tissues, so that they soon perish for want of food. Their being placed in a locality which is not adapted for them is generally fatal.

Many writers have mentioned cases of this kind. Fabricius, of Hilden, Tulpius, Lister, Paykull, Rosen, Thompson, Bateman, Lemaout, and others, have given examples of them. The *Ephémérides des curieux de la nature* contains some of these cases, and Mr. Hope has collected together all the instances of this kind, which appeared to him to be authentic.

The cavities of the body, which are attacked by these animals, are first the alimentary canal, then the nostrils, the auditory canal, and the lachrymal duct.

These insects belong especially to the Coleoptera, amongst which the principal that have been mentioned, are: *Sphodrus leucothalmus*,[1] Clairv., the *Dytiscus marginatus*, the *Oxyporus subterraneus*,[2] Fabr., the *Pœderus elongatus*, Fabr., the *Staphylinus politus*, the *S. punctulatus*, and the *S. fuscipes*, Fabr., the *Dermestes lardarius*, Linn., the *Geotrupes vernalis*,[3] Latr., the *Blaps mortisaga*,[4] Oliv., the *Tenebrio molitor*, Linn., the *Forficula auricularia* and *F. minor*, Linn.

Amongst the Myriopoda or *thousand feet*, the *Geophilus electricus*[5] has been particularly named.

[1] *Carabus leucothalmus*, Linn.
[2] *Staphylinus subterraneus*, Linn.
[3] *Scarabœus vernalis*, Linn.
[4] *Tenebrio mortisaga*, Linn.
[5] *Scolopendra electricus*, Linn.

Amongst the Lepidoptera or Butterflies, have been mentioned, the *Aglossa pingualis* and *A. farinalis*, Latr., and the Cabbage butterfly, *Pieris brassicæ*, Schr.[1]

Mr. Hope has given the name of *canthariasis* to the injuries produced by the Coleoptera and the Myriopoda; Messrs. Kirby and Spence had previously given the name of *solechiasis*, or *scholechiasis*, to those which were caused by the Lepidoptera.

It is easy to explain the entrance of those insects into the stomach and intestines, which feed upon lard, fat, flour, and other substances, which serve for food; but it is more difficult to account for their introduction into the other natural cavities.

The presence of these insects in the alimentary canal seldom produces much inconvenience, especially when the animals, or their larvæ, are small and few in number. Sometimes they are partly or entirely digested, at other times they merely act as foreign bodies, deranging the stomach and the intestines. The *Cantharides*, the *Mylabra*, or the *Meloe*, when swallowed incautiously, or when they have been given for criminal purposes, may produce a kind of poisoning, and even death.

Adult insects, which are rejected by vomiting, or which are passed by the bowels, never appear to have been long in the body, nor is there any evidence that it was there they underwent their metamorphoses. They have probably been swallowed after their transformation.

The introduction of these larvæ into the other natural cavities of the body is usually attended with serious symptoms.

M. Scoutetten relates the case of a farmer of Metz, who experienced a very disagreeable irritation in the nostrils, accompanied with an abundant secretion of mucus. In addition to this he had frequent headaches, and the pain which was at first bearable soon became very severe, and increased in intensity with every paroxysm. The mucus discharge was mixed with blood and exhaled a fetid odour. This was followed by an involuntary discharge of water from the eyes, nausea, and vomiting. Sometimes the pain was so intense that the patient was afraid he should lose his senses. The features became distorted, the jaws contracted, and the temporal arteries pulsated violently.

---

[1] *Papilio brassicæ*, Linn.
—To what insect does the larva belong which takes up its abode in the cribriform-plate of the ethmoid bone, and produces the disease known by the name *Péenash* in the north-west of India? The larva is small, articulated, and terminates in a spiral tail; the mouth and eyes are very distinct. (Taruck-Chander-Lahory.)

The senses of hearing and of sight were so sensitive that the least noise or light was quite unbearable. At other times the patient became completely delirious, pressed his head between his hands, and did not know how to endure himself. These paroxysms occurred five or six times during the day, and as often during the night. One of them continued for fifteen days almost without interruption. After lasting a year, his sufferings were suddenly terminated by the expulsion of a living *Scolopendra electrica* 2¼ inches in length.[1]

Mr. Hope only mentions one case of death caused by the presence of a meal-worm, *Tenebrio molitor*, in the nasal fossæ.

CHAPTER II.

ANIMALS INJURIOUS AS FOOD.

MANY animals are mentioned, whose flesh is injurious when taken as food, and which can produce symptoms resembling those of poisoning; but these animals are not, correctly speaking, *venomous* or *poisonous* animals; none of them are provided with a poison or with an *organ* for the secretion of poison. The majority only act in this manner under particular circumstances. Others are rather indigestible than directly injurious.

These animals consist of: 1, *Fishes*; 2, *Mollusca*; and 3, *Crustacea*.

1. FISHES.—It has long been known that many persons have been more or less ill after eating certain species of *Fish*. These disorders in some cases have terminated in death. Adanson saw negroes die after severe vomiting and convulsions from eating of the *Ostracions* or *Trunk Fishes*. Dr. Praeger mentions four cases of poisoning followed by death, which happened to sailors, belonging to Danish, Dutch, and French vessels, from partaking of these fish. One of them had only eaten the liver.

The Fish, nevertheless, are not *poisonous* animals. What then is the cause of their injurious effects?

1. It has been supposed that it depended upon some morbid condition of the flesh, which predisposed it to undergo rapid decomposition (Burrows), and in consequence gave rise to symptoms resembling *poisoning*. This opinion has been founded upon seeing half the fish, which was eaten while it was fresh,

---

[1] A similar instance is recorded in *Histoire de l'Académie des Sciences* for the year 1708, Paris, 1709, p. 12.

producing no ill effects, while the other half, which was eaten on the next day or the day after, has been followed by serious disturbances. The injurious effects which are produced by the *Tunny, Thymnus vulgaris,* Cuv., after its flesh has began to change, is well known. (Cuvier and Valenciennes.)

2. Other persons have believed that at the period of spawning, or at all times, the animal contains certain portions which cannot be eaten with impunity, while all the rest can. They endeavour in this way to account for the different effects which have been observed. For example, the *Barbel* is very injurious at the period of reproduction. Its injurious properties depend upon the ova.[1] M. Moquin-Tandon knew a young man at Toulouse, who had acute gastric pains, and who vomited a certain quantity of blood after eating half a *Barbel.*

3. Some naturalists have suggested that the injuries of *Fish* depended upon the substances upon which they had fed; that they had swallowed mineral, animal, or vegetable substances, which were of a dangerous nature. Some have spoken of submarine copper, sulphate of baryta, sulphate of iron, the salts of iodine, &c.; narcotic fruits or plants have been mentioned. Crabs, Annellides, Starfishes, microscopic Medusæ, eggs, &c., have also been named. It is said that the *Balistes* are very indigestible, and even poisonous, after they have fed upon certain Zoophytes.

4. Several medical men have thought that the very preparation which *Fish* undergo is sufficient to engender injurious properties in their flesh. Persons have been mentioned who could not eat fried *Fish* without vomiting. (Louyer-Willermay.)

5. Lastly, other medical men have maintained that the injurious effects depended upon the state of the person who was affected, and not even on the nature of the *Fish* which had been eaten.

It is very probable that all these suppositions are correct. Several of the causes which have been suggested may occur simultaneously.

Are there, however, *Fish* which are dangerous at all times, and under every circumstance? If we are to place any reliance on the statements of travellers and naturalists, certain species possess this character at the moment they are caught, both when they are in spawn and when they are not in spawn, whatever may be their age, the nature of their food, or the way in which they are cooked. The species which have been men-

---

[1] *Ova choleram causant,* Tim.

tioned as being the most dangerous belonging to the genera *Meletta*,[1] *Sphyræna*,[2] *Caranx*,[3] *Scarus*,[4] *Diodon*,[5] and *Gneion*.[6]

Most of the so termed *poisonous Fishes* are only so at times; that is to say, when they have fed upon certain animals at the period of reproduction, or under certain other peculiar circumstances. Such are the *File fish*, the *Conger eel*, the *Mackerel*, and the *Herring*.

It is more particularly in hot climates that it is necessary to guard against the ill effects of these *Fish*. M. Fonssagrives observes that the species, which are to be most dreaded are inhabitants of the tropical seas, and that the species which are dangerous in our climates become still more so in those regions.

The first symptom produced by eating these Fish is disorder of the stomach; this is followed by pain in the epigastrium, accompanied by a feeling of oppression and dyspnæa. General symptoms supervene, ushered in by shiverings and cold sweats. The countenance becomes injected and swollen, and red spots or vesicular eruptions break out over the body. These eruptions are often followed by an irritation or itching, which is sometimes quite unbearable. The patient has constant nausea, pain, vomiting, and spasmodic affections of the bowels, simulating cholera, deafness, and imperfect vision; he becomes comatoze and passes into a peculiar state of insensibility. When the patient escapes death, his convalescence is long and difficult.

2. MOLLUSCA.—Two cases of poisoning are recorded from *Snails* which had been collected; the one series from a *belladonna* plant, the other from the *sumac, coriaria myrtifolia*, Linn. *Mussels*[7] and *Oysters*[8] are the species of mollusca which most frequently produce these accidents. There is great difficulty in explaining the way in which they act, and various suggestions have been put forth; such as the presence of copper in the rocks on which they live, their having been attached to the copper bottoms of vessels, the

---

[1] For example, the *poisonous Meletta, Meletta venenosa*, and *M. Thrissa*, Valenc.
[2] The *large Sphyræna, Sphyræna Curacuda*, Cuv., and the *S. Becuna*, Lacep.
[3] *Caranx fallax*, Cuv.
[4] *Scarus capitaneus*, Cuv.
[5] *Diodon tigrinus*, Cuv.
[6] *Gneion maculatum*, Bibron.
[7] See p. 175.
[8] See pp. 86, 168.

presence of a small crab, which lodges within their valves, the spawn of the Star fishes, or of certain Medusa, which they had eaten (Lamouroux), a peculiar disease to which they may be liable, the fermentation and decomposition of their tissues, and even the *phases of the moon*, &c.

3. CRUSTACEA.—Certain *Crustacea* produce similar disorders to those which have just been described. Amongst these animals the principal are the *Land Crab, Gecarcinus ruricola*, (is it when they have eaten the fruit of the manchineal tree?)[1] and the *Hermit Crab, Pagurus Bernhardus.*

Prawns and *Shrimps* have also been mentioned, but it must be by the merest accident that these *Crustacea*, as well as the *Hermit Crab*, can produce any injurious effects.

BOOK V.

POISONOUS ANIMALS.

THE name of *Poisonous Animals* is given to all those creatures which produce a poison. These animals are provided with special glands for the secretion of the poisonous fluid, and with an apparatus for its transmission; some convey the poison by means of the mouth, or by some part of the mouth modified for that purpose; while others are provided with a special organ. This division of the poisonous animals into those which transmit the poison by means of their mouth, and into those which are provided with a special apparatus for that purpose, will be found in the works of some of the older writers.

Amongst the animals which are injurious, but not poisonous, it has been previously seen that some possess a saliva which appears to have properties that are very analogous to a poison; such is the case in the *Reduvina* and the *Gnats*.[2]

SECTION I.

ANIMALS WHICH CONVEY THEIR POISON BY THE MOUTH.

THE animals which convey their poison by means of the mouth, or by means of some part of the mouth, have special

[1] *Delectatur fructibus mancinellæ et inde sæpe venenatus fertur.* (Linn.)
[2] See pp. 222, 230.

teeth or *fangs* in the interior of this cavity provided for that purpose, or they have, placed by the side of it, *claw-shaped antennæ* or *foot-jaws*, which, like the fangs, are connected with the organ which secretes the poison.[1]

CHAPTER I.

POISONOUS ANIMALS WITH FANGS.

THE poisonous animals provided with fangs are the *Ophidia* or Serpents. The most dangerous are the *Vipers*. MM. Dumeril place them in the sub-order Solenoglypha, characterised by the possession of an upper jaw, which has the two anterior teeth hollowed out into a canal.

§ I. Vipers.

1. COMMON VIPER.—The *Common Viper* or *Asp*[1] is a serpent to be carefully avoided. It belongs to the family Viperina.

Habitat.—The *Common Viper* is frequently found in the Cevennes, in Lozere, and Aveyron. It especially abounds at Montmorency, and in the Forest of Fontainebleau; it usually keeps near the roads and footpaths, in stumps of trees, on bits of rock, or beneath stones and bushes.

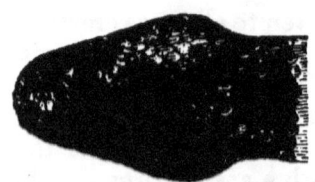

Fig. 76.- *Common Viper.*

Description.—It varies from 1 to $2\frac{1}{4}$ feet in length; the body at its thickest part is nearly an inch in diameter; the general colour is brown or of a reddish tinge, passing into an ashen or blackish

---

[1] It is stated that certain Mollusca, as, for example, the *Cones* and the *Pleurotoma*, inflict bites which inflame and become dangerous. It is supposed by some that this depends upon a poison which the animals introduce into the wound. Whence, however, it may be asked, does this poison come? M. Loven supposes that the hooks or teeth with which the tongue is armed are deeply buried in the wound, and produce the subsequent inflammation. Captain Beecher was wounded by a specimen of the *Conus aulicus*, and the wound swelled and became very painful. Has the animals, as M. Loven supposes, the power of discharging these lingual teeth?

[2] *Vipera aspis*, Merrem; *Coluber aspis*, Linn.; *Vipera Cherseax*, Latr.

[It appears from the description in the text, and from what is said of the other species, that this is not the *Common Viper* of England. The species which is known in this country as the *Common Viper* or Adder, as it is frequently termed, is that which is mentioned in the next page under the title of *Vipera Berus*, and which is described in Bell's *British Reptiles*, 2nd edit., p. 61, under the name of *Pelias Berus*, and which is the only species of Viper that is met with in Great Britain. (Ed.)]

band on the back, and a row of irregular dark spots on the sides; specimens of a uniform colour are rare; the belly is of a slate colour; the head of the *Viper* is of a subtriangular form, somewhat larger than the neck, obtuse and truncated anteriorly, and covered with granulated scales; the muzzle is covered by six small scales, two of which are perforated by the nostrils, which form two black spots; on the upper part are two black lines united in the form of a V; the upper jaw is whitish and spotted with black, while the lower is of a yellow colour; the eyes, which are very small, active, and bright, are bordered with black; the tongue is long, forked, of a black or greyish colour, soft and retractile; the scales are imbricated and carinated, characters which distinguish them from those of the Colubridæ.

The males are generally smaller than the females.

This reptile is fond of heat, especially moist heat; it hunts after shrew mice, field mice, and even moles, destroying a large number of these animals; it also feeds upon lizards, frogs, small molluscous animals, insects, and worms. It hides itself in the day and pursues the animals upon which it lives during the night time.

The *Viper* appears to be a timid animal; its movements are abrupt, sluggish, and irregular; the instincts of the animal are but feebly developed; it is incapable of being taught like the Colubridæ, and when retained in captivity it refuses its food.

At the approach of winter it retires into holes in old buildings, into the decayed trunks of trees, into the earth, or under moss; several of them are usually rolled up together, and in this manner they pass the cold weather in a torpid state.

The male has a double penis, which increases in size during copulation, and fixes the two sexes so firmly together that, if they are disturbed during the act, the male, which is weaker than the female, is carried away backwards by the latter.

The *Viper* is ovoviviparous. (Aristotle.) The young are born with the fragments of egg case adhering to them; the eggs, just before they hatched, are as large as those of the wren.

2. OTHER SPECIES.—There are two other species of *Viper* in Europe—the *Ammodytes* and the *Berus*. The following table gives the characters which distinguish them from the *Common Viper*:

Head				
	no plates.			
	Snout	truncated	. . . . .	1. *Vipera Aspis.*
		elongated	. . . . .	2. *Vipera Ammodytes.*
	with plates	. . . .		3. *Vipera Berus.*

The *Vipera Ammodytes*, which has a *horn* on the muzzle,[1] (fig. 77,) inhabits the mountains of Dauphiné; the head is separated from the body by a distinct neck; the muzzle is prolonged into a soft, obtuse, elevated point.

Fig. 77.—*Vipera Ammodytes.*

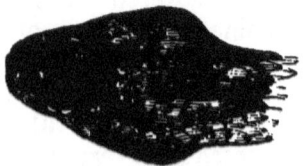

Fig. 78.—*Vipera Pelius.*

The *Vipera Berus* (Daud), or *small Viper*,[2] (fig. 78), is found in the neighbourhood of Paris. It was this species which bit M. Constant Duméril in the Forest of Sénart in September, 1851.

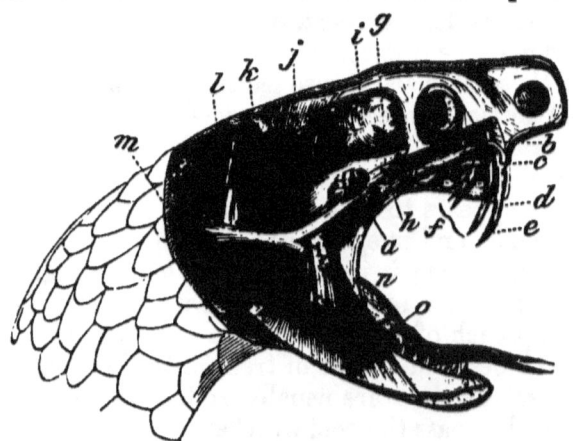

Fig. 79.—*Head of a Viper.*[3]

The body is elongated, the neck much constricted, and with a brown line along the back; it has a large pentagonal plate hollowed out anteriorly on the summit of the head;[4] behind

[1] *Coluber Ammodytes*, Linn.; *Echidna Ammodytes*, Merrem.
[2] *Pelius Berus*, Merrem; *Coluber Berus*, Linn.
[3] Head of *Pelius Berus* [Common English Viper].—*a*, poison gland, seen through an opening in the external pterygoid muscle; *b*, its duct; *c*, termination of the duct at the base of the poison fang; *d*, poison fang; *e*, external opening; *f*, fangs of replacement; *g*, external pterygoid muscle; *h*, internal pterygoid muscle; *i*, lachrymal gland; *j*, anterior temporal muscle; *k*, elevator muscle of the lower jaw; *l*, depressor muscle of the lower jaw; *m*, retractor muscle of the lower jaw; *n*, tongue; *o*, its laryngeal opening; *p*, its bifurcation.
[4] In the *Common Viper* [that is, of France, *Vipera aspis*,] there is a small hexagonal plate at the same part.

this are two oblong irregularly pentagonal plates. The head is somewhat convex. (fig. 79.)

Naturalists consider that the present species differs sufficiently from the two first to form a distinct genus. (Pelius.)

3. POISON APPARATUS.—This consists of—1, the *Gland*; 2, the *Duct*; 3, the *Poison Fang*.

1. *Gland.*—This is situated by the side of the head, behind and partly below the globe of the eye, above the superior maxillary and transverse bones, in front of the anterior temporal muscle; it is embraced by the external pterygoid muscle, which forms over it, especially anteriorly, a strong tendinous covering; it is rather an assemblage of lobes than a gland, properly so called. The substance of the gland is soft and yellow,

Fig. 80.—*Poison Apparatus.*[1]

and has a spongy appearance; examined beneath the microscope it presents a series of oval dilatations or lobules composed of a granular tissue; these dilatations are arranged very regularly along the course of the excretory ducts, like the barbs of a feather, along the two sides of its axis. The number of these lobes varies in different individuals; M. Leon Soubeiran has generally found from 6 to 8, independently of a certain number of secondary lobes placed at the commencement of the principal duct.

2. *Duct.*—The duct of the poison gland is a narrow cylindrical canal; it passes from behind forwards in a nearly horizontal direction and terminates in the fang of the same side; towards its middle portion, just below the inferior margin of the orbit, the canal forms an oval dilatation. It is this enlargement, which is very slight in the *Vipera aspis*, that has been described under the name of the *poison reservoir*. M. Soubeiran has recently examined this part, and he finds that its walls contain a number of simple follicles, which open into the cavity, and form a special glandular apparatus placed in the course of the excretory canal, like the prostate of the

---

[1] Poison apparatus of *Pelius Berus* [Common English Viper].—*a*, pinnated and ramified gland; *b b*, its duct; *c*, reservoir placed in the course of the duct; *d*, fang, cut vertically; *e*, basal orifice, receiving the duct of the gland; *f*, its terminal orifice.

gasteropoda in the course of their deferent canal. The follicles which he has described appear to be most numerous towards the posterior extremity; they are very long, and appear to be separated from each other.

3. *Poison Fang.*—The *fang* is a tooth moulded into the form of a tube; it is much longer than the other teeth, and is placed in the upper jaw; there is one on either side the mouth. They are very pointed and curved, the convexity being placed anteriorly, and provided with a narrow canal, which commences at the anterior surface of the base and terminates by an extremely narrow elongated aperture on the same surface of the apex of the fang. A fine canal passes through the convexity and connects the two apertures. This canal is sometimes obliterated.

The two lower thirds of the *fang* are invested by a strong fold of the gum (*saccus*, Mead). They extend backwards, and form a groove or case, which receives and conceals the tooth when not in use.

These organs are firmly attached, and, as it were, anchylosed to the superior maxillary bones. The latter bones are very small and very short, but enjoy great freedom of motion. There are two muscles which govern these movements; these are the external pterygoid, which elevates the bone, and the internal pterygoid, which depresses it.

Immediately behind the *fangs* are two or three smaller teeth, or the forms of teeth, destined to replace those which are in use when lost (Rosa); these are unattached, and are enclosed in the fold of gum previously mentioned.

In a state of repose the *fangs* are concealed; but they are withdrawn from the fold of the gum and elevated when the animal is about to use them. But it was an error to suppose, in consequence of this, that the teeth themselves are moveable; it is the maxillary bone to which the fang is united that alone moves. The remaining teeth in the upper part of the mouth are attached to the palate, where they form a double row.

4. ACTION ON MAN.—1. *Bite.* Redi appears to have been the first who accurately described the effects of the *Viper*. Mead and Fontana described still more carefully the bite and the poisonous action of this dangerous serpent.

Vipers habitually employ the formidable weapon with which they are armed to destroy the small animals upon which they live. They avoid man, but when trod upon or handled they become enraged and defend themselves with their poison fangs.

When a *Viper* is struck it first coils itself up, leaving its head in the centre or at the summit of the coil, and drawn a little back, as if for the purpose of reconnoitring. Speedily the animal uncoils itself like a spring. Its body is then launched out with such rapidity, that, for a moment, the eye cannot follow it. In this movement the *Viper* clears a space nearly equal to its own length, for it must be observed that it never quits the ground, where it remains supported on its tail, or on the posterior part of its body, ready to coil itself up again and launch itself forth afresh to aim a second blow, if the first should fail. To do this the Viper distends its mouth, draws back its fangs, arranges them in the right direction, and then plunges them into its enemy by the blow of its head or of its upper jaw, which strikes the object like a hammer; when this is done the fangs are immediately withdrawn. The lower jaw, which is closed at the same moment, serves as a point of resistance and favours the entrance of the poison fangs; but this assistance is very slight, and the animal, as has just been stated, acts by striking rather than by biting. There are, however, times when the Viper bites without coiling itself up, and then launching itself forth. This occurs, for instance, when the creature meets with some small animal, which it destroys at its leisure, and without rage, or when it is seized by the tail or the middle of the body, when it turns round and plunges in its fangs. As the teeth are buried in the tissues of the body the poison is driven down the canals which pass through them by the action of the muscles[1] which close the mouth, and this injection takes place with all the more force in proportion to the vigour and rage of the serpent and to the supply of poison with which it is furnished.

2. *Wound.*—The wounds inflicted by the *Viper* have a peculiar appearance, which allows them to be recognised by mere inspection, and to be distinguished from those of a non-venomous serpent, as, for example, from those of a Colubra. In fact, all serpents which are not furnished with fangs produce a number of punctures formed by the teeth of the two jaws, which are arranged in two curved lines, with the concavities looking towards each other. In the bite of the *Viper* there are only two large punctures corresponding to the two poison fangs.[2]

These wounds inflame, become red and swollen, and sometimes livid; at other times they are surrounded with vesicles or watery bulla.

---

[1] The external pterygoid muscle, in contracting for the purpose of raising the fang at the same time, compresses the gland which it covers.

[2] Plutarch mentions the presence of *two* hardly perceptible *punctures* which the *Asp* had inflicted on the arm of Cleopatra.

The general symptoms which accompany the wound have been frequently described. The person at first experiences pain in the part which has been bitten, which gradually extends itself throughout the limb, and even to the internal organs. The swelling, the redness, and the lividity, spread to the neighbouring parts; faintings come on, the pulse becomes rapid, small, and irregular. There are gastric derangements, bilious vomitings, difficult respiration, profuse cold sweats; disturbance of the vision and of the intellect, and convulsions, which are almost always followed by general jaundice. There is sometimes acute pain in the region of the umbilicus. The blood which issues from the wound often becomes black; after a time it changes into a sanies; and lastly, in some instances, which are fortunately very rare, gangrene comes on.

In weak, sickly, or timid persons, and in those who have just eaten, the symptoms increase more rapidly, and are more severe than in those who are strong, healthy, courageous, and who at the time are fasting.

The bite of the *Viper* is generally dangerous.

Ambrose Paré relates, that during his residence at Montpellier with Charles IX. he was bitten in the extremity of his index finger, when examining a *Viper*. He felt a sharp pain, but that the immediate application of a ligature and tincture of opium cured it in a few days.

When Bernard de Jussieu was herborizing in the month of July, 1747, on the hills of Montmartre, one of his pupils seized a *Viper*, which he mistook for a Colubra; the serpent bit him in three places (on both thumbs, and on the index-finger of the right hand). At first there was swelling and inflammation, afterwards faintings, and a yellowness, which was limited to the fore arm. There were no other derangements.

It would be easy to multiply similar examples. At the same time it must not be supposed that these bites are never fatal. In certain cases they may cause death.

Bedard relates in his lectures the case of a young man in the neighbourhood of Angers, who, happening to fall down in a meadow, was bitten in several places by a *Viper*, and died in consequence in the course of a few hours.

A woman bitten in the thigh died at the end of thirty-seven hours.

M. Dusoard mentions eleven cases, four of which were fatal.

Matthiole records a case which proves that a *Viper*, even when cut in two, may still bite when handled incautiously. A countryman falling down in a meadow, happened to divide one of those snakes in the middle; he seized the portion of the trunk to which the head was attached in an awkward manner, and was in consequence bitten in the finger, and died from the effects of the wound.[1]

Redi and Saviard speak also of severe bites inflicted by *Vipers* whose heads were separated from the body.

Dr. Scoutetten mentions a similar instance. In July, 1837, a young man in the neighbourhood of Metz, when seeking for worms for the purpose of fishing, saw two serpents, which he mistook for *Colubra*. He cut them in pieces with a pickaxe; soon afterwards, having taken hold of one of the heads, he felt himself bitten in the right index finger; he shook his hand violently, and it was only after several efforts that he succeeded in disengaging it.

[The common Viper, says Bell,[2] is everywhere deservedly feared on account of its venom, which, although less virulent than that of many other species, is yet sufficiently so to produce severe symptoms, and sometimes, in the warmer climates, even fatal results. In this country I have never seen a case which terminated in death, nor have I been able to trace to an authentic source any of the numerous reports of such a termination which have at various times been confidently promulgated. At the same time the symptoms are frequently so threatening, that I cannot but conclude that in very hot weather, and when not only the reptile is in full activity and power, but the constitution of the victim in a state of great irritability and diminished power, a bite from the Common Viper would very probably prove fatal. The remedies usually employed are the external application of oil, and the internal administration of ammonia.]

§ II. Foreign Serpents.

The principal foreign serpents which are poisonous are—
1. the *Cerastes;* 2. the *Crotali;* 3. the *Bothrops;* 4. the *Naia*.

1. The CERASTES or *horned Serpents*, are allied to the Vipers. They differ from them in their supra orbital plates, rising up into pointed processes, and assuming the appearance of a pair of small horns.

The principal species are the *Cerastes of Egypt, Cerastes Ægyptiacus* (fig. 81), and the *Cerastes of Persia, Cer. Persicus*. These animals are justly dreaded; the first species, which is also met

---

[1] Matthiole says *on the spot*, but this is hardly credible.
[2] Bell's *British Reptiles*, 2nd ed. p. 62, London.

with in the Sahara of Algeria, and in Morocco, is said to cause death in a few hours.

2. The CROTALI, or *Rattle Snakes*, are serpents belonging to the family Crotalidæ; they are large and strong, and may attain a length of more than six feet. They have all the upper part of their bodies covered with simple scales. The end of the tail is furnished with several horny rings, which lock loosely into each, and produce a rattling noise as the animal moves along, and hence the name of Rattle Snakes. Their poison fangs are very long, and the poison reservoir of considerable size.

Fig. 81.—*Cerastes Ægyptiacus.*

The principal species are—the *Crotalus Durissus* (fig. 82) of South America; the *Crotalus horridus* of Tropical America, particularly of Mexico, Guiana, and Brazil; and the *Crotalus miliaris* from Oregon. The latter species is said to be the most dangerous.

Fig. 82.—*Crotalus Durissus.*

The *Crotali* naturally inspire a feeling of dread, for their poison will destroy an ox or a horse almost instantaneously. Dogs will resist its influence somewhat longer. A *Crotalus*, about three feet long, killed one of these animals in fifteen minutes; a second at the end of two hours; and a third at the end of three. Four days afterwards it wounded a dog, which only survived thirty seconds, and another which only lived four minutes. Three days afterwards a frog perished in two seconds, a chicken in eight minutes, and a white amphisbena also in eight minutes. (Halm.)

M. Rousseau rapidly destroyed pigeons by forcing into their pectoral muscles the fangs of a *Crotalus* which had been dead two days.

These animals only attack man when provoked. Their poison produces death in two or three minutes; but if remedies are applied immediately death may be averted. According to Sir Everard Home, when a finger has been bitten it passes into a complete state of mortification; in other cases, the edges of the wound become gangrenous, the cellular tissue is destroyed, and the muscles are greatly inflamed. According to Laurenti, the bite of these terrible serpents produces swelling of the body and of the tongue, the mouth seems on fire, the thirst is excessive, and the person dies in the course of a few minutes in a state of frightful agony. In the case of the unfortunate Drake, who was bitten in the hand, and in whom the wound was cauterised an hour afterwards, there were faintings, stertorous breathing, scarcely any pulse, and involuntary evacuations; the eyes were closed, the pupils contracted, the body cold, and the limbs insensible; he died at the end of nine hours. (Philorel.)

When the patient is so fortunate as to escape death, he sometimes feels the effect of the injury for the remainder of his life. Lesseur, who was wounded at Simon, eight years afterwards, when he was in Paris, felt a great weight in the limb which had been wounded.

M. Alfred Dugès was bitten on the 21st of August, 1857, at Silao, in Mexico, by a young *Crotalus*,[1] about eight inches long, on the upper part of the second joint of the index-finger of the left hand; he felt a most agonising pain at the moment, as if some caustic had been applied to a recent wound; the part was strongly ligatured, and the wound cauterised with nitrate of silver; there was great exhaustion, cold sweats, a feeling of intense anxiety about the region of the heart, and the mouth was very clammy; at the end of an hour the wound was cauterised a second time, on this occasion with the bromide of iron; the hand by this time was very much swollen, and the arm painful up to the axilla; cataplasms and embrocations of olive oil were applied to the limb. On the 22nd, the finger and the back of the hand were greatly enlarged, and could not bear the least pressure; its condition might be compared to that of a large chilblain. On the 23rd, the swelling and the pain had somewhat subsided. On the 24th and 25th, the hand became of a deep brown colour, and was still much swollen. On the 27th, the colour was less intense, but the patient still felt pain in closing the finger. (A. Dugès.)

3. The *Bothrops*, or *Javelin Snakes*, also belong to the family of the Crotolidæ; they are characterised by the possession of cavities hollowed out behind the nostrils, and by a small cor-

[1] It was the *Crotalus triseriatus*, Wiegm., a variety of the *Cr. Durissus*.

neous spine at the extremity of the tail. The scales are carinated, and there are no large plates on the head.

The most formidable species is the *Javelin Snake, properly so called,* or *Yellow Viper of Martinique*.[1]

This serpent inhabits Martinique and St. Lucia. In 1826, a reward of two shillings was offered in these islands for every head of one of these snakes. In the neighbourhood of Fort Royal, 700 were killed in three months. (Rufz.) This serpent is about six feet long; its colour varies from a clear yellow to a dark brown; the head is large.

The wound of the *Javelin Snake* is always fatal to the smaller mammalia; sometimes it will also destroy the larger ones, such as the ox.

The negroes who work in the plantations, and the soldiers on duty at Martinique, are often wounded by these dangerous reptiles. M. Blot has recorded three cases (a negro, a negress, and a mulatto,) in which death occurred almost immediately after the bite was inflicted. M. Guyon saw several soldiers perish; death generally occurs in three, twelve, or twenty-four hours, or some days, after the accident.

The person who is bitten usually feels an acute pain, which is followed by a livid swelling; his body loses its warmth, and his sensibility diminishes or becomes extinguished; at the same time he experiences extreme lassitude, and a general feeling of illness, the pulse and the respiration become feeble, the ideas wonder, coma comes on, a blue tint spreads over the surface of the skin; sometimes there is intense thirst, paralysis, and occasionally a congested state of the lungs, which is followed by a more or less copious and bloody expectoration. (Guyon.)

Fig. 83.—*Poison Fang.*

Another species of *Javelin*

---

[1] *Bothrops anceolatus,* Wagl., *Vipera lanceolata,* Daud., *V. Mægera,* Shaw, *Trigonocephalus lanceolatus,* Opp., commonly called the *Yellow Serpent of the Antilles.*

[2] Poison apparatus of *Bothrops Jararaca*—*a*, fang; *b*, its terminal opening; *c*, its basal opening; *d*, poison canal; *e*, maxillary bone; *f*, pterygoid bone; *g*, tendon of external pterygoid muscle; *h*, tendon of internal pterygoid muscle.

Snake, the *Jararaca*,[1] is found in Brazil, which inflicts much injury upon the natives.

Dr. Auzoux presented to M. Tandon a prepared head of the last-named serpent, from which the accompanying drawing has been taken (fig. 83).

4. The *Naia*, or *Spectacled Serpents*,[2] [called also the Hooded Snakes,] have the body large anteriorly, and forming a kind of disc, owing to the singular power which these animals possess of expanding the first pair of ribs. These serpents are met with in Arabia and in India.

The principal species is the *Spectacled Serpent, properly so called*,[3] or the *Cobra de Capello*. It has, on the cervical expansion of the body, a brown mark in the form of a pair of of spectacles.

This group also contains the *Haje Serpent*,[4] which appears to be the true *Asp* of the ancients, celebrated as having caused the death of Cleopatra.

The *Naia* produce most dangerous wounds; the subtility of of the poison is such that death is almost instantaneous.

A chicken, bitten by one of these animals, brought by an Indian juggler, vomited; its limbs became rigid, and it died in about ten minutes. A second chicken, slightly bitten twice, died in eight minutes.

Some years ago, one of the keepers of the reptiles at the Zoological Gardens in London was wounded by one of these snakes; the man died in about half an hour. One of the most remarkable phenomena which he exhibited before his death, was a paralysis of the inspiratory muscles of the thorax. (Quain.)

[Early on the morning of the 20th of October, when in a state of inebriety, the man took out the Cobra and put it round his waist; after playing with it some time, the animal bit him at the root of the nose. He was brought into the University College Hospital about forty minutes after the accident; the patient's face was slightly livid, the respiration imperfect; he walked with difficulty from the cab to the ward, and pointed to his throat as the seat of pain; he could not speak, had difficulty in standing, and was unable to swallow.

---

[1] *Bothrops Jararaca*, Dumer, *Cophias Jararaca*, Neuw.
[2] The three previous genera are Solenoglypha, like the *Vipers*; the Naias are Pteroglypha, characterised by having the poison fang grooved and not perforated at its base.
[3] *Naja tripudians*, Merrem, *Coluber Naja*, Linn.
[4] *Naja Haje*, Schleg., *Coluber Haje*, Linn.

The fangs had wounded the right side of the nose, between the nasal bone and the inner canthus of the eye; artificial respiration was resorted to for fifty minutes, and subsequently galvanism; but stupor rapidly followed upon faintness, paralysis of the extremity set in, and the patient died in a comatose state fifty-five minutes after admission.[1]

Dr. Patrick Russel, in his work on Indian Serpents, published by order of the East India Company in 1796, mentions four cases of recovery after the persons had been bitten by a Cobra.]

CHAPTER II.

POISONOUS ANIMALS ARMED WITH ANTENNÆ IN THE FORM OF CLAWS, OR WITH FOOT JAWS.

THE venomous animals which inoculate their poison by means of antennæ terminating in a pair of pincers are the *Arachnida*, and those which perform the act by means of foot-jaws are the *Scolopendridæ*. All of them belong to classes of animals which have no teeth or upper and under jaws like those of the Vertebrata; their jaws consist of lateral pieces which move in a horizontal direction. Sometimes the animal has attached to the head appendages or talons, improperly regarded as mandibles; these are the *clawed antennæ* which produce and inject the poison. Sometimes they have a pair of small dilated feet, placed very close to the mouth, and terminating in a strong hook; these are the *foot-jaws*.

§ I. Spiders.

Spiders, and the web which they form, have been previously noticed.[2]

1. The CAVE SPIDER.[3]—This species is very common in France and Italy.

The body is about half an inch in length, covered with hair, of a dark grey colour; it has a number of triangular black spots along the middle of the back and the abdomen; its mandibles are green or of a steel blue colour.

2. OTHER SPECIES.—The most important are:—

1. The *Mygales*[4] (*Crab Spiders and Mason Spiders*), remarkable for the terminal insertion of their palpi.

[1] *Lancet*, 1852, vol. 2, p. 397.
[2] See p. 98.
[3] *Segestria cellaris*, Latr., *Aranea Florentini*, Rossi, *Segestria perfida* Walck.
[4] *Mygale*, Walck.

POISONOUS ANIMALS.

2. The *Clubiones*, in which the eyes are arranged in two lines.[1]

3. The *Theridions*, especially the *Malmignatte*[2] of Corsica and Italy, and the *Mactans*[3] of South America.

4. The *Pholci*, particularly the *Phalangioides*, or *Domestic Spider with long feet*.[4]

5. The *Epeira*, amongst which there is the *Aranea diadema*, Linn.[5]

Lastly. The *Tarantula*, which is considered in a separate section.

3. POISON APPARATUS (fig. 84).—Nature has provided the *Spiders* with two *chelicers* or *antennæ*, terminating in a pair of claws, and placed in front of the mouth; these constitute the poison apparatus.

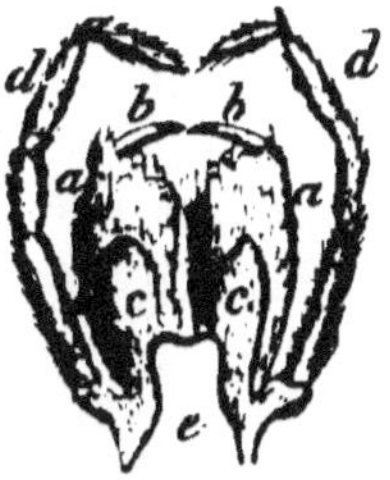

The secreting glands are placed at the base of these claws, and extend more or less into the region of the head; these are vasiform tortuous tubes, terminating in a blind extremity, and surrounded by a layer of muscular fibres, having a spiral arrangement; towards the anterior part, these glandular tubes are suddenly narrowed and form a slender excretory duct, which passes through the claw and terminates at its extremity.

Fig. 84.—*Mouth*.[6]

The chelicers consists of three pieces, a lower, a middle, and a terminal piece. The first piece is short; the middle is large and stout, and furnished with numerous hairs; towards its termination, and on its inner side, is a double row of hard conical scaly points, having the appearance of teeth; there are three of these teeth on each side, and a seventh which is placed lower down. The third piece, which is termed the hook or *claw*, is moveable, and articulated to the middle piece. The claw is

Fig. 85.—*Gland and Claw*.[7]

---

[1] The *Clubiona Nutrix*, Latr., is especially dangerous.
[2] *Theridion* 13-*guttatum*, Walck., *Aranea* 13-*guttata*, Rossi.
[3] *Theridion mactans*, Walck., *Aranea mactans*, Fabr.
[4] *Pholcus phalangioides*, Walck.
[5] *Epira diadema*, Walck. There is a species of *Epira* in New Holland which the natives make use of as food.
[6] *a a*, mandibles or clawed antennæ; *b b*, their claws; *c c*, jaws; *d d*, enormous maxillary palpi.
[7] *a*, poison gland; *b*, part of the canal placed in the mandible; *c*, claw;

of a conical form, curved inwards, very pointed, and perfectly smooth; when not in use it is folded inwards, and lies between the two rows of teeth as in a groove. Near the point of the claw, and on its under surface, is a narrow opening to allow of the exit of the poison. Leeuwenhoek was the first who pointed out this aperture, which is very narrow, and not easily seen. Mead erroneously denied its existence.

4. ACTION ON MAN.—When a spider bites it drives both claws into its victim, and at the same time a drop of poison is distilled into each of the wounds.

Much has been said of the poison of the *Spider*. Latreille has stated that the bite of one of a moderate size is sufficient to kill a house fly in a few minutes. Other observers have informed us that the bite of one of the large *Spiders* of South America (*Mygale*) would destroy a humming bird, or even a pigeon.

Are *Spiders*, especially those of Europe, dangerous to man? Is it true that the wounds of several species have been followed by serious results, and even by death itself?

Martin Lister saw some of these bites accompanied by inflammation. Is this fact quite certain? Schurig mentions the case of a bite having produced chlorosis. Cromstock speaks of another which caused St. Vitus's Dance. But these writers and these instances are scarcely to be depended on. Turner, Scaliger, Flacourt, Brogiani, and others, also regarded *Spiders* as very dangerous animals.

On the other hand, François Bon states that he had been bitten more than once, but that he had never felt the least ill effects from it, and he believed, therefore, that these animals were not poisonous. Robert, Boyle, and Amoreux entertained the same opinion. De Geer, remembering that Clerck had been often bitten by Spiders without experiencing any inconvenience, concluded that they are *not poisonous*. Lastly, H. Cloquet observed that the poison of these animals had no effect upon himself.

It is, however, certain that in hot climates, *Spiders* are able to produce, especially in young children and in women, a certain amount of local pain, which is followed by a small livid inflamed spot, and sometimes even by a pustule. Sometimes there is only a red spot, which is hardly perceptible; while at other times there is a true tumour. It is seldom that the bites are accompanied by general symptoms, but when this is

d, its terminal opening; *e*, groove bounded by the teeth, and receiving the claw when not in use.

the case the symptoms are similar to those which are produced by other poisons.

Latreille considers it is necessary to be careful of Spiders, especially the large species, when they are met with in hot climates. Rossi asserts that the *Malmignatte* can produce serious disturbances and even death. The latter assertion seems to be an exaggeration. It is, however, supported by several modern observers (Cauro, Graells, Lambotte). A medical man of the name of Bonifacio mentioned a case of this kind to M. Moquin Tandon (1852). According to Thiebaud de Berneaud, in the Island of Elba this Spider is as much dreaded as the Scorpion.

M. Abbot declares that the bite of the *Malmignatte* of America is exceedingly dangerous.

Are we to admit with Fabricius, that the *hunting Spider* of South America can cause a violent attack of fever in man? Must we also give credence to the following statement of Adanson? This celebrated naturalist states that in Senegal he felt for a *whole year* a kind of painful shivering, the course of which was indicated by a red line along the back and on the chest, where a large species of *Spider* had *passed*[1] while he was changing his shirt.

It has been previously mentioned[2] that the *Tegenaria medicinalis* and the *Clubione medicinalis* have vesicating properties. It is also asserted that the latter is narcotel and irritates the bladder. M. Ozanam has published a memoir on the employment of Spiders in medicine.

TARANTULA.—The Spiders known under the name of *Tarantula* are especially mentioned as being exceedingly poisonous.

These animals belong to the genus *Lycosa* of Latreille; they are characterised by having the eyes arranged in an elongated quadrilateral form, the two hinder ones not being supported on eminences, and by the first pair of feet being longer than the second. The abdomen of the *Tarantula* is oval, and the whole body is covered with a thick coating of down.

Most of them live upon the ground, where they form holes, which they enlarge as they grow older, and line with a coating of silk. Some reside in walls or in cavities of rocks. They keep close to their dwelling, watching for their prey, upon which they dart with astonishing rapidity. They can run very quickly.

The number of species of the Lycosa is very considerable.

---

[1] The animal, therefore, had not *bitten* him!
[2] See p. 128.

Two species only require to be noticed, the *common Tarantula*, and the *Tarantula* with a *black abdomen*.

The *common Tarantula*[1] inhabits the south of Italy. It is very common in Apulia and in Calabria. It is about an inch in length. Its body is entirely black, with the under surface of the abdomen red, with a black band across the middle of it.

The *Tarantula with a black abdomen*[2] is found in the South of France. It is smaller than the former. The under surface of the abdomen is black, with the exception of the margins, which are red.

A number of fabulous tales, all of them equally absurd, have been related of the *Tarantula*. Many medical men have written concerning this Spider. Estimable observers, amongst whom may be mentioned Baglivi, have given a long account of the dangers which attend them.[3] Ancient authors have declared that the poison of the *Tarantula* has brought on in man symptoms resembling those of a milignant fever. According to others it only produces erysipelatous spots and slight cramps or tinglings. Many think that the bites of this Spider produce convulsive attacks which compel the patients to perform a wild and irregular kind of dance. This disease has even received the name of *tarantism*. The patients have been called *tarantolati*. It has been seriously asserted that the supposed malady could only be cured by the aid of music. Some medical men have even carried the absurdity so far as to name those airs which are best adapted to soothe the tarantolati. Samuel Hafenreffer, professor at Ulm, in his treatise on diseases of the skin, has not failed to mention them.

The fear which was formerly inspired by the *Tarantula* has been overcome in the present day. Serrao, physician to the king of Naples, endeavoured to undeceive the public with regard to *tarantism*, and the remedies which had been proposed for the disease. The abbe Bertholon relates that a countryman having consented to be bitten by the Tarantula, the only effect was a slight swelling, which disappeared in twenty-four hours. Epiphane Ferdinand declared, in 1621, that in twenty years he had never known a person in Naples die from the bite of the *Tarantula*. Dr. Laurent, who inhabited that city for a long time, declares that the *Tarantula* only produces a sharp

---

[1] *Lycosa Tarantula*, Latr., *Aranea Tarantula*, Linn.

[2] *Lycosa melanogastra*, Latr., *Tarantula Narbonensis*, Walck.

[3] It appears that Baglivi was acquainted with the *Tarantula* with *the black abdomen*. Chabrier, of Montpellier, has made some curious observations on the same species.

pain, such as is caused by the bite of a bee, and that this is followed by a slight inflammation, which is occasionally accompanied by a small pustule, which, however, is easily removed by the application of simple emollients, or even pure water. (Merat.) We are acquainted in the present day with well-authenticated instances of serious disorders and convulsions, produced by the bites of these animals. As the *Tarantula* are Spiders of a large size and inhabitants of hot countries, it is only prudent to guard against being bitten by them.

Dr. Salvatore, of Renzi, some years back read, at the Academy of Medicine at Paris, a memoir in which he related the case of a harvestman who was bitten in the foot; while fast asleep he suddenly woke up with a feeling of acute pain in the injured part. He soon began to feel giddy, then oppression and feebleness of the muscular system, and afterwards general prostration and delirium. The effect of *music* was tried! The patient danced, he perspired abundantly, and was cured.

Epiphane Ferdinand maintains that tarantism is a true disease. M. Ozanam has very recently reproduced this opinion. He considers that the disease is characterised by a peculiar condition of the nervous system, over which music has a salutary effect.

§ II. Scolopendra.

The SCOLOPENDRA are insects belonging to the order Myriopoda and to the family Chilopoda. They are commonly termed *Millipides*.[1]

The characters of this genus are an elongated depressed body, composed of not less than twenty articulations; the antennæ are somewhat longer than the head, setaceous, and formed of seventeen segments; there are four pairs of small simple eyes, and twenty-one pairs of feet, of which the last are inclined towards the median line, and form a kind of tail.

The *Scolopendra* run very quickly; they avoid the light, hiding beneath stones, the beams of houses, and the bark of old worm-eaten trees. These animals feed on the earth-worm and on small insects.

The species which is most dreaded in the South of France and of Europe is the *Scolopendra cingulata*.

These insects vary considerably in size; the largest of the Scolopendra of Europe do not measure more than five inches in length, while those of India attain to eight inches. [The largest British species rarely exceed two inches in length.]

---

[1] *Centipedes, Millepeda* of the older writers.

2. POISON APPARATUS (fig. 86).—The mouth of the *Scolopendra* is composed of a square-shaped lip, of two mandibles, of two palpi, or small *foot jaws*, and of a second lip formed by another pair of dilated *foot jaws*, which are joined together at their commencement. The latter (*forcipes*)[1] are the organs which constitute the formidable weapons of the animal.

The poison gland is lodged in the interior of these organs towards their base.[2] It is oval, oblong, and provided with a long narrow excretory canal. The forceps terminate in a strong pointed moveable hook; the claw is provided with a small oblong aperture on its under surface, which allows of the exit of the poison.[3]

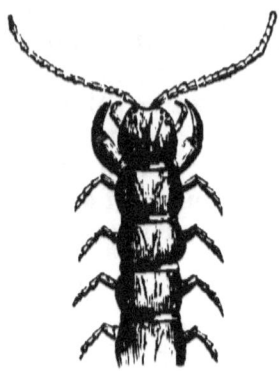

Fig. 86.—*Scolopendra*.[4]

This opening in the Scolopendra, Scopoliana, is close to the point on its under surface, and not within the curve, which is strongly carinated; a very slender canal passes from it to the base of the claw.

3. ACTION ON MAN.—The bite of the *Scolopendra* pierces the skin and inoculates its poison like that of the Spider. The claws are raised and seize the tissue one on either side, they are then pressed horizontally together and inflict

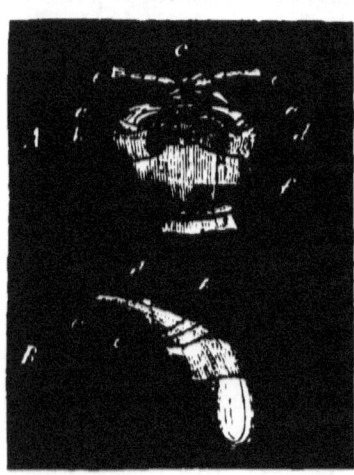

Fig. 87.—*Head and claw*.[5]

---

[1] *Pressores seu forcipes*, Leeuwenh.

[2] M. Lespés has studied the poison apparatus of a tropical species of *Scolopendra*, which was found alive at Bordeaux in a bundle of ox hides which had come from Pondichery. The gland reached halfway up the large joint of the claw, resting against its external portion; it was oblong, obtuse at the base, narrowed anteriorly, and presented at that part an oblique canal, which passed to the claw. Its tissue was very soft, of a pinkish hue, and punctated. Its canal was tolerably large and not quite equal in length to the large diameter of the gland. The hook was strong, curved, and pointed.

[3] Leeuwenhoek and Mead have described the claw of the Scolopendra from the East Indies. They represent the opening the same as it has been described above. In a Scolopendra, observed by M. Lespes, the opening was also below, but at the base of the claw.

[4] Head and anterior part of the *Scolopendra Scopoliana*, Koch.

[5] *A*, head of *Scolopendra Scopoliana*, seen from below: *a a*, the claws;

two lateral wounds, into each of which a drop of poison is discharged.

"The Millepedes," says Ambroise Paré, "excite considerable irritation, redness, and swelling in the part they have bitten."

The inhabitants of hot climates have a great dread of the *Scolopendra*. The species which are found in these countries, being larger than those of the North, secrete a greater quantity of poison, and probably also one that is more dangerous.

In general the *Scolopendra* of our climates have but little danger attached to them. Amoreux says that those in the neighbourhood of Montpellier are *free from poison*. This talented naturalist is evidently mistaken. These insects in the South of France secrete a poison like the rest of their class; only it is small in quantity, and not very active.

M. Moquin Tandon knew the case of a medical student, who, when herborizing at Maguelonne, in 1826, was bitten in the finger; the wound caused severe pain, and the part was very perceptibly swollen, but there were no other ill effects. The next day the finger was in its usual state; only there was a dark spot where it had been punctured.

M. Robelin, prosector to the faculty of Sciences at Montpellier, was bitten in the second joint of the middle finger by a large *Scolopendra* (4¼ inches in length). He felt a very acute pain, which was followed by swelling of the whole limb. He was compelled to carry his arm in a sling; and in spite of the wounds being cauterised, the symptoms lasted nearly eight days.

The bites of the *Scolopendra* often occasion a febrile condition, accompanied with shiverings.

Some foreign species, amongst others the *Scolopendra morsitans*, Linn., inflict wounds which are still more painful, and cause still more serious symptoms.

Worbe declares that there exists a species in Senegal which often produces very serious disturbances; but that, contrary to the common opinion, it does not cause death. A young Frenchman who had recently arrived at the Isle of St. Louis laid on a mattrass placed in an office, when one night he awoke in violent pain, uttered a piercing cry, and, getting up hurriedly, complained of horrible tortures over his knee. In a few minutes the part was swollen as large as the fist, having a black point in its centre (probably two). The usual remedies were employed,

b, the jaws; *c*, maxillary palpi; *d*, labrum; *e e*, portions of the antennæ; *f*, inferior arch of first ring; *B*, foot jaw from the right side, seen from below: *a*, poison gland; *b*, its canal; *c*, opening of claw; *d*, inferior groove; *e*, oblique course of groove.

and in five hours the pain and the swelling had disappeared. (Worbe.)

In the following case death was the result: In 1828 an officer of the garrison at Cayenne came out of a dancing-room and drank some water out of a small jug. It was dark, and a Scolopendra, which was probably lodged in the neck of the jug entered the mouth and attacked the pharynx. The surgeon of the regiment extracted the insect in bits. The pain was very acute and the swelling enormous. Fearful disturbance of the nervous system came on, and the officer died in a short time. (V. Mougeot.)

Are we to believe, with Bontius, that the *Scolopendra* of the East Indies can cause an affection resembling madness?

Some travellers have pretended that the virulent poison prepared by certain Indian tribes on the Upper Orinoco, the Rio Negro, and the Amazon, and known under the name of *curare*, contains the poison of a *Scolopendra*.[1] (De Castelnau.)

SECTION II.

ANIMALS WHICH INNOCULATE THEIR POISON BY MEANS OF A SPECIAL ORGAN.

The animals which possess a special organ for the insertion of their poisons are—1. The *Ornithorhynchus*; 2. the *Scorpions*; 3. certain *Hymenoptera*. In the first the organ is placed on the hinder feet; in the second and third it is situated at the extremity of the abdomen, sometimes externally, and fixed (*Scorpions*), sometimes internally and protractile (*Hymenoptera*).

In the *Ornithorhynchus* the poison apparatus belongs to the male; in the *Hymenoptera* it is limited to the female; in the *Scorpion* both sexes are furnished with it.

CHAPTER I.

ORNITHORHYNCHUS.

The *Ornithorhynchus*, *Ornithorhynchus paradoxus*, is a mammalian animal belonging to the order Edentata, and to the tribe Monotremata.

[1] The *Iuli*, which also belongs to the *Myriopoda*, according to some writers, are venomous insects. The European species, *Iulus terrestris*, it is true, secrete a scented substance which has been compared to the deutoxide of nitrogen. This substance causes little or no irritation. In the Antilles there is an *Iulus*, whose secretion can produce a tolerably acute inflammation of the eyes. (Salé.)

It inhabits the rivers and marshes of New Holland, in the neighbourhood of Port Jackson.

It is a very curious animal, remarkable for the elongated, depressed, fish-like form of its body, and for its curious flattened beak, furnished at its margins with transverse laminæ, and bearing a close resemblance to the bill of a duck. The teeth are only present at the back part of the mouth, two on each side in both the upper and under jaws; they are rootless, with flattened crowns, and are composed of numerous small vertical tubes. The tail is compressed; the feet have a membrane which unites the toes, and stretches beyond the claws in the anterior, but terminates immediately after its commencement in the posterior feet.

1. *Poison apparatus.*—This apparatus consists of a gland, an excretory canal, and a spur.

The gland is placed beneath the skin, on the external surface of the femur;[1] it is large, triangular, convex above, concave below, smooth, composed of several lobes, and covered with a delicate but firm membrane; it is of a brown colour. From this arises a small canal with thick walls; it descends behind the thigh and leg, becomes narrower, and terminates in a small sac situated in an excavation of the foot. This sac, which is about $\frac{2}{10}$ of an inch in diameter, is a reservoir in which the poison accumulates; from the centre of it another very minute membranous canal passes off, which communicates with the inoculating organ.

This organ is a large, conical, pointed spur, which is attached to the tarsus, and furnished with a canal. It consists of a layer of horny material and a bone of the same form placed within the latter. (Van der Hœven.) Its orifice is near the point on the convex surface. It is of a tolerable size, and of an oval form. (Blainville, Meckel.)

2. *Action on man.*—According to Van der Hœven the poison of the *Ornithorynchus* exercises no injurious influence upon man, although its effects are often very disagreeable. Such, at least, is the opinion which is generally entertained at Port Jackson.

When the animal is attacked, it endeavours to strike with its hind feet and wound with its spurs. The wound which it inflicts causes acute pain, accompanied by inflammation. The part swells, but there is no instance known of death having ensued. Sir J. Jamison, of Botany Bay, having wounded an *Ornithorynchus* with his gun, a person who was with him was

[1] *Glandula femorales,* Meckel.

struck in taking up the animal. In a short time the limb was swollen, and all the symptoms were present which are produced by the bite of a venomous animal; in spite of the immediate application of remedies, the wound continued painful for a long time, and the person lost the use of his limb for more than a month. (Van der Hœven.)

CHAPTER II.

SCORPIONS.

Scorpions belong to the class Arachnida, to the order Pedipalpi, and to the family Scorpionidæ. The head is confounded with the thorax, the body is elongated, and the abdomen terminates abruptly in a long tail, composed of six joints, of which the last is reflected, and terminates in a hooked claw.

The *Scorpions* are characterised by their enormous palpi, of which the first or basal joint has the form of a rounded concave jaw, and at their termination a pair of pincers.

Beneath the body, near the commencement of the abdomen, there are two peculiar appendages, called the *combs*.[1] These organs consist of a *stem* or basal portion, composed of two slender *rods*, closely united together, and a series of *teeth*, which are attached to and are capable of moving on a corresponding number of *bulbs* or marginal tubercles. Writers are not agreed upon the uses of these curious appendages. Amoreux compares them to a pair of ventral fins, and states that they move in unison with the feet. Tulk thinks they are intended to trim the palpi, the tarsi, and the end of the tail. Treviranus regards them as venereal organs. Leon Dufour believes that they serve to grasp and stimulate the genital organs.

The *Scorpions* inhabit warm climates; they are not found on mountains, or where the sub-alpine plants grow. (L. Dufour.) They live on the ground, under stones and pieces of wood, in dark, moist situations. They frequent the cellars and underground parts of houses. They only emerge from their hiding-places in the evening or at night time.

These creatures feed upon wood-lice, spiders, and small insects. They are especially carnivorous animals, even devouring their own species, the old ones eating the young. The *Scorpions* move slowly and deliberately, carrying their clawed palpi stretched out in front of them, as if feeling for any obstacles

---

[1] *Pectines duo subtus inter pectus et abdomen.* (Linn.)

that may be in their way. The tail is then straight, and trails along the ground. When they are irritated the palpi are immediately retracted, for the purpose of defending the head; at the same time the tail is curved on to the back, and becomes rigid. The animal vibrates the poison spine backwards and forwards in front of its mouth, prepared to strike at any moment. At first the *Scorpions* retreat backwards, like the crabs and some of the spiders, but they soon advance with boldness and impetuosity. The extremity of the tail is provided with a number of strong muscles, which provide for it various movements. These animals possess both strength and courage. A small *Scorpion* will often attack and destroy a spider larger than itself. It seizes it with one or both of its claws, and then strikes it on the head. If the spider endeavours to surround the *Scorpion* with its threads, when the latter has killed the spider, he cuts off all its feet with its pincers, and conveys the mutilated body to his mouth, and either eats it entire or sucks the soft parts, and then abandons the carcase. (Adanson.)

Small birds which have been wounded by a Scorpion stagger, tremble, appear to be suffocating, and turn round as if they were giddy. They soon fall down, become convulsed, and die. Dogs have been known to perish in about five hours, after a general swelling of the body, vomitings, and convulsions. (Adanson.)

The males are smaller than the females; the penis is double, and placed near the combs. The females have two vulvæ. During copulation they are placed upon their backs.

The eggs are 40 (Redi) or 60 (L. Dufour) in number. The period of gestation lasts a year. The animal is ovoviviparous. During the first few days the female carries her young on her back.

1. SPECIES.—The principal species are—1. The *Common;* 2. the *Palmated;* 3. the *Red;* 4. the African *Scorpion*. The following is a summary of their characters:—

Eyes lateral
- 2 pairs (9 teeth) . . . . . . 1. Common Scorpion.
- 3 pairs comb with { 8 teeth . . 2. Palmated Scorpion.
-                   { 28 teeth . . 3. Red Scorpion.
- 5 pairs (13 teeth) . . . . . . 4. African Scorpion.

The *Common European Scorpion*[1] (fig. 88) is common in the whole of the South of France. It is an inch and a half in length. It is of a more or less dark brown colour.

---

[1] *Scorpio Europæus*, Linn., *Sc. flavicaudus*, Geer.

The *palmated Scorpion*[1] inhabits Algeria; it is about the same colour as the common species.

Fig. 88.—*Common Scorpion.*

The *red Scorpion*[2] is found at Souvignargues, Cette, Narbonne, and Port Vendres. It is met with most frequently in the vegetable zone which includes the olive. It is from 3 to 3¼ inches in length; it is of a clear yellow colour, with the spine of the tail of a blackish colour. This species is remarkable for the number of teeth on the combs, there being from thirty to thirty-three.

The *African Scorpion*[3] is peculiar to Algeria. It is six inches long, and of a blackish brown colour.

2. POISON APPARATUS (fig. 89).—This terrible instrument of the Scorpion occupies the last joint of the tail (*in canda venenum*). It consists of a dilated portion and a spine.

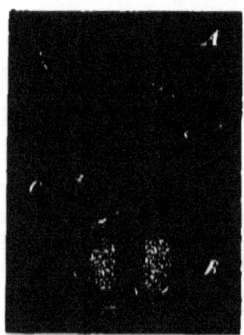

Fig. 89.
Glands and Spine.[4]

The dilated portion, improperly called *ampulla*, is a kind of oval knot covered with a few hairs; it is convex below, and has a slight medium longitudinal groove; at this part there is a kind of raphe, which indicates the line of separation between the two glands which secrete the poison. When an incision is carefully made at this part, the dilated portion may be penetrated without injury to its contents, in consequence of a very delicate, almost linear, space which separates the internal parts. (L. Dufour.)

The dilatation is formed by two closely approximated subhemispherical bodies; that is to say, they are flat on the side which is next the central space, and convex on the opposite side. Each of these bodies is drawn out into a slender neck towards the spine.

These bodies have been supposed to be hollow capsules,

---

[1] *Sc. palmatus*, Ehr., *Buthus palmatus*, Koch.

[2] *Sc. Occitanus*, Amor., *Buthus Occitanus*, Leach; commonly called the *white* or *yellow Scorpion*.

[3] *Scorpio Tunetanus*, Redi, *Sc. Afer*, partim Linn., *Sc. funestus*, Ehr. This and the preceding species belong to the section *Andronectus*.

[4] *A*, spine and dilatation containing the poison; *B*, section of the dilatation towards its centre, showing the two glands surrounded by a muscular coat.

whose walls are composed of a multitude of minute glands, closely impacted together, and communicating with each other. M. Leon Dufour, however, asserts that they are solid, and consist of a white opaque fibro-cartilaginous structure. He adds, that when carefully torn, four or five vessels may be seen, principally in the convex portion; some of these are simple, others of them are branched and ramify between the muscles. These vessels, of which it is not easy to determine the precise distribution, are not simple markings, as the mere inspection of them might lead one to suppose, since they can be raised up with the point of a needle. They all converge to a central or median trunk, which gradually narrows as it enters the neck. They are therefore secreting organs with regard to their branches, and excretory organs as regards their trunk. The latter part is composed of an external contractile coat, containing an elastic tube, which may be traced into the spine. (L. Dufour.)

Jean Muller discovered a layer of flat, smooth, muscular fasciculi around these bodies. M. Blanchard has given a drawing of these fibres, which are directed from before backwards.

The spine is a kind of strong terminal *claw*, which is elongated, slightly curved, and very pointed.[1] Near the point, and somewhat towards the under surface, are two small openings[2] of an oblong form, obtuse next the point, and narrowed at the opposite extremity. These openings appear to be rather closer to each other on the convex than on the concave margin.

M. Leon Dufour believes that each gland is provided with an excretory canal, and that the two, passing parallel to each other, terminate separately in one of the small apertures of the spine. M. Blanchard states that there is only one canal for the two glands. The delicate dissections and accurate drawings of this skilful anatomist leave no doubt that such is the case.

When the *Scorpion* is about to strike, an exceedingly minute drop of the poison is seen to exude at the extremity of the spine, the discharge taking place before this is introduced into the flesh of the victim; but the secretion becomes more abundant when the point meets with the resisting body. (Blanchard.) The poison is expelled by the contraction of the surrounding muscular fibres.

[1] *Mucro arcuatus*, Linn.
[2] Galen did not consider that the spine of the *Scorpion* was perforated. Leeuwenhoek, Vallisneri, Ghedini, and Linnæus mention three apertures; Mead and Maupertuis saw very distinctly two lateral openings in the red Scorpion.

T

3. ACTION ON MAN.—The wound of the *Scorpion* generally produces a dark red spot, which gradually enlarges and becomes black in the centre. This spot lasts for seven or eight days, rarely as long as a fortnight. Ambrose Paré has accurately described the effects of one of these wounds. "There comes on," he says, "an inflammation in the wounded part, accompanied with much redness, pain, and swelling. The patient has sweats and chills, like a person attacked with fever, and a creeping sensation over the surface of the body.

The experiments of Redi, Fallopius, Morgagni, and Amoreux, have shown that the *Scorpions* of Europe are not dangerous. The *common* species only produces local and trifling disturbances.

The *red*, which is larger, produces more serious effects. Maupertuis killed a dog in five hours by causing him to be bitten under the belly.

If we are to believe Dr. Maccari, who has had the courage to experiment upon himself, severe and even fatal consequences may ensue in man. The poison of the last species is more active in proportion to the age of the animal.

It will be readily supposed, from what has been said, that the *African Scorpion*, which is remarkable for its great size, can inflict serious wounds. Mallet de la Brossiere witnessed alarming symptoms in two persons who were wounded at Tunis. The symptoms generally consist of pain and swelling in the wounded part, vomiting, accompanied with fever and a nervous trembling.

Dr. Guyon has related several cases which were followed by death in Algeria. It should be mentioned that in these cases the wound occurred on the head.

Bontius declares that the wound of the great Scorpion of India, a species which is often confounded with that of Africa, but which is much larger, produces insanity.

According to M. Cassan, at St. Lucia, in the torrid zone, there is a large Scorpion whose poison causes death in a very short time.

It may be stated generally that Scorpions are dangerous in proportion to their size, their age, the state of irritation they may be in, and the temperature of the climate in which they reside. The wounds, however, even of the largest species are rarely fatal.

CHAPTER III.

HYMENOPTERA.

The poisonous Hymenoptera are—1. The *Bees;* 2. The *Humble Bees;* 3. The *Wasps.* The *Bees* and the *Humble Bees* belong to the family Mellifera, and the *Wasps*[1] to the Diploptera.

§ I. Bees.

The *Common* or *Honey Bee, Apis Mellifica*, Linn., has already been mentioned when speaking of honey and wax.[2]

1. Poison Apparatus (fig. 90).—This apparatus is only

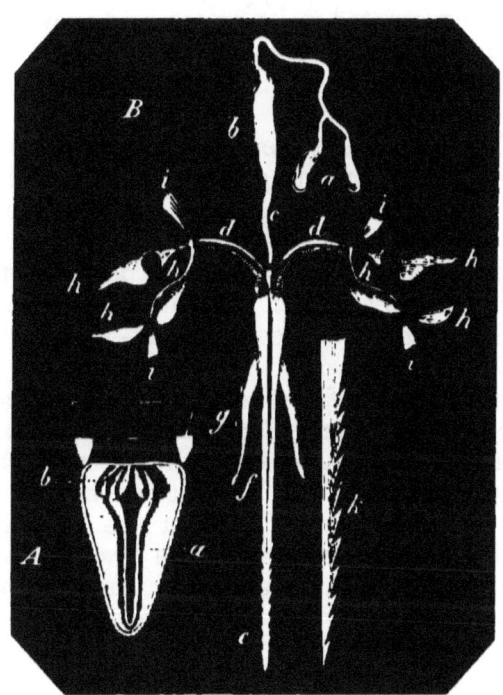

Fig. 90.—*Poison Apparatus.*[3]

present in the females and in the workers; the males are not

---

[1] The *Scoliidæ*, the *Pompilini*, and the other Hymenoptera furnished with a sting, may also attack man.

[2] See p. 195.

[3] *A*, extremity of the abdomen, with the sting retracted; *a*, sting in its case; *b*, its base, composed of cartilage and muscles; *B*, poison apparatus; *a*, poison glands; *b*, poison reservoir; *c*, its excretory canal; *d d*, extremities of the two darts forming the sting; *e*, the darts conjoined; *f*, sheath of the sting opened above; *g*, scaly appendages forming together a cleft piece;

provided with it. The ancients believed that they were provided with a sting, but that they disdained to make use of it.

The poison apparatus consists of *glands* for secreting the poison, and of a *sting* for its inoculation. In order to understand the structure of these organs, the extremity of the abdomen must be carefully dissected.

Glands.—These organs are two in number, having the form of simple flexible tubes terminating in a blind extremity;[1] their ultimate structure resembles that of the salivary glands.. Each of these bodies gives rise to a small canal; these canals unite together and form a single very tortuous duct, which opens into the reservoir; this is a tolerably large oblong fusiform sac, sometimes slightly constricted in its centre, and provided with very thin muscular membranes and contractile walls. At the opposite extremity of the reservoir is an excretory canal, which leads to the base of the sting.

Sting.—This is placed at the posterior extremity of the body.

When not in use the sting is completely enclosed in the abdomen; it can be protruded and retracted at the will of the animal, and can also be moved in any given direction so as to encounter the object which the insect is desirous of stinging.

The sting of a *Bee* has been accurately described by Swammerdam and Reaumur; it is composed of—1, a *base;* 2, a *case;* 3, a *dart.*

1. The *base* consists of several cartilaginous pieces; Swammerdam reckons eight, and Reaumur six. Audouin observes that the latter writer overlooked two pieces which had been described by Swammerdam. M. Dumeril has recognized the presence of a ninth piece placed on the median line, and having the form of the letter V. The branches of the latter piece are directed forwards and articulated with the case; their office is, possibly, to draw the latter inwards. The other eight pieces are arranged four on each side; they are united together by a strong membrane, and the whole constitutes a kind of envelope, which, by its external circumference, is attached to the last segment of the abdomen, while its internal surface surrounds the sting. Connected with the eight pieces are four muscles, two of which are protractors, and two retractors.

h h, eight cartilaginous pieces which support the base of the darts and attach them to the abdomen; *i i*, protractor and retractor muscles of these pieces; *k*, extremity of a dart magnified to show the point and the teeth placed along its outer edge.

[1] In some neighbouring genera the tubular glands are ramified.

Belonging also to the base of the sting are two long whitish membranous appendages, each of which is grooved, accompanies the sheath, and partly covers it. Swammerdam considers that these bodies are destined to move the case inwards and outwards. Reaumur believes that they prevent the soft parts of the abdomen from coming in contact with the case, and *vice versa*.

2. The *case* is a horny covering, dilated towards its base, and gradually diminishing to the extremity, which is very pointed. The case is incomplete; that is to say, it does not form a perfectly closed cylinder; it is a half canal, or is grooved, longitudinal, and inferiorly.

3. The *dart* is a double organ; it consists of two long delicate setæ, which are received into the case, but do not entirely fill it; they are placed close to each other on their inner surfaces, which are smooth, but traversed throughout their entire length by a delicate groove. The apices are extremely pointed, and furnished on their outer edges with ten small teeth directed from before backwards. These setæ separate and diverge towards the base; they are articulated with the cartilaginous pieces; they are accompanied on their under surface by the case, which also divides into two branches.

2. Action on man.—*Wound.*—When a *Bee* wishes to make use of its weapon, it protrudes its sting by the contraction of the muscles which attach it to the last segment of the abdomen. The case, which is pointed, penetrates the body which is attacked, and thus furnishes a point of resistance to the base. The muscles of the latter act upon the setæ, which are buried deeper in the skin, and are sometimes so firmly fixed by means of their teeth, that when the animal wishes to escape, the whole of the sting is torn from its body and mutilates the rectum and the oviduct; the sting then remains in the wound, and the animal soon dies. In the act of penetration the sting has a quivering motion, which lasts for some minutes. (Kunzmann.)

If the sting merely caused a puncture of the skin, the wound would not be followed by any injurious effects; but the instrument discharges a certain quantity of poison. The reservoir containing the poison contracts, and its contents are driven along the excretory canal, and enter the space produced by the divergence of the setæ at their base; it then passes along the canal formed between the setæ, and by that means enters the wound.

That it is the poison of the *Bee*, and not merely the wound, which produces the pain and inflammation in the part, is proved by taking a small quantity of the fluid on the point of a needle and inserting it into the skin, when the same symptoms are immediately produced as those which arise from the wound made by the *Bee* itself. (Audouin.)

Dr. Kunzmann has noticed that when the abdomen has been cut off from a live *Bee*, twelve hours afterwards, the least touch is sufficient to cause the sting to protrude with the same force and rapidity as if the animal was still alive, and the person may be wounded just as effectually as when that is the case.

The effect of the bite is usually slight, consisting of only transient pain; sometimes, however, it causes swellings, papillary eruptions, erysipelas, and even a phlegmonous inflammation, followed by suppuration and gangrene. When the sting remains in the wound, the irritation appears to be much greater than at other times.

Fabrice, of Hilden, relates the case of a young girl who was wounded near the ear; the swelling extended over the head, and was followed by an abscess.

Zacutus saw the sting of a *Bee* produce gangrene around the wound.

In the *Raccoglitore medico di Fano* is recorded the case of a man, thirty-six years of age, of a sanguine temperament, and athletic form, who was stung by three or four *Bees* on the back of the hand; immediately his sight became dim, he lost his strength, and his body was covered with a profuse perspiration; the face was greatly injected, there were violent pains in the head, a feeling of oppression, with general disturbance of the system, and the fear of death. He was put to bed, and an eruption of small vesicles, similar to those produced by a nettle, broke out on the lower extremities, accompanied with inflammation and intense fever; in an hour afterwards all these symptoms disappeared as if by magic.

Debrest, de Cusset, mentions the case of a villager, about thirty years of age, who was stung by a *Bee* below the eyebrow; he fell to the ground, his face became inflamed, and, after losing a large quantity of blood from the nose, died in a few minutes. Is this case well authenticated?

It may be readily supposed that if a person is wounded by several *Bees* at once, if, for instance, he should be attacked by a swarm, that the results might be serious. (Amoreux.)

In the *Archives Génerales de Médicine*, is the case of a man who died after being wounded by a number of *Bees* on the chest and face.[1]

At the siege of Massa, the crusaders were attacked by swarms of *Bees*, which the besieged threw upon them with their hives. This novel kind of foe greatly incommoded the besiegers.

Kunzmann recommends that in extracting the sting immediately after it has been inserted it should not be taken hold of by the dilated extremity of the sheath, which is always filled with poison, and would therefore communicate more of it to the wound; it should be grasped below this part without compressing it as it is drawn from below upwards.

§ II. Humble Bee.

The *Humble Bees* are larger than the Bees, and are remarkable for their transverse upper lip, and for their false proboscis, which is shorter than the body. The principal species are the—*Lapidary* or *Red-tailed Bee;* the *Moss* or *Carder Bee;* and the *Common Humble Bee*.

The *Red-tailed Bee, Bombus lapidarius,* has the body black, with the last three segments of the abdomen red; it makes its nest on the ground, at the bottom of old walls and between tones.

The *Moss* or *Carder Bee, Bombus muscorum,* is of a yellow colour, with the hairs of the thorax of a fawn colour.

The *Common Humble Bee, Bombus terrestris,* is black, with the posterior portion of the thorax and base of the abdomen yellow; the thorax is black, with a bright yellow band anteriorly; the basal segment of the abdomen black, second yellow, third black, and the three posterior ones white.

The sting of these insects is more powerful than that of the *Bee*, and occasions more pain and severe inflammation. The poison glands are not single, but double.

In 1679, several persons in Poland were stung by large *Humble Bees;* the wounds produced swellings and inflammation, which could only be arrested by deep scarification.

§ III. Wasps.

The *Wasps* have their lower lip the same length as their mandibles, and their wings are folded up when in a state of repose. The two species which are to be guarded against in France [and also in England] are the *Common Wasp* and the *Hornet*.

---

[1] Dr. Kunzmann mentions the death of a horse.

The *Common Wasp, Vespa vulgaris,* is rather less than an inch in length; it is of a black colour, with yellow in front of the head, and a black spot in the middle; it has several yellow spots on the thorax, and a band of the same colour, with three black spots on the posterior margin of each segment.

The *Hornet, Vespa Crabro,* is more than an inch in length; the head is of a fawn colour, with yellow in front; the thorax black, marked with spots of a fawn colour; the abdominal segments of a blackish brown, with a yellow band with two or three black spots.

The pain from the sting of the *Wasp* is sharp, but that from the *Hornet* is very severe. (Amoreux.)

Reaumur tested the effect of these insects on himself and on his servant. "Being stung by a *Wasp,*" says this celebrated naturalist, "I thought I might gain something from his infliction by bearing it with a good grace. I allowed the animal to wound me at his leisure; when he had withdrawn his sting of his own accord, I irritated and placed him on the hand of a domestic, who was not expecting to be stung, but the wound did not cause him much pain. I then made the *Wasp* sting me a second time, when I scarcely felt it. The poisonous fluid was nearly exhausted by the former experiments, and I could not induce the *Wasp* to make a fourth wound. This experiment, and some others, which people will probably not care to repeat, have taught me that where the animals are undisturbed the sting is never left in the wound. The sting is flexible, and is not driven straight in, but forms a curved or zigzag wound. If the insect is compelled to withdraw it suddenly, the friction is sufficient to retain the sting, which is somewhat hooked, and tears it off. On the other hand, if the animal is not disturbed it withdraws the sting gradually. The sting of the *Hornet* is more severe than that of the *Wasp;* in this country, however, it is not of that importance which it is represented by some writers, who prescribe for it all the remedies which they make use of against the most dangerous poisons."

A lady, says Richerand, was wounded by a Hornet on the middle finger of the left hand. The pain was very severe; in a few moments her whole body was swollen; the skin became inflamed and covered with wheals, and a violent fever set in. Cabanis treated the patient successfully. In a few hours the swelling, redness, and fever subsided. On the fourth day, nothing remained of all this disturbance, but a small black spot which marked the situation of the wound.

Haldanus relates a case where the wound of a Wasp, on the hand, was followed by a total prostration of strength and desquamation over the whole surface of the body.

Lansoni speaks of a woman who was wounded on the cheek, and had, in consequence, an ulcer, which lasted for three months.

Facts of this kind are far from common, and cases of death are still more rare.

In 1776 a gardener at Nancy, when eating an apple, which contained a *Wasp*, was bitten on the soft palate. It produced a violent inflammation, pain, and great swelling. The man died in a few hours.

Chaumeton mentions the case of a young man who was wounded in the throat by a *Wasp*, which he had not perceived, at the bottom of a glass. The effects were exceedingly rapid. The throat inflamed, and the young man died suffocated.

In a communication from Montbard to the *Patrie*, of September 19th, 1858, it is stated, that "the youngest son of M. L., a brickmaker, died from the sting of a *Wasp*. The unfortunate youth, who was sixteen years of age, was drinking from a bottle, when a *Wasp*, which he had not seen, got into his throat and wounded him. He died suffocated from the swelling, which ensued before any assistance could be procured."

Some of the cases which are related of severe injuries arising from the sting of the *Bee* are no doubt to be referred to those of the *Wasp* and *Hornet*.

It is an old saying that the stings of twenty-seven *Wasps* are sufficient to kill a man, and those of six *Hornets* a horse.[1]

SECTION III.

ANIMAL POISONS.

THESE *poisons* are fluids secreted by special glands and provide the animal with the means of attack or defence.

A *poison* differs from a *virus*, in the latter being a morbid and accidental formation, transmitting the original disease from one individual to another, and which is reproduced by the disease it has occasioned.

Poisons are diminished in intensity during their action, which

---

[1] Several writers have related the case of a mare and her foal being destroyed by a swarm of *Wasps* which the former had disturbed from near the bush to which she was fastened.

is always more or less prompt; they are decomposed in the production of their specific effects. A *virus* remains for some time in a state of apparent inaction, to acquire after a longer or shorter time its greatest intensity; it increases in virulence by the production of its morbid effects.[1]

The ancients supposed that in poisonous animals there were two poles of antagonism, one of which was seated in the poison apparatus, the other in the head. Charras pretends that the disorder produced by the *Viper* consisted principally in *its opening the door to the irritated spirits.*

The various *poisons* are not identical; there are probably several kinds; some, even in very small quantities, produce great pain, while others cause only a very slight amount of pain. The danger of their inoculation is not in proportion to the ill effects they give rise to. Some act upon the entire organism, while others act only locally. There are those which are almost invariably fatal; while others only cause trifling disorders.

Some writers have asserted that each poison according to its nature acts on a particular system of organs. The ancients believed that the *poison of the Asp* was somniferous. Fontana maintains that that of the *Viper* acts on the nervous system, and coagulates the blood. According to MM. Brainard and Burnett, that of the *Crotalus* disorganises the blood globules, and renders the blood more liquid. According to Amoreux that of insects more especially affects the skin.

In all cases the poisoning when it is virulent commences in the neighbourhood of the wound, from whence it spreads and becomes general. Death sometimes occurs very rapidly (*Crotalus*). In other cases it only takes place after a longer or shorter interval (*Viper*). Whatever may be the rapidity of the poisoning it is never instantaneous. There requires a certain time for the effects to be developed either in the part which was bitten or in the system generally.

The action of these *poisons* varies very much according to circumstances which serves to explain some of the contradictions that are met with in different writers. Their action appears to be increased by an increase in the temperature,[2] by the

---

[1] Linnæus defines a *poison* as follows: "VENENUM *est quod perexigua dos corpori humano ingestum aut extus admotum, vi quadam peculiari, effectus producit violentissimos, qui in perniciem sanitatis et vitæ tendunt.*" (Exanth. xiv.)

[2] It is stated that in France the *Viper* is more to be dreaded in summer than in autumn.

vigour and anger of the animal, and also at the period of heat. It is, on the contrary, diminished by cold, by weakness, by age, and by disease, and also when several wounds have been inflicted.

The *poisons* are harmless when taken into the stomach, but they are dangerous when introduced by inoculation. The ancients were aware of this distinction. Celsus distinctly says that no injury arises from swallowing these *poisons*.[1] This fact was, however, only clearly established by the experiments of Redi, Fontana, and Charras. It is also well known that boars and herons habitually feed upon *Vipers* without experiencing any inconvenience from it.

The *poisons* do not lose their properties by drying.[2] Mangili killed pigeons with *poison* which had been dry for eighteen months. Naturalists and others with good reason dread wounds which might be caused by the fangs of the *Crotalus* or the *Viper* long after the animals have been dead.

It is believed that immersion in alcohol does not destroy the noxious properties of the *poison*. M. Joly killed sparrows by wounding them with the fangs of a *Viper*, which had been preserved in spirits. It appears, however, that long immersion in this fluid ultimately destroys the poisonous properties. Duvernoy having taken some of the poison from a *Crotalus durissus*, preserved in a jar, on the end of a lancet, and having introduced it under the skin of the ear and thigh of a rabbit, no effects were produced.

1. OPHIDIANS.—The *poisons* of the Ophidia are the most terrible and the best known.

That of the *Viper* was first thoroughly investigated by Fontana, who made more than six thousand experiments in reference to this subject.

The quantity of poison contained in each apparatus of the *Viper* was estimated by Fontana at something more than $\frac{7}{10}$ of a grain, or a grain and a half for the two. M. Tandon calculates that there is as much as one grain in each. Into every wound the animal discharges about $\frac{3}{10}$ of a grain of the poison.

The *poison of the Viper* (venenum Viperæ) when fresh has something of an oleaginous consistence. Redi compares it to oil of sweet almonds. The poison is almost colourless, slightly opalescent by reflected light, or of a pale yellow colour. That

---

[1] " *Venenum serpentis non gustu, sed vulnere nocet.*" (Celsus.)—Galen relates the case of a man whose servant was wishing to kill him gave him wine in which he had steeped a *Viper*, and this cured him of his disease.

[2] M. Paul Gervais, however, states that he wounded a young dog with the fangs of a dried *Crotalus*, and that they produced no poisonous effects.

of the different species of *Crotalus* is green, and that of the *Javelin snake* transparent. (Guyon.)

At the moment of its secretion the *poison* of serpents is neither acid nor alkaline. According, however, to Dr. Rousseau, that of a *Crotalus* slightly reddens the tincture of turnsole.

The *poison of the Viper* has no distinct flavour. According to some it is at first insipid, but afterwards leaves a somewhat astringent taste in the fauces: according to others it possesses an intolerable acridity, which it is difficult to describe.[1] It has scarcely any odour. It falls to the bottom of water, in which it preserves its viscidity for some time, but is ultimately dissolved. When dried on a plate of glass it looks like a layer of gum full of cracks.

In the dried state the poison dissolves in water; but it is insoluble in sulphuric and hydrochloric acids, which only acts partially upon it, and it assumes the condition of a liquid paste. It acts in the same manner with regard to nitric acid, except that it becomes somewhat yellower. The vegetable acids, the alkalies and oils, do not dissolve it. When heated it does not melt, but swells up, and becomes thick. Placed in contact with flame it does not ignite; when thrown upon red-hot charcoal, it only burns when it has become carbonised in the same manner as occurs with vegetable matters.

Prince Lucien Bonaparte has shown that the *poison of the Viper* consists essentially of a principle to which he has given the name *echidnine* or *viperine*. This principle presents itself under the appearance of a colourless, transparent, and rather thick varnish. It has no smell or positive flavour. It does not redden the tincture of turnsole, nor does it render the syrup of violets green. It has some resemblance to gum Arabic; but it contains nitrogen. Dissolved in a solution of caustic potash, the hydrated binoxide of copper turns it of a beautiful violet colour, a phenomenon which also occurs with gelatine and albumen.

The *poison of the Viper* appears to act much more powerfully on man than on animals.

• It is injurious to all the warm-blooded vertebrata. The larger species do not die, but the small generally succumb. Thus the horse[2] almost always resists it, the sheep often, the

---

[1] M. L.-A. de Montesquiou asserts that he has tasted it several times without ever finding that it had any distinct taste.

[2] Bosc mentions the case of two horses which were bitten in America by the *black Viper*, the one on the leg, the other in the tongue. The first

cat sometimes,¹ a pigeon dies in eight or ten minutes, and a sparrow in five.²

The animals which are bitten in the chest, abdomen, liver, or intestines die in a short space of time.

Animals wounded in the ears, the head, the periosteum, the dura-mater, the brain, the marrow of the bones, the cornea, or stomach, seldom manifest any appreciable phenomena.

When the *poison of the Viper* is applied lightly to the abraided skin of a rabbit or a guinea pig, it is not followed by death; applied to the muscular fibre or to the nerves, it produces no effect.

The *poison* of two *Vipers* injected into the jugular vein of a large rabbit produced death in less than two minutes, after giving rise to cries and convulsions. The blood becomes coagulated in the ventricles of the heart. The mysentery, the intestines, and the muscles of the abdomen are inflamed.

The *poison of the Viper* does not produce any appreciable change when applied to the warm and palpitating parts which have been removed from an animal.

The coldblooded vertebrata resist the effects of the poison longer than the warmblooded. A lizard died at the end of half an hour; in the tortoise death ensues very slowly in whatever part the animal may be bitten. The common snake and the slow-worm are not affected by it. It is the same with the eel, the snail, and the leech.

A *Viper* wounded by another *Viper* does not die. A *Viper* which sends its fangs into its lower jaw or any other part of its body, does not appear to be inconvenienced by it.³

What is the quantity of the *Viper's* poison which is requisite to kill a man? The two hundredth part of a grain inserted into the muscles is sufficient to destroy a small bird almost instantaneously; it takes six times as much to kill a pigeon. Fontana calculated that it requires more than two grains to produce death in man.⁴ As the whole apparatus only contains

---

escaped with a swelling, which lasted for some days, and a weakness which continued for some weeks; the second died in less than an hour.

¹ Is it true, as stated by Lenz, that the Hedgehog may be bitten with impunity on the snout and lips, and even on the tongue?

² Fontana says that small animals die in from fifteen to twenty seconds.

³ The bite of a *Javelin Snake* is equally harmless to himself. (Guyon.) A case is mentioned of a *Rattle Snake* dying from the effects of his own bite. (Halm.)

⁴ And eight for an ox.

two grains,[1] and that each wound only introduces the $\frac{1}{10}$ of a grain, it would follow that a person might be bitten by several *Vipers* without dying, and that one could never cause death: this, however, is contrary to what has been observed. It has been shown that under certain circumstances a single wound may be fatal. The calculation of Fontana is, therefore, excessive.

The *poison* of Serpents has been recommended in America as a remedial agent; it has been pretended, that persons who were inoculated with it were secure against the yellow fever and the black vomit. Peyrilhe states, that the *poison of the Viper* has been tried in hydrophobia. He somewhat amusingly adds, "this remedy should only be used with the consent of the patient and the approval of the magistrate." M. Desmartis, of Bordeaux, submitted to the Academy of Sciences a memoir on the employment of *poisons* in medicine. He also recommends the bite of the *Viper* against hydrophobia.

2. ARACHNIDA.—The poison of these animals has received but little attention. Orfila places that of *Spiders* amongst the list of septic poisons; but he forms his opinion rather from its effects than from its nature.

Fontana says, that of the *Scorpion* is white and viscid, and that when it is placed upon the tongue it produces a sharp and burning taste. This poison resembles gum. According to M. Blanchard it holds in suspension irregular granules; it is acid, and reddens litmus paper.

According to Amoreux, it acts on the cold-blooded animals in the same manner as on the other vertebrata. It has been seen that this is not the case with the poison of the Serpents. It is worthy of remark, that the *poison of the Viper* produces but little suffering when it is introduced into the tissues, even when it proves fatal, while that of the *Arachnida* occasions more or less pain, but seldom kills.

M. Ozanam believes that he has recognized therapeutic properties in the poison of the *Arachnida*, and that it is sometimes sudorific, and at other times anti-periodic.

3. INSECTS.—Very little is known of the *poison of the Hymenoptera*. Swammerdam believed that this poison was the bile of the animal. It is a clear, limpid fluid, which quickly coagulates when exposed to the air. It does not alter vegetable colours; it appears to be slightly styptic. Swammerdam and

[1] It has been previously mentioned that Fontana only estimated it at a grain and a half.

Ludovic, having placed some of the poison on the tongue, experienced a bitter taste, which gradually became more acrid and penetrating, extended over the whole of the mouth, as far as the fauces, and produced a flow of saliva, as if they had been chewing pellitory root. Fontana declares that this *poison* acts on the tongue like a powerful caustic. Ludovic compares the sensation to that which is produced by nitric acid on the skin. Other writers describe it as a burning sensation. According to Adanson, the *poison of the Bee* is more active in the summer than in winter.

Humours analogous to Poisons.

The viscid exudation which lubricates the skin of the *Toad*, the *Triton*, and the *Salamander*, is at present regarded as a species of *poison;* it appears to answer the purpose of repelling the enemies of those animals by its nauseous odour and disagreeable taste.[1] But these animals have no instrument for the inoculation of the fluid, and at the same time it is so situated that they cannot directly employ it as a means of attack and defence.

1. *Toad.*—The humour of the common Toad, *Bufo vulgaris*, is secreted by cutaneous glands or pustules placed on the back and in the situation of the parotid gland.

This is a thick, viscid, milky fluid, with a slight yellow tint and poisonous odour. It has a disagreeable, caustic, bitter taste; it reddens turmeric; it solidifies on exposure to the air, and when placed on a plate of glass it assumes a scaly appearance. It is soluble in alcohol, which shows that it is not an albuminous substance. According to Pelletier, it contains an acid, partly free and partly combined with a base. It is this acid to which it appears to owe its acrid properties.

In the experiments of MM. Gratiolet and Cloez, birds, such as linnets and finches, which were inoculated with this fluid, died in about six minutes, but without being convulsed. These animals opened their beaks, and staggered as if in a state of drunkenness; they lost the power of co-ordinating their movements. In a short time they closed their eyes, as if they were going to sleep, and fell down dead.

These gentlemen ascertained that this fluid destroyed birds even after it had been dried. Two milligrammes ($\frac{1}{300}$ gr.) have destroyed a linnet in fifteen minutes.

It acts equally after its acid has been saturated with potash. When a small quantity of the fluid is introduced beneath the

---

[1] According to some writers it also serves to diminish the effects of the sun's rays.

skin of smaller mammalia, such as the dog or goat, it kills them in less than an hour.

M. Vulpian has repeated and varied these experiments with the *common Toad* and *Natter Jack Toad, Bufo calamita*. He experimented on dogs and Guinea pigs, and proved that these animals died in from half an hour to an hour and a half. The symptoms which were noticed might be divided into several stages—1st, a period of excitement; 2nd, one of depression; 3rd, vomiting or attempts at vomiting; 4th, intoxication in the dog, but convulsions in the Guinea pig, and then death.

The fluid of the *Toad* acts as a poison on frogs, and generally kills them in the course of an hour. It is even sufficient if a certain quantity of it is spread on the back of these animals. The fluid has no action on the *Toads* themselves.

This *fluid* acts powerfully on the heart, and arrests its movements. MM. Gratiolet and Cloez have noticed, in the dead bodies of birds, the singular fact that the semicircular canals of the ear are always filled with blood.

It is asserted that in certain countries the Indians hunt after several species of *Toads* with pointed sticks. They transfix the animals with these sticks, and when they have collected a considerable quantity of them they place them before a large fire, but at a sufficient distance to prevent their being roasted. The heat excites the cutaneous secretion, which is collected by the Indians as it is discharged from the pustules for the purpose of poisoning their arrows.

2. *Triton*, or *Aquatic Salamander, Triton cristatus.*—The humour of this species is secreted by numerous follicles which project along the sides of the neck, back, loins, and tail. When these wart-like bodies are pressed the fluid comes out in drops. The experiment succeeds better if the animal's body is previously dried by wiping it with a cloth.

The fluid is of a white colour, or of a very faint yellow, and somewhat thicker than milk. It gives off a poisonous, penetrating, and disagreeable odour. When examined beneath the microscope it appears to consist of a number of oval globules. It thickens on exposure to the air, coagulates, and becomes of a yellow colour. It dries rapidly, and when in the dry state on a plate of glass, it appears cracked, like a thin layer of gum Arabic.[1] It does not readily mix with water; it will do so par-

---

[1] If a Triton is killed by immersion in alcohol, the middle parts of its body become covered with the milky fluid, which coagulates in the form of a very thin layer. This coating is thickest on the sides of the neck and at the commencement of the tail. (H. Gosse).

tially, but soon forms an irregular coagulum. Alcohol coagulates almost the whole of it.[1] When the fluid is placed on the tongue, it does not at first produce any effect, but in the course of a few minutes a burning sensation is felt in the fauces.

This fluid poisons much in the same manner as that of the Toad, but it also produces violent convulsions.

With only a small quantity, M. Vulpian has succeeded in killing dogs, Guinea pigs, and frogs.

This fluid acts less energetically than that of the Toad. Death took place in frogs only at the end of from six to twelve hours. When placed on the back of these animals it had no effect. (Vulpian.)

Like the milky humour of the *Toad*, it acts powerfully on the heart, but it does not destroy its irritability so completely as the latter.

The humour of the *Tritons* appears to have a stupifying rather than an exciting effect; it does not produce either nausea or vomiting. Lastly, it has no action on the *Tritons* themselves. (Vulpian.)

M. Philipaux, whilst making some experiments on the *Tritons*, was suddenly attacked with inflammation of the conjunctiva, which lasted for two days.

Two other persons, who were wiping some *Tritons*, having got some of the water in which these animals were placed on their face and eyes, met with similar results. (Vulpian.)

3. *Terrestrial Salamander, Salamandra maculata.*—This animal produces a milky fluid, which is principally contained in the warty tubercles on the loins.

The humour resembles that of the Tritons.

Lacepede says, that when a drop is placed upon the tongue it causes a burning sensation. Dugès performed some experiments with this fluid. He gave pieces of bread and small quantities of honey, mixed with the fluid, to doves and sparrows, who eat them without experiencing any inconvenience. Dugès therefore concluded that the fluid is not poisonous; but if the learned professor had administered the *poison* of the Viper or the Crotalus to these animals in the same way, he would have met with similar results. The injurious effects of the humour of the *Salamanders* are only produced when it is inoculated into a wound, and so introduced into the circulation.

[1] If a Triton is killed by immersion in alcohol, the middle portion of its body becomes covered with the milky fluid, which coagulates in the form of a very thin layer. This coating is thickest on the sides of the neck and at the commencement of the tail. (H. Gosse.)

The experiments of MM. Gratiolet and Cloez on the *terrestrial Salamander*, and which have since been repeated by M. Vulpian, leave no doubt as to the poisonous property of the milky fluid which is furnished by this animal.

When introduced beneath the skin of the wing or of the thigh of a small bird, such as a lark, for instance, it does not appear to act as a caustic. At first the animal seems not to be inconvenienced by it, but in the course of two or three minutes a singular disturbance is set up, the feathers are bristled, the bird staggers, opens its beak, and snaps it convulsively. At the same time it becomes rigid, turns its head backwards, utters plaintive cries, is agitated, and after rolling over several times it soon dies. (Gratiolet and Cloez.)

A Yellow Hammer, inoculated in the thigh, died in twenty-two hours. A Chaffinch, inoculated under the wing, died in twenty-five minutes; a pigeon, in twenty; other birds, in six or seven minutes; and a Yellow Hammer, in less than three minutes. In general death occurs the more speedily in proportion to the small quantity of blood which is lost. (Gratiolet and Cloez.)

Experiments which have been tried on small mammalia have not been attended with the same results. Guinea pigs and mice, which were inoculated in the thigh, in the course of ten minutes manifested great anxiety. At times the respiration was panting and painful. The animals continually fell off to sleep, but this was interrupted by slight convulsions, resembling electric shocks. At the end of some hours these disturbances disappeared, and the animals recovered their usual state of health. Thus a quantity of the fluid which would have been sufficient to destroy a dove, only produced slight temporary convulsions in a mouse. But, a dove being much larger than a mouse, the reason of this difference can only be referred to the nature and organization of the animals acted upon. (Gratiolet and Cloez.) In conclusion, all birds which were subjected to the action of the fluid of this *Salamander* had epileptic convulsions, but did not die.

The fluid of the *Salamander* is injurious to frogs, but produces no effect on the *Salamanders* themselves. (Vulpian.)

In general it appears to be less active than the fluid of the Toads or Tritons. During the whole period of its action, the disturbances of the heart are slight.

BOOK VI.

EXTERNAL PARASITES OR EPIZOA.

As there are creatures termed *Parasites*, which live on the surface or in the interior of other animals, feeding upon their fluids, or upon the substance of their bodies, so, also, there are some which live at the expense of man.

The human parasites are generally very small animals. Their species are not numerous, but the number of the individuals is sometimes appalling.

At different periods considerable importance has been attributed to these parasitic animals. An English medical writer who lived at the commencement of the last century, imagined that all diseases were to be referred to the presence of microscopic animals.[1] M. Raspail has lately advocated the same doctrine.

In medicine the title of *Epizoa* is given to those Parasites which derive their nourishment from the skin; they have also been named *Ectozoa* or *Ectoparasites*.

Some of the *Epizoa* are born upon that part of the body on which they reside (*Lice*), while others come from without (*Fleas*).

The Epizoa may be divided into two series: 1st, those which reside upon the surface of the skin; 2nd, those which live in the interior of it.

SECTION I.

EPIZOA LIVING ON THE SKIN.

THE Epizoa which live upon the skin are: 1, the *Louse*; 2, the *Flea*; 3, the *Chigoe*; 4, the *Ticks*; 5, the *Argas*; 6, the *Harvest Bug*.

CHAPTER I.

LICE.

THE genus *Louse* or *Pediculus* belongs to the order Hemiptera, and to the family Rostrata. Its characters are—antennæ

[1] In a summary of this work published by M. A. C. D., in 1726, there are 90 figures of insects, each of which it was imagined produced a different

as long as the thorax; a sucker inclosed in an inarticulated sheath, and armed with retractile hooks; eyes, simple one on either side behind the antennæ; abdomen more or less notched at its margins; three pairs of feet, and no wings.

There are four species of *Lice* which infest the human subject: 1. *Head louse;* 2. *Body louse;* 3. *Louse of sick persons;* 4. *Pubic louse.* The following is a summary of their characters:

Body { oblong, thorax distinct, { ash coloured (lobulated) . . 1. *Head louse.* whitish. Abdomen { lobulated. 2. *Body louse.* sinuous . 3. *Louse of sick persons.* rounded and confounded with thorax . . . . . . 4. *Pubic louse.*

1. HEAD LOUSE (fig. 91).—The *head* or *common Louse*[1] is commonly known, and has been figured in various works.

Fig. 91.—*Head Louse.*[2]

This species, as its name implies, is found on the head in people who are neglectful of their person, and especially in children. It is, however, never met with in very young children, as, for example, in those who have not been weaned. (Natalis Guillot.)

The body of the insect is flattened and somewhat transparent, smooth in the centre, slightly wrinkled at the sides, and of an ashen grey colour, with patches of black in the neighbourhood of the stigmata. When the animal is old or filled with food it has a reddish tinge. On each side, there is, generally, an indistinct line divided into a number of small spots in the direction of the segments. The head is ovo-rhomboidal and has no palpi. The antennæ are filiform, about the same length as the head, and composed of five nearly equal joints; they are in a state of constant vibration when the animal is moving about. (De Geer.) The eyes are simple, round, black, and placed very far behind the antennæ; the thorax is nearly square, one fourth the length of

---

disease; such as measles, rheumatism, gout, pleurisy, jaundice, and whitlows. With the exception of the itch insect, which appears to have been drawn from nature, all the others are purely imaginary beings.

[1] *Pediculus capitis*, De Geer, *P. humanus*, Linn., *P. cervicalis*, Leach.

[2] *A*, female seen from the back; *B*, extremity of the abdomen in the male, showing its spur; *C*, the egg or nit attached to a hair.

the abdomen, rather narrower in front than behind, and divided into three divisions by shallow indentations; the limbs consist of a hip composed of two pieces, a thigh, a leg, and a tarsus consisting of one large joint. The tarsus terminates in a stout hook, which is received into a notched projection; the two together act like a pair of pinchers, and enable the animal to fix itself to the hairs. The abdomen is of an oval form, indented and lobulated at its margins. There are eight segments and sixteen stigmata. The tracheæ are festooned, and may be seen through the skin, forming a number of curves, which alternate with the marginal lobes. Swammerdam suspected that *Lice* were androgynous, in consequence of his having found ovaries in all those which he dissected. Adanson and Lamarck fell into the same error. It would appear that Swammerdam had only met with the female. Leeuwenhoek determined the existence of the two sexes. The males have at the extremity of the abdomen, which is rounded, a horny, conical, recurved, pointed spur, with which they can inflict a wound. This spur seems to be the sheath of the genital organ. In the female the extremity of the abdomen is grooved, and during copulation she places herself on the back of the male.

Lice are oviparous, and their eggs, which are found attached to the hairs, are termed *nits* (fig. 91, *C*). They are oblong or rather slightly pyriform, of a white colour, and open at their upper part.

The young are hatched in five or six days; they cast their skin several times, and, at the end of eighteen days, are capable of reproduction. A *Louse* has been known to produce fifty eggs in the course of six days, and there were others still remaining in its body.[1] According to a calculation of Leeuwenhoek's, two females might become the grandmothers of 10,000 *lice* in the space of eight weeks; others have calculated that the second generation of a single individual might furnish 2500 *lice*, and the third generation 125,000; but the usual rate of reproduction does not advance with this frightful rapidity.

1. *Mouth* (fig. 92).—In front of the head there is a short conical fleshy projection, containing a sucker (*Rostrum*), which the animal can protrude and retract at pleasure. This sucker is only seen when in action. Leeuwenhoek has compared it to a fine thread; but, contrary to his usual habit, he observed it but very imperfectly.

---

[1] Swammerdam is stated to have found 54 eggs of different sizes in a single ovary.

Fig. 92.
Rostrum.[1]

This organ is an obtuse, subcylindrical sheath, capable of being dilated at its extremity, and then presenting six small hooks, which curve from before backwards, and which, from their position and direction, are evidently intended to retain the sucker in the skin.

In the interior of the sheath are four capillary threads, which are round, very pointed, and closely packed together.

This structure of the mouth confirms the opinion of Fabricius, who regarded the lice as degraded Hemiptera, deprived of wings. (Burmeister.)

2. *Action on man.*—*Lice* puncture those parts of the skin covered with hair and suck up its juices by means of the apparatus which has just been described. It has been supposed that the itching which these insects produce is caused by the spur of the male, and not by the oral sucker, which belongs to both sexes. But if the creature first made a wound with its spur in order that it might subsequently introduce the sucker, then the female ought also to be provided with one. According to the account of some writers the entrance of the sucker into the skin does not cause any sensation, unless it touches a nerve. Leeuwenhoek made the experiment on his own hand.

Are we to believe, with Linnæus,[2] that in rainy weather these insects descend the sides of the head?

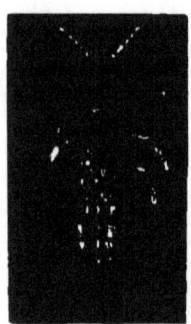

Fig. 93.
Body louse.

2. BODY LOUSE (fig. 93).—The *Body* or *clothes Louse*[3] was for a long time confounded with the former. It was De Geer who first distinguished between the two insects.

As its name implies, this *Louse* is found on different parts of the body and on the clothes.

It is somewhat larger, of a lighter colour, and less strongly marked than the *common Louse*. It has a uniform tinge of a dirty white colour.[4] The skin is not so hard, and the eyes are more prominent. (Olfers.) The junction of the thorax and abdomen is more constricted, and the former is scarcely one-third the size of the

---

[1] *A*, buccal projection beginning to be everted; *B*, the same fully extended, and become converted into a tubular rostrum; *a*, body of rostrum; *b*, hooks at its extremity; *c*, piercer, formed of four capillary threads.

[2] "*Instante pluvia, descendit ad latera capitis.*" (Linn.)

[3] *Pediculus corporis*, De Geer, *P. humanus*, Linn.

[4] A black variety is met with on the bodies of Ethiopians, *Pediculus*

latter. The marginal lobules are indistinct, and the feet are closer together and more slender.

This species causes greater irritation than the former.

3. *Lice of sick persons*.[1]—This name has been proposed for a louse which gives rise to a disease termed *phthiriasis*.

MM. Alt and Burmeister have given a minute description of this species. It is of a pale yellow colour. The head is rounded. The antennæ are longer, and the thorax larger than they are in the *body Louse*. The thorax is of a trapezoid form, and more than one-third the size of the abdomen. Its margins are nearly even.

This species seems to differ in its habits from the other *Lice*, inasmuch as it introduces itself under the skin. It is asserted that it deposits its eggs under the epidermis, and that each nest becomes a bullæ or vesicle, from whence the young *Lice* escape as soon as they are hatched to spread and multiply themselves in the surrounding parts: in this way the disease continues to spread, and its severity increases with each succeeding generation. (Raspail.)

This disease has been mentioned by several writers. Forestus speaks of a young girl who was afflicted with it, and Borellus of a soldier. Bernard Valentin relates the history of a man forty years of age, who was troubled with an intolerable itching on all parts of his body, and with large tubercles, which were filled with an enormous number of *Lice*. Bremser once met with a mass of *Lice* in a tumour on the head. M. Jules Cloquet in another invalid found some thousands of these creatures in a sub-cutaneous cavity. Cazal quotes the case of an old man, sixty-five years of age, who could not scratch himself without a swarm of these insects issuing from his neck and shoulders; they were renewed with an astonishing rapidity . . . . Dr. Jules Sichel, in 1825, published a monograph on pthiriasis, in which he enumerates the various parts in which this disease has made its appearance.

Instances of death have been mentioned, but M. Rayer regards these cases as doubtful. If, however, we are to believe the ancient writers, the king Antiochus, the philosopher Pherecydes, Sylla the dictator, Agrippa, Valerius Maximus, the emperor Arnould, cardinal Duprat, and Philip the Second, king of Spain, died from this disease. Historians state that *Lice* were seen to issue from the body of Herod as a stream

pubescens, γ *nigrescens*, Olfers; another of a brownish red has been found on the Greenlanders.

[1] *Pediculus tabescentium*, Alt, *P. subcutaneus*, Rasp.

issues from the earth. It is stated that Foucquau, bishop of Noyon, was covered with such multitudes that it was necessary to fasten his body in a leathern sack before he was buried. .(?)

4. THE PUBIC LOUSE[1] (fig. 94).—This species, which is known by the common name of *Crab Louse*, attaches itself to the hairs of the sexual organs. the arm pits, and even of the eyebrows.[2] It is never met with in the head or in the beard. Hitherto it has only been found in the white races.

Its body is large and depressed; the thorax very short. The four posterior feet are tolerably large, recurved, and so arranged as to hook themselves into the skin, so that it is extremely difficult to induce the animal to leave go its hold.[4]

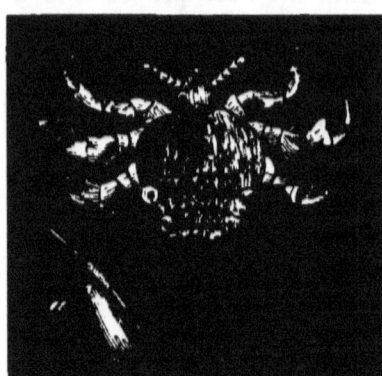

Fig. 94.—*Pubic Louse.*[3]

The eggs are oblong, and adhere to the hairs by an expansion which forms a sheath around them.

The rostrum of this species is stronger than that of the other *Lice*. The skin is covered by small red-coloured patches.

Animals which may be mistaken for Lice.

The *Lice* of other mammalia and those particular forms of *Lice* belonging to the genus Ricinus of De Geer, which infest birds, may accidentally get upon man and cause more or less irritation, but in general this is all the injury they produce. The latter species have the mouth formed for biting, and are furnished with a pair of hooked mandibles. In some instances they can bite with considerable force and give rise to a number of round or oval red spots, but these are seldom accompanied by pustules or vesicles.

The same thing may happen with certain arachnida belonging to the genus *Dermanyssus* of Dugès. These vermin are met

---

[1] *Pediculus pubis*, Linn., *P. inguinalis*. Redi, *P. Morpio*, Merrem, *P. ferus*, Olfers.—Leach proposed to form it into a distinct genus under the name of *Phthirus*.

[2] "They are found attached to the eyelids." (Celsus.)

[3] *a*, an egg attached to a hair.

[4] "They are so firmly attached to the skin that it is scarcely possible to detach them." (A. Paré.)

with in hen-roosts and pigeon-houses, even long after the birds upon which they lived have ceased to frequent these places.

Another species of arachnida belonging to the genus *Gamasus* of Latreille, gets upon the clothes, and from them upon the body; these animals do not fix themselves to one spot, but move about over the surface of the skin. Persons who are travelling in the country are occasionally tormented by them.

The *Ornithomya* (Latr.), a species of fly infesting certain birds, may also gain access to man, and attach itself to his skin by means of its claws.

CHAPTER II.

THE COMMON FLEA.

THE genus *Pulex* belongs to the Siphonoptera of Latreille, but is now approximated to the Diptera, notwithstanding that it is unprovided with wings.[1] This genus is characterised by a straight unjointed rostrum, which incloses two blades or lancets, and which is covered at its base by two scales; the eyes are two in number, and scarcely project from the sides of the head; the abdomen is compressed; the limbs are six in number, and adapted for leaping.

The COMMON FLEA[2] (fig. 95) has an oval compressed body covered with a strong chitinous integument of a shining reddish brown colour. The body is invested with a kind of armour, and when it is crushed a slight noise is heard from the resistance and rupture of the skin. The greatest diameter of the *Flea* is from the back to the belly, which both terminate in a thin sharp edge. The body is divided into twelve segments, of which three form the short thorax and seven the abdomen. The head is small, compressed, rounded above, and forms a kind of hood. In front of this are two short, nearly cylindrical antennæ, composed of four joints, of which the second is moderately long, and the third large and notched. When the *Flea* is moving about these organs are in a state of constant vibration; but when at rest they are laid along the sides and in front of the head. (De Geer.) The eyes are simple, large,

[1] Although the wings are not functionally developed, traces of them are present in the form of a pair of small scales attached to the middle segment of the thorax, and of a much larger pair appended to the third segment of the thorax, which cover the sides of the first and part of the second abdominal segments. Ed.]

[2] *Pulex hominis*, Duges, *P. irritans*, Linn., *P. vulgaris*, De Geer.

and round. Behind each there is a small aperture, which can be closed up by a moveable valve. The limbs of the *Flea* are long, strong, and spinous, and the tarsi five-jointed, terminating in a pair of strong claws. The anterior pair of limbs are placed at some distance from the others, and are inserted almost immediately beneath the head. The posterior are the strongest, and enable the animal to accomplish leaps which are greatly disproportioned to the size of its body. The abdomen is very large, and each of its segments is composed of two pieces, a superior and an inferior; this arrangement permits of the enormous distensions which the body undergoes after the animal has been sucking the blood of its prey, or after impregnation. The penultimate ring of the body supports a number of very slender spines, which are inserted in a corresponding number of minute arcolæ; this segment has received the name of *pygidium*.

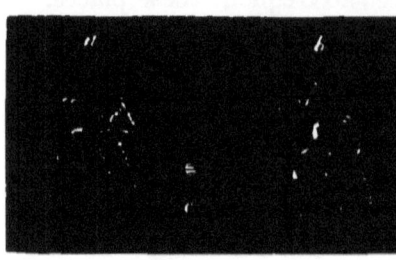

Fig. 95.—*Flea*.[1]

Fleas are bisexual. The male is only half the size of the female, and the back of the latter is the most convex. During copulation the abdomens of the insects are placed opposite to each other, the male being underneath.[2]

The female lays eight to twelve smooth oval eggs; they are slightly viscid, and of a white colour. De Geer detected a *Flea* in the act of depositing her eggs. This animal does not attach its eggs either to the hairs or to the skin, but drops them by chance upon the ground. (Rœsel.) The eggs roll about like globules of mercury. They are generally found in the crevices of the floor, in old furniture, in dirty linen, or in any place where filth has accumulated.[3]

Along with the eggs there are found a quantity of dark purple grains of various forms. These particles are not the excrements of the insect, but dried blood obtained at man's expence, and intended for the nourishment of the larvæ. (Defrance.)

At the end of four or five days in summer, and of eleven in winter, the larvæ issue forth under the form of long cylindrical

---

[1] *a*, male; *b*, female; *c*, egg.

[2] "*Femina in coitu ascendit in corpus maris.*" (Leeuwenhoek.) "*Mas sub femina jungitur.*" (Linn.)

[3] They have been met with beneath the nails of the feet.

worms, whose bodies are composed of thirteen segments plentifully furnished with hairs. The head is scaly, of a yellow colour, provided with antennæ, and the posterior extremity of the body is furnished with two hooks. The larvæ have no feet (Leeuwenhoek, Rœsel); but they are very active, twisting about in all directions, and moving along with the head erect (Defrance). At first they are white, but afterwards of a reddish colour. In eleven or fifteen days, according to the time of year, the larvæ inclose themselves in a silky, oblong, whitish cocoon, within which they are transformed into pupæ; the latter are provided with limbs placed close to the sides of the body. (Defrance.)

It takes from twelve to fifteen days before the pupæ become perfect *Fleas*.

1. *Mouth* (fig. 96).—The beak or rostellum of the common *Flea* is placed almost perpendicularly;

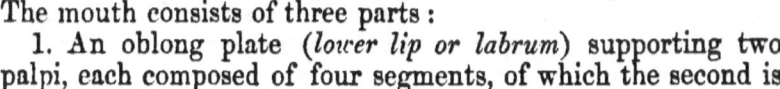

Fig. 96.—*Parts of the Mouth.*[1]

when not in use, it is curved slightly backwards and concealed between the long thigh joints of the anterior pair of limbs. The mouth consists of three parts:

1. An oblong plate (*lower lip or labrum*) supporting two palpi, each composed of four segments, of which the second is the largest.

2. Of an external articulated sheath, which supports and receives into a groove on its under surface a pair of *lancets*. The case is composed of two pieces (jaws) placed close together, oblong, concave, each supporting a palpus inserted very low down, and which is made up of four segments, of which the first is tolerably large.

3. Of two straight blades or long sharp lancets, with serrated margins. These lancets are employed in puncturing the flesh and in sucking.

2. *Action on man.*—*Fleas* produce a disagreeable itching as

---

[1] *A*, head; *a*, left jaw; *b*, the lancets or mandibles; *c*, left labial palpus; *d*, maxillary palpi; *B*, parts of the rostrum; *a a*, maxilla or inferior jaws, each with its palpus; *b b*, the lancets or mandibles; *c*, lower lip, with its two palpi; *C*, point of one of the lancets.

they move over the sensitive portions of the skin from the terminal hooks of their feet.

The puncture of these insects [1] causes a more acute sensation. When the *Flea* is about to inflict its wound, it separates the two valves of the sheath, which protects the lancets, and plunges them into the skin. It then immediately begins to suck, and fills itself with the blood.

The quantity of blood which this creature can absorb is very considerable in comparison with its size. It may be estimated by the volume of the gorged abdomen and the large amount of its excrement which partly retains the colour of the blood.

The puncture of the *Flea* leaves a small reddish spot on the skin, in the centre of which is a minute, almost microscopic aperture; in infants, in females, and in persons whose skin is exceedingly delicate, there is also a slight swelling. (Barthez.) Very rarely this tumefaction is followed by a vesicle, or by slight inflammation.

2. OTHER SPECIES.—Linnæus believed that the human *Flea* and those of other animals constituted only a single species. Bosc was the first to remark that the *Fleas* of the mole and of the fox presented some differences in their organization. Dugès has examined the *Fleas* of the dog, mouse, and bat; he has compared them with that of man, and has shown that each of them forms a distinct species. Thus, the head of the *Flea* which frequents the dog, has a number of spines below; whilst there are only four spines placed posteriorly in that of the mouse; and two which are situated anteriorly in that of the bat. In that of man there are none. The eyes are large in the latter species, of moderate size in the *Flea* of the dog, small in that of the mouse, and wanting in that of the bat.

CHAPTER III.

THE CHIGOE.

THE *Chigoe* or *Jigger* [2] is one of the most troublesome parasites known.

It is an inhabitant of tropical America, particularly Guiana and Brazil. It resides in the forests, on various shrubs and

---

[1] *Morsus pulicum.* (Sauvages).

[2] *Dermatophilus penetrans*, Guér., *Pulex penetrans*, Linn., *Sarcopsylla penetrans*, Guild. At Saint Domingo and Guiana it is commonly named

plants, and especially on the dried leaves. They are sometimes so numerous, that the clothes and body of a person who may have seated himself on the ground or on a fallen tree, are immediately covered with them.

1. DESCRIPTION.—The *Chigoe* is smaller than the common Flea, but it acquires a considerable size when gorged with blood. The insect is of an elongated oval form; it is flattened, of a reddish brown colour, with a white spot on the back. Its skin is so tough that it is torn with difficulty. The articulations of its feet are of a whitish colour.

The males are smaller than the females. The abdomen of the latter is proportionally more developed than in the other sex, and becomes of a globular form after impregnation.

The eggs are oval, oblong, and whitish. They appear to be attached to the mother by a very short funis. It is thought that when these insects do not attack the human species they deposit their eggs in the ground. (Pohl, Kollar.)

The larva of the *Chigoe* has not hitherto been detected.

2. MOUTH.—This organ is only imperfectly known; it is only ascertained that the animal possesses a long, rigid, pointed rostrum, proportionally larger than that of the common Flea.

3. ACTION ON MAN.—The *Chigoes* attack men, but it is only the females after they have become impregnated, for the purpose of depositing their young, and providing them with nutriment. These insects are found principally upon the feet, where they penetrate between the flesh and the nails. They are very rarely met with on its dorsal surface, on the hands, or on other parts of the body. Persons who travel without shoes are more exposed to these attacks than others; those who perspire much are less liable to them.

In spite of the length of its rostrum, the *Chigoe* introduces itself without causing any pain, or changing the colour of the skin, at least during the earliest portion of its sojourn. In a few days the parasite begins to develop itself, and its presence is indicated by a slight itching, which gradually increases, and ultimately becomes intolerable. When the presence of the *Chigoe* is accompanied by an appreciable amount of pain, half of its body has already penetrated the tissue. The animal at first resembles a brown speck; this speck gradually increases;

Nigua; in Brazil, *Jatecuba*, *Mygor*, and *Tunga*. The Spaniards, on their first arrival in America, named it *Chega* and *Chego;* and the French, *Pique* and *Chique*. Is it not the *Pediculus ricinoides* of Linnæus? " *Habitat in America, pedes obumbulantium intrans, sanguinem hauriens, in iis ova deponens, ulcera cacoethica causans.*" (Rolander.)

it soon assumes the appearance of a reddish swelling, in which it is difficult to recognise an abdomen.

The *Chigoe* shortly attains the size of a small pea. Its body is nothing more than an enormous sac, resembling a cyst, of a brown or livid colour, containing a sanious pus. In the interior of the abdomen are a vast number of globules, which are the eggs.

It is very difficult to make these formidable parasites quit their hold; they allow the rostrum to be broken off before they will disengage themselves from the tissue in which they have inserted it. When handled too roughly, the rostrum, head, and feet remain behind, and soon give rise to an unhealthy inflammation or ill-conditioned ulcer.[1]

The feet are sometimes entirely covered, and, as it were, eaten away by the *Chigoes*. When the animal has made its puncture, the skin presents a small white spot, surrounded by a circle of inflammation, which afterwards swells up and forms an ill-defined tumour. When the parasites are numerous and close together, the disease may present a certain amount of danger.

The *Chigoes* are sometimes found between the claws of the dog, but more particularly on the under surface of the feet of the hog; these pachyderms have been even regarded as propagators of this species of insects. (J. Goudot.)

CHAPTER IV.

TICKS.

THE *Ticks*, or *Ixodes*, are arachnidans belonging to the family of the Acaridæ or Mites, in which the palpi encase the sucker and form with it a short, projecting beak, which is truncated and somewhat dilated at its extremity.

The Ticks frequent thick woods, hooking themselves to low growing plants by their anterior feet, while the others remain extended. (Latreille.) They attach themselves to the different mammalia, and fix themselves to their skins.

These animals lay an enormous number of eggs. M. Chabrier asserts that they issue forth from the mouth.

1. SPECIES.—In France the two principal species are— 1. The *Wolf Tick;* 2. *Reticulated Tick*.

The *Wolf Tick* of the French, *Ixodes Ricinus*, Latr., *Acarus Ricinus*, Linn., *Acarus reduvius*, De Geer, is of a deep blood-

---

[1] "*Ulcera cacoethica excitat.*" (Linn.)

red colour, with the anterior scaly plate obscure; the sides of the body are margined, and provided with a few hairs.

It attaches itself to dogs.

The *reticulated Tick, Ixodes reticulatus*, Latr., *Acarus reduvius*, Schrank, *Cynorhæstes pictus*, Herm., is of an ash colour, marked with small spots and annular lines of a reddish brown. The margins of the abdomen are striated, and the palpi almost oval.

It attaches itself to oxen, sheep, and several of the domesticated mammalia.

Amongst the foreign species may be mentioned the *Nigua, Ix. Nigua*, Guér, *Acarus Nigua*, De Geer, *A. Americanus*, Linn., and the *human Tick, Ix. hominis*, Koch, a species of arachnida which is still very imperfectly known.

2. THE MOUTH.—The beak or rostrum of the *Tick* is obtuse anteriorly. It presents—1. a *supporting piece*, formed by a small scale received into a groove of the thorax, serving as a receptacle for the base of the sucker; 2. a *sheath*, composed of two very short scaly portions, concave on their inner surfaces, rounded and somewhat enlarged at their termination (each of these pieces, when seen beneath a magnifying glass, appears to be divided transversely); 3. a *sucker*, placed in the sheath, consisting of three very hard, horny, conical blades, of which the two lateral are the smallest, and cover the third; the latter is large, obtuse at its extremity, and somewhat transparent; its margins, and the whole of its inferior surface, are covered with a multitude of strong serrated teeth; in the centre it is furnished with a groove.

3. ACTION ON MAN.—M. Raspail states that, between the month of December, 1858, and the month of May, 1860, on several occasions he found young *Ticks* having but eight feet (a circumstance which proves they were adults) on the head of his daughter, who was between three and four years of age. The terrible irritation which the child suffered showed that the skin had been deeply wounded.

Some twenty years since, a young man, on his return from hunting in the neighbourhood of Melun, found on his arm a small livid swelling, as large as a lentil, and accompanied with considerable pain: it was an enormous *Tick*, which he had got in the forests.

Dr. Ernest Cosson, when travelling in Algeria, in 1856, and when he was in the oasis of Asla, in the province of Oran, was obliged to pitch his tent on a piece of ground which was frequented by sheep. The next morning his servant woke him up, having three *Ticks* close together on his right breast the size of a pea. The presence of these parasites caused him great pain.

The *Ticks* plunge their beaks into the skin in the same way as one may thrust in a trochar. The small recurved hooks which cover the surface prevent their being withdrawn from the part they have penetrated. The sucker is so firmly embedded that it can only be removed by force, and at the same time tearing away a portion of the skin which adheres to it.

These arachnida are extremely voracious, and suck up a large quantity of blood. Their body, which is capable of undergoing great distension at its sides and on the upper part, swells out and assumes the appearance of a livid excrescence.

A *Tick* has been known to penetrate a small tumour on the abdomen of a female. (Hussem.)

CHAPTER V.

ARGADES.

THE *Argades* are arachnida which are closely allied to the Ticks; they differ from them by the inferior situation of the mouth and by their free conical palpi, composed of four articulations.

These animals have an oval elliptical body; it is very flat, coriaceous, granulated, and very extensible.

They are exceedingly fond of blood. Some writers have compared them to the Bugs, which they resemble somewhat in their general appearance; they do not quit the body, however, like the latter, but fix themselves after the manner of the Ticks. They are true *Epizoa*.

1. SPECIES.—There are two principal species which require to be noticed; these are—1. the *Argas* of *Persia;* 2. the *Chinche*.

The *Argas* of *Persia*, or *Bug of Miana, Argas Persicus*, Fisch, is common at Miana, in Persia. Its size is about that of the common Bug; the body is rough, of a blood-red colour, and covered with some elevated white spots.

The *Argas* of *Chinche, Argas Chinche*, Gerv., inhabits Columbia, where it has been found by M. Justin Goudot.

It is of the same size as the former, and of a reddish colour.

2. *The mouth.*—In the *Argades* the beak resembles that of the Ixodes, but it is placed inferiorly, and is uncovered.

3. ACTION ON MAN.—For a long time it was supposed that

the *Argades* only attacked pigeons; we have, however, a European species, the *Bordered Argas, Arg. marginatus,* Latr., which frequents the dove-cots and sucks the blood of these birds.

At the present time it is well known that these parasites will attack man. In Persia it is said that they give the preference to strangers (?) The bite produces acute pain, and it has been even asserted that they may bring on consumption and death. (Fischer.)

The *Chinche* inflicts great injury in Columbia. (Goudot.)

CHAPTER VI.
HARVEST BUG.

The *Harvest bug, Leptus autumnalis,* Latr., *Acarus autumnalis,* Shaw, is also a species of Acarus.

As the Arachnida are usually provided in the perfect state with eight feet, and only six in the larval stage, Siebold, suspected that the Harvest bug, which has only six feet, was an incompletely developed animal, and it has, in fact, proved to be the larva of one of the Trombidiidæ.

The Harvest bug is very common in France; it is found on the blades of grass and other plants of moderate height, under heaps of dried leaves, in the fields and the woods; it is also met with on small shrubs, such as gooseberry bushes and furzes. Defrance met with it in gardens, on clods of earth, on trellis-work, and in the orangeries, probably waiting for an opportunity to attach themselves to some mammalia or to man. He has seen them on the ears, eyelids, and on the under surface of the belly of the dog. This parasite also attacks cats, but it does not seem to cause them much inconvenience.

1. DESCRIPTION.—The *Harvest bug* is very minute, and requires a sharp eye to detect it, unless there are several of them together. The body is oval, soft, shining, and of a bright red colour. It has short four-jointed palpi; the thorax and abdomen are distinct. The feet are slender, of equal length, and terminated by rudimentary suckers.

2. MOUTH.—According to Shaw, the *Leptus* is provided with a sucker or protractile *rostrum.* This instrument is very small, stiff, and pointed; but M. Tandon has never had the opportunity of examining it.

3. ACTION ON MAN.—Those who live in the country, especially women and children, are perfectly familiar with the Har-

vest bug. It makes its appearance, or rather renders people conscious of its presence, about the middle of July, and disappears towards the middle of September. These animals are most plentiful in hot, dry seasons. (Defrance.)

The Harvest bugs attach themselves to man, and work their way beneath his skin, near the roots of the hairs. They especially attack persons with delicate skins, appearing to prefer the legs, the inner part of the thighs, and the lower part of the abdomen; but they are also found on the chest and arms. M. Dumeril once saw more than a dozen of these animals fixed together at the base of a single hair in a child.

These animals can move about with considerable rapidity, and will mount from the feet to the head in a very short space of time. They are often stopped by the garters and the bands of the dress, when they attach themselves to the part where their progress has been arrested.

M. Dumeril considers that the Harvest bugs fix themselves by their claws, and insinuate their sucker beneath the epidermis; and that it is principally the movements of the feet and claws, which give rise to the accompanying irritation and inflammation.

The analogy between these creatures and the other parasitic arachnida, induces M. Tandon to think that the injury must be produced by the beak; but that, possibly, the saliva of the animal has some specific action, since the pain which the animals give rise to is quite disproportioned to the microscopic appearance of the instrument which they plunge into the skin.

The wound of the *Harvest bug* occasions an acute burning and insupportable itching, which deprives the person of sleep. Latreille compares it to that of the itch insect. The skin becomes swollen and red, and sometimes even of a purple colour. It forms irregular spots of a very large size, compared to that of the parasite. The persons attacked scratch themselves until they bleed, and thus increase the violence and extent of the inflammation.

The vesicles produced by these insects soon heal if they are not touched, but if they are constantly irritated they will terminate in suppuration.

John has seen these animals produce an exanthematous eruption. Moses also mentions a case of papillar and vesicular inflammation, accompanied by an insupportable itching, in a whole family, from the same cause. The circumferences of the irritable spots were covered with red patches; when examined microscopically, they appeared to contain numbers of the *Harvest bug*.

The *Chigoe* and the *Harvest bug* form a kind of transition between the external cuticular parasites and the internal cuticular parasites; that is to say, between the *Epizoa* which live upon the surface of the skin, and the *Epizoa* which reside in the substance of its tissue.

SECTION II.

EPIZOA LIVING BENEATH THE SKIN.

THE *Epizoa* which live beneath the skin are—1. the *Sarcoptus*; 2. the *Acaropsis*; 3. the *Demodex*; and 4. some species of *Acaridæ* which are imperfectly known.

CHAPTER I.

THE SARCOPTUS.

THE *Sarcoptus*, or Itch insect, is an arachnidan belonging to the family of the Acaridæ.

HISTORY.—The history of this animal is exceedingly curious. Avenzoa, an Arabian physician of the twelfth century, appears to have been the first to notice the presence of a small animal in the itch, *so small that it is scarcely visible, and is hidden beneath the epidermis, but which escapes when an opening is made.* He gave it the name of *Soab*. Rabelais twice mentions the itch Insect. He relates that one of the ancestors of Pantagruel, Enay, *was very expert in removing mites from the hands.* In another place, Panurge is asked, *but where did I get this insect which is between my fingers?* Ambroise Paré is still more explicit; he says, "The *cirons* are small animals, always hidden beneath the skin, under which they creep and move about, gnawing it away bit by bit, and producing a most troublesome irritation and itching . . . ." Scaliger, Aldrovandus, Mouffet, and especially Cestoni and Wichmann, have spoken of the itch insect. In spite, however, of these authorities, and of the tolerably accurate figures published in the *Acta eruditorum* 1682, by M. A. C. D.[1] 1726, and by De Geer in 1778,

---

[1] The anonymous author of a pamphlet, entitled *System of an English physician on the causes of all kinds of diseases, with surprising figures of the*

many practitioners, not having succeeded in finding the animal, considered its existence as very doubtful.

In 1812, Galès, of Belbèze, the chief apothecary to the hospital of Saint Louis, published a treatise on the itch, in which he declared he had seen more than three hundred of the insects, all of them having the same form, but provided sometimes with eight feet, sometimes with six, a circumstance which he referred to the difference of the sexes. Galès does not describe the animal, but he gives a drawing of it. This treatise was favourably received, and the presence of an animal in the disease in question was again admitted without opposition. The drawing given by this writer continued to be copied into various works for the space of fifteen years as an exact representation of the Parasite of the itch. Unfortunately, this drawing differed materially from the animal described by those who had first written upon it. Doubts were again entertained, and the subject was investigated more closely. Galès declared he had found the animals in the pustules themselves, where it is quite certain he *never saw them*. Alibert and Biett made a great many searches for it, but they were always unsuccessful. It was suspected that the writer of the treatise had imposed upon the public. At length M. Raspail discovered that the animal figured was nothing more than *the cheese mite*.

Persons were again incredulous, and the existence of the itch insect was denied a second time. In 1821, Mouronval published a dissertation to prove the cause of the itch was neither a maggot nor a virus. The author had examined *more than eighteen hundred* persons attacked with itch. Lastly, Dr. Lugoe offered 300 francs as a premium to any one who would undertake to demonstrate the presence of an animal in the itch.

However, in 1834, a medical student, François Renucci, a native of Corsica, who was clinical assistant to Professor Alibert, offered to extract and demonstrate the presence of the creature which had given rise to so much controversy. The experiment was perfectly successful, and some of the students who were present succeeded themselves in insolating the insect. It was proved, therefore, that the older writers were correct, and that there really is a special parasite which gives rise to the itch, and the matter was thus finally set at rest.

different varieties of minute insects which can be seen by means of a good microscope in the blood and urine of sick people, and of those who are about to become so. Paris, in-8. See p. 291.

MM. Raspail, Leroy, and Vandenkeck have studied the structure and physiology of this curious animal. Several recent writers, amongst whom it is sufficient to mention the names of MM. Aubé, Biett, Cazenave, Gras, Hébra, Piogey, and Rayer have added several important points of detail to what was previously known; but most of these gentlemen have considered the matter rather from a pathological than from a natural history point of view. M. Bourguignon presented the French Institute *An Entomological and Pathological Treatise on the Itch insect of man*. This important work received the approval of the Institute, and was ordered to be printed. Lastly, M. Lanquetin, in a valuable thesis, has recently supplied several points which were incomplete in the remarkable monograph just mentioned, and M. Robin, at the request of M. Tandon, has made a careful examination of the various parts of the rostrum with the microscope.

2. CLASSIFICATION.—Linnæus at first regarded this parasite as a well-defined species, and placed it in the genus *Acarus*, naming it *Acarus scabei*. Afterwards he associated it with the Flour mite, under the name of *Acarus Siro*. He assigned as a reason for this, that nurses often communicated the itch to children who had any irritation on the skin by *powdering them with old flour which was infested by mites*. Pallas has clearly distinguished between the *Acarus of the itch* and that which is found in *flour*. Latreille admitted the distinction, and proposed a new genus, under the name of *Sarcoptus*,[1] for the reception of the first. From that time the creature has been known as the *Sarcoptus scabei*.

The *Sarcoptus* differs from the *Acarus* in not having the body divided into two portions, and in the cephalothorax not being distinct from the abdomen; by their feet being arranged in two groups, those of the first pair being large, those of the second very small, the first pair terminating in prolongations, which support carunculæ, having the form of suckers. In the *Acari* these carunculæ are rudimentary, and without any prolongation. The *Sarcopti* are further characterised by the absence of eyes, and by a rostrum in which may be noticed two mandibles, two maxillæ, two maxillary palpi, and a lower lip.

3. DESCRIPTION.—The Itch insect (fig. 97) is extremely minute, so that it is only just visible to the naked eye; it is ·012 of an inch in length, and ·009 of an inch in breadth. The body is nearly circular, flattened, and has been compared to that of a tortoise. (P. Borel.) It is soft, shining, slightly

[1] Ζάρξ flesh, and κόπτειν to cut.

transparent, of a white colour, a little opalescent, and has a pinkish tint. The dorsal surface is convex, and the ventral somewhat less so. The margin is slightly undulating, and the surface of the abdomen is marked by more or less parallel, irregular, but often curved, lines or ridges.

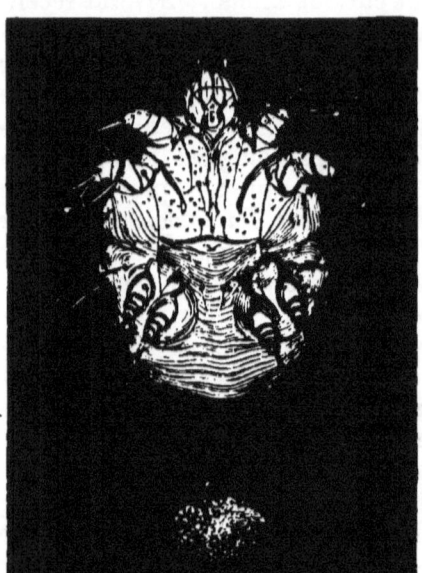

Fig. 97.—*Female Sarcoptus.*[1]

The rostrum is anterior, small, and straight; it is somewhat oval and obtuse; at its commencement there are observed two hairs.

The posterior part of the body is very obtuse, and often slightly indented towards the centre.

The limbs are eight in number, two pairs in front, and two pairs placed farther back, and at some distance from the others. The limbs are short, conical, distinctly jointed, and furnished with stiff hairs of various lengths. The two anterior pairs have the thighs divergent from each other; the feet terminate in a very slender, straight, rigid, tubular portion, provided at its extremity with a vesicular cushion or sucker. This slender portion, with its sucker, has been named the *ambulacrum* (*arolium*). The four posterior legs terminate in a long, curved, pointed thread, of a brown colour, without any sucker; these limbs are abdominal, and not thoracic, a very important and distinctive character. M. Bourguignon has ascertained that each limb consists of a hip, trochanter, small trochanter, thigh, leg, and tarsus.

The body of the insect has a few hairs scattered here and there, and on its dorsal surface are three kinds of horny appendages or spines; the first are arranged symmetrically on its central and posterior part; these are fourteen in number; they are of a conical form, are traversed by a canal, and furnished with a dilatation or basal follicle; the second are smaller, and placed near the first; the third are still more minute; they are arranged in concentric lines, have no canal, and resemble conical pointed tubercles.

[1] *a*, the egg.

The animal being soft, nature has furnished it with hard resisting parts, or *apodemata*, which perform the part of a skeleton. These apodemata have a horny appearance, are of a dull red colour, and form a solid frame work, to which the muscles are attached. On examining the *Sarcoptus* on its ventral surface, there are seen three of these apodemata, of which the central one, which is placed longitudinally, performs the office of a sternum. Anteriorly it is bifurcated, and each branch again divides into two, the innermost of which unite to form a complete ring, while the external pass to the base of the limb. The lateral apodemata are analogous to the scaly pieces named *epimera*, which in many insects give insertion to the limbs. They are composed of a long, curved portion, and of two branches, the internal passing to the anterior limb, the external to the second limb. There are also epimera having a similar arrangement at the base of the posterior limbs.

The digestive system of the *Sarcoptus* contains a mouth placed at the anterior part of the rostrum, and consisting of mandibles and maxillæ, which will be presently described. It is probably these mandibles and maxillæ that Leroy and Vandenkeck have spoken of as *teeth*.

The mouth communicates with a long and straight œsophagus. Arrived at the anterior third of the body, this canal terminates in an oblique reniform stomach, transparent, and very difficult to be seen. (Wieger.) The intestine is short and slightly undulating; it contains a number of brown granules, which occasionally accumulate towards the commencement of the rectum. The latter is nearly a straight canal. The anus may be observed on the dorsal surface in the middle of the indentation on its posterior margin.

Neither stigmata nor tracheæ are to be met with in the *Sarcoptus*. M. Bourguignon thinks that the animal respires by the mouth. It is more reasonable to suppose that in this kind of arachnida this function is fulfilled by means of the skin.

In the centre of the anterior fourth of the body, and placed against the œsophagus, may be noticed a small, oblong, transverse mass, from whence a number of extremely delicate filaments radiate. This is the nervous system.

In a state of repose the *Sarcopti* have their limbs retracted beneath their bodies, as under a carapace. When they walk they extend these organs, stretch out their ambulacra, and fasten their suckers. They can tunnel their way with considerable speed. M. Bourguignon considers that one of these insects could travel from the hand to the shoulder in less than ten minutes.

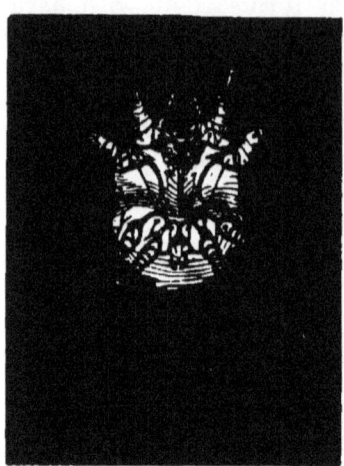

Fig. 98.—*Male.*

The *Sarcopti* are unisexual. The males (fig. 98) are scarcer than the females, the proportion being not more than one of the former to ten of the latter. We owe the discovery of the males to MM. Bourgogne and Lanquetin. The following are the characters in which they differ from the females; they are smaller (·008 inch), more oblong, flatter, of a darker colour, and more active; the rostrum is proportionally smaller and less triangular; they have not so many horny appendages on the dorsal surface; the anterior apodemata extend beyond the anterior third of the body, reaching nearly to its centre; the posterior limbs are not so wide apart, and the epimera on each side are united together; the third pair of feet are furnished with longer hairs; lastly, the fourth pair are much shorter, and have ambulacra terminated by a sucker.

The genital apparatus of the male is placed towards the middle of the body, near the third pair of limbs. It is supported anteriorly by a median apodemata, which is articulated with those of the last pair of limbs. The male organ consists of a deferent canal; of three bifurcated portions, which represent the testicles; of one or two median glandular bodies, which probably fulfil the part of prostate glands; and of a tolerably long penis, contained in a groove. The male orifice opens a little in front of the posterior margin of the body.

The vulva is placed on the ventral surface, at a short distance from the sternal apodemeta: it is a slightly sinuous opening about ·003 of an inch (Ch. Robin) in length. It communicates with a granular body, which is hardly discernible except at the period of reproduction.

At the time of heat, the males quit their dwelling-places during the night to go in search of the females. They are much more active than the latter, running about from right to left, and occasionally fighting with each other. M. Bourguignon once found two males and a single female in the same spot. The latter immediately began to fight, but as soon as they were aware they were discovered, they speedily took to flight.

These acari copulate belly to belly. (Worms.) A single union suffices for impregnation. When the eggs enlarge they are scattered through all parts of the body. The eggs (fig. 97, *a*) are quite enormous when compared with the size of the mother; when laid, they are at least one-third the length of the animal. The female usually lays one egg daily, and has several layings in succession; she can produce as many as twenty in the course of a month. The eggs are rarely placed in groups of three or four. When laid they are elipsoid or oval, slightly depressed, semitransparent, and have a whitish pearly look. They resemble the pearls of the *Unio margaritifer*. They measure ·007 of an inch in the long diameter, and ·003 of an inch in the short. It has been noticed that they are partly developed within the body. It is not until they have been laid ten or twelve days that they are hatched.

At birth the *Sarcopti* are not more than ·006 of an inch in length. They have six feet instead of eight, one of the posterior pairs being wanting. These larvæ are very active, they shelter themselves beneath the loose particles of the epidermis, and seem incapable of boring a channel for themselves. At the end of some days they are somewhat swollen, the skin becomes first wrinkled, then torn, and afterwards falls off. An additional pair of feet are developed, and the animal arrives at its perfect state.

4. THE MOUTH (fig. 99).—M. Ch. Robin has carefully examined the *rostrum* of the *Sarcoptus* (*head* of Bourguignon). There is seen, first, a pair of strong oblong mandibles, carrying towards their extremity and on their upper side a small moveable hook; this is pointed, somewhat curved, and when not in use it is received into an oblique groove, with irregular dentated margins situated on the opposite side of the prolonged portion of the organ. This prolonged portion, together with the hook just mentioned, acts like a pair of pinchers. Next are the maxillæ; these are small, narrow, and curved from without inwards. Their base is articulated to a small square piece,

Fig. 99.—*Rostrum.*[1]

[1] *A*, the rostrum, from which the two mandibles have been removed; *a a*, maxillæ; *b*, chin; *c c*, the large maxillary palpi, with three joints, and bear-

the *mentum* or chin. Their free extremity is directed abruptly from within outwards. The palpi are large pieces, supported by the maxillæ, curved, pointed, and composed of three unequal joints. The terminal joint, which is the smallest, presents externally a single long hair, while the middle joint has two. The lower lip is nearly triangular, and somewhat pointed. Towards its base and on both sides there is a very long hair; above and near to its middle portion it is provided with a lancet-shaped tongue. The whole of the *rostrum* is surrounded at its commencement by a thin sinuous margin (*camerostoma*). This margin advances on to the sides of the palpi in the form of transparent membranous plates, which are as long as the organs themselves. It is these processes which have been mistaken sometimes for *false palpi*, and sometimes for *lips*.

5. ACTION ON MAN.—The *Sarcopti* are found more especially upon the hands, in the intervals of the fingers, on the anterior surface of the wrist, on the penis, in the bend of the arm, on the breasts and on the abdomen in women, on the ankle, and, last, more rarely on other parts of the body, the face forming nearly always an exception. (Lanquetin.)

Their presence is recognised by that of the grooves. The latter will be noticed presently; their importance has been strongly insisted upon as a means of diagnosis by MM. Biett, Cazenave, and Piogey.

The *Sarcopti* give rise to an intolerable itching, causing the patients to scratch themselves violently, and thereby increase the disorder of the skin. The disease produced by the *Sarcopti* has received the name of the itch.[1]

The *Sarcoptus of the itch* is a nocturnal burrowing animal, and is admirably adapted for eating its way through our tissues, and living in them. Its great object, when it finds itself on the skin, is to discover a fitting locality for its habitation. It carefully explores the cracks and folds of the epidermis; it taps the base of the hairs where the follicle has raised the cuticular covering (Bourguignon), and if the spot seems suitable it immediately sets to work.

In the hollowing out of its gallery, the *Sarcoptus* is found to exhibit distinct preferences. It prefers the hands; it is found in this part of the body seventy times out of a hundred; it has been noticed eight times out of ten on the penis. (Piogey.)

ing three hairs; *d*, lower lip, with its small lancet-shaped tongue in the middle, and supporting two small hairs; *B*, a mandible separated; *a*, its hook.

[1] *Psora*, Linn., *scabies*, Sauvages, *zoopsordermie*, Piorry.

M. Bourguignon states that on the 4th of February, 1846, he placed a female on his left fore arm. The animal, having found a small portion of the epidermis detached between two hairs, immediately fixed itself, and in less than ten minutes had disappeared beneath the epidermis. But as the fore-arm was not to its taste, the mischievous *Sarcoptus*, availing itself of the sleep of the experimenter, during the night emerged from its retreat to seek its fortune in some other part of the body.

When a *Sarcoptus*, after several attempts, has selected a locality which suits him, he elevates himself by the long hairs attached to the posterior feet, so as to place himself at a considerable angle with the skin, and with the rostrum placed below. This position facilitates the first incision of the cuticle,[1] and the rostrum is soon buried beneath the epidermis. The little miner continues working for about a quarter of an hour. At the end of that time, he withdraws himself: it might be supposed that he was about to select some other spot, but that is not the case; it is a necessary and intentional proceeding. The animal next cuts the skin to the right and to the left of the part where he first commenced. (Bourguignon.) The object of this operation is easily understood as the original aperture would not allow its body to enter, which is so much larger than the rostrum. The *Sarcoptus*, therefore, enlarges the passage so as to allow of his passing in. From this time he is entirely buried in the skin, and does not again come out. He continues to excavate to the right and to the left of him, and in this way forms a curved passage. In this work the jaws and the palpi move horizontally, and the maxillæ nearly vertically. M. Tandon does not consider that the hook belonging to the latter can be used in the work of excavation, on account of its minute size (the supposed functions of this organ are spoken of subsequently); the lower branch, however, of the pincers may act as a kind of scoop.

The first difficulties having been overcome the parasite now rapidly advances.[2] The horny appendage and the stiff hairs support him, and furnish him with points of resistance in his diminutive gallery. They are straightened out when the animal is at work, but are laid smooth when he advances.

It is usually during the night that the animals are engaged in excavating their galleries.

[1] " *Arant enim semper inter cuticulum et cutem.*" (Casal.)
[2] " *Progrediuntur quasi Cuniculi.*" (Casal.)

The galleries (*cuniculi*, Mouffet) (fig. 100), have the appearance of white marks from one to two and a half lines in length,[1] and about two-thirds of a line in diameter. They resemble the kind of mark which is formed by a pin being drawn lightly over the skin. (Cazenave, Lanquetin.) It is not correct to compare them to a scratch.[2] These galleries are curved, undulating, or even angular; when following a natural fold of the skin they are straight. They never open into each other.

Fig. 100.—*Groove.*[3]

The colour varies with the state of the patient. In young children and in persons with a delicate skin, the galleries appear of a greyish white; in those who are dirty, and whose skin is hard and coarse, they become of a dark blackish colour. They also become of a particular colour in persons who are engaged in certain occupations. (Lanquetin.) At certain intervals, and generally where the furrows of the epidermis cross each other, the galleries are pierced by small openings, which allow the access of the external air, and mark the spot where the little miner has rested himself. These openings sometimes look like very small black dots; it is through these that the young escape.

Along the track of the galleries, or in its immediate vicinity, is a vesicle about the size of a grain of millet seed, rounded, pointed, and transparent at the summit, of a rose tint in the child, and of a dark red or brownish colour in the adult. Its base is sometimes surrounded by an inflamed areola, while at other times the part of the skin upon which it is placed is pale. These vesicles are sometimes apart, sometimes close together, and

---

[1] It is said that at the period of laying the animal excavates with great activity, and that at that time the groove may attain the length of from four to five lines.

[2] "*Canaliculum longum instar sulculi relinquunt.*" (Casal.)

[3] *a*, Sarcoptus at the end of its gallery; *b*, the dead skin of the last moult; *c c*, eggs, the first about to be hatched; *d d*, excrements; *e*, young or larva; *f*, entrance to the gallery; *g g*, small openings, through which the air gains access to the interior of the gallery.

at the end of a certain time are often confluent. In their interior is a serous or viscous fluid, transparent, and of a yellow or rose colour; sometimes there is also a small portion of blood; it is then that the vesicle has a brownish tint. Occasionally the gallery passes over the vesicle and rests upon it, an arrangement which is easily understood, from the circumstance that the gallery is beneath the *epidermis*, while the vesicle is beneath the *derm* or *cutis*. (Piogey, Lanquetin.)

The vesicle is not always present, owing to its passing through its existence in four or five days, while the gallery lasts for several months.

One end of the galleries terminates in a projection, which requires to be carefully studied. This projection[1] looks like a very small but well-defined white spot; where this communicates with the gallery, the latter appears as if it were interrupted; this arises from its being deeper at its termination. It is in this depression that the *Sarcoptus* is lodged, for it is never met with in the vesicle. (Renucci.) When the skin is carefully raised it points to the posterior part of the animal. It was in consequence of persons seeking for the *Sarcoptus* in the vesicle itself that they were unable to find it, and were therefore led to deny its existence.[2]

The males do not form a gallery; they are satisfied with excavating a space sufficient to conceal themselves in; they hide themselves beneath a raised portion of the epidermis, so small that it is scarcely visible to the naked eye. Their hiding-place is always near that of the female. (Lanquetin.)

In order to obtain a *Sarcoptus* the epidermis must be torn away with a pin or a needle at about $\frac{1}{500}$ of an inch from the white spot; the part must be dissected very gently towards the centre of the prominence already mentioned, the instrument must then be passed beneath the animalcule, and the creature carefully removed. (Renucci.) The only difficulty in the operation is to avoid killing the *Sarcoptus*. When exposed, the little parasite looks like a grain of starch; he conceals his rostrum and his limbs beneath the carapace, and pretends to be dead; if he is placed on the finger he remains for some time motionless, but he soon regains his liveliness and moves quickly away. (Renucci.)

Is the *Sarcoptus of the itch* a venomous animal? M. Tandon

[1] Acarian eminence. (Bazin.)
[2] " Hoc obiter observandum Syrones, non in ipsis pustulis, sed prope habitant." (Mouffet, 1634.) " Acarus sub ipsa pustula minime quærendus est, sed longius recessit, sequendo rugam cuticulæ observatur." (Linn.)

has no hesitation in believing that it is; his jaws are miniature representations of the antennal pincers of the spiders; they are provided with a moveable and pointed hook, which is received into a groove with dentated margins, and can be opened in accordance with the wants of the animal. In the spiders the two hooks which are external move almost horizontally from without to within, so as to antagonise each other, and so as to seize and pierce their prey. In the *Sarcoptus* these organs are placed superiorly, and act from above downwards, but without antagonising, so as to bury themselves in the tissue and inoculate it with the poison. It has not, indeed, been proved that the hook of the parasite is perforated at its extremity,[1] but it is reasonable to suppose that it is so; since that of certain acari, animals which are closely allied to it, and whose mouth differs essentially from that of the Spiders, does present a small but distinct opening. (Raspail.)

When the *Sarcoptus* is working at its gallery it does not make use of its poison; but when the animal stops in any part to eat, or for the purpose of depositing its eggs, it pierces the tissue with its jaws, and discharges some drops of liquid. This fluid acts like the poison of the Cynips, and produces a swelling or vesicle, which may be regarded as an *animal gall*:[2] this explains why the vesicles are situated deeper than the galleries. With regard to those which are not placed in the tracks of the latter, they probably arise from the absorption of the venomous fluid by the lymphatics.

6. OTHER SPECIES.—It has been supposed that in Norway there is another species of *Sarcoptus* peculiar to man, forming a different kind of gall, the animal producing thick scabs, which spread over nearly the whole of the body. Professor Boeck of Christiana observed three cases of this disease in 1852. The scabs presented masses of the *Sarcopti*, and of their excrements and eggs. M. Boeck found that these *Sarsopti* did not differ from the species which has just been described. This view has been confirmed by the observations of MM. Cazenave, Chauzit, Lanquetin, Bourguignon, and Hebra.

The *Sarcopti* of the mammalia differ from that of man; thus the species belonging to the horse, of which a good representation has been given by M. Gohier and M. Raspail, has a very straight rostrum; all the feet have carunculæ, and at the same time two rigid hairs longer than the ambulacra.

---

[1] I believe I once detected a small opening. (Moq. Tandon.)
[2] "*In ipsa pustula progeniem deposuit.*" (Linn.)

Can the itch of animals communicate itself to man?

M. Dumeril believes he has proved that a Phascolome from New Holland transmitted its itch to several persons who were employed in the Museum of Natural History.

Other examples appear to show that the *Sarcopti* of the horse, the camel, the ox, the lion, the dog, and the cat, may be developed on man, and produce a cutaneous disease similar to that which occurs on the animal from which it had been taken.

It has moreover been recently shown that the species of *Sarcoptus* which has hitherto been supposed to be peculiar to man is met with on the hog and the llama. (Lanquetin, Robin.)

CHAPTER II.

THE ACAROPSE.

ALLIED to the *Sarcoptus* is an animal discovered by Dr. Leroy de Méricourt in Newfoundland upon the person of an officer who had come from the Havannah, and of which he has published a description and drawing. M. Alexandre Laboulbène has provisionally arranged this acarus in the group *Tyroglyphus*, although he considers it must constitute a distinct genus.

Before he was acquainted with M. Laboulbène's memoir, M. Tandon had named this animal in his lectures the *Acaropse;* he therefore continues to speak of it under this title.

DESCRIPTION.—The *Acaropse of Mericourt, Acaropsis Mericourti, Tyroglyphus Mericourti,* Laboulb., *Acaropsis pectinata,* Moq. (fig. 101), is a small acarus, ·027 of an inch in length, oval, covered with long flexible hairs, and of a pale colour ; the rostrum (head, Laboulb.) is projecting, conical, and with a pointed prolongation ; the palpi are enormous,

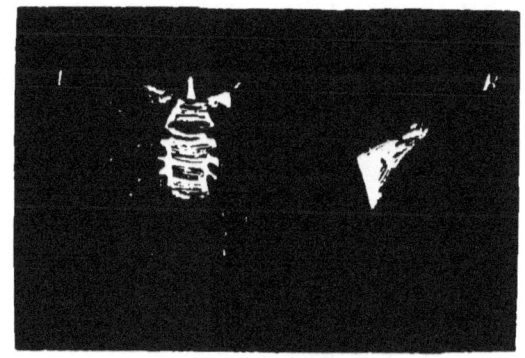

Fig. 101.—*Acaropsis.*[1]

---

[1] *A,* animal seen from its back ; *B,* right palpus.

and greatly dilated at their base; they form two oblong conical bodies, attenuated at their extremities, slightly curved, and their size is out of all proportion to that of the animal. These two palpi are extremely divergent; at the extremity is seen—1, a kind of slender hook, slightly curved from without inwards, not very pointed, and possibly articulated and moveable; 2, another hook placed internally, smaller and more slender, curved in the same direction, of an oval shape, very pointed, beautifully pectinated on its inner margin, and supporting at its base a slender curved hair, which surpasses it in length, and appears to be inserted on a small projection. The animal has no eyes; the thorax is confounded with the abdomen; the feet are eight in number, long, strong, and covered with hairs, but not having one third the thickness of the palpi. They seem to terminate in a rudimentary caruncule.

The animal is undoubtedly an Acarus, but it is distinguished from all the known genera by the enormous development and size of its palpi, and by the singular pectinated organ by which they are terminated. The pointed rostrum appears to be composed of modified jaws, which are straight, pointed, and form a beak.

Ought not the enormous didactile arms, described as palpi, to be considered as antennæ converted into pincers?

2. ACTION ON MAN.—The *Acaropsis Mericourti* was noticed in a patient with an exanthematous eruption. Three individuals were procured from pus which was discharged from the ear after inflammation of the auditory canal. They seemed to have lived in the pimples on the skin surrounded by a serous liquid.

Was the animal really developed in the pimple, or did it come from without? It is extremely probable that it is a species of Acarus peculiar to this exanthema.

CHAPTER III.

THE DEMODEX.

THE *Demodex folliculorum*, Owen, *Acarus folliculorum*, Simon (fig. 102), was discovered almost simultaneously by M. Gustave, Simon, and M. Henle, in 1842. M. Dujardin has studied it upon his own person, and M. Gruby carefully examined it in 1846.

1. DESCRIPTION.—The *Demodex folliculorum* is one of the lowest organised of the Arachnida, and has a worm-like form. It measures from $\frac{1}{100}$ to $\frac{2}{100}$ of an inch in length, and from $\frac{1}{100}$ to $\frac{7}{100}$ of an inch in breadth. The body is somewhat flattened, of a greyish white and semi-transparent; the head is confounded with the thorax, and forms an oblong cephalothorax; the rostrum is small, and is composed of two lateral palpi with a sucker placed between them.

Fig. 102.—*Demodex*.[1]

The last or terminal joint of the palpi appears to be notched; above the sucker is a triangular lip formed by two slender pieces placed close together; the abdomen, which is small in the young animal, is elongated in the adult, and gradually narrows and terminates in a point; it might be compared to a long tail, and gives the animal a vermiform appearance. When the *Demodex* is in motion, its diminutive feet are moved alternately and with great quickness; they are aided by the palpi and the rostrum, as well as by the vermicular contractions of the abdomen. The feet are eight in number, and are placed at equal intervals; they are short, conical, and composed of three joints, of which the last is provided with three hooks, one long and two short. The young animal has only six feet; these organs are remarkable for their shortness, scarcely reaching to the margin of the cephalothorax; they appear to be quite rudimentary, especially when they are compared with those of the Sarcopti.

When examined under a microscope with a high power, the body of the *Demodex* presents a number of minute granules, and some roundish uneven transparent corpuscles, which are possibly the eggs or the extremely young animals.

The *Demodex* is oviparous. The eggs are very large in proportion to the size of the animal; they are elongated and somewhat pointed at the ends. (Lanquetin.) M. Tandon examined one, shortly before it was hatched, when the feet and rostrum of the young animal could be seen within it.

[1] *A*, animal seen from the abdomen; *B*, rostrum; *C*, egg.

Three principal forms of this Acarus have been observed:—1, the cephalothorax, equalling one-third of the length of the abdomen, which is soft, terminated by a rounded extremity, and marked by fine transverse lines—this is probably the typical form; 2, the cephalothorax, as long as the abdomen or nearly so; 3, the cephalothorax longer than the abdomen, and the latter terminating in a point.

2. ACTION ON MAN.—The *Demodex* occurs in both sexes and at every age, excepting that of the young infant. M. Simon found them in the nose, and M. Henle in the external auditory canal. They appear to be very common, since out of every ten individuals they will be found in at least one or two. M. Gruby states that he met with them in forty persons out of sixty.

The *Demodex* is found in the normal or dilated ducts of the sebaceous glands, particularly in those of the alæ of the nose; they also live in the follicles of the hairs of the nose, especially those which are distended by epithelial cells, or by the accumulation of fatty globules; lastly, they are found in the follicles of the hairs of the face, lips, forehead, and cheeks.

The animals are placed parallel to the axis of the follicle with their heads directed towards the base of the sac. Persons whose skins are greasy and those who have freckles seem to be most liable to them.

These Arachnida generally live in small communities; as many as from fifteen to eighteen may be found in a single follicle.

The *Demodex* is entangled in the midst of the fatty and sebaceous matter.

These animals do not cause any diseased action. When they are numerous the skin swells and becomes red and wrinkled; the mouths of the follicles are much dilated, and there is a considerable amount of itching.

In order to procure these animals it is sufficient to squeeze the parts which are affected by them between the fingers, and then to examine the expressed matter beneath the microscope. [The addition of a drop of sweet oil to the small particle of sebaceous or fatty matter in which the Demodex is enclosed facilitates the finding of the animal, and serves to free it from the extraneous matter.] In the dead body, sections of the skin may be made in the direction of the length of the follicles.

CHAPTER IV.

SOME OTHER SPECIES OF ACARI.

The *Dermanysus of Bory*, *Dermanyssus Boryi*, Gerv. This species of Arachnida was observed on a lady forty years of age, and has been described and figured by Bory de Saint-Vincent.

The lady was troubled with a slight itching on every part her of body; this gradually increased, and at length became unbearable; whenever she rubbed or scratched the parts which were most irritable, a number of little acari, hardly visible to the naked eye, came forth; the largest was not half the size of a tobacco seed; they were of a brownish colour, and ran about by thousands in every direction. Several of them, when placed in a box on a piece of muslin, lived from forty-eight to fifty hours.

Did these animals really come from the body of the person? Was it not the same in this case as in a similar one related by M. Simon of a woman at Berlin, whose skin appeared to produce a number of small acari? It was found that they were the common *Dermanyssus, Avium*, which the woman got every day in passing through a hen-house.[1]

2. The *Dermanyssus of Busk*.—Is the acarus described by M. Busk to be considered as another species of *Dermanyssus* which is peculiar to man? This creature was found in some large sores on the soles of the feet of a black sailor.

The patient appeared to have contracted the disease by wearing a pair of shoes which he had lent to another negro, whose feet were ulcerated in a similar manner. The latter was an inhabitant of Sierra Leone, a circumstance which is remarkable in conjunction with the fact that in some water which was brought from the river Sirrae, on the coast of Africa, one very nearly perfect specimen, and fragments of others very similar to, if not identical with, the one noticed in the negro's foot, were found.[2]

3. Eutarsus cancriformis.—This arachnida was noticed by Dr. Hessling in 1852, in a case of plica polonica. The animal has a rounded cordiform shaped body, very obtuse, and, as it were, hollowed out in front. The feet are close together, and somewhat curved.

[1] See page 296.
[2] Küchenmeister, opus cit, vol. ii. p. 242.

4. CŒLOGNATHUS MORSITANS.—This species was also found by Dr. Hessling under the same circumstances as the preceding. The body is rigid, and somewhat pointed anteriorly and posteriorly. The feet are arranged in two groups, like those of the Sarcoptus, and armed with small hairs.

M. Hessling does not consider that either of these insects is peculiar to the disease, but that it merely afforded a favourable locality for their development.

We find, therefore, that it is especially amongst the Acari that we meet with the cuticular parasites. Messrs. Kirby and Spence have proposed to designate the diseases which these animals give rise to by the general name of *Acariasis*.

BOOK VII.

INTERNAL PARASITES OR ENTOZOA.

THE study of the *External Parasites* naturally leads to that of the *Internal Parasites*. The number of the latter animals is very considerable, if we associate with the true Parasites the animals which accidentally suck our blood or devour our organs, creatures which are sometimes[1] even more formidable than those that we are about to describe. The *Internal Parasites*, that is to say, the animals which live constantly at the expense of man, either when he is in health or in a state of disease, are not numerous, nor need they alarm us, for the disorders which they give rise to are not in general very severe. Thus, as it has been mentioned elsewhere,[2] it is one of the conditions of parasitism that the animal upon which the parasite lives must not be destroyed by it. We have seen that children sometimes support thousands of worms, and yet they do not appear to be ill. It is true that in many cases the parasite does not so much attack the organism in which it is placed as its superabundant products. (Beneden.)

In medical Natural History the term *Entozoa* is given to those parasites which live in the cavities or tissues of the body. Some writers have proposed to call them *Entoparasites*.

Most of the *Entozoa* are born externally, and are only introduced in man's body at some determinate period of their existence.

These animals may be divided into four series—1. INSECT ENTOZOA; 2. CRUSTACEOUS ENTOZOA; 3. ENTOZOIC WORMS; 4. INFUSORIAL ENTOZOA.

[1] See p. 239.
[2] See p. 242.

SECTION L.

INSECT ENTOZOA.

Œstridea.

VETERINARY surgeons and entomologists have long known that the ox, sheep, horse, dog, &c., are tormented by the larvæ of certain flies which live in their bodies as true parasites. These larvæ belong to the family *Œstridea*.

It was thought at first that these Insects were only met with in the mammalia. Condamine and Barrère state that they have found them under the skin and in the nostrils of man; but their accounts are very indefinite. Rudolphi admits the fact. Latreille relates that larvæ similar to those of the *Œstridea* had been extracted several times from the maxillary and frontal sinuses of man; these cases are, however, by no means well authenticated.

The majority of these instances, and many others which it would be easy to accumulate, are wanting in accuracy, and would equally apply to the larvæ of the Muscida as of the *Œstridea*.

Facts which unfortunately cannot be doubted, prove that the larvæ of some of the latter family, which are parasitic upon the mammalia, may occasionally be developed in man; and that it is even possible that one or two species exist which are peculiar to him.

1. CUTEREBRA NOXIALIS, Goud.—M. Justin Goudot has mentioned that a species of *Œstrus*, which he names *Cuterebra noxalis*, commits serious ravages in certain parts of America, more particularly in New Grenada.

The genus *Cuterebra* was proposed by Bracy Clark, and adopted by Latreille. Its characters are—cavity of the mouth straight and triangular, forming a small retractile proboscis; no palpi; and the antennæ with a plumose style.

The *Cuterebra noxialis* has been found in the ox, the dog, and the jaguar. Its presence in man is more rare.

Description.—The insect is eight lines in length. It has the forehead projecting, obtuse, brown, and covered with blackish hair; the antennæ are yellow, with the first joint furnished at its extremity with a small tuft of short hairs; the eyes are brown, with a blackish band in the middle; the thorax, of a blueish tinge, marked with grey and black longitudinal bands, is covered with very short black hairs; the abdomen, spotted with a beautiful blue colour, has a dirty white tinge on the first segment, and on the anterior margin of the second; the wings are brown; and the feet yellow, with hairs of the same colour (male).

The larva is known in Cayenne as the *Macaque*, and in New Grenada as the *Gusano*. It attains a length of nearly thirteen lines. Its body is smooth, and of a whitish colour. The first three segments are covered with irregularities, in the form of very small black spines; the three following have two circular rows of hooks of the same colour, more robust, and directed backwards. The mouth is armed with two hooks.

2. OTHER SPECIES.—Linnæus, in a letter to Pallas, mentions another larva of a diptera which lives in the human body. Gmelin speaks of this insect under the name of *Œstrus hominis*. This is also found in America.

The knowledge which we have of this animal is confined to its size, which is that of the common fly; and to its colour, which is a uniform brown (*totus fuscus*).

Its larva lives six months under the skin of the abdomen.

This is very probably another species of the *Cuterebra*. But is it really confined to man, or does it, like the preceding species, belong to the mammalia as well as to man? M. Justin Guidot regards it as altogether an imaginary species.[1]

The larva of an *Œstrus* was found on the head of a man in Trinity Island. It is deposited in the College of Surgeons in London. Mr. Hope has named it *Œstrus Guildingii*. Is this a distinct species from that of M. Goudot?

Lastly, several cases have been observed in Europe of *Œstridea* being found in the human body; such as the *Taon*, or *Œstrus of the ox*, and the *Œstrus of the sheep*. The one belongs to the genus *Hypoderma*,[2] the other to the genus *Cephalemyia*;[3] the first is characterised by the opening of the mouth being Y-shaped, and by the absence of palpi and antennæ; the second by the mouth being round, by tuberculiform palpi, and by antennæ consisting of a simple style.

3. ACTION ON MAN.—The *Cuterebra* are found on various parts of the body, but more especially on those which are accidentally uncovered.

Fray Pedro Simon, in his *History of the Conquest of New*

---

[1] And that it is the same with regard to the *Œstrus humanus* of Rudolphi and M. Guerin Meneville.

[2] *Hypoderma bovis*, Latr.; *Œstrus bovis*, Linn.; called by Reaumur *Wasp fly*.

[3] *Cephalemyia ovis*, Latr.; *Æstrus ovis*, Linn.; called by Reaumur *Fly of the nose-worm*.

Grenada, mentions certain larvæ which torment the human species. He says that they settle principally between the collar of the cuirass and the skin.

Arture, physician to the King of Cayenne, says, that worms, which cause considerable tumours, are sometimes found in America, on the bodies of persons who are of unclean habits.

Alexander Humboldt states, that in South America he saw Indians whose abdomens were covered with small tumours, which he presumed were caused by the larvæ of certain *Œstridea*.

Dr. Roulin has reported an interesting case which occurred at Mariquita, in Columbia. A man had on his scrotum a tumour of a conical form, measuring something more than two inches in diameter at its base, and about five or six lines in height. The apex, which was very red, presented a small opening, about a line across. Dr. Roulin having enlarged the opening with a lancet, a whitish pyriform larva issued forth, measuring as much as ten lines in length and five or six in breadth. On the thickest part of its body it had several rows of blackish spines. The larva resembles one which in those districts is met with in the skin of the cattle, chiefly on the sides of the neck and on the shoulders. Dr. Roulin saw a second larva of the same kind in another man, in the skin near the nape of the neck.

The observations published by Dr. Guyon are perfectly in accordance with the details which have just been recorded. He found parasitic larvæ in a negro on the twelfth day of a variolous eruption. In the pustules on his legs there were whitish worms, which the patient expelled by gently tapping his limbs.

M. Justin Goudot and Weddell have noticed similar instances, the first in New Grenada, and the second in Brazil. These facts have been confirmed by other cases collected by Mr. Say at Philadelphia, by Mr. Howship at Surinam, and by M. Percheron in Peru.

All these diptera appear to belong to the *Cuterebra*, but it is not ascertained that all belong to one and the same species.

When a larva begins to develop itself in any part of the skin, a slight pain is felt, and a swelling, with a minute opening, from which a small quantity of a serous fluid issues, is perceived in the neighbourhood. At this period it is easy to get rid of the parasite; a mercurial friction and a small quantity of ammonia are sufficient to kill it.

If curative means are neglected, the animal grows rapidly, buries itself deeper in the tissues, and produces a tumour, which becomes gradually larger and more painful. It is then necessary to extract the larva.

It is more particularly at five or six o'clock in the morning, and at night, that the larvæ begin to suck. M. Goudot compares the sensation which they produce to that of a number of needles being driven into the skin, only the punctures occur in jerks.

The *Œstrii* of Europe introduce themselves far more rarely into the body of man than the *Cuterebra* of America.

Wohlfart has published a remarkable case of an old man who had been troubled for several days with an intense headache, and who afterwards discharged from his nose eighteen worms; these were placed in a glass, with a small quantity of earth, and were metamorphosed at the end of a month. Wohlfart has given drawings of the larvæ, and the flies which come from them, but, unfortunately, they are very badly executed.

Latham, in England, states that he procured the larvæ of *Œstri*, similar to those of the ox, from the frontal sinus of a woman.

Bracy Clark reports that a larva of the same species had been extracted from the jaw of another woman.

In the *Journal de Vandermonde* is the case of a countrywoman, who, being exceedingly thirsty, drank some water out of a muddy pond, where a shepherd was in the habit of watering his flock. The water got into her nostrils as well as her mouth; some days subsequently, after being very ill, and when she had taken an emetic, she discharged about seventy-two small white worms, precisely similar to those which are found in the nasal fossæ of the sheep.

Robineau-Desvoidy communicated to the Entomological Society of France the case of a woman who, after suffering from violent pains and symptoms of inflammation of the neck of the bladder, expelled with the urine the larva of an *Œstrus*. This learned entomologist gives no intimation as to the genus to which the larva belonged.

Bateman speaks of three larvæ of the *Œstri* being taken from the throat of a man, and Mr. Hope of another larva found in the stomach of a dead body. Rudolphi, in Prussia, Eschricht, in Denmark, and Metaxa, in Italy, have mentioned the presence of other larvæ in the ear, beneath the skin of the forehead, and elsewhere . . . . Unfortunately, in all these cases the species of *Œstri* cannot be determined.

SECTION II.

CRUSTACEOUS ENTOZOA.

The Linguatula.

The *Linguatulæ* (*Linguatula*, Frolich) were at first considered as intestinal worms, having the general appearance, hooks, and habits of these animals. Some naturalists have classed them with the Arachnida. M. Van Beneden[1] has shown good reasons for associating them with the Crustacea. These extraordinary animals may, in fact, be regarded as Crustacea which have been degraded to the form of a helmintha.

The *Linguatulæ* are characterised by a flat, elongated, sub-articulated body, which is dilated in front, and attenuated posteriorly; an antero-inferior mouth, having two pairs of retractile hooks; an anal orifice at the opposite extremity; and no limbs.

These animals possess a complete intestinal canal, a kind of dorsal vessel, a nervous system, consisting of a rudimentary ring without cerebral ganglia, but with a moderately developed subsosophageal ganglion, from whence two principal filaments proceed in the length of the body. The sexes are separate; the male orifice is placed anteriorly, and the female posteriorly.

The *Linguatulæ* are oviparous. The young animals resemble certain crustacea which are parasitic upon fishes. (Van Beneden, Harley.)

The *Linguatulæ* are at first asexual, and live encysted in the body of different herbivorous mammalia. They pass from thence into the bodies of the carnivora which feed upon these animals, where they complete their development, and become sexual. (Leuckart.)[2]

1. LINGUATULA DENTICULATA.—This animal has been seen in the lungs, the trachea, the larynx, the nasal sinuses, and the liver of several of the mammalia; it has been found in the hare, rabbit, guinea pig, goat, and more rarely in the wolf, dog, and horse. It has received different names, derived from the animals in which it has been found.

Description (fig. 103).—The animal is from two to three lines in length, and about one line in width, oblong, tongue-

---

[1] [Van Beneden, *Recherches sur l'organization et le developpement des Linguatules—Memoires de l'Acad. Roy. de Bruxelles*, 1849.]

[2] *Linguatula serrata*, Fröl., *Tænia caprina*, Albig., *Tetragula caviæ*, Bosc., *Pentastoma serratum* et *denticulatum*, Rudol., *Pentastomum constrictum*, Siebold, *Linguatula constricta* et *ferox*, Gunth.

shaped, obtuse anteriorly, somewhat narrowed posteriorly, flat, transversely striated, and notched at its margins. Beneath the obtuse extremity is an elliptical mouth, supporting on each side a pair of hooks, differing somewhat in size, the exterior being the smallest; they are directed from before backwards.

Fig. 103.—*Linguatula*.[2]

2. ACTION ON MAN.—Siebold, in 1853, published the first account of the occurrence of this crustacea in man.

Siebold has associated with the *Linguatula* a parasite discovered in Egypt by Dr. Pruner in the small intestines of negroes, and in the body of a Giraffe,[1] and of which Dr. Bilharz has recently recorded some other instances.

Somewhat later, M. Zenker, prosector at the civil hospital at Dresden, met with cysts filled with *Linguatulæ* in eight bodies (5 males, 2 females).

Dr. Heschl, of Vienna, has confirmed the presence of this curious crustacea in our bodies.

SECTION III.

ENTOZOIC WORMS, OR HELMINTHA.

GENERAL CONSIDERATIONS.—The parasitic worms which are developed in the bodies of men and animals are termed *Helmintha*. They have also received the names of *Intestinal worms* and *Entozoa proper*. The division of Zoology which treats of these parasites is called *Helminthology*.

If the other divisions of natural history delight us by the varieties of colouring, the beauty of form, the complexity of structure, and the marvellous instincts of the creatures they include, the study of the *Helmintha* is equally interesting, especially to the medical man, when it is carefully pursued.

For a long time little was known of any of the intestinal worms excepting those which reside in the body of man, or in those of the domesticated animals; even of these only such as

---

[1] *Nematoide*, Pruner, *Nematoideum hominis viscerum*, Dies.
[2] *A*, animal seen from the ventral surface; *B*, one of the hooks.

live in the intestinal canal had been noticed, and the facts relating to their natural history were exceedingly vague. It was towards the close of the last century that men began seriously to inquire into their structure and modes of life.

In the present work only those species of *Helmintha* will be treated of which reside in and derive their nourishment from the human body. I shall therefore pass over those species which are found in the bodies of our domestic animals, as well the *Accessory worm*,[1] that is to say, those of the *Helmintha* which are peculiar to the mammalia, the fishes, or to other animals, and only become introduced into our bodies accidentally, or are placed there for the purpose of deceiving.

The *Helmintha* are invertebrata, unprovided with limbs or organs of respiration. The character which they possess in common is to lodge and nourish themselves in the human body, during a considerable portion or the whole of their existence.

These parasitic worms are sometimes solitary, and are sometimes collected together in variable numbers. They are met with in different parts of the body, as in the alimentary canal, or the ducts which open into it; in the blood vessels; in the substance of the liver; in the parenchyma of the lung, and in the structure of the brain. They have even been found in the osseous tissue, and in the midst of the fat. It is exceedingly important, even for the zoologist, to be aware of what part of the body they inhabit, since it facilitates the determination of the species. It may be said generally that the *Helmintha* almost always reside upon the mucous membranes or in the cellular tissue.

The presence of these worms occasionally produces scarcely any appreciable disorder. The animals live, as it were, in a latent state. In some cases there is a slight irritation, or a trifling amount of itching. At other times there is a feeling of weight, or increased appetite, occasionally an undefined feeling of illness, or sudden and violent pain; the person gets thin; there are pains in the intestines, hæmorrhages, chronic inflammation, and the formation of abscesses. These disorders are followed by spasmodic convulsions, chorea, epilepsy, amaurosis, apoplexy, and a disease similar to what is commonly termed the "staggers" in sheep. In some cases, which are happily very rare, these disorders terminate in death. The various diseases attendant upon the presence of the entozoa are fully

---

[1] *Vermes accessorii*. (Bremser.)

described in the excellent work of M. Davaine, entitled *Traité des Entozoaires et des maladies vermineuses.*

[The English reader will find a full account of the diseases and their treatment in Dr. Lankester's valuable translation of Küchenmeister's work on the Animal and Vegetable Parasites of the Human body, published by the Sydenham Society.]

The injurious effects of these Entozoa must not, however, be exaggerated. M. Dujardin has met with cases in which the animals were developed by thousands, and yet the persons appeared to be in good health.

The multiplication of the worms is most rapid in debilitated persons, who are living in cold and damp situations, and who are already in a bad state of health from other causes. (Grisolle.) Improper nourishment greatly favours the appearance of the *Helmintha*. Damaged food, green fruits, stale vegetables, sweets, impure water, are all of them circumstances which have considerable influence on the development of these animals. Childhood is the period of life which most favours their presence, possibly in consequence of the preponderance of the lymphatic system in the early periods of life. (Bouchut.) Some families seem to be more predisposed to verminous affections than others. It appears, also, that the nature of the constitution (*helminthous*, Req.) has great influence.

Some Entozoa are indigenous to several countries, as, for example, the *Tænia* to Germany and to Holland, and the *Bothriocephalus* to Switzerland and to Russia. (Boudin.)

The *Helmintha* are worms having generally long cylindrical bodies. Some are thread-like, others ribbon-shaped, and some resemble small leaves. In some the body is elastic, and covered by a strong integument; while others are soft, and have no distinct integument. Their bodies are either transversely striated or distinctly articulated, and of a white, greyish, yellow, or reddish colour. The contents of the alimentary canal and the ova frequently modify the colour.

One division of the Entozoa have a complete intestine, provided with a mouth and an anus. In a few the mouth presents certain hard parts; some have a ramified digestive canal, with only one orifice; others have oral suckers, and have no anal orifice or intestine.

A nervous system is only found in a small number, and is always of a rudimentary kind. Some have suckers or hooks, by means of which they can fix themselves.

The ancients believed in the spontaneous reproduction of the intestinal worms. Some were supposed to originate from imperfectly digested food; others from decomposing excrements; some from vitiated and fermented bile; and others, again, from the *crude, thickened,* and *putrifying* humours.[1]

"Worms," says Ambrose Paré, "are formed from a thick, viscous, crude matter, which, becoming corrupted in the stomach, then descends into the intestines."

The theory of spontaneous generation has been maintained in our own time by several physiologists of repute.[2] Redi, Audry, and Vallisneri strongly protested against this ancient doctrine. Thanks to the labours of many eminent naturalists of the present day,[3] this mode of reproduction is no longer admissible. It is now generally admitted that the Entozoa are produced by other Entozoa.

In these animals the sexes may be separated or united. The males are generally provided with a verge or *spiculum*, which may be single or double. Their spermatozoa are sometimes filiform, sometimes globular, diaphanous, and more or less adhesive. There are oviparous Entozoa and ovoviviparous Entozoa. The larvæ, in a great number, differ materially from the adult. Some can reproduce themselves by gemmæ or buds, giving rise to the curious phenomena of the alternation of generations. Lastly, it has been shown that at a certain period of their lives some of these animals make extended migrations, in order to reach the individual in whose body they are ultimately to reside.

The *Helmintha* of man may be divided into two series: the *cylindrical, which are provided with a visceral cavity*, and the *noncylindrical, which are deprived of a visceral cavity*. Of the first some live in the alimentary canal;[4] these consist of the genera ASCARIS, OXYURUS, TRICHOCEPHALUS, and ANCYLOSTOMA;— others reside out of the alimentary canal; these include the genera STRONGYLUS, SPIROPTERA, and FILARIA. The second are flat, and are found external to the alimentary canal; these constitute the genera THECOSOMA, DISTOMA, and FESTUCARIA; or they may have a riband-like form, and live in the canal;[5]

[1] *Ex cruda crassaque materia pituitosa putrescente.* (Avicenna.)
[2] Bremser, Lamarck, Frey, Dugés, Dujardin, Burdach, Berard, Pouchet, etc.
[3] Siebold, Van Beneden, Küchenmeister, Leuckart, Filippi, Claude Bernard, etc.
[4] This refers to the perfect state, for the larvæ of a great number live out of the alimentary canal, and even external to man.
[5] The larvæ all live external to man, and external to the digestive canal.

these are the genera Tænia and Bothriocephalus; in all, twelve genera. The following is a table of these genera, with their principal characters:—

Genera of Helmintha living in Man.

I.—CYLINDRICAL WITH A VISCERAL CAVITY.
  A. *Living in the alimentary canal (unisexual).*
   1. Ascarides. Body attenuated posteriorly, and still more so exteriorly. Mouth with three tubercles. Tail of the male narrower than that of the female.
   2. Oxyurus. Body attenuated anteriorly, and still more so posteriorly. Mouth with rudimentary tubercles, and a dilatation around it. The tail of the male somewhat thickened.
   3. Trichocephalus. Body capillary anteriorly. Mouth without tubercles. Tail of the male like that of the female.
   4. Ancylostoma. Body slightly attenuated anteriorly. Mouth with four hooks. Tail of the male cup-shaped.
  B. *Living out of the alimentary canal (unisexual).*
   5. Strongylus. Body attenuated posteriorly. Mouth with six lobes. Tail of the male cup-shaped.
   6. Spiroptera. Body attenuated anteriorly. Mouth armed with papillæ. Tail aliform.
   7. Filaria. Body equal (filiform). Mouth with three tubercles. Tail simple.
II.—NON-CYLINDRICAL AND WITHOUT A VISCERAL CAVITY.
  A. *Flat (living externally to the digestive canal).*[1]
   8. Thecosoma.[2] Unisexual. The male carrying the female in a groove on its abdomen.
   9. Distoma. Androgynous. An abdominal sucker.
   10. Festucaria. Androgynous. No abdominal sucker.
  B. *Riband-shaped (living in the alimentary canal, androgynous).*
   11. Tænia. Four rounded suckers. Genital pores marginal.
   12. Bothriocephalus. Two longitudinal fossæ. Genital pores mesial.

[1] Two species of *Distoma* are exceptional inhabitants.
[2] Body slightly flattened.

CHAPTER I.

ASCARIDES.

THE genus *Ascaris* was established by Linnæus. The term[1] is especially applicable to the *Oxyurus*,[2] which, unfortunately for the etymology of the subject, is no longer associated with the present group.

1. ASCARIS LUMBRICOIDES.—*A. gigas*, Goeze, *Fusaria lumbricoides*, Zeder. This species is one of the commonest and best known of the *Helmintha*. It is noticed by the most ancient writers. The first inquirers gave this animal the name of *Lumbricus teres*, and regarded it as identical with the Earth worm, or *Lumbricus terrestris*. They supposed it was the same worm, which, having been accidentally introduced into the alimentary canal, had become modified by its change of residence. The Lumbricus terrestris is, however, an animal having a far higher grade of organization.

The following are the characteristic differences of the two animals:—

Ascaris.	*Lumbricus.*
1. Body without setæ.	1. Body with eight rows of setæ.
2. Movements very slight.	2. Movements active.
3. Mouth with three tubercles.	3. Mouth with two unequal lips, one superior, one inferior.

In addition to these characters, the *Ascarides* have colourless blood, a rudimentary nervous system, the sexes separate, a permanent genital constriction in the female, the eggs separate and provided with a thin semitransparent covering; while the *Lumbrici* are provided with red blood, have a well-developed ganglionic nervous system (with an œsophageal ring and an abdominal cord), a genital enlargement at the period of reproduction in all the individuals, and ovigerous capsules, provided with a thick opaque covering.

The *Ascaris* of man was for a long time confounded with those of the horse and of the hog. In the present day it is well known, that although the latter parasites are closely allied, they are nevertheless distinct species.

M. Jules Cloquet has published an excellent work on the *Ascaris lumbricoides*.

---

[1] ασκαρις, a kind of worm.
[2] See the next chapter.

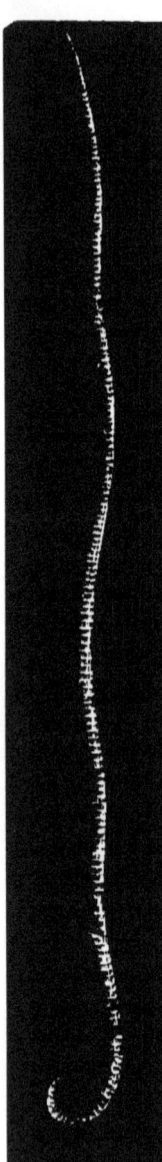

Fig. 104.
Ascaris.

Description (fig. 104).—The *Ascaris lumbricoides* is from four to twelve inches in length, and from one to four lines in circumference; it is slightly attenuated at the extremities,[1] but rather more so at the anterior. Linnæus was in error when he described the tail as triangular, or as having three surfaces; this extremity is cylindrical or awl-shaped. The surface of the body is marked by annular ridges and four longitudinal lines, one dorsal, one abdominal, and two lateral.

This worm has a somewhat polished surface, is of a whitish or milk-white colour, sometimes inclining to a dull red, or more rarely to a brown or blood-red colour. The skin is thick, strong, elastic, and almost perfectly transparent.

There is no distinct head, and consequently no neck. At the anterior extremity (fig. 104) is a somewhat triangular mouth. Around its orifice are three small tubercles, of which one is superior, and the others inferior; these are capable of being alternately divaricated and approximated. Rudolphi terms them *valves*, Cuvier *fleshy papillæ*, Blainville *nodules*, and Dujardin *valves*.[2] Some writers have unadvisedly designated the whole as the *head*. These tubercles are provided with a small cavity at the inner part of their base.

The mouth communicates with an œsophagus, which may be seen through the skin; it is long, somewhat triangular, and provided with thick muscular walls. Very narrow at its commencement, it gradually increases in size, and is then suddenly constricted. The stomach consists of two globular dilatations; its walls are thinner than those of the œsophagus. The intestine is straight, and presents some slight bendings; it becomes narrowed towards the vent. It consists of two membranes, which can be separated from each other; the external is thin, smooth, and transparent; the internal thick, rugose, and slightly coloured. The canal appears

---

[1] Linnæus says : "*Corpus teres utraque extremitate attenuatum.*"

[2] Treutler observed amongst a number of *Ascarides* in the small intestine of a female, one in which the mouth had only two tubercles.

to be surrounded by white vesicles, suspended in the cavity of the body, which are regarded by M. J. Cloquet as absorbent vessels. It is supported by two pairs of ligaments, one of which is placed superiorly, and the other inferiorly.

The anus is situated near the posterior extremity of the animal, and has the form of a transverse opening.

Each of the pairs of ligaments which have just been mentioned form a triangular canal. M. Blanchard believes that in the interior of these canals there are two vessels, one of which is deep-seated, and the other placed superficially. The two deep-seated vessels anastomose together opposite the anterior third of the œsophagus. One of them is moreover provided with a small contractile sac (heart?). The superficial vessels unite behind the preceding and anastomose with them anteriorly. This arrangement is very remarkable, and resembles that of some of the anellidæ.

The *Ascaris lumbricoides*, according to the observations of MM. Jules Cloquet and Blanchard, is provided with a nervous system, consisting of two white cords running along the sides of the body. By following the track of these nerves two ganglionic masses are met with, united together by a double cord, which surrounds the œsophagus.

Beneath the skin there are transverse fibres, placed at regular intervals, and covering a thicker layer of longitudinal fibres, from which filaments are given off, having no particular direction, and of which the majority are free and floating in the interior of the body. Many of these filaments attach themselves to the internal organs, and assist in retaining them in their proper place; they are more numerous towards the extremities than in the middle portion of the body.

The *Ascaris lumbricoides* is unisexual. M. Jules Cloquet has calculated that the females are four times as numerous as the males. The latter are smaller than the females; this circumstance is remarkable, because, as a general rule, it is contrary to what occurs amongst animals which are polygamous. Amongst the males, the caudal extremity (fig. 105, *b*) is somewhat slenderer than it is in the females; it is also slightly curved. The penis, or spiculum, is double; it is formed of two slender horny curved processes, rather less than a line in length; they are placed close to the anus, and emerge from this aperture. The testicles and the spermatic cords are filiform, and surround the alimentary canal. At the anterior third of the body in the female is a circular construction (fig. 105, *c*). Linnæus did not notice this narrowing, but stated that at this

z

part the animal had no enlargement (*clitellum*) like that which occurs in the Earth-worm, and from this alone he concluded that the *Ascaris lumbricoides* is very different from the former animal;[1] Linnæus would have found the distinction far greater if he had noticed, that there is a narrowing where in the Earth-worm there is an enlargement; and that the one is unisexual, while the other is androgynous. It is in this constriction that the vulva is placed on the right side. This orifice is very small; it communicates with a narrow vagina (*oviduct* of Blainville) from four to six lines in length, which leads to a short uterus, provided with two long flexible horns, arranged in the length of the abdomen, and formed of two distinct membranes. These horns become continuous with the ovaries, which are excessively long slender tubes, twisted upon themselves, and surrounding the alimentary canal. The ovaries closely resemble the testicles. At the period of reproduction, the horns of the uterus are filled with an enormous quantity of eggs. M. Eschricht calculates that they amount to several thousands in each individual.

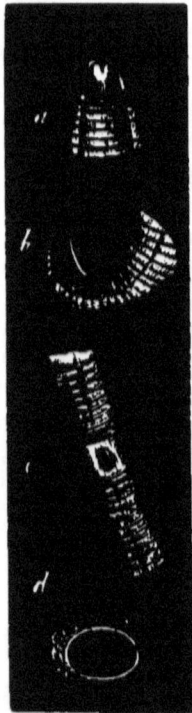

Fig. 105.
Ascaris.[2]

The eggs (fig. 105, *d*) are ovoid, and covered by a transparent envelope. Tyson and Werner, and subsequently Brera and Rudolphi, described them as being villous. Goeze and M. Jules Cloquet maintain that they are smooth.

According to the recent observations of M. Davaine, these eggs are expelled with the fæces. M. Richter, having placed them in pure water, found that at the end of eleven months they each contained a living embryo, but he did not see them hatch. (Küchenmeister.) M. Davaine has been more fortunate, and was able to follow out their development, which commenced at the end of six months. The embryo is cylindrical. The three lobes of the mouth are not present, and are characteristic of the adult worm; the caudal extremity terminates abruptly in a point.

[1] "*A Lumbrico distinctissimus.*" (Linn.)
[2] *a*, a cephalic extremity, with the three tubercles of the mouth; *b*, caudal extremity of the male, with the two spicula; *c*, genital constriction of the female with the sexual orifice; *d*, egg.

[The following is the account which Küchenmeister gives of Verloren's and Richter's experiments upon the eggs of *Ascaris marginata* and of *A. lumbricoides*.

In the early part of the month of August, 1853, Verloren put a fragment of a mature female, *Ascaris marginata*, of the dog into water, so as to preserve the eggs in the water by the prevention of evaporation. Of these he examined specimens from time to time under the microscope. The segmentation of the vitelli and the development of the young, immediately commenced. In about fourteen days the process was completed, and perfectly developed young worms made their appearance; these moved briskly within the egg shells, but did not break through them, as Verloren expected, from similar successful experiments by Schubart. With the decrease of temperature towards autumn and winter, the mobility of the embryos within the egg-shells also diminished, until at last it entirely ceased in the winter, but recommenced in the following spring, and again became very distinct in the summer months. During the whole course of the experiment a spontaneous exclusion of the embryos from the eggs never took place. In these eggs, therefore, the following remarkable peculiarities may be observed:—The eggs of other animals may, indeed, lie for a long time before the young make their appearance; as, for example, in many insects; but this always takes place within a year;[1] the eggs of many animals may also be delayed for a long time in their development, but then the development of the young cannot have commenced at all. But if this be once the case, and the young be developed, it must either be excluded soon, or it dies in a few days, whilst in the present instance, the ready-formed embryo lives more than a year in the egg-shell, like other worms in an encysted state, which live enclosed in their cyst. Both are, probably, enabled to live for a certain time unchanged in the egg-shells or cysts, both, as is well known, agreeing in being asexual, and therefore their species difficult to determine; this condition is only changed by other favourable circumstances, and the animals thereby carried on towards their development. Lastly, it is certain that the embryos of the nematode worms may pass the winter in a sort of torpid state in the open waters.

When Verloren set free the embryos artificially by crushing the eggs, they soon died, partly stifled by the fungoid struc-

[1] [That is to say, naturally, for Reaumur, by placing the eggs of the insect in an ice-house, retarded their development beyond the year.]

tures growing about them, and partly from their becoming the seat of fungoid growths. Independently of Verloren's investigations, and at a period when the experiments of that *savant* could not have been known in Germany, H. E. Richter, of Dresden, had also put the eggs of an *Ascaris lumbricoides* into water (on the 15th of November, 1854). The eggs, which were all without living embryos, and which had not even exhibited globules of segmentation, were not examined by Richter for some time after their being placed in water; but on the 15th October, 1855 (consequently after the lapse of eleven months), he found living embryos in all the eggs, of which he sent a considerable number to Haubner, Leuckart, and myself. These were employed in experiments, which unfortunately furnished no result.

When I examined dry eggs of the same worm, which Richter had sent to me, I had only the opportunity of confirming Richter's statement, that on the 15th of November, 1854, the eggs had hardly commenced any development.

All this shows that a portion of the eggs of the nematode worms issues, in the first instance, passively from the body of their previous host into the external world, and first of all passes the stage of its development, up to the formation of embryos, in the open water.][1]

2. ANOTHER SPECIES.—Mr. Bellingham has described[2] another species of *Ascaris* peculiar to man, which he discovered in Dublin, and for which he has proposed the name of *Ascaris alata*. MM. Dujardin and Diesing admit the species, although it has only been observed once. The two individuals which were found were females.

This animal was three and a half inches in length, half a line in width anteriorly, and three-fourths of a line posteriorly. At the anterior extremity it had two semi-transparent membranous *wings*, extending for about a line and a quarter, and rather straighter anteriorly than posteriorly. The body was bent anteriorly. The tail was straight and spotted with black. It resembles the species of *Ascaris* which infests the cat, *Ascaris mystax*, Rüd.

M. Diesing suspects that this worm might have been an *Ascaris lumbricoides*, whose skin had become inflated and raised up around the mouth. If this species is to be retained, the oral appendages approximate it to the genus *Oxyuris*, and justify M. Diesing's union of these genera.

[1] *Opus cit*, vol. 1, p. 310.
[2] [*Annals of Nat. Hist.*, vol. xiii. p. 173.]

[Küchenmeister rejects the *Ascaris alata*, observing that it is probably only a young individual of one of the long-known Nematoda, if, indeed, he adds, it be a worm at all.][1]

3. ACTION ON MAN.—The *Ascaris lumbricoides* inhabits every country. It is frequently found in the intestines of children, less frequently in those of adults, and hardly ever in those of old people. It is found more particularly in young persons of a lymphatic temperament, who live upon bad and indigestible food, and who inhabit low, damp, and ill-ventilated localities, circumstances which in large towns are very common to the children of the poorer classes.

M. Cruveilhier found more than a thousand in the body of a young idiot girl.

According to Petit, of Lyons, the son of a veterinary surgeon at Roanne discharged two thousand in the course of five months.

The *Ascarides* are generally met with in the small intestines. They have, however, been found in other organs, but this was an accidental occurrence. Thus M. Jules Cloquet has seen them in the large intestines. Rudolphi thinks that they are always expelled with the fæces, when they have passed into the colon.

These Helmintha may ascend to the stomach and from thence to the pharynx. It has been stated that some have passed into the larynx (Blandin, Tonnellé), and even into the bronchi (Chassaignac), giving rise to very dangerous results.[2] M. Jobert de Lamballe has mentioned the name of a person who died suffocated by one of these worms, which had penetrated into the trachea. MM. Lepelletier and Lebert have also mentioned a case of death from suffocation.

It is not extremely rare to find the *Ascaris lumbricoides* introducing itself into the nasal fossæ, and then passing out by the nostrils. Achille Richard met with a case of this kind in an infant. Martin Slabber speaks of a man who discharged one when in the act of sneezing. Bremser has described a similar instance, in which an old woman discharged one of these worms when blowing her nose. M. Cruveilhier relates the case of a patient, who, after excessive pain in one of his nostrils, to his great astonishment, drew from it a very long Ascaris.

The *Ascaris lumbricoides* may enter the biliary ducts (Tonnellé, Estevenet) and may even lodge itself in the gall-bladder.

[1] *Opus cit*, vol. 2, p. 100.
[2] These perforations often take place after death. (Cruveilhier.)

Laënnec met with it in the dead body of an infant which had vomited a large quantity of these worms, the biliary ducts were distended, and the substance of the liver looked as if it had been eaten away. M. Bouisson has recorded an instance in which a fragment of an *Ascaris* had become the nucleus of a biliary calculus.

Gmelin discovered an *Ascaris* three inches in length in the pancreatic duct.

Several of these creatures have been expelled through an opening in the umbilicus (Poussin), and others, in a case of strangulated hernia which was gangrenous, issued from an abscess in the abdominal walls. Dr. Brizet, of Chalabre, found a live *Ascaris* nearly eight inches long in a tumour in the groin, which appeared like an inflammation of the inguinal glands.

Authors have recorded cases in which the patients have had one of these worms in the maxillary sinus (Deschamps), in the frontal sinuses, in the kidneys, in the bladder (Dumeril), or in the uterus. It is, however, necessary to remark that many of these cases are incorrect, and that what has been mistaken for *Ascarides* has been either worms belonging to other genera, the larvæ of other animals, or even foreign bodies of an entirely different nature.

The instances in which the *Ascarides* have been found in the neighbourhood of the alimentary canal after it has been perforated, are extremely rare, in spite of M. Raspail's assertion to the contrary, who considers these *Helmintha* as intestinal leeches. MM. Becquerel and Bailly have mentioned an instance of perforation of the cæcum. A very curious specimen of this kind has been preserved in the Dupuytren Museum. In 1808 M. Cloquet found in the body of an infant three large *Ascarides* on the anterior surface of the sacrum, in the folds of the mesorectum. These entozoa had emerged through an ulcerated opening in the intestine, but they had not caused any inflammation.

The abscesses caused by these worms have been divided into two series: the *non-stercoraceous*, in which the perforation is so small that the fæcal matter cannot pass out, and the *stercoraceous*, which allow the excrements to filter out. (Guersant.)

The *Ascaris alata* was found in the small intestines.

CHAPTER II.

OXYURIS.

The *Oxyuris vermicularis*, Deslong., *Ascaris vermicularis*, Linn., was regarded by Linnæus as a species of *Ascaris*.[1]

It was Deslongchamps who established the genus *Oxyuris*. The meaning of the word is *pointed tail*,[2] a character which perfectly applies to the females, but not to the males.

The *Oxyurides* are distinguished from the *Ascarides* by the rudimentary condition of their three oral tubercles, and by the aliform enlargements at the mouth, which are wanting in the *Ascarides*. In reality, these characters are insufficient, and it is this which has induced M. Diesing to regard the *Oxyurides* as a section of the *Ascarides*.

1. The OXYURIS VERMICULARIS is the only species belonging to the genus which is found in man. The animal bears a strong resemblance to the Vibrio of paste made from flour.

Description (fig. 106).—The *Oxyurides* are very small *Helmintha*, measuring from three to four lines in length. Linnæus has undoubtedly confounded them with another worm, when he says they may attain the length of an inch. Their width varies from the $\frac{1}{100}$ to the $\frac{3}{100}$ of an inch. The body is filiform, attenuated at the two extremities, and provided with indistinct transverse markings; it consists of a strong, elastic, semi-transparent tissue of a snow-white colour.

Anteriorly these animals have a slightly enlarged portion, which is known as the head, and is supported by a very imperfectly defined neck. Several writers have imagined that this part is provided with two appendages or membranous contractile vesicles in the form of wings. According to MM. Dujardin and Raspail, there exists at this part a uniform ves-

Fig. 106.—*Oxyuris*.[3]

---

[1] See preceding chapter.
[2] Ὀξύς *sharp*, οὐρά tail.
[3] *a*, male; *b*, female; *c*, cephalic extremity, showing the three tubercle and the aliform dilatation; *d*, caudal extremity of the male; *e*, caudal extremity of the female; *f*, egg

icular enlargement surrounding the anterior extremity, and not independent and lateral membranous wings. When this vesicular portion is examined beneath the micrscope, it puts on the deceptive appearance of two segments of circles placed against an opaque canal. These segments are marked by transverse striæ, which have a very pleasing effect. (Raspail.) The mouth is hollowed out anteriorly into the form of a sucker, and is consequently surrounded by the vesicular enlargement which has just been mentioned (fig. 106, c). It has three slight projecting tubercles, and communicates with a short triangular œsophagus, which is provided with thick muscular walls, and is dilated into a kind of crop at its junction with the stomach; the latter is short and globular. The commencement of the intestine is enlarged, so that the alimentary canal has the appearance of three stomachal dilatations, which succeed each other—the crop, the stomach, and the intestinal dilatation. These pouches resemble globules united at their extremities.

The intestine, which is nearly straight, runs in the length of the animal, and preserves a uniform diameter up to the rectum. It is often filled with a brown, yellow, or greyish, granular matter. When the intestinal canal has arrived at the posterior part of the body it becomes enlarged, and forms a short rectum which occupies nearly the whole width of the visceral cavity. Towards its termination the canal gradually narrows, like the tail of which it fills the cone. At this part it appears to be slightly sinuous, but not spiral, as is stated by Bremser. This part is frequently empty.

A small transverse opening, the anus, which is possibly of a semicircular form, gives exit to the granules which have been previously mentioned. It is placed towards the middle part of the base of the tail; its margins are everted, and form a pair of slightly projecting lips.

M. Delle Chiaje has pointed out a longitudinal central vessel passing from the mouth to the tail.

The skin presents four longitudinal bands or fibres, which have been well described by M. Raspail. These are placed at equal intervals; they are somewhat elevated, and more opaque than the rest of the tissues, and extend from the head to the extremity of the tail. These fibres give the animal that kind of rigidity by which it is characterized. According to Dugès, the skin which fills up the intervals between the bands is composed of closely arranged fleshy fibrillæ, forming a longitudinal layer on the exterior, and a transverse layer on the interior.

According to M. Raspail, the skin, when seen beneath the microscope, appears to be composed of flattened cells having the form of transverse parallelograms separated by fibres or bands, more distinct in the transverse than in the longitudinal direction.

If the worm is divided, the pieces contract, or become coiled up. Dugès has skilfully availed himself of these contractions in the study of the different organs. On wounding or cutting a living animal, the viscera sometimes form a kind of hernial sac and become more distinct.

During life the *Oxyurides* move in an undulating and tolerably active manner. They twist themselves about in various ways in the midst of the thickened mucus by which they are surrounded. They can advance or retreat with equal facility. It is said they can even leap, and in that manner clear spaces six or eight times the length of their bodies; the vivacity of their movements is increased when they are irritated. They move out of the way of any impediment which they may meet with. They appear to avoid the light; their abode is no better lighted than that of the majority of the intestinal worms.

When they are wounded, the extremity of the body, which is nearest to the injured part, seems to turn towards the wound, to examine it, and to endeavour to remove this as the source of its suffering. (Dugès.) Every section, to whatever part of the body it may belong, continues to live for some time if it is of a suitable length. Dugès observed that the part to which the head was attached lived longer than that belonging to the tail, and this longer than a section from the middle of the body.

The *Oxyurides* prefer living in society, and are seldom found solitary. They gather together in clusters, intertwine, roll themselves up into balls, and often form masses of considerable size.

These entozoa are unisexual. The males (fig. 106, *a, d*) seem to be scarcer and smaller than the females. They are not more than from one to two lines in length. Their bodies are thread-like, with the caudal portion somewhat thickened, and bent into a spiral form. They have two spiculæ. The females (fig. 106, *b, c*) are fusiform, very attenuated posteriorly, with the caudal portion awl-shaped and straight. The sexual orifice is placed a little in front of the anterior fourth of the body; it is a transverse opening with projecting lips, which occasionally gives egress to the eggs during certain contractions of the animal. The oviduct may be compared to a straight bag, very long, and with great power of contraction, although formed by an extremely delicate membrane. It is no doubt bound down by the general covering, for when it passes out of wounds it becomes elongated and much increased in size; it occupies the whole length of the worm with the exception of the cephalic extremity and the tail; there seems to be no opening excepting that opposite the vulva. Anteriorly it becomes narrower and more twisted; posteriorly it terminates in a pointed *cul de sac*. Towards the anterior third it presents a constriction. M. Raspail shows that the anterior portion is more especially the ovary, and that the remainder corresponds to the uterus. This canal seems to consist of two folds, for Dugès has remarked that where there are wounds in the middle of the body there usually emerges a large gut and a small gut.

The *Oxyuridæ* are sometimes found twined round each other. Some of these animals are probably in the act of copulation. The observations of Dugès on the *Rhabditis* give some support to this notion. As the males and the females are not always met with at the same time, Bremser has suggested that the generation of the *Oxyurides* is analogous to that of the *Aphides*, which only produce females during the summer, while food is plentiful, but during the autumn they lay eggs, which in the following spring produce both females and males. The latter fecundate their own females, and also those of the following generation. It is difficult to decide the question. It may, however, be remarked, that the nutriment furnished by the rectum to the *Oxyurides* is always equally abundant, and if there are circumstances under which it varies it does so with great irregularity.

Dugès has on several occasions surprised the *Oxyurides* in the act of laying their eggs. The eggs are very numerous. M. Raspail has calculated that each worm may contain 3,024. The eggs (fig. 106, *f*) are elliptical or oval, flattened, provided with two coverings, and filled with a gelatinous transparent material. Their long diameter is five or six times the size of the globules of the human blood. The surface is granulated. While they are still in the animal they are constantly changing their place; some pass from before backwards, and others in the opposite direction. It is this movement which has caused several observers to mistake them for embryos, and to conclude that the *Oxyurides* were viviparous parasites. Goeze is amongst the number. But, as it is mentioned above, Dugès has seen the eggs issuing from the vulva. At the same time it is not impossible that these entozoa may be oviparous at one season, and viviparous at another, just in the same manner as the Aphides and the Planaria, although the locality in which they reside cannot be much influenced by external agents.

2. ACTION ON MAN.—The *Oxyurides* are found in infants. They are also met with in adults, but not so frequently. M. Tandon knew a tolerably robust man, fifty years of age, who had been tormented with them for ten years. M. Cruveilhier found them in a person of seventy. These worms are very common. Their presence seldom produces any serious disturbance of the health.

Notwithstanding what has been said, they are not met with in very young infants. M. Tandon's colleague, M. Natalis Guillot, physician to the Hôpital Necker, in the course of twelve years never met with the *Oxyuris vermicularis* in children before they were weaned.

These entozoa reside in large intestines, particularly in the lower part of the rectum, near the anus. Their presence causes a peculiar and disagreeable itching, especially at night when the person is going to bed.

The fæces usually contain some of the worms, which twist and move themselves about on the surface of the expelled matter, and die as soon as this becomes cold. They are never found either dead or alive in the centre of the excrements, and they soon perish when placed in any saline liquid. (Raspail.)

When the *Oxyurides* increase to an alarming extent, they ascend the intestines and pass into the cæcum. (Bremser.) Wolf, Bloch, and M. Andral state that they have found some of these animals in a cyst formed in the walls of the stomach. Brera says that he has observed them in the œsophagus of a woman. Fernel has stated that they sometimes pass into the mouth, and that during sleep they even get into the nose.

In young girls the *Oxyurides* may introduce themselves into the vagina. Sauvages gives the name of *pudendagra ab Ascaridibus* to a disease caused by the irritation of these Helmintha in the vulva. Becker, Scharf, and Bremser speak of aged females in whom the presence of the *Oxyurides* had produced a kind of nymphomania. Benedetti found these worms between the placenta and the walls of the uterus in a woman who was in the eighth month of her pregnancy.

CHAPTER III.

TRICHOCEPHALUS.

This animal was noticed by Morgagni, but, like many other discoveries, it was forgotten. During the winter of 1760-61, a student of Gottingen, who was dissecting the valve of the colon in the body of a young girl five years old, accidentally opened the cæcum, when several entozoa came out. H. A. Wrisberg and some other students considered that these worms belonged to a species not previously known. The prosector, Ch. Th. Wagler, maintained that they were *Oxyurides*[1] of a very large size. Other persons mistook them for very small *Ascarides*.[2] From this a serious discussion, or rather quarrel, arose, which might have been easily settled if the newly discovered worm had only been carefully compared either with an *Ascaris* or an *Oxyuris*. Rœderer, having heard of the dispute, had the animal in question brought to him, and having examined it with Buttner, they both came to the conclusion that it was a new species. Buttner gave it the name of *Trichiuris* (hair-tailed).

About the same time an epidemic was raging in the division of the French army stationed at Gottingen. Rœderer and Wagler give it the name of *morbus mucosus;* and as the *Trichiures* were frequently found in the bodies of the soldiers who died from it, Rœderer entertained the notion that these parasites were the cause of the disease. But all the soldiers did not have *Trichiures*, and on the other hand many persons had them, who had died from other diseases besides the *morbus mucosus*. Linnæus regarded the *Trichiuris* as a species of *Ascaris*. It was, however, soon discovered that the anterior part of the animal had been mistaken for the posterior, and it was therefore considered necessary to change the name of *Trichiuris* to that of *Trichocephalus*.[3]

1. THE TRICHOCEPHALUS OF MAN.—*Trichocephalos hominis*, Goeze, *Ascaris Trichina*, Linn., *Trichocephalus dispar*, Rudolp. As the name implies, this is the only species which is found in man.

Description (fig. 107).—The worm is from one and a half to two inches in length, and from $\frac{3}{100}$ to $\frac{6}{100}$ of an inch in width. The body is cylindrical, slender, slightly annulated, of a white or whitish, sometimes yellow, colour, and at other times of the

---

[1] See preceding chapter.
[2] See page 312.
[3] Θρìνξ τριχὸs a hair, and κεφαλὴ the head.

same colour as its food. The body looks as if it was formed of two portions; one anterior and filiform, the other posterior and somewhat thicker. The slender portion occupies two-thirds of the entire length. Some writers describe it as the neck. It does not, however, support any cephalic enlargement, but gradually narrows to a point.

The mouth (fig. 107, c) is a small round terminal opening, which it is difficult to detect.

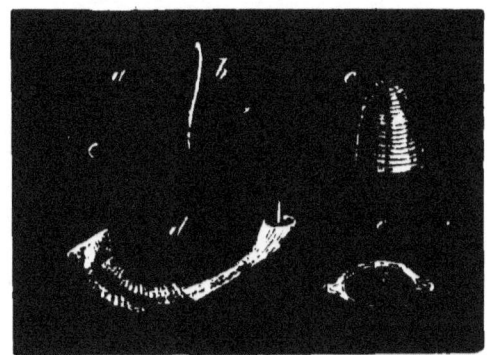

Fig. 107.—*Trichocephalus*.[1]

Wrisberg believed he had seen a small tube at this part, but neither Muller, Rudolphi, nor Bremser, was able to discover it.

The anus is placed quite at the posterior extremity of the body.

The digestive canal forms almost a straight line from the mouth to the anus. The œsophagus occupies the capillary portion. It must necessarily be of extreme tenuity. The remainder of the canal appears to be somewhat thicker, and as if it were muscular. According to Meyer there is no distinct gastric enlargement.

The *Trichocephali* are unisexual. The males (fig. 107, a) are shorter than the females; the thick portion of their body is proportionately long, and is bent into a spiral form. The spermatic vessels are situated posteriorly, and after pursuing a very tortuous course terminate at the anal aperture. At that part there is a small, subcylindrical, elongated sheath, which forms a cup at its termination, is semi-transparent, and forms a case for the spiculum. The latter is single, filiform, pointed, and capable of being retracted. The females (107, b) are always straight; never spiriform like the males. This circumstance at first led Rœderer, Wagler, and Wrisberg to look upon the two sexes as two distinct species. Pallas discovered the male in the *Trichocephalus* of a lizard, and described it under a specific name (*Tænia spiralis*); he also thinking that the spiral form indicated a distinct species. The oviduct is

[1] a, male; b, female; c, cephalic extremity with the terminal mouth; d, caudal extremity of the male with generative sheath and its spiculum; e, an egg.

placed around the alimentary canal, and opens at the junction of the capillary with the thicker portion of the body.

The eggs (fig. 107, c) are large in proportion to the size of the animal; they are elliptical, and terminated at each extremity by a small rounded nodule; the shell is strong. According to the recent observations of M. Davaine, the eggs are not hatched in the intestine of man; they are always expelled in the same condition as when they were laid.

M. Davaine has succeeded in developing the eggs in water. At the end of six months the segmentation of the yelk commences, and the embryo makes its appearance two months later. To a certain extent it possesses the form of the adult; it is about the $\frac{2}{1000}$ of an inch in length.

TRICHINA.—MM. Küchenmeister and Weiland think that the larva of the Trichocephalus is probably the small encysted entozoa discovered in 1835[1] by Prof. Owen in the dead body of an Italian, who died in St. Bartholomew's Hospital, and to which he gave the name of *Trichina spiralis*. All the voluntary muscles of the body were observed to be covered with minute white spots. Upon examining these granulations, Prof. Owen found that they were oval, and each containing a small worm. He considered the worm to be a new species, which was not referable to any known genera. Several instances of its occurrence have since been recorded by different observers. [It has been found in England, Germany, and Denmark.]

The cysts are of an elliptical figure, with the extremities more or less attenuated; they are always more opaque than the intermediate part of the cyst, which is in general sufficiently transparent to show that it contains a minute worm coiled up. The usual size of the cyst is $\frac{1}{50}$ of an inch in the long diameter, and $\frac{1}{100}$ of an inch across their middle part. (Owen.) Each cyst consists of two layers; the external is produced by the diseased tissue, and is surrounded by a vascular net work, while the interior is formed by the worm itself. (Luscha.) The worm has no organic connection with the cyst; sometimes two *Trichina*, rarely three, occur in the same cyst. By cutting off the extremity of the cyst, which may be done with a cataract needle or a fine knife, and gently pressing on the opposite extremity, the Trichina and the granular secretion with which it is surrounded will escape ; and it frequently starts out as soon as the cyst is opened. When first extracted, the Trichina is

[1] Tiedeman noticed similar vesicles as far back as 1822.

usually disposed in two or two and a half spiral coils; when straightened out it measures $\frac{1}{30}$ of an inch in length, and $\frac{1}{700}$ of an inch in diameter, and now requires for its satisfactory examination a magnifying power of at least 200 linear measurement.[1]

The worm is cylindrical and filiform, minutely annulated, terminating obtusely at both extremities, which are of unequal sizes, tapering towards one end for about one fourth part of its length, but continuing of uniform diameter from that point to the opposite extremity, which is trilabiate.

At this part, which is the mouth, a minute papilla is seen to form from time to time, and then disappear. (Luscha.) The œsophagus is very long, and extends nearly half the length of the body, a circumstance which should be borne in mind on account of its analogy with the organization of the *Trichocephalus*.

ACTION ON MAN.—The *Trichocephalus* is far from uncommon. It is found in France, England, Egypt, Ethiopia, and more rarely in Italy. In twenty-nine individuals of both sexes and various ages, who died in Dublin of different diseases, Mr. Bellingham met with it twenty-six times; in seventeen bodies Mr. Cooper, of Greenwich, found it eleven times; and in eighty individuals who died of cholera at Naples, Dr Thibault found it in all of them. M. Davaine calculates that in Paris one person in two is attacked by it.

These worms are sometimes found in considerable numbers. As many as ninety-two were taken from the cœcum of a woman, who died from colliquative diarrhœa. (Lobstein.) Bellingham found one hundred and nineteen in one body, and Rudolphi even as many as one thousand.

The Trichocephalus inhabits the cœcum, or as far as the commencement of the colon. Werner assures us that he has obtained it from the lower part of the ilium.

Its anterior extremity is usually buried in the mucous membrane of the intestine, while the remainder of its body appears free in the midst of the mucous secretion.

The animal is very common in persons attacked with typhus fever, but it is also found in a great number of other diseases. It is moreover met with in persons who are in perfect health. Its presence does not produce any serious disturbance, unless they are present in large numbers.

The history of the *Trichinæ* has been fully cleared up by the

[1] Richard Owen, F.R.S., *Lectures on the Comparative Anatomy of the Invertebrata*, p. 94, 2nd edit., Lond. 1855.

researches of Virchow and Leuckart,[1] and there is no longer any question as to its being a distinct species of entozoon.

On feeding rabbits with food containing *Trichinæ*, Virchow[2] found that in three or four weeks the animal became thin and weak, and died in the course of five or six weeks after taking the food which contained the entozoa. When the body of such an animal is examined, the muscles are found filled with thousands of *Trichinæ*, and there is no doubt that death has been produced by the progressive atrophy of the muscular system, owing to the migrations of the *Trichinæ*.

When food containing *Trichinæ* is swallowed, the entozoa become liberated from the muscular tissue in which they are lodged in the stomach, and from thence make their way into the small intestines. On the third or fourth day sperm cells and eggs are found, and the sexes have become distinct. Soon afterwards the eggs are fecundated, and are developed in the body of the females. The young are expelled from the vaginal aperture situated on the anterior half of the worm. Virchow has found them under the form of minute *Filaria* in the mesenteric glands and in the serous cavities, particularly those of the peritoneum and the pericardium; they appear to traverse the intestinal walls, in all probability by penetrating, like the Psorospermia, the epithelial cells of the intestine. Virchow has been unable to detect them in the blood or in the course of the circulation.

As they continue their migrations they are found in the primitive muscular fasiculi, where they are met with in considerable numbers three weeks after the food has been taken, and have attained nearly the same size as those which had been enclosed in the flesh eaten by the animal.

In order to be certain that the animal was not already infested by the *Trichinæ*, Virchow, on several occasions before feeding the animal, excised and examined a portion of the muscles of the back, and was unable to find a trace of the entozoa, where they were afterwards so plentiful.

The *Trichinæ* penetrate the primitive muscular fasiculi in succession. Behind them the muscle becomes atrophied while an irritation is excited around them, and on the fifth week they commence to be encysted, the sarcolemma becomes thickened and a cyst is formed around them.

Virchow prosecuted his experiments by means of the muscles of a woman who had died in the same manner as has been

[1] Gottingen Nachrichten, April 30th, 1860, p. 135.
[2] Annales des Sciences Nat., tome xiii., serie 4me, 1860, p. 109.

mentioned with regard to the rabbits, and whose body presented no other lesion than the presence of innumerable *Trichinæ*. What is most important, is the fact that these entozoa may exist even in fatal numbers, and yet not be visible to the naked eye. This was the case with the body of the female mentioned above; it is only when the cyst is in a very advanced state of cretification that they are visible to the naked eye, and this may not take place for months after the animals are first encysted.

The patient had been under the care of Professor Zeucher, of Dresden, and had been brought from the country. On making inquiries in the locality from whence the woman had come, Professor Zeucher found that a pig had been killed containing *Trichinæ*, and that the hams and sausages which had been made from it contained a large number of these entozoa. The butcher who had killed the animal and several other persons had had rheumatic and typhoid symptoms of greater or less severity, but no other person besides Professor Zeucher's patient had died in consequence.]

CHAPTER IV.

THE ANCYLOSTOMUM.

THE genus *Ancylostomum*[1] is allied to that of Strongylus, which will be noticed in the next chapter; it is characterized by having its mouth provided with a corneous armature. This genus includes only a single species.

1. THE ANCYLOSTOMUM DUODENALE, Kuch., *Ancylostoma duodenale*, Dub., was discovered, in 1838, by Dr. Angelo Dubini, in the body of a young peasant in the hospital at Milan.

Description (fig. 108).—The body of these entozoa varies from about two and a half to rather more than four and a half lines in length; it is nearly straight or slightly curved, cylindrical, and transparent at the anterior part, yellow, reddish, or brown posteriorly, and marked in the central portion with a small dark spot, which corresponds to the commencement of the intestine.

The mouth is circular, and consists of a large horny capsule, which is obliquely truncated, and is furnished at its upper part with four strong teeth in the form of hooks, which curve towards its centre; on the inferior portion are four small conical pro-

---

[1] Ἀγκυλος curved, and στόμα mouth.

jections, which are probably organs of touch. The œsophagus is clavate, and the stomach globular, and of a dark colour.

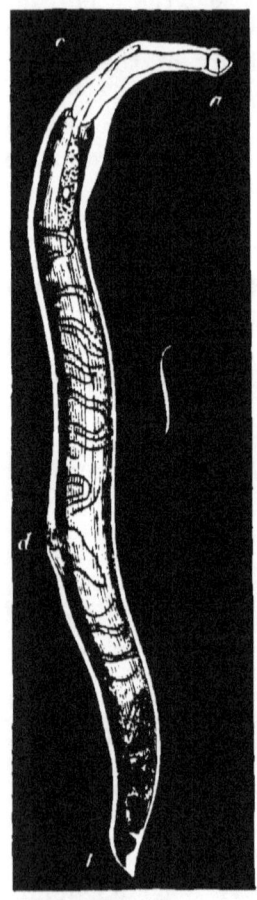

Fig. 108.
Ancylostomum Duodonale.[1]

The male is from two and a half to about four lines in length, narrowed anteriorly, and with the caudal extremity curved. At this part there is a sac with a membranous cup-like appendage, provided with eleven radiating processes, five of which are placed on either side, and one in the centre; all these processes are simple, except the central, which is bifurcated. The spiculum is long and double. The female is somewhat larger than the male, measuring from three to four and a half lines in length. One male is found to three females.

M. Dubini once found a pair *in coitu*; the male was firmly attached by means of his caudal membrane around the vulva of the female.

2. ACTION ON MAN.—Since his first discovery of the *Ancylostomum*, Dr. Dubini has met with it twenty times in one hundred bodies. MM. Pruner, Bilharz, and Griesinger, found it at Cairo, in Egypt, and M. Eschricht met with it in Iceland.

The *Ancylostomum* inhabits the duodenum and the commencement of the jejunum. The number of individuals is sometimes very considerable.

The worm is firmly attached to the mucous membrane by means of its hooks. Where it fixes itself there is a slight echymosis about the size of a lentil, in the centre of which is a white spot perforated in the middle. It is said that these entozoa sometimes give rise to intestinal hæmorrhages. M. Dubini believes that when numerous they may destroy the patient.

[Upon the latter point there seems to be no doubt. Griesinger states that from the wounds formed by the worms blood often freely enters the intestines, and that such a piece of in-

[1] Female Ancylostomum. 1, natural size; 2, highly magnified; *a*, mouth; *b*, anus; *c*, common opening of the organs of excretion; *d*, vulva; the convolutions of the genital tube are seen in the interior of body.

testine may be entirely filled with blood, which has flowed out of the punctured places. One consequence of this disorder is anæmia, and the same writer concludes that the chlorosis, so generally diffused in Egypt, which he had previously described as the Egyptian chlorosis, and which in a greater or less degree attacks at least one fourth of the population, is produced by this worm.

In the milder form of the disorder, there is paleness of the general integument and mucous membrane, palpitation of the heart, quick pulse, slight bodily lassitude without emaciation, and occasionally slight disturbances of the digestion (Gastro enteritis) occur. If this condition remains uncured for a long time it passes through many intermediate steps to the higher degree of the disorder, which closes as chlorotic marasmus. The disease often lasts for years, but in many cases its progress is very acute. Even with great care the individuals remain pallid, sickly, and miserable; slight acute diseases, which make their appearance, are very serious, and at last dysentery carries off the patient. Only occasionally a patient recovers by a change of climate and all other conditions of life. Fatiguing labour and debilitating antiphlogistic treatment hasten the end. Or the patients die from diarrhœa general dropsy without albumen in the urine, &c., in spite of all the iron and wine.][1]

CHAPTER V.

STRONGYLUS.

THE genus *Strongylus*[2] was founded in 1788 by Otto Frederick Müller in his *Zoologia Danica*.

The characters of the *Strongyli* are as follows: The body elongated, cylindrical, and attenuated posteriorly; the mouth has six tubercles; the tail is simple in the female, but in the male it terminates in a cup, in the centre of which is the double penis.

Lamark considers these animals as the most highly organized of the entozoa.

The type of the genus was the species which is found in the horse, the *Strongylus equinus* of Müller, or *Strongylus armatus* of Rudolphi.

[1] [Küchenmeister, *Opus cit*, vol. i. pp. 386-387.]
[2] Στρογγύλος, cylindrical.

1. THE STRONGYLUS OF THE KIDNEY, *Strongylus renalis*, *Strongylus gigas*, Rud., *Eustrongylus gigas*, Dies., has been long known. Gmelin regarded it as an *Ascaris*, and made two species of it. Rudolphi recognized that the parasite belonged to the genus *Strongylus* of Müller.

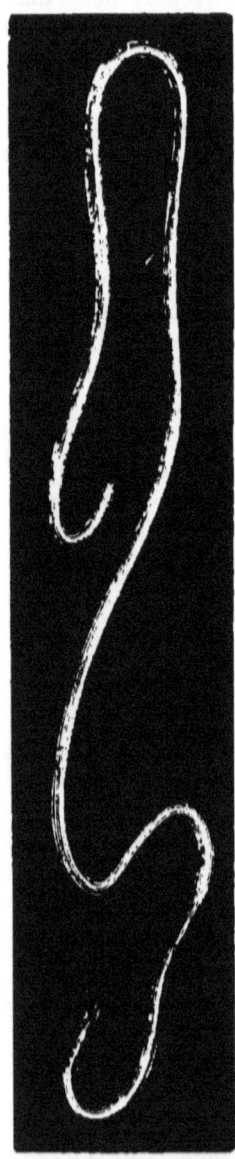

Fig. 109.—*Strongylus.*

Description.—*Strongylus renalis* (fig. 109) varies in length from six to thirty-two inches; it is said that it may even attain to the length of six feet; its thickness is equal to that of a large quill, occasionally it is equal to the diameter of the little finger. Cuvier considered it was the most voluminous of all the intestinal worms. It is, in fact, the giant of the cylindrical entozoa. Bremser speaks of a *Strongylus* from the martin which was thirty-two inches in length; this was probably a different species. But if the kidneys of this small mammal could sustain a worm of such a size, there would be nothing surprising in finding one three feet long in the human subject.

[A worm one foot eight inches in length, occupying the entire capsule of the left kidney, whose parenchyma was entirely destroyed by it, is in the Museum of the Royal College of Surgeons (No. 177a).]

The body of the *Strongylus renalis* is cylindrical, and only very slightly attenuated at the two extremities; the surface is smooth, and obscurely annulated. Bremser was not able to perceive the rings. When alive it is of a reddish hue, either of a rose tint or of a more or less intense brick red colour. Some are of a blood red colour, but this tint is soon lost when the animal is placed in spirits of wine.

The *Strongylus renalis* has no cephalic enlargement. The anterior extremity (fig. 110, *a*) is obtuse, and, as it were, truncated. The mouth is placed in its centre; it is circular, and surrounded by six tubercles.

The alimentary canal is straight, and more or less striated transversely. Numerous filaments connect it to the subcuta-

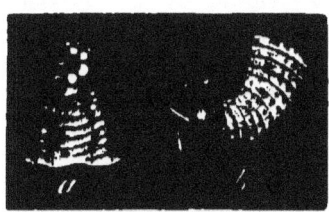

Fig. 110.—*Strongylus*.[1]

neous muscular layer. The anus is situated at the extremity of the tail.

The nervous system consists of a single nerve, of a dead white colour, passing along the ventral surface from the anterior to the posterior extremity; it is provided with a series of ganglions, from which a number of nervous filaments are distributed to the neighbouring parts.

The *Strongylus renalis* is unisexual. The males (fig. 109) are smaller than the females. The dilated portions of their caudal extremity (fig. 110, *b*) has the form of a sucker, with a smooth even margin; in the centre is a projecting vesicle, from which a long double filiform penis emerges in the shape of two rigid and pointed threads.

The female has no caudal dilatation; the tail is simply obtuse and slightly curved; the genital orifice is placed in front of the centre of the body; the ovary is single, and has the form of a tube of considerable length; it is estimated to be three or four times as long as the body.

[It commences by an obtuse blind extremity close to the anal extremity of the body, and is firmly attached to the termination of the intestine; it passes first in a straight line to the anterior extremity of the body, and when arrived within a short distance from the vulva is again attached to the parietes of the body, and makes a sudden turn backwards; it then forms two long loops about the middle of the body and returns again forwards, suddenly dilating into a uterus, which is three inches in length, and from the anterior extremity of which a slender cylindrical tube or vagina, about an inch in length, is continued, which, after forming a small convolution, terminates in the vulva at the distance of two inches from the anterior extremity of the body.][2]

This species has not been seen in coitu, but in a neighbouring species the sucker of the male was firmly applied against the female, and the two animals adhered strongly together.

SECOND SPECIES.—M. Diesing has described another species, under the name of *Strongylus longevaginatus*.

[1] *a*, cephalic extremity, showing the six tubercles; *b*, caudal extremity of the male with its pouch and the principal spiculum or penis.
[2] Richard Owen, *opus cit*, p. 108; and Art. Entozoa, Cyclopedia of Anatomy and Physiology, vol. ii. 1837.

This was found in 1845, in Transylvania, by Dr. Jovistis. The body is nearly even throughout its length, straight, and of a brownish white colour. The cephalic extremity is conical and truncated. The mouth is provided with six papillæ.

The male is from $\frac{2}{10}$ to $\frac{3}{10}$ of an inch in length, and $\frac{1}{25}$ of an inch in breadth; it is slightly attenuated anteriorly; the tail is bent, and is provided with a subcampanulated bilobed pouch, each lobe consisting of three rays. There is only one filiform penis; its sheath is composed of two long slender pieces with fine transverse striæ, and is of an orange colour.

The female is two inches in length, and $\frac{1}{25}$ of an inch in thickness; it is attenuated anteriorly and posteriorly. The genital orifice is placed beneath the end of the tail.

The *Strongylus longevaginatus* is ovoviviparous.

The distinction between this species and the *Strongylus renalis* is very marked, so that M. Diesing has no hesitation in making these worms the types of two distinct genera. The first, *Eustrongylus*, contains the *Strongylus renalis;* the second, *Strongylus*, applies to the *Strongylus longevaginatus*. The two genera are principally distinguished by the evenness of the male pouch and its having a double penis in the first, while it is bilobed and has only a single penis contained in a divided sheath in the second.

3. ACTION ON MAN.—The *Strongylus renalis*, as its name implies, is found in the kidney. It is also found in the cellular tissue surrounding the kidney, and possibly in the midst of the neighbouring muscles.

It is sometimes discharged with the urine, but that only happens with the young worm. Bremser has figured some small filiform worms, $\frac{4}{5}$ of an inch in length, which had been expelled with the urine. He supposes, with reason, that they were imperfectly developed *Strongyli*.

Dr. Artaud had a female under his care who discharged eleven of these worms through the urethra, and yet she continued to live.

The *Strongylus* of which he speaks often shows itself only in one kidney, the other remaining uninjured. It enlarges, becomes folded upon itself, causes the organ to swell and to become inflamed; it gradually destroys its substance and paralyses its functions, giving rise to the most frightful sufferings.

Strongylus longevaginatus was met with in the lung of a child six years old, in whom there were several, some free, others adherent to the substance of the lung.

CHAPTER VI.

SPIROPTERA.

The genus *Spiroptera* established by Rudolphi is principally characterised by the tail of the male being twisted into a spiral form, and furnished with marginal appendages, between which the penis emerges.

This genus comprises a large number of species which live in the bodies of the mammalia and of birds, and some few in those of fishes. M. Diesing enumerates fifty-eight species; only one of these has been found in man.

1. SPIROPTERA HOMINIS.—This worm was discovered by Dr. Barnett, of London. Rudolphi gave it the name of *Spiroptera Hominis*, which has been adopted by MM. Dujardin and Diesing.

Description.—The *Spiroptera* is from eight to ten lines in length; the body is narrow, cylindrical, and attenuated at both extremities. The head is truncated, and provided with one or two papillæ. The tail in the male is provided on either side with a delicate membranous aliform expansion, between which is the spiculum, in the form of a pointed appendage; the tail of the female is thicker, and has a short obtuse apex.

The two sexes differ in length, the male being the smallest; it is about eight lines in length, while the female is as much as ten.

This entozoon is still imperfectly known. Dr. Brighton discovered a similar but larger animal in South America. M. Diesing regards it as a variety of Dr. Barnett's entozoon.

ACTION ON MAN.—The *Spiroptera* was discharged from the bladder of a female twenty-four years of age, who had been troubled for some time with retention of urine. Dr. Lanza and Lucarelli have since found this worm in the urine of another female.

The larger variety from South America was discovered in the bladder of a female aged thirty-five.

CHAPTER VII.

FILARIA.

1. HISTORY.—The *Filaria Medinensis* has been known from the earliest times. The first person who appears to have mentioned it is Agartharchides, an historian and philosopher, born at Cnidus, and who lived between 140 and 150 years, B.C., at the time of Ptolemus Alexander.

Plutarch speaks of this entozoon in his *Table Talk*, where he says, " The people who live near the Red Sea are tormented by an extraordinary and hitherto unheard-of disease. Small worms issue from their bodies in the form of serpents, which gnaw their arms and legs; when these creatures are touched they withdraw themselves, and insinuating themselves between the muscles give rise to horrible sufferings."

Many medical men, who have not had the opportunity of examining the *Filaria medinensis* for themselves, and are only acquainted with it through the imperfect descriptions of the older writers, have put forward the most extravagant statements concerning this worm. Soranus maintains that it is a *diseased nervous plexus;* Pollux says it is a *corrupted nerve;* Ambroise Paré regards it as a *tumour produced by an ebullition of the blood;* Gui de Chauliac sees in it a *thickening of a vein;* Fragantius, a portion of *black bile;* Richerand, a *fibrous concretion;* J. D. Larrey, a *quantity of atrophied cellular tissue.*

In 1752, Henri Gallandat gave some correct ideas concerning this worm; in 1830, Dr. Brulatour; in 1844, Dr. Maissonneuve; in 1858, Dr. Cezilly; and recently, Dr. Thibaut and Dr. Benoit published minute details on the same subject. Linnæus placed this Helmintha in his genus *Gordius*.

Muller having proposed the genus *Filaria*[1] for the reception of certain entozoa, the present worm has since been arranged in that group.

The *Filaria Medinensis*, or *Dracunculus*,[2] occurs in Arabia Petra, Senegal, Congo, on the coasts of Angola, in India, and America. It is exceedingly rare in Europe, and when it does occur it has been imported from one of the countries of which it is a native.

2. DESCRIPTION.—The *Filaria medinensis* has a very simple organization. The animal varies much in length; some have been mentioned which were not more than $4\frac{1}{2}$ inches long, while Dr. Giutrac, of Bordeaux, received one from the Havannah which measured $19\frac{1}{2}$ inches. Heath states that out of seventy-four cases the smallest had this length, while the longest

[1] *Filum*, a thread, or *filarium*, a ball of thread.
[2] *Filaria Medinensis*, Gmel. (*Gordius Medinensis*, Linn., *Filaria Dracunculus*, Brems.), commonly *Worm of Medina, Guinea Worm, Worm of Senegal, Cutaneous Worm*. It was the Δρακοντιον of the Greeks, a name which the Romans translated by the word *Dracunculus*, and the French by *Dragonneau*. Amatus Lusitanus named it *Vene mitena;* Sloane, *Vena Medini;* and Kampfer, *Dracunculus Persarum*. It is called in Senegal, *Soungouf;* in Arabia, *Farentit;* in Persia, *Pejunck;* in India, *Narambo* and *Narampoo-Chalandy*.

measured 8 feet. Some writers have recorded the existence of Filaria which had attained the length of from 9½ to 16 and even 30 feet. The latter measurements are evidently exaggerated.

The body of this entozoon is slender, cylindrical, and somewhat compressed; it resembles the string of a violin. It is of the same thickness throughout its whole length, except at the posterior extremity, where it is somewhat attenuated. It is of an opaque milk-white colour, but becomes yellow when placed in alcohol. (Rudolphi.) On each side there is a longitudinal, greyish, semi-transparent line the $\frac{1}{50}$ of an inch in diameter. (Maisonneuve.)

When examined by the microscope, the body of the animal is seen to be marked by numerous transverse lines.

The anterior or cephalic extremity terminates in a bluntish point having the form of a sucker. Kampfer describes this sucker as a *proboscis;* he says that the Persians call it the *beard*, and that when it is examined by the microscope it appears to be formed of hairs. According to Fermin, Hemersand, and Lachmund, the oral extremity supports two filaments which these writers regard as hairs or *antennæ*. Bremser observes that these pretended filaments probably arise from some injury to the animal. May they not have mistaken the tail for the head, and the double penis for two antennæ? Adanson states that the mouth of the Filaria is provided with two obtuse points. M. Diesing describes this orifice as circular, and furnished with *four spinules arranged crosswise.* M. Maisonneuve declares that there are neither beard, points, or hooks. In the young animals (fig. 111, *a*) which M. Tandon examined while alive with M. Ch. Robin, the mouth did not offer any kind of appendage, but was provided with three small rounded nodules.

The tail is short, obtuse, and always curved. The transverse markings are very distinct, especially on the concave side.

According to Dr. Maisonneuve the body may be compared to a tube with thickish walls (about $\frac{7}{100}$ of an inch), consisting of two membranes, the external hard and coriaceous, the internal thin, and readily separating into very delicate longitudinal filaments, but not easily torn in the transverse direction,

In the interior of the body there is no canal or any distinct tube, but a whitish pulpy substance, which will be spoken of presently.

Analogy would lead to the notion that this creature is organised with respect to its digestive organs in the same manner as all the internal worms, especially those which are allied to it. On examining with M. Ch. Robin, young individuals taken from the body of the parent while they were still alive, M. Tandon satisfied himself of the correctness of this supposition. He distinctly saw the alimentary canal commencing at the mouth, and passing without any convolutions to the anal orifice placed at the commencement of the tail. This canal consists of a narrow œsophagus, occupying half the length of the body. The œsophagus terminates in a canal of double its size, representing the stomach and intestines; this is slightly contracted posteriorly, and terminates in a pointed conical cul de sac, which opens at the base of the tail. When the *Filaria* contracts itself, the alimentary canal is seen to be unadherent to the cutaneous envelope; its walls are thinner than those of the œsophagus; the anus is transverse, and surrounded by a projecting contractile lip.

Dr. Dariste and Doumeing have witnessed very distinct vermicular movements in the *Filaria*.

Patients are said to feel the movements of the animal, which cause them considerable pain. M. Malgaigne has noticed that if the animal is drawn out and becomes broken off, that it suddenly retracts itself within the limb. He therefore observes that in order to extract the animal without difficulty it must be killed by means of some application.

The *Filaria medinensis* is ovoviviparous and very prolific. (Jacobson, Robin.)

When the body of an adult specimen is opened it is seen to contain the pulpy matter which has already been referred to; this substance, when examined by the microscope, presents, according to M. Guitrar, a multitude of transparent elongated depressed bodies, partly folded upon themselves, and which this gentleman regards as *small unbranched vessels*. M. Jacobson has seen these transparent bodies moving rapidly about, and has recognised in them a prodigious number of small active worms. MM. Mac Clelland, Ch. Robin, and Benoit, have confirmed this view of them. It appears that after the *Filaria* has been fecundated, that the excessive development of the generative organs, the exclusion of the eggs, and the growth of young, ultimately obliterate the alimentary canal, already singularly contracted in so slender an animal, and that the individual henceforth becomes converted into a thread-like sac filled with diminutive worms.

When examined in the interior of the mother, the young (fig. 111, *A*) are rolled up sometimes with the tail projecting, and at other times coiled up. The body (fig. 111, *B*) is not cylindrical, but flattened. Just before the period of birth the body is the $\frac{5}{1000}$ of an inch in length, and the $\frac{1}{1000}$ in diameter. Its anterior extremity is somewhat narrowed, and terminates in a mouth provided with three tubercles (fig. 111, *a*). The anus (fig. 111, *B* and *b*) is situated about the posterior fourth of the body, where there is a slight enlargement. From this part the body suddenly contracts, and forms a very slender and very pointed tail. The tail is $\frac{1}{1000}$ of an inch in length, not curved, somewhat rigid, but capable of being bent in every direction; there is a marked difference between it and that of the adult animal; it bends abruptly opposite the anus after death. The surface of the body is finely ridged over the whole of its surface. These traces of segmentation are situated at regular distances from each other.

The young worms will live for some days in water at the ordinary temperature. (Jacobson, Maissonneuve.) They move about in it with great rapidity. They may be left in a drop of water until it dries up so as to deprive them of motion, and they will subsequently recover their activity upon the addition of fresh water, six or twelve hours after their desiccation. (Deville, Robin.) In order that the experiment should succeed, it is necessary that the desiccation should be incomplete: when they have been rendered absolutely dry, they do not recover their vitality.

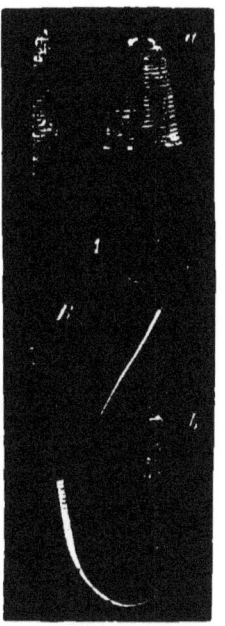

Fig. 111.—*Filaria.*[1]

3. OTHER SPECIES.—Some writers have described three other species of *Filaria* living in man. These are:—

1st. *Filaria oculi* (*F. lachrymalis* of some writers), which is not uncommon in the negroes on the Angola coast, where it is called *Loa*; it is also met with at Guadeloupe; it has been seen by Mongin at Cayenne, and by Blot at Martinique.

This entozoon is from 1 inch and $\frac{4}{10}$ to 1 inch and $\frac{9}{10}$ in length, filiform, slender, pointed at one end, and obtuse at the other; it is tolerably firm, and of a white or yellowish colour.

---

[1] Young *Filaria Medinensis.*—*A*, individual coiled up, as seen in the body of its parent; *B*, the same uncoiled in a drop of water; *a*, the head, with its three nodules and the mouth; *b*, the commencement of the tail and the anus.

M. Guyon approximates this animal to the *Strongylus;* others consider it is a young *Filaria medinensis.*

2. The *Filaria lentis,* Dies. (*F. oculi humani,* Nordm.), noticed by M. Nordmann, in 1831.

This species is from $\frac{3}{10}$ to $\frac{6}{10}$ of an inch in length, and the $\frac{1}{500}$ in width. The body is filiform, thickened posteriorly, and provided with a pointed tail; it is transparent and partly coiled up in a spiral form.

The alimentary canal may be seen through the integument, and is surrounded by the folds of the oviduct.

This animal is very imperfectly known; only the female has been seen.

Is this species to be considered as really distinct from the preceding?

3. *Filaria lymphatica* (*Hamularia lymphatica,* Treutl., *Tentacularia subcompressa,* Zeder, *Trichosoma subcompressa,* Rüd., *Filaria bronchialis,* Dies.). This species was discovered in 1790, by Treutler, who formed a new genus for its reception, under the name of *Hamularia,* characterized by the presence of two *filamentary tentacula* or oral hooks. Further observations have shown that in this case the tail was mistaken for the head, and the double male organ for appendages belonging to the mouth; the new genus was therefore suppressed and the worm transferred to the *Filaria.*

This worm is from $\frac{19}{25}$ to $\frac{17}{25}$ of an inch in length; it is cylindrical, filiform, slightly narrowed anteriorly, somewhat compressed at the sides, semi-transparent posteriorly, and of a blackish-brown colour with white spots. After it is dead the extremities are somewhat curved.

The male possesses a double penis, which resembles a pair of slightly curved pointed hooklets.

According to M. Weinland this species does not differ from the *Strongylus longevaginatus.*

4. ACTION ON MAN.—The negroes are often tormented with the *Filaria Medinensis;* and Europeans who visit India are equally liable to its attacks. M'Gregor relates that an English regiment arrived at Bombay in the month of September, 1789; at that time not one of these men was attacked by the worms, but at the period of the monsoons 300 soldiers were ill with it. It has already been stated, that where the worm has been met with in Europe, the individuals had always come from the countries inhabited by the worm. Dr. Brulator met with two cases at Bordeaux; both the patients had come from Bombay: the same was the case with a patient of Dr. Thibaut; Dr.

Maisonneuve noticed it in an old soldier who had resided at Senegal; Professor Malgaigne in a sailor under similar circumstances. Kæmpfer has recorded the case of a man who was attacked with the worm long after he had returned from the coast of Africa, and who, up to that time, had never had the slightest symptom of the complaint.

The *Filaria Medinensis* lodges beneath the skin in the cellular tissue, and sometimes between the muscles. It most frequently selects some part of the lower extremities, such as the foot or leg, and works its way upwards towards the thigh. Kæmpfer extracted two of these worms from the scrotum. Baillie has seen it in the testicle. The worm is also found, but more rarely, in the arm, elbow, neck, or even the head. Carter noticed it in the chin of a woman. M. Clot-bey met with it in the frenum of the tongue. In one of the plates belonging to the *Voyage aux Indes orientales* of Jean Hugens (Theodore de Bry's edition) is the representation of an Indian having a *Filaria* extracted from the leg by winding it round a stick, and another in whom it is being removed from the eye[1] by the same means. According to Dr. Cezilly, in Senegal, the *Filaria* is frequently developed in the parietes of the chest, principally upon the ribs. He once saw it in the mammary gland.

Are we to admit, with Nysander, that the *Guinea worm* can introduce itself into the bones?

Out of 181 cases published by M'Gregor, the worm occurred 134 times in the feet, 33 times in the legs, 11 times in the thighs, 2 in the scrotum, and once in the hand.

The worm has never been found in the visceral cavities.

The *Filaria Medinensis* sometimes occurs singly, while at other times there are several of them. Heath noticed that out of 74 patients several had as many as two, three, four, or even five. Bosmann says they may amount to as many as nine or ten. Arthus mentions a case in which there were twelve. Chapotin treated a patient who had thirteen. Andry cites a case of twenty-three. Hemersand saw thirty in the cook of a vessel. Pouppeé-Desportes mentions a case in which he counted fifty.

The *Guinea worm* having gained an entrance into the body, takes a long time to become developed. This period varies from two months to a year or more. M. Maisonneuve mentions an incubation of six months; M. Ficipio one of eight; M. Thibaut another of eight and a half; MM. Labat and

---

[1] Is this the same, or is it not rather the *Filaria oculis* or *F. lentis?*

Bernier mentions a case in which this period extended over fifteen months; and M. Cezilly has recorded cases in which two, nine, ten, fifteen, and sixteen months elapsed. Kæmpfer speaks of a case in which two years had passed by.

The presence of the *Filaria* is announced by a sensation of itching in the part; at first this is slight, but it gradually increases until it becomes quite unbearable. The part affected resembles a varicose vein, and can be moved under the skin. This kind of subcutaneous knot gradually extends, and the pain becomes excruciating. For the greater part of the time there is no derangement of the general health, but sometimes there are shiverings alternating with attacks of heat. At other times there is fever and a feeling of anxiety. A small abscess forms, which is often pointed, and terminated by a vesicle or by a black point surrounded by a brownish areola. When it opens a kind of serous liquid, or sometimes a small quantity of pus, comes out, and occasionally a white slender thread. The tumour may be transformed into a diffuse inflammation, but this seldom happens.

Is the presence of the *Filaria* ever fatal? The cases which have been mentioned are rare, and, at the same time, inconclusive. Gallandat mentions the case of a negro who was attacked in the scrotum, and Clarke of a child who had *Filariæ* in the right thigh and foot. Both these cases are imperfect, and it does not appear that death was caused by the worms. (Cezilly.)

The *Filaria oculis* resides in the lachrymal gland and in the globe of the eye. In 1768, Bajon extracted one of these worms from the eye of a young negress about six or seven years of age. Dr. Guyon extracted another from the eye of a negress in Guinea.

The worm is seen winding about and moving around the globe of the eye, in the cellular tissue which unites the conjunctiva with the sclerotic. Sometimes its presence does not occasion any disagreeable sensation (Bajon); while at other times it causes very acute pain (Mongin). Occasionally it is accompanied by a constant watering of the eye.

The *Filaria of the crystalline lens*, as its name implies, is found in that part of the eye. It was found for the first time by M. Græfe, after an operation for cataract in the liquor of Morgagni. M. Normann detected two *Filariæ* coiled up together, by means of the microscope, half an hour after the operation. The following year the same observer met with another *Filaria* in a crystalline lens which had become opaque, and had been extracted by professor Jüngken. Lastly,

M. Gescheidt, of Dresden, obtained it from the crystalline lens of a man sixty-one years of age, who had been operated on by Professor Ammon; there were three specimens of the worm, of which one was coiled up in a spiral form.

The *Filaria lymphatica* occurs in the bronchial glands. It was found in the body of a man aged twenty-eight, who died from phthisis, brought on by onanism, venereal excesses, and mercurial medicines.

5. GENERAL REMARKS.—How do the *Filariæ* introduce themselves into the human body?

Valmont de Bomare pretends that the *Guinea worm* is produced by an insect which introduces its eggs beneath the skin. Dr. Chisalm also supposes that this *Filaria* is introduced in the form of an egg. It has been shown that this animal is ovoviviparous.

MM. Maisonneuve and Deville, when examining a furunculous tumour produced by a *Filaria*, found in some a whitish looking fluid which came from thousands of small living worms, precisely resembling those which have been previously described. The young *Filariæ* are therefore deposited in the part inhabited by their parents; there they become developed, and thus render the disease more dangerous and more prolonged.

But from whence do these worms come, and how do they gain access to the individual in whom they appear for the first time?

The resemblance of the *Guinea worm* to the *Gordius aquaticus* or hair worm of our ponds and rivers led Meyer to suppose that the entozoon was the latter animal which had penetrated the cellular tissue. This opinion has been recently revived by Dr. Cezilly. Linnæus had, however, already distinctly defined the two species, although he placed them in the same genus.

This illustrious naturalist nevertheless supposed that the *Filaria* normally lived *out of man's body* in the morning dew, and that it introduced itself parasitically into the naked legs of the slaves.[1] This explanation is rendered extremely probable from what we know of the habits of the *Gordius aquaticus*, of several other species, and of the *Mermis*, which constitutes a closely allied genus. It is well known that these animals are *erratic* worms which reside in water or moist earth, that they afterwards introduce themselves into the body of an insect, where they undergo a certain amount of development, that they then emerge from the body of their victim, copulate, and

[1] This is also the opinion of Joerdens, Chapotin, Leath, Ilcat, Oken, &c.

return into the water or into moist earth [where they deposit their eggs].

Dr. Carter believes that the *Guinea worm* is an inhabitant of marshes, and that it enters the body by penetrating the skin. He relates the case of a school at Bombay, of which the pupils went to bathe in a pond in the neighbourhood: out of fifty children twenty-one were attacked by the *Guinea worm*; some of them had as many as four or five. In confirmation of this view may be adduced the case of the negroes, who, being in the habit of entering the water more frequently than the whites, and generally having their feet naked, are far more subject to the attacks of the worm than Europeans.

It is difficult to explain how the young worms can penetrate the skin, since they have neither jaws, mandibles, or osseous pieces attached to the mouth. Some have supposed that the *Guinea* worm is taken into the body with the drink.[1] The larvæ are swallowed when the brackish waters of certain rivers are drank. Dr. Cezilly rejects this explanation on account of the absence of the worm in the visceral cavities, and because of their being constantly found in the subcutaneous cellular tissue; there are, however, other worms which enter the body by means of the digestive organs, but which do not reside in them.

CHAPTER VIII.

THECOSOMA.

THE existence of entozoa in the blood was long doubted, but in the present day it can no longer be questioned. These worms are even somewhat numerous, when considered in relation to the entire animal series. They are found both in the warm-blooded and cold-blooded animals,[2] and belong to genera which differ essentially from each other. These parasites are collectively termed the *Hæmatozoa*, or *Sanguicola*.[3]

Amongst these parasites, the genus which forms the subject of the present chapter is one of the most curious. The animal which is the type of it was found in Egypt in 1851, by Dr. Bilharz, who regarded it as a species of *Distoma*. M. Weinland has formed a special genus of it, founded principally upon its unisexual character, and on the extraordinary difference which

---

[1] Burckhardt, Bilharz.
[2] They have been seen in the dog, rat, field mouse, horse, dolphin, seal, crow, rook, heron, lizard, frog, pike, tench, gudgeon, &c.
[3] Under this term are included the Helmintha and Infusoria.

exists between the male and the female. He gave the new genus the name of *Schistozoma*, a term which had been previously applied by Geof. St.-Hilaire to a particular form of monster. M. Tandon therefore proposed for it the name of *Thecosoma*.[1]

1. THECOSOMA HÆMATOBIUM, *Distoma hæmatobium*, Bilh.— Dr. Bilharz first discovered the male of this curious species, and three months afterwards the female. The two sexes are so dissimilar, both as regards size and form, that they may easily be regarded as two distinct animals. The male carries the female in a kind of canal under its belly.

Description.—The male *Thecosoma* is from $\frac{2}{10}$ to $\frac{3}{10}$ of an inch in length. It is soft, smooth, and of a white colour; the anterior part (trunk) is depressed, and lancet-shaped; it is somewhat convex above, and plane or concave below; the posterior part (tail) is round and eight or nine times longer than the trunk. In front of the cephalic portion is a kind of cup, placed somewhat inferiorly, and of a triangular form. Beneath the body is another cup, of the same size as the preceding, but of a circular form. These two cups are covered with fine granules. The alimentary canal appears to be divided into two portions.

Commencing from the vicinity of the cup, on the under surface of the abdomen, is a longitudinal groove, in which the female is lodged, like a sword in its sheath; the cephalic portion is placed anteriorly, and the tail posteriorly, the latter being free.

The genital pore of the male is situated between the groove and the tail.

The female is much smaller than the male, especially with regard to its thickness, it being very slender, and somewhat transparent. The body is flattened, and does not consist of two distinct portions, like that of the male; its tail has no groove.

M. Tandon believes that the sexes have been mistaken, and that it is the female which is the largest, and carries the male on the under surface of her abdomen. The presence of the two cups, or depressions, indicates its alliance with the genus Distoma.

2. ACTION ON MAN.—The *Thecosoma* inhabits the vena portæ, and the mesenteric, hepatic, and intestinal veins. The worm is by no means uncommon, since out of 363 autopsies, Dr. Griesinger met with it 117 times. It occurs most frequently from June to August, and is scarcest from September to January.

[1] Θηκή a case, and σῶμα a body.

CHAPTER IX.

● FLUKES.

EVERY medical man is familiar with the name of the *liver Fluke*, but few have had the opportunity of seeing it.

Linnæus at first regarded the *Fluke* as a *Slug*, while Goeze considered it to be a *Planaria*. In the *Systema Naturæ* the great Swedish naturalist created the genus *Fasciola*[1] for the reception of this entozoon and two other parasites, which are found in fish and in the calamary. He, however, confounded the human *Fluke* with that of animals. Clericus and Dœveren showed that the human *Fluke* was different to that of the mammalia. Gmelin adopted this separation. Subsequently Retz (1786) and Zeder (1800) needlessly changed the name of Fasciola for that of Distoma.[2]

1. LIVER FLUKE [*Distoma hepaticum*], *Fasciola hepatica*, Linn.,[3]—is found in France. According to Moulin it is not uncommon in Holland, Sweden, Norway, and even in Greenland.

Description (fig. 112).—The *liver Fluke* is from $\frac{8}{10}$ to $\frac{11}{10}$ of an inch in length, rarely exceeding the latter measurement; its breadth varies from $\frac{2}{10}$ to $\frac{3}{10}$ of an inch. The body is flat, oval, and somewhat oblong, more contracted anteriorly than posteriorly, and obtuse at its terminations; the margins of the body are exceedingly narrow. Linnæus compares the animal to a pumpkin seed, Bremser to the blade of a lancet, and Cuvier to a small leaf. It is of a soft consistence, and of a greyish livid brown colour. The body is capable of contracting and extending itself either partially or in its entire length, much after the manner of a leech, but with greater energy and regularity.

Fig. 112.—*Fluke*.

The anterior part of the *Fluke* is contracted, and forms a kind of cylindrical neck, which is paler than the rest of its body,

---

[1] *Fasciola*, a band.
[2] This denomination is, moreover, incorrect, for these worms have not *two* mouths. F. Muller (1787) very properly restored the Linnæan name.
[3] *Fasciola hominis*, Gmel., *Distoma hepatica*, Retz., D. *hepaticum*, Abilg. [It is the *Distoma hepaticum* of English authors, a name which has also been retained by Kuchenmeister in his *Manual of Animal and Vegetable Parasites*].

and often of a yellowish white colour. At the anterior extremity is a cup-like depression (*acetabulum*), directed obliquely downwards, and having a somewhat triangular form. Within this depression is the oral aperture. Towards the anterior third of the ventral surface, is another depression (fig. 112, *a*), whose position varies somewhat; several writers have supposed that this was also perforated. According to some it was a second sucker, while others considered it was either the anus, or the aperture of the female organs. Linnæus described the two cups as *pores;* this opinion has been adopted by those helminthologists who either proposed or accepted the inappropriate term of *Distoma*. Observation has shown that the second depression is not furnished with any opening, but is a shallow sub-triangular sucker, by means of which the animal attaches itself.

Somewhat further back are some white opaque spots, and a fasciculus of vessels or tubes of a brown colour.

The body of the *Distoma* has no visceral cavity; it is a small parenchymatous mass, without any apparent muscular fibres, and is covered with a fine closely adherent skin.

From the oral sucker an œsophagus passes off, which soon divides into two slender branches, which descend on either side of the abdominal cup. These branches approach each other, and communicate by a system of transverse vessels, and are then continued to the posterior extremity of the body. In their course the canals give off a number of branches from their exterior, which subdivide and terminate near the margins of the animal; these branches are placed at an equal distance from the two surfaces of the body, and, what is remarkable, the terminal divisions are of nearly the same diameter as those which are first given off. Deslongchamps regarded the whole of this apparatus as a *ramified intestine;* it is rather a branching stomach, analogous to that of the small leeches, which are parasitic upon the mollusca. There are as many branches as there are subdivisions, and an extremely delicate network of minute vessels are sent off, which ramify principally over the dorsal surface of the animal. These minute vessels communicate in the manner of veins, and give rise to a number of transverse branches, which communicate with a longitudinal vessel situated in the median line. The latter, which is of a large size, is regarded as an urinary apparatus; it commences opposite the abdominal sucker, passes beneath the skin, and enlarges in its course to the posterior extremity of the body, where it terminates in an open orifice.

The bile forms the exclusive nourishment of the *Distoma*.

This entozoon is androgynous; MM. Mehlis and Blanchard have well described its double genital apparatus. A little in front of the abdominal sucker is a small elongated appendage (fig. 112, *a*), twisted once or once and a half times upon itself, and capable of being retracted; this is the penis, which has been mistaken by some naturalists for a tentacle or cirrhus. Its base communicates with a pouch, which serves it as a case when it is retracted (*receptacle of the cirrhus*, Rudolphi). Passing backwards from the pouch is a straight canal, placed near the middle of the animal, which terminates in an oval seminal vesicle, filled with a white semifluid humour. A seminal duct, which is common to all the branches, secreting the white fluid, terminates at the posterior part of the vesicle. To the right and left of the vesicle there are also some after branches belonging to the testicle. More externally are two long canals communicating with the sheath of the penis; these are probably deferent canals or accessory ducts of the testicles. Except at the period of reproduction, only a small opening is seen at the part which is occupied by the penis.

The opening of the female organs is close to, and behind the base of, the male organ. According to Deslongchamps, it is difficult to perceive the opening, especially in the adult. The vulva communicates with an oviduct, which is at first situated in the median line, is slender and tortuous, but afterwards increases in thickness, becomes twisted, and forms several enlargements, which pass from right to left; it then again becomes slender, and placed in the median line, and reaches an oval cavity, which is possibly the uterus; from behind this there passes off to the right and to the left two slender horizontal canals; these soon divide into two portions, one of which passes forwards, and the other backwards, parallel to the margin of the animal. These canals give off a great number of branches externally, and represent the ovaries.

The *Distoma* is oviparous; its eggs (fig. 112, *b*) are extremely small, elliptical, and semitransparent. At one end there is a kind of oblique lid.

The *Distoma* undergo a very curious series of transformations; but these have only been traced in those species which do not infest the human body. At birth these worms have a ciliated body, resembling that of the infusoria; in its interior another animal becomes developed, which has the form of a locomotive sac. These young sacciform larvæ (*nurses*) continue to live for a certain time. They are sexless individuals, but can nevertheless reproduce themselves by the process of *gemmation*; they

PARASITIC WORMS.

give rise to another series of beings of an oblong form, and provided with a tail (*Cercaria*). The latter introduce themselves into the bodies of other animals, where they become transformed into the fully developed *Fluke*, capable of reproducing itself by a true act of *generation*.[1]

2. OTHER SPECIES.—Four other species of *Fluke* have been detected in the human body; these are the *Distoma lanceolatum*, *Distomum ophthalmobium*, *Distoma heterophyes*, and the *Distoma Buskii*. The following are their characters, compared with those of the *Distoma hepaticum*:

Intestine { ramified . . . . 1. *Distoma hepaticum*.
{ simple, subanterior. . . . . . 2. *Distoma lanceolatum*.
Abdominal sucker { { scarcely larger than
{ subcentral, { the mouth. 3. *Distoma ophthalmobium*
{ much larger than
{ the mouth. 4. *Distoma heterophyes*.
Undescribed species . . . . 5. *Distoma Buskii*.

Distoma lanceolatum.[2]—This species was first described by MM. Bucholz and Mehlis. It is rarer than the first, with which it has been often confounded. Chabert met with it in France, in a young girl twelve years of age, from whom he expelled a large number of the worms by the use of his empyreumatic oil.

The size of this *Fluke* is smaller than that of the *Distoma hepaticum*. Its body is from the $\frac{2}{10}$ to the $\frac{4}{10}$ of an inch in length, and from $\frac{1}{25}$ to the $\frac{1}{10}$ of an inch in breadth; its form is lancet-shaped, it is very flat, tolerably transparent, and of a whitish colour. The oral sucker is proportionally larger than in the preceding species, and about the same size as the ventral sucker; they are both circular.

The intestines are straight and unbranched.

The penis has not a spiral form.

The eggs may be seen through the integuments, and are of a brown or black colour, according to their stage of development.

Distoma ophthalmobium.—M. Gescheidt, of Dresden, met with this species of *Fluke* once in Germany.

This worm is from ·009 in. to ·196 in. in length, and ·006 in. in breadth. The body is of a lanceolate oval form. The two suckers are circular; the posterior is farther from the cephalic extremity than in the other species, being nearly in the centre of the body.

---

[1] Steenstrup, Van Beneden, de Fillippi, Wagener.
[2] *Fasciola lanceolata*, Moq. Tand.

Distoma heterophyes.[1]—We are indebted to Dr. Bilharz for a knowledge of this curious species. He met with it twice in Egypt, in 1851.

This *Fluke* is about ·039 in. in length, and ·019 in. in breadth. The body is oval, somewhat more dilated at its posterior than at its anterior part, depressed, and of a reddish colour. It has a small funnel-shaped oral sucker, which opens more inferiorly than anteriorly. The ventral sucker is *twelve times* the size of the former.

In consequence of the transparency of the animal the dilated œsophagus is seen anteriorly, and in the median line the urinary canals.

The sac of the penis may be also seen, bearing a strong resemblance to one of the suckers, surrounded by seventy-two horny filaments. The testicles are placed posteriorly.

The eggs are of a red colour.

Distoma Buskii.—[In the winter of 1843, fourteen flukes were found by M. Busk in the *duodenum* of a Lascar who died in the Seaman's Hospital. There were none in the gall, bladder, or gall ducts. These flukes were much thicker and larger than those of the sheep, being from an inch and a half to near three inches in length. They resembled the *Distoma hepaticum* in shape, but were like the *Distoma lanceolatum* in structure; the double alimentary canal, as in the latter variety, being not branched, and the entire space between it towards the latter part of the body being occupied by a branched uterine tube. Two specimens of this fluke are in the Museum of King's College].[2]

3. ACTION ON MAN.—The *Liver fluke* is found in the gall bladder, the hepatic ducts, and perhaps also in the substance of the liver. The presence of these animals produces great dilatation of the biliary ducts; their internal surface becomes covered with a thick dark coloured mucous secretion. Sometimes this mucosity hardens and becomes converted into a kind of osseous matter. Fortassin mentions the case of a woman in whose liver there were more than two hundred *Flukes*. Dr. Bilharz has described a curious disease which occurs at Cairo, produced by the presence of these entozoa, consisting of fungus-like excrescences of the mucous membrane of the bladder. According to M. Siebold, a *Fluke* has been seen in a tumour on the foot by Dr. Giesker. M. Dujardin says that

---

[1] *Fasciola heterophyes*, Tand.
[2] Kuchenmeister, *opus jam cit*, vol. i. p. 437.

this species was found on one occasion by M. Duval in the vena portæ.[1]

The *Distoma lanceolatum* also inhabits the liver.

The *Distomum ophthalmobium* lives between the crystalline lens and its capsule. Gescheidt once found four of these parasites in the eye of a child five years old.

The *Distoma heterophyes* was found on two occasions in large quantities in the intestines of a boy.

The *Distoma Buskii* was found in the duodenum.

CHAPTER X.

FESTUCARIA.

THE genus *Festucaria*[2] was first established by Schrank (1788). In 1800 Zeder gave it the name of *Monostoma*,[3] which Rudolphi and other writers have adopted, although it is a more recent and less appropriate name.

The genus *Festucaria* differs from that of Distoma in the absence of the ventral sucker. In the previous chapter it was seen that this sucker had been mistaken for a mouth. Hence the reason of the name *Distoma* being applied to the Flukes, and that of *monostoma* to those parasites which were supposed to have only one mouth. In reality, both genera have but a single mouth.

1. FESTUCARIA LENTIS, *Monostomum lentis*, Nord.—This small worm, which is very imperfectly known, is the only species which has been found in man.

Description.—The *Festucaria lentis* is ·003 of an inch long. It might be mistaken for the Fasciola oculis. Its body is depressed, it has a single sucker, the mouth is anterior and terminal in its position, and there is a small anal pore towards the caudal extremity. Below and behind the oral sucker is the opening of the male genital organ, which consists of a protractile penis. Close to this is the opening of the female organs, which it is difficult to detect.

ACTION ON MAN.—All that is known about this worm is that it was discovered in Germany, by Professor Jüngken, in the crystalline lens of an old woman who had cataract. He obtained eight specimens.

---

[1] This example probably referred to the *Thecosoma hæmatobium*: see p. 369.

[2] Probably from *festuca*, a branch.

[3] Μόνος one, and στόμα a mouth.

CHAPTER XI.

TÆNIA.

Two kinds of flat worms are met with in the human body, belonging to two different genera; these are the *Tænia* and the *Bothriocephalus*. These animals have been known to medical men from the earliest times, but they have not always been distinguished from one another. In most works they have been confounded together under the name of *Solitary worm* or *Tænia*. The name of *solitary worm* was given to it from the belief, which was long entertained, that these parasites lived singly. The word *Tænia*[1] signifies a *ribbon* or *band*, and is derived from the general form of their body.

1. COMMON TÆNIA, *Tænia Solium*, Linn.—This species, which is familiarly known as the *Solitary* or *Tape worm*, is a very common entozoon. It is found in France, Italy, Holland, Germany, and England. It has also been observed in Egypt, and is so common in Abyssinia that it is only absent as it were by chance. Whenever a slave is sold he is always provided with a plentiful supply of *cousso*.

Description (fig. 113).—The body of the animal is flat and narrow, resembling a piece of tape, and is composed of segments, which are joined together at their extremities. The body is very long, but it is very difficult to determine its actual dimensions. "I believe," says Bremser, "that no one has ever yet seen an entire *Tape worm*, that is to say, provided with both its head and the whole of its tail; for it often happens that the last segments, which are usually filled with eggs, become detached, and passed off from the body with the stools before the anterior segments nearest to the head are completely developed. For this rea-

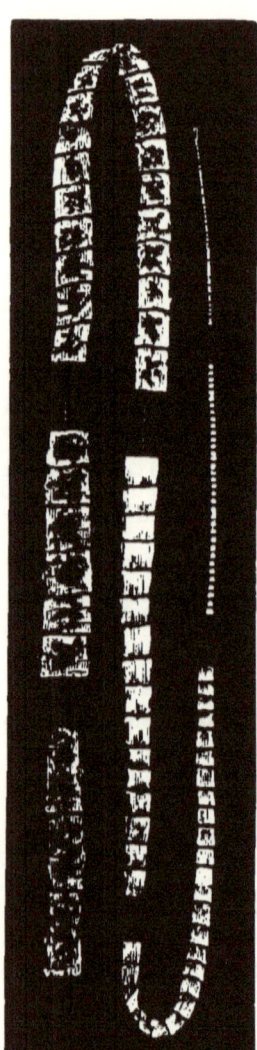

Fig. 113.
Common Tænia.

[1] Ταινία, *Tænia*.

son it is impossible to determine what is the precise length which this worm can attain if all its segments remained attached together." The *Tæniæ* which are found in dead bodies are not any the more entire. Writers have varied exceedingly as to the dimensions which they have assigned to this entozoon. Some state that they measure from 9 to 12 feet. Bremser says that specimens 25 feet in length are not uncommon. Robin found in the body of a man who, shortly before his death, had evacuated a part of a *Tænia* measuring more than three-and-twenty feet, one of these worms folded up immediately below the pylorus, one portion of it extending the whole length of the intestine to the vicinity of the anus. The animal, when it was unfolded and the portion added which had been previously discharged, measured thirty-two feet. The average length of the *Common Tænia* may be estimated at from 12 to 15 feet. M. A. Foster says its dimensions vary from 14 inches to 32 feet.

The body of the *Tænia* gradually narrows from behind forwards, until it becomes a mere thread. Thus the width of the animal varies considerably. At the anterior part it is scarcely ·025 inch in width, while towards the posterior part it is often as much as ·2 to ·4 inch. Bremser observes that when a *Tænia* is measured it is necessary to notice whether it is in a state of contraction or not, for without that precaution the measurements will not be correct. The thickness of the animal is also very variable. Some are thin, and in consequence they are almost transparent, while others are tolerably thick.

The parenchyma of this entozoon is soft, and almost white; it contains a number of microscopic calcareous granules disseminated through nearly every part of it.

According to Linnæus, the *Tænia* has no head. Its anterior extremity presents, however, a small enlargement, which usually receives that name (fig. 114). This enlargement is generally very small, and is difficult to distinguish with the naked eye. Bremser only met with one individual which had a large and very apparent head. But even what Bremser terms large, did not measure more than ·078 of an inch; in

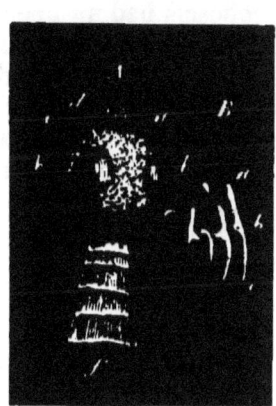

Fig. 114.—*Head*.[1]

[1] *A*, head; *a*, anterior part, somewhat attenuated; *b b*, oscula; *c*, double crown of tusks; *d*, proboscis; *e*, commencement of neck; *f*, first articulations; *B*, hooks; *a*, haft; *b*, guard; *c*, claw.

general the head is not more than ·039 or ·058 of an inch in diameter. The form of the head varies, but it is always more or less globular; occasionally it is ovoid; it is provided with four circular projections, placed at equal distances from one another, and arranged in a crucial form. In the living animal each projection has a circular disk (*oscula*) in its centre, surrounded by a rim of denser material than the rest of the tissue, and which appears to be of a muscular nature. These mouths have been compared to small suckers. While it is alive, the *Tænia* continually elongates and retracts, the mouth bearing papillæ; Bremser remarks that the animal always extends the opposite projections, and at the same time retracts the other two.

Between and in front of the mouth is a convex protuberance forming a kind of rudimental proboscis, which, however, is not perforated, but is surrounded by a double row of *hooks*. These bodies are of a horny nature, and vary in number from 12 to 15 in each row. Each hook consists of a stem or handle, which is almost straight, of moderate thickness, and forms nearly half its length; of a curved pointed claw; and of a guard or tubercular projection placed at the junction of the stem with the claw. This projection serves as a point of resistance during the backward and forward movements of the hook; it is generally surrounded by a sheath. The hooks alternate with obtuse appendages, which are nothing more than the disarticulated stems. According to Bremser a *Tænia* loses its hooks as it becomes old. Some writers have supposed that the proboscis had an opening in the centre of the double crown of hooks which represented the mouth. According to this view the openings in the disks would be accessory mouths; it was in accordance with this idea that Virey gave the animal the name of *Pentastoma*, or five-mouthed. It has been previously mentioned that the projection is not perforated.

The head is supported upon a short slender neck, which has no visible articulations. This neck, as well as the head, appears to be composed of a gelatinous looking material.

Beyond the neck is the body, composed of segments or *Zoonites*,[1] (fig. 115). These segments are very numerous. M. Eschricht possesses a *Tænia* in which there are more than 1000. Adanson asserts that the worm may have as many as 1240. The segments are united together in a single linear series.[2] The first segments are always shorter than they are wide; as they grow in size their length increases proportionally much

[1] See page 59.
[2] These zoonites are generally from ·472 in. to ·787 in. in length, and from ·275 in. to ·472 in. in breadth.

more than their width. They soon become of a square form, and afterwards oblong, and ultimately their length is equal to twice their width.[1] Individuals are occasionally met with in which some of the segments are wider than they are long, followed by others in which these proportions are reversed; a circumstance which proves the irregular contraction of the *Tænia*. In some cases these unequal contractions arise from the sudden destruction of the animal by placing it in spirits of wine. At other times the contractions are still more marked, and produce actual monstrosities. (Rayer, Follin.) In general, however, the segments which are most developed are longer than they are wide. The last segments are only slightly united together and readily separate.

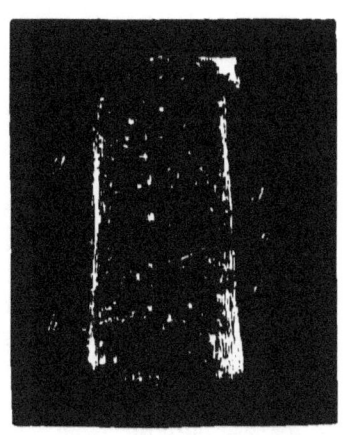

Fig. 115.—*Separate segments.*[2]

Each segment has four borders and two surfaces. The anterior border unites with the previous segment; it is always thinner than the posterior and generally narrower. The posterior border is thickened, and appears to project; it is either undulating or indented. The lateral margins are seldom straight or parallel, but incline slightly towards each other. One of them is provided with an opening, which will be described presently. These borders form with the posterior a projecting angle, which gives the animal the appearance of being notched at its sides. The two surfaces are flat, but sometimes they project slightly towards the centre.

The entozoon is covered with a very thin skin, which is intimately united to the subjacent tissue, so that it can only be taken off in strips, and then only on the largest segments.

The digestive system of the *Tænia* consists of four slender canals, which pass from the mouths. These canals, which look like so many white lines, soon unite to form two, which pass along the whole length of the two sides of the animal. They take a parallel course at a short distance from each lateral margin. At the posterior part of the segments they com-

[1] "*Animalia composita simplici catena.*" Linn.
[2] *a*, genital openings; *d*, deferent canal and testicle; *f*, oviduct; *g h*, ovaries.

municate by means of transverse branches which run along the posterior margin. The lateral canals are provided with valves, which prevent the nutrient fluid moving in a retrograde direction. Carlisle endeavoured to inject one of these canals from behind forward, but the fluid would not pass; in order to succeed it must be injected from one of the mouths.

M. Blanchard has described a circulatory system in the *Tænia*, consisting of four slender vessels, two corresponding to each surface, and communicating together by means of very delicate branches. Some recent observations tend to show that these canals are urinary vessels. (Van Breneden.)

Nervous centres are said to have been discovered in the head of this entozoon. These consist of two cerebral ganglions united together by a slender commissure, and of two long cords which are given off from the ganglions and can be traced along the margins of the different segments. A small ganglion is also stated to exist beneath each mouth, which is connected by a delicate filament with the cerebral ganglion. M. Dumeril, who has dissected a large number of *Tæniæ*, and has noticed these lateral cords, does not regard them as nerves, but as ligaments.

Beneath the general integuments some longitudinal muscular fibres are said to be present, which are not intercepted at the articulations.

When the *Teniæ* are examined in the living state, and when they are surrounded by the mucous secretion of the intestines, they are seen to move about with an undulating motion.[1] Deslongchamps having placed some of the young *Tæniæ* in tepid water, states that they swam about in the same manner as leeches. A. Richard relates, that, having immersed a living *Tenia* in tepid milk, it executed very distinct movements, which were renewed when the liquid was changed.

The *Teniæ* are androgynous, each adult segment containing both male and female organs (fig. 116). An opening situated at the side constitutes the sexual aperture; the orifice is very distinct, and pierces a prominent papilla. It is in the middle segments that this opening is seen most clearly, and is stated to be surrounded by a small projecting margin. For a long time these apertures were regarded as mouths or suckers which were intended to fix the animal to the intestine and to suck up its food.[2] The great length of the entozoon, the extreme tenuity of the alimentary canals, the size of the last segments,

[1] Gomes, Deslandes.
[2] "*Singulo articulo proprium os.* Linn.

and the prominence of the genital pore, which is able to apply itself with a certain force in the manner of a sucker, gave some show of probability to this opinion. The pores are placed sometimes on one side, sometimes on the other, but without any regular alternation. Sometimes there are two, three, or even four, arranged consecutively on the same side, while there will be only one or two on the opposite side. When examined with a magnifying glass, the genital pore resembles a cup-shaped depression. In the centre is a minute aperture from which a short small spiculum is occasionally seen to project; this opening leads to a horizontal tortuous (*deferent*) canal; the latter is of an opaque white colour, and terminates in the testicle, which is placed towards the middle of the segment. Behind the male orifice, and frequently confounded with it, is the opening of the female organs. This opening communicates with a canal (*vagina*) which passes parallel to the deferent canal, but which is longer and becomes connected with a granular, irregularly lobed organ, having a grape-like form. This organ, which some authors have described as a ramified intestine, is the ovary.

Fig. 116.—*Sexual organs.*[1]

When a *Tænia* has attained a certain stage of development, its ovaries enlarge and become very apparent. At this period individuals have been found folded up so to place some of the genital pores opposite to each other; a circumstance which has led some writers to think that the animals were in the act of copulating. The invertebrata, however, which can procreate of themselves, do not copulate. In these animals there is an internal communication between the ova and spermatozoa. Copulation takes place in all those androgynous animals which are deprived of this communication, but then it occurs between two or more individuals.

The *Teniæ* are oviparous. They deposit their eggs (fig. 116, *B*) in incalculable numbers, each segment containing hundreds.

[1] *A*, double sexual apparatus; *a*, genital depression; *b*, spiculum; *c*, female orifice; *d*, testicle; *e*, deferent canal; *f*, oviduct; *g*, axis of ovary; *h*, grape-like ovaries; *B*, egg.

The egg has a rounded form, and is of a white colour. It is provided with three coverings; an exterior one which is of a kind of albuminous layer, a middle one which is hard and resisting, and an internal one which is very thin and easily torn. The embryo may be seen in the interior, having its head armed with three pairs of spines which resemble those of the adult; only they are proportionally larger. The eggs are liberated in three ways: 1. The impregnated segments separate from each other[1] (fig. 114). These zoonites have been mistaken for a distinct species of worm, and received the name of *Cucurbitini* (*Vermes cucurbitini, cucumerini*), from having been compared to the seeds of the pumpkin. (Lamarck.) Andry regards them as the eggs of the animal. In reality they are ovigrous capsules, but at the same time they retain their vitality and possess a very distinct motion. (Siebold, Mignot.) The vitality of the segments is speedily extinguished, they become decomposed, and the eggs are set at liberty. 2. The eggs are discharged through the genital pore in the usual manner; the latter process does not occur so frequently as the former. Goeze only noticed it once. Lamarck states that by lightly pressing some of the segments the eggs can be discharged. 3. Under certain circumstances the ovary and the segment burst at the sides, and the zoonite becomes perforated. Masars de Cazeles mistook a *Tænia* perforated in this manner for a new species, to which he gave the name of *Tænia fenestrata*.

M. Weinland has described, under the name of *abietina*, a variety of the *Common Tænia*, which was sent from North America to Professor Agassiz, and in which the ovaries were ramified in a peculiar manner.

2. OTHER SPECIES. The other species of *Tæniæ* which have been noticed in the human body are:—the *Tænia nana*, the *Tænia flavopunctata*, the *Tænia Echinococcus*, and the *Tænia inermis*. The following are their characters:—

Head				
with hooks	Segments	very numerous. Sexual orifices	alternate	1. *Tænia solium*.
			unilateral — Uniform colour.	2. *Tænia nana*.
			Spotted.	3. *Tænia flavopunctata*.
		3 or 4		4. *Tænia Echinococcus*.
without hooks				5. *Tænia inermis*.

[1] When a *Tænia* has attained a certain stage of development the adult segments filled with eggs are continually cast off from the posterior extremity of the worm.

The *Tænia nana*[1] was found in considerable numbers in Egypt in 1851 by Dr. Bilharz, in the small intestines of a young man who had died from meningitis.

This entozoon is very small, not being more than half an inch in length, and not thicker than a needle. The segments are proportionally somewhat large. The head is large, obtuse anteriorly, and supported upon a long neck. Its proboscis is pyriform, and the mouths projecting.

The eggs are globular and furnished with a thick, smooth, yellow shell, through which the three pairs of hooks with which the embryo is provided can be readily seen.

The *Tænia flavopunctata* was discovered in Massachusets in 1842, by Dr. Erza Palmer, and described, unfortunately, from portions without the head by professor Weinland. It came from an infant nine months old, who was however in good health, had been weaned at six months, and fed in the usual manner.

It was mistaken at first for a *Bothriocephalus*.

The worm is from 8 to 12 inches in length, and from ·078 to ·118 of an inch in width. It is of a whitish colour, with a distinct yellow spot in the centre of each segment. The segments are very regular, excepting towards the posterior extremity, where they are so much contracted anteriorly that they are almost of a triangular form.

The most remarkable character of this species is the situation of the sexual orifices, which are all situated on one side, as is the case in the *Tæniæ* of several of the mammalia. The ovary does not consist of a central stem with lateral branches, but of a mass of germs in the centre of each segment.

The eggs are spherical and transparent, and have a yellow spot in the centre. They are provided with three coverings, of which the innermost is resisting, and breaks under pressure at acute angles; the second is thicker and wrinkled.

The *Tænia Echinococcus* is a species which is still imperfectly known; it is often met with in Iceland, where it is found in large numbers in the intestines of the dog; it is believed that it is also found in the human subject. M. Tandon considers that the latter statement is extremely doubtful.

This *Tænia* is extremely small, being almost of microscopic dimensions. Its length is hardly more than ·118 of an inch; it has only three or four segments, of which the last is already fully developed, being impregnated and filled with eggs. It has from 28 to 36 hooks.

[1] *Tænia Egyptiaca*. Bilh.

The penis is seen at the side, behind the middle of the segment. Its ovary is large and winding.

The eggs are spherical.

The segments after their separation become as large as the entire *Tænia*.

The *Tænia inermis*[1] was discovered, in 1855, by M. Kuchenmeister. It is an inhabitant of Europe, and appears to be not uncommon in Germany. It is found in the small intestines. An individual of this species was recently obtained from a pork butcher of Louvain, and another from a young girl of Liege. (Van Beneden.)

This *Tænia* closely resembles the *Common Tænia*, with which it has been confounded. It is, however, clearly distinguished by the absence of the hooks and the simplicity of its ovaries. Those who first noticed it probably mistook it for an individual of the common species in which the hooks had become lost either through accident or age.

The head of the *Tænia inermis* is somewhat larger than that of the *Tænia communis*, and is very obtuse, and as it were truncated. It has neither hooks nor proboscis; the suckers are very large; and the segments separate very readily. Its ovaries consist of a longitudinal canal, which gives off something like sixty lateral parallel branches, which are either simple or bifurcated, but never dendritic.

The eggs are oval and smooth.

Some writers have mentioned the following species as parasitic upon man; further information is still required concerning them.

1. The *Tænia of the Cape*, *Tænia Capensis*, is mentioned by Kuchenmeister as having been obtained from a Hottentot. M. Weinland considers it is a variety or monstrosity of the *Tænia communis* or the *Tænia inermis*. M. Leuchart thinks it is the same as the latter. [Kuchenmeister has founded this species upon the characters of the separated segments, not having seen either the head or the neck of the worm. He himself expresses a doubt as to whether it is really a distinct species.]

2. The *Tænia tropica* is common in the Indies, one half of the negroes being affected with it. It is seldom met with in Europeans. It has, however, been noticed in those who have resided on the coasts of Guinea, and who were at the same time

---

[1] *Tænia mediocanellata*, Kuch. This name cannot be retained, as it is badly compounded, one of its roots not being a Latin word.

affected with the *Filaria Medinensis*.[1] It has never been seen in the Malay race. It is said not to have hooks?

M. Van Beneden approximates this species to the *Tænia inermis*.

3. The *Tænia serrata*, which is very common in the dog, is it ever found in man as some medical men have stated?

4. M. Eschricht says he received a *Tænia canina*,[2] Linn., which had been passed by a negro slave. Is this fact correct?

3. ACTION ON MAN.—The *Tæniæ* usually inhabit the small intestines. When they are numerous or greatly developed they descend into the large intestines. It is very rarely that they ascend into the stomach. Aubert, of Geneva, has described a tumour in a testicle, caused by the presence of a *Tænia* (!)

This entozoon is sometimes solitary, while at other times there are several of them together. Two or three are often met with in the same patient. Rudolphi mentions a case in which there were four. M. Barth had charge of a patient who had six; M. Monod succeeded in expelling fourteen at the same time, and De Haen cured a woman aged thirty who had eighteen. The name of *Solitary Worm* by which this creature is generally known is, therefore, very ill chosen.

These worms gain access to the intestinal canal in the larval state.[3] The cephalic hooks are at this time directed forwards and can easily penetrate the mucous tissues. They are then moved from before backwards, the claw penetrating at the same time, and, by this means, the head of the worm is buried in the thickness of the mucous membrane. (Van Beneden.)

M. Sappey found a *Tænia serrata* in the intestines of a dog where the head had penetrated the epidermis, and was resting in contact with the subjacent layer of the mucous membrane. He succeeded in dissecting out the worm with a portion of the epidermal layer remaining around its neck like a collar.

The presence of the *Tæniæ* gives rise to a feeling of uneasiness, to a sensation of weight, to flatulency, and to pains in the abdomen; the latter are usually slight, especially at the commencement of the disease. The patient is subject to shiverings; he has a feeling of anxiety, and has an inordinate desire for food, while at the same time he gets thin.

M. Van Beneden suspects that it was the larvæ of the *Tænia Echinococcus* which produced the terrible epidemic,

---
[1] See p. 360.
[2] *T. cucumerina*, Bloch.
[3] See chapter xiii. on the cystic helmintha.

which destroyed one sixth of the inhabitants of Iceland. (Schleisner.)[1]

When the person has expelled a large number of the fragments of a *Tænia* the parasite ultimately perishes. During the treatment of a patient the anterior portion of the worm, and more especially the head, is anxiously sought for. The patient is often supposed to have discharged only a number of segments, while, in reality, he has got rid of the most active and important portion of the worm. By a careful examination of the fæcal matter the head can sometimes be detected. Out of a hundred persons affected with *Tænia*, who were treated by Bremser, only one of them detected the expulsion of the head of the worm, and yet ninety-nine out of the hundred were cured.

Some writers have asserted that a *Tænia* will live for ten years, a statement which appears to be very doubtful. Patients, however, have been known to discharge portions of *Tæniæ* during that space of time, but in all probability they came from different individuals.

CHAPTER XII.

BOTHRIOCEPHALUS.

THE genus *Bothriocephalus* was established by Bremser. It differs essentially from that of *Tænia*. The head has two fossæ or pits instead of the four mouths, and has no circlet of hooks.

1. BOTHRIOCEPHALUS LATUS.[2]—This entozoon inhabits the north of Europe, where it is more common than the *Tænia solium;* it is found more particularly in Russia, Poland, and Sweden. M. Küchenmeister says he has met with it in Hamburg, but only in Jews. It has also been observed in France. Two years ago Professor Grisolle succeeded in expelling a very long one from one of his patients. Mr. Jackson has twice met with this worm in England. In general the *Bothriocephalus* is common where the Tænia is rare, and vice versâ.

[Mr. Jackson's cases occurred in America, one of the patients being an Englishman. In the College of Surgeons, No. 204 of the Natural History series, is a specimen of the *Bothriocephalus latus*, which was procured by the late Sir Anthony Carlisle from a

---

[1] M. Siebold considers it was caused by the *Tænia serrata*.
[2] Βόθριον a pit, and κεφαλή the head.

female who was a native of Switzerland. Professor Quekett has kindly informed me that five other specimens have since been added to the collection. Three of these were purchased at the sale of the late Mr. Gardener's collection. One of them was said to have come from a person belonging to the Russian embassy, another from a person who had been travelling in Switzerland, and the history of the third was unknown. The fourth specimen occurred in the practice of Dr. Gull: the patient was a little girl five years old, who resided at Woolwich, where there is always a number of foreign sailors. The fifth came into the possession of Mr. Camplin, and was passed by a lady who was a native of Russia, and who, after a residence of some years in England, paid a temporary visit to her native country. In all the cases, therefore, in which the history of the disease can be traced, with the exception of that which came under the notice of Dr. Gull, the Geographical distribution of the worm is most rigidly maintained. In the case of the child residing by the water-side, the presence of foreigners readily explains the mode in which the worm might have been conveyed to this country, and impure drinking water would suggest itself as the means of transmission from one individual to another.]

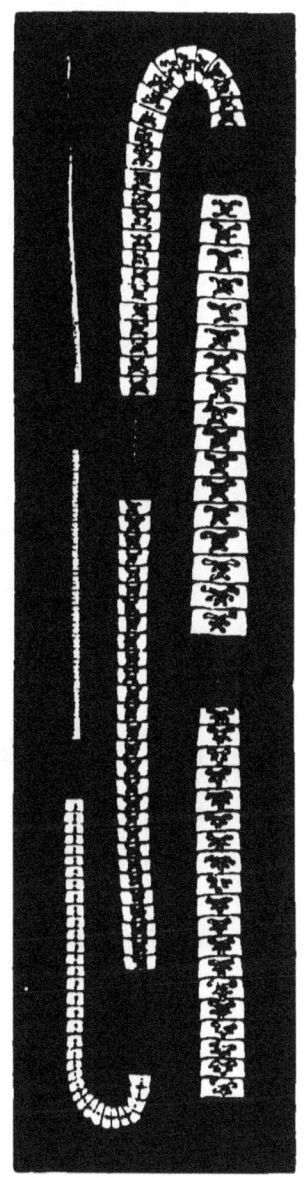

Fig. 117.
Bothriocephalus atus.

Description.—The *Bothriocephalus latus* (fig. 117) is also one of the flat, articulated entozoa. Its usual length is from 6 to 20 feet. Bremser mentions the case of a young Swiss who expelled three pieces, of which the longest measured twenty-five Vienna feet. Other writers mention 60 feet. Goeze asserts that he received a specimen from Bloch which measured more than 230 feet. Boerhave declares that he expelled a Bothriocephalus from a Russian which was not less than 1200 feet in length? The greatest width of this worm is from the ·393 of an inch to the 1·220 of an inch. Rudolphi, however, asserts that he saw one which was 3·296 inches in width. It is difficult to admit the correctness of this measurement.

The *Bothriocephalus* is generally of a greyish white or yellowish colour; it never has the milky whiteness of a Tænia. The middle of the last segments are more or less of a brown colour arising from the presence of the eggs. When this worm is put into alcohol it assumes a grey colour. From this circumstance it received the name of *Tænia grisea*, which was given to it by Pallas.

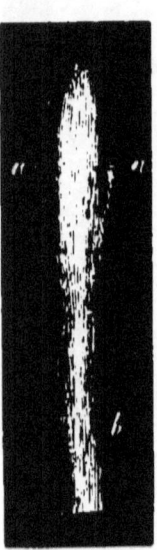

Fig. 118.
Head.

The head of the *Bothriocephalus* (fig. 118) is very small (about ·093 inch), oblong, somewhat depressed, and obtuse; there are two oblong, lateral depressions or pits placed opposite to each other, which Rudolphi justly regards as the oral apertures.

[Küchenmeister examined five heads of the Bothriocephali, only one of which was, however, tolerably fresh. The two lateral pits (the analogues of the sucking discs of the Tænia) are fissuriform; they appear, like the sucking discs on the feet of flies and mites, on leeches, &c., rather to affect the adhesion in accordance with the well-known laws of partial or total vacua, than to have anything to do with the nourishment, which is probably introduced through the entire skin. An actual opening on the head of the *Bothriocephalus* could not be detected any more than in the other *Cestoidea*.[1]]

The neck is sometimes very apparent and distinctly developed, while at other times it can be scarcely discerned. Bremser has figured two heads with well-developed necks, and a third in which it is almost absent. The neck appears to possess no articulations, but by means of the microscope a number of closely arranged ridges can be perceived.

The segments or zoonites are at first nearly square, but they soon become wider than they are long. At the posterior part of the body the transverse greatly exceeds the longitudinal

---

[1] Küchenmeister, *opus cit.* vol. i. p. 97.

diameter (fig. 119). M. Eschricht calculated that a single *Bothriocephalus* contains 10,000 segments.

At the posterior extremity of the animal there is sometimes observed a kind of incision or longitudinal rent, which divides the worm into two portions, and may give to this extremity the appearance of a head. Bremser has figured a portion of a *Bothriocephalus* with a fissure of this kind. At other times the rent is longer, and the worm appears to be furnished with two tails. M. Rayer has seen several examples of this.

As in the Tænia, filiform alimentary canals may be noticed at the anterior part, which pass in the length of the body. These canals can sometimes be seen through the skin.

According to M. Blanchard, the *Bothriocephalus* has a nervous system resembling that of the Tænia, but not so distinct.

The animal contracts and dilates itself in a very irregular manner, but its movements are generally sluggish. The head is said, however, to be distinctly movable.

About the centre of the under surface of the segments (fig. 119) is an oval or conical papilla, provided with an aperture through which there emerges a small slender somewhat pointed body,

Fig. 119.
Separate Segments.[1]

which is regarded as the penis. Behind this body is another smaller pore without a papilla. This does not always exist; it is supposed to be the vulva, and, like the penis, is not present in every segment; the hermaphroditism of the animal is not therefore uniform; it possesses some segments which are androgynous, while others are male and female.

According to M. Eschricht, the penis is furnished with a small sheath and communicates with a tolerably long deferent canal; this is folded several times upon itself, gradually increases in thickness, and terminates in a vesicula seminalis, having the form of an oval pouch. The testicle consists of white granules, and is furnished with three slender ducts, which terminate in the before-mentioned vesicle. The female organs are somewhat more complicated; the ovaries are oblong and very distinct, the oviduct presents itself under the form of a tortuous

---

[1] *a*, male orifice with the penis; *b*, vulva.

canal, especially at the period when the ova are mature. The uterus has two pouches or diverging horns, which communicate together.

The eggs of the *Bothriocephalus* (fig. 120) are exceedingly numerous. According to M. Eschricht, each individual has as many as ten millions. The eggs are of an elliptical form; when highly magnified they appear to be filled with granules.

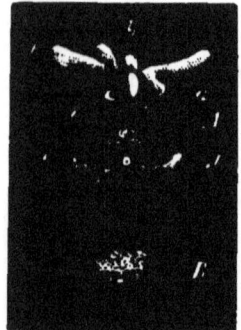

Fig 120.[1]
Sexual Organs.

The larva of the *Bothriocephalus* is unknown, as well as the circumstances under which it passes the first period of its existence. The propagation of this entozoon is supposed to occur in the same manner as that of the *Bothriocephali* of other animals. The egg produces an asexual larva, provided with a pouch-like body; this larva lives for a time in the body of some animal, and subsequently introduces itself into the human body, and is there transformed into the perfect animal.[2]

M. Van Beneden observes that the herbivorous mammalia have tape-worms which are not furnished with hooks, and that these animals cannot swallow the larvæ of these worms with the flesh of other animals, as is the case with the carnivora. It is therefore possible that the human *Bothriocephalus* is produced from a larva which does not become encysted.[3]

2. ANOTHER SPECIES.—Mayor, of Geneva, has recognised two species of the *Bothriocephalus latus*, one with short the other with long segments. The first attains a length of sixty-five feet, and is about half an inch in width; the segments are about ·078 of an inch (two millimetres) in length. The second is not more than twenty-six feet long and about ·354 of an inch in width; its segments are ·157 of an inch in length. According to this gentleman, the oil of the male fern invariably expels the *Bothriocephalus* with the long segments, while that with the short segments usually resists it, and requires to effect its expulsion that the powdered root of this plant, or a decoction of the bark of the root of the pomegranate tree, should be employed. Zoologists consider that these supposed species are mere varieties of the large *Bothriocephalus*.

[1] *A*, bisexual apparatus; *a*, male orifice with the penis; *b*, testicle; *c*, vulva; *d*, uterus with horns; *e*, tortuous oviduct; *f*, ovary; *B*, egg.
[2] See p. 396.
[3] See p. 399.

3. OBSERVATIONS.—On comparing the *Bothriocephalus latus* with the *Tænia communis*, their distinctive characters may be arranged as follows:—

The *Bothriocephalus*—1, is of a grey colour; 2, it has an elongated head, without any terminal enlargement or circlet of hooks; 3, it is furnished with two elongated fossæ; 4, the segments are wider than they are long; 5, the sexual orifices are central.

The *Tænia*—1, is white; 2, the head is globular, with a terminal enlargement and two circles of hooks; 3, it has four rounded oscula; 4, the segments are longer than they are wide; 5, the sexual orifices are marginal.

ACTION ON MAN.—Like the *Tænia*, the *Bothriocephalus* inhabits the small intestines.

The disorders which these worms produce, and the symptoms which indicate their presence, are the same in both species.

The *Tape worms* without hooks belong to the herbivora, and those with hooks to the carnivora. In man, who is omnivorous, both species are met with. As a vegetable feeder he is tormented with the *Bothriocephalus latus*, and also with the *Tænia inermis*, and as a flesh feeder with the *Tænia communis* and the *Tænia nana*.

CHAPTER XIII.

CYSTIC HELMINTHA.

UNDER the name of *Vesicular* or *Cystic Helmintha*,[1] are included those entozoa which terminate in a vesicle, are contained in a cyst, or are composed of the latter only. The old writers gave them the name of *Hydatids*, or *Hydatid Worms*. All these *Helmintha* are agamic, that is, are deprived of sexual organs. The reason of this will be seen hereafter.

Zoologists have distinguished three genera of the Cystic Helmintha—1, the *Cysticerci*; 2, the *Echinococci*; 3, the *Acephalocysts*.

§ I. Cysticerci.

The CYSTICERCI[2] are helmintha which are furnished with a caudal vesicle.

They become developed in the cellular tissue of the muscles,[3]

---

[1] *Cystica*, Rud.; *Vermes vesiculares*, Linn.; *Blassenwürmer* of the Germans.
[2] Κύστις a bladder, and κέρκος a tail.
[3] Werner, Himley, Demarquay.

they have also been noticed in the liver,[1] the heart,[2] the choroid plexus,[3] the brain,[4] between the sclerotic and the conjunctiva,[5] and in the anterior chamber of the eye.[6]

These animals are very minute, and are contained in a circular or oval cyst of a somewhat fibrous structure, which is developed at the expense of the organ which nourishes the parasite. This cyst contains a second, furnished with an opening, around which a third sac is adherent, and encloses the worm which is attached to it. (Follin, Robin.) This sac is of a globular, oval, pyriform shape; its parieties are thin, smooth, or granulated, semitransparent, of a whitish colour, and tolerably strong.

The head and the neck are always contained in the vesicle, but they can be partly or entirely withdrawn at the will of the animal.

The head is provided with four suckers placed on a similar number of projections, and with a terminal proboscis surrounded by a double circle of spines, just in the same manner as in the head of a Tænia. The neck varies in length, and is formed of a number of closely arranged segments.

When the head is retracted the opening has the appearance of a small navel, which appears to be surrounded with a kind of whitish coloured sphincter; beneath this spot is the retracted head and neck.

There are three principal species of the *Cysticerci*:—1, *Cesticercus cellulosæ*; 2, *Cysticercus tenuicollis*; 3, *Cysticercus Acanthotrias*.

1. The *Cysticercus Cellulosæ* (fig. 121)[7] is not commonly met with in man; it is supposed to be the same as the worm which is so frequently developed in the pig, and produces the peculiar affection which is known as measly pork; it has also been noticed in the ox.

The cysts measure from the ·590 to the ·787 of an inch in the large diameter, and from the ·198 to the ·236 in the small. The head has 32 hooks.[8] Some writers consider that the species which is met with in animals, and is furnished with from 26 to 28 hooks,[9] is a different species from that which is found in man.

[1] Leuckart.
[2] Morgagni, Rudolphi, Bouillaud, Andral, Leudet.
[3] Treutler, Fischer.
[4] Ruysch, Chomel, Dubreuil, Leudet, Calmeil, Bouchut.
[5] Estlin, Hæring, Siebold, Cunier.
[6] Sœmmering, Lugan.
[7] *Tænia cellulosæ*, Gmel.; *Hydatigera cellulosæ*, Lamk.
[8] Himley, Gervais, Ch. Robin.
[9] Davaine, Follin.

There is a variety (*albopunctatus*) which has a well-marked white spot at the opening of the vesicle.[1]

The *Cysticercus dicystus* of Laennec which was found in the brain of a man who had died of apoplexy, and in which the body terminated in a double vesicle, must be regarded as a monstrosity.

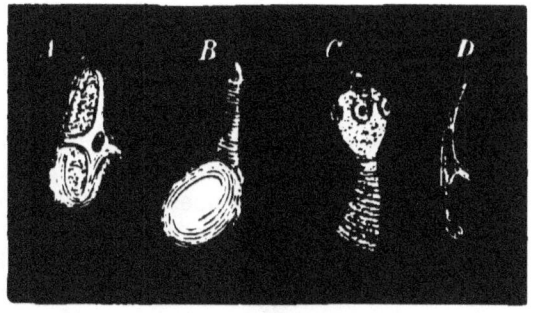

Fig. 121.—*Cysticerci.*[2]

2. The *Cysticercus Acanthotrias* (Weinl.) or *three-armed cysticercus*, was found in 1845, at Richmond, in Virginia, by Professor Wyman, in the muscles of a woman fifty years of age, who had died of phthisis.

It is nearly the ·393 of an inch long without the vesicle, which resembles that of the *Cysticercus cellulosa*.

It is characterised by having three kinds of hooks arranged in three rows, fourteen in each row; its suckers are visible to the naked eye, and its neck is distinctly articulated.

M. Weinland proposes to found a separate genus on this species under the name of *Acanthotrias*.

3. The *Cysticercus tenuicollis* (Rud.) has been seen occasionally in the liver and in the mesentery, but only very rarely. Bosc and H. Cloquet have had the opportunity of examining it. It is also found in monkeys, horses, pigs, and oxen.

The neck is long, round, and rugose. Its vesicle appears to be small in man, but in other animals it becomes very large.[3]

The following species must be regarded as doubtful, the characters which have been assigned to them not being sufficiently marked.

1. The *Cysticercus hepaticus*, Delle Chiaje, which resides in the liver, and has an oval elongated body.

2. The *Cysticercus visceralis*, Rud., which resides in the abdomen and the thorax, and has a globular body.

[1] *Tænia albo punctata*, Treutl.
[2] *A*, animal withdrawn into its vesicle; *B*, animal extended; *C*, head and neck; *D*, one of the hooks.
[3] The Tænia which produces this species is very common in the animals which are slaughtered for food. It is also found in the butcher's dog and in the shepherd's dog.

3. The *Cysticercus Fischerianus*, Laenn., which has a very slender body and a pyriform vesicle.

4. The *Cysticercus aorticus*, Notar., which has an oval body and filiform hooks.

5. The *Cysticercus vesicæ*, Crepl., in which the body is rudimental.

In March, 1859, M. Kæberle communicated to the Society of Natural History of Strasbourg, a description of what he considers to be two new species of *Cysticerci*—the *C. turbinatus* and the *C. melanocephalus*. The first is characterised by the manner in which it is coiled up and by the possession of 32 hooks; the second by a cephalic spot, and by having 24 hooks. Both animals were found in the brain.

§ II. Echinococci.

The ECHINOCOCCI[1] are worms which are enclosed in very variable numbers in a membranous cyst (sporocyst).

The *Echinococcus hominis* (fig. 122), Rud., has been described in several special memoirs.

This worm is found in several organs, but more especially in the kidneys and lungs. Zeder met with it in the brain of a young girl. Rudolphi, Eschricht, and Lebert have seen it in the liver. Morgagni once found it in the heart. Ludersen mentions the case of a man aged 40, who had died of dropsy, and whose spleen was transformed into a large dilated sac, containing an enormous number of *Echinococci*. Collet has recorded the case of a woman, aged 47, who, in about four months, discharged 135 *Echinococci* in coughing. Albers and Boch have both seen a case of goitre which was occasioned by an *Echinococcus*. (Foster.) M. Gescheidt found it between the choroid and the crystalline lens.

The cyst or capsule of the *Echinococci* varies generally in size. Some are not larger than a mustard seed, while others are of the size of a chicken's egg. This cyst causes the parenchyma of the diseased organ to recede, and induces around it the formation of a new tissue, so that the hydatid is completely embedded in an adventitious cyst. These cysts are not always solitary.

The shape of the cyst is globular, oval, or pyriform. It is composed of two membranes, the one enclosed in the other. The external (*Hydatid* of authors) consists of a structure which has the appearance of coagulated white of egg, without either fibres or cells, and is arranged in layers. (Davaine.) The in-

[1] Ἐχῖνος a hedgehog, and κόκκος a grain.

ternal cyst, corresponding to the *germinal membrane* of Goodsir, is formed of a fibrous tissue, with a number of elementary granules dispersed through it. In the interior is a clear limpid fluid, sometimes colourless, and at other times with a slight yellow or reddish tinge.

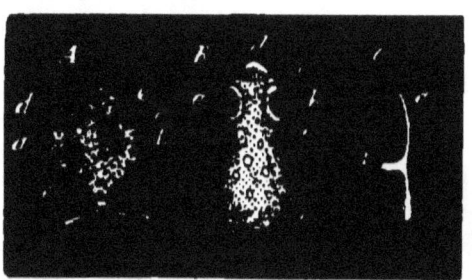

Fig. 122.—*Echinococcus*.[1]

Small corpuscles, like grains of sand, float free in the fluid; these are at first attached to the internal surface of the cyst by means of a very slender pedicle, which tears with great facility. (Davaine.) When examined beneath the microscope, these corpuscles are seen to be elongated, more or less ovoid, globular, or pyriform in shape, and depressed. Each of these is a small intestinal worm. Its anterior extremity is furnished, like that of the Cysticerci, or the Tænia, with four suckers and a double row of hooks. Germs are also developed on the external surface of the first membrane, and sometimes in its substance. They usually become detached, like the first-mentioned bodies, when they have attained the size of a hemp seed. At the end of a certain time they form in their interior the second membrane, and it is from this that the young *Echinococci* are produced. (Davaine.)

Some writers consider that the *Echinococcus* of the monkey, the dog, the ox, and the sheep, is a distinct species from that of man, and have given it the name of the *Echinococcus veterinorum*, Rud.

Others go even further, and admit that each of the animals which have been named is infested with a distinct species.

§ III. Acephalocysts.

The ACEPHALOCYSTS, *Acephalocystis* (fig. 123),[2] described by Laennec, are growths in the form of membranous cysts, but which are without head, mouth, or alimentary canal, even in the embryonal condition.

[1] *A*, animal attached to the internal wall of the sporocyst, the head and neck retracted within its body; *a*, the head; *b*, the mouths; *c*, the circlets of hooks; *d*, the proboscis; *e*, the body; *f*, the pedicle; *B*, the animal developed; *a*, the head; *b*, the oscula; *c*, the circle of hooks; *d*, the proboscis; *e*, the neck; *f*, the body; *C*, one of the hooks; *a*, the claw; *b*, the guard; *c*, the handle.

[2] a priv. κεφαλή the head, κύστις a bladder.

The *Acephalocysts* are found in the liver, spleen, and kidneys. Béclard met with them in the bladder, Cullerier in the substance of the bones, and M. Rostan in the arachnoid membrane. Dr. Carrère found one which weighed over three ounces and a half (119 grammes), in the brain of a young man.

Many naturalists have considered these cysts as true Helmintha, but an organization of such extreme simplicity belongs to the class Monadaria (Blainville), and is allied to the Volvocidæ. (Leuckart.)

[The last statement in the preceding paragraph will scarcely be admitted, since there are few naturalists in the present day who have any doubts as to the vegetable nature of the Volvocidæ.]

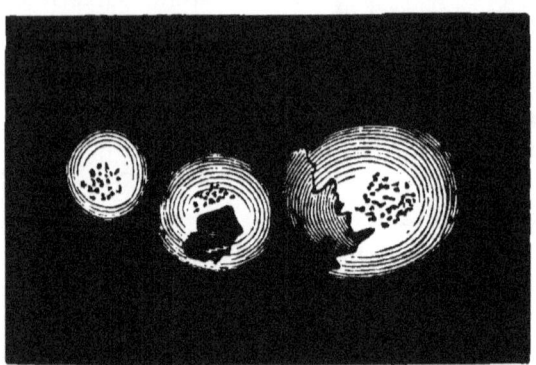

Fig. 123.—*Acephalocysts.*

Goeze and Rudolphi do not admit their animal nature; and Cuvier and Meckel held the same opinion. These vesicles have, however, separate and independent life, which may be traced through its several stages. (Dujardin.)

The membranous, tremulous, semi-transparent vesicles which are found encysted in various parts of the body, are therefore to be regarded as *hydatid Helmintha*.

The true *Acephalocysts* are simple spherical non-adherent bodies, often containing other vesicles, enclosed the one within the other.

In the present state of the science, the *Acephalocysts* must not be regarded as a special genus of Helmintha, but as *Cysticerci* and *Echinococci*, which are incompletely developed, that is to say, whose evolution has been arrested. It is not uncommon to find some of these cysts contain both unarmed vesicles and larvæ furnished with hooks, and which consequently possess the characters both of an *Acephalocyst* and of an *Echinococcus*. (Van Beneden.)

§ IV. Transformations of the Cystic Helmintha.

The *Cystic* or *hydatid Helmintha*, that is to say, the *Cysticerci* and the *Echinococci* become transformed into the flat Helmintha. The first are incompletely developed or larval stages of the second.

A knowledge of these transformations has afforded a ready explanation of the origin of verminous diseases.

The history of this discovery possesses the greatest possible interest for the medical practitioner as well as for the naturalist. More than a century ago, Abilgaard noticed that a particular species of parasite, known as the *Schistocephalus dimorphus*, which infests certain fishes belonging to the family of the *Gasterostei* or *Stickle-backs*, is sometimes found in the water-fowl, which feed upon the latter, but that the parasite has then passed into a further stage of development. M. Creplin, in 1829, by carefully comparing the intestinal worm of the Gasterostei, which annually ascend the tributary rivers of the Baltic, with those of the piscivorous birds which frequent these streams, clearly proved that the *Schistocephalus dimorphus* only acquires its *sexual organs* (that is to say, becomes a perfect animal) when it has been developed in the interior of the bird.

The changes which this worm undergoes consist only in its attaining a larger size, and in the appearance of the sexual organs. Other changes of a more complicated and curious character, amounting to a true metamorphosis, have been noticed by M. Van Beneden in other worms, such as the *Bothriocephali* of fishes. Many fishes are inhabited by small entozoa, known under the name of *Scolices*. These worms have neither hooks nor suckers, and are entirely deprived of sexual organs. At a later period the *Scolices* are furnished with four cephalic suckers, armed with a series of hooks, and are converted into *Tetrarhynci*. These remain in their cyst until the fish in whose intestines they are lodged are eaten by some larger species. The worm then emerges from its cyst, makes its way through the intestine of the devourer, and fixes itself to its mesentery. At a subsequent period, if, in its turn, this fish is devoured by another, as, for instance, by a shark, the worm becomes elongated, its body flattened, segments are formed, the sexual organs are developed, and the entozoon is transformed into a *Bothriocephalus*.

These remarkable facts serve to explain the great resemblance which M. Siebold has pointed out between the head of the *Cysticercus fasciolaris*, which lives in the mouse, and the head of the *Tænia crassicollis*, which inhabits the cat. One is led to the conclusion that the two parasites are identical. In fact, they only differ from each other in the presence of a small cavitary vesicle in the first, and in the greater length of the second. M. Siebold introduced several species of *Cysticerci* into the stomachs of dogs and rabbits; he found that after a time the worm lost the caudal vesicle, elongated, became flattened, divided into segments, and was transformed into a *Tænia*.

Siebold gave encysted *Echinococci* to dogs mixed with their food. He showed that in some of these cases the last segment became dilated into the vesicle, and the entozoon was developed into a *Cysticercus*; but, in a large number the worm became elongated, flattened, articulated, and was converted into a *Tænia*.

Küchenmeister, in 1835, by some experiments which he performed upon a woman condemned to death for assassination, showed that when the *Cysticercus cellulosæ* passed into the human intestines, it became developed into the *common Tænia*. He administered to the woman a number of *Cysticerci* obtained from a pig: twelve were given in some blood puddings, and eighteen in rice, eighty-four hours before death; fifteen in vermicelli soup, thirty-six hours before; twelve mixed with sausage-meat, twenty-four hours before; and eighteen in soup, twelve hours before. The woman had, therefore, swallowed seventy-five *Cysticerci*. The examination of the body was made forty-eight hours after execution. Four small individuals of the *Tænia communis* were found attached to the mucous membrane of the abdomen. In the water with which the intestines had been washed six other young *Tæniæ* were found, but they were not furnished with hooks.

It appears, therefore, that the *Cysticercus cellulosæ* becomes converted into the *common Tænia* in the alimentary canal of man.

Similar experiments were made by Leuckart, who administered a number of the *Cysticerci* from the pig to a young man thirty years of age. At the end of two months this man had *Tæniæ*.

M. A. Humbert, of Geneva, even went so far as to experiment upon himself. On December the 11th, 1854, he swallowed fourteen fresh *Cysticerci* in the presence of MM. Vogt and Moulinié. Early in the month of March, 1855, he felt the presence of *Tæniæ*, and discharged large fragments of them.[1] (Bertholus.)

On the other hand, it has been proved that the mature eggs of the *Tæniæ* give rise to the development of *Cysticerci* in the

[1] Similar experiments made with other *Cysticerci* on dogs fully confirm these results.

tissues of animals.[1] Pigs have been fed with the eggs of the *Tænia communis* when the animals have become *measly*.

The *Cysticerci* found in the butchers' shops, and at the pork butchers,[2] are the principal source of the *common Tape worm*. These hydatids are consumed with the flesh of the pig (an animal which is so often infested by them) especially when this is eaten raw, or merely salted and smoked, or when it is only half-cooked. More rarely they are found in the flesh of the ox and some other animals.

According to the report of the medical men of Vienna persons who are employed in butchers' shops and in kitchens are those who are most frequently affected with *Tape worms*.[3] In Abyssinia, where the people are in the habit of eating raw meat, this parasite is very common. (Auber, Siebold.) The Carthusian monks of the same country, who neither eat meat nor drink milk, are entirely free from the worm. (Ruppell, Reinlein.) At Stettin *Tæniæ* were found in seven children, for whom raw meat had been prescribed. (Scharlau.)

The following are then the successive transformations which the *Tænia communis* undergoes before arriving at its perfect state.

The egg encloses a short unarticulated embryo, which, when it is hatched, is furnished with three pairs of hooks (*hexacanthi*), of which the two central are for the purpose of fixing it to the tissues of the animal selected by the parasite for its abode.

Once it is attached to an animal, as for instance a pig, this kind of rudimental larva becomes, or more correctly speaking engenders by an *agamic* process, a new individual enclosed within its parent; the latter becomes encysted in the infected animals, like a caterpillar in its coccoon, where it becomes transformed into a chrysalis. (Van Beneden.)

This second larva has a head with four suckers, a double circle of hooks, and a moderately long neck, which terminates in a membranous enlargement or vesicle with delicate walls, and filled with serum; within this the young animal can withdraw itself, or entirely close itself up. This kind of minute worm resides in large numbers in the cellular tissues, on the fat, beneath the skin, in the midst of the muscles, and in the peritoneum.

[1] Küchenmeister, Van Beneden, Gurlt, Eschricht, Leuckart, &c.
[2] A piece of pork weighing four drachms and a half, which Küchenmeister obtained from a pork butcher in Saxony contained 133 *Cysticerci*.
[3] Pork butchers and butchers are very subject to the *common Tape worm*. (Deslandes.)

The animal lives in its cyst like a Cynips in a gall-nut.

In this second state the larva forms the *Cysticercus cellulosæ*; it is the *hydatid* stage.

The larva is capable of producing other individuals similar to itself by the process of *gemmation*, but not by a true act of *generation*. When the pig becomes measly it contains millions of individuals.

If this larva and its progeny cannot escape from the tissues in which they have become encysted, their development does not pass beyond the condition of the *Cysticercus*.

When the *Cysticercus* enters the alimentary canal of man, it attaches itself by means of its hooks and its suckers to the surface of the mucous membrane. It soon loses its vesicle, which becomes degenerated by exosmosis, and assumes the appearance of a flattened appendage. The animal becomes more transparent, lengthens, assumes a flattened form, and produces a number of segments, which constitute special organisms placed end to end, and enjoying a community of life, but each of which, at the same time, is provided with all the elements essential to its individuality.[1] This long chain of zoonites may be regarded as another form of agamic reproduction.

This third stage corresponds to the perfect animal, and constitutes the *Tænia*.

It has been seen that the larvæ, when they emerge from the egg, are neither flat nor vesicular, and that the *Cysticerci* are flat worms furnished with an *Hydatid* termination. The *Acephalocysts* may be described as large *Hydatids* without the flat anterior body, while the *Tæniæ*, on the contrary, have long flat bodies without the terminal *Hydatid*.

In the course of two or three months a *Tænia* may attain the length of several yards.

Each segment is both male and female. At the period of procreation the ovaries are enlarged and become distended with an enormous number of eggs. After this the articulations separate from each other, and each of these becomes an independent organism.

The fourth stage is that of the *Cucurbitins*,[2] or separated segments.

These are passed out with the excrements; they continue to live for some days; they then decompose, and the eggs which they contain are dispersed abroad.

[1] *" Tænia natos suos nepotes concatenata serie longitudinaliter producunt."* (Linn.)

[2] See page 382.

The eggs retain for a long time the power of germinating; they resist the effects both of high and low temperatures, of dryness and humidity, and also of water and of alcohol. At length they pass either with the food or the drink into the interior of some animal or of man : they then become hatched, and give rise to a new generation of *Cysticerci*, which in their turn are developed into *Tæniæ*.[1]

These four states of the *Helmintha*—the *rudimentary*, the *vesicular*, the *flat*, and the *disjointed*—have been named by M. Van Beneden the *protoscolex*, the *deutoscolex*, the *strobila*, and the *proglottis*.[2] These names had previously been used in a generic sense, when each of the forms to which they refer was regarded as a distinct species of animal. M. Van Beneden would now make use of them as general terms, a useless innovation, since we have already the terms *larva*, *Cysticercus*, *Tænia*, and *cucurbitin*.[3]

The first *larva* or *protoscolex*, and the *Cysticercus* or *deutoscolex*, live in the substance of the different tissues. The *Tænia* or *strobilis* resides in the alimentary canal. The *cucurbitins* or *proglottis* emerge from this cavity. The first *larvæ* and the *Cysticerci* developed within them are compelled to become encysted. The *Tæniæ* and the *cucurbitins*, meeting with no obstacle or hindrance, do not form a cyst. The first become elongated, develop themselves, but remain adherent ; the second separate, move away, and become locomotive.

The first *larvæ* and the *Cysticerci* are very short, and furnished with an imperfectly articulated neck, and have no sexual organs ; they propagate themselves by *gemmation*. The *Tæniæ* are very long, form distinct zoonites, and are androgynous ; they reproduce by a true act of *generation*. Lastly, the *cucurbitins* are disarticulated zoonites, that is to say, single individuals, formed at the expense of a multiple individual ; these disseminate the mature eggs.

These remarkable transformations occur therefore in one and the same species ; germs which emigrate, larvæ which repro-

[1] M. Siebold is of the opinion that the *Cysticercus cellulosæ* give rise to different kinds of *Tæniæ*, according to the animal into which it is transported. Thus it becomes *Tænia serrata* in the dog, *Tænia crassipes* in the fox, *Tænia marginata* in the wolf, and *Tænia crassicollis* in the martin. M. Van Beneden justly considers that the *Cysticercus cellulosæ* can only give rise to the *Tænia communis*.

[2] *Scolex*, O. F. Müller; *strobila*, Saars; *proglottis*, Dujardin. The name *strobila* is applied in botany to that form of fruit which is commonly known as a *cone*.

[3] We have also those of *hydatid* and *zoonite*.

duce themselves, parts which are repeated, organisms which become individualized, and zoonites which become isolated.

What takes place in the development of the *Tænia communis* also occurs in other *Tæniæ*. Just as the *Cysticercus cellulosæ* is transformed into the *Tænia communis*, so the *Echinococcus veterinorum* is metamorphosed into the *Tænia echinococcus*.[1] Unfortunately our present knowledge does not enable us to trace these transformations in all the species. There are *Tæniæ* whose *larvæ* are not known, and there are *larvæ* whose *Tæniæ* are not ascertained; which, for example, are the *Cysticerci* that produce the *Tænia nana*, the *Tænia flavopunctata*, and the *Tænia inermis?* And, again, which is the *Tænia* that gives rise to the *Cysticercus Acanthotrias?*

The following conclusions may be drawn from the preceding facts:—

1. The *vesicular Helmintha* or *hydatids* are the *larvæ* (*scolex*) of the *flat Helmintha*.

2. The *Acephalocysts* are vesicular Helmintha, whose development is incomplete or arrested.

3. The larvæ assume the forms of *Echinococci* or of *Cysticerci*.

4. The larvæ attain the perfect or flat state (*strobilis*) by passing from one animal of a lower grade to another which is more elevated.

5. The same thing occurs between animals and man.

6. A difference in the locality influences their development. A residence in the alimentary canal is necessary for their complete development.

7. Certain *vesicular Helmintha* which become diverted from their proper migrations never arrive at the perfect state; they live as larvæ and perish sexless.

8. The *vesicular Helmintha* are of no sex, because the larvæ have none.

9. The *vesicular Helmintha* multiply themselves by gemmæ or buds.

10. The *flat Helmintha* reproduce themselves by sexual generation; they are androgynous and form eggs.

11. The *cucurbitins* or *zoonites* (*proglottis*) are segments

---

[1] Transformations which are equally curious occur in animals. The *Cysticercus fasciolaris* of the mouse produces the *Tænia crassicollis* of the cat; the *Cysticercus pissiformis* of the rabbit, the *Tænia serrata* of the dog; the *Cysticercus longicollis* of the field mouse, the *Tænia Crassipes* of the fox; the *Cœnurus cerebralis* of the sheep, the *Tænia cœnurus* of the wolf, &c.

of the *flat Helmintha*, which become separated and isolated when the eggs are mature.

12. The gemmæ, eggs, or larvæ of the *flat Helmintha* pass from an animal into man's body, or from one animal to another, by means of the food or the drink.

CHAPTER XIV.
ZOOLOGICAL VIEWS.

THE division of the Helmintha into those which reside in the alimentary canal, and into those which live out of it, although a convenient classification for the medical practitioner, is quite insufficient for the zoologist. Moreover, it is not altogether correct. It has been seen that the *Ascaris lumbricoides*, although it is a true intestinal worm, yet that it is occasionally found in the bladder, the nasal cavities, and in the meso-rectum, &c. The *Flukes* are also met with external to the intestine as well as in its interior.

The twelve genera that have been described, when considered in relation to their structure, present three distinct types of organization; these are represented by the *Ascaris*, the *Fluke*, and the *Tænia*.

In the first type the animal is vermiform, possesses a visceral cavity, and has a more or less complete alimentary canal, which is provided with a mouth and an anus. The sexes are always separate.

In the second type the body is short and flat, it has no visceral cavity, the digestive organs are incomplete, there is a minute pore which takes place of a mouth, and the anus is either rudimentary or absent; the animal is almost always androgynous.

In the third type, the body is flat, and composed of segments placed end to end, the visceral cavity is absent, the digestive organs are incomplete, the mouth is represented by absorbing pores, the anus is wanting; the animal is androgynous.

The *cucurbitins*, or separated zoonites of this third type, possess many of the characters which belong to the second, for a series of *Flukes* placed end to end would resemble a *Tænia*.

The Helmintha which form the first section belong to the genera *Ascarides*, *Oxyuris*, *Tricocephalus*, *Ancylostoma*, *Strongylus*, *Spiroptera*, and *Filaria*. The Helmintha which form the second belong to the genera *Thecosoma, Distoma,* and *Festucaria.* Lastly, the third includes the genera *Tænia* and *Bothriocephalus.*

Zoologists have placed these three types of animals in different orders or in different classes. Linnæus arranged the two first amongst the *Intestina,* and the third amongst the *Zoophyta.* Zeder, Rudolphi, and Bremser term the Entozoa belonging to the first type *Nematoidea,* those of the second *Trematoda,* and those of the third *Cestoidea.* Cuvier divides these animals into two orders: the *Cavitary,* which includes and corresponds, therefore, to the *Nematoidea,* and into the *Parenchymata,* which includes the others; he subdivides the latter into the *Trematoda* and *Tænioidea.* M. Milne Edwards considers them all as *Entomozoairia* or *Annelida,* but he divides them into three separate classes, each of which corresponds to one of the types that have been spoken of. These are the *Helmintha,* the *Turbellaria,* and the *Cestoidea.* M. Tandon accords with these views of the learned professor of the Museum of Natural History. He admits of these three groups which constitute his sixth, seventh, and eighth classes of worms, *Annelida* or *Entomozoaria,* belonging to the subkingdom Zoonites. He considers, however, that it is desirable to retain the older titles by which they have been distinguished. For this reason he has given the name of *Nematoidea* to the first group, *Trematoda* to the second, and *Cestoidea* to the third. There is a less amount of relationship between the *Nematoidea* and the *Trematoda* than there is between the latter and the *Cestoidea.*

The most perfectly organized of the intestinal worms are unquestionably the *Nematoidea,* and amongst these the *Ascarides* and the *Strongyli.*

The following table contains all the species which are met with in man. The number of these species amounts to twenty-nine; amongst them there are ten species which are either imperfectly known, or their presence in man has not been clearly established. These are distinguished by an asterisk.

[In the original table, M. Tandon has included five other species under the title of doubtful Helmintha; these have been omitted; while the *Trichina* is not included amongst the perfect worms, but is inserted with a query as to its being the young of *Tricocephalus dispar.* The grounds upon which the *Trichina* is raised to the rank of a distinct species are given at page 352. M. Tandon has also placed an asterisk before *Distoma Buskii;* the distinctive characters of this species having been given at page 374, this has been removed.]

Species of Helmintha living in Man.

I.—NEMATOIDEA.

1. Ascaris lumbricoides.
*2. Ascaris alata.
3. Oxyurus vermicularis.
4. Tricocephalus dispar.
5. Trichina spiralis.
6. Ancylostomum duodenalis.
7. Strongylus renalis.
8. Strongylus longevaginatus.
9. Spiroptera hominis.
10. Filaria medinensis.
*11. Filaria oculi.
*12. Filaria lentis.
*13. Filaria lymphatica.

II.—TREMATODA.

14. Thecosoma sanguicola.
15. Distoma hepaticum.
16. Distoma lanceolatum.
*17. Distoma opthalmobium.
18. Distoma heterophyes.
19. Distoma Buskii.
20. Festucaria lentis.

III.—CESTOIDEA.

21. Tænia communis.
    Larva, *Cysticercus cellulosæ*.
22. Tænia nana.
    Larva, ...
23. Tænia flavopunctata.
    Larva, ...
*24. Tænia echinococcus.
    Larva, *Echinococcus veterinorum*.
*25. Tænia inermis.
    Larva, ...
*26. Tænia acanthotrias.[1]
    Larva, *Cysticercus Acanthotricus*.
*27. Tænia tenuicollis.[2]
    Larva, *Cysticercus tenuicollis*.
*28. Tænia dentalis.[3]
    Larva, *Echinococcus hominis*.[4]
*29. Bothriocephalus latus.
    Larva, ...

SECTION IV.

INFUSORIAL ENTOZOA.

THE infusorial animalculæ, which are the most diminutive of living beings, are developed in all climates, in every possible locality, and at every period of the year. They are found in the bodies of living beings, and in the midst of inorganic substances.

---

[1] Perfect state not known.
[2] Perfect state not been observed in man.
[3] Perfect state doubtful in man.
[4] The Tænia Capensis and the Tænia tropica are not well defined. The *Cysticercus hepaticus, visceralis, Fischerianus, aorticus,* and *vesicæ,* are too imperfectly characterised to be included in the table.

Parasitic infusoria, whose presence is either the cause or the result of certain disorders, are met with in the human body, sometimes when it is in a healthy state, and at other times when it is in a state of disease.

Lebert has justly remarked that these animalcules are principally found in wounds where the discharge has been retained or has decomposed. They are found in the mucus of the intestinal canal (Leeuwenhoek, Pouchet); in stale or infected secretion of the vagina (Donné, Dujardin); in the tartar of the teeth (Mandl.); and in the milk (Fuchs).

The species which are most deserving of notice belong to the genera—1, *Paramecium;* 2, *Cercomonas;* 3, *Trichomonas; Virgulina;* 5, *Vibrio.* The following is a summary of the characters of these genera:

Infusoria
- with a mouth . . . . 1. *Paramecium.*
- without a mouth.
  - One large vibratile cilium . . .
    - A tail. 2. *Cercomonas.*
    - No tail. 3. *Trichomonas.*
  - No vibratile cilium.
    - A tail. 4. *Vergulina.*
    - No tail. 5. *Vibrio.*

1. PARAMECIUM.—This genus consists of flattened oblong infusoria, provided with a longitudinal fold which leads to the mouth. The body is covered with fine cilia.

On examining with the microscope some pus obtained from a small ulceration of the rectum, and the mucous secretion of this part of the intestines, in a sailor who had survived an attack of cholera, but who had subsequent derangement of the digestive organs, Dr. Malmstein, of Stockholm, found in these secretions, besides pus cells and blood globules, a large number of infusoria, which he has described and figured under the name of *Paramecium coli.*

He afterwards observed the same infusoria in a woman who had chronic inflammation of the large intestines. The patient having died, M. Malmstein found the infusoria were more abundant on those parts of the mucous membrane which had undergone the least amount of change than where the disease was further advanced, or in the pus which it had given rise to.

These animalculæ are very active; they present themselves in large numbers, as many as from twenty to twenty-five were found in a single drop of mucus. They die very quickly when removed from the intestine.

2. CERCOMONAS, *Cercomonas Davainei,* M. Tandon.—M. Davaine, in 1853, discovered in the warm dejections of cholera patients a species of *Cercomonas,* which occurred in large numbers.

Subsequently the same gentleman met with this animalcule on two occasions in the evacuations of patients attacked with simple diarrhœa. The cholera was still prevalent.

The animalcules are $\frac{3}{10}$ of an inch in length. The body is ovoid or pyriform, but somewhat variable in shape, and very pointed at the two extremities. The integument is soft, and of a white colour. One or two very small corpuscles, or nucleolar bodies, may sometimes be seen in the interior. Anteriorly is a very slender, long, flexible vibratile filament, which commences abruptly from the anterior margin; this is detected by the motion it produces in the water, but it can only be seen at intervals, and by prolonged examination. At the opposite extremity is another filament, which is thicker at its commencement where it becomes blended with the posterior part; it is about the same length or a little longer than the body; it is rigid, nearly straight, and sometimes attaches itself to surrounding objects; when this is the case the *Cercomonas* vibrates to and fro like the pendulum of a clock.

The *Cercomonads* are extremely active, a circumstance which renders it very difficult to determine their characters.

These animalcules die as soon as the fluids in which they are contained become cold; this proves that their formation does not depend upon the decomposition of the fluids. They are true parasites, which live in the intestines of man when certain conditions are present that are requisite for their existence. (Davaine.)

Another species of *Cercomonas* was found on one occasion in a young man in a well-marked case of typhoid fever, and without any symptoms of cholera. This was also discovered by M. Davaine.

This second species differs somewhat from the first; it is smaller and more oval; its anterior cilium is of the same length and equally flexible; it commences less abruptly. The caudal filament arises somewhat from the side; it is proportionally smaller, and is not blended with the posterior part of the body. This *Cercomonas* has an undulatory motion in the length of its body, which sometimes appears to be slightly wavy. This species might be termed the *Cercomonas obliqua*.

3. TRICHOMONAS, *Trichomonas vaginalis*, Duj.—This species was discovered by M. Donné in the mucus of the vagina (fig. 124).

The *Trichomonads* assemble together and form irregular masses with the particles of thickened mucus.

Some writers do not admit the animal nature of these minute

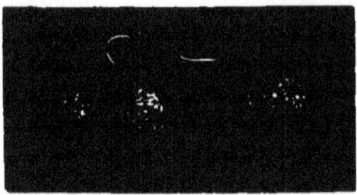
Fig. 124.—*Trichomonas vaginalis.*

objects.[1] They regard them as detached epethelial cells. Others have adopted the views of MM. Donné and Dujardin.[2] Some have even looked upon these animalcules as Acari.[3] The *Trichomonas vaginalis* is $\frac{1}{1000}$ inch in its long diameter. The body is globular, oval, or pyriform, unequal, slightly granular, gelatinous, transparent, and colourless, or of a milky appearance. They often adhere to other bodies. They have an anterior flabelliform filament (sometimes two, rarely three), thick at its base, flexible, and about $\frac{1}{1000}$ of an inch in length; there are also four or five short cilia placed on one side of it at its commencement.

Some have assigned to this animalcule a small, oblique, terminal mouth. MM. Scanzoni and Kolliker have not observed it, but they believed they had seen a shallow, oblique groove at the anterior part, near the cilia.

The *Trichomonas vaginalis* is not found in recently secreted mucus, but only in that which is beginning to decompose. Whenever this animalcule is met with the vaginal mucus encloses bubbles of air, which give it a frothy appearance. (Donné.)

[The *Trichomonas vaginalis* only occurs in women with gonorrhœal discharge, or with an abundant vaginal secretion mixed with mucus and pus corpuscles; never in a normal and healthy vaginal secretion, but only in pathological conditions. The mucus, however, need not be frothy, as Donné supposes, so long as it is not quite normal.[4]]

4. VIRGULINA, *Virgulina tenax.*—This animalcule is found in the tartar of the teeth. A small portion must be mixed with a drop of distilled water, which has been previously warmed, and examined with a magnifying power of from 400 to 500 diameters.

These animalcules vary in size from the $\frac{2}{1000}$ of an inch upwards, and move about rapidly. (Mandl.)

They are found in large quantities in patients who have been put upon a low diet for some months. They also form the greatest portion of thickened mucus of the tongue in persons who are troubled with indigestion.

[1] MM. Labert, Valentin, J. Vogel, Siebold, L. Wagner.
[2] MM. Raspail, Scanzoni, Kolliker.
[3] MM. Froriep, Ehrenberg.
[4] Küchenmeister, *opus cit,* vol. i. p. 7.

The *Virgulina tenax* has an elongated, membranous, transparent body, somewhat thickened, and truncated at its anterior part; it is furnished with a tail one third or one fourth shorter than the body.

M. Mandl. is of opinion that these animalcules contain a calcareous element in their tissues, which assists in hardening the tartar.

5. VIBRIO, *Vibrio rugula*, Müll.—Leeuwenhoek first noticed this animalcule in his own digestions during a slight illness.

Müller, who has described and figured it, saw it by thousands in an infusion of flies.

Dujardin found it in an infusion of crushed hemp seed, of Neufchatel cheese, of stale gelatine, and of the liver of the sheep.

M. Pouchet detected it in the dejections of cholera patients, where it was present in myriads. It was not found in the vomited matters.

Dr. Hassall also found the *Vibrios* in the dejections of cholera, and in the intestinal secretions some time after death.

These animalcules are hardly visible. They are from $\frac{3}{10,000}$ to $\frac{5}{10,000}$ of an inch in length, and from $\frac{2}{100,000}$ to $\frac{3}{100,000}$ of an inch in width. (Dujardin.) The body is cylindrical, attenuated at each extremity, sometimes straight, sometimes with from five to eight inflexions, and semitransparent. Its vacuoles are distinct, globular, and hyaline.

This animalcule moves about with great activity in an undulating or serpentine manner. Leeuwenhoek compared these movements to those of an eel.

Some naturalists question the animal nature of these minute bodies.

In all persons, whether ill or well, two other species of *Vibrios* are met with in the mucus of the mouth, mixed with the scales of epithelium and large granular molecules. These are the *Vibrio Bacillus* and the *Vibrio lineola* of Müller. The first is $\frac{1}{1000}$ of an inch in length, very flexible, and very slender, and contains a number of well-defined oval vacuoles. The econd, which measures about $\frac{3}{10,000}$ of an inch in length, is thick, somewhat bent, and the vacuoles are globular, but indistinct.

The blue and the yellow colours which, under some circumstances, are found in milk, are caused by the *Vibrio cyanogenus* and the *Vibrio xanthogenus* of Fuchs.

INDEX.

A.

Abd-el-Kader, 28.
Acanthia ciliata, 222.
――――― lectularia,
――――― rotundata, 222.
Acaridæ, 307.
Acaropsis, 307, 319.
――――― Mericourtii, 319.
――――― pectinata, 319.
Acanthrotriæs, 393.
Acarus, 309.
――― Americanus, 303.
――― autumnalis, 305.
――― domesticus, 130.
――― folliculorum, 319, 320 321.
――― nigua, 303.
――― reduvius, 302.
――― ricinus, 302.
――― scabei, 309.
――― Siro, 309.
Acephala, 51, 62, 86.
Acephalocysts, 391, 395, 400, 402.
Acetum cantharidis, 133.
Achatina carinata, 86.
Acipenser, 181.
――――― Huso, 182.
――――― Ruthenus, 182.
――――― stellatus, 182.
――――― Sturio, 182.
Aconitum Napellus, 206.
Actiniæ, 235.
Actinizoaria, 60, 62.
Adipose tissue, 41.
African, 34.
Aglossa farinalis, 243.
――――― pingualis, 243.
Alcyonium Lyncurium, 91.
Album Græcum, 66.
――― nigrum, 66.
Albumen, 179.
Alcyonia, 91.
Alcyonium Lyncurium, 91.

Allantoidians, 62.
Allocotyledons, 58.
Alimentary canal, 43.
Ambergris, 110, 125, 126.
Ambra cinerea, 126.
Ambreine, 127.
American, 26, 31, 33.
Ammodytes, 249.
Amphibia, 54.
Anallantoidians, 62.
Anatomy of Man, 3.
Ancyclostoma, 333, 334.
――――― duodenale, 353.
Ancylostomum duodenale, 353, 405.
Angle, facial, 5.
Andromeda Mariana, 205.
Animal, definition of, 37.
――― organization of, 37.
Animal charcoal, 161.
――― kingdom, 35.
Annelida, 60, 137, 404.
Anolius bullaris, 69.
Ant, 65, 213.
――― fire, 213.
――― flaming, 213.
――― red, 213.
Antelope Dorcas, 185.
――――― rupicapra, 184.
Anthremis musæorum, 130.
Anthropomorpha, 35.
Aphides, 154, 196.
Aphis, 155.
――― Chinensis, 155.
――― Pistaciæ, 156.
Apis Mellifica, 196, 275.
――― unicolor, 204.
Arachnida, 62, 98, 260, 286.
Aranea, 98.
――― diadema, 261.
――― Florentina, 260.
――― guttata, 260.
――― mactans, 261.
Araneidæ, 98.

Argades, 304.
Argas, 291.
—— of Persia, 304.
—— Persicus, 304.
—— Chinche, 304.
—— marginatus, 305.
Armadillo officinalis, 70.
Aromia Moschata, 110.
Articulata, 57, 60, 62.
Arteries, 45.
Artificial teeth, 81.
Ascarides, 334, 335, 403, 404.
Ascaris, 333, 335.
—— alata, 340, 405.
—— gigas, 335.
—— marginata, 339.
—— mystax, 340.
—— lumbricoides, 335, 405.
—— vermicularis, 334.
Asp, 248, 253, 282.
Ass, 65, 66, 67.
Astacus flaviatilis, 96, 176.
Australian, 26, 31.
Autumn fly, 234.
Azalea Pontica, 205.

B.

Badger, 65, 66, 67, 110.
Balæna Australis, 93.
—— Mysticetus, 93.
Balistes, 245.
Barbel, 67, 245.
Bat, 64, 65.
Batrachia, 62.
Bear, 66.
Beaver, 65, 118, 119.
Bedeguar, 149, 153.
Bee, 275.
—— eater, 66.
—— humble, 275, 279.
—— moss or carder, 279.
—— red-tailed, 279.
Beef, 163.
Bezoars, 67, 68.
Bigaye, 233.
Bile, 95.
Biline, 95.
Bizigaye, 233.
Blaps mortisaga, 242.
Blattidæ, 214.
Blood, 160.
—— transfusion of, 161.

Blood globules, 37, 40.
Blumenbach—characteristics of man, 1 ; races of men, 28.
Boat-fly, 224.
Bombycidæ, 234.
Bombus lapidarus, 279.
—————— muscorum, 279.
—————— terrestris, 279.
Bombax globosum, 100.
Bombyx Pityocampa, 234.
Bone of cuttle fish, 82, 83.
————————— composition of, 83.
Bones, 159, 160.
Bone black, 160.
Boschesman, 15.
Bothriocephali, 397.
Bothriocephalus, 332, 334, 386, 404.
——————— latus, 386, 405.
Bothrops, 255, 257.
———— Jararaca, 258.
———— lanceolatus, 258.
Bory de Saint Vincent—races of men, 28.
Brachinidæ, 214.
Brain, human, 5.
—— average weight of, 5, 6, 7, 9.
Branchiæ, 45.
Breeze-fly, 234.
Brosmius vulgaris, 102.
Bryozoa, 62.
Buffon—characteristics of man, 1.
Bufo calamita, 288.
—— vulgaris, 287.
Bug, 65.
—— ciliated, 222.
—— common, 219.
—— of miama, 304.
—— round, 222.
Burbot, 102.
Bull, 65, 67.
Bustard, 67.
Butea frondosa, 78.
Buthus Occitanus, 272.
———— palmatus, 272.
Butter, 190.
Byron, brain of, 6.

C.

Cachlot, 92, 94, 126.
Cactus Bonplandii, 71.
—— cochinellifera, 71.
—— opuntia, 71.

INDEX. 413

Calculi cancrorum, 97.
Callichroma muscata, 131.
Calliphora vomitoria, 237.
Callochalia esculenta, 185.
—————— fucifaga, 185.
—————— nidifica, 185.
Calmar, 56.
Calves, 164, 165.
Camel, 65, 66, 67, 68.
Cameleon, 65.
Cantharidin, 131.
Cantharides, 127, 128, 243.
—————— collecting of, 130.
Cantharis dubia, 132.
—————— vesicatoria, 128.
Capalan, 102.
Caranx, 246.
Carabidæ, 214.
Carbo animalis, 161.
Carcinas mænas, 176.
Cardium edule, 173.
Carmine, 76.
Carp, 65, 66.
Caryophyllia, 89.
Cases, 154.
Casowary, 65.
Castoreum, 110, 119.
—————— glands of, 120.
—————— American, 121.
—————— Canadian, 121.
—————— Hudson's Bay, 121.
—————— Russian, 121.
Castor Fiber, 118.
Cat, 66.
Caucasian race, 28, 30, 31, 32.
Cavia Capensis, 122.
Cavitaria, 404.
Cellular tissue, 41.
Celto-Scyth Arabs, 26.
Cephalopoda, 110, 125.
Ceratum cetacei, 94.
Cerastes, 255.
—————— Ægyptiacus, 255.
—————— Persicus, 255.
Cerate, 210.
Ceratum, 210.
Cercaria, 373.
Cercomonas, 406, 407.
—————— Davainei, 406.
Cerine, 210.
Cerocoma, 128, 135.
—————— Schœfferi, 135.
Ceroleine,
Cervus Alces, 181.

Cervus, Capreolus, 166.
—————— Dama, 181.
—————— Tarandus, 181.
Cestoidea, 404.
Cetacea, 92, 126.
Cetonia aurata, 131, 136.
Chamois, 184.
Chevrotain, 114.
Chigoe, 291, 300.
Chinche, 304.
Chinese gall, 154, 155.
—————— musk, 113.
Chrysomela, 131.
Cicadæ, 214.
Cimex lectularius, 219.
Civet, 110.
—————— scent of, 116.
Classification of animals, 52; Aristotle, 53; Linnæus, 53; Lamarck, 55; Cuvier, 56; Moquin-Tandon, 62.
Clubione medicinalis, 263.
Clubiones, 261.
Cobra de Capello, 259.
Coccus cacti, 71.
—————— illicis, 77.
—————— lacca, 76, 78.
—————— Polonicus, 76, 78.
Cochineal, 68, 71, 83.
Cochinella, 76.
Cockle, edible, 173.
Cockroach, 65.
Cod, 67, 101, 102.
—————— oil, 103; varieties of, 103, 104.
Cœlognathus morsitans, 300, 324.
Cœnurus cerebralis, 402.
Coluber Ammodytes, 250.
—————— Berus, 250.
Conger eel, 102.
Conops calcitrans, 234.
Common gall, 148.
Coral, 87.
—————— composition of, 88.
—————— varieties of, 88.
Corallium nobile, 87.
—————— rubrum, 87.
Cornu ustum, 181.
Cow, 66.
Crab, 97.
—————— land, 245.
—————— river, 96.
Crabs' eyes, 97.
—————— stones, 97.
Crane, 66, 67.

Cray fish, 96, 102.
Creamometer, 191.
Creeping gnat, 233.
Cricket, 165.
Cromwell, brain of, 5.
Crotalus durissus, 256.
———— horridus, 256.
———— miliaris, 256.
Croton lacciferum, 78.
Crow, 66.
Crowned gall, 151.
Crustacea, 62, 96, 213, 244.
Cuckoo, 67.
Cucumerini, 382.
Cucurbitini, 382.
Cucurbitins, 400, 401, 402.
Culex annulatus, 233.
———— pipiens, 230.
Cuterebra noxialis, 325.
Cuttle-bone, 82, 83.
Cuttle-fish, 67, 81, 82.
Cuvier—races of men, 28.
Cynanchum excelsum, 136.
Cynips, 148, 149.
———— gallæ tinctoriæ, 148.
———— quercus folii, 150.
———— quercus tojæ, 150.
———— rosæ, 153.
Cysticerci, 391, 396, 398.
Cysticercus, 401.
———————— Acanthrotias, 393.
———————— aorticus, 384.
———————— cellulosæ, 392, 398, 400, 402, 405.
———————— dicystus, 393.
———————— fasciolaris, 397, 402.
———————— Fischerianus, 394.
———————— hepaticus, 393.
———————— longicollis, 402.
———————— melanocephalus, 394.
———————— pisiformis, 402.
———————— tenuicollis, 393.
———————— turbinatus, 394.
———————— vesicæ, 394.
———————— visceralis, 394.

D.

Daman of the Cape, 122, 123.
Dasjespis, 123.
Decatoma, 128.
Decoctum gallæ, 155.
Delphinus globiceps, 189.

Delphinus marginatus, 189.
Demodex, 307, 320.
———— folliculorum, 320, 321.
Dentalium, 66.
Dermanyssus, 296.
———————— avium, 323.
———————— Boryi, 323.
———————— of Busk, 323.
Dermatophilus penetrans, 300.
Dermestes lardarius, 130, 242.
Desman, 110.
———— of Muscovy, 40.
Deutoscolex, 401.
Diodon, 246.
———— tigrinus, 246.
Diplolepis rosæ, 153.
Dippel's animal oil, 189.
Diptera, 227, 230, 237.
Distoma, 333, 334, 404.
———— Buskii, 373, 374, 405.
———— hæmatobium, 369.
———— hepaticum, 370, 405.
———— heterophyes, 373, 374, 405.
———— lanceolatum, 373, 405.
———— opthalmobium, 373, 405.
Distylium racemosum, 155.
Dog, 65, 66.
Dog-fish, 108.
Dormouse, 65.
Dorse, 102.
Dracunculus, 360.
———————— Persarum, 360.
Dsaanja, 110.
Dsehija, 110.
Duck, 65, 66.
Dugong, 189.
Dumeril—races of man, 28.
Dupuytren, brain of, 5.
Dyticus marginatus, 242.

E.

Eagle, 65, 66, 67.
———— ray, 106, 107.
Ear, 50.
Earth worm, 65.
Echinococci, 391, 394, 396, 398, 402.
Echinococcus hominis, 394, 405.
———————— veterinorum, 395.
Ectoparasites, 291.
Ectozoa, 291.
Eel, 65, 66.
Eel-pout, 65, 66.

Eggs, 193, 194, 195, 196.
Eider duck, 211.
Elementary bodies in animals, 38.
Elephant, 65, 66, 67, 80.
────── tusks of, 81.
Elephas Africanus, 80.
────── Indicus, 80.
Emplastrum cantharidis, 133.
Encephalon, 6, 7, 8.
Entomozoaria, 404.
Entozoa, 324, 330.
Epeira, 261.
Epicauta adspersa, 132.
────── cavernosa, 132.
Epizoa, 291.
Erucæ, 234.
Ethiopian race, 29.
Eustrongylus gigas, 356.
Eutarsus cancriformis, 323.
Eutoma, 234.
Eye, 50.

F.

Facial angle, 5.
────── in Chinese, 5.
────── European, 5.
────── Negro, 5.
Falcon, 65.
Fallow deer, 65, 66.
Fasciola, 370.
────── hepatica, 370.
Fat, 186.
Feathers, 211.
Fel bovinum, 95.
── tauri, 95.
Festicularia, 333, 334.
Festucaria, 375, 404.
────── lentis, 378, 404, 405.
Ficus religiosa, 78.
────── Indica, 78.
Filaria, 333, 334, 359, 403.
────── bronchialis, 364.
────── dracunculus, 360.
────── lachrymalis, 363.
────── lentis, 364, 405.
────── lymphatica, 364, 405.
────── Medinensis, 360, 465.
────── oculi, 363, 405.
Fishes, 244.
Flesh, 162.
────── of articulata, 163, 176.
────── of fish, 163, 167.

Flesh of game, 163, 166.
────── of mollusca, 163, 168.
────── of poultry, 163, 166.
────── of radiata, 163, 176.
Flamingo, 66.
Flea, 291, 297.
Flies, 213, 237.
Fly, flesh, 237.
── bluebottle, 237.
── golden, 237.
── hominivorous, 237.
Fluke, 370, 403.
Forficula auricularia, 242.
────── minor, 242.
Fox, 65, 66.
── shark, 102.
Frigate bird, 65.
Frog, 67.

G.

Gaduine, 105.
Gadus, 102.
────── Æglefinus, 102.
────── Brosme, 102.
────── Callarias, 102.
────── Carbonarius, 102.
────── Lota, 102.
────── Merlangus, 102.
────── Merlucius, 102.
────── minutus, 102.
────── Molva, 102.
────── Morrhua, 102.
Galls, 100, 148, 149.
Gall of Aleppo, 152.
── artichoke, 152.
── crowned, 152.
── gooseberry seed, 151.
── horned, 152.
── Hungarian, 152.
── Piedmont, 152.
── smooth, 152.
── squamous, 152.
Gamasus, 297.
Gasteropoda, 62, 83.
Gasterostei, 397.
Gastric glands, 44.
Gazelle, 185.
Gecarcinus ruricola, 267.
Gelatine, 179, 180.
Genette, 110.
Geophilus electricus, 242.
Geotrupes vernalis, 242.

Glandular tissue, 41.
Glossina morsitans, 228.
Gnats, 230.
Gnat, ringed, 233.
Gneion, 246.
Goat, 65, 66, 67.
Goatsucker, 64.
Goose, 211.
Goldfinch, 65.
Gordius, aquaticus, 367.
—————— Medinensis, 360.
Gorgonia antipathes, 89.
—————— nobilis, 87.
Grasshopper, 65.
Great cachelot, 92.
Grebe, 211.
Greenland whale, 93, 188.
Green or officinal leech, 140.
Grouse, 66.
Guinea worm, 360.
Gryllus Ægyptius, 163.
—————— migratorius, 163.
—————— Tartaricus, 163.

H.

Haddock, 102.
Hæmenteria, 141, 144.
—————— Ghiliani, 141.
—————— Mexicana, 141.
—————— officinalis, 141.
Hæmopis, 215, 218.
—————— sanguisuga, 215.
Hair, 210.
Hairy galls, 149.
Haje serpent, 259.
Hake, 102.
Hare, 65, 66, 67.
Harvest bug, 291, 305.
Hawk, 65, 66, 67.
Heart, 45.
Hedgehog, 64, 65, 66.
Helicidæ, 83, 84.
Helicinea, 85.
Hen, 211.
Hermit crab, 247.
Heron, 65.
Helix, 83.
—— Algira, 175.
—— aperta, 175.
—— arbustorum, 175.
—— aspersa, 85.
—— cespitum, 175.
—— ericetorum, 175.

Helix hortensis, 175.
—————— lineata, 175.
—————— melanostoma, 175.
—————— nemoralis, 85.
—————— Pisana, 175.
—————— Pomatia, 84, 85.
—————— stagnalis, 86.
—————— sylvatica, 174.
—————— variabilis, 175.
—————— vermiculata, 85.
Helmintha, 330, 332, 334, 401, 402, 404.
—————— cystic, 391, 396.
—————— hydatid, 896.
Hippobosca equina, 227.
Hippoboscidæ, 227.
Hippocolle, 184.
Hippopotamus, 81.
—————— amphibius, 81.
—————— tusks of, 81.
Hirudo, 137.
—————— medicinalis, 140.
—————— officinalis, 140.
—————— sanguisuga, 215.
—————— troctina, 141.
Hirundo esculenta, 185.
—————— fucifaga, 185.
Hirundiniculture, 147.
Holothuria edulis, 177.
—————— tubulosa, 177.
Homarus vulgaris, 176.
Homo, 2.
—— ferus, 2.
—— Lar, 26.
—— sapiens, 2, 26.
—— Troglodytes, 26.
Honey, 196, 202.
—————— adulteration of, 206.
—————— bee, 196, 197.
—————— poisonous, 208.
Horned gall, 157.
Hornet, 279.
Horse, 64, 65, 66, 67, 68.
—————— fly, 227.
—————— leech, 215, 216, 217, 218.
Human kingdom, 35.
Humantis, 109.
Huso, 182.
Hycleus, 128.
Hydatids, 391, 400.
Hymenoptera, 148, 153, 196, 268, 275, 286.
Hyraceum, 110, 122, 123, 124.
Hyrax Capensis, 122.

I.

Ibex, 68.
Iguana cærulea, 163.
—— cornuta, 163.
—— delicatissima, 163.
—— fasciata, 163.
—— tuberculata, 163.
Indian elephant, 80.
—— hog, 67.
—— ink, 82.
Insects, 296.
Intestines, 43.
—————— divisions of, 44.
Isinglass, varieties of, 183.
Isis nobilis, 87.
Itch insect, 309.
Iulus, 268.
—— terrestris, 268.
Ivory, 80, 81.
—— black, 81.
Ixodes, 302.
———— hominis, 303.
———— Nigua, 303.
———— Ricinus, 302.

J.

Jararaca, 258.
Javelin bat, 212.
———— snakes, 257.
Jaws, 42.
Jigger, 300.
Juvenis bovinus, 21.
———— lupinus, 21.
———— ovinus, 21.
———— ursinus, 21.

K.

Kabardin, 113.
Kermes, 76, 77.
Kingfisher, 65, 66.
Kite, 65, 66.
Kranchil, 114.

L.

Lac, 79.
Lacerta agilis, 69.
—— Scincus, 68.

Lactodensimetre, 191.
Lactoscope, 192.
Lamb, 163.
Lamprey, 65.
Lapis porci Ceylonici, 67.
—————— Malaccensis, 67.
—— porcinus, 67.
Lard, 186, 187, 188.
Larinus odontalgicus, 159.
—————— subrugosus, 157.
Lark, 65, 66.
Latham—on the races of men, 31, 32.
Leblanc (Mademoiselle), 21.
Leech, 100, 139, 142, 143, 144, 146.
—— dragon, 140, 141.
—— green, 100.
—— grey, 139, 140, 141, 142.
Leptus autumnalis, 305.
Liebig's soup, 177.
Life, average duration of, 17.
—— table of, for England, 18.
Ling, 102.
Linnæus—characters of man, 2.
————— on the races of men, 27.
Lion, 65, 66.
Linguatula, 329.
—————— denticulata, 329.
Liparis auriflua, 234.
—— canifolia, 234.
Liver, 44.
Lizard, 60, 65, 66, 67.
Lota vulgaris, 102.
Louse, 291.
—— body, 292, 294.
—— head, 292.
—— pubic, 292, 296.
—— of sick persons, 292, 295.
Lucilia hominivora, 238.
Lunga, 45.
Lydus, 128.
Lymnæus stagnalis, 86.
Lytta adspersa, 132.
—— dubia, 132.
—— segetum, 132.
—— Syriaca, 132.
—— vidua, 132.

M.

Macaque, 326.
Magpie, 65.
Male organs, 47.

E E

Malmignatte, 261.
Man, 1.
—— erect position, 11.
—— height of, 14.
—— original state of, 20.
—— species of, 25, 26.
—— weight of, 15.
Mandibles, 42.
Marabout, 211.
Marmot, 65.
Martin, 66.
Maxillæ, 42.
Medicinal leech, 140.
Medusæ, 235.
Meletta, 240.
Meloe, 127, 128, 136, 243.
—— Algeria, 137.
—— autumnalis, 137.
—— bimaculata, 136.
—— cichorii, 134.
—— Gallicus, 137.
—— mailis, 137.
—— Proscarabæus, 137.
—— punctatus, 137.
—— rugosus, 137.
—— Schæfferi, 135.
—— variegatus, 137.
Merlangus carbonarius, 102.
——————— vulgaris, 102.
Merlucius vulgaris, 102.
Mermis, 367.
Milk, 189.
—— preservation of, 193.
—— of ass, 190, 191.
—— of cow, 190.
—— of goat, 190, 191.
—— of sheep, 190, 191.
—— of mare, 190, 191.
—— of woman, 190, 191.
Millipedes, 265.
Mistura spiritus Vini Gallici, 196.
Mole, 64, 65, 66.
Molva vulgaris, 102.
Mollusca, 244, 246.
Mongolian race, 29, 31, 32.
Monk-fish, 109.
Monkey, 65, 66, 67.
Monostomum lentis, 375.
Montpellier drops, 100.
Morbus mucosus, 348.
Morrhua Æglefinus, 102.
————— Callarius, 102.
————— minuta, 102.
Moschus Altaicus, 114.

Moschus Javanicus, 114.
———— Kranchil, 114.
———— moschiferus, 110.
Mouse, 65, 66.
Mucilage of snails, 86.
Mule, 60.
Musaraigne, 110, 213.
Musca Cæsar, 238.
—— carnaria, 237.
—— vomitoria, 237.
Muscles, 51.
Muscular tissue, 41.
Musk, 100, 110.
—— deer, 111, 113.
—— ox, 110.
—— rat, 110.
Musquitoes, 233.
Mussel, 66, 246.
—— common, 172.
Mutton, 163.
Mygale, 260, 262, 263.
—— Muscovita, 110.
Mylabris, 128, 134, 243.
———— bimaculata, 136.
———— cichorii, 134.
———— cyanescens, 135.
———— Indica, 135.
———— oleæ, 135.
———— punctum, 135.
———— pustulata, 135.
———— Sidæ, 135.
———— variabilis, 135.
Myricine, 210.
Mytilus edulis, 172.

N.

Naia, 255, 299.
Naja Haje, 25.
—— tripudians, 259.
Napu, 114.
Navicella elliptica, 179.
Negro, 5.
Nematoidea, 62, 604, 605.
Nematoideum hominis viscerum, 330.
Nepa, 226.
—— cinerea, 226.
Nervous system, 34.
—— tissue, 41.
Nightingale, 66.
Noctonecta glauca, 224.
Noxious animals, 212.
Nutgalls, 153.

INDEX.

O.

Oculina, 89.
——— virginea, 89.
Œnas, 128.
Œstridea, 325.
Œstrus bovis, 326.
——— Guildingei, 326.
——— hominis, 326.
——— ovis, 326.
Oil, 188.
— of dugong, 189.
— of porpoise, 189.
— of whale, 188.
Oniscus asellus, 70.
Ophidia, 283.
Opuntia cochenillifera, 71.
——— Tuna, 71.
——— vulgaris, 71.
Orang-outang, 10.
Organic world, divisions of, 36.
——— tissues, 41.
Organs of motion, 51.
——— of nutrition, 42.
——— of relation, 49.
Ornithorynchus, 268.
Ostracion, 244.
Ostrea cristata, 168.
——— edulis, 168.
——— hippopus, 168.
——— lacteola, 168.
——— lamellosa, 168.
——— Mediterranea, 168.
——— plicata, 168.
——— rosacea, 168.
Ostreaculture, 169.
Ostrich, 65, 66, 67, 187, 211.
Otter, 66, 67.
Ovis Aries, 185.
Ox, 66, 67, 68, 164, 165.
— gall, uses of, 95.
Oxyporus subterraneus, 242.
Oxyuris, 333, 334, 403.
——— vermicularis, 343, 405.
Oyster, 86, 168, 169, 246.

P.

Pachydermata, 80.
Pæderus elongatus, 242.
Pagurus Bernhardus, 247.
Palinurus vulgaris, 176.
Pallulinia Australis, 205.

Pancreas, 44.
Papilio brassicæ, 243.
Paramecium, 406.
——— coli, 406.
Parenchyma, 404.
Partridge, 66, 67.
Peacock, 67.
Pearl oyster, 66.
Pediculus, 291.
——— capitis, 292.
——— cervicalis, 292.
——— corporis, 294.
——— humanus, 292.
——— inguinalis, 296.
——— morphio, 296.
——— pubescens, 294.
——— pubis, 296.
——— subcutaneus, 295.
——— tabescentium, 295.
Pee-wit, 66, 67.
Pelias Berus, 240.
Pelican, 65.
Penguin, 211.
Pentastoma, 376.
Perdix cinerea, 166.
——— petrosa, 166.
——— rubra, 166.
——— saxatilis, 166.
Phalangioides, 261.
Phalæna processionea, 234.
——— quercus, 234.
Phasianus Colchicus, 166.
——— Gallus, 193.
Pheasant, 65, 66.
Pholci, 261.
Phthiriasis, 295.
Phyllostoma haustatum, 212.
Physalia pelagica, 236.
Physcter macrocephalus, 92.
Pig, 66, 164, 265.
— stone, 67.
Pigeon, 64, 65, 66, 67.
Pithecus Lar, 21.
Pike, 66, 67.
Platessa flesus, 167.
——— vulgaris, 167.
Plover, 64.
Polistes Lecheguana, 205.
Porcupine, 65.
Pork, 163, 165.
Potentilla alba, 77.
——— reptans, 77.
Portuguese man of war, 286.
Poulp, 56, 126.

Processionary moths, 234.
Protoglottis, 401.
Protoscolex, 401.
Ptinca, 130.
Pulex, 297.
—— hominis, 297.
—— irritans, 297.
—— penetrans, 300.
—— vulgaris, 297.
Pulmones preparati, 66.
Pupipara, 227.
Pupivora, 148.
Pygocentrus, 214.

Q.

Quercus coccifera, 77.
—— Pyrenaica, 150.
—— sessiflora, 150.
Quail, 65, 67.
Quetelet—weight of man, 16.

R.

Rabbit, 65.
Races of men, 27.
Radiata, 57, 58, 61, 62.
—— flesh of, 176.
Raia Aquila, 107.
—— batis, 107.
—— clavata, 106.
—— Pastinaca, 107.
Rana esculenta, 178.
—— temporaria, 178.
Rat, 65, 213.
Rays, 106, 213.
Red coral, 83.
Reduviidæ, 222.
Reduvina, 222.
Reduvius personatus, 222.
—— serratus, 224.
Reproduction, modes of, 48.
—————— fissiparous, 46.
—————— gemmiparous, 46.
—————— organs of, 46.
—————— sexual, 46.
Reptilia, 62.
Respiration, 45.
Rhamnus Jujuba, 78.
Rhinoceros, 65, 66, 67.
Rhizostoma Aldrovandi, 236.
—————— Cuvierii, 236.

Rodentia, 118.
Roebuck, 66.
Rorqual, 188.
Ruminantia, 110.
Russian musk, 113.

S.

Salamander, 65, 87.
Salamandra maculata, 289.
Salar Ausonii, 167.
Salivary glands, 44.
Salmo fario, 167.
—— salar, 167.
Salmon, 66.
Sanguisuga interrupta, 141.
—————— medicinalis, 140.
—————— officinalis, 140.
Sarcophaga carnaria, 237.
Sarcopsylla penetrans, 300.
Sarcoptus, 307, 318.
—— scabei, 309.
Saunders (Mr.)—eruption of molar teeth, 13.
Scarabæus, 65.
—————— vernalis, 242.
Scarus, 246.
—— capitaneus, 246.
Schistocephalus dimorphus, 397.
Scink, 68.
Scolices, 397.
Scleranthus perennis, 77.
Scolopendra, 265.
—————— cingulata, 265.
—————— electrica, 244.
—————— Scopoliana, 266.
Scolopendridæ, 260.
Scomber Scombrus, 167.
—————— capitaneus, 246.
Scorpio Europæus, 271.
—— Occitanus, 272.
—— palmatus, 272.
Scorpion, 64, 65, 268, 270.
—— African, 271.
—— common, 271.
—— palmated, 271.
—— red, 271.
Seed lac, 79.
Segestria cellaris, 260.
Sepia, 82.
—— officinalis, 81.
Sepiadæ, 81.
Sepiostaire, 82.

Sepium, 82, 83.
Serpent, 68, 248, 255.
Serrasalmes, 214.
Sewruga, 182.
Shad, 65.
Shark, 102.
—— oil of, 108, 109.
Sheep, 67, 68, 164, 165.
—— skin of, 185.
Shell lac, 79.
Sight, 49.
Silkworm, 67.
Simulium reptans, 233.
Silphidæ, 214.
Size of fœtus, 12, 14.
Skate, 106, 107.
—— oil of, 105, 106, 107.
Skeleton, 52.
Skin, 184.
Slug, 65.
Smell, 49.
Smooth gall, 150.
Snail, 66, 83, 174, 246.
Snipe, 66.
Solea vulgaris, 167.
Solitary worm, 376.
Soulouque, 30.
Spermaceti, 91, 94.
Sphærodus leucothalmus, 242.
Sphyræna Becuna, 246.
—— —— Caracauda, 246.
Spider, 64, 67, 98, 99, 262.
—— cave, 260.
—— web of, 91, 98.
Spiroptera, 333, 334, 359, 403.
—— —— hominis, 359, 405.
Spodium Græcum, 66.
Sponge, 89.
—— composition of, 90.
—— nature of, 90.
—— brown, 91.
—— common, 90.
—— fine Archipelago, 91.
—————— hard, 91.
—————— Syrian, 91.
—————— gelatine, 91.
—————— Grecian, 91.
—————— Marseilles, 91.
—————— Salonica, 91.
—————— white of Syria, 91.
Spongia officinalis, 89.
—— —— spiculæ of, 90.
Sporocyst, 394.
Squalus, 108.

Squalus Acanthias, 108.
—— Catulus, 108.
—— Centrina, 109.
—— Mustelus, 109.
—— Squatina, 109.
—— Vulpes, 109.
Stag, 65, 66, 67.
—— horn of, 180.
Staphilinus fuscipes, 242.
——————— politus, 242.
——————— punctatus, 242.
Sterlet, 182.
Stick lac, 79.
Stickle back, 397.
Stigmata, 46.
Stomach, 43.
Strobila, 401.
Strongylus, 333, 334, 355, 403.
—— —— gigas, 356, 405.
—— —— longivaginatus, 357, 405.
—— —— renalis, 356, 405.
Struthio camelus, 187.
Sturgeon, 181.
Sturio, 182.
—— stellatus, 182.
Suet, 186, 187.
Sus scropha, 81.
Swallow, 65, 66.
—— esculent, 185; nests of, 185.
Swan, 65, 66.
Syrupus cocci, 76.

T.

Tabanus bovinus, 234.
Table of the animal kingdom, 62.
Tænia, 332, 334, 376, 404.
—— Acanthotrias, 405.
—— Ægyptiaca, 383.
—— canina, 385.
—— Capensis, 384.
—— communis, 399.
—— crassipes, 402.
—— crassicollis, 397, 402.
—— cucumerina, 385.
—— dentalis, 405.
—— Echinococcus, 382, 383, 405.
—— fœnestrata, 382.
—— flavopunctata, 382, 383, 405.
—— inermis, 382, 384, 405.
—— mediocanellata, 384.

Tænia nana, 382, 383, 405.
—— serrata, 385, 402.
—— Solium, 376, 382, 405.
—— tenuicollis, 405.
—— tropica, 403.
Tænioidea, 404.
Tannin, 153.
Tapeworm, 376.
Tapir, 67.
Tarantula, 263.
Taste, 49.
Teeth, 13.
—— eruption of, 13.
Tegenaria medicinalis, 182.
Tench, 65.
Tenebrio molitor, 242.
Testudo Europea, 178.
—— Græca, 178.
—— marginata, 178.
—— Mauritanica, 178.
Tetrao lagopus, 166.
—— tetrix, 166.
—— urogallus, 166.
Tetraonix, 128.
Tetrarhynci, 397.
Thecosoma, 333, 334, 368, 404.
—— hæmatobium, 369.
—— sanguicola, 405.
Theridian mactans, 261.
Thornback, 106.
Thread lac, 79.
Ticks, 291, 302.
Tick of wolf, 302.
—— reticulated, 302.
Tiedman on the human brain, 6.
Tinctura cantharides, 133.
—— castorei, 122.
—— Gallæ, 153.
Tincture of cantharides, 133.
—— of galls, 153.
Titmouse, 64.
Toad, 64, 65, 66, 287.
—— common, 288.
—— Natter Jack, 288.
Tooth powder of French codex, 83.
Torpedo, 213.
Tortoise, 65, 66, 67.
—— sea, 67.
Touch, 49.
Tracheæ, 45.
Transfusion, 161.
Trahala, 100, 156, 157, 158, 189.
Trahalose, 158.
Tree-frog, 64, 65.

Trematoda, 405.
Trepang, 177.
Trichina, 350.
—— spiralis, 350, 405.
Trichomonas, 406.
—— vaginalis, 407.
Tricocephalus, 333, 334, 348, 351, 403.
—— dispar, 405.
Tricula, 156.
Triton, 289.
—— custatus, 288.
Trombediidæ, 305.
Trout, 66.
Trunk-fish, 244.
Tsetse, 228.
Tunny, 245.
Turbellaria, 404.
Turbot, 167.
Turpentine gall, 156.
Tyroglyphus Mericourtii, 269.

U.

Unguentum cantharidis, 133.
—— Gallæ compositum, 153.

V.

Vampire, 212.
Vampyrus spectrum, 212.
Vegetable wax, 206.
Vena Medini, 334.
—— mitena, 334.
Veins, 45.
Veneridæ, 172.
Vermes accessorii, 331.
—— cucumerini, 382.
—— cucurbitini, 382.
Vesicating insects, 100.
Vespa Crabro, 280.
—— vulgaris, 280.
Vespertilio vampyrus, 212.
Vibrio, 406.
—— Bacillus, 409.
—— cyanogenus, 409.
—— lineola, 409.
—— regula, 409.
—— xanthogenus, 409.
Victor, 23.
Viper, 68, 248, 283.
—— common, 248.
Vipera ammodytes, 249.

INDEX.

Vipera aspis, 248.
—— Berus, 248.
—— lanceolata, 258.
—— Mægera, 258.
Virgulina, 406.
—— tenax, 408.
Viverra civetta, 115.
—— Zibetha, 117.
Volvocidæ, 396.
Volvox, 60, 62.

W.

Water scorpion, 226.
—— wagtail, 64.
Wax, 206, 209, 210.
—— organs, 207.
Weasel, 65, 66.
Weight of brain, 7.
—— of child at birth, 14.
Wild boar, 81.
—— boy of Aveyron, 23.
—— cat, 64, 65.
Whale, 64.

Whalebone, 211.
—— —— whale, 93.
Whiting, 65, 67, 102.
Wolf, 65, 66.
Woodcock, 66.
Woodlouse, 68, 69, 70.
Wren, 64.

Y.

Yeh, 29.

Z.

Zebra. 184.
Zebud, 228.
Zebeth, 117.
—— scent of, 117.
Zimb, 228.
Zoonites, 59, 60, 62, 376, 402.
Zoophyta, 60, 404.
Zoophytes, 61, 62, 245.

www.ingramcontent.com/pod-product-compliance
Lightning Source LLC
Chambersburg PA
CBHW020534300426
44111CB00008B/658